PLA

PHAEDRUS

Oklahoma Series in Classical Culture

PLATO'S PHAEDRUS

A Commentary for Greek Readers

PAUL RYAN

INTRODUCTION BY MARY LOUISE GILL

UNIVERSITY OF OKLAHOMA PRESS : NORMAN

Library of Congress Cataloging-in-Publication Data
Ryan, Paul, 1929–
Plato's Phaedrus : a commentary for Greek Readers / Paul Ryan ; introduction
by Mary Louise Gill.
    pages   cm. — (Oklahoma series in classical culture ; volume 47)
Includes bibliographical references and index.
ISBN 978-0-8061-4259-3 (pbk. : alk. paper)
1. Plato. Phaedrus.
I. Title.
B380.R83 2012
184—dc23

                                                              2011046329

Plato's Phaedrus: A Commentary for Greek Readers is Volume 47
in the Oklahoma Series in Classical Culture.

The paper in this book meets the guidelines for permanence and durability
of the Committee on Production Guidelines for Book Longevity of the Council
on Library Resources, Inc. ∞

CONTENTS

PREFACE

The first version of this commentary was made about twenty years ago at the University of Pittsburgh, when Professor Mary Louise Gill invited me to participate in a very small class (one student) in the *Phaedrus*. Later I revised it for her use in teaching the dialogue at Harvard and again when she first taught it at Brown. The student for whom it was first written combined a keen intellect and determination to succeed with less formal instruction in Greek than would ordinarily be expected as preparation for reading a work of the scope and subtlety of *Phaedrus*. I have kept the needs of that kind of student in mind while making the two revisions mentioned above and the one I made in preparation for publication. The work is unashamedly didactic. I do not shrink from repeating what seems important. References to Smyth's *Greek Grammar* and the lexicon of Liddell, Scott, and Jones abound. Access to those works and to Denniston's *Greek Particles* is recommended for efficient use of the commentary. Other grammatical and lexical works are cited only when they seem to have something interesting to add. Hardened Platonists will quickly see that I am not a historian of philosophy. I am, however, very interested in what Plato means as well as how he says it, and I direct students to interpretations and interpretive works where that seems likely to improve their understanding, but I remain convinced that the direct route to what Plato meant lies through an accurate and judicious grasp of what he wrote.

Accordingly, I give perhaps more than the usual amount of attention to the logical connection, nuance, and emphasis lent by particles. Students at an early stage in reading Greek tend to lose time in staring at sentences as if they were isolated boulders in a running stream. That is not the case: they are stones, big and little, cunningly fitted into a seamless wall. In a Socratic dialogue some of them arrive with naïve earnestness, others bearing countless shades of irony; some look back to what has come before, others forward, still others, Janus-like, face both ways. All are sensitive to their context, and the reader must be so too. If he or she, aided by the particles, keeps in mind what has come before and even peeks ahead from time to time, not only will the product be better, but the process will be easier and more satisfying.

Many commentaries on the elementary to intermediate level of this one accept the text that accompanies them as a given and confine themselves to expounding it. This one discusses textual difficulties with some frequency, and I should explain my motives for that and clarify my limitations. First, I think it good that undergraduates have it impressed upon them in a moderately hands-on way that the text we are reading was not revealed to us from on high, but is the product of a long process involving the errors and attempts at correction of fallible human beings all the way from antiquity to them and their teacher and me. Moreover the difficulties we shall discuss have been selected as being either crucial in interpretation or because they are intrinsically interesting as illustrations of the kinds of accidents that happen to a text in manuscript transmission or the kinds of well-intentioned distortions it can undergo at the hands of scholars. Sometimes I leave the upshot open, more often I indicate a preference—not ex cathedra but by way of advice. I have consulted no manuscripts (my defective vision alone would forbid it), only the *apparatus critici* of Burnet and Moreschini. I assume on the part of the student only access to the *apparatus* of Burnet, which is available with his text in this book.

I am solely responsible for any errors that remain in this work. That said, I am very pleased to offer thanks first to Professor Gill and her students—Wendy Teo in particular—for salutary objections mingled with encouragement during its long and fitful gestation. Of the scholars listed in my bibliography I am particularly grateful to the learned commentary of G. J. De Vries, which has been my constant ally and adversary. If I rather frequently cite him in disagreement, it is because he cannot be ignored. No doubt I could have profited much from the recent commentary on *Phaedrus* by Harvey Yunis, but unfortunately it appeared too late for me to take it into account. I thank Professor Alan Boegehold for calling to my attention the substance of the note on 229b7–9 and the second note on 237a5. I benefited from the report of Professor Margaret Graver, who read an earlier draft at the request of the University of Oklahoma Press; and the detailed critique of my second reader, who chose to remain anonymous, influenced my treatment for the better throughout. Finally—and sadly—I dedicate this commentary to the memory of Karen Hoover, the student for whose benefit its first, brief, rude version was made back in 1989. Her bright light was extinguished all too soon.

Abbreviations

C.   J. L. Cooper, *Attic Greek Prose Syntax* (after K. W. Krüger), Ann Arbor, 1998 [cited by section numbers and letters].

D.   J. D. Denniston, *The Greek Particles*, 2nd ed., Oxford, 1939.

GMT   W. W. Goodwin, *Syntax of the Greek Moods and Tenses*, 1875; repr. New York, 1965 [cited by section number].

KG   R. Kühner and B. Gerth, *Ausfürliche Grammatik der Griechischen Sprache*, Zweiter Teil, 2 vols., 3rd ed., 1898; repr. Munich, 1963 [cited by volume and page number].

LSJ   H. G. Liddell, R. Scott, and H. S. Jones, *A Greek-English Lexicon*, 9th ed., Oxford, 1951.

S.   H. W. Smyth, *Greek Grammar*, 2nd ed., 1920; revised by Gordon Messing, Cambridge, Mass., 1956 [cited by section number].

V.   G. J. De Vries, *A Commentary on the Phaedrus of Plato*, Amsterdam, 1969.

Page numbers and letters (a–e) from Stephanus's 1578 edition continue to be printed in the margins of texts and translations of Plato and used for reference. The three manuscripts that John Burnet considered primary for his text of *Phaedrus*—the only three I mention in my notes—are B, a manuscript in the Bodleian Library at Oxford, written by one John the Calligrapher in 895 for the use of the Byzantine scholar Arethas; T, from the library of St. Mark's in Venice, dated from the late eleventh or early twelfth century but almost certainly copied from a codex roughly contemporary with B; and W, in the Staatsbibliothek at Vienna, which is dated to the twelfth century by some scholars but earlier by others. Quotations and citations of other Platonic dialogues in this commentary will, unless otherwise indicated, be to John Burnet's volumes in the

Oxford Classical Text series, except for dialogues in volume 1. There the
edition of E. A. Duke et al., which has supplanted Burnet's in the series
and is currently available, will be cited. The names of the dialogues will
be abbreviated as follows:

Alc. I	*Alcibiades*	*Meno*	*Meno*
Ap.	*Apology*	*Mx.*	*Menexenus*
Chr.	*Charmides*	*Parm.*	*Parmenides*
Cra.	*Cratylus*	*Phd.*	*Phaedo*
Crito	*Crito*	*Phlb.*	*Philebus*
Euthyd.	*Euthydemus*	*Plt.*	*Politicus*
Euthyp.	*Euthyphro*	*Prt.*	*Protagoras*
Grg.	*Gorgias*	*Rep.*	*Republic*
Ion	*Ion*	*Sph.*	*Sophist*
La.	*Laches*	*Sym.*	*Symposium*
Laws	*Laws*	*Tht.*	*Theaetetus*
Lys.	*Lysis*	*Tim.*	*Timaeus*

Works Cited

Adam and Adam. *Platonis Protagoras*, edited with commentary by J. Adam and A. M. Adam, Cambridge, 1893.

Asmis. *"Psychagogia* in Plato's *Phaedrus"* by Elizabeth Asmis, Illinois Classical Studies 11 (1986): 153–72.

Ast. *Lexicon Platonicum sive Vocum Platonicarum Index* by Frederick Ast, Leipzig, 1855; repr. Bonn, 1956.

Austin and Olson. *Aristophanes: Thesmophoriazusae*, edited with introduction and commentary by Colin Austin and S. Douglas Olson, Oxford, 2004.

Barrett. *Euripides: Hippolytus*, edited with introduction and commentary by W. S. Barrett, Cambridge, 1964.

Bluck. *Plato's Meno*, edited with introduction and commentary by R. S. Bluck, Cambridge, 1964.

Boegehold. *When a Gesture Was Expected* by Alan Boegehold, Princeton, 1999.

Bowra. *Pindari Carmina cum Fragmentis*, edited by Maurice Bowra, Oxford, 1935 with numerous reprintings.

Brown and Coulter. "The Middle Speech of Plato's Phaedrus" by Malcolm Brown and James Coulter, *Journal of the History of Philosophy* 9.4 (1971): 405–23.

Burkert. *Greek Religion* by Walter Burkert, translated by John Raffin, Cambridge, Mass., 1985.

Burnet. *Plato's Euthyphro, Apology of Socrates, and Crito*, edited with commentary by John Burnet, Oxford, 1924.

Burnet. *Plato's Phaedo*, edited with commentary by John Burnet, Oxford, 1911.

Camp. *The Archaeology of Athens* by John M. Camp, New Haven, 2001.

Campbell. "On Plato's Use of Language" in vol. 2 of *Plato's Republic*, edited by Benjamin Jowett and Lewis Campbell, Oxford, 1894.

Campbell. *The Theaetetus of Plato*, with revised text and English notes by Lewis Campbell, 2nd ed., Oxford, 1883.

Chantraine. *Grammaire Homérique* by Pierre Chantraine, 2 vols., Paris, 1948 [cited by section number].

Collard and Cropp. *Euripides: Fragments*, edited and translated by
    Christopher Collard and Martin Cropp, 2 vols., Cambridge, Mass., 2008.

Denniston. *Greek Prose Style* by J. D. Denniston, Oxford, 1952.

Denyer. *Plato: Protagoras*, edited with commentary by Nicholas Denyer,
    Cambridge, 2008.

des Places. *Études sur quelques particules de liaison chez Platon* by E. des
    Places, Paris, 1929.

Dickey. *Greek Forms of Address from Herodotus to Lucian* by Eleanor
    Dickey, Oxford, 1996.

Dimock. "Ἀλλά in Lysias and Plato's Phaedrus" by George E. Dimock,
    American Journal of Philology 73.4 (1952): 381–96.

Dodds. *Euripides: Bacchae*, edited with introduction and commentary by
    E. R. Dodds, Oxford, 1960.

Dodds. *The Greeks and the Irrational* by E. R. Dodds, Berkeley and Los
    Angeles, 1959.

Dodds. *Plato: Gorgias*, edited with introduction and commentary by E. R.
    Dodds, Oxford, 1959.

Dover. *Aristophanes: Clouds*, edited with introduction and commentary by
    K. J. Dover, Oxford, 1968.

Dover. *Greek Homosexuality* by K. J. Dover, Cambridge, Mass., 1978; rev.
    ed., 1989.

Dover. *Plato: Symposium*, edited with introduction and commentary by
    Kenneth Dover, Cambridge, 1980.

Ferrari. *Listening to the Cicadas: A Study of Plato's Phaedrus* by G. R. F.
    Ferrari, Cambridge, 1987.

Fowler. *Phaedrus*, translated by H. N. Fowler in Plato I, Loeb Classical
    Library, Cambridge, Mass., 1914.

Fraenkel. *Aeschylus: Agamemnon*, edited and translated by E. Fraenkel, 3
    vols., Oxford, 1950.

Gildersleeve. *Syntax of Classical Greek from Homer to Demosthenes* by
    B. L. Gildersleeve, 2 vols., New York, 1900 [cited by volume and section
    number].

Gow. *Theocritus*, edited with translation and commentary by A. S. F. Gow, 2
    vols., Cambridge, 1950.

Guthrie. *A History of Greek Philosophy* by W. K. C. Guthrie, 6 vols.,
    Cambridge, 1961–82.

Hackforth. *Plato's Phaedrus*, translated with introduction and commentary by R. Hackforth, Cambridge, 1952.

Hamilton. *Plato: Phaedrus and the Seventh and Eighth Letters*, translated by W. Hamilton, Harmondsworth, 1973.

Helmbold and Rabinowitz. *Phaedrus*, translated with introduction by W. C. Helmbold and W. G. Rabinowitz, New York, 1956.

Henderson. *Aristophanes' Lysistrata*, edited with introduction and commentary by Jeffrey Henderson, Oxford, 1987.

Hermeias. *Hermeias von Alexandrien: In Platonis Phaedrum Scholia*, edited by P. Couvreur, Paris, 1901; repr. Hildesheim, 1971.

Jebb. *Sophocles: Oedipus Coloneus*, edited with commentary by Richard Jebb, Cambridge, 1990 with numerous reprintings.

Jebb. *Sophocles: Oedipus Tyrranus*, edited with commentary by Richard Jebb, Cambridge, 1885 with numerous reprintings.

Kennedy. *The Art of Persuasion in Greece* by George Kennedy, Princeton, 1963.

Kerferd. *The Sophistic Movement* by G. B. Kerferd, Cambridge, 1981.

Linforth. "The Corybantic Rites in Plato" by Ivan Linforth, *University of California Publications in Classical Philology* 13.5 (1946): 121–62.

Linforth. "Telestic Madness in Plato" by Ivan Linforth, Phaedrus 244DE," *University of California Publications in Classical Philology* 13.6 (1946): 162–72.

Nehamas and Woodruff. *Phaedrus*, translated by Alexander Nehamas and Paul Woodruff in *Plato: Complete Works*, edited by John M. Cooper, Cambridge, Mass./Indianapolis, 1997.

Nightingale. *Genres in Dialogue* by Andrea Wilson Nightingale, Cambridge, 1995.

Nilsson. *Geschichte der griechischen Religion* by M. P. Nilsson, vol. 1, Munich, 1940; 2nd ed., 1955.

Page. *Poetae Melici Graeci*, edited by Denys Page, Oxford, 1962.

Page. *Sappho and Alcaeus* by Denys Page, Oxford, 1955.

Plass. "Play and Philosophical Detachment in Plato" by Paul Plass, *Transactions of the American Philological Society* 98 (1967): 343–64.

Renehan. *Studies in Greek Texts* by Robert Renehan, Göttingen, 1976.

Richardson. *The Iliad: A Commentary*, edited by G. S. Kirk, vol. 6 by Nicholas Richardson, Cambridge, 1993.

Riddell. *A Digest of Platonic Idioms* by J. Riddell, 1876; repr. Amsterdam, 1967.

Robin. introduction by Léon Robin to Budé *Phaedrus*, edited by Claudio Moreschini and translated by Paul Vicaire, Paris, 1994.

Rowe. *Plato: Phaedrus*, with translation and commentary by C. J. Rowe, Warminster, 1986.

Thompson. *The Phaedrus of Plato*, edited with commentary by W. H. Thompson, London, 1868; repr. 1973.

Tod. *A Selection of Greek Historical Inscriptions* by M. N. Tod, 2nd ed., Oxford, 1946.

Travlos. *Pictorial Dictionary of Ancient Athens* by John Travlos, New York, 1980.

Verdenius. "Notes on Plato's *Phaedrus*" by W. J. Verdenius, Mnemosyne, 4th series, 8 (1955): 265–89.

West. *Elegi et Iambi Cantati ante Alexandrum*, edited by M. L. West, 2 vols., Oxford, 1971–72; rev. ed. of vol. 1, 1989.

West. *Hesiod: Theogony*, edited with prolegomena and commentary by M. L. West, Oxford, 1966.

Wycherley. "The Scene of Plato's Phaedrus" by R. E. Wycherley, *Phoenix* 17 (1963): 88–98.

INTRODUCTION

Mary Louise Gill

Plato's strange and beautiful *Phaedrus* depicts Socrates and Phaedrus taking a walk outside the city walls into the countryside, finding a shady place under a plane tree by a freshwater spring, and settling down to talk about love, rhetoric, and (implicitly) philosophy.

The dialogue breaks into two dissimilar parts. The first part is written in a grand style with lavish imagery and play of character and includes three speeches about erotic love, one purportedly by the speechwriter Lysias and two composed on the spot by Socrates in competition with him. The second part adopts a quite different style, featuring Socrates engaged in short exchanges with his interlocutor, and the discussion, though sometimes lighthearted, is a fairly technical inquiry into the nature of rhetoric using the earlier speeches as illustrations of good and bad speaking and writing.

Dramatic Setting

The two men are alone, but the countryside is teeming with other voices and especially the noisy cicadas overhead—our lost brethren who learned to sing and forgot to eat and drink, whose descendants became cicadas dear to the Muses, nine goddesses devoted to poetry, song, and dance.[1] Now when these cicadas die, Socrates cautions Phaedrus, they will report to the Muses news of our conversation—whether we spoke well or poorly, or perhaps napped lazily in the noonday sun. Through the mouths of Socrates and Phaedrus, many other voices are heard in this landscape as well, voices of well-known orators, doctors, tragic and lyric poets, but most notably the voice of the prominent speechwriter Lysias, whose

speech about love Phaedrus clutches under his cloak, intending to practice it in the open air with Socrates as his captive audience. At the end
of the dialogue we learn that perhaps Plato's contemporary with a rival
school, the speechwriter Isocrates, is in some sense also there.

The place is inhabited by more exotic beings too: gods and nymphs
and mythical or legendary creatures whose traces can be seen around the
spring or who come to life in the stories Socrates tells along the way—
about local gods, Olympian gods, and a god and god-king of ancient
Egypt. As the two men walk along the river toward their resting place,
Phaedrus notices a spot where he thinks that Oreithyia, daughter of the
legendary Athenian King Erechtheus, was abducted by Boreas, the North
Wind. This story sets the stage for the upcoming discussion of *erōs* ('erotic
love'), since the word in Greek includes in its meaning what we now call
seduction and rape. The many foreign sights and sounds, discussed by
two men reclining in the shade of a plane tree in the countryside, suggest
that Socrates and Phaedrus have come to a magical place away from the
everyday.

Socrates, though in some respects the philosopher we know from other
Platonic dialogues—walking barefoot, claiming that his sole expertise
is the art of love, and seeking self-knowledge—is in other respects quite
unlike his usual self. A man who rarely leaves town (with the exception of
two tours of military duty and occasional visits to the Piraeus), who says
that the trees have nothing to teach him, and who famously hates long
speeches, would today follow Phaedrus to Megara and back, so "sick" is he
"with passion for hearing speeches." Plato's Socrates elsewhere denigrates
the senses, saying that they mislead and confuse us, but today he revels in
the landscape, remarking at length on the beauty of the plane tree in full
bloom, the fragrance of the Agnus castus shrub nearby, the coolness of the
water, the freshness of the air, and the echoes of the cicadas' song.[2] All of
Socrates' senses are stimulated by his surroundings. As Phaedrus remarks,
Socrates is ἀτοπώτατος—strange, quite literally 'out of place.' In reading
the Phaedrus one should ask what motive Plato might have for presenting
Socrates with unusual traits in this unfamiliar setting.

Dramatic Date

Perhaps there is some actual time when the conversation between Socrates
and Phaedrus could have occurred, but Plato appears to go to consider-

able lengths to make any dramatic date hard to square with details of this dialogue and others featuring Phaedrus and other historical figures mentioned as present in Athens at the time of the conversation—in particular, the prose writers Lysias and Isocrates and the tragic poets Sophocles and Euripides. The nebulous time frame, like the exotic setting, seems designed to transport us away from the everyday.

Let us review the main evidence relevant to the dialogue's dramatic date. Phaedrus appears as a character in three of Plato's dialogues: the *Protagoras*, the *Symposium*, and the *Phaedrus*. The *Protagoras* presents a great gathering of sophists at the home of Callias, and its dramatic date is widely agreed to have been about 433/432 B.C.E. Phaedrus was there in the train of the sophist Hippias and so would probably have been a young man of at least eighteen, born around 450. The *Symposium* has a dramatic date of 416 and recounts a dinner party celebrating Agathon's first victory in a tragic competition. According to the proposed date of Phaedrus's birth, he would have been in his mid-thirties on the occasion of the *Symposium*. That evening the guests decide to forego the usual heavy drinking and entertainment by a flute girl, since they are still hung over from their celebrations the night before, and choose instead to give speeches in praise of Eros, god of erotic love. In the *Symposium* Phaedrus is said to have proposed the topic, complaining that Eros has not received the praise he deserves. The complaint would be disingenuous if the conversation in the *Phaedrus* had already occurred, given the three speeches about love in the *Phaedrus*.[3] Socrates also appears to refer to the dinner party in the *Phaedrus*, when he says that Phaedrus has in his lifetime composed or caused to be composed more speeches than anyone, with the possible exception of Simmias of Thebes.[4] These indications put the dramatic date of the *Phaedrus* after the dinner party honoring Agathon's victory in a tragic composition in 416.

Soon after the party, on the eve of the ill-fated Sicilian expedition (415–413 B.C.E.), some men went on a drunken rampage, profaned the Eleusinian mysteries, and mutilated the herms (statues of the god Hermes at crossroads and protecting sanctuaries and private doorways).[5] Phaedrus was one of those accused of profaning the mysteries, and at a trial in 415 he was exiled from Athens until a general amnesty in 403.[6] Thus the conversation could not have occurred between 415 and 403. A dramatic date for the *Phaedrus* after his return from exile between 403 and Socrates' death in 399 is unlikely, because Sophocles and Euripides are treated in the *Phaedrus* as still living, but both tragic poets died in 406.

One might suppose that the conversation took place in the interval after the dinner party and before Phaedrus's exile (416/415), but that date is problematic because Phaedrus says at the beginning of the *Phaedrus* that he has been with Lysias that morning. Lysias moved to the Greek colony in Thurii with his brother Polemarchus around 430 and returned to Athens when the Athenians were ousted from the colony in 412, by which time Phaedrus was already in exile. A date before Lysias's departure in 430 is ruled out, because at the end of the *Phaedrus* Socrates speaks of Isocrates (born in 436) as a young man, but he would have been a child of five or six years old when Lysias left Athens—too young to be a budding orator. Kenneth Dover makes a case that Lysias returned from Thurii to Athens for a visit between 418 and 416.[7] If Socrates' conversation with Phaedrus took place in the year or so before the dinner party at Agathon's in 416, Phaedrus's complaint in the *Symposium* that Eros has been unfairly ignored would be surprising but of course not impossible. We might avoid that incongruity by adopting Dover's suggestion and conjecture a date at the end of Lysias's visit in late 416, shortly after the dinner party and before the mystery trial.

There remains, however, one significant discrepancy. Phaedrus is represented in the *Phaedrus* as a boy or young man, addressed by Socrates as ὦ νεανία, ὦ παῖ, and with other young men as ὑμεῖς οἱ νέοι. At the start of his second speech about love Socrates asks: "Where, then, is the boy [παῖς] to whom I was speaking?" and Phaedrus replies: "Here he is, always right by your side, whenever you want him." Yet judging from the biographical material just surveyed, which puts the dramatic date of the dialogue in late 416, Phaedrus would have been a middle-aged man, too old to be properly called a "boy" or "young man." It has been claimed that these forms of address present no problem but simply express the coquetry of an older man toward a younger man.[8] Certainly Phaedrus and Socrates engage in playacting in the first part of the dialogue, especially in their elaborate flirtation, but this playacting adds to the impression that Plato orchestrated the timing of the *Phaedrus*, much as he designed its setting, to take his readers outside ordinary time and place into an enchanted world of make-believe.

Date of Composition

Scholars now generally agree that Plato wrote the *Phaedrus* after the *Republic* and around the same time as the *Parmenides* and *Theaetetus*, before the group of late dialogues including the *Sophist, Politicus, Philebus, Laws,* and probably *Timaeus.* The *Phaedrus* relates to the late dialogues *Sophist* and *Politicus* in that it introduces the dialectical techniques of collection and division used in those dialogues. Furthermore, the discussion of rhetoric in the second part of the dialogue explores the application of theoretical knowledge to practical situations—especially the use of rhetoric to persuade an audience of something on a particular occasion—and this interest in practical knowledge connects the *Phaedrus* to the *Politicus.* At the same time, Socrates' second speech in the first part of the dialogue harkens back to works composed earlier, such as the *Phaedo,* the conversation Socrates had with friends in his prison cell on the last day of his life. In his speech he speaks of separate immaterial forms, which explain features that things have in our changing world; he argues for the immortality of the soul; and he appeals to the doctrine of recollection, the idea that we gained knowledge of forms while our souls were disembodied and in this life bring that latent knowledge to the surface when stimulated by sense perception or questioning. Since the doctrine of recollection fades out after the *Phaedrus* and Plato appears to revise his theory of forms in the late dialogues in response to the critique of the theory in the *Parmenides,* the *Phaedrus* stands in a pivotal position looking both forward and back.

Since the *Phaedrus* looks both forward and back, there is reason to regard it as a transitional dialogue, after the great works of Plato's middle period, before the late dialogues, and in proximity to the *Parmenides* and *Theaetetus*—a conclusion also supported by stylistic evidence.[9] The three dialogues—*Parmenides, Phaedrus,* and *Theaetetus*—though quite different from one another in their content, themselves form a striking triad with regard to the age and role of Socrates, who is represented as very young in the *Parmenides* (dramatic date around 450 when Socrates would have been about eighteen or nineteen), middle-aged in the *Phaedrus* (at some indeterminate date), and old in the *Theaetetus* (dramatic date shortly before Socrates' trial and death at age seventy in 399). Socrates plays distinctive parts in these three dialogues. Unlike the Socratic dialogues (such as the *Apology, Euthyphro, Laches,* and *Charmides,* traditionally dated early in Plato's career) in which Socrates avows his ignorance and through cross-examination reduces others to puzzlement, Socrates in the *Parmenides* exchanges roles with the philosopher Parmenides. Here the youthful Socrates advocates a theory of forms similar to that in the *Phaedo,* Parmenides cross-examines him, and Socrates proves unable to rescue his theory. We have already noted Socrates' strangeness in the *Phaedrus,* his difference in several respects from the figure we know in the Socratic dialogues. In the *Theaetetus* the elderly Socrates reverts to his familiar role in the Socratic dialogues, claiming to know nothing and examining the views of others. After the *Theaetetus* Socrates serves only once more as the main speaker in a Platonic dialogue (*Philebus*), and his place is elsewhere taken over by speakers whose mode of teaching differs from the one we customarily associate with him.[10] In thinking about the *Phaedrus* in relation to other dialogues, the question arises again: in what ways is Socrates' role atypical and why?

Love and Rhetoric

The *Phaedrus* explores two explicit topics, love and rhetoric, and the dialogue appears to challenge us to discover how these themes fit together. When Phaedrus and Socrates arrive at the shade of the plane tree, Phaedrus produces the document he has hidden under his cloak and reads aloud Lysias's speech about love. Lysias argues that you should give your favors to someone who is not in love with you rather than someone who loves you, because a nonlover is sober and will look after your interests, whereas a lover is mentally deranged and will embarrass you by sleeping in doorways and generally making a fool of himself.[11]

Socrates enters a competition with Lysias and gives two speeches of his own on the same topic. In his first speech Socrates faults love as a mental derangement, as Lysias did, but his speech displays much greater coherence. First he defines love as an unreasoning desire to take pleasure in beauty, a desire that overwhelms the lover's better judgment, and then relies on that definition to demonstrate love's harmful effects on a boy's soul, body, and property.[12] Socrates wears a cloth over his head throughout his first speech, and so he should, because his speech is as shameful as it is persuasive. Since Socrates' second speech shows that he knows the truth about love and he defines it very differently, his first speech is an instance of what he later calls true rhetoric—a persuasive speech by someone who knows the truth about his subject matter but may misrepresent what it is.[13] In this first speech at least, Socrates is playing the role of a true rhetorician, someone who knows the truth but misleads his audience.

As soon as he finishes, Socrates announces that he must retract his speech and then replaces it with his magnificent Palinode.[14] This time with head unveiled, Socrates displays the true nature of love and defines it as a species of divine madness that frees the lover from conventional behavior and ensures his greatest good fortune. In this vividly sensual speech, Socrates compares the soul to a winged charioteer (reason) and pair of horses (spirit and appetite) and describes a *Fantasia*-like parade of divine souls, with their well-matched steeds, up the vault of heaven to get a full view of the stable realities beyond the heavens, food for the best part of the soul—reason, the charioteer. Other souls, whose teams are poorly matched, lose control of their unruly horse, get trampled by the stampede in their zeal to outstrip their rivals, and are deprived of any view at all. Souls allowed to enter human bodies in their first incarnation at least glimpse the forms of beauty, justice, and moderation before they lose their wings and tumble to earth to be born into a mortal body. Human souls differ from one another, depending on which god they followed and how much they saw, and the extent of their vision in turn depends on how well the charioteer controlled his team and especially his unruly horse (appetite). When someone falls in love, the beauty of the beloved reminds the lover of the form of beauty he beheld when disembodied, and the wings of his soul begin to sprout anew. In turn a boy properly loved experiences a "back-love" in which he sees himself in the lover as in a mirror and joins in the ecstatic experience. Their shared life can spare the inspired lover and beloved from cycles of rebirth.

The second part of the dialogue seems more typically Socratic. Here Socrates investigates rhetoric and defines it as a way of leading the soul (ψυχαγωγία) by means of speeches (διὰ λόγων), both in public and private. He lists three conditions for rhetorical expertise: natural ability (φύσις), knowledge (ἐπιστήμη), and practice (μελέτη).[15] The second part of the *Phaedrus* focuses mainly on the sorts of knowledge a successful orator needs. The true rhetorician (as opposed to ordinary ones like Lysias) should in the first place know the truth about his subject matter, even if he plans to mislead his audience; second, he must know the various elements and strategies of rhetorical composition; third, he must know how to combine the elements effectively into a persuasive speech, and that demands knowing his audience, since his speech aims to persuade them. The task of composing a speech for an occasion and audience also calls for practical expertise in timing. The speaker must select the sorts of components appropriate for the occasion and know when to use them, how much time to spend on them, and how to put all the components together into a unified, moving speech. While technical books on rhetoric can spell out the elements of the art and strategies for using them, give general rules about types of audiences and types of speeches, and describe what sort of speech is likely to succeed with what sort of audience and why, books cannot prepare the student to use the knowledge effectively on particular occasions. To achieve rhetorical expertise, a speaker must hone his skills through practice. The practiced orator adjusts the parts of his speech to suit not only the development of his topic but also the needs of his audience at different stages of his presentation, so that his overall strategy achieves his objective, persuasion.

In order finally to decide which discourses are spoken and written artfully and which are not, Socrates gives his notorious critique of writing, a critique that has provoked scholars to question Plato's attitude about his own philosophical writings. Socrates begins with a story. The Egyptian god Toth made many discoveries useful to human culture, including numbers, calculation, geometry, astronomy, draughts and dice, and also writing (γράμματα). According to Socrates, the god took his arts and displayed them to the god-king Thamus and urged him to distribute them to all Egyptians. Toth explains the purpose of each art, and Thamus praises or faults his inventions. When they get to the art of letters, Toth claims that he has discovered a potion (φάρμακον) that will make the Egyptians wiser and improve their memories, but Thamus is not impressed, objecting that far from benefiting humans, the art of letters will have the opposite effect and cause forgetfulness by removing the impetus for people to use their memory. By relying on writing from outside (ἔξωθεν), they will not recollect from inside (ἔνδοθεν) using their own resources. According to Thamus, Toth has found merely a potion of reminding (ὑπομνήσεως), not of memory, and consequently those exposed to writing will merely seem wise without being wise.

Taking Thamus's side, Socrates claims that writing has a lot in common with painting, since both seem alive, but if you ask questions of a painting or a piece of writing, they do not respond, and when attacked they need their author to defend them. Furthermore, a discourse once written rolls around everywhere without discriminating between those who understand and those who have no business with it. Writing does, however, have a legitimate brother—a living, breathing discourse written in the soul of the audience by an author with knowledge, a discourse able to defend itself and knowing when to speak and when to remain silent. According to Socrates the best sort of discourse is spoken, not written, by someone who knows the truth about his subject matter and the character of his audience, and on the basis of that knowledge and his familiarity with rhetorical elements composes a simple or complex speech that speaks to his listener(s) and persuades them of something, either the truth or something resembling the truth. Socrates claims that a serious person should not take his own writing seriously, but write things playfully and store up reminders (ὑπομνήματα) for his forgetful old age. What should we make of this critique for Plato's own works, such as the *Phaedrus*? Is the *Phaedrus*—a written work—simply playful, not serious?

Unity of the *Phaedrus*

While criticizing Lysias's poorly constructed speech, Socrates offers the following description of artful discourse: "Every discourse must be composed like an animal, with a body of its own, so that it is neither without a head nor without feet, but has middle parts and extremities written to fit [πρέποντα] one another and the whole" (264c2–5).

This standard of unity invites us to ask about the unity of the *Phaedrus* itself and why it seemingly fails to measure up to its own compositional ideal. Why is the first part so lush, with extensive use of the setting and drama, and the second so spare? The speeches about love in the first part serve as examples of good and bad rhetoric in the second part, but why choose love as the topic of the speeches in preference to any other rhetorical topic? The unity of the *Phaedrus* has been much discussed, and various solutions have been proposed.[16] This introduction offers a suggestion, but readers of the *Phaedrus* should consider and assess alternatives.

Plato toys with two sorts of compositions in this work, one spoken, the other written. The first is Socrates' discourse with Phaedrus one glorious day when they walk together into the countryside along the banks of the Ilissus and sit down under a plane tree while the cicadas sing overhead— an exercise in true rhetoric (ψυχαγωγία). Socrates the philosopher is disguised today as a true rhetorician, and Phaedrus is his audience. This is a live discourse on a particular occasion, and Socrates spends much of the early part of the dialogue discovering who Phaedrus is, his interests and passions, and the special nature of his psychic malady. His analysis of Phaedrus's psyche appears to apply a technique spelled out in the second part of the dialogue, called the "true method" and attributed to the famous doctor Hippocrates. Using this method the doctor and true rhetorician study the beneficiary of their art (human body or soul) in preparation for determining an appropriate therapy to cure its ailment.

Socrates quickly learns that Phaedrus has a complex soul (a soul whose reason, spirit, and appetite are not well integrated) and so gives him a complex speech in a colorful, variegated style. Socrates speaks first to Phaedrus's appetite by flirting with him and responds to Phaedrus's zeal for competition by challenging Lysias with his own first speech about love. Then he reaches magnificent heights of emotional appeal in the Palinode and finally speaks to Phaedrus's reason with hardheaded arguments about rhetoric in the second part of the dialogue.[17] The *Phaedrus* fits together as a whole with parts well adjusted to one another on the supposition that Socrates' discourse speaks in different places to different parts of Phaedrus's soul—his appetite, spirit, and reason. On this reading of the dialogue, Socrates' whole discourse is an example of true rhetoric designed to persuade Phaedrus to give up his unhealthy infatuation with Lysias and Lysias's commonplace rhetoric and to pursue a more productive form of rhetoric instead, one in which the speaker knows the truth, though he may persuade his audience of something false.

But then there is the beautifully flawed free-standing written work we have before us—the dialogue *Phaedrus*—which stands there like a picture to be viewed by readers again and again down through the ages, a work of Platonic philosophy. This second composition does not merely image the first in writing. Whereas the author of the live discourse is Socrates and his audience is Phaedrus, the author of the written discourse is Plato (who writes all the parts) and we readers are his audience. The two discourses also perform different functions—the first aims to persuade its audience, the second to provoke its audience to ask questions. Plato does not know us as individuals as Socrates comes to know Phaedrus, but he need not know us in the same way. Our individuality does not interfere with his project, because he assumes an audience with simple well-integrated souls and aims to move the controlling part of our souls: our reason.[18]

For Plato's chosen readers the *Phaedrus* is a fascinating work—a work that moves us, though not in the way that Socrates' persuasion moves Phaedrus. The written work prods us to ask many questions of our absent author. Wherein lies the unity of the *Phaedrus*, the written work? Why does Socrates say that most of the Palinode was said in play, with the exception of the (rather tedious) division of four sorts of madness at the start, which prepares for the introduction of collection and division later in the dialogue? What should we make of the proof of the soul's immortality, separate forms, and doctrine of recollection in the Palinode, which harken back especially to the *Phaedo* and apparently count among its "playful" bits? How seriously should we take the critique of writing, also characterized as "playful"?

True Rhetoric and Philosophy

The *Phaedrus* explores an idea, important for rhetoric, that people are easily misled by similarities and become confused when different things are called by the same name. The main example of such ambiguity in the *Phaedrus* is "love," used both for the vulgar derangement blamed in the first two speeches and for the divine madness praised in Socrates' Palinode. The two emotions called "love" have some features in common, and that similarity promotes the ambiguity and justifies their collection into a more inclusive form, madness. Socrates displays the difference between the two sorts of love by dividing madness into human and divine, then human madness into several varieties—including gluttony, drunkenness, and vulgar love—and divine madness into four sorts, of which true love is one. In this way he reveals the gulf between vulgar love, a mental illness, and true love inspired by the gods. An expert orator, who knows the truth about his subject matter and its relations to similar objects, can use that knowledge either to persuade his audience of the truth or to mislead them by exploiting the similarities.

Another ambiguous term is "philosophy." The dialogue is purportedly about true rhetoric, and some scholars identify that with Platonic philosophy. The two arts are akin but not the same. The relation between true rhetoric and philosophy comes into question at the end of the dialogue, when Phaedrus mentions Socrates' young friend (and Plato's later rival) Isocrates, whom Socrates credits with much greater talent than Lysias and the other orators and describes as blessed by nature with a certain philosophy (τις φιλοσοφία), a divine impulse that may propel him to greater things. Especially if commentators are right that Socrates' shameful first speech parodies Isocrates, this mention of him at the end sheds light on the larger project of the *Phaedrus*, since both Isocrates and Plato appropriated the term "philosophy" (φιλοσοφία) for their teaching, yet their modes of teaching were very different.[19] How does philosophy differ from true rhetoric, φιλοσοφία from τις φιλοσοφία? Plato moves his audience in the *Phaedrus* precisely by stimulating us to ask these questions and to use our inner resources in answering them—an exercise in Platonic philosophy.

True rhetoric resembles philosophy in using many of the same dialectical techniques, such as collection and division, to discover the truth about the topic under discussion, and both arts use discourse to intervene in the lives of their audience. Because of the similarity, an audience might easily mistake true rhetoric for philosophy, especially when Isocrates calls his own practice φιλοσοφία. Yet it makes all the difference whether a writer or speaker knows the truth about his subject matter and relies on it to persuade his audience of the truth or of something false that looks like the truth, as Socrates does in his first speech, perhaps parodying Isocrates, or uses discourse—even sometimes misleading discourse—to uncover the truth or help others find it.

The choice of love as a topic of the speeches in the *Phaedrus* seems highly relevant to the distinction between true rhetoric and philosophy. Erotic love is a profound attraction felt by a lover toward his beloved, and his love intervenes in the life of the beloved, pressing the beloved to pay attention and respond. The vulgar lover, condemned by Lysias and by Socrates in his first speech, attempts to turn the beloved toward himself and to persuade him to return his affection with sexual favors. The divinely inspired lover in the Palinode has a different aim: instead of turning the beloved's soul toward himself, the lover turns his beloved toward the realities both of them once saw when their souls were disembodied.[20]

We might think of Plato's writing as the product of his divinely inspired love—Plato is the lover, and we (the audience) are his beloved. His written works make no attempt to turn us toward him: our author always hides, speaking to us through others' voices. Nor does he try to persuade us of anything. Instead Plato puzzles us and presses us to ask questions, and in this way undertakes to turn our souls toward that unearthly beauty that Socrates describes in his Palinode. Plato himself frequently uses deception, as he does at the end of the *Phaedrus* in Socrates' denigration of writing, but the aim is not to bring us to believe the false conclusions his main speaker propounds—for instance, that writing is of little worth except as a reminder in one's forgetful old age, or that true rhetoricians are genuine philosophers—but to shake us free of those misconceptions by prodding us to ask questions and to answer them ourselves. In responding to the stimulus we engage in Platonic philosophy.

Notes

1. On the importance of the cicadas for Plato's project in the *Phaedrus*, see Ferrari; and on the many alien voices and their significance, see Nightingale, chap. 4.
2. Ferrari 16–17 compares Socrates' extravagant description of the landscape at 230b2–c5 to the sort of medical analysis we find in the Hippocratic treatise *Airs, Waters, Places*. The medical analogy comes into the foreground in the second part of the dialogue.
3. To be sure, the first two speeches fault love, but Socrates' second speech gives love high praise.
4. Simmias was a friend of Socrates and present in the prison on the day Socrates died, represented in the *Phaedo*.
5. Thucydides, *History of the Peloponnesian War* 6.27–29, discusses these events in the larger context of the Sicilian expedition.
6. The epigraphic evidence about Phaedrus and the mystery trial is preserved in *SEG* (*Supplementum epigraphicum graecum*) xiii.17.112; cf. Andocides, *De mysteriis* 1.15.
7. K. J. Dover, *Lysias and the Corpus Lysiacum* (Berkeley: University of California Press, 1968), 32–33, 41–42, 43, but Dover admits the possibility that Plato created an impossible situation for this dialogue.
8. V. 6–7, though De Vries himself thinks that Plato may have had no precise historical situation in mind. E. Asmis ("*Psychagogia* in Plato's *Phaedrus*," *Illinois Classical Studies* 11 [1986]: 153–72, esp. 166n15) suggests that Phaedrus's youth and beauty are just as lasting as Agathon's: Agathon accompanied Pausanias to

the gathering of sophists in the *Protagoras* and is described as "still a young lad" and "beautiful," and perhaps Pausanias's boyfriend (παιδικά). Agathon remains a handsome youth in the *Symposium*. See Dover's *Greek Homosexuality*.

9. C. M. Young ("Plato and Computer Dating," *Oxford Studies in Ancient Philosophy* 12 [1994]: 227–50) discusses recent books on stylometry and the chronology of Plato's dialogues. Young's table (p. 240) indicates the consensus among scholars using different criteria for the closeness in compositional date of the *Parmenides*, *Phaedrus*, and *Theaetetus* (scholars differ about the order of the dialogues within that group).

10. A. A. Long ("Plato's Apologies and Socrates in the *Theaetetus*," in *Method in Ancient Philosophy*, ed. J. Gentzler [Oxford: Clarendon, 1998], 113–36) calls attention to the progression in the *Parmenides*, *Phaedrus*, and *Theaetetus* and argues that the three dialogues present Plato's farewell to Socrates.

11. There is a scholarly question as to whether the Lysias speech was written by Lysias himself and incorporated by Plato into the *Phaedrus* or whether it is Plato's parody of Lysias. Dover, *Lysias and the Corpus Lysiacum*, 69–71, 90–93, 194, thinks that no technical criteria allow us to decide one way or the other.

12. For similarities in content and organization between Socrates' first speech and the speeches of Isocrates, see M. Brown and J. Coulter, "The Middle Speech of Plato's *Phaedrus*," *Journal of the History of Philosophy* 9 (1971): 405–23; and on style (with special attention to rhythm) see Asmis, "*Psychagogia* in Plato's *Phaedrus*," esp. 160–62.

13. Some scholars think that Socrates' nonlover is nobler than Lysias's. Yet, given that Socrates' nonlover presents a well-argued condemnation of the lover but misrepresents what love is, he is at least as unscrupulous as Lysias's nonlover and actually more cunning. That he strikes so many commentators as morally superior is a testimony to the success of his tactics. Cf. Asmis, "*Psychagogia* in Plato's *Phaedrus*," esp. 172.

14. In the interlude between his two speeches Socrates connects his upcoming speech with the lyric poet Stesichorus, who spoke disparagingly of Helen (the prime example of a woman abducted) and lost his sight, but then purified himself by writing a *Palinode* in which he rejected his false account and gave a different story about Helen's location during the Trojan War—whereupon he immediately regained his sight.

15. These three criteria were staples of rhetorical theory. From the fifth century, see *Protagoras* DK (= Diels and Kranz, *Die Fragmente der Vorsokratiker*) 80B3 and 80B10. They are also stated by Isocrates in his early work *Against the Sophists* 14–18, dated around 390 B.C.E.

16. See e.g. C. Griswold, *Self-Knowledge in Plato's* Phaedrus (New Haven, Conn.: Yale University Press, 1986), esp. 1–9, 138–56, 157–65; C. J. Rowe, "Argument and Structure of Plato's *Phaedrus*," *Proceedings of the Cambridge Philological Society* 32 (1986): 106–25; M. Heath, "The Unity of Plato's *Phaedrus*," *Oxford Studies in*

17. *Ancient Philosophy* 7 (1989): 151–73; and the exchange between Rowe and Heath in the 1989 issue of *Oxford Studies*. The proposal in this introduction shares most in common with Asmis, "*Psychagogia* in Plato's *Phaedrus*."

17. On this interpretation Lysias's speech cannot figure as part of Socrates' persuasive discourse, since Phaedrus reads it to Socrates, not Socrates to Phaedrus. Instead, the reading contributes to Socrates' diagnosis of Phaedrus's psychic malady— Phaedrus's beaming face while reading the speech is a symptom of his condition. At this stage of the discussion Socrates is more interested in Phaedrus's reaction to Lysias's poorly constructed speech than its contents.

18. The best evidence for the distinction between simple (well-integrated) souls and complex (poorly integrated) souls is Socrates' question early in the dialogue about his own soul (230a3–6).

19. See Isocrates, *To Demonicus* 3 and *Antidosis* 270–71. This topic is discussed by J. M. Cooper, "Plato, Isocrates, and Cicero on the Independence of Oratory from Philosophy," orig. 1986; repr. in Cooper's *Knowledge, Nature, and the Good* (Princeton: Princeton University Press, 2004), 65–80; and Nightingale, chap. 1. For authors who argue that Socrates' first speech parodies Isocrates, see n12 above.

20. Cf. Socrates' speech quoting the wise woman Diotima, who teaches him the secrets of love in the *Symposium* (esp. 209e5–211d1).

PLATO'S
PHAEDRUS

ΦΑΙΔΡΟΣ

ΣΩΚΡΑΤΗΣ ΦΑΙΔΡΟΣ

ΣΩ. Ὦ φίλε Φαῖδρε, ποῖ δὴ καὶ πόθεν; a

ΦΑΙ. Παρὰ Λυσίου, ὦ Σώκρατες, τοῦ Κεφάλου, πορεύ-
ομαι δὲ πρὸς περίπατον ἔξω τείχους· συχνὸν γὰρ ἐκεῖ
διέτριψα χρόνον καθήμενος ἐξ ἑωθινοῦ. τῷ δὲ σῷ καὶ
ἐμῷ ἑταίρῳ πειθόμενος Ἀκουμενῷ κατὰ τὰς ὁδοὺς ποιοῦμαι 5
τοὺς περιπάτους· φησὶ γὰρ ἀκοπωτέρους εἶναι τῶν ἐν τοῖς
δρόμοις. b

ΣΩ. Καλῶς γάρ, ὦ ἑταῖρε, λέγει. ἀτὰρ Λυσίας ἦν, ὡς
ἔοικεν, ἐν ἄστει.

ΦΑΙ. Ναί, παρ' Ἐπικράτει, ἐν τῇδε τῇ πλησίον τοῦ
Ὀλυμπίου οἰκίᾳ τῇ Μορυχίᾳ. 5

ΣΩ. Τίς οὖν δὴ ἦν ἡ διατριβή; ἢ δῆλον ὅτι τῶν λόγων
ὑμᾶς Λυσίας εἱστία;

ΦΑΙ. Πεύσῃ, εἴ σοι σχολὴ προϊόντι ἀκούειν.

ΣΩ. Τί δέ; οὐκ ἂν οἴει με κατὰ Πίνδαρον '' καὶ ἀσχολίας ὑπέρτερον '' πρᾶγμα ποιήσασθαι τὸ τεήν τε καὶ 10
Λυσίου διατριβὴν ἀκοῦσαι;

ΦΑΙ. Πρόαγε δή. c

ΣΩ. Λέγοις ἄν.

ΦΑΙ. Καὶ μήν, ὦ Σώκρατες, προσήκουσα γέ σοι ἡ ἀκοή·

a 5 ἀκουμένῳ Β Τ (cf. Symp. 176 b, 6)   b 6 οὖν δὴ Β : οὖν Τ
b 10 ποιήσασθαι Par. 1811 : ποιήσεσθαι Β Τ   τεήν G : σήν Β Τ

ὁ γάρ τοι λόγος ἦν, περὶ ὃν διετρίβομεν, οὐκ οἶδ' ὅντινα
5 τρόπον ἐρωτικός. γέγραφε γὰρ δὴ ὁ Λυσίας πειρώμενόν
τινα τῶν καλῶν, οὐχ ὑπ' ἐραστοῦ δέ, ἀλλ' αὐτὸ δὴ τοῦτο
καὶ κεκόμψευται· λέγει γὰρ ὡς χαριστέον μὴ ἐρῶντι μᾶλλον
ἢ ἐρῶντι.

ΣΩ. ᾺΩ γενναῖος. εἴθε γράψειεν ὡς χρὴ πένητι μᾶλ-
10 λον ἢ πλουσίῳ, καὶ πρεσβυτέρῳ ἢ νεωτέρῳ, καὶ ὅσα ἄλλα
d ἐμοί τε πρόσεστι καὶ τοῖς πολλοῖς ἡμῶν· ἢ γὰρ ἂν ἀστεῖοι
καὶ δημωφελεῖς εἶεν οἱ λόγοι. ἔγωγ' οὖν οὕτως ἐπιτεθύ-
μηκα ἀκοῦσαι, ὥστ' ἐὰν βαδίζων ποιῇ τὸν περίπατον Μέ-
γαράδε καὶ κατὰ Ἡρόδικον προσβὰς τῷ τείχει πάλιν ἀπίῃς,
5 οὐ μή σου ἀπολειφθῶ.

ΦΑΙ. Πῶς λέγεις, ὦ βέλτιστε Σώκρατες; οἴει με, ἃ
228 Λυσίας ἐν πολλῷ χρόνῳ κατὰ σχολὴν συνέθηκε, δεινότατος
ὢν τῶν νῦν γράφειν, ταῦτα ἰδιώτην ὄντα ἀπομνημονεύσειν
ἀξίως ἐκείνου; πολλοῦ γε δέω· καίτοι ἐβουλόμην γ' ἂν
μᾶλλον ἤ μοι πολὺ χρυσίον γενέσθαι.

5 ΣΩ. Ὦ Φαῖδρε, εἰ ἐγὼ Φαῖδρον ἀγνοῶ, καὶ ἐμαυτοῦ
ἐπιλέλησμαι. ἀλλὰ γὰρ οὐδέτερά ἐστι τούτων· εὖ οἶδα ὅτι
Λυσίου λόγον ἀκούων ἐκεῖνος οὐ μόνον ἅπαξ ἤκουσεν, ἀλλὰ
πολλάκις ἐπαναλαμβάνων ἐκέλευέν οἱ λέγειν, ὁ δὲ ἐπείθετο
b προθύμως. τῷ δὲ οὐδὲ ταῦτα ἦν ἱκανά, ἀλλὰ τελευτῶν
παραλαβὼν τὸ βιβλίον ἃ μάλιστα ἐπεθύμει ἐπεσκόπει, καὶ
τοῦτο δρῶν ἐξ ἑωθινοῦ καθήμενος ἀπειπὼν εἰς περίπατον
ᾔει, ὡς μὲν ἐγὼ οἶμαι, νὴ τὸν κύνα, ἐξεπιστάμενος τὸν
5 λόγον, εἰ μὴ πάνυ τι ἦν μακρός. ἐπορεύετο δ' ἐκτὸς τείχους ἵνα μελετῴη. ἀπαντήσας δὲ τῷ νοσοῦντι περὶ λόγων
ἀκοήν, ἰδὼν μέν, ἰδών, ἥσθη ὅτι ἕξοι τὸν συγκορυβαντιῶντα,
c καὶ προάγειν ἐκέλευε. δεομένου δὲ λέγειν τοῦ τῶν λόγων
ἐραστοῦ, ἐθρύπτετο ὡς δὴ οὐκ ἐπιθυμῶν λέγειν· τελευτῶν

c 9 ὃ W : ὃ T : ὃ B   a 4 πολὺ B : πολὺν T   a 6 εὖ B : εὖ
δ' T   b 5 πάνυ τι Schanz : πάνυ τις BT   b 6 τῷ] τῳ ci. Stephanus
b 7 ἰδὼν μὲν ἰδὼν BT : ἰδὼν μὲν ἰὼν G : ἰδὼν μὲν ἰόντα vulg. : alterum
ἰδὼν del. t Hermann : om. Schanz

δὲ ἔμελλε καὶ εἰ μή τις ἑκὼν ἀκούοι βίᾳ ἐρεῖν. σὺ οὖν,
ὦ Φαῖδρε, αὐτοῦ δεήθητι ὅπερ τάχα πάντως ποιήσει νῦν ἤδη
ποιεῖν.   5
ΦΑΙ. Ἐμοὶ ὡς ἀληθῶς πολὺ κράτιστόν ἐστιν οὕτως
ὅπως δύναμαι λέγειν, ὥς μοι δοκεῖς σὺ οὐδαμῶς με ἀφήσειν
πρὶν ἂν εἴπω ἀμῶς γέ πως.
ΣΩ. Πάνυ γάρ σοι ἀληθῆ δοκῶ.
ΦΑΙ. Οὑτωσὶ τοίνυν ποιήσω. τῷ ὄντι γάρ, ὦ Σώ- d
κρατες, παντὸς μᾶλλον τά γε ῥήματα οὐκ ἐξέμαθον· τὴν
μέντοι διάνοιαν σχεδὸν ἀπάντων, οἷς ἔφη διαφέρειν τὰ τοῦ
ἐρῶντος ἢ τὰ τοῦ μή, ἐν κεφαλαίοις ἕκαστον ἐφεξῆς δίειμι,
ἀρξάμενος ἀπὸ τοῦ πρώτου.   5
ΣΩ. Δείξας γε πρῶτον, ὦ φιλότης, τί ἄρα ἐν τῇ ἀρι-
στερᾷ ἔχεις ὑπὸ τῷ ἱματίῳ· τοπάζω γάρ σε ἔχειν τὸν λόγον
αὐτόν. εἰ δὲ τοῦτό ἐστιν, οὑτωσὶ διανοοῦ περὶ ἐμοῦ, ὡς
ἐγώ σε πάνυ μὲν φιλῶ, παρόντος δὲ καὶ Λυσίου, ἐμαυτόν σοι e
ἐμμελετᾶν παρέχειν οὐ πάνυ δέδοκται. ἀλλ' ἴθι, δείκνυε.
ΦΑΙ. Παῦε. ἐκκέκρουκάς με ἐλπίδος, ὦ Σώκρατες, ἣν
εἶχον ἐν σοὶ ὡς ἐγγυμνασόμενος. ἀλλὰ ποῦ δὴ βούλει
καθιζόμενοι ἀναγνῶμεν;   5
ΣΩ. Δεῦρ' ἐκτραπόμενοι κατὰ τὸν Ἰλισὸν ἴωμεν, εἶτα 229
ὅπου ἂν δόξῃ ἐν ἡσυχίᾳ καθιζησόμεθα.
ΦΑΙ. Εἰς καιρόν, ὡς ἔοικεν, ἀνυπόδητος ὢν ἔτυχον· σὺ
μὲν γὰρ δὴ ἀεί. ῥᾷστον οὖν ἡμῖν κατὰ τὸ ὑδάτιον βρέχουσι
τοὺς πόδας ἰέναι, καὶ οὐκ ἀηδές, ἄλλως τε καὶ τήνδε τὴν 5
ὥραν τοῦ ἔτους τε καὶ τῆς ἡμέρας.
ΣΩ. Πρόαγε δή, καὶ σκόπει ἅμα ὅπου καθιζησόμεθα.
ΦΑΙ. Ὁρᾷς οὖν ἐκείνην τὴν ὑψηλοτάτην πλάτανον;
ΣΩ. Τί μήν;

d 4 ἕκαστον TW : om. B   d 6 ἐν B : ὃ ἐν T   e 1 δὲ καὶ
λυσίου B : δὲ λυσίου T : δ' ἐκείνου Badham   e 2 δείκνυ Hirschig
e 5 καθιζόμενοι B T : καθεζόμενοι Vind. 89 Stallbaum   a 2 καθιζησόμεθα B T W Bekk. Anecd. i. 101 : καθιζώμεθα Stephanus

b   ΦΑΙ. Ἐκεῖ σκιά τ' ἐστὶν καὶ πνεῦμα μέτριον, καὶ πόα καθίζεσθαι ἢ ἂν βουλώμεθα κατακλινῆναι.

ΣΩ. Προάγοις ἄν.

ΦΑΙ. Εἰπέ μοι, ὦ Σώκρατες, οὐκ ἐνθένδε μέντοι ποθὲν
5 ἀπὸ τοῦ Ἰλισοῦ λέγεται ὁ Βορέας τὴν Ὠρείθυιαν ἁρπάσαι;

ΣΩ. Λέγεται γάρ.

ΦΑΙ. Ἆρ' οὖν ἐνθένδε; χαρίεντα γοῦν καὶ καθαρὰ καὶ διαφανῆ τὰ ὑδάτια φαίνεται, καὶ ἐπιτήδεια κόραις παίζειν παρ' αὐτά.

c   ΣΩ. Οὔκ, ἀλλὰ κάτωθεν ὅσον δύ' ἢ τρία στάδια, ᾗ πρὸς τὸ ἐν Ἄγρας διαβαίνομεν· καὶ πού τίς ἐστι βωμὸς αὐτόθι Βορέου.

ΦΑΙ. Οὐ πάνυ νενόηκα· ἀλλ' εἰπὲ πρὸς Διός, ὦ Σώ-
5 κρατες, σὺ τοῦτο τὸ μυθολόγημα πείθῃ ἀληθὲς εἶναι;

ΣΩ. Ἀλλ' εἰ ἀπιστοίην, ὥσπερ οἱ σοφοί, οὐκ ἂν ἄτοπος εἴην, εἶτα σοφιζόμενος φαίην αὐτὴν πνεῦμα Βορέου κατὰ τῶν πλησίον πετρῶν σὺν Φαρμακείᾳ παίζουσαν ὦσαι, καὶ οὕτω δὴ τελευτήσασαν λεχθῆναι ὑπὸ τοῦ Βορέου ἀνάρπαστον

d γεγονέναι—ἢ ἐξ Ἀρείου πάγου· λέγεται γὰρ αὖ καὶ οὗτος ὁ λόγος, ὡς ἐκεῖθεν ἀλλ' οὐκ ἐνθένδε ἡρπάσθη. ἐγὼ δέ, ὦ Φαῖδρε, ἄλλως μὲν τὰ τοιαῦτα χαρίεντα ἡγοῦμαι, λίαν δὲ δεινοῦ καὶ ἐπιπόνου καὶ οὐ πάνυ εὐτυχοῦς ἀνδρός, κατ' ἄλλο
5 μὲν οὐδέν, ὅτι δ' αὐτῷ ἀνάγκη μετὰ τοῦτο τὸ τῶν Ἱπποκεν- ταύρων εἶδος ἐπανορθοῦσθαι, καὶ αὖθις τὸ τῆς Χιμαίρας, καὶ ἐπιρρεῖ δὲ ὄχλος τοιούτων Γοργόνων καὶ Πηγάσων καὶ

e ἄλλων ἀμηχάνων πλήθη τε καὶ ἀτοπίαι τερατολόγων τινῶν φύσεων· αἷς εἴ τις ἀπιστῶν προσβιβᾷ κατὰ τὸ εἰκὸς ἕκαστον, ἅτε ἀγροίκῳ τινὶ σοφίᾳ χρώμενος, πολλῆς αὐτῷ σχολῆς δεήσει. ἐμοὶ δὲ πρὸς αὐτὰ οὐδαμῶς ἐστι σχολή· τὸ δὲ

b 2 ἢ ἂν] ἢ ἐὰν W : ἢ ἂν B : ἢ ἐὰν T   βουλώμεθα TW : βουλό- μεθα B   κατακλιθῆναι BTW   c 2 τὸ ἐν Ἄγρας scripsi (τὰ ἐν Ἄγρας Bratuscheck) : τὸ τῆς ἄγρας BTW : τὸ τῆς ἀγραίας rec. b Eustathius τίς T : τί B   c 7 (ἂν) αὐτὴν Ast   d 1 ἢ ἐξ... ἡρπάσθη secl. Bast   e 1 πλήθη... ἀτοπίαι BTW : πλήθει... ἀτοπίᾳ Athenaeus vulg.   θ 4 αὐτα BW : ταῦτα T

αἴτιον, ὦ φίλε, τούτου τόδε. οὐ δύναμαί πω κατὰ τὸ Δελ- 5
φικὸν γράμμα γνῶναι ἐμαυτόν· γελοῖον δή μοι φαίνεται
τοῦτο ἔτι ἀγνοοῦντα τὰ ἀλλότρια σκοπεῖν. ὅθεν δὴ χαίρειν 230
ἐάσας ταῦτα, πειθόμενος δὲ τῷ νομιζομένῳ περὶ αὐτῶν, ὃ
νυνδὴ ἔλεγον, σκοπῶ οὐ ταῦτα ἀλλ' ἐμαυτόν, εἴτε τι θηρίον
ὂν τυγχάνω Τυφῶνος πολυπλοκώτερον καὶ μᾶλλον ἐπιτεθυμμένον, εἴτε ἡμερώτερόν τε καὶ ἁπλούστερον ζῷον, θείας τινὸς 5
καὶ ἀτύφου μοίρας φύσει μετέχον. ἀτάρ, ὦ ἑταῖρε, μεταξὺ
τῶν λόγων, ἆρ' οὐ τόδε ἦν τὸ δένδρον ἐφ' ὅπερ ἦγες ἡμᾶς;
ΦΑΙ. Τοῦτο μὲν οὖν αὐτό.   b
ΣΩ. Νὴ τὴν Ἥραν, καλή γε ἡ καταγωγή. ἥ τε γὰρ
πλάτανος αὕτη μάλ' ἀμφιλαφής τε καὶ ὑψηλή, τοῦ τε ἄγνου
τὸ ὕψος καὶ τὸ σύσκιον πάγκαλον, καὶ ὡς ἀκμὴν ἔχει τῆς
ἄνθης, ὡς ἂν εὐωδέστατον παρέχοι τὸν τόπον· ἥ τε αὖ 5
πηγὴ χαριεστάτη ὑπὸ τῆς πλατάνου ῥεῖ μάλα ψυχροῦ ὕδατος,
ὥστε γε τῷ ποδὶ τεκμήρασθαι. Νυμφῶν τέ τινων καὶ Ἀχελῴου ἱερὸν ἀπὸ τῶν κορῶν τε καὶ ἀγαλμάτων ἔοικεν εἶναι.
εἰ δ' αὖ βούλει, τὸ εὔπνουν τοῦ τόπου ὡς ἀγαπητὸν καὶ   c
σφόδρα ἡδύ· θερινόν τε καὶ λιγυρὸν ὑπηχεῖ τῷ τῶν τεττίγων
χορῷ. πάντων δὲ κομψότατον τὸ τῆς πόας, ὅτι ἐν ἠρέμα
προσάντει ἱκανὴ πέφυκε κατακλινέντι τὴν κεφαλὴν παγκάλως
ἔχειν. ὥστε ἄριστά σοι ἐξενάγηται, ὦ φίλε Φαῖδρε.   5
ΦΑΙ. Σὺ δέ γε, ὦ θαυμάσιε, ἀτοπώτατός τις φαίνῃ.
ἀτεχνῶς γάρ, ὃ λέγεις, ξεναγουμένῳ τινὶ καὶ οὐκ ἐπιχωρίῳ
ἔοικας· οὕτως ἐκ τοῦ ἄστεος οὔτ' εἰς τὴν ὑπερορίαν ἀπο- d
δημεῖς, οὔτ' ἔξω τείχους ἔμοιγε δοκεῖς τὸ παράπαν ἐξιέναι.
ΣΩ. Συγγίγνωσκέ μοι, ὦ ἄριστε. φιλομαθὴς γάρ εἰμι·
τὰ μὲν οὖν χωρία καὶ τὰ δένδρα οὐδέν μ' ἐθέλει διδάσκειν,

e 6 δή B T W Proclus (in Alc. p. 289, 5) : δέ Vind. 80   a 4 ὂν
T W : om. B : ὢν vulg.   ἐπιτεθυμμένον B T W (sed μ prius in ras.
B) : ἔτι τεθυμμένον ci. Ruhnken   b 4 καὶ ὡς B T W : καὶ οὕτως ci.
Heindorf : καὶ Schanz   b 7 ὥστε γε B T W : ὥς γε Aristaenetus
vulg.   c 2 ἡδύ T W : ἤδη B   ὑπηχεῖ τῷ T W : ὑπηχεῖτο B
c 4 προσάντει T W : προσάντε B   c 6 σὺ W : οὐ B T

5 οἱ δ᾽ ἐν τῷ ἄστει ἄνθρωποι. σὺ μέντοι δοκεῖς μοι τῆς
ἐμῆς ἐξόδου τὸ φάρμακον ηὑρηκέναι. ὥσπερ γὰρ οἱ τὰ
πεινῶντα θρέμματα θαλλὸν ἤ τινα καρπὸν προσείοντες
ἄγουσιν, σὺ ἐμοὶ λόγους οὕτω προτείνων ἐν βιβλίοις τήν τε
e Ἀττικὴν φαίνῃ περιάξειν ἅπασαν καὶ ὅποι ἂν ἄλλοσε βούλῃ.
νῦν δ᾽ οὖν ἐν τῷ παρόντι δεῦρ᾽ ἀφικόμενος ἐγὼ μέν μοι
δοκῶ κατακείσεσθαι, σὺ δ᾽ ἐν ὁποίῳ σχήματι οἴει ῥᾷστα
ἀναγνώσεσθαι, τοῦθ᾽ ἑλόμενος ἀναγίγνωσκε.
5 ΦΑΙ. Ἄκουε δή.

Περὶ μὲν τῶν ἐμῶν πραγμάτων ἐπίστασαι, καὶ ὡς νομίζω
συμφέρειν ἡμῖν γενομένων τούτων ἀκήκοας· ἀξιῶ δὲ μὴ διὰ
231 τοῦτο ἀτυχῆσαι ὧν δέομαι, ὅτι οὐκ ἐραστὴς ὤν σου τυγχάνω. ὡς ἐκείνοις μὲν τότε μεταμέλει ὧν ἂν εὖ ποιήσωσιν,
ἐπειδὰν τῆς ἐπιθυμίας παύσωνται· τοῖς δὲ οὐκ ἔστι χρόνος
ἐν ᾧ μεταγνῶναι προσήκει. οὐ γὰρ ὑπ᾽ ἀνάγκης ἀλλ᾽
5 ἑκόντες, ὡς ἂν ἄριστα περὶ τῶν οἰκείων βουλεύσαιντο, πρὸς
τὴν δύναμιν τὴν αὑτῶν εὖ ποιοῦσιν. ἔτι δὲ οἱ μὲν ἐρῶντες
σκοποῦσιν ἅ τε κακῶς διέθεντο τῶν αὑτῶν διὰ τὸν ἔρωτα
καὶ ἃ πεποιήκασιν εὖ, καὶ ὃν εἶχον πόνον προστιθέντες
b ἡγοῦνται πάλαι τὴν ἀξίαν ἀποδεδωκέναι χάριν τοῖς ἐρω-
μένοις· τοῖς δὲ μὴ ἐρῶσιν οὔτε τὴν τῶν οἰκείων ἀμέλειαν
διὰ τοῦτο ἔστιν προφασίζεσθαι, οὔτε τοὺς παρεληλυθότας
πόνους ὑπολογίζεσθαι, οὔτε τὰς πρὸς τοὺς προσήκοντας
5 διαφορὰς αἰτιάσασθαι· ὥστε περιῃρημένων τοσούτων κακῶν
οὐδὲν ὑπολείπεται ἀλλ᾽ ἢ ποιεῖν προθύμως ὅτι ἂν αὐτοῖς
οἴωνται πράξαντες χαριεῖσθαι. ἔτι δὲ εἰ διὰ τοῦτο ἄξιον
c τοὺς ἐρῶντας περὶ πολλοῦ ποιεῖσθαι, ὅτι τούτους μάλιστά
φασιν φιλεῖν ὧν ἂν ἐρῶσιν, καὶ ἕτοιμοί εἰσι καὶ ἐκ τῶν λόγων

d 5 σὺ recc. : οὐ B : οὖ T   δοκεῖς T : δοκεῖ B   d 6 ἐμῆς T W :
om. B   d 7 προσείοντες t recc. : προσιόντες B T W   e 2 δ᾽ οὖν
T : οὖν B   e 3 κατακείσεσθαι T : κατακεῖσθαι (sic) B   e 7 γενομένων τούτων B : τούτων γενομένων T   a 2 μεταμέλει ὧν T :
μεταμελειῶν B   b 5 αἰτιάσασθαι] αἰτιᾶσθαι Cobet   c 1 τοὺς
T : τοῦ pr. B   c 2 ἕτοιμοί εἰσι καὶ T W et in marg. b : om. B

καὶ ἐκ τῶν ἔργων τοῖς ἄλλοις ἀπεχθανόμενοι τοῖς ἐρωμένοις
χαρίζεσθαι, ῥᾴδιον γνῶναι, εἰ ἀληθῆ λέγουσιν, ὅτι ὅσων ἂν
ὕστερον ἐρασθῶσιν, ἐκείνους αὐτῶν περὶ πλείονος ποιήσονται, 5
καὶ δῆλον ὅτι, ἐὰν ἐκείνοις δοκῇ, καὶ τούτους κακῶς ποιή-
σουσιν. καίτοι πῶς εἰκός ἐστι τοιοῦτον πρᾶγμα προέσθαι
τοιαύτην ἔχοντι συμφοράν, ἣν οὐδ' ἂν ἐπιχειρήσειεν οὐδεὶς d
ἔμπειρος ὢν ἀποτρέπειν; καὶ γὰρ αὐτοὶ ὁμολογοῦσι νοσεῖν
μᾶλλον ἢ σωφρονεῖν, καὶ εἰδέναι ὅτι κακῶς φρονοῦσιν, ἀλλ'
οὐ δύνασθαι αὑτῶν κρατεῖν· ὥστε πῶς ἂν εὖ φρονήσαντες
ταῦτα καλῶς ἔχειν ἡγήσαιντο περὶ ὧν οὕτω διακείμενοι 5
βουλεύονται; καὶ μὲν δὴ εἰ μὲν ἐκ τῶν ἐρώντων τὸν βέλτιστον αἱροῖο, ἐξ ὀλίγων ἄν σοι ἡ ἔκλεξις εἴη· εἰ δ' ἐκ τῶν
ἄλλων τὸν σαυτῷ ἐπιτηδειότατον, ἐκ πολλῶν· ὥστε πολὺ
πλείων ἐλπὶς ἐν τοῖς πολλοῖς ὄντα τυχεῖν τὸν ἄξιον τῆς σῆς e
φιλίας.

Εἰ τοίνυν τὸν νόμον τὸν καθεστηκότα δέδοικας, μὴ
πυθομένων τῶν ἀνθρώπων ὄνειδός σοι γένηται, εἰκός ἐστι
τοὺς μὲν ἐρῶντας, οὕτως ἂν οἰομένους καὶ ὑπὸ τῶν ἄλλων 232
ζηλοῦσθαι ὥσπερ αὐτοὺς ὑφ' αὑτῶν, ἐπαρθῆναι τῷ λέγειν
καὶ φιλοτιμουμένους ἐπιδείκνυσθαι πρὸς ἅπαντας ὅτι οὐκ
ἄλλως αὐτοῖς πεπόνηται· τοὺς δὲ μὴ ἐρῶντας, κρείττους
αὑτῶν ὄντας, τὸ βέλτιστον ἀντὶ τῆς δόξης τῆς παρὰ τῶν 5
ἀνθρώπων αἱρεῖσθαι. ἔτι δὲ τοὺς μὲν ἐρῶντας πολλοὺς
ἀνάγκη πυθέσθαι καὶ ἰδεῖν ἀκολουθοῦντας τοῖς ἐρωμένοις
καὶ ἔργον τοῦτο ποιουμένους, ὥστε ὅταν ὀφθῶσι διαλεγόμενοι ἀλλήλοις, τότε αὐτοὺς οἴονται ἢ γεγενημένης ἢ μελ- b
λούσης ἔσεσθαι τῆς ἐπιθυμίας συνεῖναι· τοὺς δὲ μὴ ἐρῶντας
οὐδ' αἰτιᾶσθαι διὰ τὴν συνουσίαν ἐπιχειροῦσιν, εἰδότες ὅτι
ἀναγκαῖόν ἐστιν ἢ διὰ φιλίαν τῳ διαλέγεσθαι ἢ δι' ἄλλην

c 4 ὅτι ὅσων T W : ὁπόσον B : οἵ γ' ὅσων Hermann   c 5 ποιήσονται
B : ποιήσωνται T   d 5 οὕτω rec. b : οὗτοι B T   d 6 βουλεύονται
Stephanus : βούλονται B T W : βεβούλευνται Heindorf   d 7 αἱροῖο
T : αἱροῖτο B   a 2 τῷ λέγειν B T : τῳ λέγειν t : τὸ λέγειν D :
τῷ ἔχειν Badham : alii alia   a 3 οὐκ ἄλλως T W : οὐ καλῶς B
a 5 ἀντὶ T : ἂν B   b 4 τῳ b t : τῷ B T

5 τινὰ ἡδονήν. καὶ μὲν δὴ εἴ σοι δέος παρέστηκεν ἡγουμένῳ
χαλεπὸν εἶναι φιλίαν συμμένειν, καὶ ἄλλῳ μὲν τρόπῳ διαφορᾶς γενυμένης κοινὴν ⟨ἂν⟩ ἀμφοτέροις καταστῆναι τὴν
c συμφοράν, προεμένου δέ σου ἃ περὶ πλείστου ποιῇ μεγάλην
ἄν σοι βλάβην ἂν γενέσθαι, εἰκότως ἂν τοὺς ἐρῶντας μᾶλλον ἂν φοβοῖο· πολλὰ γὰρ αὐτούς ἐστι τὰ λυποῦντα, καὶ
πάντ' ἐπὶ τῇ αὐτῶν βλάβῃ νομίζουσι γίγνεσθαι. διόπερ
5 καὶ τὰς πρὸς τοὺς ἄλλους τῶν ἐρωμένων συνουσίας ἀποτρέπουσιν, φοβούμενοι τοὺς μὲν οὐσίαν κεκτημένους μὴ χρή-
μασιν αὐτοὺς ὑπερβάλωνται, τοὺς δὲ πεπαιδευμένους μὴ
συνέσει κρείττους γένωνται· τῶν δὲ ἄλλο τι κεκτημένων
d ἀγαθὸν τὴν δύναμιν ἑκάστου φυλάττονται. πείσαντες μὲν
οὖν ἀπεχθέσθαι σε τούτοις εἰς ἐρημίαν φίλων καθιστᾶσιν,
ἐὰν δὲ τὸ σεαυτοῦ σκοπῶν ἄμεινον ἐκείνων φρονῇς, ἥξεις
αὐτοῖς εἰς διαφοράν· ὅσοι δὲ μὴ ἐρῶντες ἔτυχον, ἀλλὰ δι'
5 ἀρετὴν ἔπραξαν ὧν ἐδέοντο, οὐκ ἂν τοῖς συνοῦσι φθονοῖεν,
ἀλλὰ τοὺς μὴ ἐθέλοντας μισοῖεν, ἡγούμενοι ὑπ' ἐκείνων μὲν
ὑπερορᾶσθαι, ὑπὸ τῶν συνόντων δὲ ὠφελεῖσθαι, ὥστε πολὺ
e πλείων ἐλπὶς φιλίαν αὐτοῖς ἐκ τοῦ πράγματος ἢ ἔχθραν
γενέσθαι.

Καὶ μὲν δὴ τῶν μὲν ἐρώντων πολλοὶ πρότερον τοῦ σώματος ἐπεθύμησαν ἢ τὸν τρόπον ἔγνωσαν καὶ τῶν ἄλλων
5 οἰκείων ἔμπειροι ἐγένοντο, ὥστε ἄδηλον αὐτοῖς εἰ ἔτι τότε
βουλήσονται φίλοι εἶναι, ἐπειδὰν τῆς ἐπιθυμίας παύσωνται·
233 τοῖς δὲ μὴ ἐρῶσιν, οἳ καὶ πρότερον ἀλλήλοις φίλοι ὄντες
ταῦτα ἔπραξαν, οὐκ ἐξ ὧν ἂν εὖ πάθωσι ταῦτα εἰκὸς ἐλάττω
τὴν φιλίαν αὐτοῖς ποιῆσαι, ἀλλὰ ταῦτα μνημεῖα καταλει-

b 8 ἂν add. Hirschig   c 2 ἄν σοι BT : δή σοι Schanz   ἂν
γενέσθαι B : γενέσθαι T   εἰκότως ἂν BT : εἰκότως δὴ Schanz
μᾶλλον ἂν B : μᾶλλον T   c 5 τὰς BTW : τῆς corr. Ven. 184 ·   τῶν
ἐρωμένων] τὸν ἐρώμενον Heindorf   d 2 ἀπεχθέσθαι . . . τούτοις]
ἀπέχθεσθαι . . . τούτοις BTW : ἀπέχεσθαι . . . τούτοις vulg. : ἀπέχεσθαι
. . . τούτων al. Stallbaum   d 6 ὑπ'] σ' ὑπ' Schanz auctore Heindorf
e 2 γενέσθαι T : γενήσεσθαι B   e 5 αὐτοῖς εἰ ἔτι B : εἰ ἔτι αὐτοῖς T :
εἰ ἔτι Hermann   τότε T : om. B   a 3 μνημεῖα] σημεῖα ci.
Heindorf

φθῆναι τῶν μελλόντων ἔσεσθαι. καὶ μὲν δὴ βελτίονί σοι
προσήκει γενέσθαι ἐμοὶ πειθομένῳ ἢ ἐραστῇ. ἐκεῖνοι μὲν 5
γὰρ καὶ παρὰ τὸ βέλτιστον τά τε λεγόμενα καὶ τὰ πραττόμενα ἐπαινοῦσιν, τὰ μὲν δεδιότες μὴ ἀπέχθωνται, τὰ δὲ
καὶ αὐτοὶ χεῖρον διὰ τὴν ἐπιθυμίαν γιγνώσκοντες. τοιαῦτα b
γὰρ ὁ ἔρως ἐπιδείκνυται· δυστυχοῦντας μέν, ἃ μὴ λύπην
τοῖς ἄλλοις παρέχει, ἀνιαρὰ ποιεῖ νομίζειν· εὐτυχοῦντας δὲ
καὶ τὰ μὴ ἡδονῆς ἄξια παρ᾽ ἐκείνων ἐπαίνου ἀναγκάζει
τυγχάνειν· ὥστε πολὺ μᾶλλον ἐλεεῖν τοῖς ἐρωμένοις ἢ 5
ζηλοῦν αὐτοὺς προσήκει. ἐὰν δέ μοι πείθῃ, πρῶτον μὲν οὐ
τὴν παροῦσαν ἡδονὴν θεραπεύων συνέσομαί σοι, ἀλλὰ καὶ
τὴν μέλλουσαν ὠφελίαν ἔσεσθαι, οὐχ ὑπ᾽ ἔρωτος ἡττώμενος c
ἀλλ᾽ ἐμαυτοῦ κρατῶν, οὐδὲ διὰ σμικρὰ ἰσχυρὰν ἔχθραν ἀναιρούμενος ἀλλὰ διὰ μεγάλα βραδέως ὀλίγην ὀργὴν ποιούμενος, τῶν μὲν ἀκουσίων συγγνώμην ἔχων, τὰ δὲ ἑκούσια
πειρώμενος ἀποτρέπειν· ταῦτα γάρ ἐστι φιλίας πολὺν χρό- 5
νον ἐσομένης τεκμήρια. εἰ δ᾽ ἄρα σοι τοῦτο παρέστηκεν, ὡς
οὐχ οἷόν τε ἰσχυρὰν φιλίαν γενέσθαι ἐὰν μή τις ἐρῶν τυγχάνῃ,
ἐνθυμεῖσθαι χρὴ ὅτι οὔτ᾽ ἂν τοὺς ὑεῖς περὶ πολλοῦ ἐποιού- d
μεθα οὔτ᾽ ἂν τοὺς πατέρας καὶ τὰς μητέρας, οὔτ᾽ ἂν πιστοὺς
φίλους ἐκεκτήμεθα, οἳ οὐκ ἐξ ἐπιθυμίας τοιαύτης γεγόνασιν·
ἀλλ᾽ ἐξ ἑτέρων ἐπιτηδευμάτων.

Ἔτι δὲ εἰ χρὴ τοῖς δεομένοις μάλιστα χαρίζεσθαι, 5
προσήκει καὶ τοῖς ἄλλοις μὴ τοὺς βελτίστους ἀλλὰ τοὺς
ἀπορωτάτους εὖ ποιεῖν· μεγίστων γὰρ ἀπαλλαγέντες κακῶν
πλείστην χάριν αὐτοῖς εἴσονται. καὶ μὲν δὴ καὶ ἐν ταῖς
ἰδίαις δαπάναις οὐ τοὺς φίλους ἄξιον παρακαλεῖν, ἀλλὰ e
τοὺς προσαιτοῦντας καὶ τοὺς δεομένους πλησμονῆς· ἐκεῖνοι
γὰρ καὶ ἀγαπήσουσιν καὶ ἀκολουθήσουσιν καὶ ἐπὶ τὰς θύρας
ἥξουσι καὶ μάλιστα ἡσθήσονται καὶ οὐκ ἐλαχίστην χάριν

b 5 τοῖς ἐρωμένοις BT Stobaeus : τοὺς ἐρωμένους vulg. b 6 αὐτοὺς B Stobaeus : αὐτοῖς T δέ μοι BT : δ᾽ ἐμοὶ Ven. 184 d 6 καὶ
τοῖς ἄλλοις BT : καὶ τῶν ἄλλων Aldina : κἂν τοῖς ἄλλοις Badham
e 2 προσαιτοῦντας BT : προσαιροῦντας G

5 εἴσονται καὶ πολλὰ ἀγαθὰ αὐτοῖς εὔξονται. ἀλλ' ἴσως
προσήκει οὐ τοῖς σφόδρα δεομένοις χαρίζεσθαι, ἀλλὰ τοῖς
μάλιστα ἀποδοῦναι χάριν δυναμένοις· οὐδὲ τοῖς προσαιτοῦσι
234 μόνον, ἀλλὰ τοῖς τοῦ πράγματος ἀξίοις· οὐδὲ ὅσοι τῆς σῆς
ὥρας ἀπολαύσονται, ἀλλ' οἵτινες πρεσβυτέρῳ γενομένῳ τῶν
σφετέρων ἀγαθῶν μεταδώσουσιν· οὐδὲ οἱ διαπραξάμενοι
πρὸς τοὺς ἄλλους φιλοτιμήσονται, ἀλλ' οἵτινες αἰσχυνό-
5 μενοι πρὸς ἅπαντας σιωπήσονται· οὐδὲ τοῖς ὀλίγον χρόνον
σπουδάζουσιν, ἀλλὰ τοῖς ὁμοίως διὰ παντὸς τοῦ βίου φίλοις
ἐσομένοις· οὐδὲ οἵτινες παυόμενοι τῆς ἐπιθυμίας ἔχθρας
πρόφασιν ζητήσουσιν, ἀλλ' οἱ παυσαμένου τῆς ὥρας τότε
b τὴν αὑτῶν ἀρετὴν ἐπιδείξονται. σὺ οὖν τῶν τε εἰρημένων
μέμνησο καὶ ἐκεῖνο ἐνθυμοῦ, ὅτι τοὺς μὲν ἐρῶντας οἱ φίλοι
νουθετοῦσιν ὡς ὄντος κακοῦ τοῦ ἐπιτηδεύματος, τοῖς δὲ μὴ
ἐρῶσιν οὐδεὶς πώποτε τῶν οἰκείων ἐμέμψατο ὡς διὰ τοῦτο
5 κακῶς βουλευομένοις περὶ ἑαυτῶν.

Ἴσως ἂν οὖν ἔροιό με εἰ ἅπασίν σοι παραινῶ τοῖς μὴ
ἐρῶσι χαρίζεσθαι. ἐγὼ μὲν οἶμαι οὐδ' ἂν τὸν ἐρῶντα
πρὸς ἅπαντάς σε κελεύειν τοὺς ἐρῶντας ταύτην ἔχειν τὴν
c διάνοιαν. οὔτε γὰρ τῷ λαμβάνοντι χάριτος ἴσης ἄξιον,
οὔτε σοὶ βουλομένῳ τοὺς ἄλλους λανθάνειν ὁμοίως δυνατόν·
δεῖ δὲ βλάβην μὲν ἀπ' αὐτοῦ μηδεμίαν, ὠφελίαν δὲ ἀμφοῖν
γίγνεσθαι. ἐγὼ μὲν οὖν ἱκανά μοι νομίζω τὰ εἰρημένα·
5 εἰ δ' ἔτι ⟨τι⟩ σὺ ποθεῖς, ἡγούμενος παραλελεῖφθαι, ἐρώτα.

ΦΑΙ. Τί σοι φαίνεται, ὦ Σώκρατες, ὁ λόγος; οὐχ
ὑπερφυῶς τά τε ἄλλα καὶ τοῖς ὀνόμασιν εἰρῆσθαι;

e 8 προσαιτοῦσι Ast : προσερῶσι B : ἐρῶσι T W   a 2 γενομένῳ T :
γενόμενοι B   a 6 σπουδάζουσιν] σπουδάσουσιν ci. Stephanus (colent
Ficinus)   a 8 παυσαμένου G. Hermann : παυσάμενοι BT : παυομένης
Laur. 2643 : παυσαμένοις Winckelmann : alii alia   b 6 ἂν οὖν T :
μὲν οὖν B   b 7 μὲν T : δὲ B   c 1 τῷ T : τῷ λόγῳ BW   ἴσης
T : οισης (sic) B : οἴσεις W   c 3 δεῖ T : αἰεὶ B   ἀπ' B : ἐπ' T
c 5 δ' ἔτι τι Heindorf : δέ τι BT   σὺ ποθεῖς Ven. 189 : σὺ ὑποθεις
T : σὺ ὑποθῇς B   ἐρώτα T : ἔρωτα B

ΣΩ. Δαιμονίως μὲν οὖν, ὦ ἑταῖρε, ὥστε με ἐκπλαγῆναι. d
καὶ τοῦτο ἐγὼ ἔπαθον διὰ σέ, ὦ Φαῖδρε, πρὸς σὲ ἀποβλέπων, ὅτι ἐμοὶ ἐδόκεις γάνυσθαι ὑπὸ τοῦ λόγου μεταξὺ
ἀναγιγνώσκων· ἡγούμενος γὰρ σὲ μᾶλλον ἢ ἐμὲ ἐπαΐειν
περὶ τῶν τοιούτων σοὶ εἱπόμην, καὶ ἑπόμενος συνεβάκχευσα 5
μετὰ σοῦ τῆς θείας κεφαλῆς.

ΦΑΙ. Εἶεν· οὕτω δὴ δοκεῖ παίζειν;

ΣΩ. Δοκῶ γάρ σοι παίζειν καὶ οὐχὶ ἐσπουδακέναι;

ΦΑΙ. Μηδαμῶς, ὦ Σώκρατες, ἀλλ' ὡς ἀληθῶς εἰπὲ e
πρὸς Διὸς φιλίου, οἴει ἄν τινα ἔχειν εἰπεῖν ἄλλον τῶν
Ἑλλήνων ἕτερα τούτων μείζω καὶ πλείω περὶ τοῦ αὐτοῦ
πράγματος;

ΣΩ. Τί δέ; καὶ ταύτῃ δεῖ ὑπ' ἐμοῦ τε καὶ σοῦ τὸν 5
λόγον ἐπαινεθῆναι, ὡς τὰ δέοντα εἰρηκότος τοῦ ποιητοῦ,
ἀλλ' οὐκ ἐκείνῃ μόνον, ὅτι σαφῆ καὶ στρογγύλα, καὶ ἀκριβῶς ἕκαστα τῶν ὀνομάτων ἀποτετόρνευται; εἰ γὰρ δεῖ,
συγχωρητέον χάριν σήν, ἐπεὶ ἐμέ γε ἔλαθεν ὑπὸ τῆς ἐμῆς
οὐδενίας· τῷ γὰρ ῥητορικῷ αὐτοῦ μόνῳ τὸν νοῦν προσ- 235
εἶχον, τοῦτο δὲ οὐδ' ⟨ἂν⟩ αὐτὸν ᾤμην Λυσίαν οἴεσθαι ἱκανὸν
εἶναι. καὶ οὖν μοι ἔδοξεν, ὦ Φαῖδρε, εἰ μή τι σὺ ἄλλο
λέγεις, δὶς καὶ τρὶς τὰ αὐτὰ εἰρηκέναι, ὡς οὐ πάνυ εὐπορῶν
τοῦ πολλὰ λέγειν περὶ τοῦ αὐτοῦ, ἢ ἴσως οὐδὲν αὐτῷ μέλον 5
τοῦ τοιούτου· καὶ ἐφαίνετο δή μοι νεανιεύεσθαι ἐπιδεικνύμενος ὡς οἷός τε ὢν ταὐτὰ ἑτέρως τε καὶ ἑτέρως λέγων
ἀμφοτέρως εἰπεῖν ἄριστα.

ΦΑΙ. Οὐδὲν λέγεις, ὦ Σώκρατες· αὐτὸ γὰρ τοῦτο καὶ b
μάλιστα ὁ λόγος ἔχει. τῶν γὰρ ἐνόντων ἀξίως ῥηθῆναι

d 3 ἐδόκεις Τ: δοκεῖς Β   d 7 δὴ δοκεῖ Τ W: δὴ Β : δεῖ Schanz
e 3 τούτων μείζω Β : μείζω τούτων Τ   e 7 καὶ ἀκριβῶς fort. non
legerunt Plutarchus Hermias   e 8 ἀποτετόρνευται Β : ἀποτετόρνωται
Τ   a 1 μόνῳ Β Τ: μόνον W   a 2 ἂν ante αὐτὸν addidi : ante
ᾤμην add. Thompson: post οἴεσθαι add. Ast   a 3 καὶ οὖν Hermann : καὶ δὴ οὖν Stephanus: δικαιοῦν Β: δίκαιον οὖν Τ W   a 4 λέγεις
Τ: λέγῃς Β   a 7 ταὐτὰ Heindorf: ταῦτα Β Τ   b 2 ἀξίως]
ἀξίων Madvig

ἐν τῷ πράγματι οὐδὲν παραλέλοιπεν, ὥστε παρὰ τὰ ἐκείνῳ
εἰρημένα μηδέν' (ἂν) ποτε δύνασθαι εἰπεῖν ἄλλα πλείω καὶ
5 πλείονος ἄξια.

ΣΩ. Τοῦτο ἐγώ σοι οὐκέτι οἷός τ' ἔσομαι πιθέσθαι·
παλαιοὶ γὰρ καὶ σοφοὶ ἄνδρες τε καὶ γυναῖκες περὶ αὐτῶν
εἰρηκότες καὶ γεγραφότες ἐξελέγξουσί με, ἐάν σοι χαριζόμενος συγχωρῶ.

c ΦΑΙ. Τίνες οὗτοι; καὶ ποῦ σὺ βελτίω τούτων ἀκήκοας;

ΣΩ. Νῦν μὲν οὕτως οὐκ ἔχω εἰπεῖν· δῆλον δὲ ὅτι τινῶν
ἀκήκοα, ἤ που Σαπφοῦς τῆς καλῆς ἢ Ἀνακρέοντος τοῦ
σοφοῦ ἢ καὶ συγγραφέων τινῶν.   πόθεν δὴ τεκμαιρόμενος
5 λέγω; πλῆρές πως, ὦ δαιμόνιε, τὸ στῆθος ἔχων αἰσθάνομαι
παρὰ ταῦτα ἂν ἔχειν εἰπεῖν ἕτερα μὴ χείρω.   ὅτι μὲν οὖν
παρά γε ἐμαυτοῦ οὐδὲν αὐτῶν ἐννενόηκα, εὖ οἶδα, συνειδὼς
ἐμαυτῷ ἀμαθίαν· λείπεται δὴ οἶμαι ἐξ ἀλλοτρίων ποθὲν
d ναμάτων διὰ τῆς ἀκοῆς πεπληρῶσθαί με δίκην ἀγγείου.
ὑπὸ δὲ νωθείας αὖ καὶ αὐτὸ τοῦτο ἐπιλέλησμαι, ὅπως τε
καὶ ὧντινων ἤκουσα.

ΦΑΙ. Ἀλλ', ὦ γενναιότατε, κάλλιστα εἴρηκας.   σὺ γὰρ
5 ἐμοὶ ὧντινων μὲν καὶ ὅπως ἤκουσας μηδ' ἂν κελεύω εἴπῃς,
τοῦτο δὲ αὐτὸ ὃ λέγεις ποίησον· τῶν ἐν τῷ βιβλίῳ βελτίω
τε καὶ μὴ ἐλάττω ἕτερα ὑπέσχησαι εἰπεῖν τούτων ἀπεχόμενος, καί σοι ἐγώ, ὥσπερ οἱ ἐννέα ἄρχοντες, ὑπισχνοῦμαι
χρυσῆν εἰκόνα ἰσομέτρητον εἰς Δελφοὺς ἀναθήσειν, οὐ
e μόνον ἐμαυτοῦ ἀλλὰ καὶ σήν.

ΣΩ. Φίλτατος εἶ καὶ ὡς ἀληθῶς χρυσοῦς, ὦ Φαῖδρε,
εἴ με οἴει λέγειν ὡς Λυσίας τοῦ παντὸς ἡμάρτηκεν, καὶ οἷόν
τε δὴ παρὰ πάντα ταῦτα ἄλλα εἰπεῖν· τοῦτο δὲ οἶμαι οὐδ'
5 ἂν τὸν φαυλότατον παθεῖν συγγραφέα.   αὐτίκα περὶ οὗ
ὁ λόγος, τίνα οἴει λέγοντα ὡς χρὴ μὴ ἐρῶντι μᾶλλον ἢ

b 4 μηδέν' ἂν Aldina : μηδένα ΒΤ (μηδ' ἂν marg. t)   b 6 τ' Β :
γε Τ   πιθέσθαι Β : πείθεσθαι Τ   c 5 πως] περ Aldina   d 7 ἕτερα
ὑπέσχησαι scripsi : ἕτερα ὑπόσχες Badham (secl. εἰπεῖν): ἑτέρᾳ ὑποσχέσει
ΒΤ : ἕτερα ἐπιχείρει Schanz : alii alia   e 4 πάντα ταῦτα Β : ταῦτα
πάντα Τ : ταῦτα G   e 6 τίνα ΒΤ : τί vulg.

ἐρῶντι χαρίζεσθαι, παρέντα τοῦ μὲν τὸ φρόνιμον ἐγκω-
μιάζειν, τοῦ δὲ τὸ ἄφρον ψέγειν, ἀναγκαῖα γοῦν ὄντα, εἶτ' **236**
ἀλλ' ἄττα ἕξειν λέγειν; ἀλλ' οἶμαι τὰ μὲν τοιαῦτα ἐατέα
καὶ συγγνωστέα λέγοντι· καὶ τῶν μὲν τοιούτων οὐ τὴν
εὕρεσιν ἀλλὰ τὴν διάθεσιν ἐπαινετέον, τῶν δὲ μὴ ἀναγκαίων τε καὶ χαλεπῶν εὑρεῖν πρὸς τῇ διαθέσει καὶ τὴν 5
εὕρεσιν.

ΦΑΙ. Συγχωρῶ ὃ λέγεις· μετρίως γάρ μοι δοκεῖς εἰρηκέναι. ποιήσω οὖν καὶ ἐγὼ οὕτως· τὸ μὲν τὸν ἐρῶντα
τοῦ μὴ ἐρῶντος μᾶλλον νοσεῖν δώσω σοι ὑποτίθεσθαι, τῶν **b**
δὲ λοιπῶν ἕτερα πλείω καὶ πλείονος ἄξια εἰπὼν τῶνδε
[Λυσίου] παρὰ τὸ Κυψελιδῶν ἀνάθημα σφυρήλατος ἐν
Ὀλυμπίᾳ στάθητι.

ΣΩ. Ἐσπούδακας, ὦ Φαῖδρε, ὅτι σου τῶν παιδικῶν 5
ἐπελαβόμην ἐρεσχηλῶν σε, καὶ οἴει δή με ὡς ἀληθῶς ἐπι-
χειρήσειν εἰπεῖν παρὰ τὴν ἐκείνου σοφίαν ἕτερόν τι ποικιλώτερον;

ΦΑΙ. Περὶ μὲν τούτου, ὦ φίλε, εἰς τὰς ὁμοίας λαβὰς
ἐλήλυθας. ῥητέον μὲν γάρ σοι παντὸς μᾶλλον οὕτως ὅπως **c**
οἷός τε εἶ, ἵνα μὴ τὸ τῶν κωμῳδῶν φορτικὸν πρᾶγμα
ἀναγκαζώμεθα ποιεῖν ἀνταποδιδόντες ἀλλήλοις [εὐλαβήθητι],
καὶ μὴ βούλου με ἀναγκάσαι λέγειν ἐκεῖνο τὸ " εἰ ἐγώ, ὦ
Σώκρατες, Σωκράτην ἀγνοῶ, καὶ ἐμαυτοῦ ἐπιλέλη- 5
σμαι," καὶ ὅτι " ἐπεθύμε μὲν λέγειν, ἐθρύπτετο δέ·"
ἀλλὰ διανοήθητι ὅτι ἐντεῦθεν οὐκ ἄπιμεν πρὶν ἂν σὺ εἴπῃς
ἃ ἔφησθα ἐν τῷ στήθει ἔχειν. ἐσμὲν δὲ μόνω ἐν ἐρημίᾳ,
ἰσχυρότερος δ' ἐγὼ καὶ νεώτερος, ἐκ δὲ ἁπάντων τούτων **d**
" σύνες ὅ τοι λέγω," καὶ μηδαμῶς πρὸς βίαν βουληθῇς
μᾶλλον ἢ ἑκὼν λέγειν.

---

b2 εἰπὼν τῶνδε Τ W : εἰπόντος Β : εἰπὼν τῶν τοῦ fecit t   b3 Λυσίου
seclusi   b4 στάθητι Β Τ : ἐστάθη Photius : ἔσταθι Cobet   c 1 ἐλήλυθας Τ : ἐλήλυθα Β   c 2 ἵνα Β : ἵνα δὲ Τ   c 3 ἀναγκαζώμεθα
Β : ἀναγκαζόμεθα Τ   εὐλαβήθητι secl. Cobet   c 7 διανοήθητι Τ :
διανοήθητε Β   c 8 μόνω Β W : μόνω μὲν Τ   d 2 ὅ τοι] ὅ σοι
hoc loco Β Τ (at cf. Menon. 76 d)   βίαν Τ : βίας Β W

ΣΩ. Ἀλλ', ὦ μακάριε Φαῖδρε, γελοῖος ἔσομαι παρ'
5 ἀγαθὸν ποιητὴν ἰδιώτης αὐτοσχεδιάζων περὶ τῶν αὐτῶν.

ΦΑΙ. Οἶσθ' ὡς ἔχει; παῦσαι πρός με καλλωπιζόμενος·
σχεδὸν γὰρ ἔχω ὃ εἰπὼν ἀναγκάσω σε λέγειν.

ΣΩ. Μηδαμῶς τοίνυν εἴπῃς.

ΦΑΙ. Οὔκ, ἀλλὰ καὶ δὴ λέγω· ὁ δέ μοι λόγος ὅρκος
10 ἔσται. ὄμνυμι γάρ σοι—τίνα μέντοι, τίνα θεῶν; ἢ βού-
e λει τὴν πλάτανον ταυτηνί;—ἦ μήν, ἐάν μοι μὴ εἴπῃς τὸν
λόγον ἐναντίον αὐτῆς ταύτης, μηδέποτέ σοι ἕτερον λόγον
μηδένα μηδενὸς μήτε ἐπιδείξειν μήτε ἐξαγγελεῖν.

ΣΩ. Βαβαῖ, ὦ μιαρέ, ὡς εὖ ἀνηῦρες τὴν ἀνάγκην ἀνδρὶ
5 φιλολόγῳ ποιεῖν ὃ ἂν κελεύῃς.

ΦΑΙ. Τί δῆτα ἔχων στρέφῃ;

ΣΩ. Οὐδὲν ἔτι, ἐπειδὴ σύ γε ταῦτα ὀμώμοκας. πῶς
γὰρ ἂν οἷός τ' εἴην τοιαύτης θοίνης ἀπέχεσθαι;

237 ΦΑΙ. Λέγε δή.

ΣΩ. Οἶσθ' οὖν ὡς ποιήσω;

ΦΑΙ. Τοῦ πέρι;

ΣΩ. Ἐγκαλυψάμενος ἐρῶ, ἵν' ὅτι τάχιστα διαδράμω
5 τὸν λόγον καὶ μὴ βλέπων πρὸς σὲ ὑπ' αἰσχύνης διαπορῶμαι.

ΦΑΙ. Λέγε μόνον, τὰ δ' ἄλλα ὅπως βούλει ποίει.

ΣΩ. Ἄγετε δή, ὦ Μοῦσαι, εἴτε δι' ᾠδῆς εἶδος λίγειαι,
εἴτε διὰ γένος μουσικὸν τὸ Λιγύων ταύτην ἔσχετ' ἐπωνυμίαν, "ξύμ μοι λάβεσθε" τοῦ μύθου, ὅν με ἀναγκάζει
10 ὁ βέλτιστος οὑτοσὶ λέγειν, ἵν' ὁ ἑταῖρος αὐτοῦ, καὶ πρότερον
b δοκῶν τούτῳ σοφὸς εἶναι, νῦν ἔτι μᾶλλον δόξῃ.

Ἦν οὕτω δὴ παῖς, μᾶλλον δὲ μειρακίσκος, μάλα καλός·
τούτῳ δὲ ἦσαν ἐρασταὶ πάνυ πολλοί. εἷς δέ τις αὐτῶν

---

e 3 μηδενὸς μήτε T : μηδενός τ' B ἐξαγγελεῖν G : ἐξαγγέλλειν
BT a 7 λίγειαι T : λιγιαι B a 8 γένος τὸ Λιγύων μουσικὸν
Dionysius : γένος τι μουσικὸν Heraclitus : γένος μουσικὸν τὸ λιγὺ ὂν
Stobaeus ἔσχετ' ἐπωνυμίαν B T Stobaeus : ἔσχετε τὴν ἐπωνυμίαν
Dionysius, Heraclitus b 2 μειρακίσκος B T : μειρακίσκος ἁπαλὸς
vulg.

αἰμύλος ἦν, ὃς οὐδενὸς ἧττον ἐρῶν ἐπεπείκει τὸν παῖδα ὡς
οὐκ ἐρῴη. καί ποτε αὐτὸν αἰτῶν ἔπειθεν τοῦτ᾽ αὐτό, ὡς μὴ 5
ἐρῶντι πρὸ τοῦ ἐρῶντος δέοι χαρίζεσθαι, ἔλεγέν τε ὧδε—

Περὶ παντός, ὦ παῖ, μία ἀρχὴ τοῖς μέλλουσι καλῶς
βουλεύσεσθαι· εἰδέναι δεῖ περὶ οὗ ἂν ᾖ ἡ βουλή, ἢ παντὸς C
ἁμαρτάνειν ἀνάγκη. τοὺς δὲ πολλοὺς λέληθεν ὅτι οὐκ
ἴσασι τὴν οὐσίαν ἑκάστου. ὡς οὖν εἰδότες οὐ διομολογοῦνται
ἐν ἀρχῇ τῆς σκέψεως, προελθόντες δὲ τὸ εἰκὸς ἀποδιδόασιν·
οὔτε γὰρ ἑαυτοῖς οὔτε ἀλλήλοις ὁμολογοῦσιν. ἐγὼ οὖν 5
καὶ σὺ μὴ πάθωμεν ὃ ἄλλοις ἐπιτιμῶμεν, ἀλλ᾽ ἐπειδὴ σοὶ
καὶ ἐμοὶ ὁ λόγος πρόκειται πότερα ἐρῶντι ἢ μὴ μᾶλλον εἰς
φιλίαν ἰτέον, περὶ ἔρωτος οἷόν τ᾽ ἔστι καὶ ἣν ἔχει δύναμιν, ὁμολογίᾳ θέμενοι ὅρον, εἰς τοῦτο ἀποβλέποντες καὶ d
ἀναφέροντες τὴν σκέψιν ποιώμεθα εἴτε ὠφελίαν εἴτε
βλάβην παρέχει. ὅτι μὲν οὖν δὴ ἐπιθυμία τις ὁ ἔρως,
ἅπαντι δῆλον· ὅτι δ᾽ αὖ καὶ μὴ ἐρῶντες ἐπιθυμοῦσι τῶν
καλῶν, ἴσμεν. τῷ δὴ τὸν ἐρῶντά τε καὶ μὴ κρινοῦμεν; 5
δεῖ αὖ νοῆσαι ὅτι ἡμῶν ἐν ἑκάστῳ δύο τινέ ἐστον ἰδέα
ἄρχοντε καὶ ἄγοντε, οἷν ἑπόμεθα ᾗ ἂν ἄγητον, ἡ μὲν ἔμ-
φυτος οὖσα ἐπιθυμία ἡδονῶν, ἄλλη δὲ ἐπίκτητος δόξα,
ἐφιεμένη τοῦ ἀρίστου. τούτω δὲ ἐν ἡμῖν τοτὲ μὲν ὁμο-
νοεῖτον, ἔστι δὲ ὅτε στασιάζετον· καὶ τοτὲ μὲν ἡ ἑτέρα, e
ἄλλοτε δὲ ἡ ἑτέρα κρατεῖ. δόξης μὲν οὖν ἐπὶ τὸ ἄριστον
λόγῳ ἀγούσης καὶ κρατούσης τῷ κράτει σωφροσύνη ὄνομα·
ἐπιθυμίας δὲ ἀλόγως ἑλκούσης ἐπὶ ἡδονὰς καὶ ἀρξάσης ἐν 238
ἡμῖν τῇ ἀρχῇ ὕβρις ἐπωνομάσθη. ὕβρις δὲ δὴ πολυώνυμον
—πολυμελὲς γὰρ καὶ πολυμερές—καὶ τούτων τῶν ἰδεῶν

b 5 αἰτῶν T W Heraclitus : ἐρῶν B   c 1 βουλεύσεσθαι T : βουλεύ-
εσθαι B   δεῖ B : ἃ δεῖ T   παντὸς B Simplicius : ἅπαντος T
c 4 προελθόντες t : προσελθόντες B T   c 5 ἀλλήλοις B : ἄλλοις ex
ἀλλήλοις T   c 7 πότερα T : πότερον (sed a s. v.) W : om. B
c 8 οἷόν τ᾽] οἷόν τι ci. Heindorf   ἔχει T : εἶχε B   d 6 αὖ]
δὴ Schanz   d 8 ἡδονῶν T : δηλον ων B   a 3 πολυμελὲς
. . . καὶ πολυμερές scripsi : πολυμελὲς . . . καὶ πολυειδές B Stobaeus :
πολυμερὲς . . . καὶ πολυειδές T : πολυειδὲς . . . καὶ πολυμελές V

ἐκπρεπὴς ἢ ἂν τύχῃ γενομένη, τὴν αὑτῆς ἐπωνυμίαν ὀνο-
5 μαζόμενον τὸν ἔχοντα παρέχεται, οὔτε τινὰ καλὴν οὔτ'
ἐπαξίαν κεκτῆσθαι. περὶ μὲν γὰρ ἐδωδὴν κρατοῦσα τοῦ
λόγου τε τοῦ ἀρίστου καὶ τῶν ἄλλων ἐπιθυμιῶν ἐπιθυμία
b γαστριμαργία τε καὶ τὸν ἔχοντα ταὐτὸν τοῦτο κεκλημένον
παρέξεται· περὶ δ' αὖ μέθας τυραννεύσασα, τὸν κεκτημένον
ταύτῃ ἄγουσα, δῆλον οὗ τεύξεται προσρήματος· καὶ τἆλλα
δὴ τὰ τούτων ἀδελφὰ καὶ ἀδελφῶν ἐπιθυμιῶν ὀνόματα τῆς
5 ἀεὶ δυναστευούσης ᾗ προσήκει καλεῖσθαι πρόδηλον. ἧς δ'
ἕνεκα πάντα τὰ πρόσθεν εἴρηται, σχεδὸν μὲν ἤδη φανερόν,
λεχθὲν δὲ ἢ μὴ λεχθὲν πάντως σαφέστερον· ἡ γὰρ ἄνευ
λόγου δόξης ἐπὶ τὸ ὀρθὸν ὁρμώσης κρατήσασα ἐπιθυμία
c πρὸς ἡδονὴν ἀχθεῖσα κάλλους, καὶ ὑπὸ αὖ τῶν ἑαυτῆς συγγενῶν ἐπιθυμιῶν ἐπὶ σωμάτων κάλλος ἐρρωμένως ῥωσθεῖσα
νικήσασα ἀγωγῇ, ἀπ' αὐτῆς τῆς ῥώμης ἐπωνυμίαν λαβοῦσα,
ἔρως ἐκλήθη.

5 Ἀτάρ, ὦ φίλε Φαῖδρε, δοκῶ τι σοί, ὥσπερ ἐμαυτῷ,
θεῖον πάθος πεπονθέναι;
ΦΑΙ. Πάνυ μὲν οὖν, ὦ Σώκρατες, παρὰ τὸ εἰωθὸς εὔροιά
τίς σε εἴληφεν.
ΣΩ. Σιγῇ τοίνυν μου ἄκουε. τῷ ὄντι γὰρ θεῖος ἔοικεν
d ὁ τόπος εἶναι, ὥστε ἐὰν ἄρα πολλάκις νυμφόληπτος προϊόντος
τοῦ λόγου γένωμαι, μὴ θαυμάσῃς· τὰ νῦν γὰρ οὐκέτι πόρρω
διθυράμβων φθέγγομαι.
ΦΑΙ. Ἀληθέστατα λέγεις.

a 4 ἐπονομαζόμενον Stobaeus   a 6 κεκτῆσθαι B : κεκλῆσθαι T
a 7 τε T Stobaeus : om. B   b 5 ᾗ B T : ὃ Stobaeus   b 7 πάντως
Stobaeus Ven. 189: πᾶν πως B T   b 8 τὸ ὀρθὸν B T Dionysius
ad Cn. Pompeium : τἀγαθὸν in marg. B² Dionysius de Demosthene
c 1 ἀχθεῖσα B T pr. loc. Dionysius Hermias : ἄγουσα in marg. B² alt.
loc. Dionysius   ὑπὸ αὖ om. marg. B² alt. loc. Dionysius   ἑαυτῆς
B² T Dionysius Stobaeus : ἑαυτῇ B   c 2 ἐρρωμένως B² T Dionysius
Stobaeus : ἐρώμενος pr. B   ἐρρωμένως... νικήσασα secl. G. Hermann
c 3 ἀγωγῇ B T : ἀγωγὴ Dionysius   ἐπωνυμίαν B T pr. loc. Dionysius :
ἐπιθυμίαν marg. b alt. loc. Dionysius

ΣΩ. Τούτων μέντοι σὺ αἴτιος. ἀλλὰ τὰ λοιπὰ ἄκουε· 5
ἴσως γὰρ κἂν ἀποτράποιτο τὸ ἐπιόν. ταῦτα μὲν οὖν θεῷ
μελήσει, ἡμῖν δὲ πρὸς τὸν παῖδα πάλιν τῷ λόγῳ ἰτέον.

Εἶεν, ὦ φέριστε· ὃ μὲν δὴ τυγχάνει ὂν περὶ οὗ βου-
λευτέον, εἴρηταί τε καὶ ὥρισται, βλέποντες δὲ δὴ πρὸς αὐτὸ
τὰ λοιπὰ λέγωμεν τίς ὠφελία ἢ βλάβη ἀπό τε ἐρῶντος e
καὶ μὴ τῷ χαριζομένῳ ἐξ εἰκότος συμβήσεται. τῷ δὴ
ὑπὸ ἐπιθυμίας ἀρχομένῳ δουλεύοντί τε ἡδονῇ ἀνάγκη που
τὸν ἐρώμενον ὡς ἥδιστον ἑαυτῷ παρασκευάζειν· νοσοῦντι
δὲ πᾶν ἡδὺ τὸ μὴ ἀντιτεῖνον, κρεῖττον δὲ καὶ ἴσον ἐχθρόν. 5
οὔτε δὴ κρείττω οὔτε ἰσούμενον ἑκὼν ἐραστὴς παιδικὰ 239
ἀνέξεται, ἥττω δὲ καὶ ὑποδεέστερον ἀεὶ ἀπεργάζεται· ἥττων
δὲ ἀμαθὴς σοφοῦ, δειλὸς ἀνδρείου, ἀδύνατος εἰπεῖν ῥητορικοῦ, βραδὺς ἀγχίνου. τοσούτων κακῶν καὶ ἔτι πλειόνων
κατὰ τὴν διάνοιαν ἐραστὴν ἐρωμένῳ ἀνάγκη γιγνομένων τε 5
καὶ φύσει ἐνόντων [τῶν] μὲν ἥδεσθαι, τὰ δὲ παρασκευάζειν,
ἢ στέρεσθαι τοῦ παραυτίκα ἡδέος. φθονερὸν δὴ ἀνάγκη
εἶναι, καὶ πολλῶν μὲν ἄλλων συνουσιῶν ἀπείργοντα καὶ b
ὠφελίμων ὅθεν ἂν μάλιστ' ἀνὴρ γίγνοιτο, μεγάλης αἴτιον
εἶναι βλάβης, μεγίστης δὲ τῆς ὅθεν ἂν φρονιμώτατος εἴη.
τοῦτο δὲ ἡ θεία φιλοσοφία τυγχάνει ὄν, ἧς ἐραστὴν παιδικὰ
ἀνάγκη πόρρωθεν εἴργειν, περίφοβον ὄντα τοῦ καταφρονη- 5
θῆναι· τά τε ἄλλα μηχανᾶσθαι ὅπως ἂν ᾖ πάντα ἀγνοῶν
καὶ πάντα ἀποβλέπων εἰς τὸν ἐραστήν, οἷος ὢν τῷ μὲν
ἥδιστος, ἑαυτῷ δὲ βλαβερώτατος ἂν εἴη. τὰ μὲν οὖν κατὰ
διάνοιαν ἐπίτροπός τε καὶ κοινωνὸς οὐδαμῇ λυσιτελὴς ἀνὴρ c
ἔχων ἔρωτα.

Τὴν δὲ τοῦ σώματος ἕξιν τε καὶ θεραπείαν οἵαν τε καὶ
ὡς θεραπεύσει οὗ ἂν γένηται κύριος, ὃς ἡδὺ πρὸ ἀγαθοῦ

---

d6 καν B: ἂν T   e3 δουλεύοντι B: ἢ δουλεύοντι T   e5 μὴ
T: om. B   a2 ἥττων BT: ἥττον V   a6 ἐνόντων T Stobaeus:
ἐν ὄντων B   τῶν BT Stobaeus: secl. Nutzhorn: τοῖς Heindorf
b8 ἑαυτῷ T Stobaeus: τῷ ἑαυτῷ B   ἂν V: om. BT

5 ἠνάγκασται διώκειν, δεῖ μετὰ ταῦτα ἰδεῖν. ὀφθήσεται δὴ
μαλθακόν τινα καὶ οὐ στερεὸν διώκων, οὐδ' ἐν ἡλίῳ καθαρῷ
τεθραμμένον ἀλλὰ ὑπὸ συμμιγεῖ σκιᾷ, πόνων μὲν ἀνδρείων
καὶ ἱδρώτων ξηρῶν ἄπειρον, ἔμπειρον δὲ ἀπαλῆς καὶ ἀνάν-
d δρου διαίτης, ἀλλοτρίοις χρώμασι καὶ κόσμοις χήτει οἰκείων
κοσμούμενον, ὅσα τε ἄλλα τούτοις ἕπεται πάντα ἐπιτη-
δεύοντα, ἃ δῆλα καὶ οὐκ ἄξιον περαιτέρω προβαίνειν, ἀλλὰ
ἐν κεφάλαιον ὁρισαμένους ἐπ' ἄλλο ἰέναι· τὸ γὰρ τοιοῦτον
5 σῶμα ἐν πολέμῳ τε καὶ ἄλλαις χρείαις ὅσαι μεγάλαι οἱ
μὲν ἐχθροὶ θαρροῦσιν, οἱ δὲ φίλοι καὶ αὐτοὶ οἱ ἐρασταὶ
φοβοῦνται.

Τοῦτο μὲν οὖν ὡς δῆλον ἐατέον, τὸ δ' ἐφεξῆς ῥητέον,
e τίνα ἡμῖν ὠφελίαν ἢ τίνα βλάβην περὶ τὴν κτῆσιν ἢ τοῦ
ἐρῶντος ὁμιλία τε καὶ ἐπιτροπεία παρέξεται. σαφὲς δὴ
τοῦτό γε παντὶ μέν, μάλιστα δὲ τῷ ἐραστῇ, ὅτι τῶν φιλτά-
των τε καὶ εὐνουστάτων καὶ θειοτάτων κτημάτων ὀρφανὸν
5 πρὸ παντὸς εὔξαιτ' ἂν εἶναι τὸν ἐρώμενον· πατρὸς γὰρ καὶ
μητρὸς καὶ συγγενῶν καὶ φίλων στέρεσθαι ἂν αὐτὸν δέξαιτο,
240 διακωλυτὰς καὶ ἐπιτιμητὰς ἡγούμενος τῆς ἡδίστης πρὸς
αὐτὸν ὁμιλίας. ἀλλὰ μὴν οὐσίαν γ' ἔχοντα χρυσοῦ ἤ τινος
ἄλλης κτήσεως οὔτε εὐάλωτον ὁμοίως οὔτε ἀλόντα εὐμεταχείριστον ἡγήσεται· ἐξ ὧν πᾶσα ἀνάγκη ἐραστὴν παιδικοῖς
5 φθονεῖν μὲν οὐσίαν κεκτημένοις, ἀπολλυμένης δὲ χαίρειν.
ἔτι τοίνυν ἄγαμον, ἄπαιδα, ἄοικον ὅτι πλεῖστον χρόνον
παιδικὰ ἐραστὴς εὔξαιτ' ἂν γενέσθαι, τὸ αὑτοῦ γλυκὺ ὡς
πλεῖστον χρόνον καρποῦσθαι ἐπιθυμῶν.

Ἔστι μὲν δὴ καὶ ἄλλα κακά, ἀλλά τις δαίμων ἔμειξε τοῖς
b πλείστοις ἐν τῷ παραυτίκα ἡδονήν, οἷον κόλακι, δεινῷ θηρίῳ
καὶ βλάβῃ μεγάλῃ, ὅμως ἐπέμειξεν ἡ φύσις ἡδονήν τινα οὐκ

---

c 5 μετὰ T : με B   δὴ Hirschig : δὲ BT   d 1 κόσμοις BT :
σχήμασιν Plutarchus   d 3 ἃ δῆλα b t : ἄδηλα BT   d 4 ἐν
κεφάλαιον] ἐν κεφαλαίῳ Ast   e 3 δὲ T : γε B   e 5 εὔξαιτ'
T : εὔξετ' B   e 6 μητρὸς καὶ T Stobaeus : μητρὸς B   a 5 ἀπολλυμένης BT : ἀπολλυμένοις vulg.   a 6 ἄοικον T Stobaeus :
οἶκον B

ἄμουσον, καί τις ἑταίραν ὡς βλαβερὸν ψέξειεν ἄν, καὶ ἄλλα
πολλὰ τῶν τοιουτοτρόπων θρεμμάτων τε καὶ ἐπιτηδευμάτων,
οἷς τό γε καθ' ἡμέραν ἡδίστοισιν εἶναι ὑπάρχει· παιδικοῖς δὲ 5
ἐραστὴς πρὸς τῷ βλαβερῷ καὶ εἰς τὸ συνημερεύειν πάντων
ἀηδέστατον. ἥλικα γὰρ δὴ καὶ ὁ παλαιὸς λόγος τέρπειν τὸν c
ἥλικα—ἡ γὰρ οἶμαι χρόνου ἰσότης ἐπ' ἴσας ἡδονὰς ἄγουσα
δι' ὁμοιότητα φιλίαν παρέχεται—ἀλλ' ὅμως κόρον γε καὶ ἡ
τούτων συνουσία ἔχει. καὶ μὴν τό γε ἀναγκαῖον αὖ βαρὺ
παντὶ περὶ πᾶν λέγεται· ὃ δὴ πρὸς τῇ ἀνομοιότητι μάλιστα 5
ἐραστὴς πρὸς παιδικὰ ἔχει. νεωτέρῳ γὰρ πρεσβύτερος
συνὼν οὔθ' ἡμέρας οὔτε νυκτὸς ἑκὼν ἀπολείπεται, ἀλλ' ὑπ'
ἀνάγκης τε καὶ οἴστρου ἐλαύνεται, ὃς ἐκείνῳ μὲν ἡδονὰς ἀεὶ d
διδοὺς ἄγει, ὁρῶντι, ἀκούοντι, ἁπτομένῳ, καὶ πᾶσαν αἴσθησιν
αἰσθανομένῳ τοῦ ἐρωμένου, ὥστε μεθ' ἡδονῆς ἀραρότως αὐτῷ
ὑπηρετεῖν· τῷ δὲ δὴ ἐρωμένῳ ποῖον παραμύθιον ἢ τίνας
ἡδονὰς διδοὺς ποιήσει τὸν ἴσον χρόνον συνόντα μὴ οὐχὶ ἐπ' 5
ἔσχατον ἐλθεῖν ἀηδίας—ὁρῶντι μὲν ὄψιν πρεσβυτέραν καὶ
οὐκ ἐν ὥρᾳ, ἑπομένων δὲ τῶν ἄλλων ταύτῃ, ἃ καὶ λόγῳ
ἐστὶν ἀκούειν οὐκ ἐπιτερπές, μὴ ὅτι δὴ ἔργῳ ἀνάγκης ἀεὶ e
προσκειμένης μεταχειρίζεσθαι, φυλακάς τε δὴ καχυποτόπους
φυλαττομένῳ διὰ παντὸς καὶ πρὸς ἅπαντας, ἀκαίρους τε
ἐπαίνους καὶ ὑπερβάλλοντας ἀκούοντι, ὡς δ' αὔτως ψόγους
νήφοντος μὲν οὐκ ἀνεκτούς, εἰς δὲ μέθην ἰόντος πρὸς τῷ 5
μὴ ἀνεκτῷ ἐπαισχεῖς, παρρησίᾳ κατακορεῖ καὶ ἀναπεπταμένῃ
χρωμένου;

Καὶ ἐρῶν μὲν βλαβερός τε καὶ ἀηδής, λήξας δὲ τοῦ
ἔρωτος εἰς τὸν ἔπειτα χρόνον ἄπιστος, εἰς ὃν πολλὰ καὶ
μετὰ πολλῶν ὅρκων τε καὶ δεήσεων ὑπισχνούμενος μόγις 10

b 5 ἡδίστοισιν B: ἡδίστοις T Stobaeus   c 1 δὴ Stobaeus
Aristaenetus: om. BT   τέρπειν B ex emend. T: τέρπει T
c 7 ἑκὼν ἀπολείπεται B: ἀπολείπεται ἑκών T   d 5 διδοὺς T: αἰδοὺς
B: διαιδοὺς W   e 2 φυλακάς T: φύλακας B   καχυποτόπους T:
καχυπὸ τόπους B: καχυπόπτους vulg.   e 3 ἀκαίρους τε ἐπαίνους T:
ἀκαίρους τε καὶ ἐπαίνους B: ἐπαίνους τε καὶ ἀκαίρους W   e 5 νήφοντος
T: νήφοντες B   e 6 ἐπαισχεῖς ci. Heindorf: ἐπ' αἴσχει BT

241 κατεῖχε τήν γ' ἐν τῷ τότε συνουσίαν ἐπίπονον οὖσαν φέρειν
δι' ἐλπίδα ἀγαθῶν. τότε δὴ δέον ἐκτίνειν, μεταβαλὼν ἄλλον
ἄρχοντα ἐν αὑτῷ καὶ προστάτην, νοῦν καὶ σωφροσύνην ἀντ'
ἔρωτος καὶ μανίας, ἄλλος γεγονὼς λέληθεν τὰ παιδικά. καὶ
5 ὁ μὲν αὐτὸν χάριν ἀπαιτεῖ τῶν τότε, ὑπομιμνῄσκων τὰ
πραχθέντα καὶ λεχθέντα, ὡς τῷ αὐτῷ διαλεγόμενος· ὁ δὲ ὑπ'
αἰσχύνης οὔτε εἰπεῖν τολμᾷ ὅτι ἄλλος γέγονεν, οὔθ' ὅπως τὰ
τῆς προτέρας ἀνοήτου ἀρχῆς ὁρκωμόσιά τε καὶ ὑποσχέσεις
b ἐμπεδώσῃ ἔχει, νοῦν ἤδη ἐσχηκὼς καὶ σεσωφρονηκώς, ἵνα
μὴ πράττων ταὐτὰ τῷ πρόσθεν ὅμοιός τε ἐκείνῳ καὶ ὁ αὐτὸς
πάλιν γένηται. φυγὰς δὴ γίγνεται ἐκ τούτων, καὶ ἀπεστερηκὼς ὑπ' ἀνάγκης ὁ πρὶν ἐραστής, ὀστράκου μετα-
5 πεσόντος, ἵεται φυγῇ μεταβαλών· ὁ δὲ ἀναγκάζεται διώκειν
ἀγανακτῶν καὶ ἐπιθεάζων, ἠγνοηκὼς τὸ ἅπαν ἐξ ἀρχῆς, ὅτι
οὐκ ἄρα ἔδει ποτὲ ἐρῶντι καὶ ὑπ' ἀνάγκης ἀνοήτῳ χαρίζεσθαι,
c ἀλλὰ πολὺ μᾶλλον μὴ ἐρῶντι καὶ νοῦν ἔχοντι· εἰ δὲ μή,
ἀναγκαῖον εἴη ἐνδοῦναι αὐτὸν ἀπίστῳ, δυσκόλῳ, φθονερῷ,
ἀηδεῖ, βλαβερῷ μὲν πρὸς οὐσίαν, βλαβερῷ δὲ πρὸς τὴν
τοῦ σώματος ἕξιν, πολὺ δὲ βλαβερωτάτῳ πρὸς τὴν τῆς
5 ψυχῆς παίδευσιν, ἧς οὔτε ἀνθρώποις οὔτε θεοῖς τῇ ἀληθείᾳ
τιμιώτερον οὔτε ἔστιν οὔτε ποτὲ ἔσται. ταῦτά τε οὖν χρή,
ὦ παῖ, συννοεῖν, καὶ εἰδέναι τὴν ἐραστοῦ φιλίαν ὅτι οὐ μετ'
εὐνοίας γίγνεται, ἀλλὰ σιτίου τρόπον, χάριν πλησμονῆς,
d ὡς λύκοι ἄρνας ἀγαπῶσιν, ὡς παῖδα φιλοῦσιν ἐρασταί.

Τοῦτ' ἐκεῖνο, ὦ Φαῖδρε. οὐκέτ' ἂν τὸ πέρα ἀκούσαις ἐμοῦ
λέγοντος, ἀλλ' ἤδη σοι τέλος ἐχέτω ὁ λόγος.

a 1 γ' T : om. B   οὖσαν T : om. B   a 2 ἐκτίνειν B : ἐκτεί-
νειν pr. T : ἐκτείνει G   μεταβαλὼν B T : μεταλαβὼν corr. Coisl.
a 7 ὅτι T : οὔτ' εἰ B   b 1 ἐμπεδώσῃ B T W : ἐμπεδώσει vulg.
b 3 ἀπεστερηκὼς B T : ἀπειρηκὼς corr. Coisl. : ἀπεστυγηκὼς G. Hermann   b 5 διώκειν T : διώκων B   c 2 δυσκόλῳ φθονερῷ secl.
Spengel   c 4 τοῦ B T Stobaeus : om. vulg.   d 1 ἄρνας
ἀγαπῶσιν B T : ἄρνα φιλοῦσ' vulg. : αἶγ' ἀγαπῶσιν schol. Hermogenis :
ἄρν' ἀγαπῶσ' Bekker   d 3 ἀλλ' ἤδη B : ἀλλὰ δὴ T   τέλος B T :
πέρας vulg.

ΦΑΙ. Καίτοι ᾤμην γε μεσοῦν αὐτόν, καὶ ἐρεῖν τὰ ἴσα περὶ τοῦ μὴ ἐρῶντος, ὡς δεῖ ἐκείνῳ χαρίζεσθαι μᾶλλον, λέγων ὅσα αὖ ἔχει ἀγαθά· νῦν δὲ δή, ὦ Σώκρατες, τί ἀποπαύῃ;

ΣΩ. Οὐκ ᾔσθου, ὦ μακάριε, ὅτι ἤδη ἔπη φθέγγομαι ἀλλ' οὐκέτι διθυράμβους, καὶ ταῦτα ψέγων; ἐὰν δ' ἐπαινεῖν τὸν ἕτερον ἄρξωμαι, τί με οἴει ποιήσειν; ἆρ' οἶσθ' ὅτι ὑπὸ τῶν Νυμφῶν, αἷς με σὺ προύβαλες ἐκ προνοίας, σαφῶς ἐνθουσιάσω; λέγω οὖν ἑνὶ λόγῳ ὅτι ὅσα τὸν ἕτερον λελοιδορήκαμεν, τῷ ἑτέρῳ τἀναντία·τούτων ἀγαθὰ πρόσεστιν. καὶ τί δεῖ μακροῦ λόγου; περὶ γὰρ ἀμφοῖν ἱκανῶς εἴρηται. καὶ οὕτω δὴ ὁ μῦθος ὅτι πάσχειν προσήκει αὐτῷ, τοῦτο πείσεται· κἀγὼ τὸν ποταμὸν τοῦτον διαβὰς ἀπέρχομαι πρὶν 242 ὑπὸ σοῦ τι μεῖζον ἀναγκασθῆναι.

ΦΑΙ. Μήπω γε, ὦ Σώκρατες, πρὶν ἂν τὸ καῦμα παρέλθῃ. ἢ οὐχ ὁρᾷς ὡς σχεδὸν ἤδη μεσημβρία ἵσταται ἡ δὴ καλουμένη σταθερά; ἀλλὰ περιμείναντες καὶ ἅμα περὶ τῶν εἰρημένων διαλεχθέντες, τάχα ἐπειδὰν ἀποψυχῇ ἴμεν.

ΣΩ. Θεῖός γ' εἶ περὶ τοὺς λόγους, ὦ Φαῖδρε, καὶ ἀτεχνῶς θαυμάσιος. οἶμαι γὰρ ἐγὼ τῶν ἐπὶ τοῦ σοῦ βίου γεγονότων λόγων μηδένα πλείους ἢ σὲ πεποιηκέναι γεγενῆσθαι ἤτοι αὐτὸν λέγοντα ἢ ἄλλους ἑνί γέ τῳ τρόπῳ προσαναγκάζοντα —Σιμμίαν Θηβαῖον ἐξαιρῶ λόγου· τῶν δὲ ἄλλων πάμπολυ κρατεῖς—καὶ νῦν αὖ δοκεῖς αἴτιός μοι γεγενῆσθαι λόγῳ τινὶ ῥηθῆναι.

ΦΑΙ. Οὐ πόλεμόν γε ἀγγέλλεις. ἀλλὰ πῶς δὴ καὶ τίνι τούτῳ;

d 4 γε μεσοῦν αὐτόν V : γε μεσοῦν αὐτοῦ B T : σε μεσοῦν αὐτοῦ Hermann   d 6 λέγων B T : λέγοντα Stephanus : λέγονθ' Schanz   e 5 ἐνθουσιάσω T : ἐνθυσιάσω B   a 4 ἡ δὴ t Suidas : ἤδη B T   ἡ δὴ . . . σταθερά secl. Ruhnken   a 6 ἀποψυχημεν (sic) B : ἀποψύξῃ ἴωμεν T : ἀποψύχῃ ἄπιμεν Phrynichus   b 1 λόγων T : om. B W   πεποιηκέναι B t : πεπονηκέναι pr. T   γεγενῆσθαι] γενέσθαι H. Richards   b 2 τῳ B T : om. vulg.   b 3 ἐξαιρῶ Heindorf : ἐξαίρω B T   λόγου B T : τοῦ λόγου W   b 4 γεγενῆσθαι] γενήσεσθαι Badham

ΣΩ. Ἡνίκ᾽ ἔμελλον, ὦγαθέ, τὸν ποταμὸν διαβαίνειν, τὸ
δαιμόνιόν τε καὶ τὸ εἰωθὸς σημεῖόν μοι γίγνεσθαι ἐγένετο
c —ἀεὶ δέ με ἐπίσχει ὃ ἂν μέλλω πράττειν—καί τινα
φωνὴν ἔδοξα αὐτόθεν ἀκοῦσαι, ἥ με οὐκ ἐᾷ ἀπιέναι πρὶν ἂν
ἀφοσιώσωμαι, ὥς δή τι ἡμαρτηκότα εἰς τὸ θεῖον. εἰμὶ δὴ
οὖν μάντις μέν, οὐ πάνυ δὲ σπουδαῖος, ἀλλ᾽ ὥσπερ οἱ τὰ
5 γράμματα φαῦλοι, ὅσον μὲν ἐμαυτῷ μόνον ἱκανός· σαφῶς
οὖν ἤδη μανθάνω τὸ ἁμάρτημα. ὡς δή τοι, ὦ ἑταῖρε,
μαντικόν γέ τι καὶ ἡ ψυχή· ἐμὲ γὰρ ἔθραξε μέν τι καὶ
πάλαι λέγοντα τὸν λόγον, καί πως ἐδυσωπούμην κατ᾽ Ἴβυκον,
μή τι παρὰ θεοῖς

d   ἀμβλακὼν τιμὰν πρὸς ἀνθρώπων ἀμείψω·
νῦν δ᾽ ᾔσθημαι τὸ ἁμάρτημα.
    ΦΑΙ. Λέγεις δὲ δὴ τί;
    ΣΩ. Δεινόν, ὦ Φαῖδρε, δεινὸν λόγον αὐτός τε ἐκόμισας
5 ἐμέ τε ἠνάγκασας εἰπεῖν.
    ΦΑΙ. Πῶς δή;
    ΣΩ. Εὐήθη καὶ ὑπό τι ἀσεβῆ· οὗ τίς ἂν εἴη δεινότερος;
    ΦΑΙ. Οὐδείς, εἴ γε σὺ ἀληθῆ λέγεις.
    ΣΩ. Τί οὖν; τὸν Ἔρωτα οὐκ Ἀφροδίτης καὶ θεόν τινα ἡγῇ;
10   ΦΑΙ. Λέγεταί γε δή.
    ΣΩ. Οὔ τι ὑπό γε Λυσίου, οὐδὲ ὑπὸ τοῦ σοῦ λόγου, ὃς
e διὰ τοῦ ἐμοῦ στόματος καταφαρμακευθέντος ὑπὸ σοῦ ἐλέχθη.
εἰ δ᾽ ἔστιν, ὥσπερ οὖν ἔστι, θεὸς ἤ τι θεῖον ὁ Ἔρως, οὐδὲν
ἂν κακὸν εἴη, τὼ δὲ λόγω τὼ νυνδὴ περὶ αὐτοῦ εἰπέτην ὡς
τοιούτου ὄντος· ταύτῃ τε οὖν ἡμαρτανέτην περὶ τὸν Ἔρωτα,
5 ἔτι τε ἡ εὐήθεια αὐτοῖν πάνυ ἀστεία, τὸ μηδὲν ὑγιὲς λέγοντε

b 9 τε καὶ Β Τ : del. ci. Schanz : μοι καὶ V (om. mox μοι) : καὶ Proclus
τὸ Β Τ Proclus : om. al.   c 1 ἀεὶ . . . πράττειν secl. Heindorf,
at legit Proclus   ὃ Β Τ : ἃ Proclus   c 3 δή Proclus : om. Β Τ
c 5 μὲν Β : om. Τ   ἱκανός Τ : ἱκανῶς Β   c 6 ὡς δή τοι ὦ Τ W :
ὡς δε ποιω Β W² (ε et π s. v.)   d 1 ἀμβλακὼν Β : ἀμπλακὼν Τ
τιμὰν Τ : τιμᾶν Β   d 7 οὗ τις Τ : οὔ τις Β : οὔ τί (et mox δεινότερον)
Proclus   d 11 οὔ τι Τ : ὅτι Β : οὗτοι Heindorf   e 3 τὼ δὴ λόγω
τὼ Τ : τῷ δὲ λόγῳ τῷ Β   e 5 ἔτι τε Τ : εἴτε Β

μηδὲ ἀληθὲς σεμνύνεσθαι ὡς τὶ ὄντε, εἰ ἄρα ἀνθρωπίσκους 243
τινὰς ἐξαπατήσαντε εὐδοκιμήσετον ἐν αὐτοῖς. ἐμοὶ μὲν οὖν,
ὦ φίλε, καθήρασθαι ἀνάγκη· ἔστιν δὲ τοῖς ἁμαρτάνουσι περὶ
μυθολογίαν καθαρμὸς ἀρχαῖος, ὃν Ὅμηρος μὲν οὐκ ᾔσθετο,
Στησίχορος δέ. τῶν γὰρ ὀμμάτων στερηθεὶς διὰ τὴν Ἑλένης 5
κακηγορίαν οὐκ ἠγνόησεν ὥσπερ Ὅμηρος, ἀλλ' ἅτε μουσικὸς
ὢν ἔγνω τὴν αἰτίαν, καὶ ποιεῖ εὐθὺς—

> Οὐκ ἔστ' ἔτυμος λόγος οὗτος,
> οὐδ' ἔβας ἐν νηυσὶν εὐσέλμοις,
> οὐδ' ἵκεο Πέργαμα Τροίας· b

καὶ ποιήσας δὴ πᾶσαν τὴν καλουμένην Παλινῳδίαν παρα-
χρῆμα ἀνέβλεψεν. ἐγὼ οὖν σοφώτερος ἐκείνων γενήσομαι
κατ' αὐτό γε τοῦτο· πρὶν γάρ τι παθεῖν διὰ τὴν τοῦ Ἔρωτος
κακηγορίαν πειράσομαι αὐτῷ ἀποδοῦναι τὴν παλινῳδίαν, 5
γυμνῇ τῇ κεφαλῇ καὶ οὐχ ὥσπερ τότε ὑπ' αἰσχύνης
ἐγκεκαλυμμένος.

ΦΑΙ. Τουτωνί, ὦ Σώκρατες, οὐκ ἔστιν ἅττ' ἂν ἐμοὶ εἶπες
ἡδίω.

ΣΩ. Καὶ γάρ, ὠγαθὲ Φαῖδρε, ἐννοεῖς ὡς ἀναιδῶς εἴρησθον c
τὼ λόγω, οὗτός τε καὶ ὁ ἐκ τοῦ βιβλίου ῥηθείς. εἰ γὰρ
ἀκούων τις τύχοι ἡμῶν γεννάδας καὶ πρᾶος τὸ ἦθος, ἑτέρου
δὲ τοιούτου ἐρῶν ἢ καὶ πρότερόν ποτε ἐρασθείς, λεγόντων
ὡς διὰ σμικρὰ μεγάλας ἔχθρας οἱ ἐρασταὶ ἀναιροῦνται καὶ 5
ἔχουσι πρὸς τὰ παιδικὰ φθονερῶς τε καὶ βλαβερῶς, πῶς οὐκ
ἂν οἴει αὐτὸν ἡγεῖσθαι ἀκούειν ἐν ναύταις που τεθραμμένων
καὶ οὐδένα ἐλεύθερον ἔρωτα ἑωρακότων, πολλοῦ δ' ἂν δεῖν
ἡμῖν ὁμολογεῖν ἃ ψέγομεν τὸν Ἔρωτα; d

ΦΑΙ. Ἴσως νὴ Δί', ὦ Σώκρατες.

ΣΩ. Τοῦτόν γε τοίνυν ἔγωγε αἰσχυνόμενος, καὶ αὐτὸν
τὸν Ἔρωτα δεδιώς, ἐπιθυμῶ ποτίμῳ λόγῳ οἷον ἁλμυρὰν

---

a 1 μηδὲ T : μήτε B   a 7 ποιεῖ] ἐποίει H. Richards   a 9 οὐδ'
ἔβας T : οὐδὲ βὰς B   b 6 τῇ T : om. B   c 2 τὼ λόγω T · τῷ
λόγῳ B   c 7 τεθραμμένων corr. Coisl. : τεθραμμένον B T

5 ἀκοὴν ἀποκλύσασθαι· συμβουλεύω δὲ καὶ Λυσίᾳ ὅτι τάχιστα
γράψαι ὡς χρὴ ἐραστῇ μᾶλλον ἢ μὴ ἐρῶντι ἐκ τῶν ὁμοίων
χαρίζεσθαι.

ΦΑΙ. Ἀλλ' εὖ ἴσθι ὅτι ἕξει τοῦθ' οὕτω· σοῦ γὰρ εἰπόντος
τὸν τοῦ ἐραστοῦ ἔπαινον, πᾶσα ἀνάγκη Λυσίαν ὑπ' ἐμοῦ
e ἀναγκασθῆναι γράψαι αὖ περὶ τοῦ αὐτοῦ λόγον.

ΣΩ. Τοῦτο μὲν πιστεύω, ἕωσπερ ἂν ᾖς ὃς εἶ.

ΦΑΙ. Λέγε τοίνυν θαρρῶν.

ΣΩ. Ποῦ δή μοι ὁ παῖς πρὸς ὃν ἔλεγον; ἵνα καὶ τοῦτο
5 ἀκούσῃ, καὶ μὴ ἀνήκοος ὢν φθάσῃ χαρισάμενος τῷ μὴ
ἐρῶντι.

ΦΑΙ. Οὗτος παρά σοι μάλα πλησίον ἀεὶ πάρεστιν, ὅταν
σὺ βούλῃ.

ΣΩ. Οὑτωσὶ τοίνυν, ὦ παῖ καλέ, ἐννόησον, ὡς ὁ μὲν
244 πρότερος ἦν λόγος Φαίδρου τοῦ Πυθοκλέους, Μυρρινουσίου
ἀνδρός· ὃν δὲ μέλλω λέγειν, Στησιχόρου τοῦ Εὐφήμου,
Ἱμεραίου. λεκτέος δὲ ὧδε, ὅτι Οὐκ ἔστ' ἔτυμος λόγος ὃς ἂν
παρόντος ἐραστοῦ τῷ μὴ ἐρῶντι μᾶλλον φῇ δεῖν χαρίζεσθαι,
5 διότι δὴ ὁ μὲν μαίνεται, ὁ δὲ σωφρονεῖ. εἰ μὲν γὰρ ἦν
ἁπλοῦν τὸ μανίαν κακὸν εἶναι, καλῶς ἂν ἐλέγετο· νῦν δὲ τὰ
μέγιστα τῶν ἀγαθῶν ἡμῖν γίγνεται διὰ μανίας, θείᾳ μέντοι
δόσει διδομένης. . ἥ τε γὰρ δὴ ἐν Δελφοῖς προφῆτις αἵ τ' ἐν
b Δωδώνῃ ἱέρειαι μανεῖσαι μὲν πολλὰ δὴ καὶ καλὰ ἰδίᾳ τε καὶ
δημοσίᾳ τὴν Ἑλλάδα ἠργάσαντο, σωφρονοῦσαι δὲ βραχέα ἢ
οὐδέν· καὶ ἐὰν δὴ λέγωμεν Σίβυλλάν τε καὶ ἄλλους, ὅσοι
μαντικῇ χρώμενοι ἐνθέῳ πολλὰ δὴ πολλοῖς προλέγοντες εἰς
5 τὸ μέλλον ὤρθωσαν, μηκύνοιμεν ἂν δῆλα παντὶ λέγοντες.
τόδε μὴν ἄξιον ἐπιμαρτύρασθαι, ὅτι καὶ τῶν παλαιῶν οἱ τὰ

d 8 οὕτω· σοῦ Schanz : οὕτως σοῦ t : οὕτως οὐ ΒΤ   e 4 τοῦτο
Β : τούτου Τ   e 7 πάρα Cobet (secl. mox πάρεστιν)   a 3 λεκτέος
ΤW: om. Β   λόγος Β: ὁ λόγος Τ   a 8 γὰρ δὴ Τ : γὰρ * * Β : γὰρ
Aristides   b 4 ἐνθέῳ Τ: ἐν θεοῖς Β   b 5 ὤρθωσαν Ven. 189
corr. V Aristides : ὀρθῶς ΒΤ

ὀνόματα τιθέμενοι οὐκ αἰσχρὸν ἡγοῦντο οὐδὲ ὄνειδος μανίαν·
οὐ γὰρ ἂν τῇ καλλίστῃ τέχνῃ, ᾗ τὸ μέλλον κρίνεται, αὐτὸ c
τοῦτο τοὔνομα ἐμπλέκοντες μανικὴν ἐκάλεσαν. ἀλλ' ὡς
καλοῦ ὄντος, ὅταν θείᾳ μοίρᾳ γίγνηται, οὕτω νομίσαντες
ἔθεντο, οἱ δὲ νῦν ἀπειροκάλως τὸ ταῦ ἐπεμβάλλοντες
μαντικὴν ἐκάλεσαν. ἐπεὶ καὶ τήν γε τῶν ἐμφρόνων, 5
ζήτησιν τοῦ μέλλοντος διά τε ὀρνίθων ποιουμένων καὶ τῶν
ἄλλων σημείων, ἅτ' ἐκ διανοίας ποριζομένων ἀνθρωπίνῃ
οἰήσει νοῦν τε καὶ ἱστορίαν, οἰονοϊστικὴν ἐπωνόμασαν,
ἣν νῦν οἰωνιστικὴν τῷ ὦ σεμνύνοντες οἱ νέοι καλοῦσιν· d
ὅσῳ δὴ οὖν τελεώτερον καὶ ἐντιμότερον μαντικὴ οἰωνιστικῆς,
τό τε ὄνομα τοῦ ὀνόματος ἔργον τ' ἔργου, τόσῳ κάλλιον
μαρτυροῦσιν οἱ παλαιοὶ μανίαν σωφροσύνης τὴν ἐκ θεοῦ τῆς
παρ' ἀνθρώπων γιγνομένης. ἀλλὰ μὴν νόσων γε καὶ πόνων 5
τῶν μεγίστων, ἃ δὴ παλαιῶν ἐκ μηνιμάτων ποθὲν ἔν τισι
τῶν γενῶν ἡ μανία ἐγγενομένη καὶ προφητεύσασα, οἷς ἔδει
ἀπαλλαγὴν ηὕρετο, καταφυγοῦσα πρὸς θεῶν εὐχάς τε καὶ e
λατρείας, ὅθεν δὴ καθαρμῶν τε καὶ τελετῶν τυχοῦσα ἐξάντη
ἐποίησε τὸν [ἑαυτῆς] ἔχοντα πρός τε τὸν παρόντα καὶ τὸν
ἔπειτα χρόνον, λύσιν τῷ ὀρθῶς μανέντι τε καὶ κατασχομένῳ
τῶν παρόντων κακῶν εὑρομένη. τρίτη δὲ ἀπὸ Μουσῶν 245
κατοκωχή τε καὶ μανία, λαβοῦσα ἁπαλὴν καὶ ἄβατον ψυχήν,
ἐγείρουσα καὶ ἐκβακχεύουσα κατά τε ᾠδὰς καὶ κατὰ τὴν
ἄλλην ποίησιν, μυρία τῶν παλαιῶν ἔργα κοσμοῦσα τοὺς
ἐπιγιγνομένους παιδεύει· ὃς δ' ἂν ἄνευ μανίας Μουσῶν ἐπὶ 5
ποιητικὰς θύρας ἀφίκηται, πεισθεὶς ὡς ἄρα ἐκ τέχνης ἱκανὸς

c 4 ἐπεμβαλόντες Aristides   c 6 ποιουμένων secl. Schanz :
ποιουμένην Stephanus   c 7 ποριζομένων] ποριζομένην Stephanus
ἀνθρωπίνῃ οἰήσει pr. B Aristides : ἀνθρωπίνην οἰήσει corr. b (νοήσει
voluit) : ἀνθρωπίνη νοήσει T   c 8 οἰονοϊστικὴν W Aristides : οἰωνιστικὴν B : οἷον νοϊστικὴν T   d 5 γε B T : τε Aristides   d 7 γενῶν,
ἡ B T : γενῶν ἣν Hermann   e 2 δὴ T : om. B   e 3 ἑαυτῆς
ἔχοντα B T : αὐτὴν ἔχοντα Aristides : ἑαυτῆς seclusi (glossema ἔξω
ἄτης fuisse suspicor)   a 2 κατοκωχή W : κατοικωχή B : κατακωχή
T : κατοχή vulg.   a 6 ποιητικὰς B T Aristides Stobaeus (poeticas
Seneca) : ποιητικῆς Proclus Synesius : secl. Cobet   πεισθεὶς B T
Stobaeus : secl. Cobet   ὡς ἄρα B T : ἄρα ὡς Stobaeus

ποιητὴς ἐσόμενος, ἀτελὴς αὐτός τε καὶ ἡ πυίησις ὑπὸ τῆς
τῶν μαινομένων ἢ τοῦ σωφρονοῦντος ἠφανίσθη.

b   Τοσαῦτα μέν σοι καὶ ἔτι πλείω ἔχω μανίας γιγνομένης
ἀπὸ θεῶν λέγειν καλὰ ἔργα.   ὥστε τοῦτό γε αὐτὸ μὴ φοβώμεθα, μηδέ τις ἡμᾶς λόγος θορυβείτω δεδιττόμενος ὡς πρὸ
τοῦ κεκινημένου τὸν σώφρονα δεῖ προαιρεῖσθαι φίλον· ἀλλὰ
5 τόδε πρὸς ἐκείνῳ δείξας φερέσθω τὰ νικητήρια, ὡς οὐκ ἐπ'
ὠφελίᾳ ὁ ἔρως τῷ ἐρῶντι καὶ τῷ ἐρωμένῳ ἐκ θεῶν ἐπιπέμπεται.
ἡμῖν δὲ ἀποδεικτέον αὖ τοὐναντίον, ὡς ἐπ' εὐτυχίᾳ τῇ μεγίστῃ
c παρὰ θεῶν ἡ τοιαύτη μανία δίδοται· ἡ δὲ δὴ ἀπόδειξις ἔσται
δειυοῖς μὲν ἄπιστος, σοφοῖς δὲ πιστή. δεῖ οὖν πρῶτον ψυχῆς
φύσεως πέρι θείας τε καὶ ἀνθρωπίνης ἰδόντα πάθη τε καὶ
ἔργα τἀληθὲς νοῆσαι· ἀρχὴ δὲ ἀποδείξεως ἥδε.
5 Ψυχὴ πᾶσα ἀθάνατος. τὸ γὰρ ἀεικίνητον ἀθάνατον· τὸ
δ' ἄλλο κινοῦν καὶ ὑπ' ἄλλου κινούμενον, παῦλαν ἔχον
κινήσεως, παῦλαν ἔχει ζωῆς. μόνον δὴ τὸ αὐτὸ κινοῦν, ἅτε
οὐκ ἀπολεῖπον ἑαυτό, οὔποτε λήγει κινούμενον, ἀλλὰ καὶ
τοῖς ἄλλοις ὅσα κινεῖται τοῦτο πηγὴ καὶ ἀρχὴ κινήσεως.
d ἀρχὴ δὲ ἀγένητον. ἐξ ἀρχῆς γὰρ ἀνάγκη πᾶν τὸ γιγνόμενον
γίγνεσθαι, αὐτὴν δὲ μηδ' ἐξ ἑνός· εἰ γὰρ ἔκ του ἀρχὴ
γίγνοιτο, οὐκ ἂν ἔτι ἀρχὴ γίγνοιτο. ἐπειδὴ δὲ ἀγένητόν
ἐστιν, καὶ ἀδιάφθορον αὐτὸ ἀνάγκη εἶναι. ἀρχῆς γὰρ δὴ
5 ἀπολομένης οὔτε αὐτή ποτε ἔκ του οὔτε ἄλλο ἐξ ἐκείνης
γενήσεται, εἴπερ ἐξ ἀρχῆς δεῖ τὰ πάντα γίγνεσθαι. οὕτω
δὴ κινήσεως μὲν ἀρχὴ τὸ αὐτὸ αὑτὸ κινοῦν. τοῦτο δὲ οὔτ'
ἀπόλλυσθαι οὔτε γίγνεσθαι δυνατόν, ἢ πάντα τε οὐρανὸν
e πᾶσάν τε γῆν εἰς ἓν συμπεσοῦσαν στῆναι καὶ μήποτε αὖθις
ἔχειν ὅθεν κινηθέντα γενήσεται. ἀθανάτου δὲ πεφασμένου

b 1 μέν σοι T Aristides: μέντοι B   b 6 ὅ om. V Stobaeus   d 3 ἔτι
ἀρχὴ Buttmann (et sic ut videtur Iamblichus : cf. Timaeum Locrum ap.
Theodoretum εἰ γὰρ ἐγένετο, οὐκ ἂν ἦν ἔτι ἀρχά) : ἀρχὴ Vind. 89 Cicero
(ut videtur) : ἐξ ἀρχῆς B T Simplicius Stobaeus   d 4 ἀδιάφθορον T
Proclus : ἀδιάφορον B : ἄφθορον Stobaeus   e 1 γῆν εἰς ἓν Philoponus :
γένεσιν B T Hermias Syrianus Stobaeus : γῆν in marg. t   e 2 ἔχειν
Stobaeus : ἔχειν στῆναι B T   δὲ T Alexander Stobaeus : om. B

τοῦ ὑφ' ἑαυτοῦ κινουμένου, ψυχῆς οὐσίαν τε καὶ λόγον
τοῦτον αὐτόν τις λέγων οὐκ αἰσχυνεῖται. πᾶν γὰρ σῶμα,
ᾧ μὲν ἔξωθεν τὸ κινεῖσθαι, ἄψυχον, ᾧ δὲ ἔνδοθεν αὐτῷ 5
ἐξ αὐτοῦ, ἔμψυχον, ὡς ταύτης οὔσης φύσεως ψυχῆς· εἰ
δ' ἔστιν τοῦτο οὕτως ἔχον, μὴ ἄλλο τι εἶναι τὸ αὐτὸ ἑαυτὸ
κινοῦν ἢ ψυχήν, ἐξ ἀνάγκης ἀγένητόν τε καὶ ἀθάνατον ψυχὴ 246
ἂν εἴη.

Περὶ μὲν οὖν ἀθανασίας αὐτῆς ἱκανῶς· περὶ δὲ τῆς ἰδέας
αὐτῆς ὧδε λεκτέον. οἷον μέν ἐστι, πάντη πάντως θείας
εἶναι καὶ μακρᾶς διηγήσεως, ᾧ δὲ ἔοικεν, ἀνθρωπίνης τε 5
καὶ ἐλάττονος· ταύτῃ οὖν λέγωμεν. ἐοικέτω δὴ συμφύτῳ
δυνάμει ὑποπτέρου ζεύγους τε καὶ ἡνιόχου. θεῶν μὲν οὖν
ἵπποι τε καὶ ἡνίοχοι πάντες αὐτοί τε ἀγαθοὶ καὶ ἐξ ἀγαθῶν,
τὸ δὲ τῶν ἄλλων μέμεικται. καὶ πρῶτον μὲν ἡμῶν ὁ ἄρχων b
συνωρίδος ἡνιοχεῖ, εἶτα τῶν ἵππων ὁ μὲν αὐτῷ καλός τε καὶ
ἀγαθὸς καὶ ἐκ τοιούτων, ὁ δ' ἐξ ἐναντίων τε καὶ ἐναντίος·
χαλεπὴ δὴ καὶ δύσκολος ἐξ ἀνάγκης ἡ περὶ ἡμᾶς ἡνιόχησις.
πῇ δὴ οὖν θνητόν τε καὶ ἀθάνατον ζῷον ἐκλήθη πειρατέον 5
εἰπεῖν. ψυχὴ πᾶσα παντὸς ἐπιμελεῖται τοῦ ἀψύχου, πάντα δὲ
οὐρανὸν περιπολεῖ, ἄλλοτ' ἐν ἄλλοις εἴδεσι γιγνομένη. τελέα
μὲν οὖν οὖσα καὶ ἐπτερωμένη μετεωροπορεῖ τε καὶ πάντα c
τὸν κόσμον διοικεῖ, ἡ δὲ πτερορρυήσασα φέρεται ἕως ἂν
στερεοῦ τινος ἀντιλάβηται, οὗ κατοικισθεῖσα, σῶμα γήϊνον
λαβοῦσα, αὐτὸ αὑτὸ δοκοῦν κινεῖν διὰ τὴν ἐκείνης δύναμιν,
ζῷον τὸ σύμπαν ἐκλήθη, ψυχὴ καὶ σῶμα παγέν, θνητόν τ' 5
ἔσχεν ἐπωνυμίαν· ἀθάνατον δὲ οὐδ' ἐξ ἑνὸς λόγου λελογισμένου, ἀλλὰ πλάττομεν οὔτε ἰδόντες οὔτε ἱκανῶς νοήσαντες

a 6 ἐοικέτω δὴ γρ. t Hermias Stobaeus : ἔοικε τῳ δὴ T : ἔοικε τῷ δὴ
B : ἔοικε δή τῳ V : ἔοικε δὴ τῇ vulg.   a 8 πάντες αὐτοί τε T : καὶ
πάντες αὐτοὶ B   b 2 αὐτῷ BT : αὐτῶν al.   b 5 τε T : om. B
b 6 ψυχὴ πᾶσα Simplicius : πᾶσα ἡ ψυχὴ B : ἡ ψυχὴ πᾶσα T : ψυχὴ γὰρ
πᾶσα Eusebius   b 7 οὐρανὸν BT : ἄνθρωπον V : οὖν Herwerden :
secl. Badham   c 1 οὖν T : om. B   μετεωροπολεῖ Syrianus
πάντα B : ἅπαντα T   c 7 πλάττομεν Proclus corr. V : πλαττομένου
BT   οὔτε ἰδόντες T : οὔτ' εἰδότες B Proclus

d θεόν, ἀθάνατόν τι ζῷον, ἔχον μὲν ψυχήν, ἔχον δὲ σῶμα, τὸν
ἀεὶ δὲ χρόνον ταῦτα συμπεφυκότα. ἀλλὰ ταῦτα μὲν δή,
ὅπῃ τῷ θεῷ φίλον, ταύτῃ ἐχέτω τε καὶ λεγέσθω· τὴν δὲ
αἰτίαν τῆς τῶν πτερῶν ἀποβολῆς, δι' ἣν ψυχῆς ἀπορρεῖ,
5 λάβωμεν. ἔστι δέ τις τοιάδε.

Πέφυκεν ἡ πτεροῦ δύναμις τὸ ἐμβριθὲς ἄγειν ἄνω μετε-
ωρίζουσα ᾗ τὸ τῶν θεῶν γένος οἰκεῖ, κεκοινώνηκε δέ πῃ
μάλιστα τῶν περὶ τὸ σῶμα τοῦ θείου [ψυχή], τὸ δὲ θεῖον
e καλόν, σοφόν, ἀγαθόν, καὶ πᾶν ὅτι τοιοῦτον· τούτοις δὴ
τρέφεταί τε καὶ αὔξεται μάλιστά γε τὸ τῆς ψυχῆς πτέρωμα,
αἰσχρῷ δὲ καὶ κακῷ καὶ τοῖς ἐναντίοις φθίνει τε καὶ διόλ-
λυται. ὁ μὲν δὴ μέγας ἡγεμὼν ἐν οὐρανῷ Ζεύς, ἐλαύνων
5 πτηνὸν ἅρμα, πρῶτος πορεύεται, διακοσμῶν πάντα καὶ ἐπι-
μελούμενος· τῷ δ' ἕπεται στρατιὰ θεῶν τε καὶ δαιμόνων,
247 κατὰ ἕνδεκα μέρη κεκοσμημένη. μένει γὰρ Ἑστία ἐν θεῶν
οἴκῳ μόνη· τῶν δὲ ἄλλων ὅσοι ἐν τῷ τῶν δώδεκα ἀριθμῷ
τεταγμένοι θεοὶ ἄρχοντες ἡγοῦνται κατὰ τάξιν ἣν ἕκαστος
ἐτάχθη. πολλαὶ μὲν οὖν καὶ μακάριαι θέαι τε καὶ διέξοδοι
5 ἐντὸς οὐρανοῦ, ἃς θεῶν γένος εὐδαιμόνων ἐπιστρέφεται
πράττων ἕκαστος αὐτῶν τὸ αὑτοῦ, ἕπεται δὲ ὁ ἀεὶ ἐθέλων
τε καὶ δυνάμενος· φθόνος γὰρ ἔξω θείου χοροῦ ἵσταται.
ὅταν δὲ δὴ πρὸς δαῖτα καὶ ἐπὶ θοίνην ἴωσιν, ἄκραν ἐπὶ τὴν
b ὑπουράνιον ἀψῖδα πορεύονται πρὸς ἄναντες, ᾗ δὴ τὰ μὲν θεῶν
ὀχήματα ἰσορρόπως εὐήνια ὄντα ῥᾳδίως πορεύεται, τὰ δὲ
ἄλλα μόγις· βρίθει γὰρ ὁ τῆς κάκης ἵππος μετέχων, ἐπὶ
τὴν γῆν ῥέπων τε καὶ βαρύνων ᾧ μὴ καλῶς ἦν τεθραμμένος
5 τῶν ἡνιόχων. ἔνθα δὴ πόνος τε καὶ ἀγὼν ἔσχατος ψυχῇ

---

d1 τι T : τὸ B   d2 δή T : ἤδη B   d8 ψυχή BT : om.
Plutarchus   e2 αὔξεται BT : ἄρδεται Proclus   μάλιστά γε b :
μάλιστά τε B : μάλιστα T   e3 καὶ τοῖς ἐναντίοις secl. Schanz
a5 εὐδαιμόνων B T Syrianus Damascius : καὶ δαιμόνων Badham : εὐδαι-
μόνως Schanz   a7 θείου χοροῦ B Alexander : χοροῦ θείου T
a8 καὶ B : τε καὶ T   ἐπὶ T Proclus : ὑπὸ B   b1 ὑπουράνιον B
Proclus : ὑπουρανίαν W (sed ε supra ὑ): οὐράνιον T   ᾗ δὴ Proclus : ἤδη
BT   b3 κάκης T : κακῆς B   b4 ἦν recc. : ᾗ BT

πρόκειται. αἱ μὲν γὰρ ἀθάνατοι καλούμεναι, ἡνίκ' ἂν πρὸς
ἄκρῳ γένωνται, ἔξω πορευθεῖσαι ἔστησαν ἐπὶ τῷ τοῦ οὐρανοῦ
νώτῳ, στάσας δὲ αὐτὰς περιάγει ἡ περιφορά, αἱ δὲ θεωροῦσι c
τὰ ἔξω τοῦ οὐρανοῦ.

Τὸν δὲ ὑπερουράνιον τόπον οὔτε τις ὕμνησέ πω τῶν τῇδε
ποιητὴς οὔτε ποτὲ ὑμνήσει κατ' ἀξίαν. ἔχει δὲ ὧδε—τολμητέον γὰρ οὖν τό γε ἀληθὲς εἰπεῖν, ἄλλως τε καὶ περὶ ἀλη- 5
θείας λέγοντα—ἡ γὰρ ἀχρώματός τε καὶ ἀσχημάτιστος καὶ
ἀναφὴς οὐσία ὄντως οὖσα, ψυχῆς κυβερνήτῃ μόνῳ θεατὴ
νῷ, περὶ ἣν τὸ τῆς ἀληθοῦς ἐπιστήμης γένος, τοῦτον ἔχει
τὸν τόπον. ἅτ' οὖν θεοῦ διάνοια νῷ τε καὶ ἐπιστήμῃ ἀκη- d
ράτῳ τρεφομένη, καὶ ἁπάσης ψυχῆς ὅσῃ ἂν μέλῃ τὸ
προσῆκον δέξασθαι, ἰδοῦσα διὰ χρόνου τὸ ὂν ἀγαπᾷ τε καὶ
θεωροῦσα τἀληθῆ τρέφεται καὶ εὐπαθεῖ, ἕως ἂν κύκλῳ ἡ
περιφορὰ εἰς ταὐτὸν περιενέγκῃ. ἐν δὲ τῇ περιόδῳ καθορᾷ 5
μὲν αὐτὴν δικαιοσύνην, καθορᾷ δὲ σωφροσύνην, καθορᾷ δὲ
ἐπιστήμην, οὐχ ᾗ γένεσις πρόσεστιν, οὐδ' ἥ ἐστίν που ἑτέρα
ἐν ἑτέρῳ οὖσα ὧν ἡμεῖς νῦν ὄντων καλοῦμεν, ἀλλὰ τὴν ἐν e
τῷ ὅ ἐστιν ὂν ὄντως ἐπιστήμην οὖσαν· καὶ τἆλλα ὡσαύτως
τὰ ὄντα ὄντως θεασαμένη καὶ ἑστιαθεῖσα, δῦσα πάλιν εἰς
τὸ εἴσω τοῦ οὐρανοῦ, οἴκαδε ἦλθεν. ἐλθούσης δὲ αὐτῆς ὁ
ἡνίοχος πρὸς τὴν φάτνην τοὺς ἵππους στήσας παρέβαλεν 5
ἀμβροσίαν τε καὶ ἐπ' αὐτῇ νέκταρ ἐπότισεν.

Καὶ οὗτος μὲν θεῶν βίος· αἱ δὲ ἄλλαι ψυχαί, ἡ μὲν 248
ἄριστα θεῷ ἑπομένη καὶ εἰκασμένη ὑπερῆρεν εἰς τὸν ἔξω
τόπον τὴν τοῦ ἡνιόχου κεφαλήν, καὶ συμπεριηνέχθη τὴν
περιφοράν, θορυβουμένη ὑπὸ τῶν ἵππων καὶ μόγις καθορῶσα

---

c 1 νώτῳ στάσας Proclus : νώτωι* στάσας T : νώτωι ἱστάσας B
θεωροῦσι corr. Ven. 189 : θεωροῦσαι B T   c 7 οὖσα ψυχῆς T Simplicius : ψυχῇ οὖσα B : ψυχῆς Stobaeus : οὖσα Madvig   θεατὴ νῷ
Clemens Proclus : θεατῇ νῷ B : θεατῇ νῷ χρῆται T W   d 1 τόπον T
Simplicius : τρόπον B   ἀ::ηράτῳ τρεφομένη W Damascius : ἀκήρατος
στρεφομένη B et os s v. W² : ἀκηράτῳ vel ἀκήρατος στρεφομένη T
d 2 ὅσῃ B : ὅσῃ T   μέλῃ G : μέλλῃ B T   d 3 δέξασθαι T :
δέξεσθαι B   d 6 καθορᾷ μὲν T : καθορῶμεν B   d 7 οὐδ' ἥ B : οὐ
δὴ T : οὐδ' ᾗ vulg.

31

5 τὰ ὄντα· ἡ δὲ τοτὲ μὲν ἦρεν, τοτὲ δ' ἔδυ, βιαζομένων δὲ τῶν
ἵππων τὰ μὲν εἶδεν, τὰ δ' οὔ. αἱ δὲ δὴ ἄλλαι γλιχόμεναι
μὲν ἅπασαι τοῦ ἄνω ἕπονται, ἀδυνατοῦσαι δέ, ὑποβρύχιαι
συμπεριφέρονται, πατοῦσαι ἀλλήλας καὶ ἐπιβάλλουσαι, ἑτέρα
b πρὸ τῆς ἑτέρας πειρωμένη γενέσθαι. θόρυβος οὖν καὶ
ἅμιλλα καὶ ἱδρὼς ἔσχατος γίγνεται, οὗ δὴ κακίᾳ ἡνιόχων
πολλαὶ μὲν χωλεύονται, πολλαὶ δὲ πολλὰ πτερὰ θραύονται·
πᾶσαι δὲ πολὺν ἔχουσαι πόνον ἀτελεῖς τῆς τοῦ ὄντος θέας
5 ἀπέρχονται, καὶ ἀπελθοῦσαι τροφῇ δοξαστῇ χρῶνται. οὗ
δ' ἕνεχ' ἡ πολλὴ σπουδὴ τὸ ἀληθείας ἰδεῖν πεδίον οὗ ἐστιν,
ἥ τε δὴ προσήκουσα ψυχῆς τῷ ἀρίστῳ νομὴ ἐκ τοῦ ἐκεῖ
c λειμῶνος τυγχάνει οὖσα, ἥ τε τοῦ πτεροῦ φύσις, ᾧ ψυχὴ
κουφίζεται, τούτῳ τρέφεται. θεσμός τε Ἀδραστείας ὅδε.
ἥτις ἂν ψυχὴ θεῷ συνοπαδὸς γενομένη κατίδῃ τι τῶν ἀληθῶν, μέχρι τε τῆς ἑτέρας περιόδου εἶναι ἀπήμονα, κἂν ἀεὶ
5 τοῦτο δύνηται ποιεῖν, ἀεὶ ἀβλαβῆ εἶναι· ὅταν δὲ ἀδυνατήσασα ἐπισπέσθαι μὴ ἴδῃ, καί τινι συντυχίᾳ χρησαμένη
λήθης τε καὶ κακίας πλησθεῖσα βαρυνθῇ, βαρυνθεῖσα δὲ
πτερορρυήσῃ τε καὶ ἐπὶ τὴν γῆν πέσῃ, τότε νόμος ταύτην
d μὴ φυτεῦσαι εἰς μηδεμίαν θήρειον φύσιν ἐν τῇ πρώτῃ
γενέσει, ἀλλὰ τὴν μὲν πλεῖστα ἰδοῦσαν εἰς γονὴν ἀνδρὸς
γενησομένου φιλοσόφου ἢ φιλοκάλου ἢ μουσικοῦ τινος καὶ
ἐρωτικοῦ, τὴν δὲ δευτέραν εἰς βασιλέως ἐννόμου ἢ πολεμικοῦ
5 καὶ ἀρχικοῦ, τρίτην εἰς πολιτικοῦ ἤ τινος οἰκονομικοῦ ἢ
χρηματιστικοῦ, τετάρτην εἰς φιλοπόνου ⟨ἢ⟩ γυμναστικοῦ ἢ
περὶ σώματος ἴασίν τινος ἐσομένου, πέμπτην μαντικὸν βίον
e ἤ τινα τελεστικὸν ἕξουσαν· ἕκτῃ ποιητικὸς ἢ τῶν περὶ
μίμησίν τις ἄλλος ἁρμόσει, ἑβδόμη δημιουργικὸς ἢ γεωργικός,
ὀγδόῃ σοφιστικὸς ἢ δημοκοπικός, ἐνάτῃ τυραννικός. ἐν δὴ

b 2 οὗ δὴ T : ουδη B   b 5 οὗ δ' ἕνεχ' ἡ corr. D : οὐδὲν ἔχει B :
οὗ δὴ ἕνεχ' ἡ T   b 6 οὗ secl. Madvig   c 3 ψυχῇ T : ψυχῆ B
c 4-5 κἂν αἰεὶ τοῦτο ... αἰεὶ ἀβλαβῆ TW : εἰ τοῦτο ... κἂν αἰεὶ βλάβη B
c 6 χρησαμένη T : χρησαμένη B   d 1 θήρειον T : θηρείαν B   d 6 ἢ
add. Badham   d 7 τινος Hermann : τινα B T   e 3 δημοκοπικός
T : δημοτικός B   δὴ B : δὲ T

τούτοις ἅπασιν ὃς μὲν ἂν δικαίως διαγάγῃ ἀμείνονος μοίρας
μεταλαμβάνει, ὃς δ᾽ ἂν ἀδίκως, χείρονος· εἰς μὲν γὰρ τὸ 5
αὐτὸ ὅθεν ἥκει ἡ ψυχὴ ἑκάστη οὐκ ἀφικνεῖται ἐτῶν μυρίων—
οὐ γὰρ πτεροῦται πρὸ τοσούτου χρόνου—πλὴν ἡ τοῦ φιλοσο- **249**
φήσαντος ἀδόλως ἢ παιδεραστήσαντος μετὰ φιλοσοφίας,
αὗται δὲ τρίτῃ περιόδῳ τῇ χιλιετεῖ, ἐὰν ἕλωνται τρὶς ἐφεξῆς
τὸν βίον τοῦτον, οὕτω πτερωθεῖσαι τρισχιλιοστῷ ἔτει ἀπέρχονται. αἱ δὲ ἄλλαι, ὅταν τὸν πρῶτον βίον τελευτήσωσιν, 5
κρίσεως ἔτυχον, κριθεῖσαι δὲ αἱ μὲν εἰς τὰ ὑπὸ γῆς δικαι-
ωτήρια ἐλθοῦσαι δίκην ἐκτίνουσιν, αἱ δ᾽ εἰς τοὐρανοῦ τινα
τόπον ὑπὸ τῆς Δίκης κουφισθεῖσαι διάγουσιν ἀξίως οὗ ἐν
ἀνθρώπου εἴδει ἐβίωσαν βίου. τῷ δὲ χιλιοστῷ ἀμφότεραι b
ἀφικνούμεναι ἐπὶ κλήρωσίν τε καὶ αἵρεσιν τοῦ δευτέρου
βίου αἱροῦνται ὃν ἂν θέλῃ ἑκάστη· ἔνθα καὶ εἰς θηρίου
βίον ἀνθρωπίνη ψυχὴ ἀφικνεῖται, καὶ ἐκ θηρίου ὅς ποτε
ἄνθρωπος ἦν πάλιν εἰς ἄνθρωπον. οὐ γὰρ ἥ γε μήποτε 5
ἰδοῦσα τὴν ἀλήθειαν εἰς τόδε ἥξει τὸ σχῆμα. δεῖ γὰρ ἄνθρωπον συνιέναι κατ᾽ εἶδος λεγόμενον, ἐκ πολλῶν ἰὸν αἰσθήσεων εἰς ἓν λογισμῷ συναιρούμενον· τοῦτο δ᾽ ἐστιν c
ἀνάμνησις ἐκείνων ἅ ποτ᾽ εἶδεν ἡμῶν ἡ ψυχὴ συμπορευθεῖσα
θεῷ καὶ ὑπεριδοῦσα ἃ νῦν εἶναί φαμεν, καὶ ἀνακύψασα εἰς
τὸ ὂν ὄντως. διὸ δὴ δικαίως μόνη πτεροῦται ἡ τοῦ φιλοσόφου διάνοια· πρὸς γὰρ ἐκείνοις ἀεί ἐστιν μνήμῃ κατὰ δύναμιν, 5
πρὸς οἷσπερ θεὸς ὢν θεῖός ἐστιν. τοῖς δὲ δὴ τοιούτοις ἀνὴρ
ὑπομνήμασιν ὀρθῶς χρώμενος, τελέους ἀεὶ τελετὰς τελού-
μενος, τέλεος ὄντως μόνος γίγνεται· ἐξιστάμενος δὲ τῶν
ἀνθρωπίνων· σπουδασμάτων καὶ πρὸς τῷ θείῳ γιγνόμενος, d
νουθετεῖται μὲν ὑπὸ τῶν πολλῶν ὡς παρακινῶν, ἐνθουσιάζων
δὲ λέληθεν τοὺς πολλούς.

b 3 θέλῃ BT : ἐθέλῃ Eusebius   b 4 βίον T : βίον B   b 7 ⟨τὸ⟩
κατ᾽ εἶδος Heindorf   ἰὸν BT : οἷον rec. b : ἰόντ᾽ Badham   c 1 ξυναι-
ρούμενον BT : ξυναιρουμένων Heindorf   c 6 θεὸς B : ὁ θεὸς T
(utrumque traditum fuisse testatur Hermias)   θεῖός BT : θεός
quoque traditum fuisse testatur Hermias

Ἔστι δὴ οὖν δεῦρο ὁ πᾶς ἥκων λόγος περὶ τῆς τετάρτης
5 μανίας—ἣν ὅταν τὸ τῇδέ τις ὁρῶν κάλλος, τοῦ ἀληθοῦς
ἀναμιμνῃσκόμενος, πτερῶταί τε καὶ ἀναπτερούμενος προ-
θυμούμενος ἀναπτέσθαι, ἀδυνατῶν δέ, ὄρνιθος δίκην βλέπων
ἄνω, τῶν κάτω δὲ ἀμελῶν, αἰτίαν ἔχει ὡς μανικῶς διακεί-
e μενος—ὡς ἄρα αὕτη πασῶν τῶν ἐνθουσιάσεων ἀρίστη τε
καὶ ἐξ ἀρίστων τῷ 'τε ἔχοντι καὶ τῷ κοινωνοῦντι αὐτῆς
γίγνεται, καὶ ὅτι ταύτης μετέχων τῆς μανίας ὁ ἐρῶν τῶν
καλῶν ἐραστὴς καλεῖται. καθάπερ γὰρ εἴρηται, πᾶσα μὲν
5 ἀνθρώπου ψυχὴ φύσει τεθέαται τὰ ὄντα, ἢ οὐκ ἂν ἦλθεν
250 εἰς τόδε τὸ ζῷον· ἀναμιμνῄσκεσθαι δὲ ἐκ τῶνδε ἐκεῖνα οὐ
ῥᾴδιον ἀπάσῃ, οὔτε ὅσαι βραχέως εἶδον τότε τἀκεῖ, οὔθ' αἱ
δεῦρο πεσοῦσαι ἐδυστύχησαν, ὥστε ὑπό τινων ὁμιλιῶν ἐπὶ
τὸ ἄδικον τραπόμεναι λήθην ὧν τότε εἶδον ἱερῶν ἔχειν.
5 ὀλίγαι δὴ λείπονται αἷς τὸ τῆς μνήμης ἱκανῶς πάρεστιν·
αὗται δέ, ὅταν τι τῶν ἐκεῖ ὁμοίωμα ἴδωσιν, ἐκπλήττονται
καὶ οὐκέτ' ⟨ἐν⟩ αὑτῶν γίγνονται, ὃ δ' ἔστι τὸ πάθος ἀγνο-
b οῦσι διὰ τὸ μὴ ἱκανῶς διαισθάνεσθαι. δικαιοσύνης μὲν οὖν
καὶ σωφροσύνης καὶ ὅσα ἄλλα τίμια ψυχαῖς οὐκ ἔνεστι
φέγγος οὐδὲν ἐν τοῖς τῇδε ὁμοιώμασιν, ἀλλὰ δι' ἀμυδρῶν
ὀργάνων μόγις αὐτῶν καὶ ὀλίγοι ἐπὶ τὰς εἰκόνας ἰόντες
5 θεῶνται τὸ τοῦ εἰκασθέντος γένος· κάλλος δὲ τότ' ἦν ἰδεῖν
λαμπρόν, ὅτε σὺν εὐδαίμονι χορῷ μακαρίαν ὄψιν τε καὶ
θέαν, ἑπόμενοι μετὰ μὲν Διὸς ἡμεῖς, ἄλλοι δὲ μετ' ἄλλου
θεῶν, εἶδόν τε καὶ ἐτελοῦντο τῶν τελετῶν ἣν θέμις λέγειν
c μακαριωτάτην, ἣν ὠργιάζομεν ὁλόκληροι μὲν αὐτοὶ ὄντες καὶ
ἀπαθεῖς κακῶν ὅσα ἡμᾶς ἐν ὑστέρῳ χρόνῳ ὑπέμενεν, ὁλό-
κληρα δὲ καὶ ἁπλᾶ καὶ ἀτρεμῆ καὶ εὐδαίμονα φάσματα
μυούμενοί τε καὶ ἐποπτεύοντες ἐν αὐγῇ καθαρᾷ, καθαροὶ

---

d 5 ἦν BT Stobaeus: ᾗ al.: ἵν' vulg.   d 6 τε καὶ BT Stobaeus:
secl. Schanz   d 9 μανικῶς T: μανικὸς B   e 4 καλεῖται BT:
γίγνεται Stobaeus   a 3 ὥστε B γρ. t: οὔτε T   a 7 οὐκέτ'
ἐν αὑτῶν Hirschig: οὐκέτ' αὑτῶν BT: οὐκέθ' αὑτῶν vulg.   b 4 ὀλίγοι
Bt: ὀλίγοις T   b 8 τῶν B: om. T   ἣν recc.: ἢ B: ᾗ T
c 1 ὠργιάζομεν W: ὀργιάζομεν BT   c 4 αὐγῇ T: αυτη B

ὄντες καὶ ἀσήμαντοι τούτου ὃ νῦν δὴ σῶμα περιφέροντες 5
ὀνομάζομεν, ὀστρέου τρόπον δεδεσμευμένοι.

Ταῦτα μὲν οὖν μνήμῃ κεχαρίσθω, δι' ἣν πόθῳ τῶν τότε
νῦν μακρότερα εἴρηται· περὶ δὲ κάλλους, ὥσπερ εἴπομεν,
μετ' ἐκείνων τε ἔλαμπεν ὄν, δεῦρό τ' ἐλθόντες κατειλήφαμεν d
αὐτὸ διὰ τῆς ἐναργεστάτης αἰσθήσεως τῶν ἡμετέρων στίλβον
ἐναργέστατα. ὄψις γὰρ ἡμῖν ὀξυτάτη τῶν διὰ τοῦ σώματος
ἔρχεται αἰσθήσεων, ᾗ φρόνησις οὐχ ὁρᾶται—δεινοὺς γὰρ ἂν
παρεῖχεν ἔρωτας, εἴ τι τοιοῦτον ἑαυτῆς ἐναργὲς εἴδωλον 5
παρείχετο εἰς ὄψιν ἰόν—καὶ τἆλλα ὅσα ἐραστά· νῦν δὲ
κάλλος μόνον ταύτην ἔσχε μοῖραν, ὥστ' ἐκφανέστατον εἶναι
καὶ ἐρασμιώτατον. ὁ μὲν οὖν μὴ νεοτελὴς ἢ διεφθαρμένος e
οὐκ ὀξέως ἐνθένδε ἐκεῖσε φέρεται πρὸς αὐτὸ τὸ κάλλος,
θεώμενος αὐτοῦ τὴν τῇδε ἐπωνυμίαν, ὥστ' οὐ σέβεται προσορῶν, ἀλλ' ἡδονῇ παραδοὺς τετράποδος νόμον βαίνειν
ἐπιχειρεῖ καὶ παιδοσπορεῖν, καὶ ὕβρει προσομιλῶν οὐ δέ- 5
δοικεν οὐδ' αἰσχύνεται παρὰ φύσιν ἡδονὴν διώκων· ὁ δὲ 251
ἀρτιτελής, ὁ τῶν τότε πολυθεάμων, ὅταν θεοειδὲς πρόσωπον
ἴδῃ κάλλος εὖ μεμιμημένον ἤ τινα σώματος ἰδέαν, πρῶτον
μὲν ἔφριξε καί τι τῶν τότε ὑπῆλθεν αὐτὸν δειμάτων, εἶτα
προσορῶν ὡς θεὸν σέβεται, καὶ εἰ μὴ ἐδεδίει τὴν τῆς σφό- 5
δρα μανίας δόξαν, θύοι ἂν ὡς ἀγάλματι καὶ θεῷ τοῖς παιδικοῖς. ἰδόντα δ' αὐτὸν οἷον ἐκ τῆς φρίκης μεταβολή τε
καὶ ἱδρὼς καὶ θερμότης ἀήθης λαμβάνει· δεξάμενος γὰρ τοῦ b
κάλλους τὴν ἀπορροὴν διὰ τῶν ὀμμάτων ἐθερμάνθη ᾗ ἡ
τοῦ πτεροῦ φύσις ἄρδεται, θερμανθέντος δὲ ἐτάκη τὰ περὶ
τὴν ἔκφυσιν, ἃ πάλαι ὑπὸ σκληρότητος συμμεμυκότα εἶργε
μὴ βλαστάνειν, ἐπιρρυείσης δὲ τῆς τροφῆς ᾤδησέ τε καὶ 5
ὥρμησε φύεσθαι ἀπὸ τῆς ῥίζης ὁ τοῦ πτεροῦ καυλὸς ὑπὸ
πᾶν τὸ τῆς ψυχῆς εἶδος· πᾶσα γὰρ ἦν τὸ πάλαι πτερωτή.

c 5 ἀσήμαντοι] fort. ἀπήμαντοι H. Richards   νῦν δὴ T : νῦν B
c 6 δεδεσμευμένοι T : δεδεσμευμένον B   a 5 μὴ ἐδεδίει Cobet : μὴ
'δεδίει Schanz : μὴ δεδιείη B (sed εἴη punctis notatum) : μὴ δεδίει T
b 2 ᾗ . . . ἄρδεται ante ἐθερμάνθη transp. ci. Ast   ᾗ ἡ T : ἢ B

c ζεῖ οὖν ἐν τούτῳ ὅλη καὶ ἀνακηκίει, καὶ ὅπερ τὸ τῶν ὀδοντοφυούντων πάθος περὶ τοὺς ὀδόντας γίγνεται ὅταν ἄρτι
φύωσιν, κνῆσίς τε καὶ ἀγανάκτησις περὶ τὰ οὖλα, ταὐτὸν
δὴ πέπονθεν ἡ τοῦ πτεροφυεῖν ἀρχομένου ψυχή· ζεῖ τε καὶ
5 ἀγανακτεῖ καὶ γαργαλίζεται φύουσα τὰ πτερά. ὅταν μὲν
οὖν βλέπουσα πρὸς τὸ τοῦ παιδὸς κάλλος, ἐκεῖθεν μέρη ἐπιόντα καὶ ῥέοντ᾽—ἃ δὴ διὰ ταῦτα ἵμερος καλεῖται—δεχομένη
[τὸν ἵμερον] ἄρδηταί τε καὶ θερμαίνηται, λωφᾷ τε τῆς ὀδύνης
d καὶ γέγηθεν· ὅταν δὲ χωρὶς γένηται καὶ αὐχμήσῃ, τὰ τῶν
διεξόδων στόματα ᾗ τὸ πτερὸν ὁρμᾷ, συναυαινόμενα μύσαντα
ἀποκλῄει τὴν βλάστην τοῦ πτεροῦ, ἡ δ᾽ ἐντὸς μετὰ τοῦ
ἱμέρου ἀποκεκλῃμένη, πηδῶσα οἷον τὰ σφύζοντα, τῇ διεξόδῳ
5 ἐγχρίει ἑκάστη τῇ καθ᾽ αὑτήν, ὥστε πᾶσα κεντουμένη κύκλῳ
ἡ ψυχὴ οἰστρᾷ καὶ ὀδυνᾶται, μνήμην δ᾽ αὖ ἔχουσα τοῦ
καλοῦ γέγηθεν. ἐκ δὲ ἀμφοτέρων μεμειγμένων ἀδημονεῖ τε
τῇ ἀτοπίᾳ τοῦ πάθους καὶ ἀποροῦσα λυττᾷ, καὶ ἐμμανὴς
e οὖσα οὔτε νυκτὸς δύναται καθεύδειν οὔτε μεθ᾽ ἡμέραν οὗ ἂν
ᾖ μένειν, θεῖ δὲ ποθοῦσα ὅπου ἂν οἴηται ὄψεσθαι τὸν ἔχοντα
τὸ κάλλος· ἰδοῦσα δὲ καὶ ἐποχετευσαμένη ἵμερον ἔλυσε μὲν
τὰ τότε συμπεφραγμένα, ἀναπνοὴν δὲ λαβοῦσα κέντρων τε
5 καὶ ὠδίνων ἔληξεν, ἡδονὴν δ᾽ αὖ ταύτην γλυκυτάτην ἐν τῷ
252 παρόντι καρποῦται. ὅθεν δὴ ἑκοῦσα εἶναι οὐκ ἀπολείπεται,
οὐδέ τινα τοῦ καλοῦ περὶ πλείονος ποιεῖται, ἀλλὰ μητέρων
τε καὶ ἀδελφῶν καὶ ἑταίρων πάντων λέλησται, καὶ οὐσίας
δι᾽ ἀμέλειαν ἀπολλυμένης παρ᾽ οὐδὲν τίθεται, νομίμων δὲ
5 καὶ εὐσχημόνων, οἷς πρὸ τοῦ ἐκαλλωπίζετο, πάντων κατα-
φρονήσασα δουλεύειν ἑτοίμη καὶ κοιμᾶσθαι ὅπου ἂν ἐᾷ τις
ἐγγυτάτω τοῦ πόθου· πρὸς γὰρ τῷ σέβεσθαι τὸν τὸ κάλλος
b ἔχοντα ἰατρὸν ηὕρηκε μόνον τῶν μεγίστων πόνων. τοῦτο

c 1 ζεῖ t : ζῇ B : ζῇ T   ὀδοντοφυούντων B t : ὀδόντων φυόντων T
c 3 φυωσιν B : φύωσι T : φυῶσι Bekker   κνῆσίς T : κίνησίς BW
c 4 ζεῖ T : ζῇ B   c 8 τὸν ἵμερον secl. olim Stallbaum   d 5 ἑκάστη
Ruhnken : ἑκάστῃ B T   e 4 συμπεφραγμένα T : συμπεπραγμένα B
e 5 ὠδίνων] ὀδυνῶν Badham   a 6 ἂν T : ἐὰν B

δὲ τὸ πάθος, ὦ παῖ καλέ, πρὸς ὃν δή μοι ὁ λόγος, ἄνθρωποι
μὲν ἔρωτα ὀνομάζουσιν, θεοὶ δὲ ὃ καλοῦσιν ἀκούσας εἰκότως
διὰ νεότητα γελάσῃ. λέγουσι δὲ οἶμαί τινες Ὁμηριδῶν ἐκ
τῶν ἀποθέτων ἐπῶν δύο ἔπη εἰς τὸν Ἔρωτα, ὧν τὸ ἕτερον 5
ὑβριστικὸν πάνυ καὶ οὐ σφόδρα τι ἔμμετρον· ὑμνοῦσι δὲ
ὧδε—

    τὸν δ᾽ ἤτοι θνητοὶ μὲν Ἔρωτα καλοῦσι ποτηνόν,
    ἀθάνατοι δὲ Πτέρωτα, διὰ πτεροφύτορ᾽ ἀνάγκην.

τούτοις δὴ ἔξεστι μὲν πείθεσθαι, ἔξεστιν δὲ μή· ὅμως δὲ ἥ c
γε αἰτία καὶ τὸ πάθος τῶν ἐρώντων τοῦτο ἐκεῖνο τυγχάνει ὄν.
    Τῶν μὲν οὖν Διὸς ὀπαδῶν ὁ ληφθεὶς ἐμβριθέστερον
δύναται φέρειν τὸ τοῦ πτερωνύμου ἄχθος· ὅσοι δὲ Ἀρεώς
τε θεραπευταὶ καὶ μετ᾽ ἐκείνου περιεπόλουν, ὅταν ὑπ᾽ 5
Ἔρωτος ἁλῶσι καί τι οἰηθῶσιν ἀδικεῖσθαι ὑπὸ τοῦ ἐρωμένου,
φονικοὶ καὶ ἕτοιμοι καθιερεύειν αὑτούς τε καὶ τὰ παιδικά.
καὶ οὕτω καθ᾽ ἕκαστον θεόν, οὗ ἕκαστος ἦν χορευτής, ἐκεῖ- d
νον τιμῶν τε καὶ μιμούμενος εἰς τὸ δυνατὸν ζῇ, ἕως ἂν ᾖ
ἀδιάφθορος καὶ τὴν τῇδε πρώτην γένεσιν βιοτεύῃ, καὶ
τούτῳ τῷ τρόπῳ πρός τε τοὺς ἐρωμένους καὶ τοὺς ἄλλους
ὁμιλεῖ τε καὶ προσφέρεται. τόν τε οὖν Ἔρωτα τῶν καλῶν 5
πρὸς τρόπου ἐκλέγεται ἕκαστος, καὶ ὡς θεὸν αὐτὸν ἐκεῖνον
ὄντα ἑαυτῷ οἷον ἄγαλμα τεκταίνεταί τε καὶ κατακοσμεῖ, ὡς
τιμήσων τε καὶ ὀργιάσων. οἱ μὲν δὴ οὖν Διὸς δῖόν τινα e
εἶναι ζητοῦσι τὴν ψυχὴν τὸν ὑφ᾽ αὑτῶν ἐρώμενον· σκοποῦσιν οὖν εἰ φιλόσοφός τε καὶ ἡγεμονικὸς τὴν φύσιν, καὶ
ὅταν αὐτὸν εὑρόντες ἐρασθῶσι, πᾶν ποιοῦσιν ὅπως τοιοῦτος
ἔσται. ἐὰν οὖν μὴ πρότερον ἐμβεβῶσι τῷ ἐπιτηδεύματι, 5
τότε ἐπιχειρήσαντες μανθάνουσί τε ὅθεν ἄν τι δύνωνται καὶ
αὐτοὶ μετέρχονται, ἰχνεύοντες δὲ παρ᾽ ἑαυτῶν ἀνευρίσκειν

b 4 οἶμαί Τ : οἱ μέν Β   b 6 ὑβριστικὸν πάνυ Β : πάνυ ὑβριστικὸν
Τ Stobaeus   b 8 δ᾽ ἤτοι Τ : δή τοι Β Stobaeus   b 9 πτεροφύτορ᾽
Stobaeus : πτερόφυτον Β : πτερόφοιτον Τ   d 2 ζῇ recc. : ζῆν ΒΤ
d 3 βιοτεύῃ corr. Coisl. : βιοτεύει ΒΤ   d 4 καὶ τοὺς Β : καὶ πρὸς
τοὺς Τ   d 5 prius τε Β : γε Τ   e 1 δῖόν D : δι᾽ ὅν Β : διιόν Τ

253 τὴν τοῦ σφετέρου θεοῦ φύσιν εὐποροῦσι διὰ τὸ συντόνως
ἠναγκάσθαι πρὸς τὸν θεὸν βλέπειν, καὶ ἐφαπτόμενοι αὐτοῦ
τῇ μνήμῃ ἐνθουσιῶντες ἐξ ἐκείνου λαμβάνουσι τὰ ἔθη καὶ
τὰ ἐπιτηδεύματα, καθ᾽ ὅσον δυνατὸν θεοῦ ἀνθρώπῳ μετα-
5 σχεῖν· καὶ τούτων δὴ τὸν ἐρώμενον αἰτιώμενοι ἔτι τε μᾶλλον
ἀγαπῶσι, κἂν ἐκ Διὸς ἀρύτωσιν ὥσπερ αἱ βάκχαι, ἐπὶ τὴν
τοῦ ἐρωμένου ψυχὴν ἐπαντλοῦντες ποιοῦσιν ὡς δυνατὸν
b ὁμοιότατον τῷ σφετέρῳ θεῷ. ὅσοι δ᾽ αὖ μεθ᾽ Ἥρας εἵποντο,
βασιλικὸν ζητοῦσι, καὶ εὑρόντες περὶ τοῦτον πάντα δρῶσιν
τὰ αὐτά. οἱ δὲ Ἀπόλλωνός τε καὶ ἑκάστου τῶν θεῶν οὕτω
κατὰ τὸν θεὸν ἰόντες ζητοῦσι τὸν σφέτερον παῖδα πεφυκέναι,
5 καὶ ὅταν κτήσωνται, μιμούμενοι αὐτοί τε καὶ τὰ παιδικὰ
πείθοντες καὶ ῥυθμίζοντες εἰς τὸ ἐκείνου ἐπιτήδευμα καὶ
ἰδέαν ἄγουσιν, ὅση ἑκάστῳ δύναμις, οὐ φθόνῳ οὐδ᾽ ἀνελευ-
θέρῳ δυσμενείᾳ χρώμενοι πρὸς τὰ παιδικά, ἀλλ᾽ εἰς ὁμοιότητα
c αὑτοῖς καὶ τῷ θεῷ ὃν ἂν τιμῶσι πᾶσαν πάντως ὅτι μάλιστα
πειρώμενοι ἄγειν οὕτω ποιοῦσι. προθυμία μὲν οὖν τῶν ὡς
ἀληθῶς ἐρώντων καὶ τελετή, ἐάν γε διαπράξωνται ὃ προθυμοῦνται ᾗ λέγω, οὕτω καλή τε καὶ εὐδαιμονικὴ ὑπὸ τοῦ
5 δι᾽ ἔρωτα μανέντος φίλου τῷ φιληθέντι γίγνεται, ἐὰν
αἱρεθῇ· ἁλίσκεται δὲ δὴ ὁ αἱρεθεὶς τοιῷδε τρόπῳ.
    Καθάπερ ἐν ἀρχῇ τοῦδε τοῦ μύθου τριχῇ διείλομεν ψυχὴν
ἑκάστην, ἱππομόρφω μὲν δύο τινὲ εἴδη, ἡνιοχικὸν δὲ εἶδος
d τρίτον, καὶ νῦν ἔτι ἡμῖν ταῦτα μενέτω. τῶν δὲ δὴ ἵππων
ὁ μέν, φαμέν, ἀγαθός, ὁ δ᾽ οὔ· ἀρετὴ δὲ τίς τοῦ ἀγαθοῦ
ἢ κακοῦ κακία, οὐ διείπομεν, νῦν δὲ λεκτέον. ὁ μὲν τοίνυν
αὐτοῖν ἐν τῇ καλλίονι στάσει ὢν τό τε εἶδος ὀρθὸς καὶ
5 διηρθρωμένος, ὑψαύχην, ἐπίγρυπος, λευκὸς ἰδεῖν, μελανόμ-

a 5 τούτων recc. : τοῦτον Β Τ   a 6 κἂν] χἂν Madvig   b 1 ἥρας
t : ἡμέρας Β Τ   c 3 τελετή corr. Par. 1808 : τελευτή Β Τ   ἐάν
γε διαπράξωνται Hermias : ἐάν τ᾽ ἐνδιαπράξωνται Β Τ : ἐάν γ᾽ εὖ διαπράξωνται G. Hermann   c 4 ᾗ λέγω Heindorf : ἣν λέγω Τ : ην δ᾽
ἐγὼ Β   c 5 γίγνεται Τ : γίγνηται Β   c 6 ὁ αἱρεθεὶς secl. Badham
c 7 διείλομεν Heindorf : διειλόμην Β Τ   d 1 ἵππων Τ : ἵππω Β
d 4 αὐτοῖν Τ : αὐτῶν Β

ματος, τιμῆς ἐραστὴς μετὰ σωφροσύνης τε καὶ αἰδοῦς, καὶ
ἀληθινῆς δόξης ἑταῖρος, ἄπληκτος, κελεύσματι μόνον καὶ
λόγῳ ἡνιοχεῖται· ὁ δ' αὖ σκολιός, πολύς, εἰκῇ συμπεφορη- e
μένος, κρατεραύχην, βραχυτράχηλος, σιμοπρόσωπος, μελάγχρως, γλαυκόμματος, ὕφαιμος, ὕβρεως καὶ ἀλαζονείας ἑταῖρος,
περὶ ὦτα λάσιος, κωφός, μάστιγι μετὰ κέντρων μόγις ὑπεί-
κων. ὅταν δ' οὖν ὁ ἡνίοχος ἰδὼν τὸ ἐρωτικὸν ὄμμα, πᾶσαν 5
αἰσθήσει διαθερμήνας τὴν ψυχήν, γαργαλισμοῦ τε καὶ πόθου
κέντρων ὑποπλησθῇ, ὁ μὲν εὐπειθὴς τῷ ἡνιόχῳ τῶν ἵππων, 254
ἀεί τε καὶ τότε αἰδοῖ βιαζόμενος, ἑαυτὸν κατέχει μὴ ἐπι-
πηδᾶν τῷ ἐρωμένῳ· ὁ δὲ οὔτε κέντρων ἡνιοχικῶν οὔτε
μάστιγος ἔτι ἐντρέπεται, σκιρτῶν δὲ βίᾳ φέρεται, καὶ πάντα
πράγματα παρέχων τῷ σύζυγί τε καὶ ἡνιόχῳ ἀναγκάζει 5
ἰέναι τε πρὸς τὰ παιδικὰ καὶ μνείαν ποιεῖσθαι τῆς τῶν
ἀφροδισίων χάριτος. τὼ δὲ κατ' ἀρχὰς μὲν ἀντιτείνετον
ἀγανακτοῦντε, ὡς δεινὰ καὶ παράνομα ἀναγκαζομένω· τελευ- b
τῶντε δέ, ὅταν μηδὲν ᾖ πέρας κακοῦ, πορεύεσθον ἀγομένω,
εἴξαντε καὶ ὁμολογήσαντε ποιήσειν τὸ κελευόμενον. καὶ
πρὸς αὐτῷ τ' ἐγένοντο καὶ εἶδον τὴν ὄψιν τὴν τῶν παιδικῶν
ἀστράπτουσαν. ἰδόντος δὲ τοῦ ἡνιόχου ἡ μνήμη πρὸς τὴν 5
τοῦ κάλλους φύσιν ἠνέχθη, καὶ πάλιν εἶδεν αὐτὴν μετὰ
σωφροσύνης ἐν ἁγνῷ βάθρῳ βεβῶσαν· ἰδοῦσα δὲ ἔδεισέ
τε καὶ σεφθεῖσα ἀνέπεσεν ὑπτία, καὶ ἅμα ἠναγκάσθη εἰς
τοὐπίσω ἑλκύσαι τὰς ἡνίας οὕτω σφόδρα, ὥστ' ἐπὶ τὰ c
ἰσχία ἄμφω καθίσαι τὼ ἵππω, τὸν μὲν ἑκόντα διὰ τὸ μὴ
ἀντιτείνειν, τὸν δὲ ὑβριστὴν μάλ' ἄκοντα. ἀπελθόντε δὲ
ἀπωτέρω, ὁ μὲν ὑπ' αἰσχύνης τε καὶ θάμβους ἱδρῶτι πᾶσαν
ἔβρεξε τὴν ψυχήν, ὁ δὲ λήξας τῆς ὀδύνης, ἣν ὑπὸ τοῦ 5

d 6 καὶ secl. Badham   d 7 ἀληθινῆς om. Heraclitus   κελεύσματι t Heraclitus: κελεύματι ΒΤ   e 2 βραχυτράχηλος ΒΤ:
βαρυτράχηλος V   e 4 περὶ ὦτα λάσιος κωφός Τ: περὶ ὦτα λασιοκωφος
B Photius Synesius: περιωτάλσιος ὑπόκωφος Heraclitus   e 6 αἰσθήσει
dub. Heindorf: secl. Herwerden   a 1 κέντρων] πτερῶν Herwerden
a 5 ⟨τῷ⟩ ἡνιόχῳ Herwerden   b 1 τελευτῶντε Τ: τελευτῶντες Β

χαλινοῦ τε ἔσχεν καὶ τοῦ πτώματος, μόγις ἐξαναπνεύσας
ἐλοιδόρησεν ὀργῇ, πολλὰ κακίζων τόν τε ἡνίοχον καὶ τὸν
ὁμόζυγα ὡς δειλίᾳ τε καὶ ἀνανδρίᾳ λιπόντε τὴν τάξιν καὶ
d ὁμολογίαν· καὶ πάλιν οὐκ ἐθέλοντας προσιέναι ἀναγκάζων
μόγις συνεχώρησεν δεομένων εἰς αὖθις ὑπερβαλέσθαι. ἐλ-
θόντος δὲ τοῦ συντεθέντος χρόνου [οὗ] ἀμνημονεῖν προσποιουμένω ἀναμιμνήσκων, βιαζόμενος, χρεμετίζων, ἕλκων
5 ἠνάγκασεν αὖ προσελθεῖν τοῖς παιδικοῖς ἐπὶ τοὺς αὐτοὺς
λόγους, καὶ ἐπειδὴ ἐγγὺς ἦσαν, ἐγκύψας καὶ ἐκτείνας τὴν
κέρκον, ἐνδακὼν τὸν χαλινόν, μετ᾽ ἀναιδείας ἕλκει· ὁ δ᾽
e ἡνίοχος ἔτι μᾶλλον ταὐτὸν πάθος παθών, ὥσπερ ἀπὸ ὕσ-
πληγος ἀναπεσών, ἔτι μᾶλλον τοῦ ὑβριστοῦ ἵππου ἐκ τῶν
ὀδόντων βίᾳ ὀπίσω σπάσας τὸν χαλινόν, τήν τε κακηγόρον
γλῶτταν καὶ τὰς γνάθους καθῄμαξεν καὶ τὰ σκέλη τε καὶ
5 τὰ ἰσχία πρὸς τὴν γῆν ἐρείσας ὀδύναις ἔδωκεν. ὅταν δὲ
ταὐτὸν πολλάκις πάσχων ὁ πονηρὸς τῆς ὕβρεως λήξῃ,
ταπεινωθεὶς ἕπεται ἤδη τῇ τοῦ ἡνιόχου προνοίᾳ, καὶ ὅταν
ἴδῃ τὸν καλόν, φόβῳ διόλλυται· ὥστε συμβαίνει τότ᾽ ἤδη τὴν
τοῦ ἐραστοῦ ψυχὴν τοῖς παιδικοῖς αἰδουμένην τε καὶ δεδιυῖαν
255 ἕπεσθαι. ἅτε οὖν πᾶσαν θεραπείαν ὡς ἰσόθεος θεραπευόμενος οὐχ ὑπὸ σχηματιζομένου τοῦ ἐρῶντος ἀλλ᾽ ἀληθῶς
τοῦτο πεπονθότος, καὶ αὐτὸς ὢν φύσει φίλος τῷ θεραπεύοντι, ἐὰν ἄρα καὶ ἐν τῷ πρόσθεν ὑπὸ συμφοιτητῶν ἤ
5 τινων ἄλλων διαβεβλημένος ᾖ, λεγόντων ὡς αἰσχρὸν ἐρῶντι
πλησιάζειν, καὶ διὰ τοῦτο ἀπωθῇ τὸν ἐρῶντα, προϊόντος
δὲ ἤδη τοῦ χρόνου ἥ τε ἡλικία καὶ τὸ χρεὼν ἤγαγεν εἰς
b τὸ προσέσθαι αὐτὸν εἰς ὁμιλίαν· οὐ γὰρ δήποτε εἵμαρται

c8 λιπόντε Τ : λιπόντα Β   d2 δεομένων ΒΤ : δεομένοιν Heindorf   d3 οὗ secl. Heindorf   d6 ἐπειδὴ Τ : ἐπεὶ δὲ Β
ἐκτείνας Τ : ἐντείνας Β   e8 φόβῳ Τ : φόβον Β   τότ᾽ Β : ποτ᾽ Τ
e9 δεδιυῖαν Bekker : δεδυῖαν Β (sed κῦι supra versum) : δεδοικυῖαν Τ
a2 ὑποσχηματιζομένου Τ : ὑποσχημένου Β (σχηματιζο in marg. b)
a3 φίλος ΒΤ : φίλος εἰς ταὐτὸν ἄγει τὴν φιλίαν vulg.   a6 ἀπωθῇ
corr. Coisl. : ἀπωθεῖ ΒΤ   ἐρῶντα t : ἔρωτα ΒΤ   b1 προσέσθαι
corr. Coisl. : προέσθαι ΒΤ

κακὸν κακῷ φίλον οὐδ' ἀγαθὸν μὴ φίλον ἀγαθῷ εἶναι.
προσεμένου δὲ καὶ λόγον καὶ ὁμιλίαν δεξαμένου, ἐγγύθεν
ἡ εὔνοια γιγνομένη τοῦ ἐρῶντος ἐκπλήττει τὸν ἐρώμενον
διαισθανόμενον ὅτι οὐδ' οἱ σύμπαντες ἄλλοι φίλοι τε καὶ 5
οἰκεῖοι μοῖραν φιλίας οὐδεμίαν παρέχονται πρὸς τὸν ἔνθεον
φίλον. ὅταν δὲ χρονίζῃ τοῦτο δρῶν καὶ πλησιάζῃ μετὰ
τοῦ ἅπτεσθαι ἔν τε γυμνασίοις καὶ ἐν ταῖς ἄλλαις ὁμιλίαις,
τότ' ἤδη ἡ τοῦ ῥεύματος ἐκείνου πηγή, ὃν ἵμερον Ζεὺς c
Γανυμήδους ἐρῶν ὠνόμασε, πολλὴ φερομένη πρὸς τὸν
ἐραστήν, ἡ μὲν εἰς αὐτὸν ἔδυ, ἡ δ' ἀπομεστουμένου ἔξω
ἀπορρεῖ· καὶ οἷον πνεῦμα ἤ τις ἠχὼ ἀπὸ λείων τε καὶ
στερεῶν ἁλλομένη πάλιν ὅθεν ὡρμήθη φέρεται, οὕτω τὸ 5
τοῦ κάλλους ῥεῦμα πάλιν εἰς τὸν καλὸν διὰ τῶν ὀμμάτων
ἰόν, ᾗ πέφυκεν ἐπὶ τὴν ψυχὴν ἰέναι ἀφικόμενον καὶ ἀναπτερῶσαν, τὰς διόδους τῶν πτερῶν ἄρδει τε καὶ ὥρμησε d
πτεροφυεῖν τε καὶ τὴν τοῦ ἐρωμένου αὖ ψυχὴν ἔρωτος
ἐνέπλησεν. ἐρᾷ μὲν οὖν, ὅτου δὲ ἀπορεῖ· καὶ οὔθ' ὅτι
πέπονθεν οἶδεν οὐδ' ἔχει φράσαι, ἀλλ' οἷον ἀπ' ἄλλου
ὀφθαλμίας ἀπολελαυκὼς πρόφασιν εἰπεῖν οὐκ ἔχει, ὥσπερ 5
δὲ ἐν κατόπτρῳ ἐν τῷ ἐρῶντι ἑαυτὸν ὁρῶν λέληθεν. καὶ
ὅταν μὲν ἐκεῖνος παρῇ, λήγει κατὰ ταὐτὰ ἐκείνῳ τῆς ὀδύνης,
ὅταν δὲ ἀπῇ, κατὰ ταὐτὰ αὖ ποθεῖ καὶ ποθεῖται, εἴδωλον
ἔρωτος ἀντέρωτα ἔχων· καλεῖ δὲ αὐτὸν καὶ οἴεται οὐκ ἔρωτα e
ἀλλὰ φιλίαν εἶναι. ἐπιθυμεῖ δὲ ἐκείνῳ παραπλησίως μέν,
ἀσθενεστέρως δέ, ὁρᾶν, ἅπτεσθαι, φιλεῖν, συγκατακεῖσθαι·
καὶ δή, οἷον εἰκός, ποιεῖ τὸ μετὰ τοῦτο ταχὺ ταῦτα. ἐν οὖν
τῇ συγκοιμήσει τοῦ μὲν ἐραστοῦ ὁ ἀκόλαστος ἵππος ἔχει 5
ὅτι λέγῃ πρὸς τὸν ἡνίοχον, καὶ ἀξιοῖ ἀντὶ πολλῶν πόνων
σμικρὰ ἀπολαῦσαι· ὁ δὲ τῶν παιδικῶν ἔχει μὲν οὐδὲν εἰπεῖν, 256

b 3 προσεμένου T : πρὸς ἐμὲ νου B   λόγον καὶ B : λόγον τε καὶ T
b 8 τοῦ Eusebius : τούτου BT   c 1 τότ' ἤδη BT : τότε δὴ
Eusebius   c 4 ἀπορρεῖ T : ἀπορεῖ B   λείων] σκληρῶν Herwerden
d 3 οὔθ' BT : οὐδ' Buttmann   d 5 ὀφθαλμίαν Ast   d 6 alterum
ἐν secl. Cobet   e 6 λέγῃ Bekker : λέγει BT : λέγοι Eusebius : λέξει
Herwerden

σπαργῶν δὲ καὶ ἀπορῶν περιβάλλει τὸν ἐραστὴν καὶ φιλεῖ,
ὡς σφόδρ' εὔνουν ἀσπαζόμενος, ὅταν τε συγκατακέωνται,
οἷός ἐστι μὴ ἂν ἀπαρνηθῆναι τὸ αὑτοῦ μέρος χαρίσασθαι
5 τῷ ἐρῶντι, εἰ δεηθείη τυχεῖν· ὁ δὲ ὁμόζυξ αὖ μετὰ τοῦ
ἡνιόχου πρὸς ταῦτα μετ' αἰδοῦς καὶ λόγου ἀντιτείνει.
ἐὰν μὲν δὴ οὖν εἰς τεταγμένην τε δίαιταν καὶ φιλοσοφίαν
νικήσῃ τὰ βελτίω τῆς διανοίας ἀγαγόντα, μακάριον μὲν
b καὶ ὁμονοητικὸν τὸν ἐνθάδε βίον διάγουσιν, ἐγκρατεῖς αὑτῶν
καὶ κόσμιοι ὄντες, δουλωσάμενοι μὲν ᾧ κακία ψυχῆς ἐνεγίγνετο, ἐλευθερώσαντες δὲ ᾧ ἀρετή· τελευτήσαντες δὲ δὴ
ὑπόπτεροι καὶ ἐλαφροὶ γεγονότες τῶν τριῶν παλαισμάτων
5 τῶν ὡς ἀληθῶς Ὀλυμπιακῶν ἓν νενικήκασιν, οὗ μεῖζον
ἀγαθὸν οὔτε σωφροσύνη ἀνθρωπίνη οὔτε θεία μανία δυνατὴ
πορίσαι ἀνθρώπῳ. ἐὰν δὲ δὴ διαίτῃ φορτικωτέρᾳ τε καὶ
c ἀφιλοσόφῳ, φιλοτίμῳ δὲ χρήσωνται, τάχ' ἄν που ἐν μέθαις
ἤ τινι ἄλλῃ ἀμελείᾳ τὼ ἀκολάστω αὐτοῖν ὑποζυγίω λαβόντε
τὰς ψυχὰς ἀφρούρους, συναγαγόντε εἰς ταὐτόν, τὴν ὑπὸ
τῶν πολλῶν μακαριστὴν αἵρεσιν εἱλέσθην τε καὶ διεπρα-
5 ξάσθην· καὶ διαπραξαμένω τὸ λοιπὸν ἤδη χρῶνται μὲν
αὐτῇ, σπανίᾳ δέ, ἅτε οὐ πάσῃ δεδογμένα τῇ διανοίᾳ πράττοντες. φίλω μὲν οὖν καὶ τούτω, ἧττον δὲ ἐκείνων, ἀλλή-
d λοιν διά τε τοῦ ἔρωτος καὶ ἔξω γενομένω διάγουσι, πίστεις
τὰς μεγίστας ἡγουμένω ἀλλήλοιν δεδωκέναι τε καὶ δεδέχθαι,
ἃς οὐ θεμιτὸν εἶναι λύσαντας εἰς ἔχθραν ποτὲ ἐλθεῖν. ἐν
δὲ τῇ τελευτῇ ἄπτεροι μέν, ὡρμηκότες δὲ πτεροῦσθαι ἐκβαί-
5 νουσι τοῦ σώματος, ὥστε οὐ σμικρὸν ἆθλον τῆς ἐρωτικῆς
μανίας φέρονται· εἰς γὰρ σκότον καὶ τὴν ὑπὸ γῆς πορείαν
οὐ νόμος ἐστὶν ἔτι ἐλθεῖν τοῖς κατηργμένοις ἤδη τῆς ὑπου-

a 4 ἂν T : om. B Eusebius   a 6 λόγου corr. Coisl. : λόγους B T
a 7 ἐὰν T : ἃ B   a 8 νικήσῃ T : νικήσει B   b 2 μὲν ᾧ T : μὲν ὡς B
b 3 δὲ ᾧ T : δὲ ω B   δὲ δὴ T : δὲ B   c 1 τάχ' ἄν B T : τάχα W
c 3 ξυναγαγόντε B : συναγαγόντες T   τὴν ὑπὸ B : τὴν ὑπὸ τὴν T
c 4 εἱλέσθην Eusebius : εἱλέτην B T   διεπραξάσθην Eusebius : διεπράξαντο B T   c 7 φίλω μὲν T : φιλῶμεν B   d 2 ἡγουμένω recc. :
ἡγουμένων B T   δεδέχθαι T : δέχθαι B   d 7 ὑπουρανίου B T
Eusebius : ἐπουρανίου Ven. 184 : ὑπερουρανίου Buttmann

ρανίου πορείας, ἀλλὰ φανὸν βίον διάγοντας εὐδαιμονεῖν
μετ᾽ ἀλλήλων πορευομένους, καὶ ὁμοπτέρους ἔρωτος χάριν, e
ὅταν γένωνται, γενέσθαι.

Ταῦτα τοσαῦτα, ὦ παῖ, καὶ θεῖα οὕτω σοι δωρήσεται ἡ
παρ᾽ ἐραστοῦ φιλία· ἡ δὲ ἀπὸ τοῦ μὴ ἐρῶντος οἰκειότης,
σωφροσύνῃ θνητῇ κεκραμένη, θνητά τε καὶ φειδωλὰ οἰκονο- 5
μοῦσα, ἀνελευθερίαν ὑπὸ πλήθους ἐπαινουμένην ὡς ἀρετὴν
τῇ φίλῃ ψυχῇ ἐντεκοῦσα, ἐννέα χιλιάδας ἐτῶν περὶ γῆν 257
κυλινδουμένην αὐτὴν καὶ ὑπὸ γῆς ἄνουν παρέξει.

Αὕτη σοι, ὦ φίλε Ἔρως, εἰς ἡμετέραν δύναμιν ὅτι καλλίστη καὶ ἀρίστη δέδοταί τε καὶ ἐκτέτεισται παλινῳδία, τά
τε ἄλλα καὶ τοῖς ὀνόμασιν ἠναγκασμένη ποιητικοῖς τισιν διὰ 5
Φαῖδρον εἰρῆσθαι. ἀλλὰ τῶν προτέρων τε συγγνώμην καὶ
τῶνδε χάριν ἔχων, εὐμενὴς καὶ ἵλεως τὴν ἐρωτικήν μοι
τέχνην ἣν ἔδωκας μήτε ἀφέλῃ μήτε πηρώσῃς δι᾽ ὀργήν,
δίδου τ᾽ ἔτι μᾶλλον ἢ νῦν παρὰ τοῖς καλοῖς τίμιον εἶναι.
ἐν τῷ πρόσθεν δ᾽ εἴ τι λόγῳ σοι ἀπηχὲς εἴπομεν Φαῖδρός b
τε καὶ ἐγώ, Λυσίαν τὸν τοῦ λόγου πατέρα αἰτιώμενος παῦε
τῶν τοιούτων λόγων, ἐπὶ φιλοσοφίαν δέ, ὥσπερ ἀδελφὸς
αὐτοῦ Πολέμαρχος τέτραπται, τρέψον, ἵνα καὶ ὁ ἐραστὴς
ὅδε αὐτοῦ μηκέτι ἐπαμφοτερίζῃ καθάπερ νῦν, ἀλλ᾽ ἁπλῶς 5
πρὸς Ἔρωτα μετὰ φιλοσόφων λόγων τὸν βίον ποιῆται.

ΦΑΙ. Συνεύχομαί σοι, ὦ Σώκρατες, εἴπερ ἄμεινον ταῦθ᾽
ἡμῖν εἶναι, ταῦτα γίγνεσθαι. τὸν λόγον δέ σου πάλαι c
θαυμάσας ἔχω, ὅσῳ καλλίω τοῦ προτέρου ἀπηργάσω· ὥστε
ὀκνῶ μή μοι ὁ Λυσίας ταπεινὸς φανῇ, ἐὰν ἄρα καὶ ἐθελήσῃ

d 8 διαχαγόντας Eusebius   e 2 γίγνωνται H. Richards   e 3 θεῖα
οὕτω B : οὕτω θεῖα T   a 1 χιλιάδας T : χιλιάδες B   γῆν corr.
Coisl. : την B : τὴν T   a 2 καλινδουμένην Herwerden   γῆς T :
της B   a 4 δέδοταί T : δέδοκταί B   a 7 τὴν ἐρωτικήν μοι B :
τὴν μοι ἐρωτικὴν T   a 8 ἔδωκας B : δέδωκας T   a 9 τ᾽ T : δ᾽ B
b 1 ἐν T : om. B   ἀπηχὲς Hermias : ἀπηνὲς B T   b 3 ἀδελφὸς
Bekker : ἀδελφὸς B T   b 4 τέτραπται T W : γέγραπταί τε τέτραπται B

πρὸς αὐτὸν ἄλλον ἀντιπαρατεῖναι. καὶ γάρ τις αὐτόν, ὦ
5 θαυμάσιε, ἔναγχος τῶν πολιτικῶν τοῦτ' αὐτὸ λοιδορῶν
ὠνείδιζε, καὶ διὰ πάσης τῆς λοιδορίας ἐκάλει λογογράφον·
τάχ' οὖν ἂν ὑπὸ φιλοτιμίας ἐπίσχοι ἡμῖν ἂν τοῦ γράφειν.

ΣΩ. Γελοῖόν γ', ὦ νεανία, τὸ δόγμα λέγεις, καὶ τοῦ
d ἑταίρου συχνὸν διαμαρτάνεις, εἰ αὐτὸν οὕτως ἡγῇ τινα
ψοφοδεᾶ. ἴσως δὲ καὶ τὸν λοιδορούμενον αὐτῷ οἴει ὀνειδίζοντα λέγειν ἃ ἔλεγεν.

ΦΑΙ. Ἐφαίνετο γάρ, ὦ Σώκρατες· καὶ σύνοισθά που
5 καὶ αὐτὸς ὅτι οἱ μέγιστον δυνάμενοί τε καὶ σεμνότατοι ἐν
ταῖς πόλεσιν αἰσχύνονται λόγους τε γράφειν καὶ καταλείπειν
συγγράμματα ἑαυτῶν, δόξαν φοβούμενοι τοῦ ἔπειτα χρόνου,
μὴ σοφισταὶ καλῶνται.

ΣΩ. Γλυκὺς ἀγκών, ὦ Φαῖδρε, λέληθέν σε ὅτι ἀπὸ τοῦ
e μακροῦ ἀγκῶνος τοῦ κατὰ Νεῖλον ἐκλήθη· καὶ πρὸς τῷ
ἀγκῶνι λανθάνει σε ὅτι οἱ μέγιστον φρονοῦντες τῶν πολιτικῶν μάλιστα ἐρῶσι λογογραφίας τε καὶ καταλείψεως
συγγραμμάτων, οἵ γε καὶ ἐπειδάν τινα γράφωσι λόγον,
5 οὕτως ἀγαπῶσι τοὺς ἐπαινέτας, ὥστε προσπαραγράφουσι
πρώτους οἳ ἂν ἑκασταχοῦ ἐπαινῶσιν αὐτούς.

ΦΑΙ. Πῶς λέγεις τοῦτο; οὐ γὰρ μανθάνω.

258 ΣΩ. Οὐ μανθάνεις ὅτι ἐν ἀρχῇ ἀνδρὸς πολιτικοῦ [συγ-
γράμματι] πρῶτος ὁ ἐπαινέτης γέγραπται.

ΦΑΙ. Πῶς;

ΣΩ. "Ἔδοξέ" πού φησιν "τῇ βουλῇ" ἢ "τῷ δήμῳ"
5 ἢ ἀμφοτέροις, καὶ "ὃς (καὶ ὃς) εἶπεν"—τὸν αὐτὸν δὴ λέγων
μάλα σεμνῶς καὶ ἐγκωμιάζων ὁ συγγραφεύς—ἔπειτα λέγει

---

c 4 αὐτὸν BT: αὐτῶν vulg. : αὐτῷ Heindorf   d 1 ἡγεῖ τινα B :
τινὰ ἡγεῖ T   d 2 ὀνειδίζοντα Postgate : ὀνειδίζοντα νομίζοντα B :
νομίζοντα TW   d 9 ὅτι . . . e 1 ἐκλήθη secl. Heindorf   e 5 ἐπαινέτας BT: ἐπαινοῦντας V   e 7 λέγεις τοῦτο B : τοῦτο λέγεις T
a 1 ἀρχῇ secl. Madvig : ἀνδρὸς secl. Herwerden (et mox συγγράμματος)
συγγράμματι seclusi : συγγράμματος vulg.   a 4 φησι B : φησὶν
αὐτῶν τὸ σύγγραμμα TW : φησιν αὐτὸ τὸ σύγγραμμα vulg.   a 5 καὶ
ὃς add. Winckelmann

δὴ μετὰ τοῦτο, ἐπιδεικνύμενος τοῖς ἐπαινέταις τὴν ἑαυτοῦ
σοφίαν, ἐνίοτε πάνυ μακρὸν ποιησάμενος σύγγραμμα· ἤ σοι
ἄλλο τι φαίνεται τὸ τοιοῦτον ἢ λόγος συγγεγραμμένος;

ΦΑΙ. Οὐκ ἔμοιγε. b

ΣΩ. Οὐκοῦν ἐὰν μὲν οὗτος ἐμμένῃ, γεγηθὼς ἀπέρχεται
ἐκ τοῦ θεάτρου ὁ ποιητής· ἐὰν δὲ ἐξαλειφθῇ καὶ ἄμοιρος
γένηται λογογραφίας τε καὶ τοῦ ἄξιος εἶναι συγγράφειν,
πενθεῖ αὐτός τε καὶ οἱ ἑταῖροι. 5

ΦΑΙ. Καὶ μάλα.

ΣΩ. ·Δῆλόν γε ὅτι οὐχ ὡς ὑπερφρονοῦντες τοῦ ἐπιτηδεύματος, ἀλλ᾿ ὡς τεθαυμακότες.

ΦΑΙ. Πάνυ μὲν οὖν.

ΣΩ. Τί δέ; ὅταν ἱκανὸς γένηται ῥήτωρ ἢ βασιλεύς, ὥστε 10
λαβὼν τὴν Λυκούργου ἢ Σόλωνος ἢ Δαρείου δύναμιν ἀθά- c
νατος γενέσθαι λογογράφος ἐν πόλει, ἆρ᾿ οὐκ ἰσόθεον
ἡγεῖται αὐτός τε αὐτὸν ἔτι ζῶν, καὶ οἱ ἔπειτα γιγνόμενοι
ταὐτὰ ταῦτα περὶ αὐτοῦ νομίζουσι, θεώμενοι αὐτοῦ τὰ συγγράμματα; 5

ΦΑΙ. Καὶ μάλα.

ΣΩ. Οἴει τινὰ οὖν τῶν τοιούτων, ὅστις καὶ ὁπωστιοῦν
δύσνους Λυσίᾳ, ὀνειδίζειν αὐτὸ τοῦτο ὅτι συγγράφει;

ΦΑΙ. Οὔκουν εἰκός γε ἐξ ὧν σὺ λέγεις· καὶ γὰρ ἂν τῇ
ἑαυτοῦ ἐπιθυμίᾳ, ὡς ἔοικεν, ὀνειδίζοι. 10

ΣΩ. Τοῦτο μὲν ἄρα παντὶ δῆλον, ὅτι οὐκ αἰσχρὸν αὐτό d
γε τὸ γράφειν λόγους.

ΦΑΙ. Τί γάρ;

ΣΩ. Ἀλλ᾿ ἐκεῖνο οἶμαι αἰσχρὸν ἤδη, τὸ μὴ καλῶς λέγειν
τε καὶ γράφειν ἀλλ᾿ αἰσχρῶς τε καὶ κακῶς. 5

ΦΑΙ. Δῆλον δή.

ΣΩ. Τίς οὖν ὁ τρόπος τοῦ καλῶς τε καὶ μὴ γράφειν;
δεόμεθά τι, ὦ Φαῖδρε, Λυσίαν τε περὶ τούτων ἐξετάσαι καὶ

a 7 ⟨τὸ⟩ μετὰ Krische   b 3 ἐξαλειφθῇ Τ : ἐξαλιφῇ Β   c 7 τινα
οὖν Β : οὖν τινα Τ   c 8 αὐτὸ] αὐτῷ Ast   d 4 οἶμαι Β : οἶμαί
σε Τ : οἶμαί γε vulg.   d 8 τι ΒΤ : τοι vulg.

ἄλλον ὅστις πώποτέ τι γέγραφεν ἢ γράψει, εἴτε πολιτικὸν
10 σύγγραμμα εἴτε ἰδιωτικόν, ἐν μέτρῳ ὡς ποιητὴς ἢ ἄνευ
μέτρου ὡς ἰδιώτης;

e   ΦΑΙ. Ἐρωτᾷς εἰ δεόμεθα; τίνος μὲν οὖν ἕνεκα κἄν
τις ὡς εἰπεῖν ζῴη, ἀλλ᾽ ἢ τῶν τοιούτων ἡδονῶν ἕνεκα; οὐ
γάρ που ἐκείνων γε ὧν προλυπηθῆναι δεῖ ἢ μηδὲ ἡσθῆναι,
ὃ δὴ ὀλίγου πᾶσαι αἱ περὶ τὸ σῶμα ἡδοναὶ ἔχουσι· διὸ καὶ
5 δικαίως ἀνδραποδώδεις κέκληνται.

ΣΩ. Σχολὴ μὲν δή, ὡς ἔοικε· καὶ ἅμα μοι δοκοῦσιν ὡς
ἐν τῷ πνίγει ὑπὲρ κεφαλῆς ἡμῶν οἱ τέττιγες ᾄδοντες καὶ
259 ἀλλήλοις διαλεγόμενοι καθορᾶν καὶ ἡμᾶς. εἰ οὖν ἴδοιεν καὶ
νὼ καθάπερ τοὺς πολλοὺς ἐν μεσημβρίᾳ μὴ διαλεγομένους
ἀλλὰ νυστάζοντας καὶ κηλουμένους ὑφ᾽ αὑτῶν δι᾽ ἀργίαν
τῆς διανοίας, δικαίως ἂν καταγελῷεν, ἡγούμενοι ἀνδράποδ᾽
5 ἄττα σφίσιν ἐλθόντα εἰς τὸ καταγώγιον ὥσπερ προβάτια
μεσημβριάζοντα περὶ τὴν κρήνην εὕδειν· ἐὰν δὲ ὁρῶσι
διαλεγομένους καὶ παραπλέοντάς σφας ὥσπερ Σειρῆνας
b ἀκηλήτους, ὃ γέρας παρὰ θεῶν ἔχουσιν ἀνθρώποις διδόναι,
τάχ᾽ ἂν δοῖεν ἀγασθέντες.

ΦΑΙ. Ἔχουσι δὲ δὴ τί τοῦτο; ἀνήκοος γάρ, ὡς ἔοικε,
τυγχάνω ὤν.

5   ΣΩ. Οὐ μὲν δὴ πρέπει γε φιλόμουσον ἄνδρα τῶν τοιούτων
ἀνήκοον εἶναι. λέγεται δ᾽ ὥς ποτ᾽ ἦσαν οὗτοι ἄνθρωποι τῶν
πρὶν Μούσας γεγονέναι, γενομένων δὲ Μουσῶν καὶ φανείσης
ᾠδῆς οὕτως ἄρα τινὲς τῶν τότε ἐξεπλάγησαν ὑφ᾽ ἡδονῆς,
c ὥστε ᾄδοντες ἠμέλησαν σίτων τε καὶ ποτῶν, καὶ ἔλαθον
τελευτήσαντες αὑτούς· ἐξ ὧν τὸ τεττίγων γένος μετ᾽ ἐκεῖνο
φύεται, γέρας τοῦτο παρὰ Μουσῶν λαβόν, μηδὲν τροφῆς
δεῖσθαι γενόμενον, ἀλλ᾽ ἄσιτόν τε καὶ ἄποτον· εὐθὺς ᾄδειν,

---

d 10 ὡς ποιητὴς et mox ὡς ἰδιώτης secl. Badham   e 1 ἕνεκα κἄν
B : ἕνεκ᾽ ἄν T : ἕνεκα Stobaeus   e 3 μηδὲ B T : μὴ V Stobaeus
a 1 καὶ ἡμᾶς T Stobaeus: om. B   καὶ νὼ Stobaeus : καινῶ B T
b 5 γε T Stobaeus : om. B   b 6 δ᾽] δὴ malit Heindorf   c 4 γενόμενον post δεῖσθαι B T Stobaeus: post εὐθὺς transp. Badham

ἕως ἂν τελευτήσῃ, καὶ μετὰ ταῦτα ἐλθὸν παρὰ Μούσας 5
ἀπαγγέλλειν τίς τίνα αὐτῶν τιμᾷ τῶν ἐνθάδε. Τερψιχόρᾳ
μὲν οὖν τοὺς ἐν τοῖς χοροῖς τετιμηκότας αὐτὴν ἀπαγγέλ-
λοντες ποιοῦσι προσφιλεστέρους, τῇ δὲ Ἐρατοῖ τοὺς ἐν τοῖς d
ἐρωτικοῖς, καὶ ταῖς ἄλλαις οὕτως, κατὰ τὸ εἶδος ἑκάστης
τιμῆς· τῇ δὲ πρεσβυτάτῃ Καλλιόπῃ καὶ τῇ μετ᾽ αὐτὴν
Οὐρανίᾳ τοὺς ἐν φιλοσοφίᾳ διάγοντάς τε καὶ τιμῶντας τὴν
ἐκείνων μουσικὴν ἀγγέλλουσιν, αἳ δὴ μάλιστα τῶν Μουσῶν 5
περί τε οὐρανὸν καὶ λόγους οὖσαι θείους τε καὶ ἀνθρωπίνους
ἱᾶσιν καλλίστην φωνήν. πολλῶν δὴ οὖν ἕνεκα λεκτέον τι
καὶ οὐ καθευδητέον ἐν τῇ μεσημβρίᾳ.

ΦΑΙ. Λεκτέον γὰρ οὖν.

ΣΩ. Οὐκοῦν, ὅπερ νῦν προυθέμεθα σκέψασθαι, τὸν λόγον e
ὅπῃ καλῶς ἔχει λέγειν τε καὶ γράφειν καὶ ὅπῃ μή, σκεπτέον.

ΦΑΙ. Δῆλον.

ΣΩ. Ἆρ᾽ οὖν οὐχ ὑπάρχειν δεῖ τοῖς εὖ γε καὶ καλῶς
ῥηθησομένοις τὴν τοῦ λέγοντος διάνοιαν εἰδυῖαν τὸ ἀληθὲς 5
ὧν ἂν ἐρεῖν πέρι μέλλῃ;

ΦΑΙ. Οὑτωσὶ περὶ τούτου ἀκήκοα, ὦ φίλε Σώκρατες, οὐκ
εἶναι ἀνάγκην τῷ μέλλοντι ῥήτορι ἔσεσθαι τὰ τῷ ὄντι δίκαια 260
μανθάνειν ἀλλὰ τὰ δόξαντ᾽ ἂν πλήθει οἵπερ δικάσουσιν,
οὐδὲ τὰ ὄντως ἀγαθὰ ἢ καλὰ ἀλλ᾽ ὅσα δόξει· ἐκ γὰρ τούτων
εἶναι τὸ πείθειν ἀλλ᾽ οὐκ ἐκ τῆς ἀληθείας.

ΣΩ. "Οὔτοι ἀπόβλητον ἔπος" εἶναι δεῖ, ὦ Φαῖδρε, 5
ὃ ἂν εἴπωσι σοφοί, ἀλλὰ σκοπεῖν μή τι λέγωσι· καὶ δὴ
καὶ τὸ νῦν λεχθὲν οὐκ ἀφετέον.

ΦΑΙ. Ὀρθῶς λέγεις.

ΣΩ. Ὧδε δὴ σποπῶμεν αὐτό.

ΦΑΙ. Πῶς; 10

c 6 τερψιχόρᾳ Β Τ Stobaeus : τερψιχόρη vulg.　　d 3 μετ᾽ αὐτὴν
Β Stobaeus : μετὰ ταύτην Τ　　d 7 ἴασιν Β : ἴασιν Τ (corr. t :
πέμπουσι suprascr. b)　　δὴ οὖν ἕνεκα W : δὴ ουνεκεν Β : δὴ οὖν
ἕνεκεν Τ　　e 4 γε Β : τε Τ　　a 5 ὦ Τ : ὃ Β　　a 6 λέγωσι
Β Τ : λέγουσι Schaefer

b ΣΩ. Εἴ σε πείθοιμι ἐγὼ πολεμίους ἀμύνειν κτησάμενον
ἵππον, ἄμφω δὲ ἵππον ἀγνοοῖμεν, τοσόνδε μέντοι τυγχάνοιμι
εἰδὼς περὶ σοῦ, ὅτι Φαῖδρος ἵππον ἡγεῖται τὸ τῶν ἡμέρων
ζῴων μέγιστα ἔχον ὦτα—

5 ΦΑΙ. Γελοῖόν γ' ἄν, ὦ Σώκρατες, εἴη.

ΣΩ. Οὔπω γε· ἀλλ' ὅτε δὴ σπουδῇ σε πείθοιμι, συντιθεὶς
λόγον ἔπαινον κατὰ τοῦ ὄνου, ἵππον ἐπονομάζων καὶ λέγων ὡς
παντὸς ἄξιον τὸ θρέμμα οἴκοι τε κεκτῆσθαι καὶ ἐπὶ στρατιᾶς,
ἀποπολεμεῖν τε χρήσιμον καὶ πρός γ' ἐνεγκεῖν δυνατὸν
c σκεύη καὶ ἄλλα πολλὰ ὠφέλιμον.

ΦΑΙ. Παγγέλοιόν γ' ἂν ἤδη εἴη.

ΣΩ. Ἆρ' οὖν οὐ κρεῖττον γελοῖον καὶ φίλον ἢ δεινόν τε
καὶ ἐχθρὸν [εἶναι ἢ φίλον];

5 ΦΑΙ. Φαίνεται.

ΣΩ. Ὅταν οὖν ὁ ῥητορικὸς ἀγνοῶν ἀγαθὸν καὶ κακόν,
λαβὼν πόλιν ὡσαύτως ἔχουσαν πείθῃ, μὴ περὶ ὄνου σκιᾶς
ὡς ἵππου τὸν ἔπαινον ποιούμενος, ἀλλὰ περὶ κακοῦ ὡς
ἀγαθοῦ, δόξας δὲ πλήθους μεμελετηκὼς πείσῃ κακὰ πράττειν
10 ἀντ' ἀγαθῶν, ποῖόν τιν' ἂ(ν) οἴει μετὰ ταῦτα τὴν ῥητορικὴν
d καρπὸν ὧν ἔσπειρε θερίζειν;

ΦΑΙ. Οὐ πάνυ γε ἐπιεικῆ.

ΣΩ. Ἆρ' οὖν, ὦ ἀγαθέ, ἀγροικότερον τοῦ δέοντος λελοιδορήκαμεν τὴν τῶν λόγων τέχνην; ἢ δ' ἴσως ἂν εἴποι· "Τί
5 ποτ', ὦ θαυμάσιοι, ληρεῖτε; ἐγὼ γὰρ οὐδέν' ἀγνοοῦντα
τἀληθὲς ἀναγκάζω μανθάνειν λέγειν, ἀλλ', εἰ τι ἐμὴ
συμβουλή, κτησάμενον ἐκεῖνο οὕτως ἐμὲ λαμβάνειν· τόδε
δ' οὖν μέγα λέγω, ὡς ἄνευ ἐμοῦ τῷ τὰ ὄντα εἰδότι οὐδέν τι
μᾶλλον ἔσται πείθειν τέχνῃ.

b 5 εἴη TW: om. B   b 6 οὔπω γε T: οὔποτε B   δὴ T: om. B
b 9 πρός γ' ἐνεγκεῖν Thompson: προσενεγκεῖν BT   c 3 γελοῖον
καὶ φίλον legit Hermias: γελοῖον BT   c 4 εἶναι ἢ φίλον BT:
non legit Hermias   c 10 τιν' ἂν Hirschig: τινα BT   d 1 ὧν
TW: ὃν B   d 2 γε B: om. T   d 5 οὐδένα B: οὐδὲν B
d 6 εἴ τι B: εἴ τις T   ἐμὴ ξυμβουλή B: ἐμῇ ξυμβουλῇ T: ἐμῇ ξυμβουλῇ χρῆται Stephanus   d 7 κτησάμενον Vahlen: κτησάμενος BT
λαμβάνειν BT: λαμβάνει al.

ΦΑΙ. Οὐκοῦν δίκαια ἐρεῖ, λέγουσα ταῦτα;　　　　　　　　e

ΣΩ. Φημί, ἐὰν οἵ γ᾽ ἐπιόντες αὐτῇ λόγοι μαρτυρῶσιν
εἶναι τέχνῃ. ὥσπερ γὰρ ἀκούειν δοκῶ τινων προσιόντων καὶ
διαμαρτυρομένων λόγων, ὅτι ψεύδεται καὶ οὐκ ἔστι τέχνη
ἀλλ᾽ ἄτεχνος τριβή· τοῦ δὲ λέγειν, φησὶν ὁ Λάκων, ἔτυμος　5
τέχνη ἄνευ τοῦ ἀληθείας ἧφθαι οὔτ᾽ ἔστιν οὔτε μή ποτε
ὕστερον γένηται.

ΦΑΙ. Τούτων δεῖ τῶν λόγων, ὦ Σώκρατες· ἀλλὰ δεῦρο　261
αὐτοὺς παράγων ἐξέταζε τί καὶ πῶς λέγουσιν.

ΣΩ. Πάριτε δή, θρέμματα γενναῖα, καλλίπαιδά τε Φαῖδρον πείθετε ὡς ἐὰν μὴ ἱκανῶς φιλοσοφήσῃ, οὐδὲ ἱκανός
ποτε λέγειν ἔσται περὶ οὐδενός. ἀποκρινέσθω δὴ ὁ Φαῖδρος.　5

ΦΑΙ. Ἐρωτᾶτε.

ΣΩ. Ἆρ᾽ οὖν οὐ τὸ μὲν ὅλον ἡ ῥητορικὴ ἂν εἴη τέχνη
ψυχαγωγία τις διὰ λόγων, οὐ μόνον ἐν δικαστηρίοις καὶ ὅσοι
ἄλλοι δημόσιοι σύλλογοι, ἀλλὰ καὶ ἐν ἰδίοις, ἡ αὐτὴ σμικρῶν
τε καὶ μεγάλων πέρι, καὶ οὐδὲν ἐντιμότερον τό γε ὀρθὸν περὶ　b
σπουδαῖα ἢ περὶ φαῦλα γιγνόμενον; ἢ πῶς σὺ ταῦτ᾽ ἀκήκοας;

ΦΑΙ. Οὐ μὰ τὸν Δί᾽ οὐ παντάπασιν οὕτως, ἀλλὰ μάλιστα
μέν πως περὶ τὰς δίκας λέγεταί τε καὶ γράφεται τέχνη,
λέγεται δὲ καὶ περὶ δημηγορίας· ἐπὶ πλέον δὲ οὐκ ἀκήκοα.　5

ΣΩ. Ἀλλ᾽ ἦ τὰς Νέστορος καὶ Ὀδυσσέως τέχνας μόνον
περὶ λόγων ἀκήκοας, ἃς ἐν Ἰλίῳ σχολάζοντες συνεγραψάτην,
τῶν δὲ Παλαμήδους ἀνήκοος γέγονας;

ΦΑΙ. Καὶ ναὶ μὰ Δί᾽ ἔγωγε τῶν Νέστορος, εἰ μὴ　c
Γοργίαν Νέστορά τινα κατασκευάζεις, ἤ τινα Θρασύμαχόν
τε καὶ Θεόδωρον Ὀδυσσέα.

ΣΩ. Ἴσως. ἀλλὰ γὰρ τούτους ἐῶμεν· σὺ δ᾽ εἰπέ, ἐν

---

e 5 τοῦ δὲ ... e 7 γένηται secl. Schleiermacher　　e 5 φησὶν ὁ Λάκων
secl. Voegelin　　ἔτυμος τέχνη TW: ἔτοιμος B　　a 1 δεῖ T: δὴ B
λόγων ⟨ἀκροᾶσθαι⟩ H. Richards　　a 4 πείθετε T: πείθεται B　　ὡς
ἐὰν B: ἕως ἂν T　　b 4 τέχνη T: τέχνῃ B　　b 6 καὶ B: τε
καὶ T　　b 7 περὶ secl. Thompson　　σχολάζοντες BTW: σχο-
λάζοντε corr. Coisl.　　c 1 Νέστορος ⟨καὶ Ὀδυσσέως⟩ Herwerden
c 2 κατασκευάζεις T: κατασκευάζῃς B　　c 3 τε T: δὲ B

5 δικαστηρίοις οἱ ἀντίδικοι τί δρῶσιν; οὐκ ἀντιλέγουσιν μεντοι;
ἢ τί φήσομεν;

ΦΑΙ. Τοῦτ' αὐτό.

ΣΩ. Περὶ τοῦ δικαίου τε καὶ ἀδίκου;

ΦΑΙ. Ναί.

10 ΣΩ. Οὐκοῦν ὁ τέχνῃ τοῦτο δρῶν ποιήσει φανῆναι τὸ
d αὐτὸ τοῖς αὐτοῖς τοτὲ μὲν δίκαιον, ὅταν δὲ βούληται, ἄδικον;

ΦΑΙ. Τί μήν;

ΣΩ. Καὶ ἐν δημηγορίᾳ δὴ τῇ πόλει δοκεῖν τὰ αὐτὰ τοτὲ
μὲν ἀγαθά, τοτὲ δ' αὖ τἀναντία;

5 ΦΑΙ. Οὕτως.

ΣΩ. Τὸν οὖν Ἐλεατικὸν Παλαμήδην λέγοντα οὐκ ἴσμεν
τέχνῃ, ὥστε φαίνεσθαι τοῖς ἀκούουσι τὰ αὐτὰ ὅμοια καὶ
ἀνόμοια, καὶ ἓν καὶ πολλά, μένοντά τε αὖ καὶ φερόμενα;

ΦΑΙ. Μάλα γε.

10 ΣΩ. Οὐκ ἄρα μόνον περὶ δικαστήριά τέ ἐστιν ἡ ἀντιλογικὴ
e καὶ περὶ δημηγορίαν, ἀλλ', ὡς ἔοικε, περὶ πάντα τὰ λεγόμενα
μία τις τέχνη, εἴπερ ἔστιν, αὕτη ἂν εἴη, ᾗ τις οἷός τ' ἔσται
πᾶν παντὶ ὁμοιοῦν τῶν δυνατῶν καὶ οἷς δυνατόν, καὶ ἄλλου
ὁμοιοῦντος καὶ ἀποκρυπτομένου εἰς φῶς ἄγειν.

5 ΦΑΙ. Πῶς δὴ τὸ τοιοῦτον λέγεις;

ΣΩ. Τῇδε δοκῶ ζητοῦσιν φανεῖσθαι. ἀπάτη πότερον ἐν
πολὺ διαφέρουσι γίγνεται μᾶλλον ἢ ὀλίγον;

262 ΦΑΙ. Ἐν τοῖς ὀλίγον.

ΣΩ. Ἀλλά γε δὴ κατὰ σμικρὸν μεταβαίνων μᾶλλον
λήσεις ἐλθὼν ἐπὶ τὸ ἐναντίον ἢ κατὰ μέγα.

ΦΑΙ. Πῶς δ' οὔ;

5 ΣΩ. Δεῖ ἄρα τὸν μέλλοντα ἀπατήσειν μὲν ἄλλον, αὐτὸν
δὲ μὴ ἀπατήσεσθαι, τὴν ὁμοιότητα τῶν ὄντων καὶ ἀνομοιότητα
ἀκριβῶς διειδέναι.

c 10 τέχνη Τ : τέχνη Β (et mox)   d 1 βούληται ἄδικον Β :
ἄδικον βούληται pr. Τ   d 7 φαίνεσθαι Β Τ : δοκεῖν φαίνεσθαι vulg.
d 8 μένοντα Τ : μὲν ὄντα Β   e 2 ᾗ τις corr. Coisl. : ἢ τις Τ : ἡ τις Β
e 3 πᾶν παντὶ Τ : πάμπαν τί Β   a 2 γε δὴ Β : δὴ Τ : μὴν Galenus

ΦΑΙ. Ἀνάγκη μὲν οὖν.

ΣΩ. Ἡ οὖν οἷός τε ἔσται, ἀλήθειαν ἀγνοῶν ἑκάστου, τὴν τοῦ ἀγνοουμένου ὁμοιότητα σμικράν τε καὶ μεγάλην ἐν τοῖς 10 ἄλλοις διαγιγνώσκειν;

ΦΑΙ. Ἀδύνατον. b

ΣΩ. Οὐκοῦν τοῖς παρὰ τὰ ὄντα δοξάζουσι καὶ ἀπατωμένοις δῆλον ὡς τὸ πάθος τοῦτο δι' ὁμοιοτήτων τινῶν εἰσερρύη.

ΦΑΙ. Γίγνεται γοῦν οὕτως.

ΣΩ. Ἔστιν οὖν ὅπως τεχνικὸς ἔσται μεταβιβάζειν κατὰ 5 σμικρὸν διὰ τῶν ὁμοιοτήτων ἀπὸ τοῦ ὄντος ἑκάστοτε ἐπὶ τοὐναντίον ἀπάγων, ἢ αὐτὸς τοῦτο διαφεύγειν, ὁ μὴ ἐγνωρικὼς ὃ ἔστιν ἕκαστον τῶν ὄντων;

ΦΑΙ. Οὐ μή ποτε.

ΣΩ. Λόγων ἄρα τέχνην, ὦ ἑταῖρε, ὁ τὴν ἀλήθειαν μὴ c εἰδώς, δόξας δὲ τεθηρευκώς, γελοίαν τινά, ὡς ἔοικε, καὶ ἄτεχνον παρέξεται.

ΦΑΙ. Κινδυνεύει.

ΣΩ. Βούλει οὖν ἐν τῷ Λυσίου λόγῳ ὃν φέρεις, καὶ ἐν 5 οἷς ἡμεῖς εἴπομεν ἰδεῖν τι ὧν φαμεν ἀτέχνων τε καὶ ἐντέχνων εἶναι;

ΦΑΙ. Πάντων γέ που μάλιστα, ὡς νῦν γε ψιλῶς πως λέγομεν, οὐκ ἔχοντες ἱκανὰ παραδείγματα.

ΣΩ. Καὶ μὴν κατὰ τύχην γέ τινα, ὡς ἔοικεν, ἐρρηθήτην 10 τὼ λόγω ἔχοντέ τι παράδειγμα, ὡς ἂν ὁ εἰδὼς τὸ ἀληθὲς d προσπαίζων ἐν λόγοις παράγοι τοὺς ἀκούοντας. καὶ ἔγωγε, ὦ Φαῖδρε, αἰτιῶμαι τοὺς ἐντοπίους θεούς· ἴσως δὲ καὶ οἱ τῶν Μουσῶν προφῆται οἱ ὑπὲρ κεφαλῆς ᾠδοὶ ἐπιπεπνευκότες ἂν ἡμῖν εἶεν τοῦτο τὸ γέρας· οὐ γάρ που ἔγωγε τέχνης τινὸς 5 τοῦ λέγειν μέτοχος.

ΦΑΙ. Ἔστω ὡς λέγεις· μόνον δήλωσον ὃ φής.

ΣΩ. Ἴθι δή μοι ἀνάγνωθι τὴν τοῦ Λυσίου λόγου ἀρχήν.

b 5 μεταβιβάζειν T Galenus : μεταβιβάζει B   c 6 ἀτέχνων . . . ἐντέχνων Heindorf : ἄτεχνόν . . . ἔντεχνον BT   d 1 τὼ λόγω T : τῷ λόγῳ B e ΦΑΙ. ''Περὶ μὲν τῶν ἐμῶν πραγμάτων ἐπίστασαι, καὶ ὡς νομίζω συμφέρειν ἡμῖν τούτων γενομένων, ἀκήκοας. ἀξιῶ δὲ μὴ διὰ τοῦτο ἀτυχῆσαι ὧν δέομαι, ὅτι οὐκ ἐραστὴς ὢν σοῦ τυγχάνω. ὡς ἐκείνοις μὲν τότε μεταμέλει''—

5 ΣΩ. Παῦσαι. τί δὴ οὖν οὗτος ἁμαρτάνει καὶ ἄτεχνον ποιεῖ λεκτέον· ἢ γάρ;

263 ΦΑΙ. Ναί.

ΣΩ. Ἆρ' οὖν οὐ παντὶ δῆλον τό γε τοιόνδε, ὡς περὶ μὲν ἔνια τῶν τοιούτων ὁμονοητικῶς ἔχομεν, περὶ δ' ἔνια στασιωτικῶς;

5 ΦΑΙ. Δοκῶ μὲν ὃ λέγεις μανθάνειν, ἔτι δ' εἰπὲ σαφέστερον.

ΣΩ. Ὅταν τις ὄνομα εἴπῃ σιδήρου ἢ ἀργύρου, ἆρ' οὐ τὸ αὐτὸ πάντες διενοήθημεν;

ΦΑΙ. Καὶ μάλα.

ΣΩ. Τί δ' ὅταν δικαίου ἢ ἀγαθοῦ; οὐκ ἄλλος ἄλλῃ
10 φέρεται, καὶ ἀμφισβητοῦμεν ἀλλήλοις τε καὶ ἡμῖν αὐτοῖς;

ΦΑΙ. Πάνυ μὲν οὖν.

b ΣΩ. Ἐν μὲν ἄρα τοῖς συμφωνοῦμεν, ἐν δὲ τοῖς οὔ.

ΦΑΙ. Οὕτω.

ΣΩ. Ποτέρωθι οὖν εὐαπατητότεροί ἐσμεν, καὶ ἡ ῥητορικὴ ἐν ποτέροις μεῖζον δύναται;

5 ΦΑΙ. Δῆλον ὅτι ἐν οἷς πλανώμεθα.

ΣΩ. Οὐκοῦν τὸν μέλλοντα τέχνην ῥητορικὴν μετιέναι πρῶτον μὲν δεῖ ταῦτα ὁδῷ διῃρῆσθαι, καὶ εἰληφέναι τινὰ χαρακτῆρα ἑκατέρου τοῦ εἴδους, ἐν ᾧ τε ἀνάγκη τὸ πλῆθος πλανᾶσθαι καὶ ἐν ᾧ μή.

c ΦΑΙ. Καλὸν γοῦν ἄν, ὦ Σώκρατες, εἶδος εἴη κατανενοηκὼς ὁ τοῦτο λαβών.

ΣΩ. Ἔπειτά γε οἶμαι πρὸς ἑκάστῳ γιγνόμενον μὴ λανθάνειν ἀλλ' ὀξέως αἰσθάνεσθαι περὶ οὗ ἂν μέλλῃ ἐρεῖν
5 ποτέρου ὂν τυγχάνει τοῦ γένους.

---

e 2 ἡμῖν T : ὑμῖν B   a 3 τοιούτων B T : ὄντων corr. Coisl. : fort.
ὀνομάτων H. Richards   ὁμονοητικῶς T Galenus : οὐ μόνον ποιητικῶς B
b 7 δεῖ B : δὴ T   b 8 πλῆθος T : εἶδος B   c 1 εἶδος addubitat
H. Richards

ΦΑΙ. Τί μήν;

ΣΩ. Τί οὖν; τὸν ἔρωτα πότερον φῶμεν εἶναι τῶν ἀμφισβητησίμων ἢ τῶν μή;

ΦΑΙ. Τῶν ἀμφισβητησίμων δήπου· ἢ οἴει ἄν σοι ἐγχω- ρῆσαι εἰπεῖν ἃ νυνδὴ εἶπες περὶ αὐτοῦ, ὡς βλάβη τέ ἐστι 10 τῷ ἐρωμένῳ καὶ ἐρῶντι, καὶ αὖθις ὡς μέγιστον ⟨ὂν⟩ τῶν ἀγαθῶν τυγχάνει;

ΣΩ. Ἄριστα λέγεις· ἀλλ' εἰπὲ καὶ τόδε—ἐγὼ γάρ τοι d διὰ τὸ ἐνθουσιαστικὸν οὐ πάνυ μέμνημαι—εἰ ὡρισάμην ἔρωτα ἀρχόμενος τοῦ λόγου.

ΦΑΙ. Νὴ Δία ἀμηχάνως γε ὡς σφόδρα.

ΣΩ. Φεῦ, ὅσῳ λέγεις τεχνικωτέρας Νύμφας τὰς Ἀχελῴου 5 καὶ Πᾶνα τὸν Ἑρμοῦ Λυσίου τοῦ Κεφάλου πρὸς λόγους εἶναι. ἢ οὐδὲν λέγω, ἀλλὰ καὶ ὁ Λυσίας ἀρχόμενος τοῦ ἐρωτικοῦ ἠνάγκασεν ἡμᾶς ὑπολαβεῖν τὸν Ἔρωτα ἔν τι τῶν ὄντων ὃ αὐτὸς ἐβουλήθη, καὶ πρὸς τοῦτο ἤδη συνταξάμενος πάντα τὸν e ὕστερον λόγον διεπεράνατο; βούλει πάλιν ἀναγνῶμεν τὴν ἀρχὴν αὐτοῦ;

ΦΑΙ. Εἰ σοί γε δοκεῖ· ὃ μέντοι ζητεῖς οὐκ ἔστ' αὐτόθι.

ΣΩ. Λέγε, ἵνα ἀκούσω αὐτοῦ ἐκείνου. 5

ΦΑΙ. " Περὶ μὲν τῶν ἐμῶν πραγμάτων ἐπίστασαι, καὶ ὡς νομίζω συμφέρειν ἡμῖν τούτων γενομένων, ἀκήκοας. ἀξιῶ δὲ μὴ διὰ τοῦτο ἀτυχῆσαι ὧν δέομαι, ὅτι οὐκ ἐραστὴς ὢν 264 σοῦ τυγχάνω. ὡς ἐκείνοις μὲν τότε μεταμέλει ὧν ἂν εὖ ποιήσωσιν, ἐπειδὰν τῆς ἐπιθυμίας παύσωνται"—

ΣΩ. Ἦ πολλοῦ δεῖν ἔοικε ποιεῖν ὅδε γε ὁ ζητοῦμεν, ὃς οὐδὲ ἀπ' ἀρχῆς ἀλλ' ἀπὸ τελευτῆς ἐξ ὑπτίας ἀνάπαλιν διανεῖν 5 ἐπιχειρεῖ τὸν λόγον, καὶ ἄρχεται ἀφ' ὧν πεπαυμένος ἂν ἤδη

c 9 ἐγχωρῆσαι codex Marcianus Galeni : συγχωρῆσαι B T   c 11 ὂν addidi auctore Heindorfio (ἀγαθῶν ὢν infra Hirschig)   d 4 ὡς T : om. B   d 6 Πᾶνα] πάντα B T : del. τ b t   λόγους T : λόγου B : λόγον al.   e 6 ἐπίστασαι B : ἐπίσταμαι T   a 2 τότε T : τὸ τότε B   a 4 ζητοῦμεν ὃς T : ζητούμενος B   a 5 διανεῖν B T : διανύειν rec. b ὁ ἐραστὴς λέγοι πρὸς τὰ παιδικά. ἢ οὐδὲν εἶπον, Φαῖδρε, φίλη κεφαλή;

b   ΦΑΙ. Ἔστιν γέ τοι δή, ὦ Σώκρατες, τελευτή, περὶ οὗ τὸν λόγον ποιεῖται.

ΣΩ. Τί δὲ τἄλλα; οὐ χύδην δοκεῖ βεβλῆσθαι τὰ τοῦ λόγου; ἢ φαίνεται τὸ δεύτερον εἰρημένον ἔκ τινος ἀνάγκης 5 δεύτερον δεῖν τεθῆναι, ἤ τι ἄλλο τῶν ῥηθέντων; ἐμοὶ μὲν γὰρ ἔδοξεν, ὡς μηδὲν εἰδότι, οὐκ ἀγεννῶς τὸ ἐπιὸν εἰρῆσθαι τῷ γράφοντι· σὺ δ' ἔχεις τινὰ ἀνάγκην λογογραφικὴν ᾗ ταῦτα ἐκεῖνος οὕτως ἐφεξῆς παρ' ἄλληλα ἔθηκεν;

ΦΑΙ. Χρηστὸς εἶ, ὅτι με ἡγῇ ἱκανὸν εἶναι τὰ ἐκείνου c οὕτως ἀκριβῶς διιδεῖν.

ΣΩ. Ἀλλὰ τόδε γε οἶμαί σε φάναι ἄν, δεῖν πάντα λόγον ὥσπερ ζῷον συνεστάναι σῶμά τι ἔχοντα αὐτὸν αὑτοῦ, ὥστε μήτε ἀκέφαλον εἶναι μήτε ἄπουν, ἀλλὰ μέσα τε ἔχειν καὶ 5 ἄκρα, πρέποντα ἀλλήλοις καὶ τῷ ὅλῳ γεγραμμένα.

ΦΑΙ. Πῶς γὰρ οὔ;

ΣΩ. Σκέψαι τοίνυν τὸν τοῦ ἑταίρου σου λόγον εἴτε οὕτως εἴτε ἄλλως ἔχει, καὶ εὑρήσεις τοῦ ἐπιγράμματος οὐδὲν διαφέροντα, ὃ Μίδᾳ τῷ Φρυγὶ φασίν τινες ἐπιγεγράφθαι.

d   ΦΑΙ. Ποῖον τοῦτο, καὶ τί πεπονθός;

ΣΩ. Ἔστι μὲν τοῦτο τόδε—

     Χαλκῆ παρθένος εἰμί, Μίδα δ' ἐπὶ σήματι κεῖμαι.
     ὄφρ' ἂν ὕδωρ τε νάῃ καὶ δένδρεα μακρὰ τεθήλῃ,
5   αὐτοῦ τῇδε μένουσα πολυκλαύτου ἐπὶ τύμβου,
     ἀγγελέω παριοῦσι Μίδας ὅτι τῇδε τέθαπται.

e ὅτι δ' οὐδὲν διαφέρει αὐτοῦ πρῶτον ἢ ὕστατόν τι λέγεσθαι, ἐννοεῖς που, ὡς ἐγῷμαι.

ΦΑΙ. Σκώπτεις τὸν λόγον ἡμῶν, ὦ Σώκρατες.

ΣΩ. Τοῦτον μὲν τοίνυν, ἵνα μὴ σὺ ἄχθῃ, ἐάσωμεν—

---

a 7 ἐραστὴς recc. : ἐρασθεὶς Β Τ   b 5 δεῖν secl. Madvig : δὴ Schanz   b 9 με Τ : μὴ Β   c 3 σῶμά τι t : σώματι Β Τ c 4 μήτε ἀκέφαλον Τ : μὴ τὸ ἀκέφαλον Β   d 3 μίδα Τ : μίδᾳ Β e 3 ἡμῶν Β : om. Τ

καίτοι συχνά γε ἔχειν μοι δοκεῖ παραδείγματα πρὸς ἅ τις 5
βλέπων ὀνίναιτ' ἄν, μιμεῖσθαι αὐτὰ ἐπιχειρῶν μὴ πάνυ τι—
εἰς δὲ τοὺς ἑτέρους λόγους ἴωμεν. ἦν γάρ τι ἐν αὐτοῖς, ὡς
δοκῶ, προσῆκον ἰδεῖν τοῖς βουλομένοις περὶ λόγων σκοπεῖν.

ΦΑΙ. Τὸ ποῖον δὴ λέγεις;   265

ΣΩ. Ἐναντίω που ἤστην· ὁ μὲν γὰρ ὡς τῷ ἐρῶντι, ὁ δ'
ὡς τῷ μὴ δεῖ χαρίζεσθαι, ἐλεγέτην.

ΦΑΙ. Καὶ μάλ' ἀνδρικῶς.

ΣΩ. Ὤιμην σε τἀληθὲς ἐρεῖν, ὅτι μανικῶς· ὃ μέντοι 5
ἐζήτουν ἐστὶν αὐτὸ τοῦτο. μανίαν γάρ τινα ἐφήσαμεν εἶναι
τὸν ἔρωτα. ἦ γάρ;

ΦΑΙ. Ναί.

ΣΩ. Μανίας δέ γε εἴδη δύο, τὴν μὲν ὑπὸ νοσημάτων
ἀνθρωπίνων, τὴν δὲ ὑπὸ θείας ἐξαλλαγῆς τῶν εἰωθότων 10
νομίμων γιγνομένην.

ΦΑΙ. Πάνυ γε.   b

ΣΩ. Τῆς δὲ θείας τεττάρων θεῶν τέτταρα μέρη διελόμενοι,
μαντικὴν μὲν ἐπίπνοιαν Ἀπόλλωνος θέντες, Διονύσου δὲ
τελεστικήν, Μουσῶν δ' αὖ ποιητικήν, τετάρτην δὲ Ἀφροδίτης
καὶ Ἔρωτος, ἐρωτικὴν μανίαν ἐφήσαμέν τε ἀρίστην εἶναι, 5
καὶ οὐκ οἶδ' ὅπῃ τὸ ἐρωτικὸν πάθος ἀπεικάζοντες, ἴσως
μὲν ἀληθοῦς τινος ἐφαπτόμενοι, τάχα δ' ἂν καὶ ἄλλοσε
παραφερόμενοι, κεράσαντες οὐ παντάπασιν ἀπίθανον λόγον,
μυθικόν τινα ὕμνον προσεπαίσαμεν μετρίως τε καὶ εὐφήμως c
τὸν ἐμόν τε καὶ σὸν δεσπότην Ἔρωτα, ὦ Φαῖδρε, καλῶν
παίδων ἔφορον.

ΦΑΙ. Καὶ μάλα ἔμοιγε οὐκ ἀηδῶς ἀκοῦσαι.

ΣΩ. Τόδε τοίνυν αὐτόθεν λάβωμεν, ὡς ἀπὸ τοῦ ψέγειν 5
πρὸς τὸ ἐπαινεῖν ἔσχεν ὁ λόγος μεταβῆναι.

ΦΑΙ. Πῶς δὴ οὖν αὐτὸ λέγεις;

e 6 βλέπων ⟨μὲν⟩ . . . μιμεῖσθαι ⟨δ'⟩ Herwerden   e 7 ἑτέρους
T : ἑταίρους B   b 2 τεττάρων θεῶν secl. Schanz   b 5 τε
BT : om. Stobaeus   b 8 λόγον corr. Par. 1808 : λόγου BT
c 4 ἔμοιγε B : ἐμοὶ μὲν T

ΣΩ. Ἐμοὶ μὲν φαίνεται τὰ μὲν ἄλλα τῷ ὄντι παιδιᾷ
πεπαῖσθαι· τούτων δέ τινων ἐκ τύχης ῥηθέντων δυοῖν εἰδοῖν,
d εἰ αὐτοῖν τὴν δύναμιν τέχνῃ λαβεῖν δύναιτό τις, οὐκ ἄχαρι.

ΦΑΙ. Τίνων δή;

ΣΩ. Εἰς μίαν τε ἰδέαν συνορῶντα ἄγειν τὰ πολλαχῇ
διεσπαρμένα, ἵνα ἕκαστον ὁριζόμενος δῆλον ποιῇ περὶ οὗ ἂν
5 ἀεὶ διδάσκειν ἐθέλῃ. ὥσπερ τὰ νυνδὴ περὶ Ἔρωτος—ὃ ἔστιν
ὁρισθέν—εἴτ' εὖ εἴτε κακῶς ἐλέχθη, τὸ γοῦν σαφὲς καὶ τὸ
αὐτὸ αὑτῷ ὁμολογούμενον διὰ ταῦτα ἔσχεν εἰπεῖν ὁ λόγος.

ΦΑΙ. Τὸ δ' ἕτερον δὴ εἶδος τί λέγεις, ὦ Σώκρατες;

e ΣΩ. Τὸ πάλιν κατ' εἴδη δύνασθαι διατέμνειν κατ' ἄρθρα
ᾗ πέφυκεν, καὶ μὴ ἐπιχειρεῖν καταγνύναι μέρος μηδέν, κακοῦ
μαγείρου τρόπῳ χρώμενον· ἀλλ' ὥσπερ ἄρτι τὼ λόγω τὸ
μὲν ἄφρον τῆς διανοίας ἕν τι κοινῇ εἶδος ἐλαβέτην, ὥσπερ
266 δὲ σώματος ἐξ ἑνὸς διπλᾶ καὶ ὁμώνυμα πέφυκε, σκαιά, τὰ δὲ
δεξιὰ κληθέντα, οὕτω καὶ τὸ τῆς παρανοίας ὡς ⟨ἐν⟩ ἐν ἡμῖν
πεφυκὸς εἶδος ἡγησαμένω τὼ λόγω, ὁ μὲν τὸ ἐπ' ἀριστερὰ
τεμνόμενος μέρος, πάλιν τοῦτο τέμνων οὐκ ἐπανῆκεν πρὶν ἐν
5 αὐτοῖς ἐφευρὼν ὀνομαζόμενον σκαιόν τινα ἔρωτα ἐλοιδόρησεν
μάλ' ἐν δίκῃ, ὁ δ' εἰς τὰ ἐν δεξιᾷ τῆς μανίας ἀγαγὼν ἡμᾶς,
ὁμώνυμον μὲν ἐκείνῳ, θεῖον δ' αὖ τινα ἔρωτα ἐφευρὼν καὶ
b προτεινάμενος ἐπήνεσεν ὡς μεγίστων αἴτιον ἡμῖν ἀγαθῶν.

ΦΑΙ. Ἀληθέστατα λέγεις.

ΣΩ. Τούτων δὴ ἔγωγε αὐτός τε ἐραστής, ὦ Φαῖδρε, τῶν
διαιρέσεων καὶ συναγωγῶν, ἵνα οἷός τε ὦ λέγειν τε καὶ
5 φρονεῖν· ἐάν τέ τιν' ἄλλον ἡγήσωμαι δυνατὸν εἰς ἓν καὶ ἐπὶ

c8 παιδιᾷ T : παιδία B   c9 πεπαῖσθαι T : πεπέσθαι B   τινῶν
. . . ῥηθέντων] τι νῶν . . . ῥηθὲν τὸ τοῖν Badham   εἰδοῖν] εἰδῶν
Galenus   d1 αὐτοῖν BT : αὐτὴν vulg.   d5 τὰ BT : τὸ Schanz
d8 δὴ T : μὴ B   e1 κατ' BT : καὶ τὰ Madvig   διατέμνειν T
Stobaeus Galenus : τέμνειν B   a1 σώματος BT : σώματι Stobaeus
πέφυκε σκαιά T Stobaeus : πέφυκες· καὶ ἃ B   τὰ δὲ Stobaeus :
τάδε ἡ BT   a2 παρανοίας BT : παροινίας Stobaeus   ἐν ἐν
Heindorf : ἐν BT : ἓν al. : om. Stobaeus   ἡμῖν T Stobaeus : ὑμῖν B
a3 τὸ BT : om. Stobaeus   a4 ἐπανῆκεν BT : ἀνῆκεν Stobaeus
ἐν αὐτοῖς BT : ἑαυτοῖς Stobaeus   a7 καὶ secl. Badham

ΦΑΙΔΡΟΣ 266 b

πολλὰ πεφυκόθ' ὁρᾶν, τοῦτον διώκω " κατόπισθε μετ'
ἴχνιον ὥστε θεοῖο." καὶ μέντοι καὶ τοὺς δυναμένους αὐτὸ
δρᾶν εἰ μὲν ὀρθῶς ἢ μὴ προσαγορεύω, θεὸς οἶδε, καλῶ δὲ
οὖν μέχρι τοῦδε διαλεκτικούς. τὰ δὲ νῦν παρὰ σοῦ τε καὶ c
Λυσίου μαθόντας εἰπὲ τί χρὴ καλεῖν· ἢ τοῦτο ἐκεῖνό ἐστιν ἡ
λόγων τέχνη, ᾗ Θρασύμαχός τε καὶ οἱ ἄλλοι χρώμενοι σοφοὶ
μὲν αὐτοὶ λέγειν γεγόνασιν, ἄλλους τε ποιοῦσιν, οἳ ἂν
δωροφορεῖν αὐτοῖς ὡς βασιλεῦσιν ἐθέλωσιν;   5

ΦΑΙ. Βασιλικοὶ μὲν ἄνδρες, οὐ μὲν δὴ ἐπιστήμονές γε ὧν
ἐρωτᾷς. ἀλλὰ τοῦτο μὲν τὸ εἶδος ὀρθῶς ἔμοιγε δοκεῖς καλεῖν,
διαλεκτικὸν καλῶν· τὸ δὲ ῥητορικὸν δοκεῖ μοι διαφεύγειν ἔθ'
ἡμᾶς.

ΣΩ. Πῶς φῄς; καλόν πού τι ἂν εἴη, ὃ τούτων ἀπο- d
λειφθὲν ὅμως τέχνῃ λαμβάνεται; πάντως δ' οὐκ ἀτιμαστέον
αὐτὸ σοί τε καὶ ἐμοί, λεκτέον δὲ τί μέντοι καὶ ἔστι τὸ
λειπόμενον τῆς ῥητορικῆς.

ΦΑΙ. Καὶ μάλα πού συχνά, ὦ Σώκρατες, τά γ' ἐν τοῖς 5
βιβλίοις τοῖς περὶ λόγων τέχνης γεγραμμένοις.

ΣΩ. [Καὶ] καλῶς γε ὑπέμνησας. προοίμιον μὲν οἶμαι
πρῶτον ὡς δεῖ τοῦ λόγου λέγεσθαι ἐν ἀρχῇ· ταῦτα λέγεις
—ἢ γάρ;—τὰ κομψὰ τῆς τέχνης;

ΦΑΙ. Ναί.   e

ΣΩ. Δεύτερον δὲ δὴ διήγησίν τινα μαρτυρίας τ' ἐπ'
αὐτῇ, τρίτον τεκμήρια, τέταρτον εἰκότα· καὶ πίστωσιν
οἶμαι καὶ ἐπιπίστωσιν λέγειν τόν γε βέλτιστον λογοδαίδαλον Βυζάντιον ἄνδρα.   5

ΦΑΙ. Τὸν χρηστὸν λέγεις Θεόδωρον;

ΣΩ. Τί μήν; καὶ ἔλεγχόν γε καὶ ἐπεξέλεγχον ὡς 267
ποιητέον ἐν κατηγορίᾳ τε καὶ ἀπολογίᾳ. τὸν δὲ κάλλιστον

b 7 πεφυκόθ'] πεφυκὸς BT Stobaeus : πεφυκότα vulg.   b 9 ἢ μὴ
T : εἰ μὴ B   c 1 δὲ νῦν B : νῦν δὲ T   c 2 μαθόντας B : μαθόντες T :
μαθόντα H. Richards   c 6 ἄνδρες Bekker : ἄνδρες BT   c 7 τὸ T :
om. B   d 7 καὶ secl. Hirschig   d 8 ἐν ἀρχῇ T : ἐπ' ἀρχῇ B :
secl. ci. Schanz   e 4 λογοδαίδαλον T (et legit Cicero) : λόγου
δαίδαλον B : λόγων Δαίδαλον Winckelmann

Πάριον Εὐηνὸν ἐς μέσον οὐκ ἄγομεν, ὃς ὑποδήλωσίν τε
πρῶτος ηὗρεν καὶ παρεπαίνους—οἱ δ' αὐτὸν καὶ παραψό-
5 γους φασὶν ἐν μέτρῳ λέγειν μνήμης χάριν—σοφὸς γὰρ ἀνήρ.
Τεισίαν δὲ Γοργίαν τε ἐάσομεν εὕδειν, οἳ πρὸ τῶν ἀληθῶν
τὰ εἰκότα εἶδον ὡς τιμητέα μᾶλλον, τά τε αὖ σμικρὰ μεγάλα
καὶ τὰ μεγάλα σμικρὰ φαίνεσθαι ποιοῦσιν διὰ ῥώμην λόγου,
b καινά τε ἀρχαίως τά τ' ἐναντία καινῶς, συντομίαν τε λόγων
καὶ ἄπειρα μήκη περὶ πάντων ἀνηῦρον; ταῦτα δὲ ἀκούων
ποτέ μου Πρόδικος ἐγέλασεν, καὶ μόνος αὐτὸς ηὑρηκέναι ἔφη
ὧν δεῖ λόγων τέχνην· δεῖν δὲ οὔτε μακρῶν οὔτε βραχέων
5 ἀλλὰ μετρίων.

ΦΑΙ. Σοφώτατά γε, ὦ Πρόδικε.

ΣΩ. Ἱππίαν δὲ οὐ λέγομεν; οἶμαι γὰρ ἂν σύμψηφον
αὐτῷ καὶ τὸν Ἠλεῖον ξένον γενέσθαι.

ΦΑΙ. Τί δ' οὔ;

10 ΣΩ. Τὰ δὲ Πώλου πῶς φράσωμεν αὖ μουσεῖα λόγων—ὡς
c διπλασιολογίαν καὶ γνωμολογίαν καὶ εἰκονολογίαν
—ὀνομάτων τε Λικυμνίων ἃ ἐκείνῳ ἐδωρήσατο πρὸς ποίησιν
εὐεπείας;

ΦΑΙ. Πρωταγόρεια δέ, ὦ Σώκρατες, οὐκ ἦν μέντοι
5 τοιαῦτ' ἄττα;

ΣΩ. Ὀρθοέπειά γέ τις, ὦ παῖ, καὶ ἄλλα πολλὰ καὶ
καλά. τῶν γε μὴν οἰκτρογόων ἐπὶ γῆρας καὶ πενίαν
ἑλκομένων λόγων κεκρατηκέναι τέχνῃ μοι φαίνεται τὸ τοῦ
Χαλκηδονίου σθένος, ὀργίσαι τε αὖ πολλοὺς ἅμα δεινὸς ἀνὴρ
d γέγονεν, καὶ πάλιν ὠργισμένοις ἐπᾴδων κηλεῖν, ὡς ἔφη,
διαβάλλειν τε καὶ ἀπολύσασθαι διαβολὰς ὁθενδὴ κράτιστος.

a 3 ἐς B : εἰς T   a 5 ἀνήρ Bekker : ἀνήρ B T   a 6 δὲ in
ras. T   b 4 τέχνην B T : τέχνη Stephanus   δεῖν corr. Par. 1808 :
δεινὰ B T   b 7-8 ἰππίαν . . . τὸν ἠλεῖον T : ἰππείαν . . . τὸν ἥλιον B
b 10 φράσωμεν B : φράσομεν T : ⟨οὐ⟩ φράσωμεν Schanz   ὡς B : ὃς T
c 2 Λικυμνιείων Ast   ἃ ἐκείνῳ ἐδωρήσατο secl. Ast   πρὸς ποίησιν
B T : προσεποίησεν Cornarius   c 3 εὐεπείας B T : εὐέπειαν Schanz
c 9 Καλχηδονίου Herwerden   ὀργίσαι τε T : ὀργίσαιτο B   ἀνὴρ
Bekker : ἀνήρ B T   d 2 ὅθεν δὴ Par. 1808 : ὅθεν δεῖ B T

τὸ δὲ δὴ τέλος τῶν λόγων κοινῇ πᾶσιν ἔοικε συνδεδογμένον
εἶναι, ᾧ τινες μὲν ἐπάνοδον, ἄλλοι δ' ἄλλο τίθενται ὄνομα.

ΦΑΙ. Τὸ ἐν κεφαλαίῳ ἕκαστα λέγεις ὑπομνῆσαι ἐπὶ 5
τελευτῆς τοὺς ἀκούοντας περὶ τῶν εἰρημένων;

ΣΩ. Ταῦτα λέγω, καὶ εἴ τι σὺ ἄλλο ἔχεις εἰπεῖν λόγων
τέχνης πέρι.

ΦΑΙ. Σμικρά γε καὶ οὐκ ἄξια λέγειν.

ΣΩ. Ἐῶμεν δὴ τά γε σμικρά· ταῦτα δὲ ὑπ' αὐγὰς μᾶλλον 268
ἴδωμεν, τίνα καὶ πότ' ἔχει τὴν τῆς τέχνης δύναμιν.

ΦΑΙ. Καὶ μάλα ἐρρωμένην, ὦ Σώκρατες, ἔν γε δὴ
πλήθους συνόδοις.

ΣΩ. Ἔχει γάρ. ἀλλ', ὦ δαιμόνιε, ἰδὲ καὶ σὺ εἰ ἄρα καὶ 5
σοὶ φαίνεται διεστηκὸς αὐτῶν τὸ ἤτριον ὥσπερ ἐμοί.

ΦΑΙ. Δείκνυε μόνον.

ΣΩ. Εἰπὲ δή μοι· εἴ τις προσελθὼν τῷ ἑταίρῳ σου
Ἐρυξιμάχῳ ἢ τῷ πατρὶ αὐτοῦ Ἀκουμενῷ εἴποι ὅτι " Ἐγὼ
ἐπίσταμαι τοιαῦτ' ἄττα σώμασι προσφέρειν, ὥστε θερμαίνειν 10
τ' ἐὰν βούλωμαι καὶ ψύχειν, καὶ ἐὰν μὲν δόξῃ μοι, ἐμεῖν b
ποιεῖν, ἐὰν δ' αὖ, κάτω διαχωρεῖν, καὶ ἄλλα πάμπολλα
τοιαῦτα· καὶ ἐπιστάμενος αὐτὰ ἀξιῶ ἰατρικὸς εἶναι καὶ
ἄλλον ποιεῖν ᾧ ἂν τὴν τούτων ἐπιστήμην παραδῶ," τί ἂν
οἴει ἀκούσαντας εἰπεῖν; 5

ΦΑΙ. Τί δ' ἄλλο γε ἢ ἐρέσθαι εἰ προσεπίσταται καὶ
οὕστινας δεῖ καὶ ὁπότε ἕκαστα τούτων ποιεῖν, καὶ μέχρι
ὁπόσου;

ΣΩ. Εἰ οὖν εἴποι ὅτι " Οὐδαμῶς· ἀλλ' ἀξιῶ τὸν ταῦτα
παρ' ἐμοῦ μαθόντα αὐτὸν οἷόν τ' εἶναι [ποιεῖν] ἃ ἐρωτᾷς; " c

ΦΑΙ. Εἰπεῖν ἂν οἶμαι ὅτι μαίνεται ἄνθρωπος, καὶ ἐκ

d4 τίθενται Τ : τιθέντες Β   a 1 ὑπ' αὐγὰς μᾶλλον ΤW : ὑπαύγασμα
καλὸν Β   a 2 πότ' ΒΤ : ποτ' vulg.   a 8 εἰπὲ Τb : εἴπερ pr. Β
a 9 Ἀκουμενῷ] ἀκουμένῳ ΒΤ   a 10 σώμασι ΒΤ : σώματι V
b 1 μὲν Τ : μὴ Β (in ras.)   b 3 ἐπιστάμενος b : ἐπισταμένους ΒΤ
ἰατρικὸς Β : ἰατρὸς Τ   b 6 δ' ἄλλο γε Τ : γε ἄλλο Β   c 1 ποιεῖν
secl. Buttmann : ἐπατειν Schleiermacher   c 2 εἰπεῖν scripsi :
εἴποιεν Stephanus : εἴποι ΒΤ   ἄνθρωπος Bekker : ἄνθρωπος ΒΤ

βιβλίου ποθὲν ἀκούσας ἢ περιτυχὼν φαρμακίοις ἰατρὸς
οἴεται γεγονέναι, οὐδὲν ἐπαΐων τῆς τέχνης.

5 ΣΩ. Τί δ' εἰ Σοφοκλεῖ αὖ προσελθὼν καὶ Εὐριπίδῃ τις
λέγοι ὡς ἐπίσταται περὶ σμικροῦ πράγματος ῥήσεις παμμήκεις
ποιεῖν καὶ περὶ μεγάλου πάνυ σμικράς, ὅταν τε βούληται
οἰκτράς, καὶ τοὐναντίον αὖ φοβερὰς καὶ ἀπειλητικὰς ὅσα τ'
d ἄλλα τοιαῦτα, καὶ διδάσκων αὐτὰ τραγῳδίας ποίησιν οἴεται
παραδιδόναι;

ΦΑΙ. Καὶ οὗτοι ἄν, ὦ Σώκρατες, οἶμαι καταγελῷεν εἴ
τις οἴεται τραγῳδίαν ἄλλο τι εἶναι ἢ τὴν τούτων σύστασιν
5 πρέπουσαν ἀλλήλοις τε καὶ τῷ ὅλῳ συνισταμένην.

ΣΩ. Ἀλλ' οὐκ ἂν ἀγροίκως γε οἶμαι λοιδορήσειαν, ἀλλ'
ὥσπερ ἂν μουσικὸς ἐντυχὼν ἀνδρὶ οἰομένῳ ἁρμονικῷ εἶναι,
ὅτι δὴ τυγχάνει ἐπιστάμενος ὡς οἷόν τε ὀξυτάτην καὶ βαρυ-
e τάτην χορδὴν ποιεῖν, οὐκ ἀγρίως εἴποι ἄν· "Ὦ μοχθηρέ,
μελαγχολᾷς," ἀλλ' ἅτε μουσικὸς ὢν πρᾳότερον ὅτι "Ὦ
ἄριστε, ἀνάγκη μὲν καὶ ταῦτ' ἐπίστασθαι τὸν μέλλοντα
ἁρμονικὸν ἔσεσθαι, οὐδὲν μὴν κωλύει μηδὲ σμικρὸν ἁρμονίας
5 ἐπαΐειν τὸν τὴν σὴν ἕξιν ἔχοντα· τὰ γὰρ πρὸ ἁρμονίας
ἀναγκαῖα μαθήματα ἐπίστασαι ἀλλ' οὐ τὰ ἁρμονικά."

ΦΑΙ. Ὀρθότατά γε.

269 ΣΩ. Οὐκοῦν καὶ ὁ Σοφοκλῆς τόν σφισιν ἐπιδεικνύμενον
τὰ πρὸ τραγῳδίας ἂν φαίη ἀλλ' οὐ τὰ τραγικά, καὶ ὁ Ἀκου-
μενὸς τὰ πρὸ ἰατρικῆς ἀλλ' οὐ τὰ ἰατρικά.

ΦΑΙ. Παντάπασι μὲν οὖν.

5 ΣΩ. Τί δὲ τὸν μελίγηρυν Ἄδραστον οἰόμεθα ἢ καὶ
Περικλέα, εἰ ἀκούσειαν ὧν νυνδὴ ἡμεῖς διῇμεν τῶν παγκάλων
τεχνημάτων—βραχυλογιῶν τε καὶ εἰκονολογιῶν καὶ ὅσα
ἄλλα διελθόντες ὑπ' αὐγὰς ἔφαμεν εἶναι σκεπτέα—πότερον
b χαλεπῶς ἂν αὐτούς, ὥσπερ ἐγώ τε καὶ σύ, ὑπ' ἀγροικίας

c 8 αὖ W : καὶ αὖ BT   ὅσα τᾶλλα (sic) τοιαῦτα καὶ διδάσκων
T : καὶ ὅσα ταλλα (sic) τοιαῦτα διδάσκων B   d 5 πρέπουσαν T :
τρέπουσαν B   d 6 γε B : τε T   e 1 ἀγροίκως Osann   e 5 πρὸ
t : πρὸς BT   a 5 οἰόμεθ' ⟨ἂν⟩ Hirschig   a 8 αὐγὰς T : αὐτὰς B

ῥῆμά τι εἰπεῖν ἀπαίδευτον εἰς τοὺς ταῦτα γεγραφότας τε καὶ
διδάσκοντας ὡς ῥητορικὴν τέχνην, ἢ ἅτε ἡμῶν ὄντας σοφωτέρους κἂν νῷν ἐπιπλῆξαι εἰπόντας· "Ὦ Φαῖδρέ τε καὶ
Σώκρατες, οὐ χρὴ χαλεπαίνειν ἀλλὰ συγγιγνώσκειν, εἴ τινες 5
μὴ ἐπιστάμενοι διαλέγεσθαι ἀδύνατοι ἐγένοντο ὁρίσασθαι
τί ποτ' ἔστιν ῥητορική, ἐκ δὲ τούτου τοῦ πάθους τὰ πρὸ
τῆς τέχνης ἀναγκαῖα μαθήματα ἔχοντες ῥητορικὴν ᾠήθησαν
ηὑρηκέναι, καὶ ταῦτα δὴ διδάσκοντες ἄλλους ἡγοῦνταί σφισιν c
τελέως ῥητορικὴν δεδιδάχθαι, τὸ δὲ ἕκαστα τούτων πιθανῶς
λέγειν τε καὶ τὸ ὅλον συνίστασθαι, οὐδὲν ἔργον ⟨ὄν⟩, αὐτοὺς
δεῖν παρ' ἑαυτῶν τοὺς μαθητάς σφων πορίζεσθαι ἐν τοῖς
λόγοις". 5

ΦΑΙ. Ἀλλὰ μήν, ὦ Σώκρατες, κινδυνεύει γε τοιοῦτόν
τι εἶναι τὸ τῆς τέχνης ἣν οὗτοι οἱ ἄνδρες ὡς ῥητορικὴν
διδάσκουσίν τε καὶ γράφουσιν, καὶ ἔμοιγε δοκεῖς ἀληθῆ εἰρη-
κέναι· ἀλλὰ δὴ τὴν τοῦ τῷ ὄντι ῥητορικοῦ τε καὶ πιθανοῦ
τέχνην πῶς καὶ πόθεν ἄν τις δύναιτο πορίσασθαι; d

ΣΩ. Τὸ μὲν δύνασθαι, ὦ Φαῖδρε, ὥστε ἀγωνιστὴν τέλεον
γενέσθαι, εἰκός—ἴσως δὲ καὶ ἀναγκαῖον—ἔχειν ὥσπερ τἄλλα·
εἰ μέν σοι ὑπάρχει φύσει ῥητορικῷ εἶναι, ἔσῃ ῥήτωρ ἐλλό-
γιμος, προσλαβὼν ἐπιστήμην τε καὶ μελέτην, ὅτου δ' ἂν 5
ἐλλείπῃς τούτων, ταύτῃ ἀτελὴς ἔσῃ. ὅσον δὲ αὐτοῦ τέχνη,
οὐχ ᾗ Λυσίας τε καὶ Θρασύμαχος πορεύεται δοκεῖ μοι
φαίνεσθαι ἡ μέθοδος.

ΦΑΙ. Ἀλλὰ πῇ δή;

ΣΩ. Κινδυνεύει, ὦ ἄριστε, εἰκότως ὁ Περικλῆς πάντων e
τελεώτατος εἰς τὴν ῥητορικὴν γενέσθαι.

ΦΑΙ. Τί δή;

ΣΩ. Πᾶσαι ὅσαι μεγάλαι τῶν τεχνῶν προσδέονται

b2 ῥῆμά τι T: ῥήματι B   b7 ῥητορική B: ἡ ῥητορική T
c3 οὐδὲν ἔργον ὄν Heindorf: οὐδὲν ἔργον Β Τ: ὡς οὐδὲν ἔργον ὄν
Hermias   c4 σφων] ἐφῶν B: σφῶιν T   c6 γε T: om. B
c8 δοκεῖς T: δοκεῖ B   d4 ῥητορικῷ T: ῥητορικὸς B   d5 ὅτου
Β Τ: ὅπου Aldina   d6 ἐλλείπῃς Τ Aristides: ἐλλίπῃς Β   ἀτελὴς
Τ: ἀτελὲς Β   d7 Λυσίας] Gorgias Ficinus: Τισίας Schaefer

270 ἀδολεσχίας καὶ μετεωρολογίας φύσεως πέρι· τὸ γὰρ ὑψηλόνουν τοῦτο καὶ πάντῃ τελεσιουργὸν ἔοικεν ἐντεῦθέν ποθεν
εἰσιέναι. ὃ καὶ Περικλῆς πρὸς τῷ εὐφυὴς εἶναι ἐκτήσατο·
προσπεσὼν γὰρ οἶμαι τοιούτῳ ὄντι 'Αναξαγόρᾳ, μετεωρο-
5 λογίας ἐμπλησθεὶς καὶ ἐπὶ φύσιν νοῦ τε καὶ διανοίας ἀφικόμενος, ὧν δὴ πέρι τὸν πολὺν λόγον ἐποιεῖτο 'Αναξαγόρας,
ἐντεῦθεν εἵλκυσεν ἐπὶ τὴν τῶν λόγων τέχνην τὸ πρόσφορον
αὐτῇ.
ΦΑΙ. Πῶς τοῦτο λέγεις;
b ΣΩ. Ὁ αὐτός που τρόπος τέχνης ἰατρικῆς ὅσπερ καὶ
ῥητορικῆς.
ΦΑΙ. Πῶς δή;
ΣΩ. Ἐν ἀμφοτέραις δεῖ διελέσθαι φύσιν, σώματος μὲν
5 ἐν τῇ ἑτέρᾳ, ψυχῆς δὲ ἐν τῇ ἑτέρᾳ, εἰ μέλλεις, μὴ τριβῇ
μόνον καὶ ἐμπειρίᾳ ἀλλὰ τέχνῃ, τῷ μὲν φάρμακα καὶ τροφὴν
προσφέρων ὑγίειαν καὶ ῥώμην ἐμποιήσειν, τῇ δὲ λόγους τε
καὶ ἐπιτηδεύσεις νομίμους πειθὼ ἣν ἂν βούλῃ καὶ ἀρετὴν
παραδώσειν.
10 ΦΑΙ. Τὸ γοῦν εἰκός, ὦ Σώκρατες, οὕτως.
c ΣΩ. Ψυχῆς οὖν φύσιν ἀξίως λόγου κατανοῆσαι οἴει
δυνατὸν εἶναι ἄνευ τῆς τοῦ ὅλου φύσεως;
ΦΑΙ. Εἰ μὲν Ἱπποκράτει γε τῷ τῶν 'Ασκληπιαδῶν
δεῖ τι πιθέσθαι, οὐδὲ περὶ σώματος ἄνευ τῆς μεθόδου
5 ταύτης.
ΣΩ. Καλῶς γάρ, ὦ ἑταῖρε, λέγει· χρὴ μέντοι πρὸς τῷ
Ἱπποκράτει τὸν λόγον ἐξετάζοντα σκοπεῖν εἰ συμφωνεῖ.
ΦΑΙ. Φημί.
ΣΩ. Τὸ τοίνυν περὶ φύσεως σκόπει τί ποτε λέγει Ἱππο-
10 κράτης τε καὶ ὁ ἀληθὴς λόγος. ἆρ' οὐχ ὧδε δεῖ διανοεῖσθαι

a 2 καὶ B: καὶ τὸ T   τελεσιουργὸν B Plutarchus: τελεσιουργικὸν
T: τελεσίεργον Badham   a 4 τοιούτῳ T: τῷ B   a 5 διανοίας
V Aristides: ἀνοίας BT: ἐννοίας al.   a 6 ὧν Tb: ὃν pr. B
b 4 ἐν T: om. B   b 7 τῇ δὲ T: τῷ δὲ B   c 2 ὅλου TW:
λόγου B   c 3 γε Heindorf: τε BT: om. Galenus   τῶν BT:
om. pr. T   c 4 πιθέσθαι T: πείθεσθαι B

περὶ ὁτουοῦν φύσεως· πρῶτον μέν, ἁπλοῦν ἢ πολυειδές d
ἐστιν οὗ πέρι βουλησόμεθα εἶναι αὐτοὶ τεχνικοὶ καὶ ἄλλον
δυνατοὶ ποιεῖν, ἔπειτα δέ, ἂν μὲν ἁπλοῦν ᾖ, σκοπεῖν τὴν
δύναμιν αὐτοῦ, τίνα πρὸς τί πέφυκεν εἰς τὸ δρᾶν ἔχον ἢ
τίνα εἰς τὸ παθεῖν ὑπὸ τοῦ, ἐὰν δὲ πλείω εἴδη ἔχῃ, ταῦτα 5
ἀριθμησάμενον, ὅπερ ἐφ' ἑνός, τοῦτ' ἰδεῖν ἐφ' ἑκάστου, τῷ τί
ποιεῖν αὐτὸ πέφυκεν ἢ τῷ τί παθεῖν ὑπὸ τοῦ;

ΦΑΙ. Κινδυνεύει, ὦ Σώκρατες.

ΣΩ. Ἡ γοῦν ἄνευ τούτων μέθοδος ἐοίκοι ἂν ὥσπερ
τυφλοῦ πορείᾳ. ἀλλ' οὐ μὴν ἀπεικαστέον τόν γε τέχνῃ e
μετιόντα ὁτιοῦν τυφλῷ οὐδὲ κωφῷ, ἀλλὰ δῆλον ὡς, ἄν
τῷ τις τέχνῃ λόγους διδῷ, τὴν οὐσίαν δείξει ἀκριβῶς τῆς
φύσεως τούτου πρὸς ὃ τοὺς λόγους προσοίσει· ἔσται δέ που
ψυχὴ τοῦτο. 5

ΦΑΙ. Τί μήν;

ΣΩ. Οὐκοῦν ἡ ἅμιλλα αὐτῷ τέταται πρὸς τοῦτο πᾶσα· 271
πειθὼ γὰρ ἐν τούτῳ ποιεῖν ἐπιχειρεῖ. ἢ γάρ;

ΦΑΙ. Ναί.

ΣΩ. Δῆλον ἄρα ὅτι ὁ Θρασύμαχός τε καὶ ὃς ἂν ἄλλος
σπουδῇ τέχνην ῥητορικὴν διδῷ, πρῶτον πάσῃ ἀκριβείᾳ γράψει 5
τε καὶ ποιήσει ψυχὴν ἰδεῖν, πότερον ἓν καὶ ὅμοιον πέφυκεν
ἢ κατὰ σώματος μορφὴν πολυειδές· τοῦτο γάρ φαμεν φύσιν
εἶναι δεικνύναι.

ΦΑΙ. Παντάπασι μὲν οὖν.

ΣΩ. Δεύτερον δέ γε, ὅτῳ τί ποιεῖν ἢ παθεῖν ὑπὸ τοῦ 10
πέφυκεν.

ΦΑΙ. Τί μήν;

ΣΩ. Τρίτον δὲ δὴ διαταξάμενος τὰ λόγων τε καὶ ψυχῆς b
γένη καὶ τὰ τούτων παθήματα δίεισι πάσας αἰτίας, προσαρ-
μόττων ἕκαστον ἑκάστῳ καὶ διδάσκων οἷα οὖσα ὑφ' οἵων

---

d 5 του T : τοῦδε B   d 6 ἀριθμησάμενον Galenus : ἀριθμησάμενος
BT : ἀριθμησαμένους Stephanus   d 7 αὐτὸ recc. : αὐτῷ BT :
οὕτω V   e 1 γε B : om. T   e 3 τῷ T : om. B   e 4 δ T :
om. B   a 10 τι T : om. B   b 2 πάσας TW : τὰς B

λόγων δι' ἣν αἰτίαν ἐξ ἀνάγκης ἡ μὲν πείθεται, ἡ δὲ
5 ἀπειθεῖ.

ΦΑΙ. Κάλλιστα γοῦν ἄν, ὡς ἔοικ', ἔχοι οὕτως.

ΣΩ. Οὗτοι μὲν οὖν, ὦ φίλε, ἄλλως ἐνδεικνύμενον ἢ
λεγόμενον τέχνῃ ποτὲ λεχθήσεται ἢ γραφήσεται οὔτε τι
c ἄλλο οὔτε τοῦτο. ἀλλ' οἱ νῦν γράφοντες, ὧν σὺ ἀκήκοας,
τέχνας λόγων πανοῦργοί εἰσιν καὶ ἀποκρύπτονται, εἰδότες
ψυχῆς πέρι παγκάλως· πρὶν ἂν οὖν τὸν τρόπον τοῦτον
λέγωσί τε καὶ γράφωσι, μὴ πειθώμεθα αὐτοῖς τέχνῃ γράφειν.
5 ΦΑΙ. Τίνα τοῦτον;

ΣΩ. Αὐτὰ μὲν τὰ ῥήματα εἰπεῖν οὐκ εὐπετές· ὡς δὲ δεῖ
γράφειν, εἰ μέλλει τεχνικῶς ἔχειν καθ' ὅσον ἐνδέχεται,
λέγειν ἐθέλω.

ΦΑΙ. Λέγε δή.

10 ΣΩ. Ἐπειδὴ λόγου δύναμις τυγχάνει ψυχαγωγία οὖσα,
d τὸν μέλλοντα ῥητορικὸν ἔσεσθαι ἀνάγκη εἰδέναι ψυχὴ ὅσα
εἴδη ἔχει. ἔστιν οὖν τόσα καὶ τόσα, καὶ τοῖα καὶ τοῖα,
ὅθεν οἱ μὲν τοιοίδε, οἱ δὲ τοιοίδε γίγνονται· τούτων δὲ δὴ
οὕτω διῃρημένων, λόγων αὖ τόσα καὶ τόσα ἔστιν εἴδη, τοιόνδε
5 ἕκαστον. οἱ μὲν οὖν τοιοίδε ὑπὸ τῶν τοιῶνδε λόγων
διὰ τήνδε τὴν αἰτίαν ἐς τὰ τοιάδε εὐπειθεῖς, οἱ δὲ τοιοίδε
διὰ τάδε δυσπειθεῖς· δεῖ δὴ ταῦτα ἱκανῶς νοήσαντα, μετὰ
ταῦτα θεώμενον αὐτὰ ἐν ταῖς πράξεσιν ὄντα τε καὶ πραττό-
e μενα, ὀξέως τῇ αἰσθήσει δύνασθαι ἐπακολουθεῖν, ἢ μηδὲν
εἶναί πω πλέον αὐτῷ ὧν τότε ἤκουεν λόγων συνών. ὅταν
δὲ εἰπεῖν τε ἱκανῶς ἔχῃ οἶος ὑφ' οἵων πείθεται, παραγιγνό-
μενόν τε δυνατὸς ᾖ διαισθανόμενος ἑαυτῷ ἐνδείκνυσθαι ὅτι
272 οὗτός ἐστι καὶ αὕτη ἡ φύσις περὶ ἧς τότε ἦσαν οἱ λόγοι,

b 7 οὗτοι] οὕτω B : οὗτοι T   d 3 τοιοίδε ... τοιοίδε T Galenus :
τοῖοι ... τοιοίδε B : τοῖοι ... τοῖοι Hermann   δὲ δὴ B : δὲ T
Galenus   d 4 οὕτω T Galenus : om. B   αὖ τόσα T : αὐτὸς ἃ B
τοιόνδε BT : τοιόνδε δὲ Galenus   d 5 μὲν οὖν T Galenus : μὲν B
d 6 ἐς B : εἰς T   d 8 αὐτὰ recc. : αὐτὸν BT : αὐτὸ Galeni cod.
Marc.   e 1 ἢ μηδὲν εἶναι Galenus : εἰ μὴ εἰδέναι B : ἢ μηδὲ εἰδέναι
T   e 2 αὐτῷ BT : αὐτῶν vulg.   e 4 τε T Galenus : δὲ B

νῦν ἔργῳ παροῦσά οἱ, ᾗ προσοιστέον τούσδε ὧδε τοὺς
λόγους ἐπὶ τὴν τῶνδε πειθώ, ταῦτα δ' ἤδη πάντα ἔχοντι,
προσλαβόντι καιροὺς τοῦ πότε λεκτέον καὶ ἐπισχετέον,
βραχυλογίας τε αὖ καὶ ἐλεινολογίας καὶ δεινώσεως ἑκάστων 5
τε ὅσα ἂν εἴδη μάθῃ λόγων, τούτων τὴν εὐκαιρίαν τε καὶ
ἀκαιρίαν διαγνόντι, καλῶς τε καὶ τελέως ἐστὶν ἡ τέχνη
ἀπειργασμένη, πρότερον δ' οὔ· ἀλλ' ὅτι ἂν αὐτῶν τις
ἐλλείπῃ λέγων ἢ διδάσκων ἢ γράφων, φῇ δὲ τέχνῃ λέγειν, b
ὁ μὴ πειθόμενος κρατεῖ. "Τί δὴ οὖν; φήσει ἴσως ὁ συγγραφεύς, ὦ Φαῖδρέ τε καὶ Σώκρατες, δοκεῖ οὕτως; μὴ ἄλλως
πως ἀποδεκτέον λεγομένης λόγων τέχνης;"

ΦΑΙ. Ἀδύνατόν που, ὦ Σώκρατες, ἄλλως· καίτοι οὐ 5
σμικρόν γε φαίνεται ἔργον.

ΣΩ. Ἀληθῆ λέγεις. τούτου τοι ἕνεκα χρὴ πάντας τοὺς
λόγους ἄνω καὶ κάτω μεταστρέφοντα ἐπισκοπεῖν εἴ τίς πῃ
ῥᾴων καὶ βραχυτέρα φαίνεται ἐπ' αὐτὴν ὁδός, ἵνα μὴ μάτην c
πολλὴν ἀπίῃ καὶ τραχεῖαν, ἐξὸν ὀλίγην τε καὶ λείαν. ἀλλ'
εἴ τινά πῃ βοήθειαν ἔχεις ἐπακηκοὼς Λυσίου ἤ τινος ἄλλου,
πειρῶ λέγειν ἀναμιμνησκόμενος.

ΦΑΙ. Ἕνεκα μὲν πείρας ἔχοιμ' ἄν, ἀλλ' οὔτι νῦν γ' 5
οὕτως ἔχω.

ΣΩ. Βούλει οὖν ἐγώ τιν' εἴπω λόγον ὃν τῶν περὶ ταῦτά
τινων ἀκήκοα;

ΦΑΙ. Τί μήν;

ΣΩ. Λέγεται γοῦν, ὦ Φαῖδρε, δίκαιον εἶναι καὶ τὸ τοῦ 10
λύκου εἰπεῖν.

ΦΑΙ. Καὶ σύ γε οὕτω ποίει. d

ΣΩ. Φασὶ τοίνυν οὐδὲν οὕτω ταῦτα δεῖν σεμνύνειν οὐδ'
ἀνάγειν ἄνω μακρὰν περιβαλλομένους· παντάπασι γάρ, ὃ

a 2 οἱ D : σοι Galenus : om. BT   a 3 ταῦτα δ' ἤδη πάντα BT :
πάντα δὴ ταῦτ' Galenus   a 6 ὅσα B Galenus : ὅς T   τε καὶ ἀκαιρίαν
TW Galenus : om. B   b 2 φήσει T : φύσει B   b 3 μὴ scripsi : ἢ BT
c 2 ἀπίῃ BT : ἀνίῃ Stallbaum : περίῃ Badham : ἴῃ Schanz   c 3 ἤ
τινος T : εἴ τινος B   c 5 ἔχοιμ' ἄν T : ἔχοιμαν B : λέγοιμ' ἄν Schanz
c 7 λόγον T : λόγων pr. B   c 8 τινων BT : δεινῶν corr. Ven. 184

καὶ κατ' ἀρχὰς εἴπομεν τοῦδε τοῦ λόγου, ὅτι οὐδὲν ἀληθείας
5 μετέχειν δέοι δικαίων ἢ ἀγαθῶν πέρι πραγμάτων, ἢ καὶ
ἀνθρώπων γε τοιούτων φύσει ὄντων ἢ τροφῇ, τὸν μέλλοντα
ἱκανῶς ῥητορικὸν ἔσεσθαι. τὸ παράπαν γὰρ οὐδὲν ἐν τοῖς
δικαστηρίοις τούτων ἀληθείας μέλειν οὐδενί, ἀλλὰ τοῦ πιθα-
e νοῦ· τοῦτο δ' εἶναι τὸ εἰκός, ᾧ δεῖν προσέχειν τὸν μέλλοντα
τέχνῃ ἐρεῖν. οὐδὲ γὰρ αὐτὰ ⟨τὰ⟩ πραχθέντα δεῖν λέγειν ἐνίοτε,
ἐὰν μὴ εἰκότως ᾖ πεπραγμένα, ἀλλὰ τὰ εἰκότα, ἔν τε κατηγορίᾳ καὶ ἀπολογίᾳ, καὶ πάντως λέγοντα τὸ δὴ εἰκὸς διωκτέον
5 εἶναι, πολλὰ εἰπόντα χαίρειν τῷ ἀληθεῖ· τοῦτο γὰρ διὰ
273 παντὸς τοῦ λόγου γιγνόμενον τὴν ἅπασαν τέχνην πορίζειν.

ΦΑΙ. Αὐτά γε, ὦ Σώκρατες, διελήλυθας ἃ λέγουσιν οἱ
περὶ τοὺς λόγους τεχνικοὶ προσποιούμενοι εἶναι· ἀνεμνήσθην
γὰρ ὅτι ἐν τῷ πρόσθεν βραχέως τοῦ τοιούτου ἐφηψάμεθα,
5 δοκεῖ δὲ τοῦτο πάμμεγα εἶναι τοῖς περὶ ταῦτα.

ΣΩ. Ἀλλὰ μὴν τόν γε Τεισίαν αὐτὸν πεπάτηκας ἀκριβῶς·
εἰπέτω τοίνυν καὶ τόδε ἡμῖν ὁ Τεισίας, μή τι ἄλλο λέγει
b τὸ εἰκὸς ἢ τὸ τῷ πλήθει δοκοῦν.

ΦΑΙ. Τί γὰρ ἄλλο;

ΣΩ. Τοῦτο δή, ὡς ἔοικε, σοφὸν εὑρὼν ἅμα καὶ τεχνικὸν
ἔγραψεν ὡς ἐάν τις ἀσθενὴς καὶ ἀνδρικὸς ἰσχυρὸν καὶ
5 δειλὸν συγκόψας, ἱμάτιον ἤ τι ἄλλο ἀφελόμενος, εἰς δικα-
στήριον ἄγηται, δεῖ δὴ τἀληθὲς μηδέτερον λέγειν, ἀλλὰ τὸν
μὲν δειλὸν μὴ ὑπὸ μόνου φάναι τοῦ ἀνδρικοῦ συγκεκόφθαι,
τὸν δὲ τοῦτο μὲν ἐλέγχειν ὡς μόνω ἤστην, ἐκείνῳ δὲ κατα-
c χρήσασθαι τῷ Πῶς δ' ἂν ἐγὼ τοιόσδε τοιῷδε ἐπεχείρησα; ὁ δ' οὐκ ἐρεῖ δὴ τὴν ἑαυτοῦ κάκην, ἀλλά τι
ἄλλο ψεύδεσθαι ἐπιχειρῶν τάχ' ἂν ἔλεγχόν πη παραδοίη
τῷ ἀντιδίκῳ. καὶ περὶ τἆλλα δὴ τοιαῦτ' ἄττα ἐστὶ τὰ
5 τέχνῃ λεγόμενα. οὐ γάρ, ὦ Φαῖδρε;

d 8 μέλειν Stephanus e Ficino : μέλει B T   θ 2 αὐτὰ τὰ Hein-
dorf: αυτὰ B: αῦ τὰ T   a 4 ἐφηψάμεθα T: ἐψηφισάμεθα B   a 6 τισίαν
Tb: τισιν pr. B   a 7 λέγειν Par. 1826: λέγει B T   b 5 ἤ τι
T (ex emend.) : εἴ τι B

ΦΑΙ. Τί μήν;

ΣΩ. Φεῦ, δεινῶς γ' ἔοικεν ἀποκεκρυμμένην τέχνην ἀνευ-
ρεῖν ὁ Τεισίας ἢ ἄλλος ὅστις δή ποτ' ὢν τυγχάνει καὶ
ὁπόθεν χαίρει ὀνομαζόμενος. ἀτάρ, ὦ ἑταῖρε, τούτῳ ἡμεῖς
πότερον λέγωμεν ἢ μὴ — 10

ΦΑΙ. Τὸ ποῖον; d

ΣΩ. Ὅτι, ὦ Τεισία, πάλαι ἡμεῖς, πρὶν καὶ σὲ παρελθεῖν,
τυγχάνομεν λέγοντες ὡς ἄρα τοῦτο τὸ εἰκὸς τοῖς πολλοῖς
δι' ὁμοιότητα τοῦ ἀληθοῦς τυγχάνει ἐγγιγνόμενον· τὰς δὲ
ὁμοιότητας ἄρτι διήλθομεν ὅτι πανταχοῦ ὁ τὴν ἀλήθειαν 5
εἰδὼς κάλλιστα ἐπίσταται εὑρίσκειν. ὥστ' εἰ μὲν ἄλλο τι
περὶ τέχνης λόγων λέγεις, ἀκούοιμεν ἄν· εἰ δὲ μή, οἷς
νυνδὴ διήλθομεν πεισόμεθα, ὡς ἐὰν μή τις τῶν τε ἀκουσομένων τὰς φύσεις διαριθμήσηται, καὶ κατ' εἴδη τε διαιρεῖσθαι e
τὰ ὄντα καὶ μιᾷ ἰδέᾳ δυνατὸς ᾖ καθ' ἓν ἕκαστον περιλαμ-
βάνειν, οὔ ποτ' ἔσται τεχνικὸς λόγων πέρι καθ' ὅσον
δυνατὸν ἀνθρώπῳ. ταῦτα δὲ οὐ μή ποτε κτήσηται ἄνευ
πολλῆς πραγματείας· ἣν οὐχ ἕνεκα τοῦ λέγειν καὶ πράττειν 5
πρὸς ἀνθρώπους δεῖ διαπονεῖσθαι τὸν σώφρονα, ἀλλὰ τοῦ
θεοῖς κεχαρισμένα μὲν λέγειν δύνασθαι, κεχαρισμένως δὲ
πράττειν τὸ πᾶν εἰς δύναμιν. οὐ γὰρ δὴ ἄρα, ὦ Τεισία,
φασὶν οἱ σοφώτεροι ἡμῶν, ὁμοδούλοις δεῖ χαρίζεσθαι
μελετᾶν τὸν νοῦν ἔχοντα, ὅτι μὴ πάρεργον, ἀλλὰ δεσπόταις 274
ἀγαθοῖς τε καὶ ἐξ ἀγαθῶν. ὥστ' εἰ μακρὰ ἡ περίοδος, μὴ
θαυμάσῃς· μεγάλων γὰρ ἕνεκα περιτέον, οὐχ ὡς σὺ δοκεῖς.
ἔσται μήν, ὡς ὁ λόγος φησίν, ἐάν τις ἐθέλῃ, καὶ ταῦτα
κάλλιστα ἐξ ἐκείνων γιγνόμενα. 5

ΦΑΙ. Παγκάλως ἔμοιγε δοκεῖ λέγεσθαι, ὦ Σώκρατες,
εἴπερ οἷός τέ τις εἴη.

c 7 γ' T : τ' B   c 9 τούτῳ B T : τοῦτο corr. Coisl. : fort. τοῦτ'
αὐτῷ Thompson   d 3 τὸ T : om. B   d 7 εἰ δὲ T : εἴδη B
d 8 νῦν δὴ T W : νῦν B   e 9 ἡμῶν Heindorf : ἡ B : ἡμῶν ἢ T :
ἡμῶν μὴ vulg.   a 2 ἢ T : ἢ B   a 3 οὐχ ὡς B T : οὐχ ὦν ci.
Heindorf   a 7 οἷός τε Heindorf : οἷος B : οἷός γε T

ΣΩ. Ἀλλὰ καὶ ἐπιχειροῦντί τοι τοῖς καλοῖς καλὸν καὶ
b πάσχειν ὅτι ἄν τῳ συμβῇ παθεῖν.

ΦΑΙ. Καὶ μάλα.

ΣΩ. Οὐκοῦν τὸ μὲν τέχνης τε καὶ ἀτεχνίας λόγων πέρι
ἱκανῶς ἐχέτω.

5 ΦΑΙ. Τί μήν;

ΣΩ. Τὸ δ' εὐπρεπείας δὴ γραφῆς πέρι καὶ ἀπρεπείας, πῇ
γιγνόμενον καλῶς ἂν ἔχοι καὶ ὅπῃ ἀπρεπῶς, λοιπόν. ἢ γάρ;

ΦΑΙ. Ναί.

ΣΩ. Οἶσθ' οὖν ὅπῃ μάλιστα θεῷ χαριῇ λόγων πέρι
10 πράττων ἢ λέγων;

ΦΑΙ. Οὐδαμῶς· σὺ δέ;

c ΣΩ. Ἀκοήν γ' ἔχω λέγειν τῶν προτέρων, τὸ δ' ἀληθὲς
αὐτοὶ ἴσασιν. εἰ δὲ τοῦτο εὕροιμεν αὐτοί, ἆρά γ' ἂν ἔθ'
ἡμῖν μέλοι τι τῶν ἀνθρωπίνων δοξασμάτων;

ΦΑΙ. Γελοῖον ἤρου· ἀλλ' ἃ φῂς ἀκηκοέναι λέγε.

5 ΣΩ. Ἤκουσα τοίνυν περὶ Ναύκρατιν τῆς Αἰγύπτου γενέσθαι τῶν ἐκεῖ παλαιῶν τινα θεῶν, οὗ καὶ τὸ ὄρνεον ἱερὸν
ὃ δὴ καλοῦσιν Ἶβιν· αὐτῷ δὲ ὄνομα τῷ δαίμονι εἶναι Θεύθ.
τοῦτον δὴ πρῶτον ἀριθμόν τε καὶ λογισμὸν εὑρεῖν καὶ
d γεωμετρίαν καὶ ἀστρονομίαν, ἔτι δὲ πεττείας τε καὶ κυβείας,
καὶ δὴ καὶ γράμματα. βασιλέως δ' αὖ τότε ὄντος Αἰγύπτου
ὅλης Θαμοῦ περὶ τὴν μεγάλην πόλιν τοῦ ἄνω τόπου ἣν οἱ
Ἕλληνες Αἰγυπτίας Θήβας καλοῦσι, καὶ τὸν θεὸν Ἄμμωνα,
5 παρὰ τοῦτον ἐλθὼν ὁ Θεὺθ τὰς τέχνας ἐπέδειξεν, καὶ ἔφη
δεῖν διαδοθῆναι τοῖς ἄλλοις Αἰγυπτίοις· ὁ δὲ ἤρετο ἥντινα
ἑκάστη ἔχοι ὠφελίαν, διεξιόντος δέ, ὅτι καλῶς ἢ μὴ
e καλῶς δοκοῖ λέγειν, τὸ μὲν ἔψεγεν, τὸ δ' ἐπῄνει. πολλὰ

b 1 ὅτι T: ὅτῳ B   b 6 δὴ . . . ἀπρεπείας om. Stobaeus
b 9 θεῷ Stobaeus: θεῶν BT   c 3 μέλοι B: μέλλοι T   c 6 ἱερόν
Stobaeus Hermias: τὸ ἱερόν BT   c 7 δὴ Stobaeus: δὲ BT
d 3 ἣν V: ὃν BT Stobaeus   d 4 θεόν] Θαμοῦν Postgate   d 5 τοῦτον T: τούτων B   ἐπέδειξεν T: ἐπέδειξε Stobaeus: ἀπέδειξε B
d 6 ἥντινα BT: ἣν δὴ Stobaeus   d 7 ἔχοι BT: ἔχει Stobaeus
e 1 δοκοῖ BT: δοκοίη Stobaeus

μὲν δὴ περὶ ἑκάστης τῆς τέχνης ἐπ' ἀμφότερα Θαμοῦν τῷ
Θεὺθ λέγεται ἀποφήνασθαι, ἃ λόγος πολὺς ἂν εἴη διελθεῖν·
ἐπειδὴ δὲ ἐπὶ τοῖς γράμμασιν ἦν, "Τοῦτο δέ, ὦ βασιλεῦ, τὸ
μάθημα," ἔφη ὁ Θεύθ, " σοφωτέρους Αἰγυπτίους καὶ μνημο- 5
νικωτέρους παρέξει· μνήμης τε γὰρ καὶ σοφίας φάρμακον
ηὑρέθη." ὁ δ' εἶπεν· "Ὦ τεχνικώτατε Θεύθ, ἄλλος μὲν
τεκεῖν δυνατὸς τὰ τέχνης, ἄλλος δὲ κρῖναι τίν' ἔχει μοῖραν
βλάβης τε καὶ ὠφελίας τοῖς μέλλουσι χρῆσθαι· καὶ νῦν
σύ, πατὴρ ὢν γραμμάτων, δι' εὔνοιαν τοὐναντίον εἶπες ἢ 275
δύναται. τοῦτο γὰρ τῶν μαθόντων λήθην μὲν ἐν ψυχαῖς
παρέξει μνήμης ἀμελετησίᾳ, ἅτε διὰ πίστιν γραφῆς ἔξωθεν
ὑπ' ἀλλοτρίων τύπων, οὐκ ἔνδοθεν αὐτοὺς ὑφ' αὑτῶν ἀναμι-
μνῃσκομένους· οὔκουν μνήμης ἀλλὰ ὑπομνήσεως φάρμακον 5
ηὗρες. σοφίας δὲ τοῖς μαθηταῖς δόξαν, οὐκ ἀλήθειαν πορί-
ζεις· πολυήκοοι γάρ σοι γενόμενοι ἄνευ διδαχῆς πολυγνώ-
μονες εἶναι δόξουσιν, ἀγνώμονες ὡς ἐπὶ τὸ πλῆθος ὄντες, b
καὶ χαλεποὶ συνεῖναι, δοξόσοφοι γεγονότες ἀντὶ σοφῶν."

ΦΑΙ. Ὦ Σώκρατες, ῥᾳδίως σὺ Αἰγυπτίους καὶ ὁποδαποὺς
ἂν ἐθέλῃς λόγους ποιεῖς.

ΣΩ. Οἱ δέ γ', ὦ φίλε, ἐν τῷ τοῦ Διὸς τοῦ Δωδωναίου 5
ἱερῷ δρυὸς λόγους ἔφησαν μαντικοὺς πρώτους γενέσθαι.
τοῖς μὲν οὖν τότε, ἅτε οὐκ οὖσι σοφοῖς ὥσπερ ὑμεῖς οἱ νέοι,
ἀπέχρη δρυὸς καὶ πέτρας ἀκούειν ὑπ' εὐηθείας, εἰ μόνον
ἀληθῆ λέγοιεν· σοὶ δ' ἴσως διαφέρει τίς ὁ λέγων καὶ ποδαπός. c
οὐ γὰρ ἐκεῖνο μόνον σκοπεῖς, εἴτε οὕτως εἴτε ἄλλως ἔχει;

ΦΑΙ. Ὀρθῶς ἐπέπληξας, καί μοι δοκεῖ περὶ γραμμάτων
ἔχειν ᾗπερ ὁ Θηβαῖος λέγει.

e 3 ἃ λόγος . . . διελθεῖν B W Stobaeus : om. T   e 6 παρέξει Stobaeus : παρέξοι B : παρέξειν T   e 8 τέχνης T Stobaeus : τῆς τέχνης B
a 2 μὲν om. Schanz   a 4 ἔνδοθεν T Stobaeus : ἔνδον B   αὐτοῖς
. . . ἀναμιμνῃσκομένοις H. Richards   a 6 εὗρες T : εὗρε B   b 1 τὸ
B T : om. Stobaeus   b 3 καὶ B : τε καὶ T   b 5 οἱ δέ γ' ὦ T :
οἶδ' ἐγὼ B : οὐδέ γ' ὦ V : σοὶ δ' ἐγὼ Stobaeus   b 6 ἔφησαν B Stobaeus : ἔφασαν T   b 8 δρυὸς T b : διὸς pr. B   c 1 δ'ἴσως T W
Stobaeus : om. B

5 ΣΩ. Οὐκοῦν ὁ τέχνην οἰόμενος ἐν γράμμασι καταλιπεῖν, καὶ αὖ ὁ παραδεχόμενος ὥς τι σαφὲς καὶ βέβαιον ἐκ γραμμάτων ἐσόμενον, πολλῆς ἂν εὐηθείας γέμοι καὶ τῷ ὄντι τὴν Ἄμμωνος μαντείαν ἀγνοοῖ, πλέον τι οἰόμενος εἶναι λόγους

d γεγραμμένους τοῦ τὸν εἰδότα ὑπομνῆσαι περὶ ὧν ἂν ᾖ τὰ γεγραμμένα.

ΦΑΙ. Ὀρθότατα.

ΣΩ. Δεινὸν γάρ που, ὦ Φαῖδρε, τοῦτ᾽ ἔχει γραφή, καὶ
5 ὡς ἀληθῶς ὅμοιον ζωγραφίᾳ. καὶ γὰρ τὰ ἐκείνης ἔκγονα ἕστηκε μὲν ὡς ζῶντα, ἐὰν δ᾽ ἀνέρῃ τι, σεμνῶς πάνυ σιγᾷ. ταὐτὸν δὲ καὶ οἱ λόγοι· δόξαις μὲν ἂν ὥς τι φρονοῦντας αὐτοὺς λέγειν, ἐὰν δέ τι ἔρῃ τῶν λεγομένων βουλόμενος μαθεῖν, ἕν τι σημαίνει μόνον ταὐτὸν ἀεί. ὅταν δὲ ἅπαξ

e γραφῇ, κυλινδεῖται μὲν πανταχοῦ πᾶς λόγος ὁμοίως παρὰ τοῖς ἐπαΐουσιν, ὡς δ᾽ αὔτως παρ᾽ οἷς οὐδὲν προσήκει, καὶ οὐκ ἐπίσταται λέγειν οἷς δεῖ γε καὶ μή. πλημμελούμενος δὲ καὶ οὐκ ἐν δίκῃ λοιδορηθεὶς τοῦ πατρὸς ἀεὶ δεῖται βοηθοῦ·
5 αὐτὸς γὰρ οὔτ᾽ ἀμύνασθαι οὔτε βοηθῆσαι δυνατὸς αὑτῷ.

ΦΑΙ. Καὶ ταῦτά σοι ὀρθότατα εἴρηται.

276 ΣΩ. Τί δ᾽; ἄλλον ὁρῶμεν λόγον τούτου ἀδελφὸν γνήσιον, τῷ τρόπῳ τε γίγνεται, καὶ ὅσῳ ἀμείνων καὶ δυνατώτερος τούτου φύεται;

ΦΑΙ. Τίνα τοῦτον καὶ πῶς λέγεις γιγνόμενον;

5 ΣΩ. Ὃς μετ᾽ ἐπιστήμης γράφεται ἐν τῇ τοῦ μανθάνοντος ψυχῇ, δυνατὸς μὲν ἀμῦναι ἑαυτῷ, ἐπιστήμων δὲ λέγειν τε καὶ σιγᾶν πρὸς οὓς δεῖ.

ΦΑΙ. Τὸν τοῦ εἰδότος λόγον λέγεις ζῶντα καὶ ἔμψυχον, οὗ ὁ γεγραμμένος εἴδωλον ἄν τι λέγοιτο δικαίως.

c 5 καταλιπεῖν Β Τ : καταλείπειν Stobaeus   c 7 ἂν Τ Stobaeus : om. Β   c 8 εἶναι] ἔχειν Heindorf : ποιεῖν Stallbaum   d 1 τοῦ τὸν Β Τ : καὶ τοῦτον Stobaeus : ἢ τὸ τον fuisse susp. Wachsmuth   d 4 γραφῇ b : γραφήν pr. Β Τ   d 6 δ᾽ ἀνέρῃ Τ : δ᾽ ἂν ἔρῃ Β : δὲ ἔρῃ Stobaeus   e 1 κυλινδεῖται Β Τ : καλινδεῖται V   e 3 γε] τε Hirschig   πλημμελούμενος Τ : πλημμενος Β   a 1 ὁρῶμεν Β Τ : ἐροῦμεν V   γνήσιον corr. Coisl. : γνήσιος Β Τ

ΣΩ. Παντάπασι μὲν οὖν. τόδε δή μοι εἰπέ· ὁ νοῦν b
ἔχων γεωργός, ὧν σπερμάτων κήδοιτο καὶ ἔγκαρπα βούλοιτο
γενέσθαι, πότερα σπουδῇ ἂν θέρους εἰς Ἀδώνιδος κήπους
ἀρῶν χαίροι θεωρῶν καλοὺς ἐν ἡμέραισιν ὀκτὼ γιγνομένους,
ἢ ταῦτα μὲν δὴ παιδιᾶς τε καὶ ἑορτῆς χάριν δρῴη ἄν, ὅτε 5
καὶ ποιοῖ· ἐφ' οἷς δὲ ἐσπούδακεν, τῇ γεωργικῇ χρώμενος ἂν
τέχνῃ, σπείρας εἰς τὸ προσῆκον, ἀγαπῴη ἂν ἐν ὀγδόῳ μηνὶ
ὅσα ἔσπειρεν τέλος λαβόντα;

ΦΑΙ. Οὕτω που, ὦ Σώκρατες, τὰ μὲν σπουδῇ, τὰ δὲ ὡς c
ἑτέρως ἂν ᾗ λέγεις ποιοῖ.

ΣΩ. Τὸν δὲ δικαίων τε καὶ καλῶν καὶ ἀγαθῶν ἐπιστήμας
ἔχοντα τοῦ γεωργοῦ φῶμεν ἧττον νοῦν ἔχειν εἰς τὰ ἑαυτοῦ
σπέρματα; 5

ΦΑΙ. Ἥκιστά γε.

ΣΩ. Οὐκ ἄρα σπουδῇ αὐτὰ ἐν ὕδατι γράψει μέλανι
σπείρων διὰ καλάμου μετὰ λόγων ἀδυνάτων μὲν αὐτοῖς
λόγῳ βοηθεῖν, ἀδυνάτων δὲ ἱκανῶς τἀληθῆ διδάξαι.

ΦΑΙ. Οὔκουν δὴ τό γ' εἰκός. 10

ΣΩ. Οὐ γάρ· ἀλλὰ τοὺς μὲν ἐν γράμμασι κήπους, ὡς d
ἔοικε, παιδιᾶς χάριν σπερεῖ τε καὶ γράψει, ὅταν [δὲ] γράφῃ,
ἑαυτῷ τε ὑπομνήματα θησαυριζόμενος, εἰς τὸ λήθης γῆρας
ἐὰν ἵκηται, καὶ παντὶ τῷ ταὐτὸν ἴχνος μετιόντι, ἡσθή-
σεταί τε αὐτοὺς θεωρῶν φυομένους ἀπαλούς· ὅταν ⟨δὲ⟩ 5
ἄλλοι παιδιαῖς ἄλλαις χρῶνται, συμποσίοις τε ἄρδοντες αὑ-
τοὺς ἑτέροις τε ὅσα τούτων ἀδελφά, τότ' ἐκεῖνος, ὡς ἔοικεν,
ἀντὶ τούτων οἷς λέγω παίζων διάξει.

ΦΑΙ. Παγκάλην λέγεις παρὰ φαύλην παιδιάν, ὦ Σώ- e

b 1 νοῦν T: νυν B   b 2 ὧν T: ω B: ἂν V   b 4 ἀρῶν B T:
δρῶν V: σπείρας Herwerden   b 6 χρώμενος ἂν τέχνῃ T: ἂν χρώμενος τέχνῃ ἂν B   c 7 γράψει ⟨ἐν⟩ Badham   c 8 μετὰ]
σπέρματα Badham   ἀδυνάτων (bis) B: ἀδυνατῶν (bis T (et sic Heindorf omissis μετὰ λόγων)   c 9 ταληθῆ B: τ' ἀληθὲς T   d 2 δὲ
om. Bekker: τε Heindorf: γε Schanz   d 5 δὲ add. Par. 1811: τε
Stephanus: om. B T   d 8 οἷς λέγω γρ. Par. 1812: οἷς λέγων B T:
ἐν οἷς λέγω Heindorf: οὗ λέγω Schanz   διάξει T: διέξει B

κρατες, τοῦ ἐν λόγοις δυναμένου παίζειν, δικαιοσύνης τε καὶ
ἄλλων ὧν λέγεις πέρι μυθολογοῦντα.

ΣΩ. Ἔστι γάρ, ὦ φίλε Φαῖδρε, οὕτω· πολὺ δ᾽ οἶμαι
5 καλλίων σπουδὴ περὶ αὐτὰ γίγνεται, ὅταν τις τῇ διαλεκτικῇ
τέχνῃ χρώμενος, λαβὼν ψυχὴν προσήκουσαν, φυτεύῃ τε καὶ
σπείρῃ μετ᾽ ἐπιστήμης λόγους, οἳ ἑαυτοῖς τῷ τε φυτεύσαντι
277 βοηθεῖν ἱκανοὶ καὶ οὐχὶ ἄκαρποι ἀλλὰ ἔχοντες σπέρμα, ὅθεν
ἄλλοι ἐν ἄλλοις ἤθεσι φυόμενοι τοῦτ᾽ ἀεὶ ἀθάνατον παρέχειν
ἱκανοί, καὶ τὸν ἔχοντα εὐδαιμονεῖν ποιοῦντες εἰς ὅσον
ἀνθρώπῳ δυνατὸν μάλιστα.

5 ΦΑΙ. Πολὺ γὰρ τοῦτ᾽ ἔτι κάλλιον λέγεις.

ΣΩ. Νῦν δὴ ἐκεῖνα ἤδη, ὦ Φαῖδρε, δυνάμεθα κρίνειν,
τούτων ὡμολογημένων.

ΦΑΙ. Τὰ ποῖα;

ΣΩ. Ὧν δὴ πέρι βουληθέντες ἰδεῖν ἀφικόμεθα εἰς τόδε,
10 ὅπως τὸ Λυσίου τε ὄνειδος ἐξετάσαιμεν τῆς τῶν λόγων
b γραφῆς πέρι, καὶ αὐτοὺς τοὺς λόγους οἳ τέχνῃ καὶ ἄνευ
τέχνης γράφοιντο. τὸ μὲν οὖν ἔντεχνον καὶ μὴ δοκεῖ μοι
δεδηλῶσθαι μετρίως.

ΦΑΙ. Ἔδοξέ γε δή· πάλιν δὲ ὑπόμνησόν με πῶς.

5 ΣΩ. Πρὶν ἄν τις τό τε ἀληθὲς ἑκάστων εἰδῇ πέρι ὧν
λέγει ἢ γράφει, κατ᾽ αὐτό τε πᾶν ὁρίζεσθαι δυνατὸς γένηται,
ὁρισάμενός τε πάλιν κατ᾽ εἴδη μέχρι τοῦ ἀτμήτου τέμνειν
ἐπιστηθῇ, περί τε ψυχῆς φύσεως διιδὼν κατὰ ταὐτά, τὸ
c προσαρμόττον ἑκάστῃ φύσει εἶδος ἀνευρίσκων, οὕτω τιθῇ
καὶ διακοσμῇ τὸν λόγον, ποικίλῃ μὲν ποικίλους ψυχῇ καὶ
παναρμονίους διδοὺς λόγους, ἁπλοῦς δὲ ἁπλῇ, οὐ πρότερον
δυνατὸν τέχνῃ ἔσεσθαι καθ᾽ ὅσον πέφυκε μεταχειρισθῆναι
5 τὸ λόγων γένος, οὔτε τι πρὸς τὸ διδάξαι οὔτε τι πρὸς τὸ
πεῖσαι, ὡς ὁ ἔμπροσθεν πᾶς μεμήνυκεν ἡμῖν λόγος.

ΦΑΙ. Παντάπασι μὲν οὖν τοῦτό γε οὕτω πως ἐφάνη.

a 1 καὶ B : τε καὶ T   a 3 καὶ om. Schanz   b 5 εἰδῇ corr.
D : ἰδῇ (sic) T : ἰδῃ B   b 6 τε BT : γε vulg.   b 7 κατ᾽ εἴδη
T : κατίδη B

ΣΩ. Τί δ' αὖ περὶ τοῦ καλὸν ἢ αἰσχρὸν εἶναι τὸ λόγους d
λέγειν τε καὶ γράφειν, καὶ ὅπη γιγνόμενον ἐν δίκῃ λέγοιτ'
ἂν ὄνειδος ἢ μή, ἆρα οὐ δεδήλωκεν τὰ λεχθέντα ὀλίγον
ἔμπροσθεν—

ΦΑΙ. Τὰ ποῖα; 5

ΣΩ. Ὡς εἴτε Λυσίας ἤ τις ἄλλος πώποτε ἔγραψεν ἢ
γράψει ἰδίᾳ ἢ δημοσίᾳ νόμους τιθείς, σύγγραμμα πολιτικὸν
γράφων καὶ μεγάλην τινὰ ἐν αὐτῷ βεβαιότητα ἡγούμενος
καὶ σαφήνειαν, οὕτω μὲν ὄνειδος τῷ γράφοντι, εἴτε τίς
φησιν εἴτε μή· τὸ γὰρ ἀγνοεῖν ὕπαρ τε καὶ ὄναρ δικαίων 10
καὶ ἀδίκων πέρι καὶ κακῶν καὶ ἀγαθῶν οὐκ ἐκφεύγει τῇ e
ἀληθείᾳ μὴ οὐκ ἐπονείδιστον εἶναι, οὐδὲ ἂν ὁ πᾶς ὄχλος
αὐτὸ ἐπαινέσῃ.

ΦΑΙ. Οὐ γὰρ οὖν.

ΣΩ. Ὁ δέ γε ἐν μὲν τῷ γεγραμμένῳ λόγῳ περὶ ἑκάστου 5
παιδιάν τε ἡγούμενος πολλὴν ἀναγκαῖον εἶναι, καὶ οὐδένα
πώποτε λόγον ἐν μέτρῳ οὐδ' ἄνευ μέτρου μεγάλης ἄξιον
σπουδῆς γραφῆναι, οὐδὲ λεχθῆναι ὡς οἱ ῥαψῳδούμενοι ἄνευ
ἀνακρίσεως καὶ διδαχῆς πειθοῦς ἕνεκα ἐλέχθησαν, ἀλλὰ τῷ
ὄντι αὐτῶν τοὺς βελτίστους εἰδότων ὑπόμνησιν γεγονέναι, 278
ἐν δὲ τοῖς διδασκομένοις καὶ μαθήσεως χάριν λεγομένοις καὶ
τῷ ὄντι γραφομένοις ἐν ψυχῇ περὶ δικαίων τε καὶ καλῶν
καὶ ἀγαθῶν [ἐν] μόνοις ἡγούμενος τό τε ἐναργὲς εἶναι καὶ
τέλεον καὶ ἄξιον σπουδῆς· δεῖν δὲ τοὺς τοιούτους λόγους 5
αὑτοῦ λέγεσθαι οἷον ὑεῖς γνησίους εἶναι, πρῶτον μὲν τὸν
ἐν αὑτῷ, ἐὰν εὑρεθεὶς ἐνῇ, ἔπειτα εἴ τινες τούτου ἔκγονοί
τε καὶ ἀδελφοὶ ἅμα ἐν ἄλλαισιν ἄλλων ψυχαῖς κατ' ἀξίαν b
ἐνέφυσαν· τοὺς δὲ ἄλλους χαίρειν ἐῶν—οὗτος δὲ ὁ τοιοῦτος

d 1 τοῦ T: τὸ B   d 2 λέγοιτ' ἂν T: λέγει τὰν B   d 3 ἢ
corr. Par. 1812: εἰ BT   d 7 γράψει B: γράφει T   νόμους τιθείς
secl. Schleiermacher   d 10 δικαίων καὶ B: δικαίων τε καὶ T
e 8 οὐδὲ ... e 9 ἐλέχθησαν secl. Schanz: ὡς οἱ ... ἐλέχθησαν secl.
Ast   ὡς οἱ] ὅσοι Schleiermacher   a 1 αὐτῶν T: αὐτῷ B
a 4 ἐν secl. ci. Heindorf   ἡγούμενος TW: om. B   a 7 ἐν αὐτῷ
B: ἑαυτῷ T

ἀνὴρ κινδυνεύει, ὦ Φαῖδρε, εἶναι οἷον ἐγώ τε καὶ σὺ εὐξαίμεθ'
ἂν σέ τε καὶ ἐμὲ γενέσθαι.

5 ΦΑΙ. Παντάπασι μὲν οὖν ἔγωγε βούλομαί τε καὶ εὔχομαι
ἃ λέγεις.

ΣΩ. Οὐκοῦν ἤδη πεπαίσθω μετρίως ἡμῖν τὰ περὶ λόγων·
καὶ σύ τε ἐλθὼν φράζε Λυσίᾳ ὅτι νὼ καταβάντε ἐς τὸ
Νυμφῶν νᾶμά τε καὶ μουσεῖον ἠκούσαμεν λόγων, οἳ ἐπέ-
c στελλον λέγειν Λυσίᾳ τε καὶ εἴ τις ἄλλος συντίθησι λόγους,
καὶ Ὁμήρῳ καὶ εἴ τις ἄλλος αὖ ποίησιν ψιλὴν ἢ ἐν ᾠδῇ
συντέθηκε, τρίτον δὲ Σόλωνι καὶ ὅστις ἐν πολιτικοῖς λόγοις
νόμους ὀνομάζων συγγράμματα ἔγραψεν· εἰ μὲν εἰδὼς ᾗ τὸ
5 ἀληθὲς ἔχει συνέθηκε ταῦτα, καὶ ἔχων βοηθεῖν, εἰς ἔλεγχον
ἰὼν περὶ ὧν ἔγραψε, καὶ λέγων αὐτὸς δυνατὸς τὰ γεγραμμένα φαῦλα ἀποδεῖξαι, οὔ τι τῶνδε ἐπωνυμίαν ἔχοντα δεῖ
d λέγεσθαι τὸν τοιοῦτον, ἀλλ' ἐφ' οἷς ἐσπούδακεν ἐκείνων.

ΦΑΙ. Τίνας οὖν τὰς ἐπωνυμίας αὐτῷ νέμεις;

ΣΩ. Τὸ μὲν σοφόν, ὦ Φαῖδρε, καλεῖν ἔμοιγε μέγα
εἶναι δοκεῖ καὶ θεῷ μόνῳ πρέπειν· τὸ δὲ ἢ φιλόσοφον ἢ
5 τοιοῦτόν τι μᾶλλόν τε ἂν αὐτῷ καὶ ἁρμόττοι καὶ ἐμμελεστέρως ἔχοι.

ΦΑΙ. Καὶ οὐδέν γε ἀπὸ τρόπου.

ΣΩ. Οὐκοῦν αὖ τὸν μὴ ἔχοντα τιμιώτερα ὧν συνέθηκεν
ἢ ἔγραψεν ἄνω κάτω στρέφων ἐν χρόνῳ, πρὸς ἄλληλα
e κολλῶν τε καὶ ἀφαιρῶν, ἐν δίκῃ που ποιητὴν ἢ λόγων
συγγραφέα ἢ νομογράφον προσερεῖς;

ΦΑΙ. Τί μήν;

ΣΩ. Ταῦτα τοίνυν τῷ ἑταίρῳ φράζε.

5 ΦΑΙ. Τί δὲ σύ; πῶς ποιήσεις; οὐδὲ γὰρ οὐδὲ τὸν σὸν
ἑταῖρον δεῖ παρελθεῖν.

ΣΩ. Τίνα τοῦτον;

b8 ἐς T: εἰς B   τὸ T: τὸν B   b9 μουσεῖον T: μουσιον
B: μουσῶν vulg.   ἐπέστελλον B: ἐπελλον T   d1 ἐφ' B: ὑφ' T
d5 τοιοῦτόν τι B: τι τοιοῦτον T   αὐτῷ καὶ T: αὐτῷ B   d8 αὖ
τὸν t: αὐτὸν BT   e1 ἐν δίκῃ T: δίκῃ B   που B: om. T   e4 ἑταίρῳ
T: ἑτέρῳ B

ΦΑΙ. Ἰσοκράτη τὸν καλόν· ᾧ τί ἀπαγγελεῖς, ὦ Σώκρατες; τίνα αὐτὸν φήσομεν εἶναι;

ΣΩ. Νέος ἔτι, ὦ Φαῖδρε, Ἰσοκράτης· ὃ μέντοι μαν- 10
τεύομαι κατ’ αὐτοῦ, λέγειν ἐθέλω. 279

ΦΑΙ. Τὸ ποῖον δή;

ΣΩ. Δοκεῖ μοι ἀμείνων ἢ κατὰ τοὺς περὶ Λυσίαν εἶναι
λόγους τὰ τῆς φύσεως, ἔτι τε ἤθει γεννικωτέρῳ κεκρᾶσθαι·
ὥστε οὐδὲν ἂν γένοιτο θαυμαστὸν προϊούσης τῆς ἡλικίας εἰ 5
περὶ αὐτούς τε τοὺς λόγους, οἷς νῦν ἐπιχειρεῖ, πλέον ἢ
παίδων διενέγκοι τῶν πώποτε ἁψαμένων λόγων, ἔτι τε εἰ
αὐτῷ μὴ ἀποχρήσαι ταῦτα, ἐπὶ μείζω δέ τις αὐτὸν ἄγοι
ὁρμὴ θειοτέρα· φύσει γάρ, ὦ φίλε, ἔνεστί τις φιλοσοφία
τῇ τοῦ ἀνδρὸς διανοίᾳ. ταῦτα δὴ οὖν ἐγὼ μὲν παρὰ τῶνδε b
τῶν θεῶν ὡς ἐμοῖς παιδικοῖς Ἰσοκράτει ἐξαγγέλλω, σὺ δ’
ἐκεῖνα ὡς σοῖς Λυσίᾳ.

ΦΑΙ. Ταῦτ’ ἔσται· ἀλλὰ ἴωμεν, ἐπειδὴ καὶ τὸ πνῖγος
ἠπιώτερον γέγονεν. 5

ΣΩ. Οὐκοῦν εὐξαμένῳ πρέπει τοῖσδε πορεύεσθαι;

ΦΑΙ. Τί μήν;

ΣΩ. Ὦ φίλε Πάν τε καὶ ἄλλοι ὅσοι τῇδε θεοί, δοίητέ
μοι καλῷ γενέσθαι τἄνδοθεν· ἔξωθεν δὲ ὅσα ἔχω, τοῖς ἐντὸς
εἶναί μοι φίλια. πλούσιον δὲ νομίζοιμι τὸν σοφόν· τὸ δὲ c
χρυσοῦ πλῆθος εἴη μοι ὅσον μήτε φέρειν μήτε ἄγειν δύναιτο
ἄλλος ἢ ὁ σώφρων.

Ἔτ’ ἄλλου του δεόμεθα, ὦ Φαῖδρε; ἐμοὶ μὲν γὰρ μετρίως
ηὖκται. 5

ΦΑΙ. Καὶ ἐμοὶ ταῦτα συνεύχου· κοινὰ γὰρ τὰ τῶν
φίλων.

ΣΩ. Ἴωμεν.

a4 τε B: δὲ T   a5 τῆς ἡλικίας T: ἰσηλικίας B   a6 τοὺς
T: om. B   a7 ἔτι τε T: εἴτε B   a8 ἐπιμείζων δέ τις αυτῷ
B: ἐπὶ μείζων δέ τις αὐτὸν T   a9 ὁρμῇ θειοτέρᾳ B   b2 ἐξαγ-
γελῶ Stallbaum   b6 εὐξαμένῳ Bekker   c1 φιλία B: φίλα T

COMMENTARY: PART 1

THE NONLOVER HAS HIS DAY

THE WALK

227a1–d5: Socrates, having encountered Phaedrus by chance near the temple of Olympian Zeus, agrees to accompany him on a walk outside the city wall if Phaedrus will repeat to him the paradoxical speech he had heard Lysias deliver earlier that morning.

227a1 Ὦ φίλε Φαῖδρε This form of address, to be sure, suggests affectionate friendship, but for less obvious aspects of the significance of the vocative expressions with which Socrates often addresses Phaedrus and is sometimes addressed by him, see second note on 228d6.

ποῖ δὴ καὶ πόθεν; That the elided verb is πορεύῃ is implied in Phaedrus's reply and shown by the full form of the greeting we see at *Lys.* 203a6–b1. If we may judge by Plato's practice, this question was as customary when two Athenians met as is the enquiry after each other's health that is exchanged by speakers of modern English. It can be simplified, as in πόθεν, ὦ Σώκρατες, φαίνῃ (*Prt.* 309a1), or combined with a conjecture, as in ἐξ ἀγορᾶς ἢ πόθεν Μενέξενος; (*Mx.* 234a1), or with a more formal greeting, worthy of a visiting *artiste*, as in *Ion* 530a1–2.

a2 Παρὰ Λυσίου . . . τοῦ Κεφάλου Cephalus was a wealthy metic from Syracuse; the discussion in Plato's *Republic* takes place in his house in the Piraeus, and he and his son Polemarchus (mentioned at 257b3–4) are prominent characters in book 1. His son Lysias, probably by a second wife, was a prominent writer of speeches for others to deliver. As a noncitizen, he could not speak in the assembly or courts himself.

a3 πρὸς περίπατον Πρός + accusative in the sense 'with a view to.'* Compare the common question πρὸς τί; ('to what end?') (S. 1695.3c).

---

* Glosses and translations enclosed in single quotation marks are by me; those enclosed in double quotation marks are from other sources, which are named in the context.

ἔξω τείχους Compare with ἐν ἄστει at b3 and e.g. ἐν ἀγορᾷ at *Ap.* 17c9 or εἰς λιμένα at *Tht.* 142a6. The article is not employed in these phrases, because designations of such frequently mentioned topographical features serve as proper nouns for people who live near them and frequently mention them. For an Athenian ἐν ἀγορᾷ was analogous to our 'in Times Square' rather than 'in the theater district.' Since the conversation in which our *Theaetetus* citation occurs takes place in Megara, εἰς λιμένα there means 'to Nisaia'; at Athens the same phrase would mean 'to Piraeus.' Such terms constitute a special case of the category "words forming a class by themselves" (S. 1141).

a3–4   συχνὸν . . . χρόνον The presence of συχνὸν enables an aorist indicative to denote duration in past time rather than simply a past occurrence. The word order also thrusts συχνὸν into prominence.

γὰρ tells us that this sentence will show the reason for Phaedrus's decision to go for a walk, which turns out to be that he has been sitting indoors since early in the morning. From 242a3–5 we can infer that it is now not long before noon.

a5   Ἀκουμενῷ Acumenus has traditionally been identified by commentators with the father of Eryximachus, Phaedrus's admirer in Plato's *Symposium*, and that is clearly the Acumenus who will be mentioned at 268a9, where it is implied that he was, like his son, a physician. Another view of the identification here seems worth considering: Dover, in his note to *Sym.* 176b5, points out that there seems to have been an Acumenus who belonged to the same generation as Phaedrus and Eryximachus and was involved, as they were, in the sacrilegious acts that preceded the sailing of the Sicilian expedition. Perhaps that is the Acumenus Phaedrus has in mind here as well as being the one who is implied to be a physician by Xenophon (*Memorabilia* 3.13.2). This Acumenus would have been a brother or cousin of Eryximachus, both of them following the family pursuit of medicine.

a6   ἀκοπωτέρους 'more refreshing' or—to maintain the negative turn of phrase—'less tiring.' At *Tim.* 89a8 Plato speaks of travel by ship as ὀχήσεις ἄκοποι, and at *Laws* 789d2 bodies swayed in a rowboat are called ἄκοπα. According to Thompson ἄκοπος is a medical term, used in the neuter as a substantive for applications to relieve lassitude and strengthen the nervous system, and Plato probably borrowed it from Hippocrates. But the word is just as likely to have passed into the vocabulary of fashionable young men of Phaedrus's generation as it is to have been taken by Plato directly from technical discourse.

τῶν   sc. περιπάτων.

a6–7   ἐν τοῖς δρόμοις   Commentators seem to assume that these were roofed colonnades, but the κατάστεγος δρόμος of the Lyceum (*Euthyd.* 273a3) was perhaps exceptional; the running tracks connected with gymnasia were more often open to the sun (Wycherley 88n2).

227b2   Καλῶς γάρ   For γάρ, see note on 228c9. Hackforth translates, "Yes, he's right in saying so."

ἀτάρ   Attic writers in general use this particle to mark an abrupt change of subject (D. 52). "Socrates is not much interested in Acumenus' precepts," De Vries infers.

b3   ἐν ἄστει   There would be no point in remarking that Lysias was 'in town' (see second note on a3), unless he lived elsewhere, probably with or near his father Cephalus in Piraeus.

b4   παρ' Ἐπικράτει = *apud Epicratem* or *chez Epicrate*; 'at Epicrates' house' in English, which lacks a compact prepositional phrase for the relation (S. 1692.2a). Epicrates is identified by commentators with a prominent democratic politician of that name, whose career is summarized, in flattering terms, in a scholium to Aristophanes' *Ecclesiazusae* 71, as that of a man of importance who aided the city in many ways and participated in restoring democracy at the time of the Thirty. The identification is likely enough, with the caveat that the name was a common one in Athens. Judging by Lysias's career and known associates, one would expect him to cultivate the friendship of such a man.

b4–5   ἐν . . . Μορυχίᾳ   The demonstrative τῇδε allows us to imagine Phaedrus pointing to the house, although it is far enough away to lead him to identify it further by its proximity to the Olympieion. Ὀλυμπίου   In LSJ (s.v. Ὀλυμπιεῖον) this form is taken as a variant on the name of the temple. De Vries, following Verdenius, rightly explains it as from the adjective Ὀλύμπιος with τοῦ ἱεροῦ understood.

οἰκίᾳ τῇ Μορυχίᾳ   Use of the adjectival derivative of a proper noun in place of the normal genitive is almost exclusively poetic and can be paralleled in Plato only by ὁ . . . Κλεινίειος οὗτος ('this Cleinian fellow')—in place of the usual ὁ τοῦ Κλεινίου—as a patronymic designation of Alcibiades at *Grg.* 482a6–7. De Vries speculates that there may be an archaic or colloquial ring to the usage in prose. "Parodic" might be more to the point here. In any case, Morychus left behind a reputation for extravagant self-indulgence. At Aristophanes' *Wasps* 506 Bdelycleon says that he wants his old father to live a βίος γενναῖος like that of Morychus, whose fondness for Copaic eels, a delicacy emblematic of high living, the poet remarks on at *Acharnians* 887 and *Peace* 1008.

b6   διατριβή can mean either the place where time is spent or, as here, the manner in which it is spent. See Burnet on *Ap.* 33e4 for a collection of citations that illustrates the semantic development of this word. For οὖν δή (or δὴ οὖν) in a question in Plato, see D. 468–69: (You have told me that you were with Lysias all morning.) 'So what was going on?' or 'What was going on, then?' In 228a–b Socrates implies, without being contradicted, that Phaedrus would have had ample opportunity for personal attention from Lysias, so the διατριβή may have been a private lesson rather than a display (ἐπίδειξις) before a group of listeners such as Gorgias had given immediately before the dialogue named for him opens. ἤ introducing the second member of a double question signifies a partial correction—usually a refinement—of the first: 'or rather,' 'or—to be more precise.' Here Socrates renders the question he has just asked more specific by suggesting a possible answer (S. 2860).

b6–7   τῶν . . . εἱστία   'Lysias was giving you a feast of his speeches.' Compare the accusative and genitive after verbs of filling and being full (S. 1369) and, in particular, *Rep.* 571d7–8: τὸ λογιστικὸν . . . ἑστιάσας λόγων καλῶν καὶ σκέψεων (of the untroubled sleep of a man who has treated his reasoning faculty to a feast of rational argument and enquiry). For 'a feast of speeches,' compare *Grg.* 447a5, where Callicles calls the ἐπίδειξις that Gorgias has just concluded an ἀστεία ἑορτή. The conceit of language as food is ubiquitous and multifaceted in the plays of Aristophanes, especially his *Birds*. There is a new tenant in the house of Morychus, and—as Thompson remarks—"the character of the entertainments had changed with the possessors."

τῶν offers a clear example of an article with the force of a possessive adjective (S. 1121).

b9–11   οὐκ ἂν . . . ἀκοῦσαι;   The reference is to *Isthmian* 1.1–3: Μᾶτερ ἐμά, τὸ τεόν, χρύσασπι Θήβα, / πρᾶγμα καὶ ἀσχολίας ὑπέρτερον / θήσομαι ('My mother, Thebes with golden shield, I shall put your concerns above even my lack of leisure'). In Plato's sentence the poetic τεήν modifies his own διατριβὴν rather than any word of Pindar, so some editors have accepted the Attic σήν offered by B and T, but the more difficult reading is quite in line with the liberal spirit in which Plato treats quotations from the poets. To quote Campbell on *Tht.* 173e5–6 (another appeal to Pindar): "Plato almost always thus inweaves quotations with his own language and accommodates the poet's measures to the rhythm of prose." Here he has taken four words from Pindar, put the first one (πρᾶγμα) last, and altered its function from direct object to predicate accusative in order to fit it into the syntax of his own sentence. To go on and employ within that sentence a form that will recall Pindar's τεόν and help fit the quotation into his own texture in a seamless way would not exceed the bounds of his practice, which is, after all, intended to recall the way such things are done in urbane conversation—not by pedants checking their references, but by people of taste and wit communicating with each other. Take ἄν with ποιήσασθαι as a potential statement in indirect discourse. The aorist form is found only in Papyrus Oxyrhynchus 1016 (see note on c7–8). All the primary manuscripts on which the text of Plato is based show ποιήσεσθαι. The future indicative (which the infinitive would represent here) with ἄν is very rare in Attic prose (GMT 197), which is doubtless why Burnet and many other editors put the papyrus reading in their texts. De Vries defends ποιήσεσθαι, citing Οὐχ ἥκει . . . οὐδ' ἄν ἥξει δεῦρο ('he hasn't come this way and he won't') at *Rep.* 615d3 as very strong evidence that Plato was open to using the construction. The difference will lie mainly in tone. Goodwin says that the colloquial style in the passage from the *Republic* makes the inclusion of ἄν "less objectionable." Perhaps the poetic ambience here is pertinent. The construction with future indicative was common in early poetry, particularly in Homer. The principal lesson to be drawn is that just because the evidence of the papyrus predates the manuscripts by a millennium or more does not mean that its reading is necessarily to be preferred.

227c1   **Πρόαγε δή** 'lead the way.' Greek is rich in transitive verbs, particularly verbs of motion, that also exhibit an intransitive usage in the active voice (KG 1.91).

c2   **Λέγοις ἄν** The potential optative may be used as a command, exhortation, or request. As Smyth (1830) indicates, the usage is not necessarily more courteous or diffident than an imperative form would be. Here, though, it would seem to provide a deliberate contrast with Phaedrus's imperative, an imperative that is rendered more emphatic by a following δή (D. 216).

c3   **Καὶ μήν** 'very well' or 'all right.' See D. 355 for the καὶ μήν of "inceptive response." The person who has been invited to speak expresses his acceptance of the invitation.

    προσήκουσα . . . ἀκοή Compare *Sym.* 177d7–8, where Socrates says that he is not likely to object to the subject that Eryximachus has proposed, because, as he maintains, matters of Eros are all he understands. Phaedrus says that what Socrates will hear is right up his alley. For ἡ ἀκοή in the sense 'the thing heard' or 'what you will hear,' see LSJ s.v. I.2.

c4–5   **οὐκ οἶδ' ὄντινα τρόπον** *Nescio quo modo*, 'somehow or other.' By this formula the speaker admits that there is something that eludes his comprehension in what he has just said or is about to say. Often there is present, as De Vries points out ad loc., an element of reluctant admiration, as in Callicles' words at *Grg.* 513c4–6: οὐκ οἶδ' ὄντινά μοι τρόπον δοκεῖς εὖ λέγειν, ὦ Σώκρατες, πέπονθα δὲ τὸ τῶν πολλῶν πάθος· οὐ πάνυ σοι πείθομαι. The implication is that even though Callicles admires Socrates' adroitness in argument, he—like many people—finds it, in some way he can't quite put his finger on, too clever by half, and is not really persuaded by him.

c5   **γέγραφε** 'has depicted.' Instead of taking, as it usually does, the written work as its object, γράφω is used here as it is in talking about painting or drawing. The object is the thing outlined or depicted, here not by lines but by written characters.

    πειρώμενον Πειράω used in the transitive sense 'make an attempt on someone's virtue or honor' (LSJ s.v. A.IV.2) can cover a broad range of behavior, from mere suggestion, such as is, perhaps, involved in Thucydides' treatment of the tyrannicides (πειραθεὶς δὲ ὁ Ἁρμόδιος ὑπὸ Ἱππάρχου in 6.54.3), to the violence that is implied by a vivid evocation of Athenian domestic life in Lysias 1.12, where a wife, who has been ordered by her husband to leave the room and take their baby with her, says, ἵνα σύ γε . . . πειρᾷς ἐνταῦθα τὴν παιδίσκην· καὶ πρότερον δὲ μεθύων εἷλκες αὐτήν ('Yes, so you can stay here and make your move on the young maidservant; this wouldn't be the first time you dragged her about when you were drunk').

c6–7   **οὐχ . . . κεκόμψευται** 'but not by a lover; he has, rather, made something clever of this very point.' Δέ signals opposition not to anything that Phaedrus has said, but to what he assumes that Socrates will think he meant. For the verb, Jowett and Campbell (on *Rep.* 376a11), cited by De Vries, pointed out that Plato never uses κομψός or its derivatives without irony. Phaedrus himself is happily oblivious of that nuance in what he is saying.

c7   **χαριστέον** exhibits the impersonal, active use of the verbal adjective; the copula ἐστί is here, as frequently, omitted with it (S. 2149.2, 2152).

c7–8   **μὴ ἐρῶντι μᾶλλον ἢ ἐρῶντι** 'to someone who isn't a lover rather than to someone who is.' Attributive participles used without an article have an indefinite force, as if accompanied by the appropriate case of the indefinite pronoun (S. 2052a or GMT 827, which is more helpful). Either the copyist who is responsible for Papyrus Oxyrhynchus 1016 or some predecessor in the tradition he followed felt a need to insert a definite article before each participle, making the unspecified—but assumed to be specifiable—individual stand for a class. The difference is small, but there was no need to make the change. Anyone who is reading *Phaedrus* in Greek should at least take a look at the transcription of this papyrus. Written in the early third century C.E., it presents a full, clear text from the opening of the dialogue through 230e and often seems to present, along with citations in writers like Athenaeus and Aristaenetus, what might be called an ancient vulgate, which differs in interesting ways from the tradition available to modern scholarship through Byzantium. The negative here is μή rather than οὐ, because the force of the participles is conditional (S. 2688, 2689).

c9   **Ὦ γενναῖος** is an exclamatory nominative (S. 1288). Socrates does not invoke the absent Lysias; he describes him with ironical admiration: 'What a gentleman (Lysias is)!' Notice the accent on omega. For ὦ conventional with vocative in Plato's time see Dickey 199ff. Exclamatory ὤ, on the other hand, is highly emotional. Plato uses it only twice: here, where it expresses Socrates' ironically heightened appreciation of Lysias's noble and beneficent nature, and at *Prt.* 309d3, where it helps express Socrates' anonymous friend's amazement at learning that Protagoras is in Athens. As one might expect, it is more frequent in drama.

c9–d1   **εἴθε . . . ἡμῶν** An optative of wish with two objects: (1) the ὡς clause, in which χαρίζομαι must be supplied (from χαριστέον in c7) to follow χρὴ; and (2) the clause in which ὅσα ἄλλα ('whatever else' or 'everything else that') is the subject of πρόσεστι.

227d1–2   **ἀστεῖοι καὶ δημωφελεῖς** Lysias's speech has already been characterized as an exercise in wit (c6–7), so the usual translations, such as 'witty' or 'charming,' seem preferable to looking in ἀστεῖοι for political overtones of dubious validity, which are, in any case, stated explicitly by δημωφελεῖς. Pairing the adjectives implies the addition of a democratic slant to the wit that Lysias's speech can be assumed to exhibit.

d2–3   **ἔγωγ᾽ . . . ἀκοῦσαι** There is here, as De Vries argues, a slight touch that is easy to miss of opposition to what came before, which is expressed by the γε element of ἔγωγε in combination with οὖν. Socrates represents himself as a bit disappointed in the nonfulfillment of his wish: 'Nevertheless I have conceived so great a desire to hear. . . .'

d4   **κατὰ Ἡρόδικον** Herodicus of Selymbria (in Thrace) is one of those who, as Plato's Protagoras (*Prt.* 316d–e) says, were σοφισταί in practice but concealed it in order to avoid the odium (τὸ ἐπαχθές) inseparable from the name. In this group he includes Homer, Hesiod, and Simonides. In *Rep.* 406a–b Socrates blames Herodicus for devising a clever regimen that would enable himself and others to live on after their lives had become painful and useless. He must be distinguished from Herodicus of Leontini, a brother of Gorgias (*Grg.* 448b5), who was also a physician, but not, presumably, a specialist in gerontology.

    προσβὰς τῷ τείχει Notice the article and compare on ἔξω τείχους at a3. For Socrates, an Athenian, the wall of Megara is not the equivalent of a proper noun. Parallels for προσβαίνω + dative in the Classical period are too scant for us to know precisely what Herodicus's method entailed, but clearly one was meant to approach, possibly touch, a wall and then return. Herodicus was from Megara before migrating to Selymbria (*Prt.* 316e1), and it would not be surprising if he framed his prescription with reference to the wall of his native city. In any case, Socrates' imaginary περίπατος is implausible and not meant to be taken seriously. The walk would be one of more than forty miles.

d5   **οὐ μή σου ἀπολειφθῶ** Οὐ μή followed by the subjunctive, usually the aorist, can have the force of an emphatic negative prediction (S. 1804, 2755). This construction can stand in various kinds of dependent sentences, including the result clause in which we find it here.

227d6–228e5: Phaedrus disclaims competence to repeat a speech of Lysias in a way worthy of its author. Socrates, though, feels sure that he had been conning the speech all morning and had set out on his walk expressly for the purpose of declaiming it. In the end, he brings Phaedrus to admit that he is carrying the text itself beneath his cloak and to promise to read it aloud as soon as they find a suitable place to sit.

228a1–2   **δεινότατος ... γράφειν** 'who is the most capable writer among our contemporaries.' For the infinitive limiting adjectives of fitness or capacity, see S. 2001–2.

τῶν νῦν Adverbs of time and place (νῦν, πάλαι, ἐνθάδε, ἐκεῖ, etc) are frequently subject to the substantive-making power of the definite article (S. 1153e). Phaedrus means 'most skilled at writing speeches.' The verb proper to writing poetry is not γράφω but ποιέω. The preceding clause shows us συντίθημι, the most general verb for literary composition; it applies to prose and poetry alike.

a3   **πολλοῦ γε δέω** 'far from it' (S. 1397).

ἐβουλόμην ... ἄν with an infinitive: an unattainable wish (S. 1789). Take γενέσθαι with both sides of the comparison.

a5–6   **ἐμαυτοῦ ἐπιλέλησμαι** Verbs of remembering and forgetting take a partitive genitive (S. 1356).

a6   **ἀλλὰ γὰρ** 'however' or 'but in fact,' i.e. 'but (what was just suggested is out of the question) for.' See D. 100–101 for possible origin of this usage.

a7   **ἀκούων** 'when he listened.' Since the imperfect tense has no participle, the present, which can also connote duration, must fill in for it.

a8   **ἐπαναλαμβάνων** is a circumstantial participle of manner that works adverbially with πολλάκις to modify ἐκέλευέν: 'he asked (him) again and again.'

οἱ is an enclitic third-person pronoun used as an indirect reflexive (S. 325d and 1225–28, especially 1228b); it refers to Phaedrus, the subject of the main verb ἐκέλευέν, of whom Socrates speaks in the third-person throughout this paragraph, and it depends on λέγειν, of which Lysias is the unexpressed subject. Lysias, who is present in the unexpressed background of *this* clause, turns up expressed as subject in the ὁ δὲ with which the following clause begins, and Phaedrus, who is present in the unexpressed background of *that* clause (as the implied agent of persuasion), turns up expressed in the τῷ δὲ with which the next clause begins. Such manipulation of the article followed by δέ is of the essence of Greek narrative. It affords a most economical way of switching between grammatical or logical subjects without material ambiguity.

228b1   **τελευτῶν** As with ἐπαναλαμβάννων in a9, the force of the participle is adverbial: 'in the end.' Phaedrus, who has been the logical subject in the preceding clause, now becomes the grammatical subject as well.

b2   **ἐπεσκόπει** It is important to observe the force of the imperfect here. And we must supply ἐπισκοπεῖν as complement for ἐπεθύμει, but that is easy enough.

b3   **τοῦτο . . . ἀπειπὼν** brings heavy participial concentration, but no congestion: ἀπειπὼν is in charge and directs the traffic; τοῦτο δρῶν is causal and tells us why Phaedrus became weary; καθήμενος expresses the manner in which he did what he was doing and tells us why he felt a need for exercise; ἐξ ἑωθινοῦ can be taken ἀπὸ κοινοῦ with the two participles it is so neatly parked between.

b4   **νὴ τὸν κύνα** Swearing by the dog, although characteristic of Socrates, was not peculiar to him. Aristophanes puts the same oath into the mouth of a slave at *Wasps* 83. Nor could it, as is sometimes suggested, have had for Socrates any great importance as a pious euphemism to avoid taking the names of the gods in vain, because he elsewhere swears freely by both Zeus and Hera. For fuller discussion of Socrates' oaths, see Dodds on *Grg.* 482b5.

b4–5   **ἐξεπιστάμενος τὸν λόγον** Socrates represents this as an aspect of Phaedrus's enthusiasm, but Aristotle (*Sophistici elenchi* 183[b] 36ff.) tells us that Gorgias and others, presumably his contemporaries, assigned their pupils λόγους ῥητορικούς to be learned by rote. He goes on to say that such teachers are like people who pretend to impart knowledge of how to prevent sore feet and then, instead of teaching shoemaking or the method of procuring suitable shoes, merely provide their pupils with a variety of different kinds of shoes. Such a teacher, he says, "has come to the aid of a want but has not transmitted an art."

b5–6   ἐπορεύετο . . . μελετῴη   Presumably because he wanted to speak
        aloud without an audience of curious passersby.

b6–7   τῷ νοσοῦντι περὶ λόγων ἀκοήν   'the man with a morbid craving
        for listening to speeches.' Νοσέω is used as freely of mental
        imbalance or flaws of character as of physical illness. Since this
        is a concrete encounter with a particular man, it does not offer
        an instance of a participle with the article used generically (see
        note on 227c7–8). Here the article tells us that this feeling about
        speeches is being represented by Socrates as a characteristic
        of himself known to Phaedrus. Notice in the apparatus that
        there is a textual tradition with the indefinite τῳ, which would
        have Phaedrus encounter 'someone' with a morbid craving for
        speeches. The run of the narrative calls for the definite article;
        Phaedrus immediately recognizes Socrates as the very man to
        meet his present needs.

b7   ἰδὼν μέν, ἰδών   Denniston (365) accounts, rather tentatively,
        for the emphatic μέν *solitarium* by suggesting that this may be a
        poetical quotation or reminiscence. That Socrates is speaking of
        himself and Phaedrus as sharers in Corybantic frenzy may also
        justify the overwrought quality of this phrase. Find a translation
        that will convey an artificial, somewhat forced enthusiasm, like
        'when he had seen him—when he had actually laid eyes on him.'
        Some editors and commentators (V., for instance) would print
        simply ἰδών, on the persuasive grounds that what our text offers
        is unprecedented and perhaps not good Greek, and Papyrus
        Oxyrhynchus 1016 does not show the second ἰδών. Still, Socrates
        in this context represents himself and Phaedrus as subject to an
        'illness' that leads to frenzy. We will find, moreover, that elsewhere
        in this introductory scene (see note on 230b2) he allows himself
        to speak in an eccentric way. Ferrari 233n8 translates "seeing him,
        seeing him," the repetition and added emphasis deriving from
        what might be called a double vision: Phaedrus has not merely
        seen the man, he has seen in him a "fellow fanatic" fallen into his
        clutches. This is interesting but perhaps excessively ingenious.

        ὅτι ἕξοι is a causal clause, which gives a reason for the pleasure.
        Causal clauses conveying an alleged or reported reason take
        the optative after secondary tenses (S. 2242). This is a kind
        of implied indirect discourse; hence, the future tense. What
        Socrates implies that Phaedrus said to himself is, 'I'm going to
        have someone with whom to dance the Corybantic dance.' Here

89

τὸν συγκορυβαντιῶντα affords an example of a participle with the article used generically (compare on 228b6–7 and 227c7–8). Socrates is here merely 'someone,' who happens to fit in with Phaedrus's already formed desire to dance the Corybantic dance, i.e. indulge his frenetic enthusiasm, over the speech. In this way he and Socrates could indulge together their morbid craving (νοσοῦντι) for such compositions. For the implications of the metaphor, see Linforth's "Corybantic Rites."

228c1   **προάγειν ἐκέλευε**   Socrates recalls 227c1.

c2   **ἐθρύπτετο** 'refused out of coyness' (LSJ s.v. II.2c).

       ὡς δὴ imparts amused skepticism to οὐκ ἐπιθυμῶν (D. 229–30).

c2–3   **τελευτῶν . . . ἐρεῖν** 'but he was even going to deliver the speech by force in the end if no one would listen willingly': a kind of mixed condition. The protasis is future-less-vivid, as the possibility would have presented itself to Phaedrus's mind, but Socrates, who is after all the speaker, knows that the condition will not be fulfilled, so in the main clause he uses ἔμελλε with a future infinitive, a substitute for a past contrary-to-fact apodosis (S. 1960, 2318). For τελευτῶν, see note on b1. The antithesis between ἑκών and βίᾳ is a common one; compare e.g. πρὸς βίαν . . . μᾶλλον ἢ ἑκὼν at 236d2–3. Physical violence is not necessarily implied any more than it is when we say that someone 'forces himself' on another in a social situation. Although καὶ could be taken with εἰ, De Vries and most recent translators rightly take it with βίᾳ: 'even by force.'

c4–5   **αὐτοῦ . . . ποιεῖν** 'ask him to do right now what he is soon going to do in any case.' Because Socrates has been speaking of Phaedrus in the third-person since a5, he can now turn to the flesh-and-blood, second-person Phaedrus walking beside him and tell him to make a request of that Phaedrus whom Socrates knows so well. For πάντως, see LSJ s.v. II.1.

c6–8   **Ἐμοὶ . . . πως** The asyndeton is dramatic and conveys emotional engagement; Phaedrus is a bit annoyed and wants to convey acquiescence under duress.

c8   **πρὶν ἂν** with subjunctive after a negative main clause: 'until' (S. 2444).

       ἀμῶς γέ πως 'somehow or other,' 'as well as I can.'

c9   **Πάνυ γάρ σοι ἀληθῆ δοκῶ** (with grating literalness) 'for I very much seem (to be) true things to you,' i.e. 'the way I seem to you is the way I really am.' In context this amounts to something like 'you're quite right about that.' This idiom, without the intensifier πάνυ, occurs at *Rep.* 567e2 also. Γάρ is of the kind Denniston (86ff.) calls "assentient"; it originated in replies in which assent is assumed and only the reason for it is expressed. Here the whole thought might be: 'Yes, your best course is indeed to repeat the speech as well as you can; for the impression I make on you (namely, that I won't let you go until you have done so) is an accurate one.' In practical translating it is rarely desirable to express all that is implied, but if you wish to take account of this type of γάρ in your version, it will usually be necessary to add the explicit assent by prefixing something like 'yes' or 'that's right' to the substance of the reply. Γάρ at 227b2 marked not assent, but approval. Socrates there is not agreeing with Phaedrus but saying that Acumenus has spoken well in giving the opinion quoted. In sentences of that sort, too, only the reason for approval is likely to be stated in Greek, but, there too, we may sometimes wish to be more explicit in our translations.

228d1   **Οὑτωσὶ** here and at d8 points to what follows. Οὗτος and its derivatives reverse their usual orientation more often than ὅδε and its derivatives refer to what precedes (KG 1.646).

d1–2   **τῷ ὄντι . . . ἐξέμαθον** 'for really, Socrates, the last thing I would want you to think is that I learned it word for word.' For παντὸς μᾶλλον, an idiom favored by Plato, see LSJ s.v. πᾶς D.III.4.

    γάρ looks back to οὑτωσὶ; Phaedrus lays out the reason for the procedure he is going to propose before he proposes it.

d3   **διάνοιαν** 'Thought,' when offered in contrast to ῥήματα, becomes 'substance' or 'content.'

d3–4   **διαφέρειν . . . ἢ** 'the case of the lover differs from.'

d4–5   **ἐν κεφαλαίοις . . . πρώτου** Phaedrus proposes to take up summarily and in the order in which Lysias presented them each of the ways in which the lover's case differs from that of the nonlover.

    ἕκαστον, which agrees in gender with ἁπάντων, replaces διάνοιαν as complement before we reach the verb—a slight anacoluthon.

    δίειμι The present indicative forms of εἶμι and its compounds are used as the future of ἔρχομαι (S. 774).

d6   **Δείξας γε πρῶτον** For γε in affirmative replies that only imply the affirmation, being more concerned to add some qualification to it, see D. 133ff., especially 135. Here it has its familiar limiting sense as well: 'Yes, you will, but only when you have revealed. . . .'

ὦ φιλότης is an abstract replacement for the concrete and familiar ὦ φίλε. Obviously Plato's Socrates enjoys being playful with affectionate forms of address in conversation with young friends. (For other variants on ὦ φίλε, see the Homeric φίλη κεφαλή at 264a8 and ὦ φιλούμενε Ἀγάθων at *Sym.* 201c8.) What is less obvious is the part such terms play in signaling a contender's confidence or lack of it in the give and take of Socratic argument. For a detailed treatment of these matters, see Dickey passim but especially 109–19, where she discusses the meaning of what she calls "friendship terms" as forms of address in Plato. Friendship terms include forms of address that are common to many Greek writers, terms such as φίλε, ἑταῖρε, φίλε ἑταῖρε, ἀγαθέ, ἄριστε, βέλτιστε, and—in appropriate contexts—θαυμάσιε and δαιμόνιε, and more *recherché* and specifically Platonic examples like φιλότης here. In the Socratic dialogues these forms tend to be used by whoever is at the moment in control of the argument or attempting to establish control. If we look back over what we have read so far, we find that Phaedrus normally addresses Socrates, when he does formally address him, merely by his name; the sole exception occurs at 227d6, where—whatever his real intentions may be—Phaedrus affects, with the help of ὦ βέλτιστε, to have an argument that will save him from attempting what Socrates has requested. In other words, a point of contention has arisen and he is trying to assert control. Socrates, on the other hand, establishes from the outset a tone of perhaps rather condescending familiarity with his ὦ φίλε Φαῖδρε in 227a1 and ὦ ἑταῖρε in 227b2. At the point we have now reached, Socrates has completely dismantled Phaedrus's sham attempt at grasping control of the first controversy in the dialogue and shown it to be nothing but social hypocrisy. Vocatives in Plato are almost always preceded by the particle ὦ. What ὦ means (if that is the proper term) is a subject of much dispute and little agreement (Dickey 199–206). In any case, avoid any temptation to carry it directly over into English, where it is not at home.

d6–7 ἐν τῇ ἀριστερᾷ It may be significant that Phaedrus carries the speech of Lysias in his left hand when we reach the division of love into left- and right-handed kinds in 266a.

228e1 παρόντος … Λυσίου, in the person of the manuscript.

καὶ is more likely to be adverbial with the participle ('actually') than it is to equal English 'too,' i.e. 'in addition to you and me,' but the latter is certainly possible.

e1–2   ἐμαυτόν . . . παρέχειν 'to hand myself over to you to practice on.' A complementary infinitive of a verb compounded with ἐν can express an action that will take place in or on whatever the infinitive depends on, which is here the reflexive pronoun.

e3   Παῦε Since the meaning intended is plainly intransitive, we might expect παύου, but Attic prose uses the present active or the aorist middle for the intransitive imperative of this verb.

e4   ἐν σοὶ ὡς ἐγγυμνασόμενος is a more analytical construction than that discussed in the note on e1–2. Compare *Alc. I* 114d5: ἐν ἐμοὶ ἐμμελέτησον ('practice on me'). De Vries is probably right in saying that the sort of practice Phaedrus would have in mind would probably have been memory training, despite his denial that he had the speech by heart.

     ὡς lets us know that it was Phaedrus's intention (expressed by the future participle) that provided the grounds for his now-vanished hope (S. 2065, 2086).

e4–5   βούλει . . . ἀναγνῶμεν is an idiomatic fusion of the two questions 'do you wish' and 'are we to read' into one (S. 1806).

229a1–c3: Socrates and Phaedrus turn down along the Ilissus and make for a tall plane tree that stands in view. Phaedrus asks whether the stretch of river they are on is the very one from which Boreas snatched Oreithyia in the myth. Socrates replies that the traditional site lies two or three stades farther downstream, near the crossing to Agra.

229a1   κατὰ τὸν Ἰλισὸν The article shows that Socrates expects Phaedrus to be familiar with the name of the river even though it has not been mentioned before in their conversation.

a2   ἐν ἡσυχίᾳ is possibly used, as De Vries suggests, in a concrete sense: 'in solitude' or 'in a quiet place.'

a3   ἀνυπόδητος ὢν ἔτυχον The tense of ἔτυχον shows that putting his shoes on is something Phaedrus failed to do in the past; that of ὢν shows that the resulting barefoot state lasts into the present. The aorist of τυγχάνω often takes a supplementary participle in the present tense, the aorists of λανθάνω and φθάνω more rarely (S. 2096).

a3–4   σὺ . . . ἀεί Going about ἀνυπόδητος was held to be characteristic of Socrates and his followers. See e.g. Aristophanes, *Clouds* 102–

4: τοὺς ἀλαζόνας, τοὺς ὠχριῶντας, τοὺς ἀνυποδήτους λέγεις / ὧν ὁ κακοδαίμων Σωκράτης καὶ Χαιρεφῶν ('you are talking about the humbugs, the palefaces, the barefoot boys, among whom are the accursed Socrates and Chaerephon').

μὲν γὰρ δὴ   Μὲν contrasts this thought with an unspoken antithesis: 'you are always barefoot (but I am not).' Γὰρ, as De Vries observes, indicates that this clause gives the reason that the preceding one switched to a singular subject rather than carrying on with the plurals ἴωμεν and καθιζησόμεθα. Δὴ is often found emphasizing γὰρ (D. 243).

a5–6   **τήνδε . . . ἡμέρας**   It is midsummer (230c2) and shortly before noon (242a4). For the accusative, compare Euripides, *Bacchae* 723–24: τὴν τεταγμένην ὥραν ('at the appointed time of day') with Dodds's note. We might expect the dative, but in a few idiomatic phrases ὥρα and καιρός seem to be used in the accusative even though no idea of duration is involved.

a7   **ὅπου καθιζησόμεθα**   'somewhere to sit.' Relative clauses of purpose regularly take the future indicative (S. 2554; GMT 565). Compare Socrates' claim at *Ap.* 37c3–4: οὐ γὰρ ἔστι μοι χρήματα ὁπόθεν ἐκτείσω ('I don't have money to pay in full').

a8   **Ὁρᾷς οὖν**   The inferential force of οὖν (S. 2964) can be quite weak; 'therefore' would be too heavy here. De Vries suggests "Well, do you see. . . ?" "Well" presumably conveys lightly some notion such as, 'You say you want to sit down, so. . . .'

πλάτανον   In *De oratore* 1.28 Cicero remarks: *Illa (platanus) . . . quae mihi videtur non tam ipsa acula, quae describitur, quam Platonis oratione crevisse.* Cicero had been a student in Athens. Perhaps in the dry tone of his suggestion that the plane tree may have grown more out of Plato's eloquence than from the nearby spring, one can detect memories of men who would be glad to show you, for a small consideration, the very tree under which Socrates and Phaedrus had reclined on that summer day more than three hundred years before. The plane tree is encountered more in literature than in life by North Americans, who are more familiar with the sycamore, a common shade tree of the same genus.

a9   **Τί μήν;**   Formally a question, this phrase is regularly used by Plato to indicate unqualified assent: 'what else?' and so 'naturally' or 'of course' (S. 2921; D. 333).

229b1–2   **πόα καθίζεσθαι**   Infinitives do not often depend on substantives in Greek, but here the context makes it clear that πόα means 'grass *suitable for*,' and infinitives are regular with adjectives like ἐπιτήδειος (S. 2001).

b2   **ἂν βουλώμεθα** The future-more-vivid protasis is employed where there is no verb of future reference in the apodosis, only a statement about suitability for something that has not yet taken place.

b4   **μέντοι** In questions of the *nonne* type (sentence questions that expect the answer 'yes'; S. 2651) μέντοι merely enlivens the expectation of a positive answer (D. 403).

b5   **ὁ Βορέας τὴν Ὠρείθυιαν** Legend made Oreithyia the daughter of King Erechtheus. In Herodotus 7.189 we read that the Athenians were advised by an oracular response to call upon their son-in-law for help. Since Boreas "according to the story of the Greeks" had carried off Oreithyia, the Athenians concluded that he was their son-in-law and approached him with sacrifice and prayer. Immediately a heavy wind blew across the Aegean and destroyed that part of the Persian fleet beached along the coast of Magnesia. Herodotus suggests that perhaps the wind began to blow before the prayers were made but adds that the Athenians were positive in giving credit to Boreas and that, when they got home, they built a shrine for him παρὰ ποταμὸν Ἰλισσόν. (Comparison with a1 will show that there was not complete consistency in Greek authors about the spelling of the river's name.)

b7   **Ἆρ' οὖν ἐνθένδε;** 'from right here?' as opposed to ἐνθένδε . . . ποθὲν: 'from somewhere hereabout?' at b4.

    γοῦν ('at any rate') is the particle of "part proof" (D. 450–51). Phaedrus advances one reason for believing that this may be the place, but it will quickly prove to be insufficient.

b7–9   **χαρίεντα . . . αὐτά** This may have been the case in the days of King Erechtheus and his daughter, but an inscription (*Inscriptiones graecae* I³ 257; photograph in Travlos fig. 442 or Camp fig. 8) discovered at the corner of Byron and Bacchus Streets in Athens directs the Archon Basileus to see to setting up a stele on each side of the Ilissus (the surviving inscription would be one of them, transported to a new location for reuse in a later age) forbidding the steeping of hides and throwing of refuse (καθάρματα) from the tanning process into the stream. Apparently a tannery located above 'the precinct of Heracles' had been polluting the Ilissus. The inscription dates from before 400 and possibly as early as 440. Given the corresponding uncertainty about the dramatic date of our dialogue (see introduction) the reader is free to imagine this pollution as either rampant on or corrected by the day Socrates and Phaedrus took their walk.

229c1   ὅσον 'approximately' (LSJ s.v. IV.3).

c2   πρὸς τὸ ἐν Ἄγρας Understand ἱερόν (LSJ s.v. ἱερός III.2): 'to the shrine in Agra.' The reading ἐν Ἄγρας is not found in the manuscripts; it was derived from the lemma of a scholiast to the *Phaedrus*. De Vries provides a defense of Burnet's use of it. Perhaps we should also understand a dative after Ἄγρας to make the whole phrase mean something like 'to the building in the sacred precinct at Agra,' but for the possibility that here, as well as in a number of passages in Homer, we have an archaic use of the genitive with ἐν see Chantraine 2.104–5. The exact location of the deme Agra is not known, but it was certainly on the southeast bank of the Ilissus. James Stuart and Nicholas Revett, surveyors and topographical artists who were sent to Greece in 1751 by the Society of Dilettanti in London, found the remains of a metroon—a shrine of Demeter—among the rocks above the river on the side away from the city. Unfortunately those remains were removed by Turks in building fortifications in 1778. Identification of this site with the shrine mentioned by Socrates is a cornerstone of the topographical interpretation offered in this note. My map is based on the section of an archeological map made by Travlos in 1959 (and printed as plate 3 of his Πολεοδοκιμὴ Ἐξέλιξις τῶν Ἀθηνῶν), which was reproduced by Wycherley in 1963. The route my dotted line suggests for the walk taken by Phaedrus and Socrates in this opening scene of the dialogue depends heavily on Wycherley's discussion. It differs radically from the route suggested by Robin in his introduction to the Budé *Phaedrus* and accepted by De Vries and others. Those who are interested in the matter should begin by reading Robin's discussion and Wycherley's article. I shall confine myself to the five points that follow: (1) Phaedrus and Socrates meet within sight of (τῇδε; 227b4) the house of Morychus, which was at some undetermined place near the Olympieion in the southeast quarter of Athens, and leave the city by the Gate of Aigeus. (The name, which comes from Plutarch's *Theseus* 12.6, is not certain, but the existence of a gate in this part of the wall, which is all that matters for our problem, is secure.) They then walk eastward until they approach

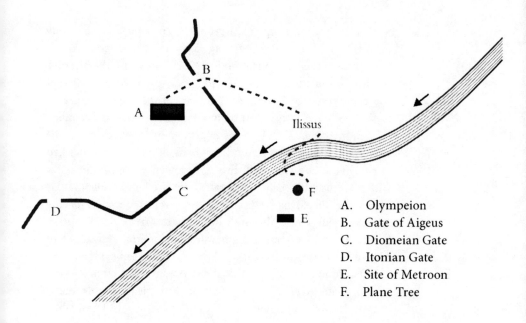

A. Olympeion
B. Gate of Aigeus
C. Diomeian Gate
D. Itonian Gate
E. Site of Metroon
F. Plane Tree

the Ilissus, whereupon they turn and walk downstream. Robin, on the other hand, has them emerging from the city on the south by either the Itonian or Diomeian Gate, turning to their left and walking upstream. One should add that he wrote before the gate tentatively identified as the Gate of Aigeus had been discovered and published. (2) Socrates and Phaedrus do not walk in the direction of Megara, but that is quite irrelevant (see second note on 227d4). I mention the point only because it has caused confusion by playing a role in previous discussions. (3) At 229a1 Socrates suggests that they turn aside and walk κατὰ τὸν Ἰλισὸν. Granted that the use of κατὰ does not necessarily imply that they will walk downstream—a riverbed always lies below any spot nearby, so there is a sense in which it is always natural to speak of going 'down along' the river, whether one intends to walk downstream or up—the downstream sense is, nevertheless, the usual one for κατά governing the name of a river in the accusative, and, unlike its opposite, it involves no special pleading. (4) If τὸ ἐν Ἄγρας was in fact located at the known site of the Metroon, the river crossing and the altar of Boreas will not have been far from that site. At 229c1 Socrates and Phaedrus are still from four hundred to six hundred yards upstream from the crossing (κάτωθεν ὅσον δύ' ἢ τρία στάδια). Without trying to correlate in a pedantic way the length of their conversation in 229c1–230a6 with the distance on the ground it might be expected to occupy, it seems likely that the plane tree stood no more than part of the way downstream to the ford. Hence the admittedly arbitrary location of the plane tree on my map. (5) Robin was uncertain as to whether the tree stood on the northwest or southeast bank of the river and marked alternative sites on his map. This is, however, the one point about which we can be certain. Socrates' declared intention (242a1) of leaving Phaedrus by crossing the river is decisive for the southeast side. He would surely intend to return to his customary haunts in the city rather than wander alone on the slopes of Mount Hymettus to the east. All that having been said, perhaps one should remind oneself that the dialogue is not reportage but fiction. Plato gives us inconsistent data that leave the dramatic date of the dialogue open. If he does not care to let us know when it took place, perhaps we ought not be too curious about where.

διαβαίνομεν   The subject is not Phaedrus and Socrates on this occasion specifically but 'we Athenians'; Socrates means the usual ford at seasons of the year when the river did not consist, as it did on that midsummer day, of mere rivulets and runnels (see ὑδάτια at b8).

c2–3   βωμὸς αὐτόθι Βορέου   See note on b5.

229c4–230a6: Phaedrus asks whether Socrates believes the myth about Boreas and Oreithyia to be literally true. Socrates replies that speculation about such matters, although fashionable among clever people, is a lengthy and time-consuming process that brings little reward. He goes on to say that it would be strange if he, who cannot yet fulfill the Delphic command, spent his time investigating other creatures rather than trying to discover what sort of beast he is himself.

229c4   Οὐ πάνυ νενόηκα   Riddell 139 says that οὐ πάνυ always means "scarcely" and cites twenty Platonic passages (omitting ours), some of which (*Tht.* 149d9, for instance) would better be translated 'not at all.' Hackforth's "I have never really noticed it" manages to straddle the two interpretations. Compare οὐ πάνυ (μοι) δέδοκται at 228e2, where either 'it is certainly not my intention' or 'it is scarcely my intention' would do, the latter being only a somewhat ironic way of conveying the former.

c5   σὺ ... εἶναι   Papyrus Oxyrhynchus 1016 shows σε in place of σύ. Moreover, its transcriber wrote, very likely following his exemplar, the form πείθει where Burnet, following the manuscripts, prints πείθῃ. Now πείθει can, of course, be read as either a second-person middle-passive or a third-person active present indicative. Assuming that either the transcriber of the papyrus or someone in the textual tradition behind him took that form to represent a third-person singular active, the second-person subject would obviously no longer do, but τὸ μυθηλόγημα could take its place, if only σύ could be taken to be a corruption of σε and so emended. This narrative, if it indeed represents approximately what happened, provides both an instructive example of how a certain kind of textual corruption might come about and a heartening indication that people in the ancient world sometimes experienced the same elementary difficulties we experience.

c7   φαίην   The force of ἄν carries over from the preceding clause.

πνεῦμα Βορέου   Boreas the wind rather than Boreas the god. Commentators often discuss this passage as if the σοφοί of whom Socrates speaks were precursors of the Stoic school of allegorical interpretation of poetry, but the down-to-earth naturalism of the interpretation he advances here makes it certain that what Plato had in mind was, as Ferrari (235n14) suggests, something much more like the reduction of the myth of Io's wandering to a mere case of kidnapping we find in the opening pages of Herodotus.

c8   σὺν Φαρμακείᾳ   Oreithyia's playmate was evidently the nymph of a spring thought to have curative powers.

c9–d1   ἀνάρπαστον γεγονέναι is a periphrasis for ἀνηρπάσθαι.

229d1–2   ἢ ... ἡρπάσθη   Some editors and commentators consider these words to be a distracting interpolation, inserted into the text by a pedant in pursuit of comprehensiveness. That is possible, but casual (or casual *seeming*) afterthoughts of this sort are one of the means by which Plato distinguishes dramatic dialogue from the meditated treatise. By his offhand manner Socrates may be, as De Vries suggests, showing how little importance he attaches to the whole matter.

d3   ἄλλως μὲν   i.e. 'apart from the disadvantages I am about to mention.'

χαρίεντα 'elegant' or something else implying a meretricious attractiveness.

d3–4   λίαν . . . ἀνδρός modifies τὰ τοιαῦτα parallel to χαρίεντα as a predicate adjective. For the predicate use of genitive of possession, see S. 1304. Understand εἶναι ἡγοῦμαι with τὰ τοιαῦτα as subject of the infinitive.

d4–5   κατ' ἄλλο μὲν οὐδέν, ὅτι δ' 'if only because.' The implication is not that this is the only reason, but that it is a sufficient reason.

d6–7   καὶ ἐπιρρεῖ δὲ The last item of a series is sometimes flanked by καί . . . δέ, especially when it is, as here, a kind of etcetera (D. 202). Here καί connects with the preceding clause, while δὲ emphasizes the important intervening word.

d7   Γοργόνων καὶ Πηγάσων There were three Gorgons but only one Pegasus, so the plurals are of the kind that indicate that the specific monsters mentioned are only examples of the kind of thing under discussion. Compare e.g. *Tht.* 169b7: Ἡρακλέες τε καὶ Θησέες ('men like Heracles and Theseus'). Here Socrates is expressing a degree of casual contempt; for that aspect of the usage, see Fraenkel on Aeschylus's *Agamemnon* 1439, where Clytemnestra refers to Chryseis in the plural, implying that she was only one of a series of trollops with whom Agamemnon consorted before Troy.

d7–e2   καὶ . . . φύσεων 'and large numbers of other impossibilities and curiosities that consist of portentous creatures of one kind or another'—to offer a not-quite-literal translation of the text transmitted by the manuscripts and printed by Burnet. Πλήθη and ἀτοπίαι are, in this reading, nominatives, parallel to ὄχλος, the latter being an abstract used concretely (I borrow the translation 'curiosities' for ἀτοπίαι from De Vries and adopt the concrete sense 'creatures' for φύσεων from LSJ s.v. V). Papyrus Oxyrhynchus 1016 offers the dative singulars πλήθει and ἀτοπίᾳ. (For the copyist of the papyrus the latter did not differ orthographically from the nominative plural, so our interpretation of it as dative or nominative depends entirely on whether we accept πλήθει or πλήθη.) If we read with the papyrus, they would be datives of respect (S. 1516), a construction that is found limiting the adjective ἀμήχανος elsewhere; indeed, at *Tht.* 184a7 we find the phrase ἀμήχανον πλήθει describing a subject for discussion (λόγος) that is 'unmanageable in magnitude.' With this reading we take all the genitives together and the two datives with ἀμήχανον: 'a host of Gorgonish and Pegasus-like beings and of other portentous creatures of one kind or another, unmanageable in their number and strangeness.' This reading seems preferable on grounds of sense and idiom, even though that of Burnet and the medieval tradition is also readable and does present the *lectio difficilior*. (When manuscripts or other text sources offer two readings that are both acceptable in terms of syntax and suitability to context, editors will, other things being equal, normally choose the one that presents features that seem odder, rarer, or less to be expected—"more difficult," in other words—on the grounds that a scribe would be more likely to strive to avoid it than spontaneously fabricate it.)

229e2   **προσβιβᾷ κατὰ τὸ εἰκὸς** "will force into agreement with probability" (Thompson). The future indicative in a protasis is emphatic and common only when the condition conveys a strong appeal, a threat, or—as here—a warning (GMT 447). For the form, see S. 539d.

e3   **ἀγροίκῳ** This word wanders rather far from the farm, sociologically speaking. It can be applied to anyone who violates urbane taste, which is not the exclusive prerogative of rustics. Here an excessive and self-conscious cleverness is in question.

e4   **πρὸς αὐτὰ** It is hard to ascertain to what the pronoun refers. Possibly the πρὸς ταῦτα of T or the πρὸς τοιαῦτα of Papyrus Oxyrhynchus 1016 is to be preferred.

e6   **γράμμα** serves as a reminder that the precept was inscribed on the temple at Delphi.

e6–230a1   **γελοῖον . . . σκοπεῖν** Socrates deftly slips from dative μοι into accusative ἀγνοοῦντα, in order to become the subject of an infinitive. This transformation is quite common in sentences in which the infinitive depends on an impersonal expression.

    δή both emphasizes the already emphatically placed adjective it follows and expresses logical connection: 'so it seems to be actually ridiculous.' For a similar use, see φθονερὸν δὴ at 239a7 (D. 237ff).

230a2   **τῷ νομιζομένῳ** 'the conventional opinion.'

a2–3   **ὃ νυνδὴ ἔλεγον** In these conversational reminders English tends to use a relative adverb ('as I was saying a moment ago') but Greek a relative pronoun.

a3–6   **εἴτε . . . μετέχον** West gives a succinct and circumspect exposition of the confusing ancient tradition about the monster Typhon (or Τυφωεύς, to employ the form of his name known to Homer and Hesiod) in his note to Hesiod's *Theogony* 820–80. What is relevant to our passage is that he became identified in the Greek mind with τυφῶν and τυφώς, names for violent winds, hurricanes, or 'typhoons,' in fact. (By serendipitous similarity in sound *tai feng*, the Chinese name for a violent storm at sea, came ready made for adoption and adaptation by classically educated Europeans.) Plato—never one to overlook a fruitful ambiguity—feels free to make Socrates evoke, as they suit his shifting purposes, either the mythological or the meteorological aspect of this creature. Since Τυφωεύς the monster was encircled by snakes from the waist down and had dragons' heads for fingers, Socrates can justly imply that he is πολύπλοκος. The snakes, moreover, with their black tongues, could speak in such a manner that the gods could understand them on the one hand and so as to imitate the sounds made by all sorts of animals on the other. Zeus struck this "marvel of miscegenation" (Nightingale 134) with a lightning bolt, so he can be called ἐπιτεθυμμένον, which can be found in LSJ under ἐπιτύφομαι, 'to be burnt up, especially by lightning.' (De Vries observes that we see here the first traces in the dialogue of Plato's liking for playing with etymology.) It is in contrast to this windy, fiery persona that Socrates uses ἀτύφου: 'un-Typhonic,' i.e. 'not puffed up or enflamed.' On θεία μοῖρα, see Bluck's long, rich note on *Meno* 100a1. The phrase might be rendered 'partaking by nature in a kind of divine and tranquil way of life.'

a4   τυγχάνω governs the supplementary participle ὄν, which has been attracted into the gender of its predicates θηρίον and ζῷον.

230a6–e5: Socrates waxes so poetic over the beauty of the natural scene in the shade of the plane tree that Phaedrus marvels at his mood and comments on how seldom he was to be found outside the city wall. Socrates explains that trees, unlike men, have nothing to teach him, but he adds that in proffering a speech Phaedrus has found the means to draw him outside the walls. They settle themselves for Phaedrus's reading of Lysias's speech.

230a6–7   ἀτάρ . . . ἡμᾶς; The implication is that Socrates and Phaedrus had been so absorbed in their conversation that they had not noticed that they were approaching the plane tree until, Voila!

There it was before them. See note on 227b2 for ἀτάρ. For ὦ ἑταῖρε, see second note on 228d6. In the conversation in 229a1–c5, which is devoted entirely to enquiries about matters of fact and plans on which there is agreement, Socrates does not address Phaedrus by name at all and Phaedrus addresses Socrates twice, both times simply by name and in asking a question that involves a change of subject, a use that comes naturally to speakers of English as well. Socrates begins the present paragraph in the same low emotional key, but he begins to show that he has warmed to his subject with ὦ Φαῖδρε at 229d3, and by the time he reaches ὦ φίλε at 229e5 he is fully engaged with its ethical implications and trying again to control the argument and persuade his young friend that what he is saying is both important and true. Although the present sentence changes the subject abruptly, ὦ ἑταῖρε maintains the master-pupil relationship between them.

a7   **ἦν** English would prefer the present, because Socrates calls attention to the tree as it stands before them now; Greek the imperfect, because what he says presupposes something already said about it (229a8–b2). This usage is sometimes called the philosophical imperfect, because it is frequently used, especially by characters in Plato's dialogues, to recall previous points in a discussion (S. 1903; GMT 40).

230b1   **Τοῦτο μὲν οὖν αὐτό** 'Yes, this is the very one.' Assentient μὲν οὖν (D. 476–77; S. 2901a) is particularly at home in replying to a question of the *nonne* type (see note on 229b4).

b2   **Νὴ τὴν Ἥραν** De Vries points out that Plato puts this "woman's oath" in Socrates' mouth six times, always accompanying expressions of admiration.

καλή γε ἡ καταγωγή Denniston (128) cites this as an example of exclamatory γε in an expression accompanied by an oath. The usage is often ironical, even sarcastic in tone, particularly after a form of καλός. An ironical touch is probably to be seen here. De Vries suggests that καταγωγή in the concrete sense 'halting place,' as a rare variant in Attic for the more common diminutive καταγώγιον, which Socrates applies to the same scene at 259a5, "helps to heighten the style."

ἥ τε The use of solitary τε to connect sentences pervades this paragraph. Since this is not ordinary prose usage in Plato's time (see D. 499 for its relative frequency in Thucydides), it contributes to the establishment of an elevated, perhaps mannered, tone.

b3   τοῦ τε ἄγνου *Vitex agnus castus* (no English name in common use) is a Mediterranean shrub with fragrant white or violet blossoms. As the subspecies element in its Linnaean name indicates, it has been thought to possess antiaphrodisiac properties. Ἄγνος, on the other hand, is not so specific and could refer merely to use in ritual without any pharmacological overtones. The transliteration of the species element in its name into Latin has led to mistaken common names like 'Chaste Lamb.'

b4–5   καὶ . . . τόπον Hackforth's "now that it is in full flower, it will make the place ever so fragrant" makes it clear that he took the first ὡς as causal (S. 2240) and the second as being of the sort that accompany superlative adjectives to heighten their force (S. 1086). This is probably less objectionable than other interpretations (usually involving "exclamatory" ὡς) that have been given to this short but rather puzzling sentence. The potential optative is less assertive and more urbane than would be the indicative.

b6   ῥεῖ μάλα ψυχροῦ ὕδατος 'flows with very cold water.' In this further addition to the mannered language of Socrates' description, the genitive is *recherché*; even in poetry the instrumental dative would be usual (LSJ s.v. ῥέω 1a). The phrase may have a rough parallel in *Phd.* 113a8–9, where we find 'a lake boiling with water and mud' (λίμνην . . . ζέουσαν ὕδατος καὶ πηλοῦ).

b7   ὥστε . . . τεκμήρασθαι is hard. Probably it is preferable to accept (with V. and Moreschini) the reading ὥς γε from the mass of later manuscripts and the epistolographer Aristaenetus (who wrote love stories in the form of letters in the fifth or sixth century C.E. in a style that is a patchwork of phrases from the elegiac poets and Plato). It gives us a sort of parenthetic afterthought: 'to judge by my foot at any rate.' Elsewhere Plato likes to use this combination (ὥς γε) with εἰρῆσθαι in similar, rather parenthetic expressions: 'to tell you the truth' (*Prt.* 339e4 and *Euthyd.* 307a1) or 'just between ourselves' (ὥς γε ἐν αὑτοῖς ἡμῖν εἰρῆσθαι, at *Prt.* 309a4).

b7–8   Νυμφῶν . . . ἱερὸν We must not be surprised to find a shrine dedicated in part to Achelous along the Ilissus. The Achelous in Boeotia, the largest river in Greece, can stand for freshwater in general, being thought to be the father of rivers: ὁ Ἀχελῷος πηγὴ τῶν ἄλλων πάντων, in the words of a scholium to *Iliad* 21.195.

b8   κορῶν Votive figurines in the form of dolls (LSJ s.v. κόρη II).

230c1   τὸ εὔπνουν 'the freshness of the air.' Plato regularly makes substantives of neuter adjectives like καλόν and ἀγαθόν, but to do so with such out-of-the-way choices as εὔπνουν here and σύσκιον at b4 (neither word is used by him elsewhere) certainly helps give this passage a studied effect. Socrates is praising Phaedrus's choice of a site for their reading. According to Aristotle (*Ars rhetorica* A 1368ᵃ 10ff.) exaggeration is a means proper to panegyric, but the reader may perhaps detect a touch of mockery. We are hard put to know how to take it—as Phaedrus will be.

c2   **θερινόν τε καὶ λιγυρὸν** are adverbial accusatives indicating manner (S. 1608).

     ὑπηχεῖ The subject is formally τὸ εὔπνουν, although it is the air itself, not its freshness, that resounds in a shrill and summerlike way to the cicadas' song.

c3   **τὸ τῆς πόας** is a more abstract and distanced way of saying ἡ πόα. Compare τὸ τοῦ θεοῦ at *Ap.* 21e4, which is a more abstract version of ὁ θεός, making it more like τὸ θεῖον. The turn is characteristic of the style of Thucydides, one of whose favorites is τὸ τῆς τύχης for 'fortune.'

c3–5   **ὅτι . . . ἔχειν** Ἱκανὴ agrees in gender with πόας, thus acknowledging the artificiality of the preceding phrase; ἐν ἠρέμα προσάντει tells us in what respect the grass is sufficient; ἔχειν might be translated 'to support.'

c5   **ἐξενάγηται** Perfect passive used impersonally. Ferrari 16–17 draws an interesting parallel between the performance Socrates has given in the paragraph now coming to an end and the sort of assessment that, according to the opening pages of the Hippocratic treatise *Airs, Waters, Places*, would be expected of a physician arriving in a place new to him. He would, as Socrates has done, comment on the quality of air, water, and vegetation.

c6   **Σὺ . . . φαίνῃ** Phaedrus expresses his bemusement in both the form of address he employs and in his adjective. With ἀτοπώτατος compare ἄτοπος at 229c6. There he could avoid being 'out of place' by aligning himself with οἱ σοφοί, but he refuses. Here he is 'very out of place' in the environs of his own city, as if, as Phaedrus will go on to say, he were indeed a foreigner being given a tour rather than a native (Ferrari, chap. 1, esp. pp. 12ff.). Yet it was Socrates who knew the facts about historic places along the Ilissus back in 229b–c—a contradiction we might keep in mind.

     ὦ θαυμάσιε This can be one of Dickey's "friendship terms" (see second note on 228d6), but here I would prefer to take it literally.

Phaedrus is genuinely puzzled by Socrates' behavior, but with ὦ
ἄριστε attached to 'excuse me' in d3 Socrates continues to assert
his control by using one of the most strongly ironical of those
terms.

230d1   **οὕτως** "to such a degree" (V.); Phaedrus is explaining why he
can advance such a paradoxical view as he has in the preceding
sentence.

ἐκ τοῦ ἄστεος employs the definite article because Athens is
being considered as an entity opposed to foreign parts, just as
with ἐν τῷ ἄστει at d5 Socrates is thinking of the city as opposed
to the countryside, whereas ἐν ἄστει at 227b3 meant merely 'in
town.' Compare 'I'm going to town' as opposed to 'I prefer the
town to the country.' For the genitive singular termination in
-εος, see S. 268 and D2a (bottom of p. 68). The transcriber of
Papyrus Oxyrhynchus 1016 wrote ἄστεως, the normal Attic prose
form, which he doubtless learned in school, just as we did.

εἰς τὴν ὑπερορίαν sc. γῆν: 'abroad' (LSJ s.v. ὑπερόριος 2).

d4   **τὰ . . . χωρία** 'the open country'; χωρίον in the sense 'field' or
farmstead' is found here and elsewhere in Plato, but you would
never know it from LSJ.

μὲν οὖν is transitional, with each particle exerting its own force;
οὖν looking backward and saying that this sentence can be
inferred from what preceded, μὲν looking forward to a contrast
with the δὲ that follows (S. 2901c).

ἐθέλει 'are willing,' a mild personification that we use
conversationally in English as well.

d5-6   **τῆς . . . φάρμακον** 'the charm to lead me out of the city.'

d6-8   **ὥσπερ . . . ἄγουσιν** From ἄγουσιν understand ἄγοντες with
πεινῶντα θρέμματα as its object, as De Vries suggests.

d7   **ἢ τινα καρπὸν** 'or perhaps a vegetable.' De Vries cites Fraenkel on
ἤ τις Ἀπόλλων at Aeschylus, *Agamemnon* 55.

230e1   **φαίνῃ περιάξειν** Although σὺ is, of course, formally the subject,
a translation like 'it looks as if you can cart me all around Attica
and . . .' (the translation of περιάξειν borrowed from Hackforth)
would catch the spirit of what Socrates is saying: the passive of
φαίνω with a future infinitive in the sense 'seem to be able to do a
thing.'

e2   **δ' οὖν** This collocation leads back to the main topic (S. 2959).
It is, whether mildly or strongly, dismissive of the subject of

discourse that it terminates. Perhaps Socrates could be led all over Attica by dangling speeches in front of him as one would lead recalcitrant donkeys or goats by means of dangling vegetables in front of them, but now it is time for him to lie down and for Phaedrus to begin his reading. There is a long-standing and unresolved controversy over whether the speech that follows is indeed by Lysias or presents a parody of his style and outlook by Plato. This commentary assumes the latter to be the case.

THE SPEECH OF LYSIAS

230e6–231e2: As the speech of Lysias begins, the nonlover points out to the boy the prudential disadvantages of yielding to a lover, a man who is in a morbid state of mind, which he will later regret, and he adds that nonlovers offer a larger field from which to choose than do lovers.

230e6   **τῶν ἐμῶν πραγμάτων** 'my situation,' i.e. 'the sexual relationship I propose and the terms on which I propose it,' as what follows makes clear. Compare the use of πρᾶγμα to allude to the liaison of Harmodius and Aristogeiton in Aeschines' *Against Timarchus* 132. Τούτων in the following line refers to this relationship, as does ὧν δέομαι in the line after. The pervasive presence of euphemisms and evasions gives parts of this speech a curiously muffled effect, as if we were reading it through cotton batting. Dover (*Greek Homosexuality*, 44) compares its circumspect language with Aeschines' reluctance to use the word πεπορνευμένος ('prostituted') in the speech mentioned above, which he calls (13) a source of "peculiar value" for assessing Athenian public attitudes toward homosexuality.

     ὡς νομίζω It is often not easy to decide whether ὡς introduces an indirect question or an indirect statement. For the development of the latter usage from the former, see S. 2578c. Here 'you have heard that I think' seems on the whole preferable.

e7   **γενομένων τούτων** is genitive absolute with conditional force and another euphemism: 'if I achieve my object.' The euphemistic use of pronouns of unexplained reference throughout these opening sentences leaves the impression that the speech represents the climax of a discussion about this subject already long in progress.

e7–231a1   **διὰ τοῦτο** prepares for the causal clause to follow. Compare on 228d1.

231a1–2   **ὅτι . . . τυγχάνω** 'because I don't really love you.'

a2   **μεταμέλει** takes dative of the person who repents and genitive of the object of his regret (S. 1467).

a3   **τῆς ἐπιθυμίας** Παύομαι can take genitive of separation (S. 1392) in the sense 'leave off' or 'cease' participating in some state or activity.

a4   ἐν ᾧ ... προσήκει   'in which repentance is called for.'

a4–5   οὐ ... ἑκόντες   De Vries cites Dimock, who points out that this speech employs "eliminative" ἀλλά after a negative expression (not *x* but *y*; S. 2776) 13 times per hundred lines, whereas the authentic speeches of Lysias use it only 5.5 times per hundred lines, "exaggeration being the soul of caricature." But the nature of the subject calls upon the speaker to repeatedly say that the nonlovers do not do what the lovers do, but something else. I mention this in illustration of the difficulties in the way of assigning the speech to Plato or to Lysias on stylistic grounds. Reasons elicit counterreasons.

a5–6   ὡς ... ποιοῦσιν   The nonlovers confer favors or benefits (εὖ ποιεῖν is central to their conception of the relationship) 'in proportion to their resources,' just as they would best take thought for their own affairs. For πρός + accusative in this sense, compare Thucydides 4.39.2 (of the Spartans at Sphacteria): ὁ γὰρ ἄρχων Ἐπιτάδας ἐνδεεστέρως ἑκάστῳ παρεῖχεν ἢ πρὸς τὴν ἐξουσίαν ('for their commander Epitades issued individual rations more sparingly than supplies justified').

a6   ἔτι δὲ is a connective empty of logical force, which is used four times in this rather brief speech, as if the speaker is able to score clever small points in the order in which he happens to think of them, but is unable or unwilling to arrange his thoughts with logical coherence or cumulative force. Hackforth translates it consistently as "again," which provides a suitably haphazard effect in English.

a8   πεποιήκασιν has in view the permanence of the benefits conferred, whereas the aorist διέθεντο in the line above pointed to individual acts in violation of self-interest on the part of the lover as they occurred.

ὃν ... προστιθέντες   The trouble one takes in performing a benefaction is something distinguishable from the loss one incurs, so it can be represented as an addition to the loss column in the account the lover keeps.

231b1   πάλαι could well represent an exaggeration characteristic of a mind on its way from desire to resentment.

ἀξίαν   i.e. equal in value.

ἀποδεδωκέναι χάριν   The χάρις the lover received can be found in LSJ s.v. III.2 (another euphemism), that which he has returned, under III.1. De Vries points out that ἀξίαν and the prefix of ἀποδεδοκέναι only make more explicit what the article conveys, namely, that this χάρις is a debt to be paid, not a gift to be given.

b3   τοῦτο is *l'affaire de coeur*, a quiet euphemism.

ἔστιν = ἔξεστιν.

b4   ὑπολογίζεσθαι means to subjoin to an account and corresponds to προστιθέντες above. For both lover and nonlover the affair is described as a strictly commercial transaction in the language of bookkeeping.

τοὺς προσήκοντας   'his relatives' (LSJ s.v. III.3).

b5   διαφορὰς   For διαφορά in the sense 'disagreement,' see LSJ s.v. III.

αἰτιάσασθαι with accusative of thing and no personal object means 'complain about.' The change from the present infinitives to this aorist seems unmotivated and has elicited Cobet's αἰτιᾶσθαι and other conjectures.

περιῃρημένων τοσούτων κακῶν is genitive absolute with temporal force.

b6   ἀλλ' ἤ   'except' (S. 2778).

αὐτοῖς (sc. τοῖς ἐρωμένοις) depends on χαριεῖσθαι.

b7   πράξαντες   'by doing.'

ἔτι δὲ   See note on a6.

b7–c1   εἰ ... ποιεῖσθαι   Ἐστί must, as is often the case, be understood with ἄξιον.

231c1   περὶ πολλοῦ ποιεῖσθαι   'to value highly,' 'make much of' (LSJ s.v. πολύς I.3).

c2   φασιν   The subject is οἱ ἐρῶντες, rather than simply 'people.' The point is not, don't be fooled by what everyone says about lovers, but rather, don't fall for their line.

φιλεῖν is here obviously a term of wider application than is ἐρᾶν but does not exclude it.

c2–3   ἐκ ... ἔργων modifies ἀπεχθανόμενοι: 'by making enemies of others as a consequence of their words and deeds' (S. 1688c). As De Vries points out, the articles are possessive (S. 1121).

c4   ῥᾴδιον γνῶναι   The main clause also lacks an expressed verb (see note on ἄξιον at b7–c1). The ὅτι clause that follows is not causal, but depends on γνῶναι as an indirect statement.

ἀληθῆ λέγουσιν has the same subject as φασιν at c2.

c5   **ἐρασθῶσιν** In prose ἐράω is deponent outside the present system.

       ἐκείνους are the new favorites, who are now preferred to αὐτῶν, their former favorites, who are to become τούτους in the following line.

       περὶ πλείονος ποιήσονται See note on c1.

c6   **καὶ** before τούτους might be translated 'in their turn.'

c7   **καίτοι** As De Vries suggests, the loosely continuative sense (D. 559ff.) is appropriate: 'and indeed.'

       εἰκός 'reasonable.'

       τοιοῦτον πρᾶγμα 'a thing as precious as your virtue,' which is a palpable euphemism.

231d1   **τοιαύτην ἔχοντι συμφοράν** 'the victim of such a misfortune'— or even 'such a disease,' i.e. the lover.

d1–2   **ἣν . . . ἀποτρέπειν** 'which no one [οὐδεὶς] who has ever experienced it would even [οὐδ'] try to avert.'

d2   **καὶ** is adverbial with αὐτοί: 'for even they themselves admit' (S. 2881).

d3–4   **ἀλλ' . . . κρατεῖν** Ἀλλά οὐ after a statement formally positive but negative in meaning, like κακῶς φρονοῦσιν, often means 'and not': these lovers 'think ineptly and are not able to control themselves.' A casual, conversational anacoluthon seems to result from Plato's writing δύνασθαι, as if we were to read it as another infinitive following ὁμολογοῦσι, instead of δύνανται, parallel to φρονοῦσιν in indirect statement following ὅτι.

d4   **εὖ φρονήσαντες** 'when they have come to their senses.' The aorist participle marks that point in time.

d5   **οὕτω διακείμενοι** i.e. being in the state they were said to acknowledge in the preceding sentence.

d6   **καὶ μὲν δὴ** marks an emphatic transition: 'and in truth' or 'and in fact.' It is "notably common in Lysias" (D. 395–96), so that the five times the collocation occurs introducing sentences in this speech could well offer another touch of parody or pastiche (see note on a6). Here it introduces a detached point that has the effect of a non sequitur. Hackforth translates it on each occurrence with "and observe this," which yields a suitably abrupt and disjointed effect.

d6–7   **τὸν βέλτιστον** As De Vries remarks, this saves moral appearances, but we have no idea what criteria the speaker may have applied in making such a judgment.

231e3–232b5: If the boy fears for his reputation, let him know that a lover is much more prone to indiscretion than is a nonlover, who chooses what is best over flaunting his success in the eyes of the world.

231e3   **τοίνυν** is another particle of mere transition: 'further' (D. 575). The familiar consequential force 'therefore' is obviously out of place here. Compare on καίτοι at c7.

     τὸν νόμον τὸν καθεστηκότα   Both the unwritten law enforced by public opinion and legal sanctions should be kept in mind. A young man who allowed himself to seem to be 'kept' could face serious penalties as well as giving a weapon to his political enemies for the rest of his life. See Dover's treatment of Aeschines' *Against Timarchus* in chap. 2 of *Greek Homosexuality.*

e4   **εἰκός ἐστι**   'it is likely.' Contrast 'it is reasonable' at c7. Here the phrase constitutes a verb of expecting and can take either an aorist infinitive of simple action (ἐπαρθῆναι at 232a2) or a present infinitive of continuing or repeated action (ἐπιδείκνυσθαι at a3 and αἱρεῖσθαι at a6), both tenses denoting future expectation (S. 1868).

232a1   **ἄν** goes with ζηλοῦσθαι to mean 'would be considered happy' (LSJ s.v. I.2). As De Vries points out, αὐτοὺς ὑφ' αὑτῶν rules out the translation 'would be envied.'

a2   **ἐπαρθῆναι τῷ λέγειν** ('to be carried away in speaking') suggests the familiar experience of saying more than one intends to say in an excited state of mind that feeds upon itself. Editors who expunge or emend τῷ λέγειν remove a nice psychological touch.

a3–4   **ὅτι ... πεπόνηται** is a euphemistic way of putting the matter. For πονέω used impersonally with dative of agent, LSJ cites only this occurrence.

a4–5   **κρείττους αὑτῶν ὄντας**   Plato's customary expression for being in control of oneself. The nonlovers can hold their tongues.

a5–6   **τὸ βέλτιστον ... αἱρεῖσθαι**   "There is a pleasant irony in this twisting of a Socratic precept into propaganda for the sensualist," as Hackforth remarks in a note ad loc.

a6   **ἔτι δὲ**   See note on 231a6. For what follows as far as b2, a vivid illustration is given in *Chr.* 154a–d, where young Charmides enters with a train of ἐρασταί in his wake and an advance guard of young men λοιδορουμένους ἀλλήλοις in their rivalry over him. At the other extreme lies the inhibited and respectful behavior of young Hippothales, would-be ἐραστής of Lysis, who lingers at the edge of a crowd that surrounds the object of his affections and maintains a bashful silence (*Lys.* 207b).

πολλοὺς is the subject of the infinitives in a7, τοὺς . . . ἐρῶντας their object.

a7   πυθέσθαι 'become aware of.'

a8   ἔργον τοῦτο The demonstrative refers to ἀκολουθοῦντας τοῖς ἐρωμένοις and is the object; the noun is predicate accusative; these fellows make a career of conspicuous wooing.

232b1   οἴονται takes its subject from πολλοὺς in a6, as does ἐπιχειροῦσιν in b3.

b1–2   ἢ γεγενημένης . . . ἐπιθυμίας Ἐπιθυμία bears the sense 'satisfaction of desire,' referring not to the person but the act. The phrase—vague, as are so many in this speech—is yet another euphemism, but the συνεῖναι that follows does not have the sexual meaning this verb so often has in this sort of context.

b3   οὐδ' must be split and taken half with ἐπιχειροῦσιν and half with αἰτιᾶσθαι; the crowd does not take the trouble to so much as blame the nonlovers.

b4–5   δι' ἄλλην τινὰ ἡδονήν Not other than φιλία (which would scarcely be called a ἡδονή), but other than the amorous trysts, which are presumed to precede or follow the social contact and provide its motive in the other case.

232b5–e2: The nonlover proceeds to list and describe the disadvantages that arise from the touchiness and possessiveness of lovers.

232b5   καὶ μὲν δὴ See note on 231d6.

εἰ . . . ἡγουμένῳ The apodosis will not turn up until we reach εἰκότως . . . φοβοῖο (c2–3). These two clauses form the exoskeleton of the sentence; between them lies its soft tissue—the indirect statement dependent on ἡγουμένῳ, which consists of the brief assertion χαλεπὸν . . . συμμένειν and a pair of conditions, each of which has genitive absolute as its protasis. There is a lot of Greek here, and the details are worthy of attention.

b6   καὶ The fear presents itself in two stages: first anxiety over the difficulty attendant upon maintaining cordial relationships in general, then the distinction made in the μὲν . . . δὲ antithesis that follows. (Φιλία is broader than ἔρως but includes it; compare on 231c2.)

ἄλλῳ . . . τρόπῳ i.e. in some way other than an erotic relationship.

b6–7   διαφορᾶς γενομένης is conditional, as is προεμένου . . . σου ln c1.

b7   <ἄν> The supplement is not necessary. This clause purports to state something true of all cases in which quarrels arise from some cause other than erotic attachment; καταστῆναι can, therefore, stand in indirect discourse for a gnomic aorist, which would, of course, not require ἄν (GMT 159). In the clause that follows, the particular case of the boy being addressed is dealt with, so γενέσθαι represents a potential optative in direct discourse and needs its ἄν, but when ἄν does arrive—in c2 and c3—it comes, like sorrow, "not in single spies but in battalions." Repetition of ἄν is not uncommon in Greek (S. 1765 and KG 1.246ff., which is rich in examples) but for one pair to tread so hard on the heels of another that all four are seen within the compass of eleven words *is* uncommon, even unprecedented. Some editors omit one of them. De Vries suggests that they constitute "a conscious trick . . . to mark some nervousness on the part of the speaker who is now dangerously near to making clear his secret intentions." Presumably he means conscious on the part of Plato, but I fail to see how the speaker is any closer to revealing "his secret intentions" here than he has been from the beginning of the speech.

καταστῆναι is to all intents and purposes a synonym for γενέσθαι (LSJ s.v. B.5).

232c1   προεμένου . . . σου Compare τοιοῦτον πρᾶγμα προέσθαι at 231c7.

περὶ πλείστου ποιῇ We have now seen the idiom περὶ πολλοῦ ποιεῖσθαι (see note on 231c1) in all three degrees of the adjective.

c2   σοι is contrasted with ἀμφοτέροις in b7. It is, therefore, emphatic and should have an accent, as Ast and Hackforth see. Compare σου in the preceding line, which requires no emphasis and is properly enclitic (S. 187a).

εἰκότως 'reasonably'; compare εἰκός ἐστι at 231c7 with note.

c3–4   καὶ πάντ' 'and everything that happens.'

c5–6   ἀποτρέπουσιν 'try to prevent,' the conative present (S. 1878; GMT 25).

c7   ὑπερβάλωνται 'outbid' (LSJ s.v. B.3).

c8   κρείττους i.e. than themselves.

γένωνται   'prove to be' or 'reveal themselves as' (Dodds on *Grg.* 496a6–7).

232d1   πείσαντες   The force is instrumental.

d2   σε serves as the subject of ἀπεχθέσθαι and the object of καθιστᾶσιν in the sense 'to bring someone or something into a certain state' (LSJ s.v. II.3).

τούτοις are those who are equipped with the advantages just mentioned.

d3   τὸ σεαυτοῦ σκοπῶν   'in considering your own affairs.'

d5   ἀρετὴν would seem to denote something that contrasts with the jealous, possessive behavior of the lover: 'simple merit,' perhaps.

ἔπραξαν ὧν ἐδέοντο   Compare ἀτυχῆσαι ὧν δέομαι at 231a1. Πράττω commonly bears this significance in this speech and erotic contexts elsewhere; Theocritus 2.143 wrote ἐπράχθη τὰ μέγιστα for 'intercourse took place.'

τοῖς συνοῦσι recalls the συνουσίαι πρὸς τοὺς ἄλλους that the lover discourages in c5.

d6   μὴ ἐθέλοντας   sc. συνεῖναι τοῖς ἐρωμένοις.

d6–7   ἡγούμενοι . . . ὠφελεῖσθαι   The nonlovers want the seal of society's approval on their judgment.

232e1   αὐτοῖς   i.e. the boys.

ἐκ τοῦ πράγματος has no specifically sexual meaning here but refers to association with the nonlover in general.

e2   γενέσθαι   For the aorist infinitive referring to future hopes or expectations in direct discourse, see note on 231e4. What is said there applies in Plato regularly after εἰκός and frequently after ἐλπίς and ἀνέλπιστον.

232e3–233d4: Love imposes bad judgment on his subjects: they desire those whom they do not yet know, and they praise without discrimination. The nonlover, on the other hand, is master of himself. His social responses are measured and appropriate; the benevolence he offers has a common basis with that offered by friends and family.

232e3–5   **Καὶ . . . ἐγένοντο** is an assertion presented as a general truth by verbs in the gnomic aorist (S. 1931).

e3   **Καὶ μὲν δὴ**   See note on 231d6.

e4–5   **τὸν τρόπον ... τῶν ἄλλων οἰκείων** There is little, if anything, in the Classical usage of τρόπος to support a translation as 'character' in any deep moral sense clearly distinguishable from more superficial 'traits' denoted by οἰκεῖα. Ὀικεῖα were the facts about a man that were determined by his οἶκος—family, friends, traditions, and material circumstances. Translations will vary, but something like 'his personal behavior and family circumstances as well' is better than trying, as some translators do, to make a contrast for which the Greeks possibly did not yet have terms. For ἄλλων as translated above, see S. 1272.

e5   **αὐτοῖς** refers to the lovers if we take it with ἄδηλον, to the boys if we take it with φίλοι. The former interpretation seems more likely, both because of word order and because the lovers' judgment is what is at issue here.

233a1   **τοῖς ... μὴ ἐρῶσιν** is the class of nonlovers, whoever they may be. If five of them, let us say, were under discussion and we knew who they were, they would be τοῖς οὐκ ἐρῶσιν (S. 2734). The dative denotes relation (S. 1495) and depends on εἰκὸς in the following line.

a1–4   **οἳ ... ἔσεσθαι** Ἀλλήλοις is used rather loosely, as if the antecedents of the relative pronoun included both ἐρῶντες and ἐρώμενοι. This ambiguity succeeds in associating the latter with the former as subjects of the shady euphemisms ταῦτα ἔπραξαν and εὖ πάθωσι. Understand ἐστί with οὐκ ... εἰκὸς to provide your sentence with a main verb. For the tense of ποιῆσαι and καταλειφθῆναι, see note on 232e2. The second ταῦτα in a2 and the one in a3 both serve to pick up ὧν (= τούτων ἅ) and repeat it as subject of these two infinitives. Αὐτοῖς is grammatically redundant, but needed rhetorically to recall τοῖς μὴ ἐρῶσιν after all that has come between. Μνημεῖα is predicate accusative. Some commentators find difficulty in its translation and give it ad hoc meanings to fit the context, but surely anything that recalls to mind what was not there a moment before, including previously formed expectations of future bliss, can be called a 'reminder.'

a4   **καὶ μὲν δὴ** See note on 231d6.

a5   **ἐκεῖνοι** The change to plural from the collective singular ἐραστῇ is quite normal (S. 1012).

a6   **παρὰ τὸ βέλτιστον** Compare 232a5–6 and note. Here τὸ βέλτιστον is much less fraught with ethical baggage.

233b1   **καὶ αὐτοὶ** The ἐρώμενοι have shown a degree of bad judgment in what they said or did, but even the ἐρασταί themselves sometimes show inferior discernment (χεῖρον . . . γιγνώσκοντες), as distinguished from their insincere praise.

b1–2 τοιαῦτα . . . ἐπιδείκνυται 'for such is Love's performance.' Plato, who did not have at his disposal the distinction between uppercase and lowercase to distinguish proper nouns, surely had Ἔρως in mind here. Ἔρως, also, is an artist of sorts; he works in human behavior, and such are the results. Since Ἔρως is the subject of the main verbs in the following sentence, τοιαῦτα must look forward.

b3 εὐτυχοῦντας δέ is quite outside the grammar of the sentence and has usurped the place of something like παρ' εὐτυχούντων δέ (which would eliminate the need for παρ' ἐκείνων) for the sake of the formal antithesis with δυστυχοῦντας μέν it provides. We shall find a good many instances of anacoluthon in this work, and they often occur, especially in some of Socrates' longer sentences, in a way that yields an effect of conversational informality or psychological verisimilitude. What we have here, though, is rhetorical anacoluthon, mannered and called into being by a desire for a purely verbal parallelism. Also, δυστυχοῦντας has been wrenched conspicuously out of normal word order to prepare the way for this bauble. Both participles are temporal and have the lovers, ἐκεῖνοι of a5, as subject. The sentence brings together, after its fashion, 232c3–4 and 233a5–b1.

b5–6 ὥστε . . . προσήκει contradicts an important part of the apologetics for these relationships; the ἐραστής was said to provide a model for the ἐρώμενος to admire and thereby improve himself. Τοῖς ἐρωμένοις depends on προσήκει: 'it is (much more) appropriate.' αὐτούς, the ἐρασταί, is the object of both infinitives.

b6 ἐὰν . . . πείθῃ 'if you are persuaded by me,' not 'if you believe me.'

233c1 τὴν . . . ἔσεσθαι The infinitive depends on μέλλουσαν, and the phrase as a whole provides a second object for θεραπεύων, which one could perhaps take in two senses: 'not indulging . . . but fostering.'

c1–5 οὐχ . . . ἀποτρέπειν This passage so obviously aspires to balanced antithesis that one can sympathize with Thompson's desire to find ταχέως between σμικρὰ and ἰσχυράν, in order to answer βραδέως and perfect this Gorgianic gimcrack.

c2   **ἐμαυτοῦ κρατῶν**   See 232a4–5. The participle, like ἡττώμενος, is circumstantial with causal force.

c2–3   **ἀναιρούμενος** 'conceiving.' See LSJ s.v. B.5, where no indication of the metaphorical usage is to be found.

c6   **εἰ δ' ἄρα** 'but if perhaps.' For ἄρα in a conditional protasis suggesting that "the possibility is one that has only just been realized," see D. 37–38.

  σοι . . . παρέστηκεν 'has occurred to you.' At 232b5, where the subject is δέος, 'has come over you' or even, reactivating the original metaphor, 'is your companion' would be better.

c7   **ἐρῶν τυγχάνῃ** 'is really in love.' Compare 231a1–2 and note.

233d1–3   **ὅτι . . . ἐκεκτήμεθα** Some such protasis as 'if that were the case' must be understood. In the triple anaphora of οὔτ' ἄν, the first recurrence connects the mothers and fathers with the sons as objects of the same verb, the second heralds its own verb, ἐκεκτήμεθα, a pluperfect that can stand parallel to the imperfect ἐποιούμεθα, because the perfect system of κτάομαι means 'to possess.'

d4   **ἐπιτηδευμάτων** Commentators and translators strain to find a convincing contrast to ἐπιθυμίας in this word. The task is daunting if we take the latter to denote a feeling, but see note on 232b1–2. If we understand it once again as a euphemism for 'satisfaction of desire,' it becomes an action, and 'other practices' both contrasts with it nicely and is vague enough to appear to respect its secret.

233d5–234b1: It is proper to give not to those most in want and most importunate, but to the most deserving, who will continue to be your friends once your bloom is past.

233d5   **Ἔτι δὲ** See note on 231a6.

d6   **τοῖς ἄλλοις** is not parallel to τοῖς δεομένοις, but is neuter and dative of respect (S. 1516).

d7   **γὰρ** The reason given does not, of course, represent the opinion of the speaker; it is the rationale offered by people who behave in this way. This playing of the *advocatus diaboli* will go on as far as εὔξονται in e5.

d8   **χάριν . . . εἴσονται** χάριν οἶδα + dative means 'to feel gratitude to' (LSJ s.v. χάρις II.2); αὐτοῖς must be understood from the context to mean 'to their benefactors.'

καὶ μὲν δὴ καὶ See note on 231d6. The additional καὶ could be translated 'in particular.'

233e1 **δαπάναις** From παρακαλεῖν we learn that the expense of entertaining is in question.

e2 **τοὺς προσαιτοῦντας** The needy are here said to do what Poverty herself planned to do, when (in *Sym.* 203b) she arrived at Aphrodite's natal festivities προσαιτήσουσα and loitered by the door.

τοὺς δεομένους πλησμονῆς 'people in need of a square meal.'

e3–4 **ἀγαπήσουσιν . . . ἥξουσι** 'will prize them and become their followers and throng their doors.'

e4–5 **χάριν εἴσονται** See note on d8.

e5–234b1 **ἀλλ' ἴσως . . . ἐπιδείξονται** Ἀλλ' ἴσως initiates rejection of the course of action that has been mockingly advanced beginning at d6; the diffidence expressed by ἴσως is, of course, ironical. In this sentence Plato's Lysias was in danger of falling into more than eleven lines in succession of clauses introduced by dative participles depending on προσήκει . . . χαρίζεσθαι and referring to the lovers and nonlovers alternately. He avoided that by interposing two blocks (234a1–5 and a7–b1) in which clauses are introduced by nominative relative pronouns, whose antecedents (datives dependent on προσήκει χαρίζεσθαι) must be supplied mentally by the reader. The entire passage is in the οὐ . . . ἀλλά (not *x* but *y*) mode.

e7 **τοῖς προσαιτοῦσι** is absolute in the sense 'to those who are importunate' (LSJ s.v. II). But we get it through emendation. De Vries, following Dimock, would keep τοῖς ἐρῶσι from T and W, which would give μόνον more point and avoid redundancy after τοῖς σφόδρα δεομένοις in e6.

234a1–2 **τῆς σῆς ὥρας** Ὥρα is the youthful bloom that, according to the convention, attracts the ἐραστής. Compare the opening sentences of the *Protagoras*: Πόθεν, ὦ Σώκρατες, φαίνῃ; ἢ δῆλα δὴ ὅτι ἀπὸ κυνηγεσίου τοῦ περὶ τὴν Ἀλκιβιάδου ὥραν; It is instructive that in translating this Cicero simply omitted the very Hellenic concept of the pursuit of ὥρα: *Inde tamen appares, Socrate? An id quidem dubium non est, quin ab Alcibiade?*

a2 **ἀπολαύσονται** The verb is deponent in the future system.

a3 **διαπραξάμενοι** The prefix δια-, as often, denotes that the action was carried to completion. One might think of this as a euphemism accompanied by a knowing wink.

a4–5   αἰσχυνόμενοι has causal force, whereas the aorist διαπραξάμενοι in a3 was temporal.

a8   παυσαμένου Hermann's emendation requires that we mentally supply σου; this may seem difficult, but it is possible. The middle of παύω would then denote 'leaving off' τινός (τῆς ὥρας here, τῆς ἐπιθυμίας in the line above) in the sense no longer possessing it; compare 231a3 with note. An interesting exercise would be to find the sense and reason in all the manuscript readings and emendations printed in Burnet's apparatus with the addition of παυσαμένης, favored by De Vries, which was conjectured by a corrector of a manuscript in the Laurentian Library and is attractive but not compelling.

234b1   τὴν αὐτῶν ἀρετὴν ἐπιδείξονται 'will show the stuff they are made of.' See note on 232d5.

234b1–c5: It is significant that nonlovers are not reproved by friends and family, as are lovers. No more than would lovers do they advocate yielding indiscriminately to everyone of their own kind; the essential thing is that there be mutual advantage without risk. Thereupon the speech ends abruptly with an offer to entertain questions.

234b3   ὡς . . . ἐπιτηδεύματος Ὡς marks the participle as giving the grounds on which the agent (οἱ φίλοι) acts (S. 2086). The ἐπιτήδευμα in question is being a lover. In the following line ὡς introduces the grounds on which the nonlovers' friends and family cannot blame him.

b3–4   τοῖς . . . ἐρῶσιν For dative of person with μέμφομαι, see LSJ s.v. 3.

b6–7   Ἴσως . . . χαρίζεσθαι The speaker seems to be reduced to bringing up straw men that are absurdly easy to knock down. Perhaps it is not surprising that he will soon come to an abrupt close.

b7–c1   ἐγὼ . . . διάνοιαν As De Vries says, this is a very sophistic argument, but the observation really applies through δυνατόν in c2.

b8–c1   ταύτην ἔχειν τὴν διάνοιαν i.e. χαρίζεσθαι.

234c1   τῷ λαμβάνοντι The object is left to our imaginations in the manner we have come to expect from this cagey speaker on a delicate topic. Χάριν would suit the context, but it would have to be taken in a sense different from χάριτος: 'favor' as opposed to 'gratitude.'

ἄξιον, like δυνατόν in the following line, agrees with something like 'this course of action,' which can be understood out of διάνοιαν. What is under consideration is the feasibility of concealing multiple affairs from all the others in his social ambience, not merely from his other lovers. Otherwise there would be no point in ὁμοίως, which must compare the feasibility of concealment in this situation with that in which there is only one lover.

c2   τοὺς ἄλλους λανθάνειν must be taken with both δυνατόν and βουλομένῳ.

ὁμοίως modifies δυνατόν; concealment, that is, is not as feasible in this situation as it would be in the case of having only one lover.

c3–4   δεῖ ... γίγνεσθαι 'but what is wanted is that there be . . .' offers a rather abrupt cooling-off from the steamy imaginings that precede, as if the clock were running out.

c3   ἀπ' αὐτοῦ See first note on 231b3.

c5   παραλελεῖφθαι Understand αὐτό (from τι) as the subject of this one-word indirect statement.

ἐρώτα Presumably this offer to take questions is part of the written speech. Does Phaedrus have the same right to make it as would Lysias, the author? See the discussion of writing later in the dialogue, in particular the paragraph beginning at 275d4.

The First Interlude

234c6–235a8: Socrates adopts a bantering tone about the speech, and when Phaedrus protests that no one in Greece could speak more effectively and say more about this subject, he expresses surprise at the notion that he was expected to admire its substance and not merely its style, which he in fact found repetitious.

234c7 τά . . . ὀνόμασιν exhibits accusative and dative of respect in tandem: 'especially in choice of words.' Socrates will use the same expression with reference to his great Palinode, the showpiece of the dialogue, at 257a4–5. For forms of ἄλλος or its adverb followed by τε καί and something more defined than ἄλλος, see S. 1273 and, particularly, 2980.

234d1 Δαιμονίως μὲν οὖν Μὲν οὖν is corrective (S. 2901b; D. 475–76): Socrates implies that ὑπερφυῶς did not put the matter strongly enough.

ἐκπλαγῆναι As De Vries points out, at *Sym.* 198b5 (τίς οὐκ ἂν ἐξεπλάγη ἀκούων;) Socrates uses the same word in expressing his ironical admiration for Agathon's speech.

d2–3 πρὸς σὲ ἀποβλέπων Prefixed ἀπο- can perform a singling-out function and transform verbs of looking into verbs of gazing fixedly. After all, looking at a person or thing with attention involves looking away from everything else. (Compare the relationship between δείκνυμι and ἀποδείκνυμι.) The participle is imperfect in tense and aspect, as is frequently the case with present participles in agreement with the subjects of aorist verbs (compare 228a7 with note); its force is causal, reinforcing διὰ σέ. Socrates is being careful to distinguish himself from Phaedrus; all three personal pronouns are visibly emphatic: ἐγὼ simply because it is expressed, the two instances of σέ because they are not enclitic. The distinction between the reactions of the two friends to the speech is marked by emphatic personal pronouns through the end of the paragraph. Compare the enclitic με in d1, where no such distinction is being made.

d3　　　γάνυσθαι is a poetic word. Commentators find a play on Phaedrus's name (see LSJ s.v. φαιδρός).

ὑπὸ τοῦ λόγου For ὑπό with the genitive in this sense after verbs of passive meaning, see S. 1698.1b. Phaedrus (the bright one) seems to Socrates to be brightened "under the influence of" (V.'s excellent suggestion for ὑπὸ) the speech.

d3–4　　μεταξὺ ἀναγιγνώσκων Μεταξύ can perform the same function with a temporal participle that ἄτε or οἷα perform with a causal one: 'while you were reading' (S. 2081).

d5　　　εἰπόμην, καὶ ἑπόμενος Picking up a finite verb by its participle in proceeding to the next clause is a common feature of λέξις εἰρομένη, the "strung together" style of Greek prose narrative that either expresses or affects artlessness, as opposed to the openly artful λέξις κατεστραμμένη or "periodic style" (Denniston, *Greek Prose Style*, 60). The device is a favorite of both Herodotus and Plato (Denniston, *Greek Prose Style*, 95).

συνεβάκχευσα Compare τὸν συγκορυβαντιῶντα at 228b7 and Linforth's article cited there. Since the most common ecstatic rites were Bacchic, βακχεύω can be used generically and need not imply any distinction from κορυβαντιάω in contexts of this sort. The verb here sums up the effect of the paragraph. Socrates represents the reading as a Corybantic experience for Phaedrus and himself in such details as his own ecstatic response (ἐκπλαγῆναι), rapt in fascination (see note on d2–3) with a Phaedrus who seems transfigured (γάνυσθαι with note on d3) and submissive to his lead. His rapture was necessarily brought about by Phaedrus's manner and shining face, since, as we shall see, nothing could have been less likely to inspire such a state of mind in him than the speech itself. However that may be, he and Phaedrus have indeed danced the Corybantic dance together; whether they danced to the same music is another question.

d6　　　τῆς θείας κεφαλῆς is in apposition with σοῦ. A comma would have been helpful. As synecdoche for the whole person, κεφαλή goes back to Homer. This paragraph exemplifies the problems that the constantly shifting—one might say shimmering—shades of irony and affection with which Plato's Socrates speaks to his friends give to a translator from a different culture with different traditions shaping its language. Do not be dismayed if you can sometimes understand, enjoy, and even explain what you despair of translating. For θεῖος applied to people, see Bluck on *Meno* 81b1, where he cites τοῖς μάντεσι τοῖς θείοις ('the inspired soothsayers' as opposed to the fraudulent ones) from *Ion* 534d1. Phaedrus's glowing aspect at d3 and his metaphorical participation in Bacchic frenzy qualify him for the epithet 'inspired.' The word brings the end of the paragraph back to the religious connotations of δαιμονίως, with which it began.

d7–8   **Εἶεν ... ἐσπουδακέναι** Phaedrus's οὕτω δὴ gives his question a palpable touch of indignation (D. 204, 209). De Vries calls εἶεν "more or less gruff," and perhaps it is. In translating Socrates' reply we must grasp the force of γάρ, which in questions that reply to a question "conveys surprised recognition of the grounds that occasioned that question" (D. 78–79): 'What? Do you think I am joking and not in earnest?' The perfect of σπουδάζω often seems to be no more than a strengthened present—what Smyth (1947) calls an "intensive perfect." But see further on 236b5–8.

234e1   **Μηδαμῶς** 'don't!'—said in the reproachful tone in which we show that we are mildly annoyed when a friend goes too far in teasing us. Obviously an imperative is needed to complete the syntax, but we need be no more specific than is Phaedrus. Socrates replies with the same word when Callicles tries to wriggle out of an elenchus at *Grg.* 497b4.

e2   **πρὸς Διὸς φιλίου** In appealing as friend to friend, Phaedrus invokes Zeus Philios.

e2–3   **τινα ... Ἑλλήνων** Phaedrus is not implying that some Scythian or Nubian might have done better. Until a few years ago someone in the United States, in discussing manufacturing, might have asked if any American could have shown more know-how without implying that possibly someone from elsewhere might have.

e3   **μείζω καὶ πλείω** When πολύς is paired with another adjective, it almost always comes first (KG 2.252 and Henderson on Aristophanes' *Lysistrata* 616–24). The reverse order constitutes a special effect that interferes with the reader's expectations and makes him look at the two adjectives separately, perhaps as when in English we say 'many and large' rather than 'many large'; here 'weightier and more numerous.' It is characteristic of Phaedrus to be most impressed by the quantity of different arguments Lysias has found. He will mention this as being at least on the same level of importance as their quality at 235b4–5 and d7 and at 236b2.

e5   **Τί δέ;** Expresses surprise, incredulity, or irritation (D. 175). It is usually, as here, followed by another question, in which the speaker reveals the reason for his feelings. Surprise is conveyed here. Socrates is still playing the rhetorical illiterate and will gradually, during the course of this paragraph, openly regain control of the discussion by rejecting both the substance and the form of Lysias's speech.

e6–8   **ὡς . . . ἀποτετόρνευται** Genitive absolute with ὡς, which is explanatory of ταύτῃ in the line above, is parallel to the causal clause ὅτι . . . ἀποτετόρνευται, which is explanatory of ἐκείνῃ: 'for this reason too . . . on the grounds that the writer . . . and not for that reason alone, because. . . .'

e6   **ποιητοῦ** is not 'poet' here but 'author' in a more general sense, the maker of the speech as opposed to Phaedrus, who merely read it aloud (LSJ s.v. II.2).

e7   **σαφῆ καὶ στρογγύλα** With a comma after these words, as in Burnet's text, we are to take it that Socrates starts to say that something (perhaps he already had ἕκαστα τῶν ὀνομάτων in mind) is clear and epigrammatic, but changes the construction when he thinks of the verb ἀποτορνεύω and the metaphorical resources it offers. Without the comma we must think of the two neuter adjectives as adverbial and parallel to ἀκριβῶς, which seems harsher and more difficult than accepting the minor anacoluthon.

e8   **ὀνομάτων** seems to mean 'phrases' or perhaps 'expressions' in this context. Opposed to ῥήματα it can mean 'words' as opposed to 'phrases' (*Ap.* 17c1) or 'nouns' as opposed to 'verbs' (*Tht.* 168b8–c1 and, spelled out very explicitly, *Sph.* 262a1–7). There is no word in Greek to mean—simply and unequivocally—'word.'

e9   **χάριν σήν** 'on account of you,' in the sense 'because you say so.' For the possessive pronominal adjective used for the objective genitive of the personal pronoun, see S. 1197.

         ἐπεὶ . . . γε is a combination that is often, but not always, to be translated 'although' (S. 2380). 'Although' will do here if we take the clause as concessive to συγχωρητέον, but 'since' will be required if we take it as explanatory of χάριν σήν. The latter seems preferable, because σήν and ἐμέ, an emphatic form emphatically positioned, seem strongly contrasted.

235a1–3 **τῷ . . . εἶναι** The two halves of this sentence deal with the two possible objects for attention that Socrates mentioned in 234e6–

8, and he takes them in reverse order, as is often the case. The first clause deals with the rhetoric of the speech and the second with its substance.

a1   αὐτοῦ refers to the speech.

a2   τοῦτο stands for the author's saying what ought to be said (τὰ δέοντα εἰρηκότος τοῦ ποιητοῦ in e6). Although τῷ ῥητορικῷ is closer, taken as the referent of τοῦτο it has the crippling disadvantage that it makes Socrates say that he was thinking, as he listened, that Lysias would think his own rhetorical performance inadequate, which is very unlikely. It is much more likely that Lysias would deprecate his own treatment of τὰ δέοντα, a phrase that, incidentally, means something far different for Phaedrus than it does for Socrates. Ast's supplement <ἄν>, wherever one may place it, is accepted by most recent translators, but 'I did not think [as I listened to his speech being read] that even Lysias himself thinks . . .' makes perfectly good sense of the transmitted text. The supplement demands 'that even Lysias himself would think [if the question occurred to him or were brought to his attention].' This refinement, too, makes perfectly good sense, but why insist on it?

a3   καὶ οὖν ('and in fact') would serve quite well as a bridge from the preceding sentence, but the collocation is very rare (D. 445), and it was introduced by emendation. Stephanus's καὶ δὴ οὖν would yield the same meaning and perhaps be easier to derive from the impossible readings of the manuscripts.

a4   εὐπορῶν in the sense 'finding a way' or 'being able' (LSJ s.v. 2) takes a genitive articular infinitive here, perhaps by analogy with verbs of aiming at or striving or with those of reaching and attaining (S. 1349, 1350).

a5   πολλὰ   i.e. many *different* things.
       μέλον is accusative absolute (S. 2076.A).

a6   νεανιεύεσθαι is strong language. One could almost fancy that Socrates remembers when Callicles, using the same verb, accused *him* of acting like an adolescent (*Grg.* 482c4).

a7   ὡς introduces a participial phrase (οἷός τε ὢν . . . εἰπεῖν), which tells us what was in Lysias's mind—his grounds for showing off. Compare 234b3 with note.

a7–8   λέγων ἀμφοτέρως   i.e. in speaking of the case of (not, of course, on the side of) both the lover and the nonlover.

235b1–d3: *Phaedrus insists that no one could make a better or fuller speech on the subject, but Socrates maintains that if he should agree with that, he would be refuted by wise men and women of the past, who even now are causing a speech better than the one he had heard to well up inside him.*

235b1   Οὐδὲν λέγεις, ὦ Σώκρατες is not particularly polite.

b1–2   **τοῦτο καὶ μάλιστα** Καί following a demonstrative makes the following word or phrase adhere closely with it (D. 307): 'this very quality in particular.' The quality in question is τοῦ πολλὰ λέγειν περὶ τοῦ αὐτοῦ from a5.

b2   **τῶν ... ῥηθῆναι** 'of the things that can be fitly said.' Ἔνεστι can mean 'is possible,' because a thing that is possible is a thing that can be (contained) in a situation. For instance at Sophocles' *Elektra* 527 Clytemnestra says of the charge that she killed Agamemnon: τῶνδ' ἄρνησις οὐκ ἔνεστί μοι ('a denial of the charge is not *in* the situation [i.e. is not possible] for me').

b3   **παρὰ** 'in addition to' and therefore 'besides' or 'apart from' (S. 1692.3a). This is an important requirement, and Phaedrus will soon casually abandon it.

b4   **<ἄν>** The supplement—otiose at a2—is necessary for grammar and sense here.

b6   **Τοῦτο ... πιθέσθαι** For accusative of thing and dative of person with πείθομαι, compare *Ap.* 25e5: ταῦτα ἐγώ σοι οὐ πείθομαι, ὦ Μέλητε. The second aorist form πιθέσθαι is more usually found in poetry.

b7   **παλαιοὶ ... καὶ σοφοὶ** Qualitative attributes are almost never linked by a conjunction. Denniston (290) says that most of the few instances that occur involve a suspect text, this being, indeed, the only example he cites without explaining away. As is his custom, Socrates brings in sponsors for whatever positive contribution he deigns to make to the discussion. This is not necessarily ironical; it can provide roots in tradition for deeply held positions he is not ready to defend by dialectic.

αὐτῶν refers to the matters discussed in Lysias's speech.

b8–9   **σοι χαριζόμενος** Socrates clearly implies that there could be no question of his agreeing out of conviction.

235c1   **βελτίω ... ἀκήκοας** Generally speaking verbs of hearing take a genitive of the person or thing that makes the sound ... but an accusative of sounds, words, or, as here, the arguments or other matter expressed in them (S. 1361). The genitive of comparison τούτων refers to the arguments in Lysias's speech.

c2   οὕτως 'offhand' (LSJ s.v. IV). Compare the use at *Grg.* 464b5, where Socrates uses the word to say that he cannot on the spur of the moment give any one name to the art for care of body that corresponds to the political art for care of soul.

c3-4   ἤ . . . τινῶν The connection of Sappho and Anacreon with discourse on love is obvious, but Socrates will certainly not recall, even dimly, any praise of the nonlover from their poems. What he may recall, however, is a notion of ἔρως consistent with the definition of it with which he will begin his treatment. There is surely irony in the adjectives: Sappho was not known for being καλή, Anacreon was not σοφός as Socrates ordinarily understood the term, but here the word need not mean more than 'skilled,' whether in love or poetry.

c4   ἤ καὶ can, but need not, introduce a climax ('or even'). More often it merely adds another possibility: 'or maybe' (D. 299; S. 2862). Rowe found a reference to Plato's earlier works in συγγραφέων τινῶν. That seems to be worthy of consideration. In the *Symposium* Socrates denies the divinity of ἔρως, but the other speakers share with the two poets an awareness of his power combined with what we will eventually find to be a profound misunderstanding of his nature.

c4-5   πόθεν . . . λέγω offers with what follows an example of the figure hypophora, i.e. a reply that anticipates an objection your opponent is likely to make: 'From where, then (as you will ask), do I get my evidence for what I am saying?'

c4   δὴ following an interrogative in a question motivated by what precedes can be connective (D. 210).

c5   πως We say 'in a way,' to take the edge off a metaphor.

    ὦ δαιμόνιε This formula of address is usually reserved for someone whose deeds or words have surprised the speaker so much that he thinks that person in some sense possessed. In addressing Phaedrus, it need evoke nothing more than the "Corybantic" stance he adopts with relation to speeches in general and the speech of Lysias in particular, the way his face glows when he reads them (γάνυσθαι; 234d3); but see second note on 228d6 as well.

    αἰσθάνομαι Socrates' confidence is based on a sensation in his breast, so—just as we can say 'I feel that' in the sense 'I think that'—Plato lets this verb introduce indirect statement.

c6   παρὰ See note on b3.

ἕτερα μὴ χείρω Socrates dwells on quality and, for now, ignores the competition to find who can say πλείω that Phaedrus is intent on promoting.

μὲν οὖν 'certainly' (S. 2901a).

c7   ἐννενόηκα 'I have invented' (LSJ s.v. II).

c8   λείπεται is impersonal (LSJ s.v. B.2). An accusative and infinitive construction follows it here: 'it remains that. . . .'

ἀλλοτρίων 'outside of myself.'

235d1   δίκην ἀγγείου See LSJ s.v. δίκη 2. In *Sym*. 175d the possibility is entertained, only to be rejected, that σοφία can be passed from person to person by physical contact, like water from one cup to another through a wick. Here it seems that one can hold σοφία of some as yet ill-defined sort as if one were a bucket. It is possible, perhaps probable, that in these two words Plato was consciously quoting Democritus. In the introduction to *Harmonics*, Ptolemy's work on music, written by the third-century Neoplatonist and polymath Porphyry we find: ἡ ἀκοὴ . . . , ὥς φησιν Δημόκριτος, ἐκδοχεῖον μύθων οὖσα μένει τὴν φημὴν ἀγγείου δίκην (Diels and Kranz, *Die Fragmente der Vorsokratiker*, 68A 126a): 'As Democritus says, the faculty of hearing, being a reservoir of stories, awaits the spoken word as would a bucket.' Both Phaedrus and Socrates have very full reservoirs and draw off almost countless stories, opinions, and prescriptions of others for mutual examination. See Nightingale's chap. 4 on "Alien and Authentic Discourse" for an account of the flood of voices that pass through them. As she points out (p. 136), ἀκούω and related words, notably ἀκοή, appear 55 times in the *Phaedrus*.

d2   αὖ καὶ Socrates had forgotten the substance of what is now welling up in his breast; 'moreover' he has 'even' forgotten the very thing that Phaedrus enquired about: the circumstances of its acquisition.

235d4–236b4: In the face of Phaedrus's delight at the prospect of hearing another speech wholly different from and even better than the speech of Lysias, Socrates protests that any speech he might make will inevitably share certain commonplaces with that of Lysias. Phaedrus agrees and offers to stipulate certain points.

235d4 Ἀλλ' is the *mais oui* ἀλλά, which conveys assent to or acquiescence in what the other person has proposed by rejecting the very possibility of disagreement (D. 16).

d5 **μηδ'** . . . **εἴπῃς** From μηδ' the negative element goes with the subjunctive εἴπῃς to make a negative command, but the conjunctive element adheres to the conditional clause: 'don't tell me even if I urge you to do so.' The tone of this sentence manages not only to convey Phaedrus's eagerness to move on to the promised speech, but also to suggest that even he can see through Socrates' convenient claim to be dull and forgetful.

d6–8 **τῶν** . . . **ἀπεχόμενος** illustrates asyndeton of the explanatory sort (D. xliii–xliv), since it serves merely to unfold the meaning of the forward-looking τοῦτο . . . ποίησον.

d7 **μὴ ἐλάττω** rings a simple change on πλείω at b4, reminding us that for Phaedrus quantity is at least as important as quality. What Socrates had actually professed to have within himself at c6 was the ability to speak ἕτερα μὴ χείρω.

ὑπέσχησαι 'you have undertaken.'

d7–8 **τούτων ἀπεχόμενος** 'while refraining from the points made in Lysias's speech.'

d8–9 **καὶ** . . . **ἀναθήσειν** Aristotle (*Constitution of Athens* 7.1) says that upon taking office Athenian archons had to swear an oath ἀναθήσειν ἀνδριάντα χρυσοῦν, ἐάν τινα παραβῶσι τῶν νόμων. Ἀνδριάντα tells us nothing about the size of the figure, and the oath does not mention Delphi. Plutarch (*Solon* 25) tried to bring the statement of Aristotle into line with this passage of Plato, but this scheme of that *grand enfant* (as Robin calls him) Phaedrus is surely the product of his own habitual vanity and inclination toward hyperbole rather than of any Athenian legal institution. Life-sized gold statues (if that is what ἰσομέτρητον means here) are out of the question; and why would the Athenians use malfeasance on the part of their officials as an occasion for enriching Delphi? For εἰς Δελφοὺς ἀναθήσειν, see LSJ s.v. ἀνατίθημι II.

235e1 **ἐμαυτοῦ ἀλλὰ καὶ σήν** Compare τεήν τε καὶ Λυσίου at 227b10–

11. That the statues were to be of themselves is in itself enough to rule out any connection with the legal obligation mentioned by Aristotle.

e2   **ὡς ἀληθῶς χρυσοῦς** The exact connotation is no doubt irrecoverable, and translations vary widely. Since the words are paired with φίλτατος, they must express some positive quality that is being attributed to Phaedrus ironically. Rowe's "worth your weight in gold" has the virtue of emerging naturally from the context.

e3   **τοῦ παντὸς ἡμάρτηκεν** Like verbs of hitting the mark, verbs of missing it take a partitive genitive.

e3–4   **οἷόν τε** is impersonal with ἐστί understood (Burnet's comma shows that he took it so). Alternatively, one could remove the comma and take οἷον as masculine in agreement with με and understand εἶναι, parallel to λέγειν, which also makes good sense and is good Greek.

e4   **παρὰ πάντα ταῦτα** i.e. denying himself every point made in the speech of Lysias; ταῦτα, like τούτων in d7, refers to the speech, which we can imagine as still visible in Phaedrus's hand.

  τοῦτο sc. τοῦ παντὸς ἁμαρτάνειν.

e5   **αὐτίκα** 'to begin with' or 'in the first place' (LSJ s.v. II).

e6–236a2   **λέγοντα ... παρέντα ... ὄντα ... ἕξειν** The distinctions in tense are clearly articulated: 'in asserting ... after he has neglected ... which are ... will be able.' For παρίημι in the sense 'neglect' or 'fail to' with the infinitives, see LSJ s.v. II.2.

236a1   **ἀναγκαῖα ... ὄντα** 'which are commonplaces in any case,' i.e. both inside and outside the specific subject matter at hand, which has just been spelled out in 235e5–7, wisdom must be praised and foolishness blamed. For γοῦν, see S. 2830.

a2   **τὰ μὲν τοιαῦτα** will be repeated as τῶν μὲν τοιούτων in a3 before it is answered with τῶν δὲ μὴ ἀναγκαίων in a4–5.

a3   **λέγοντι** It is tempting to understand μοι, but the argument is more likely to be that such commonplaces (ἀναγκαῖα) must be allowed to any speaker on this subject.

a4   **ἐπαινετέον** exemplifies the impersonal and active use of the verbal adjective (S. 2152), whereas ἐατέα and συγγνωστέα just above were personal and passive (S. 2151).

a5   **πρὸς** 'in addition to.'

a8   **ποιήσω ... οὕτως** Socrates has spoken μετρίως, showing himself reasonable. Now Phaedrus as well (καὶ ἐγώ) will show himself reasonable by making the following (οὕτως) concession.

a8–b1   τὸ . . . νοσεῖν is the object of ὑποτίθεσθαι in its meaning 'assume as a preliminary or hypothesis' (LSJ s.v. IV).

236b1–2   τῶν . . . λοιπῶν is a genitive of the sort that characteristically stands at the head of a clause and defines the area or universe of discourse within which the substance of what is said will lie. Consider Euripides' *Andromache* 361–62: τῆς δὲ σῆς φρενός— / ἕν σου δέδοικα ('as far as your disposition is concerned, I fear one thing in you'). Fraenkel (on Aeschylus's *Agamemnon* 950) calls it by the rather unfortunate name "genitive of respect," as if datives and accusatives of respect were not enough. In our passage we might say, 'as far as the rest of the points (as opposed to the one point I granted to you in the μέν clause) are concerned.' See Fraenkel on Aeschylus's *Agamemnon* 950 and KG 1.363n11 for further examples.

b2   πλείονος ἄξια corresponds to μείζω at 234e3: 'more impressive.' εἰπών is conditional.

τῶνδε, genitive of comparison, is deictic: Phaedrus gestures with the scroll from which he had read.

b3–4   παρὰ . . . στάθητι The dedications made by the Cypselids of Corinth at Olympia were a famous example of lavish largess. Phaedrus invites Socrates to be cast in bronze and stood (στάθητι: first aorist passive imperative) beside them. Compare this phrase with the idiom commented on at the end of the note on 235d8–9. There we are looking from the point of view of those setting up the dedication, and the notion of motion toward is in the background; here we see with the eyes of the proposed statue, at rest on its plinth.

236b5–237a6: Socrates now hints that he had never seriously intended to make a speech in competition with that of Lysias, but after an interval of banter and playful threats on the part of Phaedrus, he capitulates and, in preparation, veils his head in shame.

236b5–8   Ἐσπούδακας . . . ποικιλώτερον; The intensive perfect (S. 1947) of σπουδάζω is found in the sense of feeling excitement or earnestness of various kinds. Thompson's "you are seriously annoyed?" is good, since that is the form earnestness takes in someone who feels that banter and mockery at his expense have gone too far. He punctuates the sentence as an assertion rather than a question. The citation of this passage in LSJ s.v. σπουδάζω I.3 is wrong about the construction of the ὅτι clause, which is causal and gives the reason for Phaedrus's attitude.

b5   **σου τῶν παιδικῶν** At 257b4 Socrates will call Phaedrus the ἐραστής of Lysias.

b6   **ἐπελαβόμην** For ἐπιλαμβάνομαι with a genitive in the sense 'attack' (especially of verbal aggression), see LSJ s.v. III.2.

    οἴει δή ('you actually think') exhibits the basic use of δή, namely, to strengthen words, often adjectives or verbs, that admit of stronger and weaker use.

b9   **εἰς τὰς ὁμοίας λαβὰς** For the metaphor from wrestling, compare *Rep.* 544b5, where Glaucon, in asking to be allowed to go back to a previous stage of the argument and repeat a question, directs Socrates to give him the same hold he had before, as a wrestler might do: ὥσπερ παλαιστής ... τὴν αὐτὴν λαβὴν πάρεχε. The significance of ὁμοίας will become clear as the paragraph proceeds and the reader compares it with 228a5–c5. Socrates may have suggested the wrestling figure to Phaedrus by τῶν παιδικῶν ἐπελαβόμην at b5–6.

236c1–4   **ῥητέον ... ἐκεῖνο** It is best to read, following Moreschini and De Vries, δὲ after ἵνα (from T) and to restore εὐλαβήθητι to the text, moving the comma back to follow ἀλλήλοις. The structure will then run: 'For you must speak ... and so that we may not be obliged ... take care and do not deliberately force me.' Εὐλαβήθητι goes closely with μὴ βούλου and commences Phaedrus's warning about 'the low comic routine' (τὸ τῶν κωμῳδῶν φορτικὸν πρᾶγμα), which he professes to want to avoid, but actually stages with no little relish.

c4   **μὴ βούλου** The imperative of βούλομαι followed by an infinitive is often best translated by an adverb, making the infinitive into the main verb: 'do not willingly force.'

    ἐκεῖνο implies that turning another's words against him (LSJ s.v. ἀνταποδίδωμι II.4) was a well-known device in comedy.

c4–6   **εἰ ... ἐπιλέλησμαι** Compare 228a5–6.

c6   **ὅτι** Direct quotations are sometimes introduced by a pleonastic ὅτι, which serves much the same purpose as quotation marks do in our typographical conventions (LSJ s.v. II.1; KG 2.366–67).

ἐπεθύμει ... ἐθρύπτετο δέ (You will find the misprint ἐπεθύμε in Burnet's text.) Compare 228c2.

c8–d3 ἐσμὲν ... λέγειν On the opening page of Plato's *Republic* Polemarchus threatens to keep Socrates from leaving by force if necessary. An all-male social ambiance breeds such forms of humor.

236d2 σύνες ὅ τοι λέγω is quoted at *Meno* 76d3 as well and credited there to Pindar (frag. 94, Bowra). Its unspecific relevance and easy adaptability to such mock-solemn contexts as we have here probably made it a familiar tag.

μηδαμῶς ... βουληθῇς See note on μὴ βούλου at c4.

d5 ποιητὴν is used here to distinguish a writer of speeches from one who would speak extemporaneously. Compare on 234e6. The general rule is that ποιητής means 'poet' and συγγραφεύς 'prose writer.' These two apparent exceptions "prove the rule" in the proper sense of that much abused expression, i.e. they test the rule, but since there are good reasons for their exceptional status, they do not break it.

d6 Οἶσθ' ὡς ἔχει; Phaedrus's question implies that Socrates, in spite of the warning he was given in c9–d3, perhaps does not yet fully comprehend the danger that threatens him.

καλλωπιζόμενος is reminiscent of ἐθρύπτετο at 228c2 (see LSJ s.v. καλλωπίζω II.3). Both there and here the desire to be coaxed is imputed.

d7 σχεδὸν softens the assertion with mock modesty: 'I daresay I have' (LSJ s.v. IV.2).

d8 τοίνυν has its rather weak inferential sense here (D. 569–70): 'Well then (if that is the case), by all means don't say it.'

d9 Οὔκ sc. οὕτω ποιήσω. He will not acquiesce in Socrates' request: 'forget it!' perhaps.

λέγω is present of anticipation, which is found in statements of what is immediate, certain, or threatening (S. 1879). It is emphasized by καὶ δή, which in response to a command or, as here, a prohibition marks something as happening this minute (D. 251–52).

d10–e1 τίνα μέντοι ... ταυτηνί; For μέντοι in impatient questions, see D. 402–3: 'I swear by—now let's see, by whom *do* I swear? By which deity? How about this plane tree right here?' The ad hoc nature of the oath is evident; it is by no means the same sort of thing as Socrates' habitual oath by the dog.

236e1–3   ἦ μήν…ἐξαγγελεῖν   The oath contains a daunting accumulation of negatives. See S. 2760–61 for the distinction between the accumulation of simple and compound negatives within a clause.

e2   ἐναντίον + genitive = 'in the presence of' (LSJ s.v. II.1); the tree is to act as witness to the fulfillment of what is required of Socrates. For ἦ μήν to introduce the content of oaths, see S. 2865. The two future infinitives depend directly on ὄμνυμι. Thompson points out that if the speech Phaedrus threatens not to deliver had been of his own composition, he would have said ἐπιδείξεσθαι.

e4   Βαβαῖ affects alarmed admiration at Phaedrus's ingenuity and ruthlessness.

μιαρέ is a strong term of abuse often used by characters in comedy in addressing each other. Socrates employs it here in a spirit of playful exaggeration.

e4–5   τὴν . . . ποιεῖν   There is a slight brachylogy (S. 3017): 'the constraint (appropriate) for a lover of discourse to (make him) do. . . .' Compare 230d5–e1; this is a different sort of φάρμακον, more an emetic.

e6   Τί . . . στρέφῃ;   'why then do you keep twisting and turning?' (LSJ s.v. ἔχω B.IV.2 and S. 2062a). For δῆτα as both emphatic and connective after interrogatives, see D. 269–70.

e8   τοιαύτης θοίνης   Compare εἱστία at 227b7 with note.

237a5   μὴ does not adhere to βλέπων; it is a conjunction introducing a negative purpose clause to correspond to the positive one that has preceded.

ὑπ' αἰσχύνης is ambiguous at this point; the reader is still able to take it of Socrates' shame at possibly not being able to speak as well as Lysias. That is certainly how Phaedrus would take it. For covering the head in shame at losing, see Boegehold fig. 22 with discussion on p. 29. There Aias is shown on an Attic red-figure cup of the late sixth century covering his head in shame as Athena, by the vote of his fellow warriors, awards the arms of Achilles to Odysseus rather than to him.

διαπορῶμαι 'be quite at a loss' and therefore unable to proceed.

THE FIRST SPEECH OF SOCRATES

237a7–b6: Socrates prefaces his speech with an invocation of the Muses and a brief narrative passage that serves to place it in a fictional setting.

237a7–b1 Ἄγετε ... δόξῃ is a nonmetrical hymn that calls upon the Muses for aid. It is characteristic of such prayers that they avoid offending the gods, while at the same time admitting the limitations of human knowledge, by proposing alternatives as to the favorite residences of the deity being invoked, the name by which he or she may prefer to be invoked, and the origin of those names. Λίγειαι is a traditional epithet for the Muses in the poetic tradition (Μοῦσα λίγεια at *Odyssey* 24.62). Socrates here affects to be unsure whether it stems from their own musical practices (δι' ᾠδῆς εἶδος) or from the musical race of the Ligyans, who presumably served the Muses in some conspicuous way. Indeed, the commentary on the Phaedrus left by the fifth-century C.E. Neoplatonist Hermeias tells us that in battle the Ligyans fought with only part of their army, while the remainder stood aside and sang—a reputation for curious and inefficient military institutions that, as Thompson remarks, is due "to the ingenuity of Greek etymologists." We need not suppose that Plato, if he knew such tales, took them seriously. The Ligyans are mentioned by Herodotus 5.9.3 as inhabiting the hinterland north of Marseilles and can perhaps be identified with the Ligurians of northern Italy. In any case, they are people of the distant west, to whom Plato could attribute odd customs without fear of contradiction. The lack of articles in the phrase δι' ᾠδῆς εἶδος is a poetic touch, as is the tmesis in ξύμ μοι λάβεσθε, which is rightly set off as a quotation by Burnet, although no specific source can be identified. The hymn lays the groundwork for the lapses into poetic tone and manner by which Socrates will affect to shock himself in 238c–d and 241d1. Aristotle (*Rhetorica* Γ 1408[b] 12–20) says that poetical language is permissible in prose either when the speaker has wrought his audience to an emotional pitch that corresponds to it, or μετ' εἰρωνείας, ὥσπερ Γοργίας ἐποίει καὶ τὰ ἐν Φαίδρῳ. The remark is valuable, not only because it makes a distinction that was beyond the discernment of some critics in antiquity, but also for its implication about the intentions of Gorgias as Aristotle saw them. If the elevated tone of this prayer did not reveal itself clearly enough as ironical in the reading, the irony would be given away by its sudden descent into a typically Socratic self-deprecatory joke in the purpose clause at the end.

237b2 οὕτω can serve roughly the same function as the phrase 'once upon a time' in introducing exemplary tales (LSJ s.v. I.4)—which is not to be interpreted as saying that it *means* the same thing as the English phrase but only that it serves the same function in introducing a fable—because it implies that the tale is told as an illustration of something beyond itself. Imagine, for example, a fable of Aesop turned about with the moral at the beginning: the tale itself might then begin with οὕτω, implying that 'thus' or 'in this way" (i.e. in a way that exemplifies the moral) the fox and the crow behaved. Evidence for this usage consists, in the main, of (1) this passage, in which the briefly narrated setting illustrates the sort of human situation that might give rise to the speech that follows; (2) Aeschylus's *Agamemnon* 717ff., where the story of a lion cub raised in the house serves as an illustration of a complex kind of the life story of Paris; (3) Aristophanes' *Wasps* 1182, where old Philocleon, who is urged by his son to tell one of the kind of stories we tell κατ' οἰκίαν, begins οὕτω ποτ' ἦν μῦς καὶ γαλῆ ('once upon a time there lived a mouse and a ferret'); and (4) Aristophanes' *Lysistrata* 785ff., where οὕτως introduces the story of a pre-Christian hermit of a sort—a young man named Melanion, who goes off to the mountains and lives by hunting rabbits, in order to avoid the company of women, thereby illustrating the feelings of the male chorus who tell his story. They shortly give the female chorus a kick. Socrates does not imply that his story takes place in the distant and fabulous past; if he had wished to do that he would have begun with something like the expression ἦν ποτε χρόνος ὅτε . . . with which Protagoras introduces his fable in *Prt.* 320c8.

b4 αἱμύλος is poetic and not common. Plato's only other use of it occurs in *Laws* 823e6, where once again a αἱμύλος ἔρως of young men is in question, a 'crafty desire'—but for snaring birds rather than boys.

οὐδενὸς ἧττον ἐρῶν conveys a very important distinction between this man and the speaker in the speech of Lysias.

b5   **καὶ . . . αὐτό** 'and on one occasion in the course of his importunities he tried to convince the boy of this very point.' Here ποτε is close to meaning 'once upon a time' literally. The same ποτε, for instance, occurs in the passages from the *Protagoras* and from Aristophanes' *Wasps* cited in the note on b2. For a lesson in the importance of aspect, compare ἔπειθεν here, a conative imperfect (S. 1895; GMT 36) that must be translated 'was trying to persuade' rather than 'persuaded,' with the clear, crisp aorist ἔσχετ᾽ back at a8, which must be translated 'got' rather than 'had.' What began to emerge with τοῦ μύθου at a9 is now quite clear: the speech to follow will differ radically in its setting from the speech of Lysias. In that speech the reader was plunged *in medias res* into what seemed to be an ongoing debate; this one will be part of a moral tale, which has been carefully removed from the here and now.

237b7–238c4: Socrates begins by asserting the need to define what we are talking about if we are to discuss any subject productively. Love is defined as a kind of irrational desire, akin to gluttony and drunkenness. In the case of love, however, the object of desire is physical beauty.

237c1   **εἰδέναι . . . βουλή** exhibits asyndeton of the explanatory kind (D. xliii ff.); μία ἀρχὴ in b7 patently called for explanation.

c3   **τὴν οὐσίαν ἑκάστου** 'what each thing is.'

     ὡς οὖν εἰδότες 'so because they assume that they know.' Socrates takes no responsibility for the accuracy of their assumption (S. 2086).

     διομολογοῦνται is more formal and emphatic than will be ἀλλήλοις ὁμολογοῦσιν in c5: 'come to (no) common agreement.'

c4–5   **προελθόντες . . . ὁμολογοῦσιν** They proceed in the σκέψις from this slapdash starting point, and for that they pay the price one would expect: their arguments are full of internal contradictions, and they reach no agreement either within themselves or with each other. With ἀποδίδωμι the metaphor is often from business (paying back what one has borrowed), but here it is from the courts. They must pay the expected penalty for an intellectual transgression.

c5–d3   **ἐγώ . . . παρέχει** This sentence breaks into two members of very unequal length at αλλ’ in c6. The main verb of the second is the hortatory subjunctive ποιώμεθα.

c6   ὃ . . . ἐπιτιμῶμεν   Since ἐπιτιμάω basically means to assess a penalty (τιμή) against a person, it also takes accusative of thing and dative of person in the sense 'rebuke' or 'censure' (LSJ II.2).

c7   ὁ λόγος πρόκειται   "the question before us is" (Hackforth). See LSJ s.v. λόγος VIII.1 for the sense 'matter for debate or enquiry.'
ἐρῶντι ἢ μὴ   Plato frequently omits the second participle in this recurring phrase.

c8   περὶ ἔρωτος οἷόν τ' ἔστι   is a variant of the common proleptic question employing the interrogative τίς: about love, what it is. Here it manages to make ἔρως itself, rather than 'the sort of thing it is,' the subject of the thought. The whole phrase περὶ . . . δύναμιν depends on and serves to define ὅρον.

237d1–2   εἰς τοῦτο . . . ἀναφέροντες   For the force of the prefix in ἀποβλέποντες, see note on 234d2–3. Both ἀποβλέπω and ἀναφέρω are frequently used with εἰς where the context involves reference to some standard—here τοῦτο, the definition that ought to be agreed upon before proceeding.

d3   μὲν οὖν δὴ   Μὲν οὖν marks the transition from talking about the need for definitions to the defining of ἔρως (S. 2901c). Δή, which can also signal transition, merely adds emphasis here.

d5   τὸν ἐρῶντά τε καὶ μὴ   See second note on c7. For the use of τε καί, compare *Tht.* 150b3, where Socrates says if women bore sometimes dolls and sometimes living babies, the principal job of the midwife would be τὸ κρίνειν τὸ ἀληθές τε καὶ μή. English consistently distinguishes one thing from another, but Greek is willing to distinguish one thing and another.

d6–7   δύο . . . ἄγητον   In Attic "masculine" dual forms of demonstratives (see τούτω in d9) are regularly and of relatives and attributive participles (like οἷν, ἄγοντε, and ἄρχοντε here) are often of common gender and can modify or refer to a feminine dual like ἰδέα (KG 1.73–74). How should we translate ἰδέα itself? Fowler, Hamilton, and Nehamas and Woodruff all go with "principles." Nothing with any philosophical precision is to be expected in this speech, and I like Rowe's "kinds of thing," an expansion, I assume, of the simple "things" that De Vries suggested.

d8   δόξα   does not appear in her customary Platonic role as the disreputable half-sister of ἐπιστήμη. We must not look for developed Platonic psychology here; Socrates is after all delivering a speech that fills him with shame (a4–5) and that he will later repudiate.

237e2–238a2   **δόξης . . . ἐπωνομάσθη**   The two participial phrases could be taken as genitive absolutes or as objective genitives, depending on κράτει and ἀρχῇ respectively. Word order makes the absolute construction somewhat more likely.

e2   **μὲν οὖν** marks a transition that is subordinate to that of μὲν οὖν δὴ in d3.

238a2   **ἐπωνομάσθη**   Since you ἐπονομάζειν a name in the accusative to a person or thing in the dative, the name becomes the subject in the passive: 'the name hubris is given to.' The aorist is gnomic (S. 1931).

    δὲ δὴ ('but then') passes to a new point that mention of hubris has suggested (D. 259).

a3   **πολυμελὲς . . . καὶ πολυμερές**   Hybris is a creature of many limbs and many parts; we are reminded of Typhon in 230a. None of the principle manuscripts show both of these adjectives, and all of them show πολυειδές in place of one or the other. Burnet possibly arrived at his text on the grounds that the two uncommon adjectives he printed do appear, one or the other of them, in all the manuscripts he took into account, and πολυειδές, which is more common than either in Plato and suggests itself by the tenor of the immediate context, is more likely to have been substituted by a scribe for one of them than would either of them for it.

    τούτων τῶν ἰδεῶν   See 237d6–7 with note. Here 'forms'—in a nontechnical sense—seems suitable, since Socrates will go on to talk about the shapes or guises in which ὕβρις makes its appearance.

a4   **ἐκπρεπὴς . . . γενομένη**   The word order emphasizes ἐκπρεπὴς. In translating, put it inside the relative clause.

a4–5   **τὴν . . . ὀνομαζόμενον**   'called by its own name,' i.e. that of the ἰδέα of hubris that happens to be ἐκπρεπής in a given person (τὸν ἔχοντα).

a5   **παρέχεται** has the relative clause ἢ . . . γενομένη as its subject. For the sense 'make' or 'render' for oneself (governing the object τὸν ἔχοντα with his predicate ὀνομαζόμενον), see LSJ s.v. παρέχω B.V.

a6   **κεκτῆσθαι** limits ἐπαξίαν.

a7–b1   **ἐπιθυμία γαστριμαργία**   sc. ἐστί or, better, καλεῖται to join these two nominatives and give the first member of this compound sentence a verb.

238b1 ταὐτὸν τοῦτο κεκλημένον 'have this same name'—not γαστριμαργία, of course, but the corresponding γαστρίμαργος.

b2-3 τυραννεύσασα ... ἄγουσα sc. ἐπιθυμία. These two nominative participles will not turn out to be in agreement with the subject of any verb, whether expressed or understood; they constitute a *nominativus pendens* or "hanging nominative" (S. 941). This is a type of anacoluthon that results from the speaker putting the subject of his thought in the nominative case early in the sentence, but subsequently arriving at a sentence form that deprives that logical subject of its grammatical sovereignty. Here grammatical consistency demands that it be put into accusative of respect. The effect is one of conversational spontaneity.

b3 οὐ τεύξεται προσρήματος The relative pronoun can serve as an indirect interrogative (S. 339–40). The subject of τεύξεται must be taken from τὸν κεκτημένον. Plato could have made the sentence grammatical, but less informal and striking, by starting with ὁ δὲ κεκτημένος τὴν ἐπιθυμίαν περὶ μέθας τυραννεύσασαν καὶ ταύτῃ ἄγουσαν.

b3-5 καὶ ... πρόδηλον A much-vexed sentence. I suggest taking everything from τἄλλα to ὀνόματα as accusative of respect with genitive modifiers. A subject (τὸν ἔχοντα) can be supplied for καλεῖσθαι from the context, and the genitive τῆς ... δυναστευούσης will depend on the latent and idiomatic presence of ὄνομα as its internal accusative. A painfully literal translation might be, 'And in the matter of other names that are kindred to these and the names of their kindred desires, it is immediately evident that the man who has it will be called in the appropriate way by the name of the desire that is in control (of him) at any given time.' I take καλεῖσθαι as future middle with passive meaning (S. 809), but taking it as present passive will make no material difference. The distinction between 'other names' and 'the names of their kindred desires' will be the distinction made in the note on b1 between γαστρίμαργος and γαστριμαργία. Socrates actually gives none of the names and only one name of a kindred desire, preferring paraphrases for the most part.

b5 ἧς sc. ἐπιθυμίας.

b7-c4 ἡ γὰρ ... ἐκλήθη This sentence is bizarrely unbalanced: until the penultimate word, it consists of a series of participial constructions in agreement with ἐπιθυμία—one enormous subject with the predicate ἔρως ἐκλήθη (a gnomic aorist) turning up when we had almost given up looking for it. The sentence could be called dithyrambic (see note on d3) in both its headlong, breathless syntax, and the desperate fancifulness of the etymology it puts forward for ἔρως, the word toward which the sentence moves like a musical cadence to a sudden resolution. Denniston (*Greek Prose Style*, 68) uses this sentence as his prime example of periods in which "proportion between the parts is deliberately sacrificed for the sake of a pregnant and striking brevity at the end."

b7-8   ἄνευ λόγου is to be taken with ἐπιθυμία.

238c1-2   καὶ . . . κάλλος Burnet's punctuation rightly connects these words with ἐρρωμένως ῥωσθεῖσα: 'strongly strengthened in the direction of physical beauty by desires kindred to the desire for it.' Of the kindred desires we have seen, only those leading to gluttony and intemperance are named or described, and that is not without significance. In his *Eunuchus* 4.5.6 Terence employs what he calls a 'proverb' (*verbum*): *Sine Cerere et Libero friget Venus* ('without food and wine Love grows cold'), Ceres being the goddess of the crops and Liber the *interpretatio Romana* (a term that scholarship borrows from Tacitus to denote the Roman equivalents for Greek deities) for Dionysus. This proverb was passed on, most influentially through the *Adages* of Erasmus, to the Renaissance and was particularly popular among the Dutch painters of the seventeenth century. The *Venus Frigida* of Rubens in the Royal Museum at Antwerp is a striking example. Moreover the proverb, as a piece of folk wisdom, can be traced back at least into the fifth century B.C.E. On Liber's side, Euripides' *Bacchae* 773 (οἴνου δὲ μηέτ' ὄντος οὐκ ἔστιν Κύπρις); and on that of Ceres, Euripides' frag. 895 Collard and Cropp (ἐν πλησμονῇ [recall 233e2 with note] τοι Κύπρις, ἐν πεινῶντι δ' οὔ).

c2   σωμάτων makes an important distinction: the ἡδονὴν κάλλους toward which ἐπιθυμία was driven in the line above will be revealed later to be open to manifestations more permanent and valuable than bodies.

ῥωσθεῖσα is subordinate to νικήσασα and indicates means.

c3   νικήσασα ἀγωγῇ Translators either shirk translating ἀγωγῇ (Hackforth, Fowler, Hamilton) or translate it by "in its course"

(Rowe) or a variation thereof (Nehamas and Woodruff). That makes sense, but 'course,' meaning, I assume, 'onward movement in a particular direction,' does not seem to translate ἀγωγή elsewhere in Plato (I do not accept LSJ's 'movement' for an occurrence at *Rep.* 604b3, where it would be better translated 'impulse'). The transitive nature of ἄγω is perhaps respected in this noun derived from it. (Remember ἀχθεῖσα at c1 and τὸν κεκτημένον ταύτῃ ἄγουσα at b2–3.) I suggest: 'in guidance,' *ductus* in Ast's *Lexicon*.

238c5–d7: Socrates breaks off his speech, ostensibly in surprise and apprehension at the dithyrambic level of style to which it has risen, which he attributes to the influence of the place and its deities.

238c7   **Πάνυ μὲν οὖν**   Complete assent in reply to a question conveyed by assentient μὲν οὖν is a usage almost confined to Plato and not found before him; here the intensive adverb adds to the sense of enthusiasm (D. 476–77). Of this phrase Denyer says in his note on *Prt.* a4 "people start using it when Socrates starts asking questions." He then quotes an amusing passage from the corpus of Epicharmus, which satirizes the phrase as a philosophical cliché.

c7–8   **εὔροιά τίς σε εἴληφεν**   Λαμβάνω denoting possession by gods, excited states of mind, or—as here—extraordinary faculties looks back to its use with such subjects as μένος and χόλος in Homer. The metaphor in εὔροια is akin to that in 'fluency.' According to De Vries this is its first occurrence in connection with speech.

c9   **τοίνυν**   'well, then,' transitional for the most part, with a slight logical connection to what precedes. Compare 236d8 with note.

238d1   **ἐὰν . . . πολλάκις**   'if perhaps,' an Attic expression (LSJ s.v. πολλάκις III). KG 2.115 derives the usage from ὅ τι πολλάκις γίγνεται, presumably on the grounds that what often happens was felt to perhaps be so on any given occasion. For ἄρα with connective force, see D. 40–41.

   νυμφόληπτος alludes to the scene in which the conversation is taking place (230b7). Nymphs could bring about madness. In the fifth century—perhaps during Plato's childhood—a metic named Archedemus from the island of Thera took over a cave on Mount

Hymettus, decorated it, planted a garden, and had inscriptions carved that referred to him as νυμφόληπτος (Nilsson 1.231; Camp 50). This was a genuine psychological phenomenon and not merely a metaphorical manner of speaking.

d3   **διθυράμβων** The dithyramb seems to have originated in choral song connected with the worship of Dionysus. A number of scraps of evidence make it likely that it played some part in the birth of tragedy. By Plato's time it had become a byword for poetry with forced and self-conscious "rhapsodic" qualities. A look at the extensive fragment of Timotheus (Berlin Papyrus 9875), a contemporary of Plato, will show one why. Dionysius of Halicarnassus (*On the Style of Demosthenes* 7) contains a discussion of Plato's style in the *Phaedrus* that culminates in taking this word as a condemnation of Plato's style taken from his own mouth. The discussion is wholly lacking in sensitivity to irony. Compare Aristotle's allusion to the style of the *Phaedrus* in the note to 237a7–b1, another passage that Dionysius condemns without the slightest awareness of the drama in which it is playing a part.

d5   **Τούτων ... αἴτιος** 'This is *your* fault, you know.' For emphatic μέντοι with σύ, see D. 400. Socrates will repeat the accusation at 241e4, 242b4, and 242d5.

    τὰ λοιπά i.e. the rest of the speech. Socrates intends to persevere despite the danger.

d6   **ἴσως ... ἐπιόν** 'for perhaps the onset may be averted.' In Plato ἔπειμι often denotes hostile rather than simple approach. Socrates refers to the nympholepsy that seems to threaten him. In his commentary Hermeias regards this possible onset as something to be cultivated and thinks that Socrates has warned Phaedrus to be quiet lest it go away. This is interesting, but even as an ironical stance, hardly likely. It sheds light on the attitudes of the wrong fifth century.

d6–7   **ταῦτα ... μελήσει** The personal construction of μέλει, especially when the subject is a neuter pronoun, is common in poetry but rare in prose (KG 1.367).

d7   **ἡμῖν**, placed first for contrast with the gods, is dative of agent with ἰτέον, and therefore the subject in English.

    τῷ λόγῳ is dative of instrument.

238d8–239c2: Socrates continues. Now that we know what love is, we can talk about what help or harm will come to a boy from a lover. A lover is bound to be jealous and will want the boy to depend on him alone. He will attempt to deprive him of other associations, in particular those that might improve his mind.

238d8   ὦ φέριστε "A light tone of parody" (V.) is quite possible, but see second note on 228d6. Plato's readers may have recalled the address of Diomedes to Glaucus at *Iliad* 6.123: τίς δὲ σύ ἐσσι, φέριστε, καταθνητῶν ἀνθρώπων; ('And who among mortal men are you, my noble friend?').

         ὃ . . . τυγχάνει ὄν 'what it really is.' Avoid always translating τυγχάνω with supplementary participle by 'happens.'

d9   δὲ δὴ See note on a2. Here Socrates is passing from the definition of ἔρως to consideration of the ὠφελία or βλάβη it may bring.

238e1   τὰ λοιπὰ is accusative of respect: 'from now on.'

e2   ἐξ εἰκότος συμβήσεται is a variation on the usual εἰκὸς (ἐστί) συμβαίνειν.

e4   παρασκευάζειν To 'make' or 'render' someone or something in a certain state (LSJ s.v. 3). Compare on παρέχεται at a5.

         νοσοῦντι here includes only those suffering from mental disturbances. Compare on 228b6–7.

e5   καὶ ἴσον For καί instead of ἤ linking alternatives, see D. 292.

239a1   δὴ 'therefore' (D. 238).

         κρείττω is, like ἰσούμενον, accusative singular masculine modifying παιδικὰ. This particular variety of *constructio ad sensum* (masculine singular adjective modifying a neuter plural noun) seems to occur only with παιδικά (KG 1.53).

a2   ἀπεργάζεται 'tries to make' (S. 1878).

a3–4   ῥητορικοῦ Later in the dialogue this will become a technical term; here it denotes merely someone who is articulate as opposed to tongue-tied.

a4–7   τοσούτων . . . ἡδέος The syntactical skeleton of this sentence is provided by ἐραστὴν . . . ἀνάγκη . . . ἥδεσθαι . . . παρασκευάζειν. Κακῶν . . . γιγνομένων refers to the bad qualities that might emerge from the boy's circumstances and education, κακῶν . . . ἐνόντων to those (like being βραδύς rather than ἀγχίνους) that are innate to his nature. The difficulty lies in [τῶν]. In the opinion of De Vries, the objections against it are "not insuperable," but he does not tell us how to surmount them. Perhaps he found here the rare and poetic genitive after ἥδομαι, which is contrary to Plato's consistent use of the normal dative elsewhere. On the other hand, merely to delete it leaves μὲν and δὲ crying aloud for a pointed antithesis that is not there. Heindorf's conjecture τοῖς is more than tempting: τοῖς μὲν ἥδεσθαι, τὰ δὲ παρασκευάζειν gives both point and excellent sense. The antithesis will be between the bad qualities the lover finds ready made and those he helps bring about. And τῶν could have replaced τοῖς easily, not only through dittography (inadvertent repetition) of the last syllable of the preceding ἐνόντων, but, more generally, as the last house in an extensive genitive plural neighborhood that extends all the way from a4. Papyrus Oxyrhynchus 1017 (second–third century C.E.) shows τοῖς in superscript above τῶν. This may be an emendation there no less than in Heindorf, but it at least shows that someone in antiquity felt the same difficulty and came to the same conclusion. Παρασκευάζειν has a sense different from its sense in 238e4: 'to devise' or 'bring into being.' The asyndeton is of the "formal" sort in which a demonstrative that looks back to what has preceded is found at or near the beginning of a sentence (D. xliv).

a7 ἤ 'otherwise.' Compare 237c1.

φθονερὸν δὴ See on a1 and 229e6–230a1.

239b1 ἀπείργοντα is a circumstantial participle that tells us the means by which the lover will make himself αἴτιον βλάβης. Understand τὸν ἐρώμενον as its object.

b3 μεγίστης . . . εἴη The sentence might seem complete with βλάβης, were it not for πολλῶν μὲν ἄλλων in b1, but now comes μεγίστης, which is not parallel to μεγάλης, but takes us back to direct dependence on ἀπείργοντα. The text is, as De Vries says, an elliptical way of saying, μεγίστης δὲ (αἴτιον βλάβης εἶναι ἀπείργοντα) τῆς (συνουσίας) ὅθεν ἂν φρονιμώτατος εἴη ('And [the lover must perforce] be a cause of harm by debarring [his beloved] from the most important association in particular, that whence . . .').

b6–7 μηχανᾶσθαι . . . ἐραστήν In Attic writers (Plato, Aristophanes, and Xenophon in particular) verbs of effort sometimes govern a purpose clause with ὅπως ἄν and the subjunctive, instead of the usual ὅπως with the future indicative (S. 2214–15; GMT 348). For ἢ with ἀγνοῶν and ἀποβλέπων, periphrasis involving forms of εἰμί with the present participle emphasizes the adjectival nature of the participle (S. 1857, 1961): 'so that he may somehow be completely ignorant and wholly dependent on his lover.'

b7–8   **οἶος . . . εἴη** 'being such that he would. . . .' In a correlation of τοιοῦτος . . . οἶος the demonstrative is frequently omitted (LSJ s.v. οἶος II).

b8   **μὲν οὖν** The transitional use of μὲν οὖν (S. 2901c) is often found near the end of what modern editors mark off as a paragraph.

239c1–2   **ἀνὴρ ἔχων ἔρωτα** Compare the evocative parallel from the stasimon about the power of Ἔρως in Sophocles' *Antigone* 789–90: ὁ δ᾽ ἔχων μέμηνεν ('he who has it is mad'). One can 'have' love as one has a cold in the head.

239c3–240a8: The lover will prefer someone physically soft and useless in battle. He will also see with satisfaction his beloved deprived of possessions and family connections, since that will lengthen the period of the boy's dependence on him and of his own pleasure.

239c3–5   **Τὴν . . . ἰδεῖν** It is best to begin with the clause at the end, since τὴν ἕξιν and the indirect question about θεραπείαν that follows are objects of ἰδεῖν. Θεραπεύσει will have to be rendered twice, once with its cognate accusative and once with its adverb ὡς: 'What sort of care he will give and how he will give it.' The antecedent of οὗ is the boy whose σῶμα is at issue. The clause ὃς . . . διώκειν, subject of both θεραπεύσει and γένηται, offers an unflattering periphrasis for the ἐραστής. What a compact and complexly interconnected little sentence! It fairly hums with syntactic tension.

c5   **ὀφθήσεται δὴ** 'he will be seen, of course.' For δή marking what is obvious or natural, see S. 2841.

c6   **στερεὸν** Muscularity is implied.

       ἐν . . . καθαρῷ 'in full sunlight.'

c8   **ἱδρώτων ξηρῶν** Hermeias and the *Suda* tell us that 'dry sweats' are the result of dry activities in the gymnasium, while wet ones come from bathing and drinking. This looks like nothing more than a guess, but it may be right.

239d1–2   **ἀλλοτρίοις . . . κοσμούμενον** Compare *Grg.* 465b3–5, where ἡ κομμωτική (τέχνη), which seems to have combined the arts of the beautician and the fashion designer, is spoken of as deceiving (ἀπατοῦσα) by means of the following instrumental datives: σχήμασιν καὶ χρώμασιν καὶ λειότητι καὶ ἐσθῆσιν. In his note ad loc. Dodds distinguishes the first three as follows: σχήμασιν denotes "stays and padding," χρώμασιν cosmetics, and λειότητι (which may be a corruption of plural λειότησι) depilatories. Since χήτει οἰκείων implies that these boys are trying to supply qualities lacking in themselves, presumably because of their coddled way of life, κόσμοις may well be synonymous with σχήμασιν; after all, muscles would be—along with a healthy complexion—their most conspicuous deficiency. This view is lent credence by Plutarch (*Moralia* 51D [*How to Tell a Flatterer from a Friend*]), who cites our passage with σχήμασιν in place of κόσμοις.

d3   ἃ ... προβαίνειν Ἐστί must be supplied twice, once with ἃ and its predicate adjective δῆλα, and again with ἄξιον.

d4   ἓν κεφάλαιον ὁρισαμένους Ast's ἐν κεφαλαίῳ ('summarily') is attractive. With the transmitted text we can say, 'having marked off one heading [i.e. one subdivision], it is ἄξιον to proceed to another.' With Ast's conjecture the notion of being summary fits both with the rejection of περαιτέρω προβαίνειν and with the following sentence, which could stand as a summary of the soft qualities we disdain to enumerate at length.

d4-5   τὸ ... σῶμα is the object of both verbs, θαρροῦσιν taking a direct object in the sense 'feel confident in opposing' (LSJ s.v. θαρσέω 2), φοβοῦνται in the sense 'feel anxious about' (LSJ s.v. B.II.6).

d5   χρείαις ὅσαι μεγάλαι Attic for "the times that try men's souls."

d8   ὡς δῆλον This common expression involves an ellipsis of ὄν, i.e. it originates with the familiar use of ὡς with participle to indicate someone's grounds for an action or opinion or feeling.

239e1   τὴν κτῆσιν What he has, in the widest sense: money, property, and human connections such as family and friends.

239e2   ἐπιτροπεία Compare ἐπίτροπος at c1. There is a question whether these terms are to be taken in a loose, general sense or in their full legal significance. Shorter life expectancy in antiquity meant that legal guardians for minors were needed more often than among us. Many of the private orations that have survived from ancient Greece concern accusations of peculation and malfeasance against men in these positions of trust. It is not unlikely that boys frequently found themselves wards of men whose feelings toward them became more—or less—than paternal.

e5   **πρὸ παντὸς** Where English says 'above all,' Greek prefers 'in front of all.'

e6   **ἄν . . . δέξαιτο** 'he would gladly see.' For δέχομαι in this sense, see LSJ s.v. I.2 and compare *Sym.* 179a4, where Phaedrus uses the same expression to say that the lover would not mind being seen deserting his station in battle by all the world besides as much as by his beloved.

240a1–2   **τῆς . . . ὁμιλίας** puts the matter about as plainly as it could be put in public discourse.

a2   **ἀλλὰ μὴν** often merely proceeds to a new point: 'then again' (D. 344). Having money is allied to but not wholly the same as having the support and oversight of family.

a3   **ὁμοίως** often compares the case at hand with another that is merely implied—here that of the boy who lacks resources.

a3–4   **εὐμεταχείριστον** is, in this context, a rather nasty word.

a5   **οὐσίαν** must be the object of κεκτημένοις, since φθονεῖν would take genitive of the thing. Κεκτημένοις is not singular in the *constructio ad sensum* discussed in the note on 239a1, although that kind of concord will be found again in the following sentence. Consistency was evidently not required in the matter.

     ἀπολλυμένης sc. οὐσίας; a one-word genitive absolute (S. 2072a).

a6   **ἔτι τοίνυν** Either particle alone can mark transition to a new point; together they do so a bit more conspicuously: 'and furthermore.'

     ἄγαμον, ἄπαιδα, ἄοικον Destitution is hammered home with alliteration based on alpha privative. Compare οὔτε . . . ἄφρων οὔτ' ἄσκοπος οὔτ' ἀλιτήμων ('neither stupid nor lacking in foresight nor wicked'), Zeus speaking of Achilles, at *Iliad* 24.157 with Richardson's note ad loc., and Fraenkel on Aeschylus's *Agamemnon* 412. Perhaps such "privative tricola" (Richardson's phrase) in moral and religious contexts emerged from popular rhetorical practice.

     ὅτι πλεῖστον χρόνον 'for as long as possible.'

a7   **γλυκὺ** Plato chooses a word that emphasizes the voluptuousness of the lover's experience more than would the less specifically sensuous ἡδύ.

*240a9–e7: There are evil companions for whom a case can be made,
since they bring pleasure along with their bad influence; but association
with a lover older than himself entails for a boy, in addition to the
practical disadvantages already mentioned, only boredom, disgust, and
humiliation.*

240a9   **ἄλλα κακά**   i.e. other than the ἐραστής.

    τις δαίμων   It may be significant that a δαίμων, rather than a
θεός, brings about this confusion in moral values.

a9–b2   **ἔμειξε . . . ἐπέμειξεν**   The order in which these two verbs stand
invites comment. In Greek, as in Latin, it is common to repeat
the idea of a compound verb, when repetition is needed, by
using the corresponding simple verb, with which the force of the
prefix apparently continues to be felt. A long but by no means
exhaustive list of such sequences in Plato was given by Adam and
Adam in their note to ἀναστάντες in *Prt.* 311a. Here, however,
the compound picks up and repeats the idea of the simple, which
is far less common and not at all the same phenomenon. Leaving
aside cases in which the compound has acquired a meaning quite
distinct from the simple, it must add something to the simple verb
by way of conscious correction, according to examples analyzed
by Renehan 22–27, which usually implies that the simple verb
has understated or underdetermined the case and ought to be
strengthened or rendered more precise. Here I conjecture that
the prefix adds the notion that, in the case of the κόλαξ, φύσις
mixes in ἡδονή "in addition" to beastliness and harm.

240b2   **ἡ φύσις**   This alternative expression discourages attempts to be
precise about the identity of τις δαίμων above. Are the two terms
meant to apply to the same agency? If they are distinct, we must
suppose that φύσις takes no part in making the lover.

240b2–3   **ἡδονήν τινα οὐκ ἄμουσον**   'a kind of pleasure not lacking
in refinement.' Part of the job description of the κόλαξ or the
παράσιτος of later times was to have a ready wit.

b4   **θρεμμάτων**   Θρέμμα is derived from τρέφω and means anything
one feeds. De Vries remarks that it is often used "half humorously
for creatures one keeps," as for the ass at 260b8. Its range of
meaning would cover, but not be confined to, what we speak of as
a pet. The courtesan and her like, then, are domestic animals and
are viewed with more tolerance than that other professional of the
demimonde, the parasite, who is a 'fearsome wild beast.'

b5   **οἷς . . . ὑπάρχει** 'which can be very pleasant' (LSJ s.v. ὑπάρχω B.III).

    τό γε καθ᾽ ἡμέραν 'from day to day at any rate' involves the distributive use of κατά with the accusative (LSJ s.v. B.II.2). The phrase is essentially equivalent to ἐν τῷ παραυτίκα at b1. What is implied is that, as the days pass and time must be filled, these are relatively harmless diversions and do yield pleasure. The implication of γε, however, is that this course of life is second best, and there is a more ordered way to live. The phrase as a whole is accusative of respect, and it illustrates that the substantive-making power of the article extends to prepositional phrases (S. 1153c).

    ἡδίστοισιν We see these Ionic or Homeric dative plural forms here and there in Plato's works, presumably for euphony or elevation of style or both.

b6   **συνημερεύειν** Alcibiades uses this word of Socrates and himself at *Sym.* 217b7. It is as close as Classical Attic comes to "hang out together."

240c1   **γὰρ δὴ καὶ** Δή, if genuine, emphasizes the obviousness of the γάρ connection: 'for, to be sure, even the old saw has it that,' understanding λέγει out of λόγος.

c2   **ἐπ᾽ ἴσας ἡδονὰς** The proximity of ἰσότης elicits ἴσας where we might look for ὁμοίας.

c3–4   **κόρον . . . ἔχει** exhibits a rather brachylogical use of ἔχω: 'holds (the potential for) satiety.' De Vries suggests "admits" (LSJ s.v. A.I.11).

c3   **καὶ** is adverbial with the noun phrase that follows: 'even.'

c4   **τούτων** sc. ἡλίκων.

    καὶ μὴν . . . αὖ 'moreover constraint, in its turn.' This is a new reason for discontent, allied to but distinct from disparity of age and tastes.

c5   **ὃ δὴ** 'the very thing which.'

    πρός 'in addition to.'

c6   **πρός** 'in his relationship with.'

c6–e7   **νεοτέρῳ . . . χρωμένου;** This long compound sentence first states metaphorically the lover's motivation in longing for the constant company of the beloved; then—with τῷ δὲ δὴ in d4—it turns into a rhetorical question that asks, at greater length and with more concrete language, what reason the beloved could possibly have for reciprocating that longing.

c7   ἀπολείπεται is what Gildersleeve (1.167) calls the permissive passive: 'allows himself to be left alone.'

c7–d1   ὑπ' ἀνάγκης τε καὶ οἴστρου provides an instance of explanatory τε καί: the second element, rather than being added to the first, serves as a metaphorical animation of it, revealing the lover as the maiden Io turned into a cow and being pursued by the gadfly of compulsion. Io was an Argive maiden loved by Zeus and turned into a white heifer by Hera, who sent a gadfly to torment her and pursue her all over the face of the earth. Her story would have been known to Athenians through Hesiod's *Catalogue of Women* (now lost) and the tragedy *Prometheus Bound*, attributed to Aeschylus. The incongruity is more than unflattering.

240d1   ἐκείνῳ The lover is free to seek refuge in the dative, since the subject is now the gadfly that pursues him.

d2   ἄγει sc. αὐτόν. The gadfly keeps the lover on the move.

d2–3   ὁρῶντι . . . αἰσθανομένῳ The participles are temporal; the first three are in asyndeton, but the last is joined to them by καί. This seems quite normal to speakers of English, so we might need to remind ourselves that Greek, as well as Latin, normally joins either all or none of the elements of a series by conjunctions. In Greek exceptions occur most often when the last element of a series is, in effect, an etcetera (see 246e1 with note) or when the last element receives special prominence through being longer and more complex than the earlier ones. Both criteria are met here. Αἰσθάνομαι takes genitive of thing perceived, but that should not be confused with the cognate accusative, which we have here; the perception is not what is perceived, except perhaps in a special sense, which is not applicable here.

d3   ἀραρότως 'closely.' Think of a servant attentive to the least wish of his master. The word is poetic, found in tragedy but nowhere else in Plato.

d4–e7   τῷ δὲ . . . χρωμένου; The first thing to notice about the second member of the sentence is that the question is syntactically complete with ἀηδίας at d6. What follows is a series of participial modifiers in the dative in agreement with ἐρωμένῳ in d4, and all introducing reasons for the boy to feel smothered and disgusted. Since he was so conspicuously dative when his part of the sentence began with τῷ δὲ δὴ in d4, it is natural for the participles to revert to that case, even though he has in the mean time done brief service in the accusative (συνόντα in d5, as subject of ἐλθεῖν). At this point we would do well to recall that the speaker has been identified in 237b4 as being secretly a genuine lover. Self-flagellation becomes painful here. For the speech viewed from this point of view, see Ferrari 95–112.

d5 **διδοὺς ποιήσει** Perhaps the subject may have faded from the reader's attention, but it is still formally the relative pronoun in d1, which has as its antecedent the gadfly of compulsive passion, which does not bite the ἐρώμενος (see note on d7). In any case, the ἐραστής, must supplant the gadfly in the reader's mind as the agent acting on the ἐρώμενος in time to reappear as subject of the genitive participles νήφοντος, ἰόντος, and χρωμένου in e5–7. Gadflies never drink to excess. The force of διδοὺς is instrumental as it was in d2.

τὸν ἴσον χρόνον A period of time equal to that which the lover wishes to spend with him, which we were told of at c7.

μὴ οὐχὶ shows "sympathetic" οὐ, which is seen when an infinitive that is negated by μή follows a verb that is itself negated, either explicitly or, as here, by implication, since it is clearly implied that no sort of persuasion or pleasure is going to keep the boy from feeling disgust (S. 2745).

d7 **ἑπομένων . . . ταύτῃ** is genitive absolute expressing attendant circumstances: 'along with other things that accompany that.' It is clear that the boy is expected to derive no physical pleasure from these affairs. His position resembles the unbecoming one attributed to women in nineteenth- and early-twentieth-century Britain and United States by medical theory and popular prejudice: he is thought to endure what is repugnant to him for the sake of what he can gain by it. Compare—and contrast— Xenophon's *Symposium* 8.21: οὐδὲ γὰρ ὁ παῖς τῷ ἀνδρὶ ὥσπερ γυνὴ κοινωνεῖ τῶν ἐν τοῖς ἀφροδισίοις εὐφροσυνῶν, ἀλλὰ νήφων μεθύοντα ὑπὸ τῆς ἀφροδίτης θεᾶται ('nor does the boy, as does a woman, share in the pleasures of intercourse with the man; on the contrary, he looks in sobriety on his lover drunk with desire'), If a boy was seen to feel bodily pleasure, he risked "disapproval as a *pornos* and as perverted" (Dover, *Greek Homosexuality*, 52).

καὶ is adverbial: 'even in speech.'

240e1 **μὴ ὅτι** 'much less.' The clause that precedes is negative and parallel to this one (S. 2763d).

e2-3   φυλακάς ... φυλαττομένῳ When a transitive verb goes into the passive voice, its direct object becomes its subject, but a cognate or internal accusative can be retained as such. Note the accent on φυλακάς; it is not from φύλαξ. The apparatus shows that φύλακας appears in the Bodleian manuscript. There was always a tendency to substitute more common words for even marginally less common ones, but while one could be 'guarded a guarding,' he could scarcely be 'guarded guards.'

e3   διὰ παντὸς καὶ πρὸς ἅπαντας 'constantly in all his associations.'

e4   ὡς δ' αὔτως 'as likewise.' Having mentioned the disgust the boy feels at hearing himself excessively and inappropriately praised, Socrates now turns to his feelings about the blame and abuse he must undergo.
      ψόγους with its modifiers οὐκ ἀνεκτούς and ἐπαισχεῖς provides an additional object for ἀκούοντι.

e5-7   νήφοντος ... ἰόντος ... χρωμένου sc. τοῦ ἐραστοῦ, genitive absolute with temporal force. The first two members apply to distinct situations, the last merely makes explicit what is meant by ψόγους ἐπαισχεῖς.

e6   παρρησίᾳ ... ἀναπεπταμένη 'uncontrolled [LSJ s.v. κατακορής II.2] and open frankness,' presumably about intimate matters.

240e8–241d1: The lover's good will cannot be depended upon. When his desire has cooled, he will regret the promises he made and flee as eagerly as he once pursued. The boy who yields to him is doomed to exploitation and regret.

240e8-241a2   Καὶ ... ἀγαθῶν The understood subject is ὁ ἐραστής, but ἐρῶν is a true participle with temporal force: 'as long as he remains in love.'

e9   εἰς ὃν sc. χρόνον, the time during which he made many promises (πολλὰ is internal accusative with ὑπισχνούμενος, which has instrumental force).

241a1   κατεῖχε The imperfect emphasizes the difficulties he faced: 'he kept possession of' his relationship.
      ἐν τῷ τότε i.e. before the beginning of the time marked by λήξας τοῦ ἔρωτος above, while he was ἐρῶν.
      ἐπίπονον οὖσαν φέρειν 'which was painful [for the ἐρώμενος]

to bear.' Since there is no imperfect participle, the present, which can also denote continued action, must do its work. Compare on 228a7.

a2   δι' ἐλπίδα ἀγαθῶν   i.e. the promises of future benefits he has made to the ἐρώμενος.

τότε . . . ἐκτίνειν   Δὴ is purely emphatic, and the force of the accusative absolute (S. 2076.A) is temporal: 'then—when it is time to pay.'

a2–3   μεταβαλὼν . . . προστάτην   'having exchanged the ruler and overseer in himself for a new one.' Compare Euripides' *Iphigenia in Aulis* 343: μεταβαλὼν ἄλλους τρόπους ('having changed your ways'). This use of μεταβάλλω involves a brachylogy (S. 3017). The expression is a condensed form of 'having cast out one thing and got another.'

a4   μανίας is the earliest appearance in the dialogue of a word that will soon claim the limelight.

ἄλλος   'a different man.'

a5   ὁ μὲν refers to παιδικά. See second note on 239a1.

τῶν τότε   Objective genitive with χάριν. They are the ἡδοναί he has given to the ἐραστής and the promises he has received in return, τὰ πραχθέντα καὶ λεχθέντα of the clause to follow.

a6   τῷ αὐτῷ   'to the same man.' Compare on ἄλλος in a4.

a7–b1   οὔθ' ὅπως . . . ἔχει   'nor does he know how he is to make good on.' Ἐμπεδώσῃ is a deliberative subjunctive retained in a relative clause (S. 2549). The same construction will accommodate the future indicative, which many manuscripts (but not the best ones) show here.

241b1   νοῦν . . . σεσωφρονηκώς   'now that he is in his right mind and in control of himself.' Ἤδη, as it often does, refers not so much to clock or calendar time as to a point reached in a process. At this point we might recall that in the speech of Lysias the ἐραστής betrayed his παιδικά because he has found a new one. Socrates' ἐραστής would seem to have undergone a conversion of sorts—to prudence if not exactly to philosophy.

b2   πράττων...ὅμοιός   'by behaving like his former self.' Translators render this clause in a variety of ways, but syntactically its function is, of course, to tell us the lover's purpose in refusing to meet his obligations.

ὁ αὐτὸς is the same person as ἐκείνῳ, namely, the man he was before he came to his senses, τῷ πρόσθεν.

b3   ἐκ τούτων 'in consequence of these circumstances'; but other interpretations are possible.

b3–4   ἀπεστερηκὼς ὑπ' ἀνάγκης One who has committed fraud or defaulted has been made a defaulter, so we have, as often in Greek, the agent construction with an active verbal form.

b4–5   ὀστράκου μεταπεσόντος 'now that the shard has fallen with the other side up.' The metaphor comes from the children's game ὀστρακίνδα, which is described by both a scholiast ad loc. and Hermeias. Two teams were stationed on opposite sides of a line, and a shard, painted black on one side and white on the other, was thrown into the air. Team A then fled and team B pursued or vice versa, depending on whether the shard came to rest with its black or white side uppermost.

b5   ἵεται . . . μεταβαλών For the middle of ἵημι meaning 'make haste,' see LSJ s.v. II; φυγῇ is dative of manner; μεταβαλών is intransitive, in contrast to its use at a2: 'having changed sides,' to carry on the metaphor from children's games.

b6   ἀγανακτῶν καὶ ἐπιθεάζων 'with angry curses.'
   τὸ ἅπαν is adverbial with ἠγνοηκώς.

b7   οὐκ ἄρα . . . χαρίζεσθαι 'that he ought never, as he now realizes, have gratified. . . .' For ἄρα expressing "the surprise attendant on disillusionment" see D. 35–36. Sometimes we can translate it as 'after all'; sometimes it is better to leave it untranslated.
   ὑπ' ἀνάγκης 'necessarily.'

241c2   εἴη is parallel to ἔδει at b7, both of them in indirect discourse after ἠγνοηκώς . . . ὅτι. Riddell 282 gives an abundance of examples from Plato of the optative paired with the indicative in *oratio obliqua* after a secondary tense.

c5   ἧς is genitive of comparison.

c6   τε οὖν is both prospective and connective: 'so one must both reflect on the points I have made and know . . . as well' (D. 441). The collocation is almost unknown in other writers but favored by Plato.

c8   σιτίου τρόπον 'as is the case with food,' an adverbial accusative used in a quasiprepositional way, like the more common δίκην, which we saw in 235d1 and shall see again in 249d7, and the much more common χάριν, which turns up in the following phrase.
   χάριν πλησμονῆς Compare τοὺς δεομένους πλησμονῆς at 233e2.

241d1   ὡς . . . ἐρασταί is an adaptation of something like the hexameter proverb cited by De Vries from the scholia to *Iliad* 22.262: ἄρνα φιλοῦσι λύκοι νέον ὡς φιλέουσιν ἐρασταί. Socrates, who was speaking in "dithyrambic" style before he interrupted himself after 238c4, now narrowly escapes speaking in hexameters. Bekker's conjecture ἄρν' ἀγαπῶσ' would perfect the meter, but perhaps that is not necessary or even desirable (compare on e1 and 227b9–11). Socrates will again affect to take his narrow brush with speaking in verse as a sign that he ought to bring his speech to a close.

THE SECOND INTERLUDE

241d2–242a2: Phaedrus protests that Socrates has broken off his speech after having dealt with only half his subject, but Socrates insists that he has said enough and announces his intention of leaving immediately.

241d2   **Τοῦτ' ἐκεῖνο** 'There I go!' In this idiom ἐκεῖνο refers to some warning or prophecy that is thought of by the speaker as distant (here Socrates' warning at 238d1–2 that nympholepsy might make him speak in an overwrought, "poetic" manner), while τοῦτο (sometimes τόδε) refers to the fulfillment of that prophesy that has just turned up—in this case Socrates' narrow escape from breaking into epic verse in d1. The expression is colloquial, as is shown by its relative frequency in Plato and Aristophanes and rarity in tragedy before Euripides.

ἂν . . . ἀκούσαις is more urbane than would be a future indicative.

d3   **σοι** 'if you please,' an ethical dative (S. 1486).

d4   **Καίτοι . . . γε** 'and yet I *thought*.' Καίτοι is adversative (D. 556), and γε emphasizes the intervening word (D. 564). The particles help Phaedrus express his disappointment.

αὐτόν Socrates often personifies ὁ λόγος in the sense 'the argument.' Here Phaedrus picks up on his use of it in the sense 'the speech' in d3 and makes the speech the subject of μεσοῦν and, more surprisingly, of ἐρεῖν. Some editors print Hermann's σε μεσοῦν αὐτοῦ, which combines one well-attested reading (αὐτοῦ) with a conjectural σε (in place of γε) to provide a personal subject for the infinitives and participle. Take your pick. I am loath to give up γε, and the notion of a speech speaking, although more striking in Greek than in modern English, ought not be rejected on that account. Compare τὼ λόγω εἰπέτην in 242e3.

τὰ ἴσα 'just as much.' Again we see Phaedrus dwelling on quantity. Phaedrus's reading of the speech of Lysias had come to a formal close, asking for applause, which he received, although not quite in the manner he had expected, in 234d. This speech has ended abruptly in confusion and meets with a complaint.

d6   **λέγων** There is a slight and not very noticeable anacoluthon here. Phaedrus, after the impersonal clause with δεῖ, goes on as if Socrates had been the subject.

ὅσα...ἀγαθά Socrates' speech was conspicuously asymmetrical in comparison with that of Lysias; it was copious in enumerating the disadvantages of yielding to the lover, but paid no attention to the advantages of yielding to his rival, the nonlover.

νῦν δὲ δή marks a turn in a new direction, from the sterile ground of complaint toward curiosity, which will lead to further discussion: 'But since that's how it is, Socrates, *why* are you stopping?'

241e1   ἔπη Hexameter verses, that is. Bekker's emendation ἄρν' ἀγαπῶσ' would turn the proverb at d1 into a dactylic hexameter with no alteration in meaning beyond changing 'lambs' to 'lamb' (for the declension of the irregular noun ἀρήν, see S. 285). The very imperfection of the hexameter in the transmitted text, however, perhaps heightens the impression that some external influence is in the process of turning Socrates' speech into verse. There would, after all, be nothing particularly unusual or inappropriate about his merely quoting a line of verse, especially a proverb, in a speech. Ancient verse forms were stricter than ours, so that both Greeks and Romans were much more sensitive to sequences of metrical feet occurring in prose, even if they fell short of a whole line, than is a speaker of English. Patches of Dickens fall into iambic pentameters, but few readers are aware of the fact. Socrates and Phaedrus, on the other hand, could have been expected to realize immediately that Socrates had begun, in the middle of his sentence, to speak in verse, as if inspired.

e2   οὐκέτι διθυράμβους See note on 238d3.

καὶ ταῦτα ψέγων 'and that, too, in speaking critically.' The implication is that if Socrates should start to speak words of praise, it is hard to say how rapt he might become or what metrical form his speech might adopt. The idiomatic καὶ ταῦτα (S. 947) is to be preferred to taking καὶ separately as emphasizing a concessive participle (S. 2083), and ταῦτα as the sort of internal accusative with a verb of praising or blaming we shall see in ὅσα τὸν ἕτερον λελοιδορήκομεν in e5–6 and in ἃ ψέγομεν τὸν Ἔρωτα at 243d1.

e3   ἆρ' οἶσθ' ὅτι Denniston's remark (46) that "ἄρα, by itself, often has a skeptical tone" encourages us to translate flexibly: 'Do you *realize* that I will clearly become possessed. . . ?' with the emphasis indicating that although Phaedrus ought to realize it, it seems that he does not.

e4   προύβαλες 'you exposed' (LSJ s.v. III). Elsewhere Plato uses this verb for proposing subjects for study or difficult problems to solve (whence πρόβλημα in its mathematical and logical senses).

e5   ἐνθουσιάσω The future indicative here represents a potentiality that will reveal itself in the future. Socrates implies that under the influence of the Nymphs he is bound to become inspired.

οὖν lets us know that Socrates will adopt this summary procedure out of fear of what the Nymphs may do.

e8–242a1   καὶ . . . πείσεται i.e. it will proceed no further but be left to accept the fate it merits.

καὶ οὕτω "and that being so" (Hackforth). On the significance of ὁ μῦθος, see 237a9 and on 237b5.

242a1   κἀγὼ . . . ἀπέρχομαι The present of anticipation can replace the future in statements of what is "immediate, likely, certain, or threatening" (S. 1879). The presence and emphatic position of ἐγώ strongly contrasts what Socrates is going to do with what his μῦθος is going to suffer. For the relevance of this sentence to the question of the dialogue's locale, see note on 229c2.

a1–2   πρὶν . . . ἀναγκασθῆναι 'before having something worse forced on me by you.' The internal accusative with ἀναγκάζω (compare Rep. 473a5: τοῦτο μὲν δὴ μὴ ἀνάγκαζέ με) is here retained with the passive, as it is at 254b1. My translation of τι μεῖζον was suggested by the context.

242a3–d2: Phaedrus begs Socrates to stay until the heat of the day has passed. Socrates not only acquiesces but goes on to say that he will even make another speech, because his divine sign prevents him from leaving and his prophetic soul divines something of the reason.

242a3   Μήπω γε sc. ἀπέλθῃς.

πρὶν . . . παρέλθῃ 'until the heat of the day passes.' Compare this with the construction in the preceding sentence. When πρίν follows a positive main clause and means 'before,' it takes an infinitive. When it follows a main clause that is negative, either explicitly or by implication, and means 'until,' it takes a subjunctive with ἄν. An overview of πρίν introducing temporal clauses can be found in S. 2430–57.

a4   **ἵσταται** 'is standing,' because for a while around noon the sun appears to be neither rising nor sinking in the sky. It comes to a stop not literally but in the sense that a walker who reverses direction comes to a stop of a kind in turning back even though he may never cease to move.

a4–5   **ἡ δὴ καλουμένη σταθερά** Δή is frequently found with τὸ λεγόμενον and similar expressions to imply that whatever words or phrases are either formally or informally quoted are not to be taken objectively and at their face value (D. 235). Here it surrounds σταθερά with quotation marks as a quasiscientific term, not part of the urbane vocabulary of Socrates and Phaedrus, and apologizes for its redundancy in the wake of the ordinary, nontechnical ἵσταται. The effect of the two expressions is to say with no little emphasis that it is not merely μεσημβρία, a division of the day of some considerable length, but high noon.

a6   **ἐπειδὰν ἀποψυχῇ** gives definition to τάχα in its meaning 'soon' or 'presently,' not "perhaps" as Hackforth and Rowe take it. The verb is second aorist passive subjunctive. Unfamiliarity with the form will have brought about ἀποψύξῃ of T, which calls for an impersonal, intransitive sense of the third-person active that is doubtful, at least for Plato's time.

a7   **Θεῖός γ'** Exclamatory γε (D. 126–27). De Vries' observation on περὶ τῶν εἰρημένων διαλεχθέντας in a5–6 that "this wish to discuss the two speeches is interpreted by Socrates as a request for a second speech of his own" is not supported by a careful reading of this paragraph. It seems to be obvious that Socrates is already possessed by the feeling that will produce his second speech, and he pays no attention at this time to Phaedrus's request for a discussion of the two earlier speeches. Phaedrus will be responsible for Socrates' second speech only because he and his enthusiasm for Lysias's speech have brought about everything that follows his reading of it.

a8–b1   **οἶμαι . . . γεγενῆσθαι** Μηδένα is the subject of πεποιηκέναι, which governs πλείους [with its partitive genitive τῶν λόγων] γεγενῆσθαι.

a8   **ἐπὶ** with genitive in the sense 'in the time of' is idiomatic and usual.

242b2   **ἑνί γέ τῳ τρόπῳ** 'in one way or another'; for indefinite sense of εἷς, see LSJ s.v. 4.

b3   **Σιμμίαν . . . λόγου** *Phaedo* (85c–d in particular) shows Simmias as one who is not content until every human resource has been exhausted in getting to the bottom of a question and as a φιλόλογος of a more genuinely philosophical sort than is Phaedrus. For ἐξαιρῶ λόγου, compare *Sym.* 176c3–4, where Eryximachus uses the same expression to say that he leaves Socrates out of account in comparing the relative drinking capacities of his friends.

b4   αὖ in its primary sense 'anew' or 'once more' bears a great deal of weight in this clause.

b4–5   αἴτιός... ῥηθῆναι Dative of thing caused with αἴτιος, in place of the customary genitive, is hard to find parallels for, but evidently what we have in λόγῳ τινὶ here. The infinitive is complementary: 'for a speech being spoken.'

b6   Οὐ πόλεμόν γε ἀγγέλλεις offers a notable instance of litotes (S. 3032). The same words occur in the same sort of context at *Laws* 702d6. Perhaps it was a fashionable conversational turn at the time. I like Denyer's "that's hardly bad news" from his note on *Prt.* 310b4–5.

b6–7   ἀλλὰ ... τούτῳ; 'But how? And responsible for what speech?' Socrates has mentioned a speech, so Phaedrus can ask for further precision about it using a demonstrative.

b8–9   τὸ δαιμόνιόν... ἐγένετο Τε καὶ does not add τὸ εἰωθὸς σημεῖον to τὸ δαιμόνιον as if they were separate entities, but introduces the latter as an explanation of the former. Compare 240c7–d1 with note.

b9   γίγνεσθαι is complementary with εἰωθὸς.

242c1   ἀεὶ ... πράττειν The sense of ἀεὶ is distributive: 'on each occasion when it occurs.'

     Ἐπίσχει governs both με and, as a verb of hindering, the relative clause. Compare *Ap.* 31d3–4: φωνή τις γιγνομένη, ἣ ὅταν γένηται, ἀεὶ ἀποτρέπει με τούτου ὃ ἂν μέλλω πράττειν, προτρέπει δὲ οὔποτε. In this earlier description of the same phenomenon the distributive force of ἀεί is defined and emphasized in advance by the general conditional relative clause ὅταν γένηται.

c2   αὐτόθεν suggests—as does English 'on the spot'—both a local and a temporal sense.

     ἐᾷ is in the present tense because, although the voice is no longer speaking (if that is the proper word for what it does), it still does not allow Socrates to depart.

c2–3   πρὶν ἂν ἀφοσιώσωμαι See note on a3.

c3   ὥς ... θεῖον offers, as ὡς makes clear, Socrates' conjecture as to the grounds the δαιμόνιον had for restraining him. Τι is an internal accusative.

c3–4   **δὴ οὖν** An anomaly of *Phaedrus*, considering the late place in the order of Plato's works usually assigned to it, is that δὴ οὖν is found in it nearly five times as often as οὖν δή, even though the latter tended to replace the former as Plato grew older. Some statistics can be found in D. 468–69. The two are indistinguishable in meaning; both emphasize the obviousness or certainty of what is being asserted.

c4–5   **οἱ τὰ γράμματα φαῦλοι** are people who can read, but barely.

c5   **ὅσον μὲν . . . ἱκανός** As is often the case when μὲν stands alone, it looks forward to antithesis with a δὲ that the speaker feels to be too obvious to need saying: sufficient for myself alone, "but not for others," as De Vries explains. This elliptically antithetical usage accounts for the great majority of instances of μέν standing alone outside of Homer and Pindar. In his normally austere treatise on the particles, Denniston (359) allowed himself the pleasantry of referring to the usage as "μέν the widower," as opposed to "μέν the bachelor," by which he meant the solitary and emphatic usage that is common in Homer but almost completely replaced by μήν in Attic.

c6   **ὡς δή τοι** "introducing a sentence, is a Platonic idiom" (D. 552, where his reference to p. 229 would seem to imply that δή adds a touch of irony, which seems doubtful here); ὡς is comparative, referring back to ὥσπερ in c4. The soul brings to divination skill comparable to that which the barely literate bring to letters: not particularly good, but better than nothing.

c7   **καὶ ἡ ψυχή** 'the soul too,' i.e. as well as μάντεις σπουδαῖοι, whose job it is to be μαντικοί.

c7–8   **καὶ πάλαι** 'a while ago too.' Whether the interval is to be considered long or short is wholly subjective.

c8   **ἐδυσωπούμην** The citation in Plutarch's *Moralia* 748c (*Table Talk* 9.15.2) of the fragment of Ibycus (frag. 29, Page) that follows makes it clear that the line δέδοικα μή τι πὰρ θεοῖς preceded the line Burnet sets off here as a quotation. Plato, as is his custom (see note on 227b9–11), has adapted the verses and, as it were, eased into them, by softening the verb and changing the preposition to its familiar prose form. Δυσωπέομαι conveys an emotion close enough to fear to enable it to govern the construction governed by Ibycus's δέδοικα.

242d1   ἀμβλακών   Find in LSJ under ἀμπλακεῖν.

d2   νῦν . . . ἁμάρτημα   Νῦν δ' carries a great deal of weight. While Socrates was delivering his speech (λέγοντα τὸν λόγον), his prophetic soul troubled him a little (ἔθραξε . . . τι) and he experienced a vague feeling of embarrassment (πως ἐδυσωπούμην), but now he has perceived his error.

242d3–243b7: Socrates maintains that the two speeches that have been made were offensive to Eros, who is a divinity. He must deliver a third in retraction immediately if he is to avoid the punishment of blindness that was visited on Homer and, for a time, Stesichorus, because they had insulted Eros by their treatment of Helen.

242d3   δὲ δή   Here the transition and new direction might be conveyed by 'Well, what do you mean?' Phaedrus is saying, 'You have told me at length that you made a serious mistake, so what *is* it?'

d4   δεινὸν λόγον as the object of ἐκόμισας denotes a physical object, the scroll containing the speech of Lysias. With the strongly pathetic anaphora of δεινὸν, compare that of τίνα at 236d10, which merely conveyed hesitation.

d7   ὑπό τι ἀσεβῆ   'a trifle impious.' See KG 1.525, and compare *Grg.* 493c3–4: ταῦτ' ἐπιεικῶς μέν ἐστιν ὑπό τι ἄτοπα: "broadly speaking, a bit on the queer side" (Dodds), where ὑπό τι can be seen attenuating the force of the following adjective, as it does in our passage. The accusative adjectives agree with λόγον above; εὐήθης can be positive in its connotations, but here it means 'silly.' 'Simple' still has comparable radical ambiguity in English. τίς sc. λόγος.

d9   Ἀφροδίτης καὶ θεόν τινα shows the predicative use of the genitive (S. 1303–5) in tandem with the predicate accusative; sc. εἶναι.

d10   Λέγεταί γε δή gives a rather grudging assent: "He is *said* to be so, certainly," as D. 245 translates. Limitative γε is emphasized by δή. Contrast the Phaedrus of Plato's *Symposium*, whose eagerness to honor the god served as the mainspring of the competition. Apparently he is now more susceptible to the non-eros claims.

d11–e1   ὃς . . . ἐλέχθη   Socrates here attributes his first speech to Phaedrus, who, as he has already said in d4–5, compelled him to deliver it. How was Socrates' mouth 'drugged into compliance' by Phaedrus? By the influence of his Corybantic delight in intellectual discourse? By the influence of the deities of the place to which Phaedrus has brought him? By both?

242e2   ὥσπερ οὖν ἔστι 'as he, in fact, is.' See S. 2956 for confirmatory οὖν.

e4   τοιούτου i.e. κακοῦ.

τε οὖν See note on 241c6.

e5   ἀστεία 'sophisticated.' There is irony and a touch of oxymoron in modifying εὐήθεια with this word.

e5–243a1   τὸ . . . σεμνύνεσθαι stands in apposition to εὐήθεια, explaining in what sense it can be considered 'very sophisticated.' Translate λέγοντε 'while saying,' with a concessive shade of meaning.

243a1   ὡς τὶ ὄντε 'as if they are something,' i.e. something of substance and importance, something as opposed to nothing. When the indefinite pronoun has this pregnant sense, some manuscripts show it with a grave accent rather than leaving it enclitic, and some modern editors, Burnet among them, print it that way. For the usage, see LSJ s.v. τις A.II.5. For a brief overview of the rather chaotic state of practice in accentuation, see LSJ s.v. τις A.III.

a1–2   εἰ ἄρα . . . ἐν αὐτοῖς 'if, after all, by deceiving a few poor souls they are going to be held in honor among them.' Ἄρα is used in a hypothesis whose possibility is represented as having just occurred to the speaker (D. 37). For protases with the future indicative—in what Gildersleeve called "minatory and monitory" conditions—see GMT 447. They commonly express something the speaker looks upon without favor.

a4   Ὅμηρος The tradition known to late antiquity that Homer was blinded because of the anger of Helen (as distinguished from a tradition that he was blinded by the brilliance of the armor of Achilles in a vision that was granted him) may well stem from this passage. Her anger would have had to originate in the mere fact that his epics sent her to Troy with Paris, since Homer's treatment of her, especially in the *Iliad*, is refreshingly free from moralizing; he represents her as something uncanny, and the only words in condemnation of her come from her own mouth.

a5–6   διὰ τὴν Ἑλένης κακηγορίαν The only substantial fragment ascribed with certainty to Stesichorus's first poem about Helen consists of three inoffensive lines that seem to describe her wedding (frag. 10, Page). A fragment that is preserved by a scholium on Euripides' *Orestes* 249 (frag. 46, Page) is more to

Socrates' point, whether it comes from the *Helen* or some other poem by Stesichorus. It represents Aphrodite, angered at being forgotten by Tyndareus in sacrifice, as making his daughters, Clytemnestra and Helen, διγάμους τε καὶ τριγάμους . . . καὶ λιπεσάνορας ('twice married and thrice married, and forsakers of their husbands').

a6 ἠγνόησεν is parallel to ἔγνω in the following line and shares its object, τὴν αἰτίαν.

μουσικὸς 'cultured.' Examinations of invocations to the Muse or Muses in Homer and Hesiod will show that what they provided to the poet was not inspiration in some Romantic sense, but knowledge. The tone here is playfully ironical; no conclusion can be drawn as to Plato's real opinion about the relative degrees of insight of Homer and Stesichorus.

a7 ποιεῖ is a historical present (S. 1883; GMT 33), made more vivid by εὐθὺς.

a8–b1 These are the only surviving lines of the *Palinode* (frag. 15, Page). Testimonia, including *Rep.* 586c3–5, make it clear that Stesichorus originated, so far as we know, the story that the Helen fought over by the heroes at Troy was a mere εἴδωλον. Notice, however, that the second of the lines quoted here by Socrates contradicts the variation on that tale, familiar from Herodotus 2.112ff. and Euripides' *Helena*, in which she set out for Troy with Paris, but was detained in Egypt by Proteus through the whole ten years of fighting. And it is indeed hard to see how any tale such as that could be of much use in vindicating her character.

243b2–3 ποιήσας . . . ἀνέβλεψεν At Sparta Helen was a goddess with an important cult, and in the time of Stesichorus, which was probably from the late seventh to the early sixth century, Sparta had not yet adopted the austere way of life for which it later became famous. Chagrin at having offended such good patrons of choral poetry as the Spartans of his time and a desire to ingratiate himself anew provide a more likely motive than a desire to be free of temporary blindness for Stesichorus's *Palinode*.

b3 γενήσομαι 'I shall prove to be.' Compare 232c8 with note for this well-established usage.

b4 κατ' αὐτό γε τοῦτο i.e. in recanting quickly enough to avoid even temporary blindness.

b6 ὥσπερ τότε See 237a4–5.

243b8–e8: Socrates points out the vulgarity of what has been said about Eros thus far. He says that they must wash it out of their ears with fresh discourse and tells Phaedrus to advise Lysias to do the same. He prepares to deliver his Palinode by linking it delicately to the narrative frame of his previous speech.

243b8   **Τουτωνί** Demonstratives tend to weaken over time. This deictic form should point to something, as if what Socrates has just said were literally hanging in the air. It would be absurd, though, to press the meaning that far; the deictic form is called upon, because what Socrates has just said is closer than his earlier speech, which—since it in its turn is closer than the speech of Lysias—will be referred to with οὗτος in c2.

243c1   **καὶ γάρ** is assertive and connective: 'for in fact' (D.108). This time Socrates ignores Phaedrus's mania for speeches and goes on as if his friend were genuinely interested in the moral point at issue.
ὠγαθὲ Φαῖδρε See second note on 228d6.

c3   **γεννάδας ... ἦθος** 'well brought up and with gentle manners.' Γεννάδας is Doric for Attic γενναῖος (227c9).

c3–4   **ἑτέρου ... τοιούτου** 'another like himself.'

c4   **ἐρῶν ... ἐρασθείς** At 231c5 we noted that this verb is deponent in Attic prose except in the present system; ὁ ἐρώμενος is the beloved, but ὁ ἐρασθείς the former lover.
ἢ καί 'or perhaps,' suggesting an alternative, which is, I assume, what D. 306 means by "or again."
λεγόντων 'as we say,' in agreement with ἡμῶν.

c5   **μεγάλας ... ἀναιροῦνται** See note on 233c1–5.

c6–7   **πῶς ... ἡγεῖσθαι** Οὐκ must be taken with οἴει (rather than with ἄν ... ἡγεῖσθαι), and πῶς οὐκ οἴει will be needed again with πολλοῦ ... δεῖν in c8. The condition is mixed: 'for if someone should happen to hear [c3] ... how can you fail to think that he would suppose [c7] ... and can you doubt that he would be far from [c8]. ...' The subject of the infinitives throughout is the anonymous gentleman of c3.

c8   **οὐδένα** The negative element must be taken with ἑωρακότων; the ἕνα element with ἐλεύθερον ἔρωτα.
πολλοῦ δ' ἂν δεῖν For the idiom, see LSJ s.v. δέω (B) 2.

243d1   **ἅ ... Ἔρωτα** The verb of blaming takes both a direct object and an internal accusative. The clause as a whole is an internal object of ὁμολογεῖν.

d3 **Τοῦτον** i.e. the imaginary, well-bred eavesdropper of c3. For accusative of person before whom shame is felt, see LSJ s.v. αἰσχύνω B.II.3.

   τοίνυν See note on 236d8.

d4 **οἷον** apologizes for the metaphor: 'as it were.'

d6 **ἐκ τῶν ὁμοίων** is hard. It seems clear that *ceteris paribus*, the interpretation of older editors (as seen in e.g. Thompson) will not do; it would be merely distracting if Socrates were to imply that his message to Lysias does not apply if other things are not equal. What other things? I can see nothing better than the solution Fraenkel gives in his note on Aeschylus's *Agamemnon* 1423: "Here, too [i.e. in our passage of *Phaedrus*], the meaning is 'under the same conditions on the other side,' so that ἐκ τῶν ὁμοίων χαρίζεσθαι comes very near to an ἀντιχαρίζεσθαι." Since ἀντιχαρίζεσθαι means 'to show kindness in return,' the sentence would direct Phaedrus to tell Lysias to tell the boy that he should reciprocate in like manner the kindness he has been shown by an ἐραστής, and the sense of ἐκ will be that of LSJ s.v. III.8, where it with its following genitive takes the place of an adverb: here 'similarly.'

243e2 **Τοῦτο μὲν πιστεύω** The particle emphasizes a contrast with an unexpressed antithesis: 'This I believe (but I have no such confidence in other propositions).' See note on 242c5.

   ἕωσπερ ἄν ... εἶ 'as long as you are the man you are.' Socrates alludes to his characterization of Phaedrus in 242a–b. For the temporal clause, see S. 2423b.

e4 **ὁ παῖς** The παῖς of 237b2 and b7.

e5–6 **καὶ ... ἐρῶντι** Ὤν is causal; χαρισάμενος is supplementary with φθάσῃ (S. 2096).

e7–8 **Οὗτος ... βούλῃ** It is hard to take Phaedrus as merely meaning that Socrates can evoke this product of his imagination at will. The pervasive tone of erotic badinage between them surely allows us to take Phaedrus as meaning that he will always be there to fulfill in reality the role of the boy in the situation imagined in 237b.

COMMENTARY: PART II

THE PALINODE

THE KINDS OF MADNESS

243e9–244d5: The Palinode begins: madness cannot without qualification be thought a bad thing. Prophecy made in a state of madness at Delphi and Dodona has benefited Greece, and men of old showed that they distinguished this kind of prophecy from the rational kind by the names they gave them, although men of later generations have obscured this distinction through bad taste and vanity.

243e9   τοίνυν   Compare 243e3 and 243d3, and see note on 236d8.

244a1–3   **Φαίδρου . . . Ἱμεραίου**   Identification of Phaedrus in official style, i.e. with the name of his father and his deme, brings a touch of mock-solemnity to the opening of Socrates' Palinode. It also leads into an identification of Stesichorus in terms that are convenient for Socrates' rhetorical strategy. Εὔφημος is one of five names for the poet's father that survive in the ancient tradition, and it is easy to see why Plato chose it—if, indeed, he did not, as has been suggested, invent it. He was certainly as conscious of the relevance of the verb εὐφημέω to Socrates' intentions at this point of the dialogue as he was of the relevance of the noun ἵμερος, which is evoked by the name of Stesichorus's home city Himera, to the theme of both the speech to come and the dialogue in general (see 251c in particular). Socrates, in typical fashion, disclaims personal responsibility for both his speeches. For the implication that Phaedrus was the real author of his first speech, see 242e1 with note.

a3   **λεκτέος**   For the personal and passive construction of the verbal adjective, see S. 2151. The subject is λόγος of ὃν . . . λέγειν in the line above, which is quite distinct in meaning from λόγος to follow in this line, which forms part of a direct quotation from the first line of Stesichorus's *Palinode*, but here it will be 'the speech' rather than 'the story' that is not true. (Since this is a quotation from poetry, we can add the definite article in our translation of λόγος.)

a4   **παρόντος ἐραστοῦ**   Not necessarily in the flesh; the notion of physical presence has been weakened to mere availability: 'in the picture.'

a5   **διότι δή** 'just because.' For ὅτι δή implying that the reason given is inadequate, see D. 231.

a6   **ἁπλοῦν** is predicate adjective to the articular infinitive phrase: 'something simple,' a thing that is, as De Vries put it, "true without qualifications or distinctions."

    νῦν δὲ frequently, as here, opens the sentence that follows a contrary-to-fact condition: 'but as it is.'

a7–8   **θείᾳ . . . διδομένης** Since μέντοι "is normally a balancing adversative and seldom goes so far as to eliminate, or seriously invalidate, the opposed idea" (D. 405), it is easy to see how it could develop a limiting sense: 'through madness (not all madness but) the madness that is a divine gift, at any rate.'

a8   **ἤ τε . . . αἵ τ'** For repeated τε as a particularly close way to bind two phrases into one concept, see KG 2.243.

244b1   **ἱέρειαι** Homer says nothing of priestesses at Dodona. The sounds made by the rustling leaves of an oak (*Odyssey* 14.327–28 = 19.296–97) were interpreted there, presumably by the Selloi (or perhaps Helloi), priests whom Achilles mentions in *Iliad* 16.234–35, along with the memorable information that they slept on the ground and did not wash their feet—no doubt taboos and not evidence of rustic manners.

    πολλὰ δὴ καὶ καλά English has no objection to saying 'many fine things,' but Greek prefers to join the plural of πολύς to another adjective with a conjunction. Usually one should simply translate the Greek idiom into the English, but here the added emphasis given to πολλά by δὴ (D. 205) might be transmitted by a litotes: 'no small number of fine things.' Compare 234e3 and note.

b1–2   **ἰδίᾳ τε καὶ δημοσίᾳ** The oracles were consulted sometimes by representatives of cities in an official capacity, as in, for instance, many incidents narrated by Herodotus, but sometimes by individuals in a private capacity, as by Chaerephon in his famous question about Socrates (*Ap.* 21a) or by Xenophon, at the urging of Socrates, about his contemplated enlistment in the forces of Cyrus (*Anabasis* 3.1).

b2   **τὴν Ἑλλάδα** Accusative of person or persons affected as well as of the thing done may be found after ἐργάζομαι, which belongs to a class of verbs dealt with in S. 1622.

b2–3   **βραχέα ἢ οὐδέν** 'little or—rather—nothing.' As Dodds argues in *The Greeks and the Irrational* (chap. 3, n41), the implication is not that the priestesses sometimes gave brief, jejune oracles in moments of sobriety. They gave none in that state.

b3   **Σίβυλλάν** Plato and Aristophanes (*Peace* 1095) use this name in the singular; it is only later that the lady multiplies, and writers begin to speak of the Sibyl of such-and-such a place.

b4   **μαντικῇ χρώμενοι . . . προλέγοντες** Both participles express means, with προλέγοντες in the lead: 'by making many predictions to many people by the use of the mantic art.'

b5   **ὤρθωσαν** sc. αὐτούς out of πολλοῖς. The aorist is gnomic.
     μηκύνοιμεν ἄν For the combination of a future-less-vivid apodosis with a future-more-vivid protasis, see GMT 505 and S. 2326d. This example, I should think, falls into Goodwin's class in which the optative is merely a "softened" substitute for the future indicative.

b6   **τόδε . . . ἐπιμαρτύρασθαι** 'yet the following point ought to be put in evidence,' literally 'ought to be deposed to'—lawyer's language. Adversative μὴν usually "balances, implying that a fact coexists with another fact opposed to it: 'yet,' 'however'" (D. 334). Here the need to provide additional information is balanced against the futility of piling up examples of what everyone agrees to be so.

b7   **τιθέμενοι** shows us the imperfect use of the present participle again (228a7). An aorist participle would make this process too sudden and delimited; the men of old gave names over an indefinite period of time, coterminous with that envisioned by the imperfect ἡγοῦντο. Contrast ἔθεντο in c4 and ἐκάλεσαν in c5, where the giving of particular names, μανική and μαντική, is in question.

244c1–2   **οὐ γὰρ ἄν . . . ἐκάλεσαν** For the sake of clarity, 'otherwise' can often be supplied in lieu of a protasis for contrary-to-fact sentences that stand alone as this one does.
     κρίνεται 'is expounded' (LSJ s.v. II.5).
     αὐτὸ τοῦτο τοὔνομα i.e. μανία.

c2   **ἐμπλέκοντες** 'Implanting' might make a more easily apprehensible metaphor in English; LSJ abandons metaphor and suggests "connecting."

c2–3   **ὡς καλοῦ ὄντος** sc. μανίας: 'on the grounds that madness is a fine thing,' explaining οὕτω νομίσαντες. The same shift in gender has occurred by which masculine or feminine subjects often lead to neuter predicates in Plato, e.g. justice (δικαιοσύνη) is a good thing (ἀγαθόν), and the like.

c3   **θείᾳ μοίρᾳ** See 230a3–6 and note. Hackforth's "by divine dispensation" would do.

c4   **ἔθεντο** 'they assigned [the name] μανική.' See τιθέμενοι at b7 with note.

       οἱ δὲ νῦν 'but the moderns.' Socrates seems to divide history into only two periods in this passage: οἱ παλαιοί (b6) and οἱ νῦν. We might have expected οἱ ὕστεροι, but it is always tempting to attribute bad taste to one's contemporaries or immediate predecessors. Before long we shall meet posterity, the third group required by this simple scheme: τοὺς ἐπιγιγνομένους at 245a4–5.

c4–5   **τὸ ταῦ . . . ἐκάλεσαν** Plato's fantastical etymologies differ in the earnestness with which they are offered. This one had other adherents, and Plato may have thought it true. But the tripartite origin that will be advanced for οἰωνιστική in c7–d1, like that we shall find for ἵμερος in 251c6–7, are in his best vein of straight-faced parody.

c5–d1   **ἐπεὶ καὶ . . . καλοῦσιν** Take ἐπεὶ in a causal sense and closely with καὶ, since this sentence merely adds another case of "the moderns" foolishly (ἀπειροκάλως) changing the name of a kind of prophecy. It is best to observe the comma Burnet prints after ἐμφρόνων and take τήν with a τέχνην supplied from τῇ καλλίστῃ τέχνῃ in c1 and parallel to μαντικήν (τέχνην) in the preceding sentence. (If you are bent on removing the comma and taking τήν with ζήτησιν, you might try accepting Stephanus's ποιουμένην [passive] and πορίζομένην, but I do not recommend it. The distinction between the two kinds of prophetic τέχνη is essential to the argument.) "Insight" is De Vries' useful suggestion to translate νοῦν.

c6–7   **τῶν ἄλλων σημείων** The entrails of sacrificed animals, for instance.

c8   **ἱστορίαν** denotes either the activity of research or its product; 'data' might do here. Socrates says that because sane men deliberately (ἐκ διανοίας) furnish themselves (πορίζομένων) with insight and data by means of human thought (ἀνθρωπίνη οἰήσει), in the past they combined the words for insight, data, and thought and called the resulting process οἰονοϊστική. In order to lend plausibility to his assertion that this was the original form of οἰωνιστική, he keeps the real etymology of that word out of sight by using ὀρνίθων in c6, thereby avoiding οἰωνοί, the normal word for birds of omen. It is not wholly clear just how the moderns can be accused of putting on airs (σεμνύνοντες) by bringing in the omega, but it may have to do with omega being an Ionic letter in use but not yet officially adopted in Athens at any plausible dramatic date we can assign to *Phaedrus*.

244d2–5   ὅσῳ . . . γιγνομένης   No causal connection pertains between these two assertions, only a likeness in the degree of difference involved in each of them. The subject that began at b6 is being brought to a close in a manner more rhetorical than logical. The word order at the end of the sentence is very artful, designed to contrast μανία with σωφροσύνη in a way that appears paradoxical until Socrates resolves the paradox by playing the divinity card. For δὴ οὖν ('and so, clearly . . .'), see note on 242c3–4.

244d5–245a8: Socrates adds a second variety of beneficial madness, prophetic frenzy that reveals to the sufferer purifications and rites to cure illness, and a third, madness from the Muses that possesses poets and distinguishes them from poetasters.

244d5   ἀλλὰ μὴν is progressive, "marking a new stage in the march of thought" (D. 344): 'and then.'

νόσων... πόνων are objective genitives, depending on ἀπαλλαγὴν far away in e1. The resources of Greek word order allow the sentence to be introduced with the ideas of illness and suffering, its emotional subjects.

d6–7   ἅ... γενῶν   Put a comma after γενῶν. The neuter plural relative pronoun refers to antecedents of both masculine and feminine gender. Editors have added various verbs—such as ἦν as a supplement or ἔνι (= ἔνεστι) as an emendation of ἔν—to the text, but surely a verb can be understood, a liberty that is rendered easier, as Thompson saw, by the poetic resonance of the whole phrase, which recalls Euripides' *Phoenissai* 934: Κάδμου παλαιῶν Ἄρεος ἐκ μηνιμάτων ('from the ancient wrath of Ares against Cadmus'). We need not suppose that Plato's readers would have remembered this specific line; they would have perceived that something poetic was afoot through the legendary associations of the diction and the word order of παλαιῶν ἐκ μηνιμάτων. Students who come to Greek from studying Latin may accept this as normal, although it is quite rare in Greek prose. See KG 1.554–5. As De Vries points out, τῶν makes it clear that it is the famous families of legend that are in question, but Plato is deliberately unspecific: ποθὲν discourages curiosity about the origin of these bloodguilts, and τισι denies interest in just which families are involved.

d7   **οἷς ἔδει** Remove the comma before these words. They must be taken closely with the two participles that precede and supplemented mentally with αὐτὴν προφητεῦσαι. These are the particular members of the families in whom Μανία must reside and to whom she must prophesy. I personify her to point out that, while prophetic madness operated through priestesses and poetic madness will be seen to use poets for her ends, here the goddess is her own agent and operates directly on the sufferer. For this second kind of μανία, and an interpretation of this sentence that I found convincing enough to follow in most of my recommendations here, see Linforth's "Telestic Madness." The changes I made in Burnet's punctuation left the two key words μανία and ἀπαλλαγὴν at the head of their clauses, where they belong.

244e1–2   **καταφυγοῦσα . . . λατρείας** See LSJ s.v. καταφεύγω 3. Θεῶν is an objective genitive with both accusatives; λατρείας covers any sort of service to the gods from ordinary sacrifice to Dionysian or Corybantic rites with music, dancing, and extreme emotional excitement. Socrates could refer to his whole way of life as τὴν τοῦ θεοῦ λατρείαν (*Ap.* 23c1).

e2   **ἐξάντη** 'out of danger.' The word is used in the Hippocratic writings to indicate that a patient is past the crisis of a disease.

e3   **[ἑαυτῆς]** should probably be accepted into the text and taken with ἔχοντα in the sense and construction of μετέχοντα: 'having a share of her.' For Plato's boldness in using the partitive genitive with transitive verbs, see Dodds on *Grg.* 514a5–8. Linforth points out that, since Μανία is personified and an active presence in the sentence, the usual τὸν ἑαυτὴν ἔχοντα would make the absurd suggestion that he was her husband.

e4   **τῷ . . . κατασχομένῳ** Ὀρθῶς recalls the important distinction made by θείᾳ μέντοι δόσει διδομένης in a7–8 and repeated with ὅταν θείᾳ μοίρᾳ γίγνηται at c3. Κατασχομένῳ: 'possessed.' This use of the second aorist middle of ἔχω and its compounds with passive meaning is common in Homer but quite rare in Attic. See Barrett on Euripides' *Hippolytus* 27.

245a2   **κατοκωχή τε καὶ μανία**   Explanatory τε καί. See note on 240c7–d1.

ἁπαλὴν καὶ ἄβατον   To be possessed by the Muses a soul must be virginal and free from the hardening effect of previous impressions.

a3–4   **κατά . . . ποίησιν**   'in conformity with choral song and other forms of poetry.' After ἐκβακχεύουσα, which connotes the frenzy of inspiration, this phrase adds the formal requirements of art, the τέχνη of a6, which even the Μανία of the Muses must respect and allow to inform her inspiration.

a6   **ποιητικὰς θύρας**   In the absence of the article we cannot translate 'the gates of poetry'; Plato may have used the plural because he was thinking, as De Vries suggests, of separate poetic forms, or because he thought of the initiation of each composition as a fresh approach to 'poetic gates.'

a6–7   **πεισθεὶς . . . ἐσόμενος**   Πείθω, meaning 'convince' with ὡς, is followed by a substantive clause (usual) or—as here—by a participle (KG 2.9). Since πεισθεὶς adds little to what ὡς + participle alone would convey, some editors and commentators would delete it, but Plato did not pay by the word. Socrates is reporting what he conjectures to be in the mind of the would-be poet, and ἄρα indicates his skepticism as to its validity (D. 38): 'no doubt.'

a7–8   **ἀτελὴς . . . ἠφανίσθη**   The adjective is used proleptically; i.e. it describes the subject as it will be as a result of the action of the verb, as if ἠφανίσθη [a gnomic aorist] ὥστε ἀτελὴς εἶναι had been written. Compare the last example in S. 1579. Plato may have borrowed the notion of *furor poeticus* from Democritus, but he also may have developed it independently. Elsewhere (e.g. *Ap.* 22a–c) he shows it less respect and declares that the poet says many fine things under its influence, but does not know what he is saying. That point of view is not denied here, but a positive, educational effect that can be attributed to his poems is emphasized instead. The moral objections to poetry in Plato's *Republic* would, on the other hand, be harder to reconcile with its treatment in this passage.

245b1–c4: We must not fear an argument that says that the affection of the sane man ought to be preferred to that of the madman, unless it can show that love has not been sent by the gods to benefit the lover and the beloved. Our job will be to show that the lover's madness is a supremely beneficent gift from the gods; and we must begin by knowing the truth about the soul.

245b1   μέν contrasts many καλὰ ἔργα with an unspoken antithetical thought about the few or no αἰσχρὰ ἔργα of divine madness.

b2–3   ὥστε . . . φοβώμεθα When ὥστε introduces an imperative or a volitive or (as here) prohibitory subjunctive, the clause will be independent, and ὥστε can be translated 'and so' (S. 2275).

b3–4   δεδιττόμενος . . . φίλον The idea of utterance predominates over the idea of fear (perhaps because the subject is λόγος) and brings about indirect discourse: 'frighten by saying that.' The pleonasm displayed in πρὸ τοῦ κεκινημένου . . . προαιρεῖσθαι is a common device to secure emphasis. For κεκινημένος in the sense 'emotionally excited,' see LSJ s.v. κινέω B.2.

b4–5   ἀλλὰ . . . νικητήρια Τόδε refers to the content of the clause ὡς . . . ἐπιπέμπεται, ἐκείνῳ refers to the content of the clause ὡς . . . φίλον. The subject of δείξας φερέσθω is λόγος. For πρός + dative meaning 'in addition to,' see S. 1695.2.

b6   ἐκ θεῶν ἐπιπέμπεται Ἐκ in place of ὑπό when the agent is an originator is common in Herodotus and Attic tragedy but rare in Attic prose (KG 1.460). Ἐπιπέμπω seems to be the *vox propria* for occasions when gods send things to men, as in *Ap.* 31a7 and *Phd.* 62c7. Accordingly, the god should have his uppercase epsilon here.

b7   ἡμῖν δὲ ἀποδεικτέον 'but it is our job to show,' i.e. the job of Socrates and Phaedrus on this occasion, or—more generally—of anyone who rejects the λόγος of b2–6. What Socrates has said in b1–6 has made the general point that μανία is not necessarily a bad thing; now he and Phaedrus must take up the task he pointedly refrained from addressing in his first speech: they must show that ἔρως (τοιαύτη μαμία of c1) has great benefits to bestow. This distinction is pointed up by δὲ, which looks back to μέν in b1.

    ἐπ' εὐτυχίᾳ τῇ μεγίστῃ As in the case of ἐπ' ὠφελίᾳ a few lines above, the motive of an agent is expressed by ἐπί + dative (S. 1689.2c).

245c1   **παρὰ θεῶν** Παρά in place of ὑπό because the agent's action is handing something over into another's use. Compare use of ἐκ in note on b6.

c2   **δεινοῖς μὲν . . . σοφοῖς δὲ** The δεινοί are those whose superficial cleverness keeps them from seeing what matters; in their company the σοφοί shed the negative connotations they had at 229c6 and become 'wise' in a positive sense, people of insight and settled judgment.

c3   **φύσεως πέρι** follows τἀληθές. For the omission of the article in prepositional phrases, see S. 1128. For its omission with ψυχῆς, see S. 1135.
    θείας τε καὶ ἀνθρωπίνης modifies ψυχῆς rather than φύσεως, as the myth ahead will show.

c3–4   **ἰδόντα . . . ἔργα** What is involved in knowing the φύσις of a thing will be explained more fully and circumspectly in 270c10–d7.

c4   **ἀρχὴ . . . ἥδε** As the use in c1 shows, ἀπόδειξις is the entire speech, not just the deductive demonstration that follows immediately. Ἥδε is the subject; ἀρχή, as the predicate, lacks an article. This grammatical principle can often help the reader to stay on track through Plato's more closely reasoned demonstrations, such as the paragraph that is about to begin.

THE SOUL IN DEDUCTION
AND SIMILITUDE

245c5–246a2: Socrates prefaces his myth with a deductive demonstration that soul is immortal. The ever-moving, he says, is immortal, but nothing but the self-moving is ever-moving. The self-moving is, therefore, the origin or first principle of all other motion, and a first principle can neither come to be nor suffer extinction. But self-motion is an essential and unique quality of soul, so soul neither comes to be nor suffers extinction.

245c5–e2 **Ψυχὴ . . . γενήσεται** Denniston (*Greek Prose Style*, 3–5) compares this passage with the twelfth fragment of Anaxagoras. The brevity and syntactical directness of its sentences contribute to what he calls the "statuesque grandeur" of this prose. The pervasive repetition of certain words, such as ἀθάνατος, κινέω, ἀρχή, and their cognates, does not, however, yield an effect of Gorgianic wordplay, but of being simply, in Swift's well-known phrase, "proper words in proper places." Certain subjects are being discussed at some length, and no attempt is made to disguise that fact by varying the language in which they are expressed. The repetitions, to quote D. on the Anaxagoras fragment, "flood and permeate, rather than strike, the ear."

c5 **Ψυχὴ πᾶσα** can mean 'every soul' or 'all soul,' and debate over which meaning Plato intended has been carried on since antiquity. All soul, it is maintained, could be immortal in ways that allow for the extinction of the individual soul. The feeling in the present paragraph tends toward the collective sense of ψυχή, because overarching principles of universal application are being discussed, but the myth proper will follow with its individual souls that are clearly immortal. Perhaps the distinction is, as Hackforth says, "not here before Plato's mind." Scholars compare Plato's proof with a passage from the sixth-century thinker Alcmaeon of Croton. He is reported by Aristotle (*De anima* A 405^a 29ff.) to have said that the soul is immortal, because it is similar τοῖς ἀθανάτοις, and that this is true of it, because it is constantly moving and everything θεῖα is constantly moving— moon, sun, stars, and the heavens as a whole. We shall see that Plato, assuming that he was influenced by this view, added to it the very important distinction between self-motion and motion initiated from outside.

c5–6   **τὸ δ' ἄλλο ... κινούμενον** The thing, that is, that occupies an intermediate position in a chain of transmitted motion.

c7   **μόνον δὴ** 'so nothing but'; δὴ marks the obviousness of this conclusion and connects it with what precedes. See notes on 229e6–230a1.

c8   **ἀπολεῖπον** 'deserting' (LSJ s.v. A.II). The expression involves a brachylogy; it is not precisely itself, but rather its essential quality, self-motion, that τὸ αὐτὸ κινοῦν never abandons.

c9   **πηγὴ καὶ ἀρχὴ** For the absence of articles in the predicate, see note on c4; τοῦτο (i.e. τὸ αὐτὸ κινοῦν) is the subject.

245d1   **ἀρχὴ δὲ ἀγένητον** Ἀρχὴ, which was in an uncomplicated way 'the beginning' in c4, has by now emerged as something much more portentous: 'a first principle' perhaps. Its association with πηγὴ in the preceding line facilitated the transformation. It is now being used without an article like a proper noun. There is only one ἀρχή of motion, but we have not yet been told what it is.

d2   **μηδ' ἐξ ἑνός** is often a bit more emphatic than ἐκ μηδενός, in the manner of Latin *ne unus quidem*, but here little if any distinction seems to be intended.

d3   **ἔτι ἀρχὴ** is Buttmann's conjecture, made to eliminate the apparently faulty logic of the transmitted reading ἐξ ἀρχῆς, which would seem—if it is to make any sense at all—to demand to be taken temporally: 'from the beginning'; and that lacks relevance as well as being obscure. But another interpretation, favored by De Vries, is to take πᾶν τὸ γιγνόμενον in d1 as subject of the second γίγνοιτο and render: 'for if the first principle should come into being from something (else), everything that comes into being would not come into being from the first principle.' The sentence would then point out that, if its hypothesis is granted, ἐξ ἀρχῆς ... γίγνεσθαι in d1–2 lacks significance, when its correlate αὐτὴν ... ἑνος is contradicted. Another interpretation of the transmitted text is Rowe's: "For if a first principle came into being from anything, it would not do so from a first principle." I am not sure whether he means that the hypothesis involves us in an infinite regress or that the ἀρχή is unique and if it came into being from something, that thing couldn't be an ἀρχή; i.e. it must derive its existence from something that is not a first principle (Thompson). That, however, would start a hare that would demand pursuit, but Plato moves on oblivious of the chase. Cicero's translation, *nec enim esset id principium, quod gigneretur aliunde*, would seem to support Buttmann's conjecture.

d3–4 ἐπειδὴ ... εἶναι The unexpressed subject of the protasis is ἀρχή, but since it has already been made a 'thing' by its neuter predicate adjective there, it can be picked up by αὐτὸ in the main clause.

d5 ἐκείνης refers to the same thing as did αὐτή, namely ἀρχή.

d6–7 οὕτω ... κινοῦν Again the presence and absence of the article distinguishes the subject from the predicate nominative.

d8 ἤ 'otherwise,' as at 237c1 and frequently.

πάντα τε οὐρανὸν 'the whole universe' (LSJ s.v. οὐρανός I.4). The vault of the heavens, where the machinery of the universe is to be seen in all its grandeur, can bear this meaning, especially in philosophy. See, e.g. *Plt.* 269d7–8, where κόσμος and οὐρανός appear synonymous.

245e1 γῆν εἰς ἕν Burnet took this reading from the sixth-century Christian Neoplatonist John Philoponus. The manuscripts and other citations from late antiquity show γένεσιν, which is better, as De Vries, for reasons somewhat different from those that follow, argued. The distinction being made is not the common one between οὐρανός and γῆ, which is a rhetorical amplification that lacks point in this context. Socrates adds to the impossibility (the infinitives depend on an implied δυνατόν) of stopping the working of the universe the impossibility of finding the means to start it again. Since the ἀρχή cannot cease to be, even if the universe we know were to pass away, there would be *some* universe left, and it would have motion. But if the ἀρχή *could* cease to be, there would be nothing left to provide γένεσις for another.

στῆναι In a strong sense: 'come to a stop' and 'stand still'(LSJ s.v. B.II).

e2 ὅθεν ... γενήσεται 'the means of starting to move.' For the periphrastic future using γίγνομαι, see S. 1964; it is a poetic touch. The aorist participle denotes the moment of beginning to move again. For the masculine οὐρανός and the feminine γῆ or γένεσις taking a singular verb with a neuter plural predicate, see S. 1057.

e3–4　　**ψυχῆς … αἰσχυνεῖται** Τοῦτον αὐτόν stands for τὸ ὑφ' ἑαυτοῦ κινούμενον, but takes its gender from λόγον. This kind of attraction is particularly common with verbs of naming (KG 1.74). Translate τις λέγων οὐκ αἰσχυνεῖται as 'a person will feel no embarrassment in calling' (GMT 903.1). This person, in stating that being a self-moving thing is the οὐσία of the ψυχή, will give it its λόγος, so the two parts of the predicate accusative are nearly identical—an item of knowledge and its statement. Compare *Tht.* 207b8–c4, where Socrates says that a man who knows the οὐσία of a wagon by being able to go through all its hundred timbers will add a λόγος to his true opinion of it.

e5　　**αὐτῷ** is redundant but rhetorically desirable, because it adds to the notion of 'selfness.'

e6　　**ὡς … ψυχῆς** Ταύτης is self-motion attracted into the gender of its predicate. Compare on τοῦτον αὐτὸν in e3–4.

e7　　**εἶναι** For an infinitive without the article standing in apposition to and explaining an adverb (οὕτως) in this way, see S. 1987. To sum up, we have completed the ἀρχὴ ἀποδείξεως and found that the φύσις [οὐσία and λόγος in the preceding sentence] ψυχῆς is that it is τὸ ὑφ' ἑαυτοῦ κινούμενον. And on the way we learned that a thing of that sort is ἀγένητον and ἀθάνατον.

246a3–d5: Socrates describes the form of the soul in a similitude, making distinctions between those of gods and our own, and between the latter in their perfect state and the damaged state in which they enter our bodies.

246a3　　**αὐτῆς** sc. τῆς ψυχῆς, as in the following clause as well, where it begins quite unequivocally to mean the individual soul.

a4　　**πάντῃ πάντως** Nearly synonymous adverbs that reinforce one another are not uncommon in Plato. The same pair are found at *Tim.* 29c5 and in the less compact sequence πάντως καὶ πάντῃ at *Rep.* 490a2 and *Phlb.* 60c2–3. Οὐδαμῇ οὐδαμῶς is also common.
　　θείας 'superhuman.'

a5　　**εἶναι** A notion of saying carries over from λεκτέον at the end of the previous sentence and governs this infinitive, which can be translated 'needs' or 'requires' with the predicative genitive of quality διηγήσεως (S. 1320). A short and pertinent parallel is provided by Thucydides 1.142.9: τὸ δὲ ναυτικὸν τέχνης ἐστίν ('seamanship requires skill').

a6   **ταύτῃ** i.e. figuratively, through the myth to follow.

             ἐοικέτω δὴ The subject is ἡ ψυχή. The imperative is usual for laying down assumptions or demanding concessions for the sake of the argument. Here it demands that a similitude be accepted, because a description is not feasible. Ἔοικέ τῳ δή, following the reading of T, deserves consideration; it involves the indicative and an uncommon but well-attested use of δή to underline the indefiniteness of an indefinite pronoun and impart to it an air of mystery: 'it resembles a kind of . . .' (D. 213).

a6–7   **συμφύτῳ δυνάμει** The adjective insists at the outset on the organic unity of a creature of the imagination that will be, as the myth progresses, in some danger of falling into three parts in the reader's mind. The noun draws attention away from excessive curiosity about graphic details toward function.

a7   **ὑποπτέρου** modifies both nouns.

a8   **ἀγαθοὶ καὶ ἐξ ἀγαθῶν** There is no harm in translating this phrase by 'noble themselves and of noble lineage' here and even at 274a2, where the gods, who after all have a genealogy of their own, are in question, but the expression has become a conventional commendation and sometimes occurs in contexts where literal translation verges on nonsense. See, for instance, on 249e1–2.

246b1   **τὸ δὲ τῶν ἄλλων** For τό + genitive to mean the 'matter,' 'affair,' or 'situation' of someone or something, see LSJ s.v. ὁ, ἡ, τό B.II.2: 'the case of the others is mixed.'

             πρῶτον μὲν 'in the first place'; answered by εἶτα in b2.

             ἡμῶν ὁ ἄρχων is, of course, our charioteer, but in this context, the more general denotation of the term used suggests the governing element within us.

b2   **συνωρίδος ἡνιοχεῖ** Ordinarily ἡνιοχέω takes an accusative, but here it is being used as a verb of ruling (S. 1370). A συνωρίς is definitely a pair, as the description will elaborate; ζεῦγος in a7 was less determinate, since it is used sometimes of a pair, sometimes of the τέθριππον (ἅρμα) or four-horse chariot of the games. In fact, Plato opposes the two terms in *Ap.* 36d9. So, when the chariot is first mentioned it is called merely a 'team,' and although that of the human soul is clearly drawn by a pair, the case of the gods is left ambiguous (a distinction made by Myles Burnyeat in an unpublished paper).

b4   **δύσκολος** Drawing on our more accurate knowledge of physiology, we may prefer to say 'nerve-racking' rather than 'hard on the bowels.'

περὶ ἡμᾶς   'in our case' (S. 1693.3c).

b5–6   πῆ . . . εἰπεῖν This point must be elucidated, since soul per se has, after all, already been shown to be ἀθάνατον. Elucidating it will occupy Socrates through λεγέσθω in d3. Ζῷον can be applied to a very broad range of living creatures, from gods to animals.

b5   θνητόν τε καὶ ἀθάνατον Predicate adjectives. The conjunctive pairing is used where a speaker of English would prefer the disjunctive 'or.'

ἐκλήθη is a gnomic aorist; see note on 247e4. For δὴ οὖν, see note on 242c3–4: 'so clearly.'

b6   ψυχὴ . . . ἀψύχου We have already seen that soul produces motion in what would otherwise be an inert universe.

b6–7   πάντα . . . οὐρανὸν See note on 245d8. Οὐρανός, like γῆ, forms a class by itself and so does not need a definite article (S. 1141); compare πάντα τὸν κόσμον in c1–2.

b7   γιγνομένη 'manifesting itself.' For the compendious use of ἄλλοτ' ἐν ἄλλοις, see S. 1274.

b7–c3   τέλεα . . . ἀντιλάβηται The participles are temporal in force: 'as long as it is complete and has wings.' Thus the discussion begins to shift from soul itself, which remains ἀθάνατος, to soul contaminated by σῶμα. Confusion results, as we will see in c6–d2, from our uncertainty about the divine nature and attribution to it of our own somatic nature through analogy.

246c1–c2   πάντα τὸν κόσμον διοικεῖ is roughly equivalent to παντὸς ἐπιμελεῖται τοῦ ἀψύχου in b6, but the repetition is justified by Socrates now restricting this power to unimpaired soul.

c2   φέρεται The passive of φέρω often signifies moving under the guidance or influence of some agency other than the subject. No specific agent need be expressed or even clearly implied; consequently the best translation is often simply 'moves.'

c3   στερεοῦ τινος 'something solid.'

c3–6   οὗ . . . ἐπωνυμίαν The feminine subject ψυχὴ turns into the neuter subject τὸ σύμπαν not because the nature of ψυχὴ has changed, but because it is now only part of a compound thing, which is properly called by a new name, ζῷον.

c4   τὴν ἐκείνης δύναμιν Soul's power of self-motion, imparted to the body in appearance (δοκοῦν) only.

c6–7   ἀθάνατον . . . λελογισμένου Understand ἔσχεν ἐπωνυμίαν repeated with ἀθάνατον. Ζῷον remains the subject. The point, as we shall see by the end of the sentence, is that we only imagine the gods to have σώματα like ours; they are not ζῷα in the same sense.

c6   **οὐδ' ἐξ ἑνὸς**   See note on 245d2.

246d1   **θεόν** is the object of ἰδόντες and νοήσαντες, ἀθάνατόν τι ζῷον of πλάττομεν, which, for the sake of clarity, ought to be followed by a comma.

d1–2   **ἔχον δὲ . . . συμπεφυκότα**   The source of our confusion. We know that the gods are immortal and wrongly conjecture that they have bodies like ours, and then we draw a mistaken inference from those imaginary bodies not seeming to die. In reality, two essentially different kinds of creature, one simple and one compound, are being called by the one name ζῷον. Συμπεφυκότα is neuter plural, as is usual when antecedents (ψυχὴν and σῶμα) differ in gender. Compare on 245e2.

d2   **ἀλλὰ . . . μὲν δὴ** dismisses the question of how ζῷον can be called both mortal and immortal and looks forward to τὴν δὲ αἰτίαν.

d3   **ὅπῃ . . . λεγέσθω** is a conventionally pious formula; compare *Ap.* 19a6: τοῦτο μὲν ἴτω ὅπῃ θεῷ φίλον.

d3–4   **τὴν . . . ἀποβολῆς** returns to what was tantalizingly thrown into the mix without explanation by πτερορρυήσασα at c2.

d5   **λάβωμεν**   For λαμβάνω in the sense 'apprehend with the mind, understand,' see LSJ s.v. 9b.

         ἔστι δέ τις τοιάδε   'it [the αἰτία] is something such as follows.'

246d6–e4: Of all the parts of a body, wings have most in common with the divine, which is characterized by the qualities that nourish the winged soul and are opposed to those that destroy it.

246d6   **Πέφυκεν**   For πέφυκα + infinitive in the sense 'be formed or disposed by nature to do so and so,' see LSJ s.v. φύω B.II.2.

         ἡ πτεροῦ δύναμις   Abstract for concrete, the wing in respect to what it is able to do. Compare a6–7 with note.

d7–8   **κεκοινώνηκε . . . τοῦ θείου**   Τῶν περὶ τὸ σῶμα is a partitive genitive depending on ἡ πτεροῦ δύναμις, the subject of κεκοινώνηκε, which itself takes the partitive genitive τοῦ θείου (S. 1343).

246e1   **δὴ** is consecutive here (S. 2846): 'accordingly.'

e3 **καὶ τοῖς ἐναντίοις** 'and by the opposites in general,' not, of course, the opposites to the shameful and the bad, but to the qualities mentioned in e1. The expression corresponds to καὶ πᾶν ὅτι τοιοῦτον above. A similar use of καί to mean 'and in general' after a series of particulars was seen in 240d2.

THE HYPERURANIAN EXPERIENCE

246e4–247c2: The routine of the gods and of other souls who share in their activities.

246e4   **ὁ μὲν δὴ . . . Ζεύς** The treatise *On Style* attributed to Demetrius chooses this as a particularly striking use of δή, one that "placed thus at the beginning of the sentence and separating what follows from what precedes creates the impression of elevation" (*Demetrius de elocutione* 56). "Lo, mighty Zeus in his heaven," as Demetrius's editor W. Rhys Roberts translated. (The manuscripts of Demetrius lack the word ἡγεμὼν, but it is not relevant to the point he was making, and the omission need not lead us to alter the text.) It is odd to bury this abrupt and striking transition in the middle of a paragraph, as does Burnet, and many modern translators (e.g. Hackforth, Rowe, Hamilton) follow him; Nehamas and Woodruff do not.

e5–6   **διακοσμῶν . . . ἐπιμελούμενος** The two participles are not quite synonymous; Zeus must bring order to all things before he can manage them.

e6   **δαιμόνων** Plato is here interested primarily in two of the many, sometimes contradictory things that were said about δαίμονες. First, they were often thought of as following (ἕπεται) or attending upon one of the major gods, e.g. the guardian daemon who follows in the train of Zeus Xenios (*Laws* 730a). Moreover, Δίκη, Νέμεσις, and the Μοῖραι were all said to be part of Zeus's train; the Muses and Graces attend on Apollo; Kore and Triptolemus on Demeter. Second, unlike the gods, the daemons are not wholly separate from humankind. We remember that Hesiod said that after they had died, the men of the Age of Gold became pure (ἁγνοί) daemons, who roam the earth and "watch over judgments and cruel deeds" (*Works and Days* 121–26). This connection leads one to acknowledge that De Vries may be right in claiming that the daimones here are "all the nondivine souls." We will find later that all human souls are in varying degrees fallen, but many retain and all will periodically regain the ability to follow in this στρατιά. The relationship, one might say, is the inverse of that which Hesiod recounts. In this interpretation δαιμόνων here is a somewhat enigmatic foreshadowing of ὁ ἀεὶ ἐθέλων τε καὶ δυνάμενος, subject of a second ἕπεται, in 247a6-7.

247a1 **μένει ... Ἑστία** One need not look for astrological meanings or other profundities here. How is the goddess of that most fixed of locales, the hearth, to be imagined as skimming around the heavens in a chariot?

a2-3 **ὅσοι ... τεταγμένοι** According to a list that derives from Plato's pupil Eudoxus of Cnidos, the canonical twelve were Zeus, Hera, Poseidon, Demeter, Apollo, Artemis, Ares, Athena, Aphrodite, Hermes, Haephestus, and Hestia. Perhaps these were the twelve whose altar in the northern part of the Agora must have been familiar to Socrates and Phaedrus as well as to Plato himself. Certainly honoring such a Homeric pantheon would have been consistent with the policy of its dedicator Peisistratos, grandson of the tyrant. The gods who surveyed the city from the east frieze of the Parthenon were the same with one exception—Dionysus in place of Hestia, who again, it would seem, stayed home alone. With τεταγμένοι supply εἰσίν.

a3 **ἄρχοντες ἡγοῦνται** is slightly redundant: they 'lead in the vanguard.'

ἣν is a cognate accusative retained with the passive ἐτάχθη. See LSJ s.v. τάσσω 2.

a4-5 **διέξοδοι ἐντὸς οὐρανοῦ** 'excursions inside the vault of the heavens.' Throughout this passage οὐρανός sometimes means the vault or firmament of the heavens, sometimes the space between that and the earth.

a5 **ἐπιστρέφεται** 'pass back and forth over' (LSJ s.v. II.2), ἃς being the kind of internal accusative that expresses extent of space, the road traveled (S. 1581).

a6 **πράττων ... αὑτοῦ,** although the neuter γένος has preceded—a *constructio ad sensum*. By 'doing his or her own thing' Plato presumably means διακοσμῶν and ἐπιμελούμενος that aspect of the universe that is a given god's special responsibility.

ἀεὶ 'at any given time.'

a7 **φθόνος ... ἵσταται** The jealousy of the gods and the consequent need for men to remember that they were mortal are accepted as part of the way of things practically universally in Greek literature. *Timaeus* 29e, in which the demiurge is said to have lacked jealousy and to have desired that everything be as like himself as possible, provides a rare exception. "This sentence, too, seems to imply a moral condemnation of divine φθόνος," as De Vries says.

a8   ὅταν . . . ἴωσιν   The importance of the transition to this new activity is marked by δὲ δὴ responding to μὲν οὖν at a4. There is also a conscious stylistic elevation in the partial redundancy and deliberate variation in πρὸς δαῖτα and ἐπὶ θοίνην. We are meant to remember τρέφεταί τε καὶ αὔξεται at 246e2.

a8–b1   ἄκραν . . . ἁψῖδα   i.e. toward the rounded inner and earthward side of the vault of the heavens at its apex. See LSJ s.v. ἁψίς 5. For the predicate position of ἄκραν, see S. 1172, and compare the similar use of adjectives of relative position, like *summus* and *medius*, in Latin. In translating into English we make them into substantives.

247b1   πρὸς ἄναντες   'steeply uphill,' as contrasted with the smooth, effortless travel implied by the sentence in a4–7. In his little book on horsemanship Xenophon says that you must test a horse by driving it headlong uphill (πρὸς ἄναντες), downhill, and on level ground (*On Horsemanship* 3.7).

b1–2   ᾗ δὴ . . . πορεύεται   Take ῥᾳδίως with the verb and ἰσορρόπως with εὐήνια ὄντα: 'whither the chariots of the gods proceed easily because they are easy to guide in the manner of things that are well balanced.'

b3   ὁ τῆς κάκης ἵππος μετέχων   The word order is artificial. Κάκης takes an article to remind us of 246b3. We do not yet know whether it is to be understood as applying to moral character, social status, or degree of competence.

b4–5   ᾧ . . . ἡνιόχων   A conditional relative clause. Many editors, Burnet among them, accept the indicative ἦν, because the subjunctive in a conditional relative clause without ἄν seems to be absent from Attic prose. But surely a general condition is required by the sense here. The passage is highly poetic, and see GMT 540 for instances in which the manuscripts give the bare subjunctive in general conditions, as B and T, our most reliable witnesses, do here. The partitive genitive τῶν ἡνιόχων depends on the omitted antecedent of ᾧ, which is dative of agent. The antecedent itself would have probably been dative depending on βαρύνων (compare *Phd.* 117e4). The kind of training these charioteers have failed to give will be seen in 254.

b6   αἱ μὲν is not answered by αἱ δὲ at c1, which refers to the same souls, but by αἱ δὲ ἄλλαι ψυχαί at 248a1.

κ_αλούμεναι is added to make it clear that it is the gods who are in question. All soul is, after all, immortal, and in the preceding sentence ψυχῇ meant precisely the part of soul manifested in θνητὰ ζῷα (246b5); but we shall not return to that until we reach 248a.

b7–c1   ἐπὶ . . . νώτῳ Barrett on Euripides' *Hippolytus* 128 points out that when we use the word *back* metaphorically in English, we are thinking of a human back and mean the far side, but a Greek was thinking of a four-footed beast when he used νῶτον metaphorically and meant the top side, whether that be thought of as flat, like the apparent surface of the sea, or convex, like the apparent vault of the heavens. The souls of the gods have got outside the vault of heaven (ἔξω τοῦ οὐρανοῦ at c2) and are standing on the back of the universe.

247c1   στάσας echoes ἔστησαν (a gnomic aorist) in the manner of λέξις εἰρομένη. Compare on εἰπόμην . . . ἑπόμενος at 234d5.

247c3–e6: Socrates describes the experiences of the souls of the gods in the hyperuranian place, where they gaze at the forms and enjoy a feast of real knowledge of what really exists.

247c3–4   οὔτε τις . . . κατ᾽ ἀξίαν While these words may reflect the literary topos "pride of bringing something new" (V.), their emphasis lies in showing the ineffability of the experience that Socrates is about to describe. No one has sung its praises worthily and no one is going to sing them worthily—and that includes the attempt that is about to be made. In the sentence that follows, δὲ marks resignation to trying what is felt to be impossible.

c4–5   τολμητέον γὰρ οὖν 'for really one must.' "In post-Homeric Greek οὖν adds to γάρ the idea of importance or essentiality" (D. 446). This γάρ is of the familiar causal sort, but the one that follows in c6 is of the sort that D. 58ff. calls explanatory. It introduces information that has been promised by some expression that precedes, in this case ὧδε in c4. It can sometimes be translated 'namely'; De Vries suggests "to wit."

c5–6   περὶ ἀληθείας differs little from περὶ τοῦ ὄντως ὄντος—not truth as opposed to falsehood, but 'reality,' i.e. truth as opposed to appearance.

c6 λέγοντα is accusative in agreement with the unexpressed subject of τολμητέον . . . εἰπεῖν in c4–5; for accusative and infinitive following the impersonal (active) use of a verbal adjective, as if it were δεῖ, see S. 2152a.

c7–8 ψυχῆς...νῷ   Νῷ is an appositive, meant to explain the metaphor. For metaphors accompanied by their literal explanations in Plato, see Dodds on *Grg.* 447a3. Hackforth takes μόνῳ with νῷ, but it is better with κυβερνήτῃ: 'visible to the soul's steersman alone, intellect.'

c8 περὶ ἥν   The antecedent is οὐσία. The reader must supply ἐστί, as frequently in relative clauses; compare e.g. d6–7.

τὸ . . . γένος   This periphrasis does not differ materially from ἡ ἀληθὴς ἐπιστήμη: 'the real kind of knowledge,' i.e. 'knowledge that deserves to be called knowledge.'

247d1–2 ἅτ' . . . τρεφομένη   We would expect θεοῦ διάνοια, the subject of the main sentence, to stand outside this causal participial phrase, but the hyperbaton (S. 3028) of ἅτε throws more emphasis on this fact about the divine mind's nurture as necessary to its experience.

d2 ἁπάσης ψυχῆς depends on διάνοια, parallel to θεοῦ. This phrase, with the relative clause that depends on it, affords us a passing glance at the souls of mortals in a paragraph otherwise, as will be explicitly stated in 248a1, devoted to those of gods.

d2–3 τὸ προσῆκον   Since what is at issue is the nourishment of διάνοια, we may translate: 'its proper food.'

d3–4 ἰδοῦσα . . . εὐπαθεῖ   Primarily by his choice of verbs Socrates attempts to convey a sensuous experience of the intellect: it 'feels satisfaction' (LSJ s.v. ἀγαπάω III) and 'is nourished and enjoys itself' (τρέφεται καὶ εὐπαθεῖ). See note on e3. For διὰ χρόνου in the sense 'after a time,' meaning 'at last,' see LSJ s.v. διά A.II.2. The time will be the interval since its most recent journey ἔξω τοῦ οὐρανοῦ.

d4–5 ἕως . . . περιενέγκῃ   Although I agree with Hackforth that it is wrong to assume that "myth is careful to be rational and precise," I fail to see why "a period of twenty-four hours is plainly ridiculous." It seems natural to think of the hyperuranian surface as the exterior of the sphere of the fixed stars, and insofar as one gives the matter any thought at all, the apparent diurnal rotation of the heavens seems to provide a satisfactory length for this intellectual feast.

d5-6   **καθορᾷ μὲν ... καθορᾷ δὲ ... καθορᾷ δὲ**   A strong anaphora, very conspicuous and forceful. See Denniston, *Greek Prose Style*, 84–87, for more examples from Plato and on anaphora in general. It originated not as a consciously artful device of rhetoric, but as a natural expression of emotion and emphasis in speech.

d7-e1   **ἑτέρα ἐν ἑτέρῳ**   'one [knowledge] in one thing, another in another." Ἕτερος allows the same compendious use as does ἄλλος (S. 1274a).

247e1   **ὧν ... καλοῦμεν** = ἐκείνων ἃ ἡμεῖς νῦν ὄντα καλοῦμεν, by attraction of both the relative and its predicate. Νῦν means something like 'as we are circumstanced,' i.e. here on earth and not outside the phenomenal universe viewing the forms.

e1-2   **ἀλλὰ ... οὖσαν**   Take ὄντως with both οὖσαν and ὄν. Socrates means real knowledge of real being.

e3   **ἑστιασθεῖσθα**   Compare 227b6–7 for a very different sort of intellectual feast.

e4   **ἦλθεν**   The paragraph will end with a string of three gnomic aorists. One of the principal uses of the gnomic aorist is to render vivid scenes that originate in imagination rather than experience (KG 1.161). Consequently, the myth is replete with them, and I will not call attention to them per se henceforward.

e4-6   **ἐλθούσης ... ἐπότισεν**   The subject of the genitive absolute remains διάνοια, which has been the subject of all the main verbs since it appeared in d1, but the reader may have come to equate it with the ψυχή of which it is part. It would seem that among the gods, at least, the σύμφυτος δύναμις of 246a6–7 is separable into at least two parts, but doubtless to consider so would be to consider too curiously (see note on d4–5). In any case, the sentence is, as De Vries points out, "a playful reminiscence" of *Iliad* 5.368–69: ἔνθ' ἵππους ἔστησε ποδήνεμος ὠκέα Ἶρις / λύσασ' ἐξ ὀχέων, παρὰ δ' ἀμβρόσιον βάλεν εἶδαρ. The horses of Plato's gods eat the food of Homer's gods, but the gods themselves enjoy a very different diet.

e6   **ἐπ' αὐτῇ**   'in addition to it' (S. 1689.2c).

The Struggle and the Prize

248a1-b5: The other souls encounter difficulties and misfortunes in attempting to accompany those of the gods.

248a1 αἱ δὲ ἄλλαι ψυχαί See first note on 247b6. That is far away, so far that Plato repeated μὲν in the recapitulation οὗτος μὲν θεῶν βίος, which summarizes all that has intervened.

a1-6 ἡ μὲν ... τὰ δ' οὔ The experience of the first soul (ἡ μὲν) is like that of a rail passenger who gazes out the window while traveling at high speed over a rough roadbed; the second (ἡ δὲ) is plagued by the same difficulties compounded by his carriage repeatedly, and quite without warning, plunging into tunnels.

a2 ἄριστα ... εἰκασμένη Ἄριστα is an adverb and modifies both participles: those souls who are most successful in their efforts to follow and make themselves like a god. Only later (252c–253c) will we find that each of them has an affinity for a particular god.

a3-4 τὴν περιφοράν A cognate accusative retained with a passive verb.

a5 ἦρεν For the simple verb repeating the idea of the compound ὑπερῆρεν in a2, see note on 240a9–b2.

ἔδυ For conjugation of the second aorist of δύω, see S. 418.

a5-6 βιαζομένων ... ἵππων 'and because their horses are unruly' (LSJ s.v. βιάζω II.3). The black horses of the various individual souls must account for the plural.

a6 οὔ When a proclitic has nothing on which to "lean forward," it becomes oxytone (S. 180a).

a6-8 αἱ δὲ ... συμπεριφέρονται The picture evoked is reminiscent of the swirl of figures in a baroque ceiling representing, perhaps, an Apotheosis or an Assumption. Without violating the caveat expressed in the note on 247d4–5, it seems safe to say that Socrates imagines the souls emerging into the hyperuranian place through a confined area at the zenith or—more likely—the celestial pole. Αἱ δὲ ... ἄλλαι here informs us that the division of αἱ δὲ ἄλλαι at a1 into ἡ μὲν (a1) and ἡ δὲ (a5) was not exhaustive.

This new group does not succeed in seeing the longed-for sights at all.

a7   τοῦ ἄνω depends on γλιχόμεναι, which in this context may retain the notion of actually trying to cling to some part of a rival soul above.

a8   ἐπιβάλλουσαι in the sense 'jostling' (LSJ s.v. II.2) elbows in for a share of ἀλλήλας and is nearly trampled by πατοῦσαι. Plato could have added ἀλλήλαις—the dative being the case ἐπιβάλλω usually takes in this sense, but he preferred a more crowded effect.

a8–b1   ἑτέρα ... γενέσθαι Contrast the absence of φθόνος among the gods at 247a7; this is the πόνος and ἀγὼν ἔσχατος predicted at 247b5.

248b2   ἱδρὼς ἔσχατος In Greek as in English sweat provides a metaphor for labor. For ἔσχατος in the sense 'uttermost' or 'highest' degree of a thing, see LSJ s.v. 2.

οὗ 'where' (LSJ s.v. ὅς, ἥ, ὅ A.b1).

κακίᾳ is the opposite of ἀρετή. They both apply to competence as well as morality and so provide not necessarily a moral judgment, but nevertheless an assignment of responsibility to the ἡνίοχος, as at 247b3–5.

b3   χωλεύονται For a flying creature, being maimed means losing the use of a wing.

πολλαὶ ... θραύονται 'and many of them have their feathers broken in great numbers.' The causative use of the middle of transitive verbs (S. 1725) need not be restricted to things that subjects have done to or for them willingly.

b4–5   πᾶσαι ... χρῶνται These souls endure their labors before they give up and turn away, but aspect was more important than tense to Plato so he used the present participle ἔχουσαι as an imperfect (GMT 140). In the second half of the sentence time sequence is more important, so we have the aorist ἀπελθοῦσαι.

b4   ἀτελεῖς 'uninitiated' (LSJ s.v. IV). For the implications of τῆς ... θέας, see note on c2.

b5   τροφῇ δοξαστῇ "A notable expression" says Hackforth, who renders it "food of semblance." What it means is made clear by the following sentence, in which the nourishment metaphor is carried on. Compare my translation of τὸ προσῆκον in 247d2–3.

248b5–249b6: Socrates describes the goal that the souls are struggling to attain and tells what happens to those who succeed and those who in varying degrees fail.

248b5–c2 **οὐ δ' ἕνεχ' . . . τρέφεται** This sentence is cited more than once in collections and discussions of difficult ellipses in Greek prose (see Riddell 247 and KG 2.560). The consensus is that one must supply τοῦτο ἐστὶν, ὅτι to connect the first clause with the two that then become subordinate to it: 'the reason for the great eagerness . . . is this, namely, that. . . .' It is easy to understand τοῦτο as the unexpressed antecedent of οὗ and easy to understand ἐστί, but supplying ὅτι to subordinate the sentence that follows is a bolder step.

b6 **ἡ πολλὴ σπουδὴ** With an article, as opposed to the three forms of πολύς in b3: 'the great eagerness (which I have already described).'

τὸ ἀληθείας . . . οὗ ἐστιν The noun phrase is proleptic; translate as ἰδεῖν οὗ ἐστιν τὸ ἀληθείας πεδίον.

b7 **ψυχῆς τῷ ἀρίστῳ** That there are better and worse parts of the soul has been hinted in 246b1–3 and is clear by inference from 247c7–8; it will be spelled out in detail later.

ἐκεῖ = ἐπὶ τῷ τοῦ οὐρανοῦ νώτῳ (247b7–c1).

248c1 **ἥ τε τοῦ πτεροῦ φύσις** is, as De Vries says, "a semiperiphrastic turn, used to put a thing's essence in evidence."

c2 **τούτῳ** sc. τῷ λειμῶνι.

θεσμός . . . Ἀδραστείας For τε connecting sentences, see note on 230b2. Ἀδραστεία is a name for Nemesis, probably derived from alpha privative and the root of διδράσκω and meaning 'she from whom one cannot run away.' The phrase θεσμὸς Ἀδραστείας recalls χρῆμα Ἀνάγκης ('oracular pronouncement of Necessity') in frag. 115 of Empedocles, from his 'Orphic' poem *Purifications*. The same fragment speaks of human beings as fallen δαίμονες, who go through a series of incarnations occurring in cycles, the periodicity of which seems to provide a model for the reincarnations Socrates will describe. The metaphor just above, by which psychic experience is described as food and the place where it is obtained as a meadow, also has Orphic parallels. On the other hand, the metaphor in ἀτελεῖς τῆς τοῦ ὄντος θέας in b4 evokes the mysteries at Eleusis, where a distinguishing mark of an initiate was to have seen a certain sight. Plato, as is his custom, constructs his myth using materials borrowed from various religious movements current in his time in such a way as to prevent us from asserting his exclusive adherence to any of them.

c3–5 ἥτις . . . εἶναι The two infinitives in the main clause are in indirect discourse after the idea of utterance in θεσμός. The participle γενομένη is instrumental: 'by having become. . . .'

c4 τῆς ἑτέρας περιόδου 'the next circling.' Some commentators (V., for instance) understand Socrates as referring mysteriously to the periods of time that he will not explain until 248e5–249a. I prefer to look back to περιόδῳ in 247d5 and understand the 'periods' to be marked by successive journeys upward of the souls to grasp at their chance of viewing reality.

c5–6 ἀδυνατήσασα ἐπισπέσθαι The participle is causal. For the middle of ἐφέπω in the sense 'to keep up with,' see LSJ s.v. B.II.

c6 τινι συντυχίᾳ χρησαμένη: 'because it has suffered some misfortune.' See LSJ s.v. χράω (B) C.III. The indefinite pronoun used adjectivally, being an enclitic, naturally follows the noun it modifies, but in continuous discourse euphony or other rhetorical considerations sometimes override this "rule." Compare, e.g. ὑπό τινων ὁμιλιῶν at 250a3. Whatever its deeper meaning may be, on the primary level the συντυχία is likely to be the soul's encounter with and involvement in the material world as described in 246c.

c7 λήθης . . . πλησθεῖσα For possible Pythagorean connections, see Dodds on Grg. 493c3.
βαρυνθῇ, βαρυνθεῖσα Compare 234d5 and 247c1 and notes.

c8–d1 τότε . . . φυτεῦσαι sc. ἐστί and take ταύτην, the fallen soul, as the object of the infinitive. What agency would do the 'planting' is left moot.

248d2 τὴν . . . ἰδοῦσαν sc. νόμος ἐστὶ φυτεῦσαι with this and all the feminine singular objects in the string of clauses that ends with ἕξουσαν in e1.
γονὴν Not 'offspring' or 'stock,' but 'seed' (LSJ s.v. II.1) or 'birth' (LSJ s.v. III.3), the soul being a separable thing that is inserted at birth and departs at death.

d3–4 φιλοσόφου . . . ἐρωτικοῦ We must not think of these as distinct callings. One of the purposes of the myth is to equate the φιλόσοφος with the ἐρωτικός; and the φιλόκαλος is practically synonymous with the μουσικός. Consequently, when we recall that Socrates, pondering in prison on the surprising injunction that Apollo had been giving him repeatedly in his dreams (μουσικὴν ποίει καὶ ἐργάζου), concluded that philosophy was the greatest μουσική (*Phd.* 60c–61a), we see that, although he can be viewed from various points of view, it is only the philosopher who stands in the first rank among souls.

d4   **τὴν δὲ δευτέραν** and the ordinal numbers that follow are parallel to τὴν μὲν πλεῖστα ἰδοῦσαν in d2, as if that had been τὴν πρώτην.

    εἰς βασιλέως Understand γονὴν from d2 here, and with the juxtapositions of εἰς with genitive in the two following lines as well.

d4–5   **ἐννόμου . . . ἀρχικοῦ** No more than in d3 is ἢ really disjunctive; the three adjectives all offer qualities of a good king, with 'warlike' and 'royal' adhering to each other more closely than either does to 'law-abiding.'

d6   **<ἢ>** The supplement is neither necessary nor desirable; γυμναστικοῦ tells us what sort of φιλόπονος person is meant.

d7   **περὶ . . . ἐσομένου** 'of a physician'; idiomatic for indicating occupations. Compare Xenophon's *On Horsemanship* 6.3: εἰδέναι δὲ χρὴ τὸν περὶ τὸν ἵππον ὅτι ('and the groom must know that . . .').

d7–e1   **πέμπτην . . . ἕξουσαν** Weary of parallelism, Plato decides to vary the construction; we still understand φυτεῦσαι governing πέμπτην, but now, instead of telling us into what sort of person the soul will be implanted, he tells us by means of a future participle what sort of life it will lead after it has been implanted.

248e1   **ποιητικὸς** sc. βίος, as with all the nominative adjectives to the end of the sentence.

e2   **δημιουργικὸς ἢ γεωργικός** The people whose labor gave the philosopher, king, statesman, athlete, and poet leisure to follow their manner of living barely outrank the sophist, the demagogue, and the tyrant.

e3–4   **ἐν δὴ τούτοις ἅπασιν** 'among all these, then.' Sometimes δή, at the end of a passage of narrative or description, sets forth an inference and marks a transition (S. 2846).

e5   **γὰρ** This sentence does not tell us why the particular facts of the preceding sentence are true, but it does tell us why there is a long interval of time during which souls must be repeatedly reborn and move up and down the scale of μοῖραι in d2–e3.

e5–6   **τὸ αὐτὸ ὅθεν ἥκει** i.e. before the fall mentioned in c5–8.

e6   **ἡ ψυχὴ ἑκάστη** 'every single soul'—or, appropriating from the verb its negative: 'no soul at all.' The article adds strong emphasis to ἕκαστος with a noun taken as a general concept (KG 1.634).

ἐτῶν μυρίων The ten-thousand-year interval has Orphic associations stemming from the fragment of Empedocles cited in the note on c2.

249a1-2   ἡ τοῦ ... φιλοσοφίας In the socially overheated atmosphere of the gymnasia, with all their opportunities, philosophizing could easily lose its integrity and become a cover for ulterior motives. The two phrases denote the person who avoids such temptations seen from different points of view, and ἤ offers not an alternative, but an alternative way of putting the matter: "or, in other words" (V., following Verdenius).

a4   τὸν βίον τοῦτον The life of a philosopher.

οὕτω i.e. when it has successfully completed its three incarnations as a philosopher.

τρισχιλιοστῷ ἔτει Herodotus (2.123, as translated by David Grene) wrote: "The Egyptians are the first who have told this story also, that the soul of man is immortal and that, when the body dies, the soul creeps into some other living thing then coming to birth; and when it has gone through all things, of land and sea and the air, it creeps again into a human body at its birth. The cycle for the soul is, they say, three thousand years. There are some Greeks who have used this story, some earlier and some later, as though it were something of their own. I know their names but will not write them down." Pythagoras and members of his school were surely among the Greeks about whom Herodotus was so discreet. The three-thousand-year period is likely to be more than a striking coincidence. In addition Pindar in a passage that combines Pythagorean with Orphic elements (*Olympians* 2.68ff.), speaks of souls undergoing a triple probation—evidently three lives on earth and as many intervals in Hades—before being transported, if they have refrained from all injustice, to the "tower of Kronos," who rules over Islands of the Blest at the edge of the world. These are a few more ingredients mingled in the potpourri alluded to in the note on 248c2.

a4–5   ἀπέρχονται into τὸ αὐτὸ ὅθεν ἥκει of 248e5–6.

a6   κρίσεως ... κριθεῖσα A variation on the figure commented on first at 234d5.

a7–8   εἰς τοὐρανοῦ τινα τόπον is deliberately unspecific; it does not designate the same place as did εἰς ... ἀφικνεῖται at 248e5–6. For the word order, see note on 248c6; here the indefinite is tucked neatly into the middle of its noun phrase.

a8   **κουφισθεῖσαι** These souls do not receive wings, but they are relieved of the weight of their mortal bodies.

249b1   **βίου** An omitted antecedent, into the case of which a relative has been attracted, may then be expressed in the relative clause (S. 2536). In this instance, the syntactical resource permits Plato to end the sentence with an etymological figure.

ἀμφότεραι i.e. those who have been beneath the earth and those who have been lifted up.

b2   **κλήρωσίν** This assignment by lot would presumably, as in the distribution of lots in the myth of Er in Plato's *Rep.* 617d1–618b6, determine the order in which the souls make their αἱρέσεις. It implies constraints on the number of "lives" of a given kind available for choosing and also implies that there is in living well or ill an element of luck, as well as an element of responsibility for making choices.

b3–4   **ἔνθα . . . ἀφικνεῖται** The word order emphasizes ἔνθα, because it is only at this point that an issue left hanging in 248c8–d2 will be resolved.

b5–6   **οὐ γὰρ . . . σχῆμα** Combining this sentence with the passage mentioned in the preceding note shows that there must be two kinds of animal soul, permanent and temporary. Everyone will be free to think his own dog or cat one of the latter. It is, in any case, clear by now that 'all soul' (245c5) is, in practice, 'all souls'— an entity like a heap of pebbles rather than like a bucket of water. There is no soul stuff out of which souls are dipped.

249b6–d3: Even though remembering the hyperuranian experience is what distinguishes humanity from the animals, those who remember it as they should seem eccentric to their fellows.

249b6–c1   **δεῖ . . . συναιρούμενον** The general sense is clear, the exact text less so. I accept Heindorf's τὸ, because κατ᾽ εἶδος λεγόμενον seems unidiomatic without it: 'For a human being must understand a thing that is said according to class [or type], gathering it into one by reasoning, although it comes from many perceptions.' My cat Tom sits in the window and observes many occasions when it is snowing, but only I can bring them together into a single concept and give it a name. This exclusively human faculty will be enlarged upon in 265d.

249c1   τοῦτο = τὸ λεγόμενον κατ' εἶδος, the general concept.

c3   νῦν 'in our present situation.'

ἀνακύψασα Remember that in 248a even the most successful of the nondivine souls could get only their heads up εἰς τὸν ἔξω τόπον and peer at τὰ ὄντα with difficulty.

c4–5   διὸ δὴ ... διάνοια The expression of the thought is truncated; through the context we must understand that Socrates means not that the mind of the philosopher alone will become winged, but that it will become winged only after the third incarnation.

c5–6   πρὸς ... ἐστιν Πρὸς denotes physical contiguity in both clauses. Μνήμῃ is dative of means; ὤν is a circumstantial participle indicating means. Θεός is subject, θεῖος predicate nominative.

c5   κατὰ δύναμιν offers the customary recognition of human limitations.

c6–8   τοῖς δὲ ... γίγνεται The experience of a man who rightly employs reminders of things like that (τοῖς τοιούτοις ὑπομνήμασιν) is described in terms that pun on 'perfect(ed)' and 'initiated.' For the passive of τελέω in the sense 'have oneself initiated' in a rite or rites that are expressed in an internal accusative, see LSJ s.v. III. This is an initiation quite different from the mere learning of rules that left the would-be poet ἀτελὴς in 245a7.

c8   ὄντως μόνος contrasts the genuine perfection attainable in this way with that which comes through ordinary initiation. The ὑπομνήματα are not the forms themselves (ἐκείνοις of c5) but whatever can remind one who has seen them (the initiated) of the forms. Later (250c–d) we will find that beautiful things are most effective in doing that.

249d1   πρὸς is used in the same sense as at c5 and c6.

d2   παρακινῶν 'being out of his mind' (LSJ s.v. II.3).

d3   τοὺς πολλούς, where we might expect αὐτούς, emphasizes by repetition the visionary philosopher's alienation from the crowd.

THE SOUL FALLS IN LOVE

249d4–250b1: The fourth kind of divine madness is the best, and when the man who loves beauty is possessed by it he becomes a lover. He is reminded of true beauty by the beauty of this world, and he strains to fly upward. All human souls have had some experience of true being, but few can remember much. When those few see likenesses here of what they saw there, they are amazed and do not know what is happening to them.

249d4   Ἔστι... ἥκων   For the periphrasis, see S. 1961. It has the force of a perfect because of the special nature of ἥκω.

d5–e1   ἦν . . . διακείμενος   Socrates will explain what he meant by δεῦρο with ὡς . . . καλεῖται in e1–4. First, though, it occurs to him that perhaps he ought to say just what the τετάρτη μανία is. He goes about that parenthetic task with a casual air that results in an anacoluthon. He sets out with ἦν [sc. μανίαν] ὅταν, as if he is going to employ a relative clause with a temporal clause dependent on it, but when we get to what ought to be the verb governing the relative pronoun (ἔχει), we find that he has already given it a different object (αἰτίαν). This leaves ἦν stranded high and dry. If we were, for instance, to eliminate ἦν and insert γὰρ after ὅταν, we would have an explanatory sentence of a kind common in Plato, and Burnet would have had no need for his parenthetic dashes; but the effect of casual afterthought, which is reinforced by the seemingly artless but actually quite artful series of nominative participles, would be lost.

d5   τοῦ ἀληθοῦς   sc. κάλλους.

d6   πτερῶταί is a conative present (S. 1878)—not 'becomes winged' (else why would he be unable to fly upward?), but 'struggles to become winged.'

      τε καὶ connects πτερῶταί with αἰτίαν ἔχει in d8 through all the participles between. He struggles to take off (ἀναπτερούμενος is another conative present) because he is eager to fly, but he is unable and goes about looking upward and paying no attention to his surroundings.

d7   ἀδυνατῶν δέ denies the soul's ability to ἀναπτέσθαι at this point.

d7–8   ὄρνιθος...ἄνω It is more comfortable to take this as 'fixing his gaze on things above' rather than pressing the comparison too hard. Birds do not, in fact, spend any more time than many other creatures in 'looking upward,' and when they do, they must, because of the placement of their eyes, cock their heads to the side, which leads to a distracting image.

d8–e1   αἰτίαν...διακείμενος What he has just said in d2–3 lingers in Socrates' mind, and the anacoluthon mentioned in the note to d5–e1 is made to seem more natural by having him revert to it.

249e1   ἄρα is not of the sort that implies skepticism about the reported speech or thought, but of the kind for which "the context implies acceptance of the idea, but ἄρα merely denotes that its truth has not before been realized" (D. 38).

         αὕτη i.e. ἡ τετάρτη μανία.

e1–2   ἀρίστη τε καὶ ἐξ ἀρίστων seems purely conventional here, a kind of heightened superlative. See note on 246a8.

e2   τῷ κοινωνοῦντι αὐτῆς i.e. the person whose life is affected by the μανία, as opposed to the person who "has" it: the ἐρώμενος rather than the ἐραστής.

e3   γίγνεται 'turns out to be.'

         καὶ ὅτι Notice the stylistic variation from ὡς in e1.

e3–4   τῶν καλῶν is objective with ὁ ἐρῶν. It could be masculine or neuter; possibly we are not meant to decide.

e4   καθάπερ...εἴρηται in b5–6.

e5   φύσει probably means 'by its nature' (i.e. as part of its essence) rather than 'in the nature of things,' although the latter is certainly a possible interpretation.

         ἤ 'otherwise.'

250a1   τόδε τὸ ζῷον sc. ἀνθρώπινον.

         ἐκ τῶνδε ἐκεῖνα Ἐκεῖνα are the forms (a partial list at 247d6–7) seen ἔξω τοῦ οὐρανοῦ; τῶνδε are the imperfect representations of them we see around us in this life, the ὑπομνήματα of 249c7.

a1–2   οὐ ῥᾴδιον is the predicate; ἐστί must be understood.

a2   ἁπάσῃ sc. ψυχῇ: the singular, as is usual when πᾶς or ἅπας means 'every,' but plural pronouns follow in the relative clauses that split the class of those who do not find it easy into two groups.

a3   ἐδυστύχησαν might remind us of the mysterious τινι συντυχίᾳ χρησαμένη at 248c6, but that misfortune, which also produced λήθη, clearly happened before the first incarnation and led to it.

a4   ἱερῶν points once more, as De Vries says, to initiations and mysteries; it has been incorporated into the relative clause while giving its case to the pronoun (S. 2536).

a5   τὸ τῆς μνήμης   See note on 230c3. Here Plato may be making a distinction between the faculty and content of memory, but Gildersleeve (2.267), who gives a generous supply of samples of this kind of expression, warns that "the article . . . may often be left untranslated."

a6   τι . . . ὁμοίωμα is one of the τῶνδε of a1. Throughout this discussion the adverbs νῦν and τῇδε refer to the world of phenomena around us and correspond to τότε and ἐκεῖ of the ideal world.

a7   οὐκέτ' <ἐν> αὐτῶν γίγνονται 'they are no longer within themselves.' The phrase implies loss of control over themselves by being stunned, as here, or through passion, as when Socrates sees inside Charmides' himation (*Chr.* 155d4: ἐφλεγόμην καὶ οὐκέτ' ἐν ἐμαυτοῦ ἦν). For ἐν with genitive implying the ellipsis of some following dative, such as οἰκίᾳ or δόμῳ, see S. 1302 and compare note on 229c2. But is the supplement necessary? Αὐτῶν without ἐν would be a special use of genitive of possession and mean about the same thing by a different metaphorical route (C. 47.6). Compare Sophocles' *Oedipus Coloneus* 659–60: ἀλλ' ὁ νοῦς ὅταν αὐτοῦ γένηται ('but when the mind becomes its own master'), where Jebb cites our passage without the supplement. This is rarer and more poetic; it should probably be retained.

  ὃ δ' ἔστι τὸ πάθος   'what is happening to them.'

250b1–e1: There is no brightness in the earthly likenesses of justice and temperance, and they are apprehended through dull organs, but it is otherwise with beauty. We saw beauty in all its brightness among the forms of the hyperuranian world, and here on earth we apprehend whatever reminds us of it with the keenest of our senses. That makes its likeness the most manifest and most striking of all.

250b2   ὅσα . . . ψυχαῖς = ἄλλων ὅσα τίμιά ἐστι ψυχαῖς. When a relative is nominative, its genitive or dative antecedent will be assimilated to its case and frequently attracted into the relative clause (S. 2538a). (Contrast ἱερῶν at a4 with note, where without attraction the relative would have been accusative.) Here ἄλλων would, as do δικαιοσύνης and σωφροσύνης, depend on τοῖς τῇδε ὁμοιώμασιν in b3.

b3–4   **δι' ἀμυδρῶν ὀργάνων** The reader should not press the literal meaning of ὄργανα. Socrates means that the likenesses of forms such as justice and temperance, which are approached and somehow constructed through data collected by all the senses, lack the brilliance and immediacy of beauty. Although nothing specifically prevents us from thinking about beauty in landscapes, buildings, or pictures, Plato's presentation here seems designed to focus attention only on beauty in the human body. There is, for instance, no consideration given to the possibility of beauty in sound. Only sight gives us a ὁμοίωμα that is sufficiently instantaneous, whole, and striking to transport us.

b4   **αὐτῶν** depends on εἰκόνας and refers to the forms of justice and the like as experienced in the hyperuranian place.

    καὶ does not connect μόγις with ὀλίγοι; it is adverbial: 'with difficulty do even a few.'

    τὰς εἰκόνας are the ὁμοιώματα of the preceding line.

b5   **θεῶνται** 'see clearly' and, thereby, 'recognize' (LSJ 2b).

    τὸ . . . γένος is another way of putting the form that the soul has seen ἔξω τοῦ οὐρανοῦ.

    κάλλος Emphasized by standing first, the word signals the onset of an ecstatic digression.

b6   **λαμπρόν** Predicate adjective, limited by ἰδεῖν.

b6–7   **σὺν . . . θέαν** Language from the mysteries. What they, specifically the initiation at Eleusis, had in common with what Socrates is describing was chiefly that the initiate saw something and the experience changed his life.

b7   **ἑπόμενοι . . . ἡμεῖς** i.e. we philosophers, as will be seen at 252e1–3.

b8–c1   **τῶν . . . μακαριωτάτην** = πασῶν τελετῶν ταύτην ἣν θέμις ἐστὶ λέγειν μακαριωτάτην, the whole making a cognate accusative for ἐτελοῦντο.

250c1   **ὠργιάζομεν** More terminology from the mysteries. The imperfect encourages us to linger over the wonderful περίοδος, viewing reality in the company of the gods.

c2   **κακῶν . . . ὑπέμενεν** See a3–4. Here the imperfect is rather sinister.

c3   **φάσματα** The word, which may seem curiously insubstantial for entities so rich in reality, is harmonious with the mystery terminology in this context and with the primacy of the sense of sight in Plato's argument.

c4   μυούμενοί τε καὶ ἐποπτεύοντες are verbs from the mysteries. An ἐπόπτης was one admitted to the highest grade, and ἐποπτεύω is the verb for what he had done (LSJ s.v. II).

c5   ἀσήμαντοι τούτου A variety of ablatival genitive akin to that of separation is found with adjectives compounded with alpha privative (S. 1427–28) and with certain adjectives that are privative in meaning, such as ἐλεύθερος, ψιλός, and ἐρῆμος. This punning reference to the σῶμα-σῆμα identification made by the Pythagoreans shows how ready Plato is to turn from Eleusinian terminology to something quite distinct from it in concocting a myth for recollection of the forms.

περιφέροντες offers a fine example of a participle that is best translated in tandem with its verb: 'which in this life we carry about and call a body.'

c6   τρόπον is a quasiprepositional adverbial accusative: 'in the way of' (S. 1608).

c7   Ταῦτα . . . κεχαρίσθω 'let this, then, stand as our tribute to memory.' For the force of the perfect passive imperative marking a fixed decision or stating that something is to be considered completed or final, see GMT 105 and note to S. 1864c.

c7–8   δι' ἣν . . . εἴρηται offers an apology for what I called "an ecstatic digression" in the third note to b5. Socrates implies that he was carried away.

c8–d3   περὶ δὲ κάλλους . . . ἐναργέστατα What is to be the subject of the sentence is introduced in a loose and casual way, as we say, 'but as far as beauty is concerned, it. . . .'

250d1   μετ' ἐκείνων sc. φασμάτων, from c3.

ὄν is temporal and nominative, whereas στίλβον in d2 is accusative; both agree with an understood κάλλος.

κατειλήφαμεν is what S. 1948 calls an empiric perfect and Gildersleeve 1.257 a gnomic perfect. It sets forth a general truth based on experience. We have in the past apprehended beauty gleaming; therefore, as a general truth we so apprehend it.

d2   τῶν ἡμετέρων sc. αἰσθήσεων.

d3   ὀξυτάτη is predicate: 'as the keenest.'

d4–6   δεινοὺς . . . ἰόν In this way the importance of beauty in this context is reconciled with the primacy of intellect in Plato's general view.

d6   καὶ τἆλλα ὅσα ἐραστά are presumably δικαιοσύνη καὶ σωφροσύνη καὶ ὅσα ἄλλα τίμια ψυχαῖς from b1–2. Alternatives to φρόνησις, they too would dazzle us if we could see them; thus they are part of the parenthesis and Burnet's second dash should be removed.

νῦν δὲ ('but as it is') follows, as it often does, a contrary-to-fact condition.

250e1–251a7: How the response to beauty of one whose memory of his initiation is dim differs from that of one whose memory is fresh.

250e1   **μὴ νεοτελὴς ἢ διεφθαρμένος** A genuine distinction, but not necessarily a hard and fast one. Some souls may have simply passed through many lives since their last glimpse of the φάσματα; others, irrespective of the number of incarnations they have undergone, may have had their recollections erased by the experiences hinted at darkly in a3–4.

e2   **φέρεται** See note on 246c2. Here it denotes an involuntary movement of the attention, as in remembering.

   πρὸς αὐτὸ τὸ κάλλος explains ἐκεῖσε.

e3   **θεώμενος . . . ἐπωνυμίαν** involves the use of abstract for concrete: 'when he sees here on earth the name derived from it' in place of 'the thing named for it' (τὸ ἐπώνυμον).

e4   **ἡδονῇ παραδοὺς** 'yielding to pleasure'; intransitive use of a transitive verb (see note on 227c1). The similar use of the simple verb δίδωμι is common only with ἡδονῇ (LSJ s.v. V).

   τετράποδος νόμον Compare the similar and far more common prepositional use of the adverbial accusative δίκην that we saw at 249d7.

   βαίνειν In English the cock used to be said to 'tread' the hen in the days before all chickens began to live their lives in prison.

e5   **παιδοσπορεῖν** 'to ejaculate.'

251a1   **παρὰ φύσιν** This phrase has often been taken as a specific condemnation of homosexuality. It seems more likely, especially in view of the content of 250e4–5, that it rejects all sexual activity as a way of responding to the sight of beauty. Compare φύσει in 249e5. A rather circular argument in Plato's *Laws* 835dff., especially 836e, rejects the position that homosexuality does not ἀκολουθεῖν φύσει on the grounds that said position is not likely to be convincing. The main point of the passage is to show the difficulties involved in making laws about such matters.

a1–2   ὁ δὲ ... πολυθεάμων Compare μὴ νεοτελὴς ἢ διεφθαρμένος at 250e1 with note. Here we seem to have one person as seen under two aspects, the second characteristic narrowing the field that might be allowed under the first.

a3   κάλλος is the form of beauty as seen in the hyperuranian place; it is the object of εὖ μεμιμημένον, which must be understood to modify ἰδέαν as well as πρόσωπον: 'a godlike face or bodily form that imitates beauty itself well.

a4   τῶν ... δειμάτων The hyperuranian experience has not previously been spoken of in terms of fear, but the occurrence of fear and awe are, as De Vries says, "implied in the use of mystery terminology."

    ὑπῆλθεν αὐτὸν For ὑπέρχομαι (and εἰσέρχομαι) used transitively of involuntary feelings coming upon a person, see KG 1.300.

a5–6   εἰ μὴ ἐδεδίει ... θύοι ἄν Mixing a contrary-to-fact protasis with a potential apodosis is quite natural. It differs from the form with ἔθυεν ἄν more or less as the infinitive differs from the indicative in result clauses: instead of 'if he were not afraid ... he would be sacrificing' we have 'if he were not afraid ... he would (naturally) sacrifice.'

    τῆς σφόδρα μανίας For the adverb used as attributive adjective, see S. 1096.

a6   δόξαν 'reputation' (LSJ s.v. III) with the objective genitive μανίας.

    ὡς ἀγάλματι καὶ θεῷ De Vries cites *Chr.* 154c8 (describing the reaction of the other boys to the arrival of Charmides): ὥσπερ ἄγαλμα ἐθεῶντο αὐτόν.

251a7–d7: Falling in love is described as the process of regrowing the plumage the soul once had.

251a7–b1   ἰδόντα ... λαμβάνει Αὐτὸν is the possessor of κάλλος and object of ἰδόντα.

a7   οἷον ἐκ τῆς φρίκης 'as is natural after a shivering fit.' This temporal sense of ἐκ is common (S. 1688.1b).

a7–b1   μεταβολή is not parallel to, but is, rather, explained by ἱδρὼς καὶ θερμότης ἀήθης. Λαμβάνει is singular, as if the subject had been something like 'a change that consists of sweating and unwonted warmth.' Compare on 240c7–d1.

251b2–3   **ἐθερμάνθη . . . θερμανθέντος**   See first note on 234d5 and note on 247c1.

     ᾗ is instrumental; its antecedent is τὴν ἀπορροήν. The subject remains the same as that of ἰδόντα in a7, the fortunate ἀρτιτελής of a2.

     ἡ τοῦ πτεροῦ φύσις is not merely a periphrasis for τὸ πτερόν; it is equivalent to τὸ πτερὸν πεφυκὸς ὥσπερ πέφυκεν: 'the plumage being constituted as it is.' See Jebb on πέτρου φύσιν at Sophocles' *Oedipus tyrannus* 334–5.

b3   **ἄρδεται** adjacent to θερμανθέντος brings into contiguity the two essential physical conditions for eros: moisture and warmth.

     τὰ   'the area.'

b4   **τὴν ἔκφυσιν**   The growth point of the wing plumage.

b4–5   **εἶργε μὴ βλαστάνειν**   'were keeping it [τὸ πτερόν] from growing.' See S. 2739 or GMT 807 for redundant μή with an infinitive after verbs of hindering.

b5   **ἐπιρρυείσης**   'having accumulated': a second aorist passive that can be translated as active, because the verb is one of those in which English does not make the distinction.

     τῆς τροφῆς   i.e. τοῦ κάλλους τὴν ἀπορροήν from b1–2. Feeding is carried on through the eyes.

b6–7   **ὑπὸ . . . εἶδος**   The metaphor demands that we think of this activity as going on *under* the soul's skin, as it were; in this context it would seem that the whole structure is feathered, not the wings alone. Πτερόν can mean 'feather' (especially in the plural) or be a synonym for πτέρυξ ('wing'); πτερόω can mean 'furnish with feathers' or 'furnish with wings.' All we can do is translate these words as seems appropriate in a given context. I do not think that Plato's imagination troubled itself to go into the matter very far; if we attempt consistency, we evoke in our imaginations fallen souls with naked wings like plucked chickens and other grotesqueries. Most translators seem to use 'wing' when they can.

b7   **τὸ πάλαι**   i.e. in the time before a given soul's present cycle of incarnations.

251c1   **ἐν τούτῳ**   sc. τῷ χρόνῳ.

     ἀνακηκίει   The surface of the soul erupts in the tiny bumps, known as papillae, that portend the emergence of feather shafts.

c3   **φύωσιν** is present active and therefore transitive; the subject is οἱ ὀδοντοφυοῦντες. Bekker's conjecture φυῶσι, which has some support in inferior manuscripts, would let the teeth be the subject.

c4   πέπονθεν The gnomic perfect (GMT 154–55).

c4–5   ζεῖ . . . γαργαλίζεται The movement is from the metaphorical to the literal as each verb explains its predecessor. Ζεῖ at c1 evoked the pimpled and dimpled surface of boiling water; here it connotes heat and discomfort.

c7   διὰ ταῦτα ἵμερος καλεῖται The etymology (from εἶμι, μέρος, and ῥέω) is not meant to be taken seriously as such. Plato gives a somewhat different etymology of the same word in *Cra.* 419e–420a.

251d1   ὅταν... αὐχμήσῃ The subject is ἡ ψυχή. With χωρὶς understand τοῦ τοῦ παιδὸς κάλλους from c6 (V.).

d2–3   συναυαινόμενα μύσαντα ἀποκλήει 'closing because they are drying out, they shut in. . . .' Μύσαντα offers a clear example of the action of an aorist participle being coincident with that of a main verb when it defines it or is synonymous with it (S. 1872c2).

d4–5   τῇ διεξόδῳ . . . καθ᾽ αὑτήν Since the στόματα have dried and begun to close again, each βλάστη pricks against its own. There is nothing to indicate that any feather has yet appeared above the surface.

d5   κύκλῳ An adverbial use of dative of manner, meaning 'on all sides' or 'all over,' with no particular implication of circularity (LSJ s.v. 2).

d6–7   τοῦ καλοῦ sc. παιδός.

THE SOUL IN LOVE

251d7–252b1: How the mixture of pleasure and pain in growing the plumage affects the soul's values and makes it behave as it never has before.

251d7   ἀμφοτέρων μεμειγμένων is neuter, referring to the feelings of pleasure and pain that have been expressed in the preceding sentence. The participle contains the main idea and is best made into a substantive in translating: 'by a mixture of them both.' Compare the *ab urbe condita* construction in Latin.

d8   ἀποροῦσα connects Socrates' lover with his philosopher, as Robin points out.

251e1   μεθ' ἡμέραν is not exactly correlative to the genitive of 'time within which' νυκτός, but literally, 'after daybreak.' As soon as the sun rises he abandons his sleepless bed and gets on the move. While the subject remains the soul and participles in agreement with it continue to be feminine, it is forced and distracting to follow some translators, who refer to it as 'she.' It is better to think of the whole ἐραστής, body and soul, translating with 'it' and occasionally 'he,' where the context demands him, as it does in this clause.

e3   ἰδοῦσα ... ἵμερον 'when it sees him and lets desire flow in upon itself.' The participles are contemporaneous with the gnomic aorist main verb (see d2–3 with note). An ὀχετός is a sluice or water pipe. In the metaphor the pipes are ὄψις, and what flows through them is ἵμερος, composed of the ἀπορροή of b2 or the μέρη ἐπιόντα καὶ ῥέοντα of c6–7. For the reflexive usage seen in ἐποχετευσαμένη ἵμερον, see S. 1719; the indirect object ('upon itself') is not expressed here.

e4   τὰ τότε συμπεφραγμένα are the βλάστη and ἵμερος shut in with it in d3–4. In 255c we shall find that the stream of ἵμερος flows out as well as in. Like breath, it needs constant renewal; confined, it will go bad.

e5   ἡδονὴν ... γλυκυτάτην is predicate accusative, ταύτην (ἀναπνοήν) direct object.

e5–a1   ἐν τῷ παρόντι   sc. χρόνῳ: 'for the moment.' There is oscillation between pain and relief from pain.

252a1   ὅθεν δὴ   'for this reason, obviously....'

           ἑκοῦσα εἶναι   For the 'redundant' εἶναι, see S. 2012c.

           ἀπολείπεται   See 240c7 and note. Through this passage the erotically obsessed behavior that was described in the two earlier speeches is not denied, but its positive motives are emphasized, and envy—in the foreground there—is now nowhere to be seen.

a2   τοῦ καλοῦ   sc. παιδός; genitive of comparison.

a3   λέληϲται   Prose normally uses ἐπιλέληϲμαι, but the context is far from prosaic.

a3–4   οὐσίας ... ἀπολλυμένης is genitive absolute with conditional or perhaps temporal force.

a4   παρ' οὐδὲν τίθεται   'it [the subject remains the soul] thinks nothing of it.' The expression—possibly from bookkeeping—is also found in Aeschylus's *Agamemnon* 229–30 and Euripides' *Iphigenia in Tauris* 732.

a4–5   νομίμων ... εὐσχημόνων   The first adjective bears the weight of tradition, the second evokes tut-tuts and raised eyebrows; it corresponds nicely to British English 'good form.'

a5   οἷς ... ἐκαλλωπίζετο   'in which he used to take pride before this time.' See LSJ s.v. καλλωπίζω II.2, and for πρὸ τοῦ = πρὸ τούτου τοῦ χρόνου, compare e.g. *Meno* 70a5.

a6   ἑτοίμη   sc. ἐστί. The appropriate form of εἶναι is omitted particularly frequently with this adjective, δυνατός, and a few others (KG 1.40).

a7   τοῦ πόθου is concrete; 'the object of his longing.'

           γὰρ marks a rhetorical turning point. It is the first γάρ we have seen since 251b7; amid headlong description of process there was little or no occasion for giving reasons.

252b1–c2: Socrates turns to the boy of 243e9 and assures him that, whatever this experience may be called by men and by gods, its cause and nature are as he has described.

252b2   ὦ παῖ καλέ   Compare 243e9 and 237b7. This is the ideal boy in both of Socrates' speeches; and, on the level of Socrates' playful courtship of him, it is Phaedrus.

b3   θεοὶ δὲ ὃ καλοῦσιν   Θεοὶ has been pulled forward out of its place in the relative clause for the sake of the μὲν . . . δὲ antithesis with ἄνθρωποι. The Greeks assumed that the gods, like different races of men, spoke their own language. Homer gives us six items from the divine lexicon, including the hundred-handed monster Briareos (whom mortals call Aigaion) in *Iliad* 1.403–4 and the magical plant μῶλυ in *Odyssey* 10.305.

b4   **διὰ νεότητα**   As De Vries suggests, the παῖς καλός is too young to appreciate the hidden profundity of the divine name. Ironical, of course.

    γελάσῃ   The future of γελάω is consistently deponent in Plato.

    λέγουσι 'recite.'

b5   **ἀποθέτων**   Hackforth's "unpublished" walks a nice line between the two meanings 'secret' and merely 'laid by' and therefore 'not current.' Very likely the verses were made up by Plato and designed to be enigmatically Orphic.

    ἔπη 'lines' (LSJ s.v. IVc).

b6   **ὑβριστικὸν**   The outrage may be merely metrical, in which case καὶ . . . ἔμμετρον would be explanatory. The metrical irregularity lies in treating δὲ followed by initial πτ- as short, while the ultima of διὰ under the same prosodic conditions is treated (as is normal in Homer) as long.

b8   **τὸν** should be taken with ποτηνόν (= ποτανόν) as the direct object, Ἔρωτα being a predicate accusative.

b9   **ἀνάγκην** can be taken in at least two senses: as referring to love's need to grow wings, or as the wing-growing compulsion he imposes on the lover. The latter seems more convincing.

252c2   **τοῦτο ἐκεῖνο** 'just what I said.' Not the same as τοῦτ᾽ ἐκεῖνο at 241d2. There τοῦτο was pronominal; here it is adjectival. Socrates means that whether or not the reader puts any credence in the pseudo-Homeric lines above, his description has conveyed what brings lovers into being and what they experience in the process.

252c3–253c6: How lovers will vary in accordance with the nature of the god in whose train each followed.

252c3   **Τῶν . . . ὀπαδῶν** is a partitive genitive that recalls the celestial entourage described in 246e–247a. It was implied there that Zeus is the god followed by philosophers.

    ὁ ληφθεὶς sc. ὑπ᾽ ἔρωτος.

ἐμβριθέστερον is not an adjective denoting the weight of the burden, but an adverb denoting the manner in which it is borne: 'with greater dignity.' The comparison looks forward; its other term will be implied in the following sentence.

c4   τὸ ... ἄχθος 'the burden that consists of him of winged name'; genitive of material (S. 1323) that provides an oxymoron. The reference is to the name in b9, and De Vries is right in saying that the phrase shows that Plato is able to maintain an ironic distance even in the midst of enthusiastic flights.

c4–5   ὅσοι ... θεραπευταὶ sc. ἦσαν. For declension of Ares, see S. 285.1.

c6   ἀδικεῖσθαι in the lover's sense. Compare Sappho's self-questioning: τίς σε, ὦ Σάπφ', ἀδικήει; (Page, *Sappho and Alcaeus*, frag. 1.19–20).

c7   φονικοὶ ... παιδικά The sort of thing that appears in the local news day after day. Are these souls also represented as enjoying the beneficial effects of the fourth kind of divine madness? Apparently so. What follows would seem to imply as much.

252d1   καθ' ἕκαστον θεόν 'after the manner of each god.' See LSJ s.v. κατά B.IV.3.

ἦν Socrates is recalling the excursions of 246e–247b.

d2   εἰς τὸ δυνατὸν The obligatory recognition of human limitations.

d2–3   ἕως ἂν ᾖ ἀδιάφθορος See 250a3–4 and e1, and for the temporal clause, S. 2423b.

d5   τὸν ...Ἔρωτα obviously means 'the object of his passion' here (compare τοῦ πόθου in a7), so the epsilon should be printed lowercase.

τῶν καλῶν sc. παίδων, genitive of source.

d6   πρὸς τρόπου Plato did not use the article, and we need use no possessive in English: 'according to character,' leaving the question of whose character ambiguous, since it is a matter of fitting the one to the other.

ἐκεῖνον, as well as serving as object of τεκταίνεταί τε καὶ κατακοσμεῖ, is the subject of ὄντα, and αὐτὸν its predicate accusative: 'and as if that boy were himself [αὐτόν] a god for him [ἑαυτῷ].' The clause prefigures the care the lover will, as we shall see later, take to educate the boy and mold his way of living.

d7–e1   ὡς ... ὀργιάσων gives the grounds for his actions as the lover sees them: 'with the intention of revering him and celebrating his rites.' Compare 250c1 with note. For ὡς with future participles expressing intention, see S. 2065.

252e1 **μὲν δὴ οὖν** is transitional with μὲν adhering to οἱ . . . Διὸς and looking forward all the way to ὅσοι δ᾽ αὖ μεθ᾽ Ἥρας at 253b1, while δὴ οὖν "obviously then" (D. 468–69) looks backward and connects this sentence with its predecessor. Compare τε οὖν, which we just saw at d5: τε there looks forward to καὶ in the following clause, but οὖν is inferential and looks backward.

δῖόν There is no etymological connection with Διός, but the Greeks not surprisingly assumed that there was. Some editors and translators follow Plato's pun so far as to print the adjective with an uppercase delta or translate "someone Zeus-like" (Hackforth). Plato may also be punning on the name of his young friend Dion of Syracuse, who was his ἐρώμενος if anyone was.

e2 **ζητοῦσι** For ζητέω meaning 'desire' or 'want' and followed by accusative and infinitive, De Vries cites *Rep.* 2.375e7: ζητοῦμεν τοιοῦτον εἶναι τὸν φύλακα. Here τὸν ἐρώμενον is subject of the infinitive and δῖόν τινα predicate accusative.

τὴν ψυχὴν Accusative of respect is particularly common with parts of the body (S. 1601a). The ψυχή surely qualifies, being in there, as we remember, like an oyster in its shell (250c6).

e3 **ἡγεμονικὸς** We recall that Zeus was μέγας ἡγεμὼν at 246e4.

e4 **ἐρασθῶσι** See note on 231c5.

πᾶν ποιοῦσιν is an expression that usually carries negative connotations, implying that someone is a πανοῦργος, a thoroughgoing scoundrel. In his *Apology* (39a6) Plato makes Socrates disdain πᾶν ποιεῖν καὶ λέγειν to secure acquittal. Seen as a manifestation of divine madness, it becomes, if not exactly a virtue per se, at least an inevitable stage on the way to virtue.

e4–5 **ὅπως . . . ἔσται** 'to make him like that.' See S. 2211 for ὅπως + future indicative in object clauses after verbs of effort.

e5 **ἐμβεβῶσι** is a perfect subjunctive in the protasis of a present general condition: 'if they have (no) experience in.' See LSJ s.v. 5b; for the form, which is poetic, see S. 704a.

τῷ ἐπιτηδεύματι coming hard on the heels of πᾶν ποιοῦσιν ὅπως τοιοῦτος ἔσται, means primarily, as De Vries says, "the molding of the beloved," but what follows makes it clear that the remolding of the lover himself is involved as well.

e6 **τι δύνωνται** sc. μανθάνειν.

e7   ἰχνεύοντες δὲ παρ' ἑαυτῶν   Their memories of τὰ τότε provide the scent from within themselves. Hunting terms (here μετέρχονται as well as ἰχνεύοντες) are often applied metaphorically by Plato to the pursuit of either an argument or a loved one. For the latter, see e.g. the opening sentence of *Protagoras*, which was quoted in the note to 234a1–2.

e7–253a1   ἀνευρίσκειν follows εὐποροῦσι (in the sense 'to find a way' or 'be able'; see note on 235a4). The prefix must be attended to in translating it.

253a1–2   διὰ . . . βλέπειν   They succeed in the end not solely by their memories, but by being forced in an intense way (referring to the process so carefully described in 251a–252a) to look at their god in his new avatar, the παῖς καλός.

a2–3   ἐφαπτόμενοι . . . μνήμῃ   See LSJ s.v. ἐφάπτω II.2; αὐτοῦ is the god. Attend to the article with dative of means μνήμῃ. Socrates does not mean any old memory.

a3   ἐξ ἐκείνου can be taken with both ἐνθουσιῶντες and λαμβάνουσι; with the latter it does not merely mean that they receive their character traits and way of life from the god as a source, but that they conform to him in these matters; as we say, "he gets that from his father."

a5   τούτων . . . αἰτιώμενοι   Since αἰτιάομαι means to allege that someone (in the accusative) is the αἰτία of something (in the genitive), it can imply praise just as readily as blame. Τούτων refers to the lover's new way of life, which was alluded to in ἐνθουσιῶντες . . . ἐπιτηδεύματα.

a6   κἂν . . . ἀρύτωσιν   Madvig's χἂν (crasis of καὶ ἃ ἄν) would give the ordinarily transitive ἀρύτω an object, the whole providing an object for ἐπαντλοῦντες. That is very attractive, but perhaps not necessary, since the verb can be used absolutely, as in Xenophon's *Cyropaedia* 1.3.9: ἀρύσαντες ἀπ' αὐτῆς [τῆς φιάλης] τῷ κυάθῳ ('drawing from the beaker with the ladle').

  ὥσπερ αἱ Βάκχαι   The point of the comparison lies in drawing liquid from a divine source (milk and honey from Dionysus in the case of the Bacchants) and using it to 'irrigate' others.

a7   ποιοῦσιν   Understand the object τὸν ἐρώμενον.

253b2   βασιλικὸν sc. τινα. Compare 252e1–2, of which we have here, mutatis mutandis, a condensed version. When we compare the βασιλικός with ἡγεμονικὸς τὴν φύσιν (252e3), the advantage in inward qualities would seem to lie with the followers of Zeus.

Perhaps it is pertinent that in 248d the way of life that was second in dignity to the philosophical was that of the ἔννομος βασιλεύς, who was also πολεμικός. Both the retinue of Ares in 252c (with their concentration on the easily abused ideal of personal honor) and these regal followers of Hera may be Plato's somewhat perfunctory bow to essentially Dorian notions of homoeroticism as contributing to esprit de corps, which can be seen at greater length in the speeches of Phaedrus and, especially, Pausanias in his *Symposium.*

b3–4   **οὕτω κατὰ τὸν θεὸν** modifies both ἰόντες and πεφυκέναι. Just like the followers of Zeus and Hera they proceed each after his own god, and, again like them, each wants his παῖς to come to maturity in his god's image.

b4   **πεφυκέναι** 'be by nature.'

b6   **πείθοντες καὶ ῥυθμίζοντες** 'by persuasion and discipline.' **ἐκείνου** is the god.

b7   **ὅση ἑκάστῳ δύναμις** is parenthetical. The boys will differ in innate capacity.

b7–8   **οὐ φθόνῳ . . . χρώμενοι** As contrasted with the ἐραστής pilloried in Socrates' first speech as smotheringly possessive at 239a7ff. and an abusive boor in 240e.

253c1   **πᾶσαν . . . μάλιστα** Πᾶσαν πάντως makes the ὁμοιότητα as complete as possible; ὅτι μάλιστα makes the πειρώμενοι as earnest as possible.

c2   **οὕτω** We are approaching the end of this description of the process. On the heels of the emphasis pointed out in the preceding note, οὕτω now goes back to b3 and applies the whole sentence to ποιοῦσι.

c2–3   **προθυμία . . . τελετή** Reading τελετή yields 'desire and initiation' as subject. It comes from a correction in a thirteenth-century Paris manuscript. The main tradition shows τελευτή. The choice would, then, seem to be between 'desire and completion' (i.e. consummation) stated plainly and the same meaning through a metaphor of initiation, which is well prepared for in the context of the whole speech. Either pair makes a neat and particularly pointed chiasmus with διαπράξωνται ὃ προθυμοῦνται in the following clause.

c2   **μὲν οὖν** See note on 239b8.

c4   **ἢ λέγω** may well make διαπράξωνται mean something very different from what that verb meant in 234a3.

οὕτω καλή τε καὶ εὐδαιμονικὴ   Singular adjectives in agreement, as often, with the closer element in a compound subject, but also quite appropriate here, since it is really the τελετή (or τελευτή) alone that is 'so beautiful and productive of εὐδαιμονία.'

c5 γίγνεται   "falls to," as De Vries suggests.

c5-6 ἐὰν αἱρεθῇ   Thompson calls this "an explanatory repetition of ἐὰν διαπράξωνται ὃ προθυμοῦνται," but it is more than that. It turns our attention to the experience of the παῖς, making him the subject and preparing the way for the emphasis on his 'capture' in the sentence that follows.

c6 ὁ αἱρεθεὶς   This appellation, made as we turn from the fact of capture to its manner, echoes ὁ ληφθεὶς in 252c3. There is a theme of continuity here, of an experience moving through one who is captured by love to one who is captured by love's captive, or—in terms of the metaphor in a6—of one maddened by a divine fluid who then pours it into another.

253c7-e5: The account of how the beloved is caught begins with a description of the two horses of the soul.

253c7 ἐν ἀρχῇ τοῦδε τοῦ μύθου   See 246a6-7.

c7-d1 διείλομεν . . . τρίτον   Verbs of dividing can take accusative of both the thing divided and the parts into which it is divided. Compare *Plt.* 283d4: διείλωμεν . . . αὐτὴν δύο μέρη ('let us divide it [the art of measurement] into two parts'). The dual form εἴδει is avoided.

253d1-2 τῶν . . . ὁ δ' οὔ   In 246b2-3. For the tense of φαμέν, see KG 1.135-36 and GMT 28; in verbs of perceiving, knowing, or saying the present tense is sometimes made to reach back into past time.

d2-3 τοῦ ἀγαθοῦ ἢ κακοῦ   In a series sometimes the article is repeated, sometimes omitted. After collecting a multitude of instances in Plato, Riddell (237) concluded that "the object is, next to conciseness, to produce variety of expression and sound."

d3 οὐ διείπομεν   Since διαλέγω in the active is not a verb of speaking, διεῖπον is free to serve as second aorist of διαγορεύω: 'state explicitly or in detail.'

d4 ἐν τῇ καλλίονι στάσει   probably means on the right, in the position of honor and responsibility. See LSJ s.v. δεξιόσειρος, although a four-horse team is in question there.

d5 **διηρθρωμένος** Being well articulated is, in the view of Hippocrates (*Airs, Waters, Places* 24), a quality that goes along with being hard and lean (σκληρούς τε καὶ ἰσχυροὺς), whereas people who are fleshy (σαρκώδεες) are badly articulated (ἄναρθροι). 'Clean-limbed' might do nicely here. Fat does tend to conceal the exact placing of the joints and obscure the ratio of the parts of the limbs to each other.

ὑψαύχην Compare the *ardea cervix* of the admirable horse in Vergil's *Georgics* 3.79.

ἐπίγρυπος describes the line of the top of the muzzle. The term is complimentary for a horse and opposed to σιμοπρόσωπος (e2), but it is probably not complimentary when applied to Socrates' accuser Meletus in *Euthyp.* 2b11. Neither τὸ σιμόν nor τὸ γρυπόν would seem to be particularly attractive in noses, since the lover, according to Socrates (*Rep.* 474d8–9) finds it necessary to 'spin' either quality if it is present in his beloved. Aristotle tells us (*Politica* 5.1309^b 24) that εὐθύτης ('straightness') is καλλίστη in a nose.

λευκὸς ἰδεῖν Plato may be thinking of legendary teams like that of Rhesus in *Iliad* 10, but see note on e2–3. The infinitive is epexegetic, superficially like those often found with adjectives such as ἱκανός and ἄξιος.

d6 **μετὰ σωφροσύνης τε καὶ αἰδοῦς** limits the white horse's desire for τιμή just as μετὰ φιλοσοφίας limits παιδεραστήσαντες at 249a2.

d7 **ἀληθινῆς δόξης** means 'genuine glory,' not 'true opinion,' as can be seen by observing the contrasting ἀλαζονείας ἑταῖρος at e3. See LSJ s.v. δόξα III.2.

253e1 **ἡνιοχεῖται**, although formally the predicate for the whole string of nominative descriptive phrases, must be taken particularly closely with ἄπληκτος . . . λόγῳ.

e1–2 **πολύς, εἰκῇ συμπεφορημένος** This horse is massive and 'thrown together,' a big, ramshackle creature. The items in his description correspond roughly with those in that of the white horse. These two qualities, for instance, contrast with διηρθρωμένος in d5, as the preceding σκολιός contrasts with τό τε εἶδος ὀρθὸς in d4.

e2 **κρατεραύχην, βραχυτράχηλος** In this context no useful distinction is to be made between αὐχήν and τράχηλος: 'with a short, thick neck.'

e2–3   **μελάγχρως**   In the contrast between this and λευκὸς ἰδεῖν at d5 moral or spiritual qualities symbolized by black and white may play a part.

e3   **γλαυκόμματος**   See LSJ s.v. γλαυκός II.2 for citations to indicate that this gray or light blue color was not admired in eyes, despite its (perhaps erroneous) association with Athena's in Homer. Perhaps a weak, watery color is meant, contrasting with the sharp crispness implied by μελανόμματος in d5–6.

ὕφαιμος   It seems better to take this as meaning 'bloodshot' rather than as 'hot-blooded' with LSJ.

ὕβρεως καὶ ἀλαζονείας correspond to μετὰ σωφροσύνης τε καὶ αἰδοῦς and ἀληθινῆς δόξης (d6–7) respectively.

e4   **κωφός** is not to be taken literally; it corresponds to ἄπληκτος . . . λόγῳ at d7–e1 and tells us not that this horse is deaf in general, but that he is deaf to the persuasion by which the other is guided. One can imagine the charioteer shouting, like the exasperated mother of a five-year-old, "Can't you *hear*?" A question remains about the relationship, if any, between κωφός and the preceding περὶ ὦτα λάσιος. Some commentators have taken the latter as a sign of wantonness, which renders concrete what precedes. They have cited Aristophanes' *Clouds* 349, which may imply that hairiness was thought to be a sign of pederasty, but is more likely to mean merely, as the Ravenna scholiast ad loc. says, that a particular pederast, the son of Xenophantes, was shaggy. See Dover ad loc. Others think that it is preparatory to κωφός, setting out a reason for deafness. This seems unlikely, but if the notion (joke, really) that deafness resulted from a superfluity of hair around the ears was current in Athens in Plato's time, attention might be paid to Verdenius's deletion of κωφός as a gloss on what became an obscure phrase in succeeding centuries. Omission of κωφός would, incidentally, bring the strings of adjectives describing the two horses into nearly complete correspondence, but whether that is a plus or a minus is unclear, since Plato does not ordinarily strive for mechanical symmetry.

253e5–255a1: Seeing the boy for the first time sets off in the soul of the lover a violent struggle, in which again and again the charioteer acquiesces for a time in the desires of the black horse only to pull back at the last moment in repugnance, until, in the end, the black horse has itself been subjugated and filled with fear.

253e5   δ' οὖν dismisses the description of the horses and returns to the principal matter at hand, namely, the account, which was promised at c6, of how the captive is captured (S. 2959b).

τὸ ἐρωτικὸν ὄμμα refers primarily to the face of the boy, but the reader must keep in mind the primacy of light and vision in the process Socrates has described.

e5–6   πᾶσαν . . . ψυχήν It is the charioteer who initiates the proceedings; he, as Hackforth renders it, "causes a sensation of warmth to suffuse the whole soul." Αἰσθήσει is dative of manner of a bold sort. As Hackforth points out, translating it "by the (or his) perception" would require a definite article.

e6   γαργαλισμοῦ τε καὶ πόθου are what the κέντρα consist of; they are genitives of explanation (S. 1322), depending on κέντρων, itself a genitive with a verb of filling (S. 1369).

254a1   ὑποπλησθῇ i.e. when he 'begins to be filled with' the prickings of desire, as when Alcibiades was beginning to grow a beard (πώγονος ἤδη ὑποπιμπλάμενος) at *Prt.* 309a4–5. The sense imparted by ὑπο- in composition with a verb often diminishes its force, like its cognate *sub-* in Latin.

a2–3   ἑαυτὸν . . . ἐρωμένῳ For the redundant μὴ, see note on 251b4–5.

a3–4   κέντρων . . . ἐντρέπεται The horse no longer 'regards' or 'heeds' the charioteer's attempts to restrain it. Compare *Crito* 52c9, where Socrates imagines the laws of the city saying to him: οὔτε ἡμῶν τῶν νόμων ἐπιτρέπῃ ('nor do you heed us, the laws'). Burnet points out in his note ad loc. that in English as well such words as 'regard' and 'respect' originally meant to turn back and look at something. In this sense the verb takes the partitive genitive taken by verbs of remembering and caring for, like ἐπιμελέομαι or φροντίζω (S. 1356).

a4–5   πάντα πράγματα παρέχων 'making no end of trouble.'

a5   τῷ σύζυγί τε καὶ ἡνιόχῳ The article is often omitted from the second of two substantives connected by τε καί. Compare on 253d2–3.

ἀναγκάζει is a conative present. The black horse tries to make them proposition the boy, but we are not to take it that he succeeds.

a6–7   τῆς . . . χάριτος   The 'gratification' or 'delights' of love (LSJ s.v. χάρις IV).

a7   τὼ δὲ   The white horse (σύζυξ) and the charioteer.

254b1   ὡς . . . ἀναγκαζομένω   'on the grounds that they are being forced to commit dreadful crimes.' With this use of accusative of the act being forced on someone with the passive of ἀναγκάζω, compare πρὶν ὑπὸ σοῦ τι μεῖζον ἀναγκασθῆναι at 242a1–2 with note.

b2   ὅταν . . . κακοῦ   The black horse never lets up and outlasts them: κακόν as a substantive in the sense 'trouble.' Socrates is telling Phaedrus what happens repeatedly as a general rule, so the temporal clause shows ἄν with the subjunctive and is negated by μή (S. 2409a).

ἀγομένω restates that they are not acting of their own volition.

b4   πρὸς . . . εἶδον   Notice the shift to the plural; the black horse sees this sight too, but naturally the effect on him will not be the same as it is on the others.

τὴν ὄψιν is, like τὸ ἐρωτικὸν ὄμμα at 253e5, primarily the boy's face; here its brightness will be emphasized by ἀστράπτουσαν.

b5–6   τὴν τοῦ κάλλους φύσιν   Compare ἥ τε τοῦ πτεροῦ φύσις at 248c1 and note.

b6–7   καὶ . . . βεβῶσαν   This grouping is not meant as an item in a guidebook to the hyperuranian gallery, but as an association made in the memory of the charioteer of the two particular εἴδη he saw there that he is now most conspicuously betraying. For the form βεβῶσαν, see S. 704a. Κάλλος 'has stepped' onto a holy pedestal, so we could say that it 'is standing' there (LSJ s.v. βαίνω A.2).

b7–8   ἰδοῦσα . . . ὑπτία   The two participles and the predicate adjective are in formal agreement with μνήμη, even though ὁ ἡνίοχος is obviously the subject of the thought. Deponent use of the aorist passive of σέβομαι is very rare. Ἀναπίπτω is properly used of rowers, who fall back as their oars sweep forward.

254c1–2   ὥστ' . . . ἵππω   Καθίσαι could be transitive, but the horses are more likely to be its subject than its object: 'settle back [LSJ s.v. II.5] on their haunches.'

c4   θάμβους expresses a complex state of emotional shock, in which the dazzlement at the sight of the ὄψις ἀστράπτουσα plays a part along with horror at what he, the good horse, had almost done.

c5   **λήξας** 'as soon as he has recovered.'

c7   **ὀργῇ** is dative of manner ('passionately' or 'in anger'; LSJ s.v. II.2), as are **δειλίᾳ τε καὶ ἀνανδρίᾳ** in the following line.

c7–8   **πολλὰ . . . ὁμόζυγα** 'hurling a great deal of abuse both at the charioteer and at his yoke-mate.' In this sense κακίζω takes both a direct object and an internal accusative.

c8–d1   **λιπόντε . . . ὁμολογίαν** Since τάξιν λιπεῖν is a military technical term for desertion in the face of the enemy, ὁμολογίαν comes as a second object with the effect of a slight zeugma (S. 3048).

254d1   **ἀναγκάζων** is a conative present, as was ἀναγκάζει at a5. The meaning of the verb makes it particularly liable to this usage.

d2   **μόγις** 'grudgingly.'

        δεομένων is genitive absolute with temporal force. As its subject understand αὐτῶν, i.e. the charioteer and the white horse, who have already appeared in the accusative earlier in the sentence.

        ὑπερβαλέσθαι 'to postpone' (LSJ s.v. B.II).

d3–4   **προσποιουμένω** sc. αὐτώ. The charioteer and the white horse pretend to forget.

d4   **ἀναμιμνήσκων** This verb regularly takes accusative of the person reminded.

        χρεμετίζων This exclusively equine attribute comes almost as a surprise at this point. The series of participles in asyndeton is notable and expresses the determination of this horse, who has only one thing on his mind.

d5–6   **ἐπὶ . . . λόγους** refers to μνείαν ποιεῖσθαι τῆς τῶν ἀφροδισίων χάριτος from a6–7. For the use of ἐπί + accusative to express the object in view, especially when attaining the object involves movement toward it, see S. 1689.3d with N.

d6   **ἐγκύψας** usually denotes stooping to peer forward, but here it is a matter of being hunched over with the head down, in the manner of a beast pulling against resistance.

254e1   **ταὐτὸν πάθος παθών** As at b5ff., but the intensity of the struggle there is now ratcheted up by anaphora of ἔτι μᾶλλον and by devices pointed out in the next two notes and that on e4–5.

e1–2   **ὥσπερ . . . ἀναπεσών** Compare ἀνέπεσεν ὑπτία at b8. The charioteer falls back abruptly, as would a man who perceives that he is on the point of stepping into a trap. This adds vividness.

e2–4   **ἔτι μᾶλλον . . . καθήμαξεν** Another vivid touch: the charioteer pulls the bit back from the black horse's teeth and cuts into the corners of its mouth, bloodying its jaws.

τήν ... γλῶτταν refers to a6–7 again.

e4–5   τὰ σκέλη ... ἐρείσας   He forced the horse to 'sit,' as it were. Their struggle is epic: ἐρείδω is a verb common in the battle scenes of the *Iliad*, and the two words that follow it exhibit a distinctly Homeric turn of phrase, as may be seen In *Iliad* 5.397. ὀδύνῃσιν ἔδωκεν. Heroic poetry is fond of such grim understatements.

e8   συμβαίνει with accusative and infinitive: 'it comes to pass that ...' (LSJ s.v. III.b).

τότ' ἤδη   'then at last' or 'only then.'

e9   αἰδουμένην τε καὶ δεδιυῖαν   'with respect and awe.'

255a1–e4: How being served by the lover affects the soul of the beloved and awakens there feelings that correspond to the lover's own.

255a1–4   ἄτε ... θεραπεύοντι   Take ἄτε with both θεραπευόμενος and ὢν, so everything before ἐὰν in a4 is causal (S. 2085).

a1   θεραπείαν is a cognate accusative retained with a passive verb. The same pair was seen in the active at 239c3–4.

a2   τοῦ ἐρῶντος   The article is generic, and the participles in agreement with the phrase divide lovers into two classes: the lover who makes a show of being a lover, and the lover who has really experienced love.

a3   τοῦτο   i.e. the erotic μανία.

a4   ἐὰν ἄρα καὶ   'even if, let's say. ...' Here ἄρα emphasizes the hypothetical character of the notion being advanced (des Places 273) rather than the realization of a possibility, as D. 37–38 would have it.

a5   διαβεβλημένος ᾖ   'has been misled' (LSJ s.v. VI).

a5–6   ὡς ... πλησιάζειν   Understand ἐστί.

a7   δὲ   Apodotic δέ, contrasting an apodosis with a protasis that has preceded it, is common in Homer and Herodotus, uncommon— but not unknown—elsewhere (D. 177ff.). The light touch of increased emphasis it gives merely throws the transition into the main clause into slightly higher relief.

ἡλικία is not 'generation' here, but 'time of life,' thought of as something that progresses in a continuum.

τὸ χρεὼν is explained by οὐ ... εἵμαρται ... ἀγαθὸν μὴ φίλον ἀγαθῷ εἶναι in the following sentence.

	ἤγαγεν The gnomic aorist can stand in place of the present indicative in the apodosis of a present general condition (S. 2338).

ἤγαγεν The gnomic aorist can stand in place of the present indicative in the apodosis of a present general condition (S. 2338).

255b1 οὐ γὰρ δήποτε εἵμαρται Εἵμαρται takes an accusative and infinitive, and ποτε should probably be separated from δή, keeping its temporal force: 'for surely it is not ever fated that.'

b3 προσεμένου sc. τοῦ ἐρωμένου with both this participle and δεξαμένου: genitive absolute with temporal force. Compare προσέσθαι in b1: the verb seems to have been a term of art for budding "relationships."

b4 γιγνομένη goes closely with ἐγγύθεν and is causal.

b5 διαισθανόμενον 'as he becomes fully aware.'

b6 οὐδεμίαν i.e. any worth speaking of or considering; the expression is hyperbolic.

πρὸς 'in comparison with' (LSJ s.v. C.III.4). The phrase is a compendious comparison for which the full form would be πρὸς τὴν μοῖραν ἣν ὁ ἔνθεος φίλος παρέχεται.

b7–8 ὅταν...ὁμιλίαις The subject could be either the ἐρώμενος or the ἐραστής. Πλησιάζῃ here obviously implies more intimate contact than did πλησιάζειν in a6. On opportunities for erotic contact in the gymnasia, see e.g. Alcibiades' surprise and disappointment, because they came to nothing in his workouts with Socrates (*Sym.* 217c).

255c1 τότ' ἤδη See note on 254e8.

ὃν was attracted out of the gender of its antecedent ῥεύματος into that of its predicate accusative ἵμερον. The whimsical etymology that was given to ἵμερος in 251c6–7 is alluded to but not spelled out here.

c2 Γανυμήδους Ganymede's story begins in *Iliad* 20.231–35, where we are told that he was a son of Tros, the eponymous founder of Troy, that he was the handsomest of mortals, and that—because of his beauty—the gods snatched him up to be cupbearer for Zeus and live among them. In later accounts it is Zeus himself who carries the boy off, and at least by the time of the sixth-century (or possibly late-seventh-century) elegiac poems collected under the name of Theognis of Megara homoerotic intent had become explicit.

πολλὴ is predicate with φερομένη: 'in floods.'

c3 ἡ μὲν ... ἡ δ' Appositives of this sort demand a subject that can easily be divided in the mind, because it either consists of a collection of units (like στρατιά, for instance) or (like πηγή here) it consists of a nondenumerable but divisible mass (KG 1.286–87). As Cooper (47.28.3) points out, this appositive construction differs from the otherwise equivalent partitive genitive in that "the focus is on the comprehensive idea," whereas the focus would be on the parts into which it is analyzed if πηγή were to be put into the genitive.

ἀπομεστουμένου sc. τοῦ ἐραστοῦ: genitive absolute with temporal force.

c4   ἤ τις ἠχώ 'or maybe an echo.' See note on 230d7.

c4–5   ἀπὸ λείων τε καὶ στερεῶν Like rocks, for instance.

c6   διὰ τῶν ὀμμάτων goes closely with ἰόν.

c7–d1   ἀφικόμενον καὶ ἀναπτερῶσαν The subject of both participles is ῥεῦμα, and they denote the means by which it 'moistens the feather follicles.' Ἀναπτερῶσαν means 'by exciting erotically,' and we must understand an object, probably τὸν καλὸν from c6.

c7   ἤ . . . ἰέναι is an adverbial clause that indicates the manner of ἀφικόμενον; for πέφυκεν, see note on 246d6.

255d1   τὰς διόδους τῶν πτερῶν The translation (into anachronistically scientific terms) that I employed in the note on c7–d1 reflects my preference for 'feathers' here. On feathers versus wings in translating πτερά, see note on 251b6–7.

d2   ἔρωτος Ἐμπίμπλημι takes accusative of the thing filled but a partitive genitive of that with which it is filled.

d3   μὲν οὖν Affirmative (S. 2901a).

ὅτου sc. ἐρᾷ: an indirect question after ἀπορεῖ. Neuter, of course; we are not to take it that he knows that he is in love but is not sure with whom.

d3–4   οὔθ' . . . οὐδ' This sequence of negatives should lead to a climax in the second member (KG 2.290). Here that, if present, is scarcely perceptible. Editors who cannot find it have admitted Buttmann's οὐδ' to their texts in place of οὔθ' to obtain a simple 'neither . . . nor.'

d4–5   οἷον . . . ἀπολελαυκώς 'like a person who has caught an eye disease from someone else.' Take ὀφθαλμίας as genitive singular rather than accusative plural, because ἀπολαύω (like its near synonym ὀνίνημι) takes a cognate accusative of a neuter adjective (as at 256a1) but a partitive genitive of a substantive (KG 1.356).

d5   πρόφασιν is not an excuse or alleged reason here, as it was at 234a8. In the medical writers it means an "external exciting cause" (LSJ s.v. II), and that is obviously relevant in this context.

d7   **ἐκεῖνος** The ἐραστής, whereas the subject of the main verb λήγει is ὁ ἐρώμενος, as he was designated most recently in d2.

        ἐκείνῳ Dative with κατὰ ταὐτά, as it might depend on an adverb like ὁμοίως. For the reference of this and κατὰ ταὐτά (ἐκείνῳ) in the next line, compare 251d–e.

d8–e1   **εἴδωλον... ἔχων** Εἴδωλον is predicate accusative; ἀντέρωτα, the object, does not have negative connotations as does Antichrist. The force of the prefix goes back to the mirror comparison in d6; ἄντερως is, as we shall see in e3, inferior to ἔρως only in intensity.

255e1–2   **καλεῖ . . . εἶναι** The two main verbs use the same material for different constructions: αὐτὸν (i.e. ἀντέρως) is direct object of καλεῖ, but with οἴεται it is subject of εἶναι; φιλίαν also must do double duty, first as predicate accusative with καλεῖ, then as the alternative preferred to ἔρωτα, as predicate of εἶναι.

e2   **ἐκείνῳ** The ἐραστής.

e3   **φιλεῖν** means 'to kiss' here (LSJ s.v. 4).

e4   **καὶ δή** combines connection and immediacy: 'and straightway' (D. 249).

        ποιεῖ . . . ταῦτα Ταχὺ ('soon') is neuter accusative used as an adverb and can be thought of as modifying either ποιεῖ directly or the adverbial phrase τὸ μετὰ τοῦτο: 'afterward' (LSJ s.v. μετά C.II.2).

255e4–256b7: Success in the struggle to remain continent brings a victory of truly Olympic magnitude to the philosophic lovers.

255e5–6   **ἔχει... ἡνίοχον** 'has a suggestion to make to the charioteer.' The subjunctive comes by analogy with the indirect question οὐκ ἔχει ὅτι λέγῃ ('he doesn't know what to say'), in which it represents the deliberative subjunctive τί λέγω: 'what am I to say?' (GMT 572).

e6   **ἀντὶ** 'in requital for.'

256a2   **σπαργῶν δὲ καὶ ἀπορῶν** 'but swelling with passion and yet not knowing why.' Sometimes καί connects expressions that are at least mildly adversative. Denniston (292) compares the use of the English connective in the sentence, "He is seventy years old, and he walks ten miles a day."

        περιβάλλει . . . καὶ φιλεῖ Formally the subject remains the beloved's black horse, but insistence on this fact leads to a mental picture that might form part of a pornographic animated cartoon. As the sentence progresses, the ἐρώμενος, insofar as his actions are informed and determined by his black horse, seems to usurp the place of the grammatical subject in Socrates' mind. Then—with ὁμόζυξ in a5—he reverts and goes on as if he had been talking about the horse all the while.

a3   **ὡς … ἀσπαζόμενος** Intending to express his gratitude, in other words. Understand αὐτὸν ὄντα with εὔνουν.

a4   **οἷός … ἀπαρνηθῆναι** expresses result (S. 2497), literally 'he is such that he would not refuse. . . .' The infinitive is accompanied by ἄν, because the result clause forms the apodosis of a future-less-vivid condition to some unexpressed protasis like 'if he were asked.'

   τὸ αὑτοῦ μέρος is accusative of respect: 'as far as *he* is concerned.'

a5   **αὖ** 'for his part,' i.e. in contrast to the behavior of the black horse.

a6   **πρὸς ταῦτα** 'against these proceedings.'

a7   **μὲν δὴ οὖν** See note on 252e1. Here ἐὰν μὲν δὴ looks forward to ἐὰν δὲ δὴ at b7. Within the framework thus set up, μακάριον μὲν at a8 looks forward to τελευτήσαντες δὲ δὴ at b3; and within *that*, in the manner of Chinese boxes, δουλωσάμενοι μὲν at b2 looks forward to ἐλευθερώσαντες δὲ at b3.

   φιλοσοφίαν merely gives a name to τεταγμένην δίαιταν.

a8   **τὰ βελτίω τῆς διανοίας** implies a psychology based on the simple scheme of white horse and charioteer versus black horse.

   ἀγαγόντα sc. αὐτούς: 'by leading them.' Since the victory consists precisely in leading them to an ordered way of life, the aorist participle is synchronous with the main verb. Compare 251d2–3 with note.

256b2–3   **δουλωσάμενοι … ἀρετή** The relative pronouns are instrumental datives; one tends to think of the horses as their antecedents, but something more general is probably meant. The participles are causal. The tense of ἐνεγίγνετο shows that degeneration is a process.

b3   **τελευτήσαντες δὲ δὴ** The other two pairings remarked on in the note to a7 mark strongly antithetical members, but μακάριον μὲν and τελευτήσαντες δὲ δὴ merely distinguish with a certain emphasis two stages in the working out of a life informed by the best sort of μανία.

b4–5   **τῶν . . . νενικήκασιν** The Olympic wrestler had to win three falls before being crowned victor, just as the philosophical lovers had to defeat κακία in three earthly lives before returning to the heavens (249a3–4). They are, moreover, votaries of Zeus, god of Olympia.

b5   **οὗ** is genitive of comparison (S. 1431).

b6   **οὔτε . . . μανία** sc. ἐστί. De Vries is correct in saying that this is a "polar" expression—one that indicates completeness by mentioning the two ends of a spectrum—and does not imply that σωφροσύνη ἀνθρωπίνη has played any part at all in this triumph.

256b7–e2: How those who yield on occasion to the urging of their black horses, but remain friends throughout their lives, win a reward less glorious than that of the fully philosophical lovers alone.

256c1   **ἀφιλοσόφῳ** Compare on φιλοσοφίαν at a7; τε καὶ is explanatory in both phrases.

φιλοτίμῳ affords a direct link between this tripartite soul and the tripartite psychology of the *Republic*. The soul that follows a φιλότιμος way of life here resembles the citizen appropriate to a τιμοκρατία in *Rep.* 548eff. in that it is 'more self-willed' (αὐθαδέστερος) and—as it shows under the influence of wine—'rather less cultivated' (ὑποαμουσότερος) than is the philosophical soul. There as here the φιλότιμος is, as Thompson says, "put second in order of excellence to the φιλόσοφος."

τάχ' ἄν taken together with the aorist indicative main verb yields a past potentiality: 'perhaps they [the two unruly horses] may have . . .' (GMT 221).

c2   **αὐτοῖν** refers to the lover and beloved of this second rank.

c2–3   **λαβόντε . . . ἀφρούρους** 'having caught their souls off guard' (LSJ s.v. λαμβάνω 4).

c3   **εἰς ταὐτόν** can be taken in either a local or a psychological sense, ambiguous in English as in Greek.

c4–5   **εἱλέσθην τε καὶ διεπραξάσθην** These dual middles come from a citation in Eusebius and are found nowhere in the direct tradition. They look very much like conscious corrections intended to regularize the verbs in accord with the dual subject, an unnecessary refinement, as the first clause in the very next sentence shows. It would be better to abide by the manuscript readings εἰλέτην τε καὶ διεπράξαντο, take αἵρεσιν in a concrete sense, and say that 'they may have taken the course of action [LSJ s.v. αἵρεσις B.II] deemed happiest by the crowd and may have gone the limit.' For the implications of διεπράξαντο, see note on 234a3.

c6   **αὐτῇ**   i.e. ταύτῃ τῇ αἱρέσει.

σπανίᾳ is a predicate adjective, which—like its Latin counterpart *rarus*—often seems to come into idiomatic English better as an adverb.

c6-7   **ἅτε ... πράττοντες** explains σπανίᾳ.

c7   **ἐκείνων**   i.e. the pairs of philosophical lovers.

c7-d1   **ἀλλήλοιν** is to be taken with φίλω.

256d1   **διά** expresses duration: 'while they remain in love' (LSJ A.II.1), love affairs seen as a measure of time, like weeks or years.

ἔξω sc. τοῦ ἔρωτος or αὐτοῦ in its place.

d3   **λύσαντες** meaning 'rescind' or 'annul' (LSJ s.v. II.4b). A 'breakup' is in question.

d4   **ὡρμηκότες δὲ πτεροῦσθαι** 'but in the act of [or perhaps at the point of] growing plumage.'

d6   **τὴν ὑπὸ γῆς πορείαν** refers to 249a6-7. Since Phaedrus can be expected to remember what was said there, Socrates uses the definite article. The accusative expresses "the way over which" (S. 1581).

d7-8   **τοῖς ... πορείας** The state symbolized by ὡρμηκότες πτεροῦσθαι at d4 can, then, be taken as marking the beginning of the heavenly sojourn mentioned at 249a7-b1, not of the flight to view the forms; that is a hyperuranian, not a hypouranian, journey. That their reward is contrasted with journeying to darkness in the underworld makes this certain. For the genitive, see LSJ s.v. κατάρχω II.

d8   **ἀλλὰ** allows νόμος ἐστὶν to shed its negative, cross over into the second half of the sentence, and govern the two infinitives it finds there.

φανὸν 'joyous' (LSJ s.v. 3).

256e1   **ὁμοπτέρους** This indicates that their wings will be like those of the philosophical lovers, since there seems to be no point in indicating that each of the pair will have plumage like that of the other.

e2   **ὅταν γένωνται** sc. ὑπόπτεροι. There is no implication that this will happen during the present sojourn; the phrase means no more than 'sooner or later' or 'at some time or other.' Compare *Euthyp.* 7d4–5: ἐχθροὶ ἀλλήλοις γιγνόμεθα, ὅταν γιγνώμεθα. Burnet—on ὅταν ὑπομένωσιν at *Phd.* 68d9—says that "the addition of such phrases is almost a mannerism."

256e3–257b6: Socrates briefly contrasts the consequences for the boy of the love he has just described with the relationship based on worldly wisdom that was advocated, directly or by implication, in the two earlier speeches. He then ends with a prayer to Eros, begging him to turn Lysias, the begetter of those speeches, and his admirer Phaedrus away from such pursuits and to the love of wisdom.

256e3   ὦ παῖ takes the reader back to 243e9 and the beginning of the Palinode.

        θεῖα οὕτω goes in tandem with τοσαῦτα, both of them predicated of ταῦτα.

e5   σωφροσύνη θνητῇ κεκραμένη The dative is instrumental: 'diluted by mortal prudence.'

e5–6   θνητά ... οἰκονομοῦσα Emphasis is on θνητά; φειδωλὰ makes explicit one of its aspects and is to be understood under its heading. The nonlover's gifts may well be more costly than those of the lover, but they are nevertheless φειδωλά, because they are θνητά. Οἰκονομοῦσα is 'dispensing' (LSJ s.v. 2).

257a1   ἐννέα χιλιάδας ἐτῶν The number would seem to be arrived at by assuming that the earthly lives taken up every thousand years (249b) will themselves make up one thousand out of the ten-thousand-year period between returns to the winged state that even nonphilosophical souls experience (248e6).

        περὶ γῆν, as opposed to ὑπὸ γῆς in the following line, implies flitting about on the surface of the earth. Plato may also have in mind the activities, often violent, attributed to the ghosts of heroes, particularly in the vicinities of their tombs. This alternative to the underworld was not mentioned in 249a6–7; it is certainly not equivalent to the εἰς τοὐρανοῦ τινα τόπον ὑπὸ τῆς Δίκης κουφισθεῖσαι alternative at 249a7–8. Souls that have followed one of the other gods will be there, along with the followers of Zeus in the two periods of between-lives probation required of them, not souls that have lived by the dictates of σωφροσύνη θνητή.

a2   **κυλινδουμένην . . . παρέξει** For παρέχω with object and predicate accusative in the sense 'cause a thing to be in a certain state,' see LSJ s.v. A.V and compare note on 238a5.

a3–4   **Αὕτη . . . παλινῳδία** The spacious division between the demonstrative subject and the noun, which, along with its two adjectives, supplies its predicate nominative, frames the statement of dedication to Eros.

a3   **εἰς** 'up to the limits of.' The phrase, by reminding us of the limits of human power in dealing with a god, more or less takes away with one hand what ὅτι adds to the superlative adjective with the other.

a4–5   **τά . . . τισιν** See note on 234c7. The Palinode is poetic especially in its language. It is necessary to understand ποιητικῶς with τά τε ἄλλα, as De Vries recommends.

a5–6   **διὰ Φαῖδρον** Phaedrus had both read the Lysias speech and forced Socrates to compete with it, which in turn put Socrates into danger from which he could extricate himself only by a poetic Palinode à la Stesichorus.

a6   **ἀλλὰ** Hitherto Socrates has been merely addressing Eros, but with this word the prayer proper begins. Of the ἀλλά found at the opening of prayers, Denniston (15) comments that it "merely marks a gentle transition from a known present to an unknown and desired future."

a7   **ἵλεως** is Attic and formulaic with εὐμενής in prayers. Consult LSJ s.v. ἵλαος.

a7–8   **τὴν . . . ἔδωκας** No doubt Socrates alludes to the skills required for his activities as public relations consultant for Eros (*Sym.* 212b) and the god-given skill at recognizing amorous pairs he attributes to himself in *Lys.* 204c1–2: τοῦτο δέ μοί πως ἐκ θεοῦ δέδοται, ταχὺ οἵῳ τ᾽ εἶναι γνῶναι ἐρῶντά τε καὶ ἐρώμενον ('this divine gift has somehow been given to me: the ability to recognize a lover and a loved one quickly'). In Xenophon's *Symposium* 4.56ff. he claims the arts appropriate to the μαστροπός or pimp, but there he is not wholly serious.

257b1   **λόγῳ** refers to both of the earlier speeches.

    ἀπηχὲς De Vries rightly points out that this is part of Hermeias's comment rather than of his lemma and rightly prefers ἀπηνὲς ('rough, hard'), the reading of B and T. He suggests the translation "shocking."

b2   πατέρα in the sense in which the Romans used *auctor*: the person to whom belongs the praise or blame for whatever is in the genitive.

b3   τῶν τοιούτων λόγων is genitive of separation (S. 1392) with παῦε, akin to the genitive seen with λήγω several times already. Socrates means speeches like that which the dialogue attributes to Lysias; by λόγου in the preceding line he probably means all three speeches, since Lysias was, in a sense, πατήρ of the entire competition.

b3–4   ὥσπερ . . . τέτραπται At the opening of the *Republic* Polemarchus seems to be on quite easy and familiar terms with Socrates. He sustains the role of Socrates' interlocutor with good humor and a fair degree of acuity for almost five Stephanus pages before yielding to the more intellectually engaged Thrasymachus.

b4   τρέψον sc. αὐτόν.

b4–5   ὁ ἐραστὴς ὅδε αὐτοῦ Compare 236b5 and 279b3, where Lysias is referred to as Phaedrus's παιδικά. De Vries is very sensible about this sort of banter: "There is no need to take such terms too seriously, nor to attenuate their meaning too much, thereby equally taking them too seriously."

b5   ἁπλῶς contrasts with ἐπαμφοτερίζῃ.

b6   πρὸς . . . ποιῆται 'may make a life for himself with philosophical discourse in accordance with love.' See LSJ s.v. πρός C.III.5.

COMMENTARY: PART III

TOWARD AN ART OF SPEAKING

IN THE HEAT OF THE DAY

257b7–258d3: Phaedrus expresses his admiration for Socrates' speech and doubts that Lysias would dare to compose a rejoinder, especially since he recently heard a politician reproaching him for being a speech writer. Socrates then proceeds to convince Phaedrus that, although public men may pretend to despise speech writing, they practice it and look to it to win them immortal fame. And so, the two friends conclude, there can be nothing shameful about writing speeches per se.

257b7–c1   **εἴπερ . . . εἶναι** Understand ἐστί with ἄμεινον and take the accusative and infinitive phrase ταῦθ' . . . εἶναι as its predicate: 'since it is better for us that it be this way.' On εἴπερ see S. 2246.

257c1   **πάλαι** 'almost from the beginning.'

c2   **θαυμάσας ἔχω** = τεθαύμακα (S. 1963), here it governs an indirect question as well as a direct object.

   ὅσῳ . . . ἀπηργάσω Neither now nor later does Phaedrus question or comment on the strange and wonderful *content* of Socrates' speech. Ὅσῳ is dative of degree of difference (S. 1513), and τὸν λόγον has been pulled forward to stand first in the sentence. The speech, although not the grammatical subject of the main clause, is what the sentence is about.

c3   **ὀκνῶ** takes the construction of a verb of fearing here (S. 2224a).

   ἐὰν . . . ἐθελήσῃ 'if he is actually willing' or 'if he is willing at all.' Εἰ ἄρα often introduces a hypothesis that seems improbable (S. 2796), and this nuance is here made more explicit with καὶ (S. 2884). Ἐθέλω is never merely a synonym of βούλομαι; taken with the particles here, it adds up to 'dares.'

c5   **λοιδορῶν** governs both accusative of person αὐτόν and the internal accusative τοῦτ' αὐτὸ: "reproaching him on this very score" (Hackforth). Ὠνείδιζε would take dative of person (hence Heindorf's conjecture αὐτῷ), but here that is left unexpressed for us to understand out of αὐτόν.

c6   **ἐκάλει λογογράφον** explains what was meant by τοῦτ' αὐτὸ. Lysias was a professional writer of speeches for others to declaim in court. This may well have been the specific meaning of λογογράφος at the dramatic date of the dialogue, and Thucydides

1.21.1 may be λοιδορῶν when he refers to earlier prose historians, down to and including Herodotus, as λογογράφοι. The tense of ἐκάλει should be observed: 'kept calling.'

c7   ἐπίσχοι . . . τοῦ γράφειν   Ἡμῖν is an ethical dative (S. 1486). Its force might be brought out by changing the structure: 'Perhaps from now on we may find him refraining from writing out of concern for his reputation.' For ἐπίσχοι, see LSJ s.v. IV.2b. For ὑπὸ with genitive to express "internal cause," see S. 1698.1b with n1.

c8   Γελοῖόν γ᾽ . . . λέγεις   'How ridiculous is the opinion you express!' A predicate adjective in this position, especially when followed by emphatic γε, can often best be rendered by making it into a clause (S. 1169). That δόγμα means Phaedrus's opinion that Lysias may abandon speech writing (and not the unnamed politician's reported opinion that being a speech writer is somehow discreditable) is shown by the didactic, and slightly exasperated, tone of ὦ νεανία.

c8–d1   τοῦ . . . διαμαρτάνεις   For the genitive with verbs of aiming at, obtaining, or missing, see S. 1349–52.

257d1   Συχνὸν is the usual adverb, συχνῶς being comparatively rare: 'by a mile.'

d2   ψοφοδεᾶ   For the form, see S. 292d. We tend to substitute the visual metaphor 'afraid of his shadow.'

d2–3   ἴσως . . . ἔλεγεν   'and maybe you also think that the man who was railing at him was saying what he was saying in reproach.' There is no doubt that he was railing, but his motive is not so transparent. The point of καὶ is, 'You are mistaken in thinking Lysias afraid of criticism, so maybe you imagine that this man, too, has motives that he does not, in fact, have.'

d4   σύνοισθά   With the prefix Phaedrus associates Socrates' opinion with his own. De Vries suggests "you know yourself" or "you know as well as I do."

d5   σεμνότατοι   Put in the mouth of Socrates, this word would be ironical about these people's evaluation of themselves; when it is put in the mouth of Phaedrus, Plato is being ironical about Phaedrus's acceptance of that self-evaluation.

d7   συγγράμματα ἑαυτῶν   'compositions of their own,' which would include, but not be limited to, speeches.

d8   μὴ σοφισταὶ καλῶνται   See note on κατὰ Ἡρόδικον at 227d4 for another Platonic passage in which it is implied that a reputation for being a sophist was something to avoid. It became a reproach when it was associated with teaching for pay and bringing an ethically neutral professionalism to the art of persuasion in the last third of the fifth century, a time during which many of Plato's most frequently read dialogues are set. I doubt that Herodotus would have resented being called a sophist.

d9–e1 **Γλυκὺς ἀγκών . . . ἐκλήθη** Phaedrus has not noticed that people do not always say what they mean directly. No doubt the 'long bend along the Nile,' wherever it may have been, meant a tedious spell of sailing or rowing; people, therefore, called it the 'sweet bend,' as they called the treacherous Black Sea the Εὔξενος or 'Hospitable' Sea. Our passage shows that the expression became proverbial.

257e1–2 **πρὸς τῷ ἀγκῶνι** 'in addition to the matter of the bend.'

e2–3 **οἱ μέγιστον . . . πολιτικῶν** provides Socrates' less naïvely respectful version of Phaedrus's οἱ μέγιστον δυνάμενοί τε καὶ σεμνότατοι at d5. See LSJ s.v. φρονέω II.2b for μέγα φρονέω in both its complimentary and derogatory senses.

e4 **οἵ γε καὶ** 'since indeed . . . they'; in a causal relative clause (S. 2555a) γε emphasizes the pronoun; καὶ adds more emphasis. This is the Greek equivalent of Latin *quippe qui* with the subjunctive.

e5 **τοὺς ἐπαινέτας** 'their supporters,' as we shall find.

e5–6 **προσπαραγράφουσι πρώτους** 'they write in at the top.'

e7 **Πῶς . . . μανθάνω** Phaedrus's puzzlement is understandable. To make his point Socrates has extended the meaning of λογογραφία to include the writing of decrees to be voted on by the ekklesia, which lay outside the normal usage of the word, and he has pushed the meaning of ἐπαινέτης to a place that will require further context if it is to be made clear.

258a1–2 **ἐν ἀρχῇ ἀνδρὸς πολιτικοῦ [συγγράμματι]** Examination of an apparatus even as meager as Burnet's will show that there are few possible surgical procedures that have not been tried on this phrase. His own excision of συγγράμματι seems to leave too much to be supplied by the reader. Herwerden's συγγράμματος (depending on ἀρχῇ) leads to an accumulation of genitives, but that may seem to be more of an infelicity to us than it would have to Plato. Most attractive is Madvig's deletion of ἀρχῇ, which could have been attached to συγγράμματι as a kind of gloss on πρῶτος by a copyist too eager to make everything perfectly clear: ἐν ἀνδρὸς πολιτικοῦ συγγράμματι is succinct, unclogged, and complete. That is the text Moreschini prints; he also rightly punctuates the sentence as a question.

a4–5   Ἔδοξέ . . . ἀμφοτέροις Only now, presumably, will Phaedrus fully understand what sort of "speech writing" Socrates means, as he recognizes the formulaic language, which he could read at the beginning of many inscriptions giving the texts of laws that he could see around him in the city. The ἐπαινέται of 257e5 were not, after all, literary critics.

a5   ὃς <καὶ ὃς> εἶπεν 'so-and-so spoke' exhibits the use of ὅς not as a relative but as a demonstrative pronoun, which is common in Homer and survives in Attic in a few idiomatic niches, notably the familiar ὃς δέ ('and he') that we find at the beginning of clauses to make a subject of someone or something that has played a different syntactical rôle in what has preceded. See LSJ s.v. A.2.

    τὸν αὑτὸν KG 1.625 translates *sein liebes ich*: 'his own dear self.' Compare the defensive, slightly self-pitying τὸν ἐμὲ in *Tht.* 166a5. This ironical use of the article with the personal pronoun seems to occur only in the accusative case. Δὴ further deepens the ironic tone. For an example from Plato's time that will exhibit the elements of epigraphic style that Socrates is making use of here, take the beginning of a decree honoring Mytilene dating from the first half of the 360s B.C.E. (Tod 2.95):Ἔδοξεν τῆι βουλῆι καὶ τῶι δήμωι. Διόφαντος εἶπεν.

a6   λέγει is to be taken absolutely: "he proceeds with what he has to say" (Hackforth); i.e. the body of the decree will follow.

a7   ἐπιδεικνύμενος is the technical term for giving a display of rhetorical proficiency as we find it, for instance, in the opening of Plato's *Gorgias* (three times on 447, the first Stephanus page of the dialogue, along with two instances of the cognate noun ἐπίδειξις). Socrates uses it here in order to present Athenian politics as a performing art and the writing of laws as just another literary genre.

a9   λόγος συγγεγραμμένος This would be more a product of collaboration than Socrates lets on. We can infer part of the usual procedure from the scene in Aristophanes' *Thesmophoriazusae*, in which the women constitute themselves an assembly in order to deliberate on the question of how to get rid of Euripides. One of them advances, in general terms, a plan to kill him ἢ φαρμάκοισιν ἢ μιᾷ γέ τῳ τέχνῃ ('by poison or some other means') and ends her speech as follows (431–32): ταῦτ' ἐγὼ φανερῶς λέγω, τὰ δ' ἄλλα μετὰ τῆς γραμματέως συγγράψομαι ('so much I say in open assembly; the rest I will get written with the help of the secretary').

The γραμματεύς (the gender given the word by Aristophanes is, of course, an ad hoc result of his plot) is the first collaborator. The second would be the ὑπογραμματεύς or undersecretary, a permanent, professional clerk, who was conversant with legal language. Socrates is giving a simplified version of the process, because he wants to make the politicians out to be authors.

258b2   **οὗτος** sc. ὁ λόγος συγγεγραμμένος.

ἐμμένῃ Laws to be voted on were posted written on wooden tablets (σανίδες); if they were voted down the text would be wiped out (see ἐξαλειφθῇ in the following line), but if carried they would be inscribed in stone; ἀναγράφειν εἰς τὸν τοῖχον is the technical term found in Andocides' *On the Mysteries* 84. The τοῖχος in question would probably be that of the βασίλειος στοά, according to Aristotle's *Constitution of Athens* 7.1, the same passage cited in the note on 235d8–9. Only then could the decrees properly be said to ἐμμένειν.

b2–3   **ἀπέρχεται . . . ὁ ποιητής** The metaphor makes the point that was remarked on in the note to a7 even more striking, especially since it lacks the introductory ὡς or ὥσπερ usual with figurative language in prose.

b3–4   **ἐξαλειφθῇ . . . γένηται** The subject of the first verb is οὗτος (ὁ λόγος), that of the second is ὁ συγγραφεύς from a6 (or ὁ ποιητής, as he appeared more recently, in metaphorical guise). Since the switch in subjects in this conditional clause exactly parallels the one in the preceding sentence, it is not difficult.

b5   **οἱ ἑταῖροι** 'his faction,' not the same as either the βουλή or the δῆμος of a4, where the whole body is meant, just as we say that Congress passed a law, even though a large number of members may have voted against it. Socrates takes the same liberty in equating οἱ ἐπαινέται with ἡ βουλή and ὁ δῆμος in 257e–258a.

b7   **Δῆλόν γε** shows the γε that is frequent in Plato (and unknown elsewhere) when a speaker amplifies his original statement after his interlocutor has expressed agreement (D. 138).

b7–8   **ὑπερφρονοῦντες τοῦ ἐπιτηδεύματος** Verbs of caring for and disdaining qualify for inclusion in the genitive with verbs of remembering and forgetting (S. 1356). The governing verb to be understood is πενθοῦσι out of πενθεῖ in b5.

b8   **τεθαυμακότες** is an intensive perfect; see note on 234d7–8.

b9   **Πάνυ μὲν οὖν** See note on 238c7. As Denyer says on *Prt.* 310a5, "this otherwise rare formula occurs frequently in Plato and

Xenophon's Socratic works. It has a distinctly philosophical ring to judge by the pointed way people start using it when Socrates starts asking questions."

b10–c2   ἱκανὸς ... ὥστε ... λογογράφος   Ἱκανὸς (a predicate adjective here) takes an epexegetic infinitive pure and simple, but sometimes an essentially redundant ὥστε is added, possibly to render explicit a latent notion of result in constructions that normally take the infinitive alone. Compare 269d2 with note and, for many examples, see C. 65.3.1.A. Λυκούργου ... Δαρείου are all, in their respective states, associated with law codes that have come to make them seem "immortal" by Plato's time. Solon and Lycurgus had become canonical among Greeks as examples of lawgivers, but Plato's addition of the barbarian Darius to the pair is both interesting in itself and also explains the otherwise puzzling inclusion of ἢ βασιλεύς in b10. Their δύναμις is the authority to make laws and leave them for posterity. Λογογράφος finally explicitly pins on the politicians who write the laws the name that was given to Lysias and his kind in 257c6.

258c4–5   θεώμενοι ... συγγράμματα   They are all thought of as, according to the custom of Athens, reading their laws recorded on public inscriptions.

c7   τῶν τοιούτων   i.e. the politicians.

c7–8   ὅστις ... Λυσίᾳ   'whoever he may be and however hostile to Lysias.'

c8   αὐτὸ τοῦτο is an internal accusative with ὀνειδίζειν: 'to make just this reproach,' which is then defined by ὅτι συγγράφει.

c9   Οὔκουν εἰκός γε   'it certainly isn't likely;' see D. 423 and compare 276c10 with note.

       καὶ γάρ   'for in fact.' See note on 243c1.

c9–10   τῇ ... ἐπιθυμίᾳ   Dative of either person or thing is regular with ὀνειδίζειν (compare note on 257c5), unless, as in the preceding sentence, it takes a neuter pronoun as internal accusative.

258d1–2   αὐτό ... λόγους   'writing speeches in and of itself, in any case.' Αὐτός often means 'alone, all by oneself'; see Ast's *Lexicon* and Bluck on *Meno* 72c1, who speculates that this may have been the use of the word that led to Plato's special use in connection with his theory of forms, as in, e.g. αὐτῇ καθ' αὑτήν and αὐτὸ καθ' αὑτό in *Phd.* 66a.

d3   Τί γάρ;   'of course it isn't' (D. 85–86).

258d4–259b4: *Socrates and Phaedrus quickly agree that, since it is writing badly, not writing in itself, that is shameful, they ought to look into the nature of good writing and bad writing. But before they can take up this question they are brought back to an awareness of their surroundings by the sound of cicadas singing overhead. Socrates arouses Phaedrus's curiosity by alluding to a boon that the cicadas could confer on them.*

258d4   ἤδη directs us, as it often does, to the point that has been reached in the argument: 'but (now that speaking and writing per se have been shown not to be shameful) in my opinion this is where shame comes in.' Compare 241b1 with note.

d4–5   τὸ ... κακῶς The long, double articular infinitive phrase is in explanatory apposition with ἐκεῖνο.

d7   Τίς ... γράφειν Most manuscripts attribute this question to Phaedrus, but it was influentially given to Socrates by Marsilio Ficino in the fifteenth century. Since then an overwhelming preponderance of editors has followed his lead, no doubt because they think that assigning this question to Phaedrus gives him initiative in consciously shaping the discussion that, as De Vries puts it, "is not in his character." Since our sense of his character is derived from what he says in the dialogue, that argument tends toward circularity. Phaedrus everywhere shows enthusiasm for what he would take to be good writing, which is not necessarily what Socrates would mean by the term. He is about to blurt out, in e1–5, sentiments that are almost comical in their enthusiasm and equally "out of character" for the laid-back role in the discussion that prevailing views assign to him. A strong case can be made for leaving the attribution as it is in the manuscripts, with Socrates returning in d8.

d8   δεόμεθα ... ἐξετάσαι For ἐξετάζω with two accusatives in the sense 'submit someone to an examination,' see *Grg.* 515b1: ἐάν τίς σε ταῦτα ἐξετάζῃ. The construction eluded a scribe, who replaced τι with the τοι that is the reading of most manuscripts.

d9–11   εἴτε ... ἰδιώτης Two separate distinctions are made, one of content and one of form. In each the derivative of ἴδιος distinguishes the lay genre or writer from the professional. The distinctions made are rough and will not bear close scrutiny.

258e1   μὲν οὖν is of the corrective type (S. 2901b), further strengthened here by the repetition of Socrates' δεόμεθα as a question before

Phaedrus begins his own question. Why would Socrates have even asked such a thing?

κἄν The καί is adverbial. What motive would one have for so much as living?

e2   **ὡς εἰπεῖν** = ὡς ἔπος εἰπειν and alerts the reader to the coming hyperbole.

ἀλλ' ἤ For this expression separating a negation (here a rhetorical question that expects a negative reply) from an exception to it, see D. 24–25. The use of ἤ does not follow logic and probably results from analogy with expressions involving comparatives.

e2–3   **οὐ γάρ που ἐκείνων** is short for οὐδεὶς γάρ που ἂν ζῴη τῶν γε ἡδονῶν ἐκείνων ἕνεκα.

e3   **προλυπηθῆναι** Understand αὐτόν as subject out of τις in e2; ὧν depends on the prefix.

    μηδὲ 'not . . . at all' (D. 196–97)

e4   **ὀλίγου** = ὀλίγου δεῖ (S. 1399).

e6   **Σχολὴ . . . ἔοικε** Μὲν δή is probably simply a strong affirmation; possibly, though, it looks forward to καὶ, which introduces another reason for acquiescing in Phaedrus's enthusiastic demand for a discussion that had been suggested by Socrates in the first place. For such loose correlations of μέν with particles that denote mere addition, see D. 374. Socrates seems unimpressed by his friend's sudden and uncharacteristic outburst of moral fervor.

e6–7   **ὡς ἐν τῷ πνίγει** is not a comparison; ὡς, as frequently, means 'as happens.'

259a1   **καθορᾶν καὶ ἡμᾶς** 'to look down on us too,' perhaps with a touch of humility, perhaps simply relating the obvious facts. Καὶ cannot be correlative with the preceding καὶ, which connected the participles.

a1–2   **καὶ νώ** coming so soon after ἡμᾶς perhaps points up the distinction from the undoubted plural τοὺς πολλούς.

a3   **ὑφ' αὑτῶν** The direct reflexive as object of a preposition contrasts with the indirect reflexives σφίσιν at a5 and σφας at a7. Otherwise their syntactical environments are the same, since all three refer us to the subject of the main verb, but are dependent on subordinate participles.

a5   **τὸ καταγώγιον** = ἡ καταγωγή at 230b2. The diminutive seems not to be "contemptuous," as De Vries would have it, but to express affectionate amusement.

244

a6   ἐὰν δὲ ὁρῶσι contrasts delicately with εἰ οὖν ἴδοιεν at a1. The apodosis of both sentences will be potential, but there the protasis is future-less-vivid and expects that fate, whereas here Socrates begins with a future-more-vivid protasis and then fades into potentiality (KG 2.479–80).

a7–b1   διαλεγομένους ... ἀκηλήτους sc. ἡμᾶς.

a7   ὥσπερ Σειρῆνας The comparison is with σφας. We must keep in mind that the Siren song of the cicadas is, for them, a conversation (ἀλλήλοις διαλεγόμενοι at a1).

259b2   ἀγασθέντες 'out of admiration.'

b3   ἀνήκοος is not a word with a ready counterpart in standard English: perhaps 'out of the loop' will prove to be durable.

259b5–d9: Socrates recounts a myth that explains the origin of cicadas and their function as intelligence gatherers for the Muses.

259b5   μὲν δὴ is adversative and protests against the idea that a literary person like Phaedrus might be content to remain in ignorance of such a matter: 'but really' (D. 393).

b6   οὗτοι refers to τέττιγες and is the subject.

ἄνθρωποι is predicate nominative.

τῶν is partitive genitive; we must understand with it some expression meaning 'who lived' (e.g. βιωσάντων) for the adverbial πρὶν Μούσας γεγονέναι to limit. The whole amounts to a somewhat more precise version of τῶν τότε, by which it is summarily recapitulated two lines below.

b8   ἄρα 'as the story has it.' This "referential" use of ἄρα enables the speaker to disclaim personal responsibility for what he is saying. It is important in Plato, but it seems not to be recognized by D. Campbell gives a collection of examples ("On Plato's Use of Language," 207–8).

ἐξεπλάγησαν ὑφ' ἡδονῆς De Vries points out that this brings back the μανία motif.

259c1–2   ἔλαθον τελευτήσαντες αὑτούς 'they died without being conscious they were dying.' The point is that they were preoccupied with singing. Rowe's "failed to notice that they had died" either implies a degree of preoccupation that it is hard to credit or is true of everyone. The aorist participle should not be overtranslated. Aorist participles generally coincide in time with λανθάνω in any tense other than the present or imperfect (S. 2096b).

c3   φύεται is historic present. See note on 243a7.

c4   γενόμενον has temporal force: 'after they are born.'

ἄσιτόν τε καὶ ἄποτον Cicadas consume sap exuded by twigs. The popular tradition in antiquity that they live on dew, which is reflected in Aristotle's *Historia animalium* 532^b 13 and Vergil's *Eclogues* 5.77, goes back as far as the Hesiodic *Scutum* 395: ᾧ τε πόσις καὶ βρῶσις θῆλυς ἐέρση. Plato, however, is not at all interested in the details of natural history.

c6   ἀπαγγέλλειν depends, like δεῖσθαι at c4, on γέρας, with a slight zeugma in what the noun means: 'privilege' becoming more appropriate than 'reward.'

τίς τίνα Two interrogative pronouns in the same clause have a tendency to cluster.

τῶν ἐνθάδε is partitive with τίς, αὐτῶν with τίνα.

c6–d1   Τερψιχόρᾳ . . . προσφιλεστέρους These two words belong together and neatly enclose the clause. Since Τερψιχόρᾳ must wait for the adjective to make its function clear, the effect is taut, like a rubber band stretched tight. Contrast the spacious feel of the seventeen-word gap between αὕτη and παλινῳδία in 257a3–4.

259d1–2   τοὺς ἐν τοῖς ἐρωτικοῖς sc. αὐτὴν τετιμηκότας, i.e. the writers of erotic poetry in lyric meters and elegiacs. For Homer, the Muses are a plurality without distinctions. Hesiod (*Theogony* 77ff.) was the first to give them names, and it is quite possible that he made those names up, fitting them to their lineage and individual functions (West ad loc.). Their differentiation into patronesses of the various genres of verse and other arts came about gradually, and there continued to be some variation in their individual functions throughout antiquity. What Plato does with them is typical of how he uses traditional material, when, that is, he is not concerned to reject it entirely on moral grounds. Terpsichore and Urania are so etymologically pellucid that the assignment of functions to them is a foregone conclusion with which Plato does not meddle, especially since the name of the latter is so well adapted to the importance of the οὐρανός in his myth, where an experience that is eminently astronomical provides us with the philosophical basis for Calliope, or 'beautiful speaking.' The handiness for Plato's purposes of the name Erato (conventionally the Muse of choral lyric, which was considered to be ἔρατος or 'lovely') needs no comment. Some scholars find Pythagorean allusions in Plato's choice of Muses for special mention and the language he uses about them, but his treatment of them resonates richly and diversely with elements within the dialogue itself.

d3   Καλλιόπη is the only Muse set apart from the others and given a few words of description by Hesiod. She comes last in his list and is called προφερεστάτη, an epithet that, no doubt at least partly because of association with Plato's πρεσβυτάτη, is often rendered 'eldest' by translators of the *Theogony*, although there is no good reason not to give the word its normal meaning: 'most excellent.' For Hesiod Calliope is most excellent, because she attends on princes by, it would seem, making them eloquent. However, one way of serving princes is to preserve their memory, so it is easy to see how Calliope became and remained the Muse of Epic. For Plato, not surprisingly, philosophers take the place of princes as her special care; and since the half (roughly) of his dialogue we have recently entered deals with how language should be employed by the philosopher, Calliope is as suitable to be its patroness as was Urania for the Palinode and its myth. Among the Muses these two divide the functions of being περί τε οὐρανὸν καὶ λόγους . . . θείους τε καὶ ἀνθρωπίνους (d6)—and those are precisely the things philosophers are about, too.

d6   οὖσαι 'because they are.'

d7   ἰᾶσιν . . . φωνήν For ἵημι of utterance, whether speaking or singing, see LSJ s.v. 2.

   δὴ οὖν See note on 242c3–4.

d9   Λεκτέον γὰρ οὖν For assentient γάρ, see note on 228c9; γὰρ οὖν is a strengthened form of it here (D. 447).

Knowledge, Truth, and Rhetoric

259c1 260d2: Socrates embarks in earnest on an examination of what constitutes the true art of writing and speaking by asking whether the speaker must not know the truth about what he is going to expound. When Phaedrus replies with the currently fashionable doctrine that it is enough if he knows what seems to be just or good, Socrates affects to consider this opinion with respect and then subjects it to an ironical examination that ends in exposing its inadequacy.

259e1   **Οὐκοῦν** 'well then' (S. 2952).

       ὅπερ . . . σκέψασθαι At 258d7–9.

       τὸν λόγον 'speeches.' In the singular the generic article makes an individual representative of a class (S. 1123).

e4–6   **Ἆρ' οὖν . . . μέλλῃ;** Everything from τὴν to the end of the sentence serves as subject of ὑπάρχειν. The limiting sense added by γε is important and must be in the translation.

e5   **εἰδυῖαν** is best translated as the verb of a relative clause modifying διάνοιαν: 'a mind that knows.'

e6   **πέρι** in anastrophe separated from its genitive object by one or more words is more the rule than the exception. Compare *Ap.* 19c5–6: ὧν ἐγὼ οὐδὲν οὔτε μέγα οὔτε σμικρὸν πέρι ἐπαΐω.

e7   **Οὑτωσὶ** 'as follows,' in place of the usual ὧδε.

       ὦ φίλε Σώκρατες This use of a "friendship term" of address (see second note on 228d6) shows that Phaedrus, having detected, as he thinks, an inaccuracy in what Socrates has said, fancies that he is taking control of the argument.

260a1   **τὰ τῷ ὄντι δίκαια** Phaedrus disclaims on the orator's behalf the kind of knowledge that Plato's Gorgias, to his eventual undoing in the argument, claimed to be able to impart to his pupils if that should prove to be necessary (*Grg.* 460a3–4).

a2   **τὰ δόξαντ' ἄν** Ἄν gives the participle the color of a potential optative: 'what would seem just' (C. 54.6.6.D).

       πλήθει οἵπερ δικάσουσιν Just as collective singular nouns, like πλῆθος or δῆμος or στρατόπεδον, can be the subjects of plural verbs, so can such singulars be modified by plural relative clauses.

a3   **οὐδὲ . . . δόξει** This is not a mere variation on what Phaedrus has just finished saying. That dealt with forensic oratory; this with deliberative speeches in the political assemblies.

a5 **Οὔτοι ἀπόβλητον ἔπος** Socrates begins by quoting Nestor (*Iliad* 2.361: οὔ τοι ἀπόβλητον ἔπος ἔσσεται, ὅττι κεν εἴπω), but in the second half of the line he alters Nestor's customary self-complacency to suit his own ironical purpose with ὃ ἂν εἴπωσι σοφοί. These σοφοί will turn out to be those from whom Phaedrus has heard, directly and indirectly, the opinion he has just communicated. They include both the theoreticians and the practitioners of rhetoric.

a6 **ἀλλὰ . . . λέγωσι** An element of apprehension is present in σκοπεῖν, enabling it to govern the kind of subordinate clause that is normal with verbs of fearing (S. 2224a with 2225). Compare ὀκνῶ at 257c3 with note. Plato often uses the indicative in this sort of clause, when he is expressing fear that something actually is or was the case, but the subjunctive transmitted by the tradition and printed by Burnet here yields perfectly good sense: 'pay heed lest they turn out to be saying something important'; they are saying these things now and have said them in the past, but we may, to our embarrassment, discover in the future that we ought to have paid attention. For consistency Burnet ought to have printed τὶ. See note on 243a1.

a6–7 **καὶ δὴ καὶ** lays "stress on a particular instance or application of a general statement" (S. 2890): 'and in particular.'

260b1–2 **πολεμίους . . . ἵππον** 'to get a horse and ward off enemies'; the active infinitive, because Phaedrus's action would serve the city as well as himself; no article with πολεμίους because Socrates has no particular war or enemy in mind.

b2 **τοσόνδε** 'just this much,' defined by the ὅτι clause.

b3–4 **τῶν ἡμέρων ζῴων** The *vox propria* for domesticated animals, as opposed to τὰ θηρία.

b6 **Οὔπω γε** Socrates begs Phaedrus to wait for the punch line.

ἀλλ'... πείθοιμι Phaedrus has supplied an apodosis for Socrates' conditional protasis in b1–4 with his γελοῖόν γ' ἂν . . . εἴη; now Socrates proceeds to offer a new protasis, which, he implies, will really justify that conclusion. Δὴ is important: 'just when' (D. 219–20), i.e. at the point where I begin to try to persuade you in earnest, that is when the enterprise will become γελοῖον.

b7 **λόγον . . . ὄνου** The same apposition is found at *Sym.* 177d2: λόγον εἰπεῖν ἔπαινον Ἔρωτος. Following a verb of saying or any

249

expression that implies speech κατά with genitive commonly means 'against,' but it can bear quite the opposite sense under the influence of a word like ἔπαινον.

b7–8   **λέγων . . . στρατιᾶς**   sc. ἐστί with τὸ θρέμμα as its subject and παντὸς ἄξιον κεκτῆσθαι as predicate. The creature is 'supremely worth having, both at home and in the field.' Socrates, if alive today, would be kept out of the world of advertising by principle, not by want of talent.

b9   **ἀποπολεμεῖν** is a ἅπαξ λεγόμενον and perhaps a coinage by Plato. We might expect it to mean πολεμεῖν ἀφ' ἵππων but the context makes it clear that Socrates means πολεμεῖν ἀπ' ὄνων, a ludicrous image to anyone conversant with Greek warfare.

καὶ πρός γ' ('and not only that, but') carries on with the same breathless enthusiasm. For πρός as an adverb, see LSJ s.v. D. This is an emendation, an elegant one, as De Vries says. It is very lively and removes the transmitted compound προσενεγκεῖν, which does not fit the context, with a minimum of disturbance.

260c2   **ἤδη** in its basic meaning ('by this time') often marks a climax; here it strengthens the first element of παγγέλοιόν: 'utterly ludicrous.'

c3–4   **Ἆρ' οὖν . . . ἐχθρὸν** This sentence provides neutral ground between Socrates' parable and its application, which will begin at c6. If we accept Burnet's text (either as is or admitting εἶναι, which would not materially alter the sense), Socrates seems to contrast himself, willing to play the fool but benign, with someone who is clever but malign.

c6   **ἀγαθὸν καὶ κακόν** Instances like this and ἡδὺ πρὸ ἀγαθοῦ at 239c4 show that the article, while usual, is not absolutely required to make substantives of neuter adjectives.

c7   **λαβὼν** 'having hit upon.'

ὡσαύτως ἔχουσαν 'in the same state (as himself).'

περὶ ὄνου σκιᾶς This expression is proverbial for a trifle not worth considering. Socrates, who had been talking about a donkey, throws in the shadow to produce greater absurdity and a more telling contrast to κακοῦ ὡς ἀγαθοῦ in the next line. Being right about what is good and what is bad is no trifling matter. According to a story handed down by a scholium to Aristophanes' *Wasps* 191, the expression originated in a lawsuit brought by the owner of a donkey against a man, who had rented his beast but not its shadow, and yet availed himself of the latter for protection against the sun.

c9   δόξας . . . μεμελετηκώς   This man studies the results of the polls.

πείσῃ 'succeeds in persuading,' as opposed to 'sets out to persuade' (πείθῃ at c7). In sentences that convey what generally happens (or, as here, ask a question about it), after primary tenses a temporal clause that denotes continuing action takes the present subjunctive with ἄν, whereas the aorist subjunctive with ἄν (ὅταν introduces both members of this compound protasis) denotes simply occurring (completed) action and time usually before that of the main verb (S. 2409a).

260d1   ὧν . . . θερίζειν   As the apparatus shows, ὧν has aroused suspicion, but probably it is a rather bold genitive of source: 'What fruit do you suppose rhetoric would harvest from the seeds it has sown?'

d2   Οὐ πάνυ γε ἐπιεικῆ   "not a very *good* one," as Denniston (133) suggests. In replies to questions that suggest alternatives without giving any lead as to which to prefer, this use of emphatic γε is slightly colloquial.

260d3–261a6: In order to be fair to rhetoric, Socrates lets her speak in her own defense, but adds that her defense is valid only if the arguments that are about to assail her leave unscathed her claim to be an art. Phaedrus is eager to hear the arguments, so Socrates formally invokes them.

260d3   Ἆρ' οὖν   This collocation is very common in Plato. Where it can be distinguished from plain ἆρα, the question posed will be a natural inference from what has preceded. Here Phaedrus and Socrates have come to a rather rapid conclusion that rhetoric seems to sow bad seed. That might suggest that they have been unfair to her; perhaps the other side of the argument ought to be given a chance.

d5   ὦ θαυμάσιοι is a form of address suitable for people who are, in the opinion of the speaker, behaving in a manner inappropriate to the existing situation, but see second note on 228d6.

d6–7   εἴ τι ἐμὴ συμβολή   Understand ἐστί with ἐμὴ συμβολή as subject and τι as predicate: 'if my advice counts at all.'

d7   λαμβάνειν depends on ἀναγκάζω, taken by zeugma as a synonym or near synonym of κελεύω; if the learner takes the advice of the art of rhetoric, that art directs him (the subject of λαμβάνειν is supplied out of ἕνα, the positive element of οὐδέν' in d5) to try to obtain herself only οὕτως, i.e. on condition that he has already got truth in his possession (κτησάμενον ἐκεῖνο).

d7–8   τόδε ... λέγω 'but in any case, this is my boast.' As usual, δ' οὖν dismisses what went immediately before as doubtful or secondary compared with the important or unquestionable statement now being made.

d8–9   οὐδέν τι μᾶλλον De Vries wishes to take this absolutely, as equivalent to οὐδαμῶς, but there seems to be no reason not to take it in its prima facie comparative sense; the other term of the comparison (τοῦ τὰ ὄντα μὴ εἰδότος) is readily understood.

d9   ἔσται is the future of ἔστι here, not ἐστί.

τέχνη By luck, perhaps, or because he has innate talent, but not by art.

260e1   Οὐκοῦν ... ταῦτα; 'well, won't she be speaking justly in saying that?' The tone of Phaedrus's question shows that he is ready to go on defending his beloved rhetoric (S. 2951).

e2   Φημί in its strong sense: 'I agree.'

e2–3   ἐὰν ... τέχνη The arguments are represented as 'assailing' her, but the possibility is contemplated that all they will succeed in proving is that she is indeed an art. If αὐτὴν had been expressed as subject of εἶναι, its predicate also would have been in the accusative case; as it is, τέχνη takes its case from αὐτῇ. This is regular in this situation, which occurs often.

e3   ὥσπερ ... δοκῶ 'for I almost seem to hear.' Ὥσπερ ('as it were') apologizes for the slight exaggeration. This usage stands apart from the syntax of the sentence. Compare Meno 70c4: ὥσπερ αὐχμός τις τῆς σοφίας γέγονεν ('what you might call a wisdom drought has come about'). And why γὰρ? Not, certainly, because the present sentence explains the assertion of agreement made in the preceding one, but because it explains the doubt about that assertion that is implied by the condition attached to it and by the limiting γε.

e5   ἄτεχνος τριβή Elsewhere (e.g. Grg. 463b4; Phlb. 55e6; Laws 938a4) τριβή used in contrast to τέχνη is explicitly correlated with ἐμπειρία, and that gets the gist of it. Attic Greek chose as its metaphor 'rubbing along' rather than 'muddling through.'

e5–7   **τοῦ δὲ . . . γένηται** The authenticity of this sentence has been unjustly suspected, largely because Phaedrus ignores it in his reply. The article with Λάκων is generic; and notice the tense of φησὶν: this is the sort of thing the Spartan in the street normally says. We might expect γάρ, considering the logical relationship of this sentence with the preceding one, but Plato prefers the looser and perhaps more artlessly Laconian δέ (D. 169–70). For οὔτε μή ποτε . . . γένηται expressing emphatic denial that something will happen, see S. 1804.

261a1–2   **Τούτων . . . λέγουσιν** Phaedrus's ruling passion is by now familiar to us. We need not be surprised when he ignores Socrates' Laconian apothegm and makes directly for the λόγοι of 260e2. Dative of person (ἡμῖν here) must often be understood with the impersonal use of δεῖ. For ἀλλὰ ushering in a command or exhortation, see D. 13–14. Here it marks the transition from arguments in favor of an action to a demand for performing it.

a3   **θρέμματα** See note on 240b4 for the playful tone of this word. Here it further animates the λόγοι as creatures of some undefined sort.

a3–4   **καλλίπαιδά τε Φαῖδρον** Phaedrus merits the epithet as a father of discourses; see 242a8–b5.

a4   **οὐδὲ** If he does not practice philosophy sufficiently, he will 'not be a capable speaker at all.' See 258e3 with second note.

261a7–e4: Socrates defines rhetoric as an art for influencing souls by means of words in three fields of action: the courts, the assembly, and private gatherings. He answers Phaedrus's objection to the last by arguing that just as rhetoric enables opposite points of view to be expounded convincingly in grave matters under dispute in courts and public assemblies, so—as Zeno shows—can the same technique be applied in private discourse to any subject no matter how inconsequential.

261a7   **τὸ . . . ὅλον** belongs to a class of adverbial accusatives involving expressions of measure or degree (S. 1609).

a8   **ψυχαγωγία . . . λόγων** The importance of this new definition of rhetoric would be hard to exaggerate. Later (271c10ff.) we will come upon the word ψυχαγωγία again as Socrates sets out to describe a genuine rhetorical education, which, he says, begins with a knowledge of different kinds of ψυχαί, and then employs that knowledge to choose means that will lead the particular ψυχαί before the speaker at a given time to the truth. For a persuasive argument that finds in ψυχαγωγία the linchpin that holds the dialogue together, see Asmis. As she puts it: "Socrates exemplifies the right kind of psychagogia by leading the youthful Phaedrus from a fascination with the wrong kind of rhetoric to a contemplation of the right kind."

a8–9   **καὶ . . . σύλλογοι** By attraction for καὶ ἄλλοις συλλόγοις, ὅσοι δημόσιοί εἰσιν (KG 2.418).

a9   **ἐν ἰδίοις** It is this addendum that will surprise Phaedrus, and the οὐ μόνον . . . ἀλλὰ καί structure acknowledges in advance that it is not routine. Compare it with the description of his own brand of ψυχαγωγία that Plato puts into the mouth of Gorgias in *Grg.* 452e: τὸ πείθειν . . . τοῖς λόγοις καὶ ἐν δικαστηρίῳ δικαστὰς καὶ ἐν βουλευτερίῳ βουλευτὰς καὶ ἐν ἐκκλησίᾳ ἐκκλησιαστὰς καὶ ἐν τῷ ἄλλῳ συλλόγῳ παντί, ὅστις ἂν πολιτικὸς σύλλογος γίγνηται. There the relative clause at the end makes a qualification that Socrates deliberately repudiates in our passage. Here in the *Phaedrus* a rhetoric is to be sought that will apply in both small and large matters, where small and large are practically equivalent to the common antithesis between ἰδίᾳ καὶ δημοσίᾳ.

a9–b1   **σμικρῶν . . . πέρι** There is surely a tincture of irony here, as there will be in περὶ σπουδαῖα ἢ περὶ φαῦλα at b1–2. Socrates does not really regard the content of conversations such as those held between himself and his friends as trivial compared with what is discussed in the assembly and the courts.

261b1–2   **καὶ . . . γιγνόμενον** The subject is still the rhetorical τέχνη, but it turns into a 'thing' by an idiom common in Greek, when a masculine or feminine antecedent is picked up by a neuter demonstrative or a negative such as οὐδὲν here.

    τό γε ὀρθὸν is a neuter expression used adverbially in a way that developed out of neuters used in apposition to the sentence, as in S. 994. Compare *Crito* 45c–d, where Crito tells Socrates that in refusing to escape and go on living, 'you seem to me to be betraying your sons, whom you are going to desert, although you could bring them up and educate them.' He thereupon concludes: καὶ τὸ σὸν μέρος ὅτι ἂν τύχωσι τοῦτο πράξουσιν ('and for your part [i.e. as far as you are concerned] they will live without guidance'). In our sentence we might translate, 'As far as what is correct is concerned, at any rate, it is a thing no more esteemed when it is manifested in serious matters than in trivial ones.' "To put the matter in the right light" (Helmbold and Rabinowitz, quoted by V.) is a good, idiomatic rendering. Compare περὶ . . . φαῦλα with the phrase elucidated in the preceding note: the distinction between περί with genitive or accusative is sometimes barely, if at all, discernible.

b4   **λέγεταί . . . τέχνη** 'there is speaking and writing by art.' The impersonal passive, common in Latin, is rarer in Greek. If there is a battle going on, Romans are likely to say *pugnatur*, but Geeks normally prefer μάχη γίγνεται. These two verbs and the λέγεται that follows are, however, best taken as impersonal; see also πεπόνηται at 232a4.

b5   **ἐπὶ . . . ἀκήκοα** 'I haven't heard that it extends further,' the comparative of ἐπὶ πολύ in the sense 'over a great space' (LSJ s.v. πολύς IV.4a).

b6–8   **Ἀλλ' . . . γέγονας;** Ἀλλ' ἤ is a lively way of putting a question that implies surprise or incredulity about what the interlocutor has just said (D. 27). What arouses incredulity here is the unlikely notion that Phaedrus has heard the manuals on speaking of Odysseus and Nestor, but has not heard those of Palamedes.

b6   **τέχνας** has the concrete sense of handbooks or manuals, as συνεγραψάτην makes clear. For the ascription of such works to Odysseus and Nestor, see note on c4. Modern translators differ in how they take the accusative after ἀκήκοας: for instance, Rowe and Nehamas and Woodruff write "heard of," while Vicaire in the Budé writes *connais*, clearly implying that he took the verb to mean 'have heard' rather than 'have heard of,' and Hackforth reaches the same solution with "are acquainted with." Doubtless both wished to find some equivalent to 'have heard,' since the notion of being acquainted with the contents of books because one has heard them rather than read them falls oddly on modern ears. I favor 'have heard' or some equivalent, because that, the usual meaning of ἀκούω with the accusative, makes more sense in this context. Why should Phaedrus be expected to know the contents of these τέχναι if he had merely 'heard of' them?

    Παλαμήδους See note on d6.

261c2   **κατασκευάζεις** with double accusative in the sense represent someone as someone else (LSJ s.v. 6).

    ἤ τινα Θρασύμαχον For ἤ τις in the sense 'or perhaps,' see note on 230d6–8; whereas Νέστορά τινα a few words earlier meant 'a kind of Nestor.'

c2–3 **Θρασύμαχόν τε καὶ Θεόδωρον** Thrasymachus of Chalcedon, who is well known to us for his part in Plato's *Republic*, was known to his contemporaries as a sophist and theoretician of rhetoric; he will turn up again at 267c8–9 under an alias. Theodorus of Byzantium, whom we shall meet again in 266e6, was a teacher of rhetoric and author of one or more handbooks on it around the end of the fifth century.

c4 **Ἴσως . . . ἐῶμεν** What has been the point of this playful digression that is so quickly and casually dismissed? It arose in response to Phaedrus's assertion that he had never heard that rhetoric had applications outside the courts and the assembly. In asking him if he has heard only the τέχναι of Odysseus and Nestor, Socrates plays on the reputation of these two heroes as models of eloquence, a reputation that begins with Homer himself. Nestor was ἡδυεπής and a λιγὺς [compare 237a7] ἀγορητής; the sound of his voice was μέλιτος γλυκίων. As for Odysseus, we recall from *Iliad* 3 Antenor's description of his words falling as thick as the flakes of a snowstorm. Socrates pretends that their speeches were handbooks of rhetoric, which they composed in the intervals between battles before Troy. Gorgias, who lived to an age comparable to Nestor's, wrote no handbook, but his speeches were considered to be handbooks of a sort and were memorized by his pupils (see note on 228b4–5). Now the speeches of Odysseus and Nestor are mutatis mutandis of the sort that might be spoken περὶ δημηγορίας or, to a lesser degree, περὶ τὰς δίκας, so that if Phaedrus had heard only (μόνον at b6) those 'handbooks' he might well suffer from a restricted notion of the applicability of rhetoric; whereas if he had heard the clever Palamedes, who will turn out to be Zeno at d6, his view of its scope might be larger.

c5 **μέντοι** Confirmative μέντοι in questions of the *nonne* type: 'they say opposite things, don't they?' (compare d10 with note). (Burnet's text has the misprint μεντοι.)

c8 **τοῦ δικαίου τε καὶ ἀδίκου** See note on 253d2–3.

261d1 **ὅταν δὲ βούληται** corresponds to τοτὲ, but makes deliberate manipulation more explicit.

d3 **δὴ** Connective δή (S. 2846) ordinarily, like other connective particles, seeks second place in its sentence, but when a number of words go closely together and precede, it can be put as late as fourth (D. 240).

δοκεῖν Understand ὁ . . . ποιήσει from c10 with τοῦτο taken rather loosely. Socrates is careful in our present passage to distinguish the proper spheres of influence of forensic (τοῦ δικαίου τε καὶ ἀδίκου) from deliberative (ἀγαθά . . . τἀναντία) rhetoric. The latter must consider what is expedient as well as what is just.

d6   **Τὸν οὖν Ἐλεατικὸν Παλαμήδην** is a riddling way of referring to Zeno of Elea that emphasizes his inventiveness. The argument in Plato's dialogue *Parmenides* starts with Socrates' criticism of one of Zeno's famous antinomies, paradoxical arguments that attacked seemingly obvious conclusions by drawing contradictory consequences from assumptions on which they depend. In that dialogue Zeno appears as a serious follower of Parmenides, whom Plato holds in very high regard. Here his method of argument is being used to make a bridge between public and private disputation and justify the addition to the sphere of rhetoric that Socrates made in a9–b2. As for Palamedes himself, see *Rep.* 522d2–5 for his claim to be the inventor of arithmetic. In *Laws* 677d he is named with Daedalus and Orpheus among the great discoverers of the arts of civilization. Palamedes stands high in Socrates' esteem elsewhere as well: in *Ap.* 41b2–4 Socrates looks forward to perhaps meeting him in the afterlife in the company of Telamonian Aias, two heroes who will share with him the fate of having died as the result of an unjust judgment. See further on 274d2.

d8   **φερόμενα** 'in motion.'

d10   **ἡ ἀντιλογικὴ** This new name for the rhetorical τέχνη has been defined for us by the examples in c10–d1 and d7–8. It is the art of making the same thing seem to the same people to have one quality at one time and the opposite quality at another. Compare ἀντιλέγουσιν in c5. There two speakers draw opposite conclusions from the same facts, but we find in c10 that by their τέχνη each of them could take the part of the other, just as in the private sphere that same τέχνη, according to Socrates, enables Zeno to assert contradictory predicates of the same subject (compare Kerferd 60–61).

261e2 **εἴπερ ἔστιν** There is, of course, still doubt that rhetoric really is a τέχνη, although Socrates sometimes assumes that it is for the sake of the argument.

e3 **πᾶν . . . δυνατόν** I borrow, with a few modifications, Rowe's map through this broken terrain: ὁμοιοῦν πᾶν τῶν δυνατῶν <ὁμοιοῦσθαι> παντὶ <τούτων> οἷς δυνατόν <ἐστιν> ὁμοιοῦν αὐτά ('to liken every one of the things that can be likened to every one of the things to which it is possible to liken them').

e3–4 **ἄλλου . . . ἀποκρυπτομένου** is genitive absolute with temporal force.

e4 **εἰς φῶς ἄγειν** 'to expose.' The object is supplied out of the genitive absolute, the whole offering an illustration of the proverb, "It takes one to catch one."

261e5–262c4: In order to deceive efficiently, the antilogician must work from the truth to its opposite by small increments, from which it follows that he must know the truth.

261e6 **ζητοῦσιν** Understand ἡμῖν and take the participle as conditional. **φανεῖσθαι** 'will come to light,' its understood subject being 'the answer to your question.'

e6–7 **ἀπάτη . . . ὀλίγον;** Διαφέρουσι is a participle; μᾶλλον may mean 'more frequently' or perhaps 'more easily'; ὀλίγον stands for ἐν ὀλίγον διαφέρουσι.

262a2 **Ἀλλά γε δὴ** is a very rare collocation, perhaps unknown in Greek of the Classical period. Whether this or ἀλλὰ δὴ is the correct reading, some variation on the "progressive" (D. 241) significance of the latter seems appropriate: 'further' or 'again.' **κατὰ σμικρὸν** 'gradually.'

a6 **ἀπατήσεσθαι** Future middle forms used in a passive sense are quite common.

a8 **Ἀνάγκη μὲν οὖν** Use of corrective μὲν οὖν (S. 2901b) here shows that Athenians thought ἀνάγκη perceptibly more forceful than δεῖ. In general, when a respondent repeats before μὲν οὖν part of the substance of what his interlocutor has said, he strengthens the language.

a10 **τοῦ ἀγνοουμένου** denotes the particular thing of whose nature he is ignorant; he is attempting to discern the degree of likeness of a given thing to each thing among other things (ἐν τοῖς ἄλλοις) without knowing what the given thing is.

ὁμοιότητα . . . μεγάλην Understand ἑκάστῳ, depending on ὁμοιότητα.

262b3   **τὸ πάθος τοῦτο** i.e. τὸ παρὰ τὰ ὄντα δοξάζειν καὶ ἀπατᾶσθαι, as De Vries suggests.

εἰσερρύη 'slipped in.' Not a gnomic aorist, it pinpoints the moment in the past when the opinions of these misguided people were formed.

b4   **Γίγνεται γοῦν οὕτως** 'yes, that *is* what happens.' See D. 454 for emphatic γοῦν in affirmative answers.

b5   **Ἔστιν . . . ὅπως** introducing questions means 'is it possible that. . . ?' (S. 2515).

τεχνικὸς is predicate adjective to a subject that we do not begin to find until we reach ὁ μὴ ἐγνωρικὸς two lines below.

μεταβιβάζειν depends on τεχνικὸς and identifies the τέχνη in question.

b6   **ἑκάστοτε** Take with κατὰ σμικρὸν: 'at each stage' (of the exposition or argument).

b7   **ἀπάγων** is subordinate to μεταβιβάζειν and indicates means; some object such as τοὺς ἀπατωμένους is on the fringes of our consciousness.

τοῦτο See first note on b3, mutatis mutandis.

ὁ μὴ ἐγνωρικὼς illustrates the generic use of the article: 'a man who has not become acquainted with' (LSJ s.v. γνωρίζω II).

b9   **Οὐ μή ποτε** The future indicative of strong denial (S. 2755b) with the verb (τεχνικὸς ἔσται) left for us to supply.

262c1–3   **Λόγων . . . παρέξεται** And so the condition that Socrates in 260e2–3 said must be met if rhetoric was to be an art has not been met; the λόγοι he thought he heard coming there have assailed her successfully. In giving advice about what is ἀγαθόν, the rhetorically trained man has turned out to be as γελοῖος as a man who mistakes an ass for a horse; his concern for opinion a mere hunting expedition (τεθηρευκώς).

DEFINITION, COLLECTION, AND
DIVISION

262c5-e4: Phaedrus agrees with Socrates that it would be a good idea to search the three speeches that have been delivered for examples of discourse with and without art. At Socrates' request he rereads the opening sentences of the speech of Lysias.

262c5-6   ἐν οἷς = ἐν τούτοις οὕς (S. 2522).

c6   ἡμεῖς εἴπομεν The plural is not merely conventional. Socrates continues to regard the first of his two speeches as being in reality the production of Phaedrus, as he began to do in 242d11-e1.

ὧν = ἐκείνων ἅ and takes the two predicate adjectives with it into the genitive.

c8-9   ὡς . . . παραδείγματα Ὡς is causal; it introduces an opinion of Phaedrus that he regards as a fact and states in the indicative (S. 2240b). What he means by ψιλῶς is defined by the participial phrase that follows. The discussion thus far has had the bland character of abstract demonstration and has lacked the irregularities and bristliness that arguments from examples (LSJ s.v. παράδειγμα 2) might provide.

c10-d2   Καὶ μὴν . . . ἀκούοντας Any discussion of the unity of the dialogue would surely have to take this sentence into account. For adversative καὶ μήν ('and yet') see D. 367.

262d1   τὼ λόγω Which speeches are meant? The speech of Lysias and the first speech of Socrates might seem to be the obvious answer, but some scholars think that all three speeches should be included, the two of Socrates being taken as one. Certainly in Socrates' opinion the first two speeches mislead their audience, but since the Palinode is based on a myth, it, too, could be thought to "mislead" its hearers. Perhaps the potential construction of παράγοι is relevant to this issue. Need a speech actually mislead to be germane to the discussion? It may also be relevant that all three speeches do, in the end, provide material for the discussion. ὡς introduces an indirect question: 'how?' παράδειγμα means 'lesson' or 'warning' here (LSJ s.v. 3).

d2   **προσπαίζων** expresses means.

d3   **τοὺς ἐντοπίους θεούς** are the Nymphs and Achelous (230b7–8), the Muses, who are present through their agents the cicadas (259c–d) and—as we shall find later—Pan. The expression denotes a relationship that is more local and intimate than would οἱ ἐγχώριοι, the gods of the πόλις.

d4   **οἱ ὑπὲρ κεφαλῆς ᾠδοὶ** are the cicadas, of course. It would scarcely be necessary to identify them if scholars of great and generally well-deserved reputation had not, by some aberration, thought that Socrates meant birds. See De Vries for references.

d4–5   **ἐπιπεπνευκότες . . . εἶεν** The perfect optative regularly uses the periphrastic form; we shall soon see another at 263c1.

d5   **τοῦτο τὸ γέρας** i.e. the oratorical skill to have serendipitously provided themselves with texts appropriate to their discussion.

d7   **Ἔστω ὡς λέγεις** is not exactly brusque, but perhaps a bit dismissive. Phaedrus has had enough of entomological whimsy for the moment and wants to get on with the matter at hand.

d8   **Ἴθι δή μοι ἀνάγνωθι** Δή is almost always appended to φέρε, ἄγε, or ἴθι when they are used to add animation to another imperative. For the second aorist active imperative of γιγνώσκω, see S. 684.

262e1–4   **"Περὶ . . . μεταμέλει"** Plato's general practice in self-reference, as well as in quoting others, is to make minor changes to avoid the appearance of pedantry (see note on 227b9–11). The reason that procedure would be inappropriate here is obvious and perhaps relevant to what Socrates will say later about the inertness of written discourse (275d9–e3).

262e5–263c6: People agree about the meaning of some terms and disagree about that of others. Disagreement gives more scope for rhetoric, so one in possession of the rhetorical art will have some mark by which he can distinguish the two kinds of terms, and he will be quick to grasp to which of them his subject belongs.

262e5   **τί** serves as both an internal accusative with ἁμαρτάνει and as the direct object of ποιεῖ.

          οὗτος Either Lysias or the fictive speaker in his speech.

e6   **ἢ γάρ** N'est-ce-pas? (S. 2805b).

263a3   **τῶν τοιούτων** Either ὄντων or ὀνομάτων, the two emendations of τοιούτων that Burnet admitted to his apparatus, makes excellent sense. It is hard, however, to see why τοιούτων would have been substituted for either of them. It is better to accept the transmitted text as a slight extension of the sense we find in *Phd.* 73c5–7: Ἆρ' οὖν καὶ τόδε ὁμολογοῦμεν, ὅταν ἐπιστήμη παραγίγνηται τρόπῳ τοιούτῳ, ἀνάμνησιν εἶναι; λέγω δὲ τίνα τρόπον; τόνδε. ('Do we also agree that when knowledge comes about in the way I have in mind, it is recollection? What way do I mean? The following.') Here, then, Socrates will be saying, 'some of the sort of things I have in mind,' and the question Phaedrus interpolates before he is able to explain what he means takes the place of the one Socrates asks himself in the *Phaedo* passage. Verdenius cites also *Rep.* 488a, where Socrates uses the phrase τοιουτονὶ γενόμενον to ask his interlocutors to conceive of a scene that at this point exists only in his own mind. See also Riddell 53.

a6 ὄνομα . . . ἀργύρου 'the word iron or the word silver.'

a7 διενοήθημεν is a gnomic aorist.

a10 ἀλλήλοις . . . αὑτοῖς i.e. with each other in a group and with ourselves as individuals in the group. We experience internal conflict as well as disagreement.

263b1 Ἐν μὲν ἄρα τοῖς . . . ἐν δὲ τοῖς When articles associated with a μέν . . . δέ antithesis both depend on a preposition, the preposition regularly precedes any particles that may occur and the articles follow them. Ἄρα is here of the connective type, of which D. 41 says, "It is not until we come to Plato that we find ἄρα used practically as a variant for οὖν and δή, although even in Plato ἄρα perhaps conveys a slightly less formal and more conversational connexion than those particles: 'so,' instead of 'therefore' or 'then.'"

b6 μετιέναι The metaphor comes from hunting.

b7 πρῶτον μὲν is answered by ἔπειτά γε in c3.

b7–8 δεῖ . . . εἴδους 'one must have these things [i.e. the things that are easily confused and the things that are easily kept distinct] systematically divided and be in possession of some distinguishing mark for each kind.' Διῃρῆσθαι introduces a method the importance of which will emerge in 265e–266a. For translating ὁδῷ as 'systematically,' compare *Tht.* 208b4–5: τὴν γὰρ διὰ τοῦ στοιχείου ὁδὸν ἔχων ἔγραφεν, ἣν δὴ λόγον ὡμολογήσαμεν. Socrates is there saying of a person who wrote the name Theaetetus correctly, 'For he wrote in possession of the road through its elements, which we agreed is its logos.' A road, practically speaking, shares with a line the quality that in traveling along it we must come upon all the features that are on it in their proper order, whether they be milestones on a turnpike, letters in a name, the events of the Archidamian War, or the instructions in a particular manual of flute playing; so ὁδῷ means 'systematically' in the sense 'by a road through the elements.' On the other hand μέθοδος in the sense 'system for enquiry' draws its metaphor from the notion of pursuit by tracking.

263c1   **εἶδος** I can only think that this word was added by a copyist, who, thinking mistakenly that καλὸν is in need of a substantive, allowed his eye to stray in the direction of εἴδους in b8 rather than of χαρακτῆρα a few words farther back, which would at least have provided good sense. For καλὸν without an indefinite pronoun in the sense 'something fine,' compare, e.g. the use of γελοῖον in 274c4.

c3   **Ἔπειτά γε** regularly provides a close connection with what the speaker had been saying before an interruption; "perhaps Plato felt the need of a particle to carry on the flow" (D. 145–46). Here it also answers πρῶτον μὲν as noted on b7. There are two parts of ἡ ῥητορικὴ τέχνη, theory and practice.

c3–4   **πρὸς . . . λανθάνειν** 'when he comes into the presence of each, he is not unaware (that he is in its presence).' Πρός is used in the sense we noticed at 249c5–c6, and the subject of both λανθανειν and αἰσθάνεσθαι must be supplied from γιγνόμενον. For λανθάνειν used in this way—that is, doing a thing unawares, rather than escaping the notice of someone else (accusative of person) while doing it—see LSJ s.v. A.2b.

c4–5   **αἰσθάνεσθαι . . . τοῦ γένους** The omitted antecedent of οὗ is the subject of τυγχάνει, and the genitive ποτέρου . . . τοῦ γένους depends on αἰσθάνεσθαι.

263c7–264b2: The observation that eros is one of the things about which people do not agree leads to the question of whether it was defined in the speeches. Socrates—or rather, the divinities who were the true authors of his speech—turns out to have been more skillful at rhetoric than was Lysias.

263c9–10   ἢ . . . εἰπεῖν   'otherwise, do you think that you would have been able to say. . . ?'

c11   <ὄν>   The custom with regard to ellipsis of supplementary participles with τυγχάνω was roughly as follows: the participial forms of εἰμί are frequently omitted (S. 2119), and other participles are sometimes omitted in subordinate clauses when it was thought that they could be understood from some form of the same verb in the main clause. Burnet, who evidently thought that the participle should be expressed here, followed Heindorf in supplying a neuter form, which although it modifies the masculine ἔρως, is itself neuter by attraction to its modifier τῶν ἀγαθῶν, adapting the customary sequence ἔρως ἐστιν ἀγαθόν.

263d1–2   ἐγώ . . . μέμνημαι is ironical, of course. Take the negative together with πάνυ as an urbane understatement: "I have quite forgotten," as Thompson translates.

d3   ἀρχόμενος τοῦ λόγου   'at the beginning of my speech' or 'when I began to speak' (S. 2061a). Socrates did not define ἔρως at the beginning of his second speech, and he elsewhere consistently refuses to take responsibility for his first. In any case, Plato cannot be accused of inconsistency, because it will be Phaedrus who will assert that Socrates began with a definition, and Socrates, who has said that he does not remember what he said, can be represented as accepting that testimony.

d4   Νὴ Δία . . . σφόδρα   Phaedrus's vehemence is justified by his memory of the rather elaborate process that began with a theoretical statement of the need for a definition at 237c and culminated in the "dithyrambic" definition itself in 238b–c.

d6   Πᾶνα τὸν Ἑρμοῦ   There is point both in letting the presence of Pan first come to light in this context and in mentioning his paternity. At *Cra.* 408d3 we find ἤτοι λόγος ἢ λόγου ἀδελφὸς ὁ Πάν. Presumably Pan is said to be 'either speech or the brother of speech' because his father Hermes is said to have devised—i.e. been the parent of—τὸ εἴρειν ('speaking') and to have received his name from it (*Cra.* 408b1–3).

d7   ἢ οὐδὲν ... Λυσίας 'or am I completely wrong and did Lysias, too, . . . ?' Οὐδὲν λέγειν is not to be taken literally; it is the opposite of τι λέγειν in the sense 'say something of consequence.' See 260a6 with note.

        ἀρχόμενος τοῦ ἐρωτικοῦ   See note on d3.

d8-e1   ἠνάγκασεν ... ἐβουλήθη 'make us take love as some one particular thing of his own choosing.'

263e1   πρὸς τοῦτο 'with this in view.'

        συνταξάμενος 'having marshaled.' English and Greek use the same metaphor.

e2   βούλει ... ἀναγνῶμεν   See 228e4-5 with note. Like English 'do you want to read,' the expression can be taken as a very gentle substitute for an imperative. But Phaedrus will choose to take it as a genuine question, thereby, perhaps, giving a voice to the reader, who may also wonder why Socrates wants this opening read over again. The reason may lie in the discussion of proper disposition of the parts of a discourse and "organic form" to which the rereading leads.

e5   αὐτοῦ ἐκείνου   i.e. Lysias himself. Compare παρόντος δὲ καὶ Λυσίου at 228e1; Socrates is again insisting on getting things from the horse's mouth, despite a certain reluctance on Phaedrus's part.

e6-264a3   Περὶ ... παύσωνται   Notice the realistic touch in Socrates' allowing Phaedrus to read a few more words this time. See note on 262e1-4.

264a4   πολλοῦ δεῖν 'to fall far short of.' See second note on 243c8.

a5   οὐδὲ 'not at all.' See second note on 258e3.

        ἐξ ὑπτίας 'on his back' in agreement with De Vries rather than LSJ, which (s.v. ὕπτιος III.2) defines the phrase as meaning "backward." Developing an argument from its beginning is hard work; Lysias avoids that by starting at the conclusion and lazily swimming the backstroke downstream to the starting point. The figure would not bear detailed comparison with the speech, but it need undergo no such ordeal: all Socrates wants to say is that Lysias did not start at the beginning and swim upstream, as following the ὁδός (263b7) of the rhetorical τέχνη demands.

a6   τὸν λόγον is the object of διανεῖν, of which the prefix should be taken in the sense 'all the way' rather than 'across' (S. 1685.3).

a6-7   καὶ ἄρχεται ... παιδικά   Compare on 230a7.

a7-8   Φαῖδρε, φίλη κεφαλή   That this is a deliberate reminiscence of Homer's Τεῦκρε, φίλη κεφαλή (*Iliad* 8.281) is shown by this being the only one of the three occasions on which Plato uses this form of address in which he preserves Homer's word order and omits, as Homer does, the exclamatory ὦ, which is too familiar for high poetry. The address is both playful and affectionate, but see second note on 228d6.

264b1   γέ τοι δή marks that a reason, valid as far as it goes, is being given for accepting a proposition (D. 550–51).

       οὗ   The antecedent, ἐκείνου dependent on τελευτή, has been omitted.

264b3–e3: Consideration of the lack of "compositional necessity" in Lysias's speech leads to a statement of organic form as a criterion of good writing and a comparison of Lysias's speech to the epitaph of King Midas.

264b3–4   τὰ τοῦ λόγου   'the parts of the speech.'

b4–5   φαίνεται ... τεθῆναι   Δεῖν depends on φαίνεται, τεθῆναι on δεῖν.

b5   ἤ ... ῥηθέντων   The reader must understand some predicate, parallel to, but more general than, that of the preceding clause.

b6   ὡς μηδὲν εἰδότι with ἐμοὶ presents the usual Socratic self-deprecation.

       οὐκ ἀγεννῶς   'with aristocratic nonchalance.'

       τὸ ἐπιὸν   'just what came into his head.'

b7   τῷ γράφοντι is dative of agent with the perfect passive infinitive.

       ἔχεις for ἔχεις ἐν νῷ, as often.

       ἀνάγκην λογογραφικὴν   "Cogent principle of composition" (Hackforth) or 'compositional necessity,' as I render it in the section heading.

b8   οὕτως   'as he did.' Perhaps Socrates might gesture toward the scroll that Phaedrus still holds in his hand.

b9   Χρηστὸς εἶ is ironical and appropriately applied to someone who has asked the speaker to do something that is impossible or virtually so. For instance, when Theodorus (*Tht.* 161a) asks Socrates to say why Theaetetus's second definition of knowledge has turned out to be wrong, Socrates calls him χρηστός, on the grounds that he gives the impression of thinking that he, Socrates, is a sack full of arguments and can draw one out at will to prove a point. 'You are too kind,' said ironically, might do. Compare the heavier irony at 235e2 with note.

264c2–5   Ἀλλὰ ... γεγραμμένα   There are earlier statements of the need for order and internal consistency in a work of art; see e.g. *Grg.* 503e. The verbs συνίστημι and πρέπω often play a part in them, as they will at 268d5, when Socrates touches on how tragedy ought to be written. What is new here is the notion of truly organic form brought in by ζῷον, σῶμα, ἀκέφαλον, and ἄπουν. Plato sometimes lends a similar, but less developed, metaphorical sense to κεφαλή alone, as in ἵνα ἡμῖν ὁ λόγος κεφαλὴν λάβῃ at *Grg.* 505d2–3. He will employ the full metaphor again in *Plt.* 277b–c and *Phlb.* 64b. How much a part of the intellectual furniture of the educated person it became can be seen by its casual handling in the opening lines of Horace's *Ars poetica.*

      ὥσπερ ... αὑτοῦ   '(must) be put together like an animal that has a body of its very own.' Some emphasis must be given in English to convey what Cooper (51.2.12) calls the "extreme unnaturalness" of αὐτὸν αὑτοῦ.

c5   πρέποντα is subordinate to γεγραμμένα and denotes manner.

c6   Πῶς γὰρ οὔ;   It is noteworthy that Phaedrus accepts this first recorded statement of the principle of organic form as something quite unremarkable, as, indeed, Socrates seemed to expect in c2.

c7   τοῦ ἑταίρου σου   At 279b2–3 Lysias will be called Phaedrus's παιδικά.

c9   Μίδᾳ ... ἐπιγεγράφθαι   Not on Midas himself, of course, but on his funerary monument.

264d1   τί πεπονθός;   'having suffered what?' i.e. 'being in what state?' (LSJ s.v. πάσχω II). In asking Phaedrus to compare Lysias's speech to this epigram, Socrates has implied that there is something odd about it. We might say, 'What epigram? And what is the matter with it?'

d3–6   Χαλκῆ ... τέθαπται   As we will be told in e1–2, the point is that the four lines can be arranged in any order and still make sense and be syntactically consistent. Diogenes Laertius 1.90 attributes them to Cleobulus of Lindus, one of the Seven Sages, and cites two additional lines, which destroy the quality of interchangeability that Socrates is interested in here.

d3   Μίδα   For the genitive singular form, see S. 225.

d4   τεθήλῃ is perfect subjunctive of the poetic verb θάλλω.

d6   ἀγγελέω is Epic for Attic ἀγγελῶ.

264e1   οὐδὲν διαφέρει   The subject is the infinitive phrase αυτου ...

λέγεσθαι: literally, 'any given part of it being spoken first or last makes no difference.'

e3   τὸν λόγον ἡμῶν   Phaedrus continues to associate himself with Lysias.

264e4–265c4: Socrates and Phaedrus abandon the speech of Lysias for the time being and turn to discussing the two speeches of Socrates. They agree that these speeches said that love was a kind of madness, but there are two kinds of madness, human and divine, and the better sort of love is one of the four kinds of divine madness. Socrates implies that his description of this kind of love was, at best, a kind of approximation, spoken in a reverent spirit, but compounded of truth and error.

264e4   Τοῦτον . . . ἐάσωμεν   Phaedrus has begun to take the analysis of Lysias's speech rather personally, so Socrates, who has, at any rate, had enough fun with it for the time being, is ready to turn to a subject with more meat in it.

μὲν looks past the parenthetic thought that follows to δὲ in e7.

e5   καίτοι routinely introduces a reservation, so it is natural to find it in a parenthetic remark that qualifies the antithesis between balanced clauses of the μέν . . . δέ type.

e5–6   πρὸς . . . μὴ πάνυ τι   The participles are conditional. Sense and word order tell us to take μὴ with πάνυ rather than with ἐπιχειρῶν: 'If a man keeps them in view, he would profit by it, if he tries to *imitate* them, he would profit—not very much.' My crude typographical devices are meant to highlight the asyndeton between the two participial phrases as well as the striking word order. (The placing of πάνυ τι has something in common with the "contrary to expectation" [παρὰ προσδοκίαν] device that is common in the plays of Aristophanes, whereby the writer saves for the end of a clause or sentence something that reverses its meaning or otherwise alters it in an unexpected way.) As for asyndeton, Aristotle (*Rhetorica* Γ 1413[b] 17–31) discusses it and says that it is essentially a dramatic device, "appropriate to oratory: one must act the passage, not merely speak it." On dramatic, as distinguished from merely formal, asyndeton, see D. xlv. Thompson considered this an example of aposiopesis (S. 3015) and said that Socrates refrained from finishing his thought (with something to follow πάνυ τι like ἀλλὰ πολὺ μᾶλλον φυγεῖν) out of deference to Phaedrus. Aposiopesis, though, usually requires grammatical incompleteness, in order that we may know that it is there. Here the only tip-off would be the unusual word order, which, as we have seen, can be explained on other grounds.

e8   **προσῆκον ἰδεῖν** 'worth investigating' (LSJ s.v. *εἴδω A.3b).

265a2   **Ἐναντίω που ἤστην** At 262d1 we saw some reason to suppose that τὼ λόγω might contrast the speech of Lysias with the two speeches of Socrates taken as one. Here, that qualities in the speeches of Socrates are being contrasted demands that we take the dual to refer to them alone.

a4   **Καὶ μάλ' ἀνδρικῶς** Adverbial καί very frequently modifies intensifying adverbs like μάλα and πάνυ. The phrase as a whole modifies ἐλεγέτην, not χαρίζεσθαι.

a5   **μανικῶς** Understand ἐλεγέτην from a3.

    μέντοι is emphatic: μέν adds objective certainty, while τοι brings home this truth to another person; Denniston (399) suggests "really, you know."

a6   **αὐτὸ τοῦτο** A statement, that is, that the two speeches were spoken μανικῶς.

a9   **δέ γε** This collocation shows that Socrates is picking up the thread of his own discourse from a6–7, as if Phaedrus's reply had not intervened (D. 154).

    εἴδη δύο Once again the dual form εἴδει is avoided, whether by Plato or his copyists one cannot be quite sure.

a10–11   **ὑπὸ θείας . . . νομίμων** 'by a divine alteration of customary usages.' Both εἰωθότων and νομίμων have been suspected, separately, of being glosses on each other, but the authenticity of the phrase is supported by a parallel in the orator Lycurgus (*Against Leocrates* 25).

265b2–c3   **Τῆς . . . ἔφορον** This compound sentence is built around the two verbs ἐφήσαμεν and προσεπαίσαμεν, each of them preceded by a number of participial phrases in agreement with their common subject. The two members are formally joined by τε in b5 and καὶ in b6.

b2   **Τῆς . . . διελόμενοι** Both genitives depend on μέρη, τῆς θείας (sc. μανίας) being partitive, and τεττάρων θεῶν possessive: 'when we distinguished four parts of divine madness belonging to four gods.'

b3   **θέντες** 'by making' (LSJ s.v. B.2); it takes both the direct object μαντικὴν (sc. μανίαν, as with τελεστικήν, ποιητικήν, and τετάρτην in b4) and the predicate accusative ἐπίπνοιαν, which, used in a concrete sense, is modified by all five of the genitive divine names. And Burnet's comma after῎Ερωτος in b5 must be observed. The attentive reader will remember that, except in the case of poetry and the Muses, Socrates has not until now assigned any of the kinds of divine madness to a specific divine patron. Moreover, the conversation from 265a1 to this point has made what was said about love in Socrates' two speeches a bit neater and more schematic than we have seen it to be. For instance, only the mantic, telestic, and poetic were formally introduced as kinds of madness (244a5–245a8). Erotic madness, which is, of course, the most important of them all in the argument, was, beginning in 245b, assumed to be the fourth kind, but received no formal definition as such in the Palinode. In the very important discussion that is beginning here and will carry on through 266b, Socrates feels free to interpret and enlarge upon what he said earlier, particularly in the Palinode, rather than merely recalling or reproducing it. He is turning it from myth into rational discourse and becoming the first in a long line of interpreters of his Palinode.

b6   **οὐκ οἶδ' ὅπῃ** See note on 227c4–5.

b6–8   **ἴσως . . . παραφερόμενοι** Plato's usual disclaimer as to the literal truth of his myths. Notice the *variatio* of ἴσως μὲν . . . τάχα δ' ἄν, as we might say 'maybe . . . perhaps.'

b8   **κεράσαντες** implies that the ingredients for his not entirely unpersuasive speech were there for the mixing, and we found them there in the form of notions that were current from Pythagoreanism, Orphism, and the Eleusinian mysteries.

265c1   **προσεπαίσαμεν** takes a double accusative, the internal object μυθικόν τινα ὕμνον and the external object τὸν ἐμόν τε καὶ σὸν δεσπότην῎Ερωτα (LSJ s.v. προσπαίζω II). The same verb was used in a simpler way at 262d2. Rituals involving dance and song were both means of worship and kinds of παιδιά, so the ambiguity here, a very fruitful one for Plato in this context, comes ready-made. Its ramifications, which would take us beyond the reasonable bounds of this commentary, are traced by Plass.

    μετρίως τε καὶ εὐφήμως i.e. with proper reverence and not, as De Vries points out, as Lysias has done.

c4   **καὶ μάλα** See note on a4.

265c5–266c1: Socrates suggests that two procedures of some value emerged "by accident" in his speeches: the collection of particulars into a single, defined genus, followed by division of that genus, along natural lines, into species. He illustrates this by a consideration of the kinds of love that were distinguished in his two speeches.

265c5   **Τόδε . . . λάβωμεν**   Τόδε is defined by the indirect question introduced by ὡς.

       αὐτόθεν is best taken temporally: 'right away.'

c6   **ὁ λόγος** must, as De Vries points out, refer to Socrates' two speeches taken as one.

c8–9   **παιδιᾷ πεπαῖσθαι**   The dative of manner is not otiose, because the semantic field covered by the verb is more extensive than that covered by the noun.

c9   **τούτων . . . εἰδοῖν**   'but although a certain pair of forms were spoken of by accident.' The genitive absolute is concessive, setting off ἐκ τύχης against τέχνῃ. Since the demonstrative looks forward to something not yet specified (Phaedrus will ask about it in d2), it combines readily with the indefinite. Both are plural in form and modify the dual δυοῖν εἰδοῖν. Εἶδος and ἰδέα are both cognate with εἶδον and Latin *video*. Basically they both mean something like 'appearance' or 'shape.' When they are transferred from the material world into that of psychic experience, they denote something clearly defined rather than amorphous in outline; hence such translations as 'kind,' 'type,' and 'idea.' Plato, as is well known, developed a technical sense for these words that was central to his view of reality, but he by no means always uses them in that sense. Here, as we shall find, what is at issue is a method for accurate and fruitful thinking, so Thompson's translation of δυοῖν εἰδοῖν as "two forms of procedure" (simplified by Hackforth to "pair of procedures") seems quite acceptable—procedures being, in an easily apprehensible sense, intellectual forms: as opposed to random musings, they have shape and clarity of outline.

265d1   **τέχνῃ** is dative of manner and stands in pointed contrast to ἐκ τύχης, which ought to be taken as ironical.

       οὐκ ἄχαρι   Understand ἂν εἴη, the whole constituting a litotes. Hackforth's "very agreeable" is good.

d3–4   **Εἰς μίαν . . . διεσπαρμένα**   That Socrates is going on with his explanation as if Phaedrus had not interrupted with his question is shown by the connective τε. This makes it easy for ἄγειν to depend on οὐκ ἄχαρι (ἂν εἴη). Its subject is a τινά that we understand (from τις in d1) in agreement with συνορῶντα, which we might translate 'by surveying' or 'by comprehending in one overview.' (Cicero translates it using the verb *collustro*.) This same person reverts to the nominative and goes on to be the subject of ποιῇ and ἐθέλῃ in the following clause. Note ἰδέαν; Phaedrus will change to εἶδος in his reply and meet with no objection from Socrates.

d5   ἀεὶ 'on any given occasion.'

ὥσπερ . . . Ἔρωτος introduces as an example the principle (or principles) that the two speeches of Socrates had so fortuitously and fortunately provided. Νυνδὴ need not refer to the immediate past. The phrase as a whole is best taken as an adverbial accusative. Burnet's uppercase epsilon is egregious and confusing.

d5-6   ὃ ἔστιν ὁρισθέν 'what it is if or when it has been defined.' The phrase is parenthetic, the participle attracted into the gender of its predicate.

d6-7   εἶτ' . . . λόγος The implications of γοῦν must be attended to: at least one of the two definitions must be wrong, but each enables its own argument to proceed with clarity and internal consistency.

d7   διὰ ταῦτα i.e. through the procedure (εἶδος) stated in d1–5.

265e1   κατ' εἴδη . . . κατ' ἄρθρα The first κατά is distributive: 'form by form'; the second indicates conformity: 'in accordance with their natural [ᾗ πέφυκεν] joints.'

e2   κακοῦ 'bad of his kind,' i.e. 'unskillful' or 'incompetent' (LSJ s.v. 4).

e3   ἀλλ' ὥσπερ Between these words understand διατέμνειν from e1, parallel to ἐπιχειρεῖν καταγνύναι above. This ὥσπερ looks backward; Socrates will contrast the proper procedure, learned by observing how his two speeches had at first treated madness (presented under such aliases as τὸ ἄφρον τῆς διανοίας and παράνοια) in the manner of an incompetent butcher. They had begun by taking it as a single εἶδος but later the proper divisions had emerged.

ἄρτι, like νυνδὴ at d5, need not refer to the immediate past.

e3-4   τὸ μὲν ἄφρον τῆς διανοίας Genitive—sometimes called genitive of relation—of a noun with a kindred meaning often depends on adjectives compounded with alpha privative. In many cases the original notion was that of separation from whatever positive quality was denoted by the root from which the adjective was derived (S. 1428).

e4   **ἕν τι κοινῇ εἶδος** is predicate accusative with ἐλαβέτην in the sense 'take one thing [τὸ . . . διανοίας] as another' (LSJ s.v. I.6).

e4–266a1   **ὥσπερ δὲ** answers the preceding μὲν; this ὥσπερ looks forward to οὕτω in 266a2; the point of the μὲν . . . δὲ antithesis is not that the two speeches were wrong to take madness as a single εἶδος, but that that εἶδος, like the body with its two sides, can be further split into two εἴδη, which will turn out to have names with moral connotations.

266a1–2   **σκαιά, τὰ δὲ δεξιὰ κληθέντα** 'a left-hand set and the others, called the right-hand set.' The article with δέ is sometimes used with the second member of a pair, in the absence of an article or μέν with the first, in the sense 'the other' or 'another' or their respective plurals (Gildersleeve 2.517). For example, at *Tht.* 181d5–6 Socrates, in dividing change into two kinds, calls them ἀλλοίωσιν, τὴν δὲ φοράν ('alteration and the other kind, local motion').

a2   **τὸ τῆς παρανοίας** See note on 230c3. Here the same thing is meant as was meant by τὸ ἄφρον τῆς διανοίας in 265e3–4.

a2–3   **ὡς . . . ἡγησαμένω** Ἡγέομαι can take the same construction as ἐλαβέτην in 265e4, but here Plato chooses to insert ὡς between the entities that are being identified with each other.

a3   **ὁ μὲν** with the help of ὁ δ᾽ in a6 proceeds to take τὼ λόγω of 265e3 separately.

a4   **τεμνόμενος** is middle, because the speech is cutting the left-hand part off for its own use.

    τέμνων is active, because now it is merely cutting further what has already been cut off for its own use. The participle is supplementary with ἐπανῆκεν in the sense 'leave off' (LSJ s.v. ἐπανίημι II.2).

a4–5   **ἐν αὐτοῖς** is plural, because the μέρος on the left has now been chopped into pieces.

a5   **σκαιόν** By using a term of moral significance that also happens to be a synonym for ἐπ᾽ ἀριστερὰ at a3 Socrates makes a grim pun: 'a kind of love that is rightly called sinister,' we might say.

    ἐλοιδόρησεν The first speech of Socrates did indeed revile ἔρως in the person of its votary ὁ ἐρῶν.

a6   **ἐν δίκῃ** = δικαίως: a metaphorical extension of the local sense of ἐν.

a7   ὁμώνυμον... ἔρωτα   The point of the antithesis is that what has received the name love so far in this process of division—on the left side, that is—has scarcely merited being called θεῖος.

266b1   προτεινάμενος   'exhibiting it'; the speech was like a merchant holding out his wares.

b3–4   Τούτων . . . συναγωγῶν   Socrates exhibits the warmest enthusiasm for this method of division and collection. He had certainly employed its elements in earlier dialogues, but perhaps Plato had only now clarified the procedure into an εἶδος (in the sense discussed on 265c9) in his thinking. Socrates will again call himself its ἐραστής and go on to call it a gift from the gods in *Phlb.* 16b–d.

b4–5   λέγειν τε καὶ φρονεῖν   represents speaking and thinking as "the entire life of the mind" (V.). This would seem to place collection and division at the foundation of rhetoric as well as of dialectic, but we shall soon see that rhetoric as actually practiced lacks them.

b5–6   δυνατὸν . . . ὁρᾶν   'able to see unity and natural multiplicity.' This person takes disparate particulars (τὰ πολλαχῇ διεσπαρμένα from 265d3–4) as his raw material and penetrates intellectually (sees) both to the collection of genus and to its natural divisions or species. Some commentators and translators wish to take πεφυκόθ' with ἕν as well as πολλὰ by a kind of brachylogy, but Socrates felt no need to emphasize the naturalness of the process of collection in 265d, whereas he did feel that need when describing division (ᾗ πέφυκεν at 265e2, πέφυκε at 266a1). On the other hand, it is easy, often tempting, to divide a collection along lines suggested by something other than nature; inept butchers are a greater danger than inept harvesters. In the passage from the *Philebus* cited in the note to b3–4 Socrates represents the dialectical process as being 'easy to describe but very hard to apply' (δηλῶσαι μὲν οὐ πάνυ χαλεπόν, χρῆσθαι δὲ παγχάλεπον). Clearly accurate division along natural lines is where the difficulty is most likely to lie.

b6–7   κατόπισθε . . . θεοῖο   In adapting to his purposes the Homeric formula μετ' ἴχνια βαῖνε θεοῖο (four occurrences in the *Odyssey*), Plato shows his customary disdain for pedantry. Since the phrase is not a comparison in its original contexts, he substituted ὥστε (Epic for Attic ὡς) for the verb, which he did not need, his sentence already having a suitable one in διώκω. The substitution made it necessary to change ἴχνια to a singular, in order to avoid hiatus. Burnet includes κατόπισθε within quotation marks, because it is metrically consistent with what follows, and Plato does seem to have wanted it to be taken as part of the quotation.

b7   **καὶ μέντοι καὶ** offers a rather weighty progressive connection: 'yes indeed, and' (D. 413–14).

αὐτὸ The singular pronoun makes it clear that collection and division are themselves part of the overriding procedure dialectic, which Phaedrus will call τοῦτο τὸ εἶδος in c7.

266c1   **μέχρι τοῦδε** 'down to now.' Taking this phrase in light of the question that follows, Socrates implies that in the future he may have reason to call people who are able to employ collections and divisions rhetoricians as well as dialecticians.

266c1–d4: Socrates raises the question of whether those who are called rhetoricians practice this same art. When Phaedrus says they do not, Socrates says that they must try to say what it is that both belongs to rhetoric and is acquired by art.

266c1   τὰ δὲ νῦν   'but now.' Νῦν δέ is the idiomatic word order, but here the pull the second place in the sentence exerts on δέ is strong enough to break up the cohesiveness of the phrase.

c2   μαθόντας   sc. ἡμᾶς, which will serve also as the subject of καλεῖν, the object of which must be understood from τοὺς δυναμένους αὐτὸ δρᾶν in b7–8.

τί χρὴ καλεῖν   i.e. instead of διαλεκτικούς.

c2–3   ἢ . . . τέχνη   ἡ λόγων τέχνη is in explanatory apposition to ἐκεῖνο.

c2   τοῦτο refers in a loose way to the answer to the question Socrates has just raised, but since it is singular, the suggested answer will not be a group of people (parallel to διαλεκτικούς) but the art they practice. For ἤ introducing a question that contains a suggested answer to a previous question, see 227b6 with note.

c3   Θρασύμαχός   See notes on 261c2–3 and 267c8–9. Here he occurs merely as an example of a rhetorician.

c4–5   οἳ ἂν . . . ἐθέλωσιν   'if they are willing.' Observing the present general conditional relative form is important here, as is remembering that ἐθέλω is not a synonym of βούλομαι. A translation that begins 'who want' will not catch Socrates' tone or even his basic meaning.

c6   ἄνδρες   The manuscripts have ἄνδρες, which would be the predicate and require the reader to understand something like οὗτοι as subject, but scribes were so prone not to notice this crasis that the change scarcely constitutes an emendation and gives a somewhat preferable text. There is no complete agreement on the proper accentuation of this form: both in the writings of theoreticians in late antiquity and the texts of modern editors one sometimes finds ἄνδρες.

οὐ μὲν δὴ is strongly adversative in relation to the preceding μέν: 'but not by any means' (D. 393); this is slightly different from οὐ μὲν δὴ at 259b5, where the particles protest that what Phaedrus had said was, in the opinion of Socrates, not worthy of him.

c7   εἶδος   See note on εἰδοῖν at 265c9.

c8   διαφεύγειν   Speakers of English use 'escape' in precisely the same metaphorical sense.

266d1–2   τούτων ἀπολειφθὲν   'without these things' (LSJ s.v. ἀπολείπω C.II). Τούτων refers to collection and division, which are what bring it about that dialectic τέχνη λαμβάνεται.

d3   τί μέντοι καὶ ἔστι   'just what is...?' Both particles add emphasis and expressiveness to the indirect question; such particles are usually omitted in *oratio obliqua* (D. lxxiii), so their mere inclusion constitutes a kind of emphasis.

d3–4   τὸ λειπόμενον τῆς ῥητορικῆς   The genitive is not partitive and does not mean "the part of rhetoric which is being left out" (Rowe). No part of rhetoric has been mentioned, but Phaedrus has said in an unqualified way that the rhetoricians are οὐ... ἐπιστήμονες of the only things that are 'got by art' that *have* been mentioned: the two tools of dialectic. The genitive is possessive: 'that which is being left out [of the things we have mentioned that are both καλά and got by τέχνη] that belongs to rhetoric'— the missing ingredient, that is, that would make rhetoric a τέχνη even though it lacks the elements that make dialectic one.

266d5–267d9: In response to Phaedrus's suggestion that the art on which rhetoric depends might be found in the rules contained in technical handbooks on the subject, Socrates amuses himself and his friend with a rapid, maliciously ironical sampling of these rules and a parade of their most famous proponents.

266d7   [Καὶ] is bracketed, because the use of καί and γε adverbially flanking an adverb to strengthen it seems to be limited to replies in which the verb is assumed to be the same as that in the preceding question or statement and is not expressed, as in *Tht.* 147e, in reply to Theaetetus's assertion that we call numbers of a certain kind square or equilateral, Socrates replies, καὶ εὖ γε. Scholars differ on whether the use here can be viewed as an exception to that limitation. See V. ad loc. and D. 158, where καί is accepted and translated "actually."

προοίμιον has been wrested from its proper place near λέγεσθαι to announce the new turn the conversation is taking, and μέν is requisitioned from πρῶτον, after which it would normally belong (compare δεύτερον δὲ in e2), to emphasize the announcement.

266e2   διήγησίν τινα 'some kind of narration' or 'narration, I think you call it.' The effect of an indefinite added to a substantive is often slightly dismissive or even contemptuous. It can imply a casual attitude on the part of the speaker about the details of a matter beneath his notice.

e3   τρίτον . . . εἰκότα   The orators often use these terms without distinction to mean signs pointing to a probable conclusion. When a distinction is made between them, τεκμήρια seem to be things you can point to, like bloodstains or footprints, while εἰκότα are things about which you can only reason and draw inferences, like the probabilities of human conduct. The distinction is made clear by the choice of the infinitives δεικνύαι and φράζειν in Demosthenes 22.22: ἔστι τοίνυν ἀνάγκη τοὺς ἐλέγχοντας ἢ τεκμήρια δεικνύαι δι᾽ ὧν ἐμφανιοῦσι τὸ πιστὸν ὑμῖν, ἢ τὰ εἰκότα φράζειν, ἢ μάρτυρας παρέχεσθαι.

e4   ἐπιπίστωσιν 'additional confirmation.' Just how this differed from simple πίστωσις is not clear. Down to this point Socrates has touched on some of the principal terms of forensic oratory, which are common, usually under their Latin names, to the whole Western tradition of the study of rhetoric. From now on he begins to amuse himself with the authentic κομψὰ τῆς τέχνης, niceties and refinements that bubbled up out of the enthusiasm of the first generation or two active in this newfound τέχνη, but lacked the staying power imparted by usefulness in practice or teaching.

e4-5   τόν γε ... ἄνδρα   The superlative is ironical, as will be κάλλιστον in 267a2. The adjective λογοδαίδαλος is ironical in the way 'wordsmith' in place of 'writer' might be in English.

e5   Βυζάντιον serves to distinguish this man from the famous mathematician Theodorus of Cyrene, who is one of the characters in Plato's *Theaetetus*, *Sophist*, and *Politicus*. Theodorus of Byzantium, who made a brief appearance at 261c3, was a rhetorical theoretician, who seems to have elaborated finicky subdivisions for the generally accepted parts of a speech, such as the ἐπιπίστωσις Socrates has just mentioned, the ἐπεξέλεγχος he will mention in a moment, and the ἐπιδιήγησις and προδιήγησις that Aristotle (*Ars rhetorica* Γ 1414ᵇ 13ff.) says Theodorus's followers distinguished from ordinary διήγησις. Cicero, in a passage the authenticity of which has sometimes been doubted (*Brutus* 48), tells us that Lysias had begun as a rhetorical theorist but turned to writing speeches: *quod Theodorus esset in arte subtilior.* Since χρηστὸν is probably used here—as it often is in Plato—ironically, even an enthusiast for rhetoric like Phaedrus may think these distinctions excessively subtle; on the other hand, the irony may operate only between writer and reader, leaving Phaedrus a naïve admirer.

267a1–2   **καὶ... ἀπολογίᾳ** The *oratio obliqua* depends on λέγειν at 266e4, as if Phaedrus's question and Socrates' brief acknowledgment of it had not intervened. Compare καὶ ἔλεγχόν γε with what was said about καὶ καλῶς γε at 266d7; here καὶ is a conjunction rather than an adverb, and γε emphasizes the addition it makes: 'yes, and....' Ἐπεξέλεγχον stands to ἔλεγχον as ἐπιπίστωσιν stands to πίστωσιν above—as a rococo refinement on a notion that has some practical value in teaching rhetoric.

a2–3   **τὸν ... Εὐηνὸν** For κάλλιστον, see note on 266e4–5. Evenus of Paros is mentioned by Plato elsewhere as a poet (*Phd.* 60d5) and as a man who knows and can teach ἀρετή, according to the recommendation given Socrates by Callias, the rich patron of sophists (*Ap.* 20a–b). Here we find that he was also a rhetorical theorist, whose expertise would seem to have lain in devising psychological subtleties rather than the structural ones made by Theodorus.

a3   **οὐκ ἄγομεν** employs the present of anticipation, which is used in place of the future, in Greek as in English, when the speaker wants to express what is immediate or certain; in questions it indicates that the decision must be made on the spot (S. 1879a).

a4   **παρεπαίνους** Try putting a question mark after this word in place of Burnet's dash and a semicolon in place of the dash after χάριν in the next line. However one punctuates, it must be made clear that οὐκ ἄγομεν is asking a question—rhetorical perhaps, but still a question.

a4–5   **οἱ δ' ... χάριν** Since there would seem to be no reason for Evenus to put only his specimens of 'incidental blame' into meter as a mnemonic, we can assume that 'incidental praise' and 'covert allusion' were taught by him using the same device. The change in construction—as if οἱ μέν had preceded—absolves Socrates from responsibility for the factual truth of the assertions, made by "others," that Evenus both teaches incidental blame and teaches whatever he teaches in meter. Part of Socrates' stance throughout this brief history of rhetorical handbooks is to indicate only the most casual familiarity with the rhetoricians and the particulars of their theories. He reminds one of Cicero talking in public about Greek statuary and affecting nothing beyond the cursory acquaintance consistent with the education and interests of a gentleman.

a5   ἀνήρ   The ἀνήρ of the principal manuscripts would do as well. See first note on 266c6.

a6   Τεισίαν δὲ Γοργίαν τε   Adding one substantive to another with a single τε is a poeticism in which Plato indulges more frequently than most prose writers (D. 497–98). Tisias of Syracuse, whose name is often associated with that of his compatriot Corax, taught a rhetorical theory of which a written version was available to Plato and Aristotle. Cicero (De inventione rhetorica 2.6) says that a summary (now lost) of earlier rhetorical handbooks began with that of Tisias, so he may well have been the author of the first of the written τέχναι to which Phaedrus referred in 266d5–6. One among the collection of introductions to rhetoric that date from the third to the thirteenth century C.E. and are collectively called the Prolegomena tells us that Tisias was a pupil of Corax and refused to pay his fee at the end of the course. Upon being brought to court, he maintained that if he won, he would obviously not have to pay, and if he lost, he should not have to pay, because the course would have been demonstrated to be worthless. Corax replied by reversing the argument: if Tisias lost, he would obviously have to pay; if he won, he should pay, because the course would have been demonstrated to be of value. The court threw the case out, saying that it was a "bad egg from a bad crow [κόραξ]." Gorgias needs no introduction.

εὕδειν   To 'rest' or 'take their ease' in the sense be exempt from participating in our demonstration.

a6–7   οἳ πρὸ . . . μᾶλλον   In 273b–c this claim will be specifically connected to Tisias, and its consequences will be displayed.

a7–8   τά τε αὖ . . . φαίνεσθαι   Importance is what is at issue here, not length, which will be dealt with in b1–2. Isocrates (Panegyricus 8) boasts of being able τά τε μεγάλα ταπεινά ποιῆσαι καὶ τοῖς μικροῖς μέγεθος περιθεῖναι.

267b1   **καινά . . . καινῶς** The general bearing is clear, but φαίνεσθαι will not do with the adverbs; understand λέγεσθαι parallel to it and out of λόγου. Again, Isocrates (*Panegyricus* 8) boasts τά τε παλαιὰ καινῶς διελθεῖν καὶ περὶ τῶν νεωστὶ γεγενημένων ἀρχαίως εἰπεῖν.

b2   **ἄπειρα μήκη** A rather unkind way of alluding to the μακρολογία, which Socrates says that Protagoras claimed to be able to employ at will along with its opposite, βραχυλογία, in *Prt.* 335b7–8. In *Grg.* 449c1–3 Gorgias claims that nobody can say the same things ἐν βραχυτέροις than he can.

b3   **Πρόδικος** was a prominent sophist, who was present at the gathering in *Protagoras*, where Plato makes rather gentle fun of his valetudinarian ways and his enthusiasm for making quibbling distinctions between words.

b4   **ὧν δεῖ λόγων τέχνην** is quite difficult. Stephanus suggested τέχνῃ, which has been accepted by many editors in the intervening centuries. It could be interpreted as the dative (usually of person) that is governed along with genitive of thing by δεῖ (LSJ s.v. δεῖ II.2): 'what the art of speeches has need of.' Conceivably it could be instrumental with ηὑρηκέναι, in which case λόγων becomes an antecedent attracted into its relative clause: 'found by art speeches that are needed.' De Vries, who prefers to delete τέχνην altogether (as "an explanatory marginal note" that got into the text), concedes that the transmitted text can be defended as representing ηὑρηκέναι τέχνην τούτων τῶν λόγων ὧν δεῖ, where we have, presumably, τέχνην drawn into the relative clause along with λόγων, with which it is closely connected syntactically: 'has found an art for those speeches [i.e. the kind of speeches] that are needed.' That is how I read the sentence on first acquaintance, and it is still what I prefer.

b6   **Σοφώτατά γε, ὦ Πρόδικε** 'Brilliant! Prodicus.' There might be some doubt about the tone of χρηστὸν at 266e6, but Phaedrus has by now quite clearly caught the spirit of Socrates' wickedly witty compendium of the techniques of rhetoric and sees Prodicus's crashing platitude for what it is.

b7   **Ἱππίαν** Another sophist from the gathering at Callias's house in Plato's *Protagoras*, where he serves as both foil and counterpart to Prodicus. He claims to be a polymath, and the picture Plato draws of him, particularly in the two dialogues named for him, is that of, as Guthrie (3.281) says, "a somewhat bombastic, humourless, and thick-skinned character."

οὐ λέγομεν   See note on a3.

b8   αὐτῷ   i.e. to Prodicus. Perhaps it is relevant that in Prt. 337c–338b Hippias gives more long-winded but equally platitudinous advice in favor of taking a middle course between μακρολογία and βραχυλογία.

Ἠλεῖον ξένον   Hippias was a rara avis among sophists, a Dorian.

b10   Τὰ δὲ . . . λόγων   At 278b9 Socrates will speak of the spring near which he and Phaedrus have been talking as a Νυμφῶν νᾶμά τε καὶ μουσεῖον. Just as that μουσεῖον was adorned with κόραι and other ἀγάλματα (230b8), Polus's book is adorned with terms like those that follow: 'And what are we to say about Polus's gallery of linguistic exhibits, such as. . . ?' Polus is known chiefly for his bumptious and rather obtuse performance in Plato's Gorgias, which serves as a foil not only to the acuity of Socrates but also to the urbanity and gentlemanliness of Gorgias himself. He seems to have written a book on rhetoric, to which the Suda gives the name περὶ λέξεως. As Kennedy (58) writes of these do-it-yourself handbooks of rhetoric, "Great sophists such as Protagoras or Hippias or Gorgias probably did not bother with this sort of thing; it was the work of second-raters like Polus and Theodorus." Plato varies the manner in which he introduces these people: two presents of anticipation (a3, b7), a future indicative (a6), and now a deliberative subjunctive.

ὡς = οἷον, 'for example.'

267c1   διπλασιολογίαν obviously denotes some sort of repetition— perhaps mere repetition of words, as Hermeias explains it (τὸ τὰ αὐτὰ δὶς λέγειν οἷον φεῦ φεῦ), perhaps something less direct, like figura etymologica. The quotation from or—as is more likely— parody of Polus's handbook that Plato gives us in Grg. 448c rings with verbal repetition.

γνωμολογίαν   A sententious style, abounding in maxims.

εἰκονολογίαν   A style full of images and metaphors. Plato's might be so described, but one doubts that he learned that from the likes of Polus.

c2   ὀνομάτων . . . Λικυμνίων depends on μουσεῖον and is parallel to λόγων. According to Hermeias, Licymnius taught Polus about (perhaps made lists of?) such phenomena as ordinary, as opposed to metaphorical, words, compound words, and related (presumably etymologically) words, and epithets. Aristotle (*Ars rhetorica* Γ 1414ᵇ 17) deprecates his technicalities, saying that he created categories that were κενὸν καὶ ληρῶδες ('empty and silly').

c2–3   ἅ . . . εὐεπείας The subject of ἐδωρήσατο must be extracted from the adjectival Λικυμνίων. For πρός + accusative to denote the end in view, see first note 227a3.

c2   ἐκείνῳ Polus.

c4–5   Πρωταγόρεια . . . ἄττα; 'but surely that sort of thing is Protagorean, isn't it?' Μέντοι emphasizes the expectation of a positive reply to questions that expect it (D. 403). Compare 229b4 and 261c5 with notes.

c6   Ὀρθοέπειά γέ τις has sometimes been taken to mean that Protagoras wrote a book called *Correct Diction*, but it need mean no more than that he was known for discussing the subject. The predicate to be understood would be ἐστὶ Πρωταγόρεια.

   ὦ παῖ Socrates here addresses Phaedrus as if he were the imaginary boy to whom he directed the Palinode (243e9 and 252b2) except that there he added καλέ in both instances, that being appropriate to the imagined occasion.

c7   γε μὴν is progressive: 'and furthermore' (D. 349).

   ἐπὶ γῆρας καὶ πενίαν Accusative because of the idea of motion in ἑλκομένων. These piteous speeches are being 'dragged into the presence of old age and poverty,' regions into which no one would go willingly.

c8–9   τὸ τοῦ Χαλκηδονίου σθένος is a designation in Epic style, like the use of βίη in paraphrases like βίη Ἡρακληείη or βίη Διομήδεος as amplifications of the names of those heroes. The aura of legendary heroism that surrounds such names contrasts ironically with the specialty in the art of inspiring pity that this man has contributed to the art of speaking. Thrasymachus from Chalcedon on the Bosporus was a sophist known primarily as a teacher of rhetoric. The interesting fragment from one of his speeches that is preserved by Dionysius of Halicarnassus (*On the Style of Demosthenes* 3) has been overshadowed by the vivid portrait of him in the opening book of Plato's *Republic*, where he emerges as a bitter and disillusioned, but formidable man.

c9   ὀργίσαι . . . ἀνὴρ A technique that, unfortunately for democratic governments, seems fatally easy to master and transmit. Once again the breathing of ἀνήρ was altered by Bekker. Either is possible, since 'the man is skilled' and 'he is a man skilled' are both acceptable in the context. Since little credence can be given to the manuscripts on this point, the decision hinges on taste applied to the individual instance.

267d1   ὠργισμένοις   sc. αὐτοῖς, out of πολλούς.

d2   ἀπολύσασθαι διαβολὰς   This was also, we recall, the self-proclaimed task that Socrates did not have enough time to perform in Plato's version of his *Apology* (37b1–2).

ὅθενδὴ   'from whatever source.'

d3–4   κοινῇ . . . εἶναι   'there seems to be universal agreement about. . . .' Socrates has had his fun and the subject will be brought to an end rather abruptly.

d4   ἄλλοι . . . ὄνομα   Hermeias explains: τοὺς ἐπιλόγους θέλει εἰπεῖν, ὅ τινες ἐπάνοδον, οἱ δὲ ἀνακεφαλαίωσιν ὀνομάζουσι.

d5–6   Τὸ ἐν κεφαλαίῳ . . . τῶν εἰρημένων;   'Do you mean reminding the audience in summary at the end of each point involved in what has been said?' Ὑπομιμνήσκω can take accusative of person and περί with genitive of thing or, as here, accusative of both person and thing. For λέγω in the sense 'intend to say' or 'mean,' see LSJ s.v. λέγω (B) III.9.

d9   Σμικρά . . . λέγειν   And so this colorfully satirical look at the rhetorical handbooks known to Plato, which began at 266d7, comes to an end. Since they have all been lost, this passage yields the best description we have of their contents and arrangement (Kennedy 54–57).

268a1–c4: In order to shed light on the question whether knowledge of the devices in the handbooks is equivalent to possessing a rhetorical art, Socrates brings in an analogy from medicine: does knowing what procedures will produce certain effects on the body constitute being a physician? He and Phaedrus agree that it does not, unless one also knows to whom the procedures ought to be administered, and when, and for how long.

268a1–2   ταῦτα . . . ἴδωμεν   Prepositions with the accusative after a verb that does not normally denote motion often impose what is called a "pregnant" sense on the verb, causing it to denote not only its proper meaning but also the motion that naturally precedes or follows (S. 1659b). The full implication here is, 'Let us, rather, bring these matters under the light and see.'

a2   τίνα . . . δύναμιν   The subject of ἔχει is ταῦτα. Is the indirect question single or double? With πότ᾽, which Burnet prints from B and T, it is double and καὶ is connective. With the enclitic ποτ᾽, as many editors printed after Stephanus, who followed the mass of later manuscripts, καὶ following an interrogation that asks for additional information emphasizes that addition. "The effect is usually produced in English by an inflection of the voice," as D. 312–13 says: '*what* power.' The καὶ in the indirect question that asks for additional information at the end of the sentence in 266d2–4 served that function. Translator after translator prints something here that cannot be gotten from the Greek text, with the honorable exception of Hackforth, who emends τὴν to τὰ and takes τὰ τῆς τέχνης as the subject (the idiom remarked on in the note on 230c3 is found with the plural article as well). He translates, "what power the art possesses, and when." I suggest an alternative that does not involve altering the received text. Taking—along with almost everyone except Hackforth—ταῦτα, the rules and devices of the handbooks, as the subject of ἔχει and, understanding ἐστί with τίνα, translate, 'see what they are and when they have the power of the art,' the art, that is, of rhetoric, which Socrates continues to assume to be an art, unless he can prove that it is not. We have heard the names of these devices, but their nature—what they are—has not been discussed. We will get a metaphorical glimpse of it in a6, but in a8 Socrates will embarks on a demonstration by analogy that will show them to be nothing more than the preliminaries to a true understanding of rhetoric. In his reply here Phaedrus gives no direct answer to the first part of what Socrates had asked; he chooses, instead, to answer the second question in a way that lauds the power of rhetoric without addressing the harder question of what these rules and devices in the handbooks really are, just as Socrates' interlocutors in the opening of the *Gorgias* praised rhetoric while shirking the harder task of saying what it is.

a3–4   ἔν γε . . . συνόδοις   Principally the courts and the ekklesia. Δὴ stresses the limitation that γε puts on the field of application of the affirmation that the δύναμις is powerful (D. 245).

a5   ἔχει γάρ   See note on 228c9.

ὦ δαιμόνιε here expresses mild irritation not precisely because, as

De Vries would have it, Phaedrus has replied with an irrelevancy rather than answering the question, but because he confined himself to making a stab at answering what he took to be the easier half of it. See also second note on 228d6.

a6   διεστηκὸς ... ἤτριον 'Ihe warp is here taken as representative of the state of both the warp and the woof. Αὐτῶν refers to the same rhetorical handbook devices as does ταῦτα in a1; διεστηκὸς implies being loosely woven rather than having holes. Phaedrus is being asked whether he agrees with Socrates that an art woven from devices in the handbooks would not 'hold water.'

a7   Δείκνυε This imperative form, where we might expect δείκνυ from δείκνυμι, is from δεικνύω. For such forms see S. 746a. Copyists often regularized -υμι verbs into omega verbs, making it difficult in some cases to know what the writer of the Classical period actually wrote.

a9   Ἐρυξιμάχῳ ... Ἀκουμέῳ Both were physicians (227a5).
ὅτι See first note on 236c6.

a10   προσφέρειν is the medical term of art for administering a drug (LSJ s.v. 3b).

268b4   ἄλλον ποιεῖν sc. ἰατρικόν. Ἀξιῶ, which meant 'claim' with εἶναι, means 'claim to be able' with ποιεῖν.

b5   οἴει ... εἰπεῖν; sc. αὐτούς as subject of ἀκούσαντας, Eryximachus and his father.

b6   προσεπίσταται The subject is τις from a8.

b7-8   οὕστινας ... ὁπόσου; The first question shows the normal double accusative with ποιεῖν in the sense 'do something to someone.'

268c1   [ποιεῖν] ἃ ἐρωτᾷς; Ἃ ἐρωτᾷς refers to the content of the indirect questions in b7-8, and ποιεῖν, which governs it and refers back to ποιεῖν in b7, should not be bracketed. There is a question mark, because this sentence is a question parallel to that which begins with εἴ τις in a8, and the reader must understand something like τί ἂν οἴει ἀκούσαντας εἰπεῖν from b4-5 to complete the thought.
αὐτὸν can be rendered 'of himself.' Thompson's "by the light of nature" goes a bit too far; we do not know where he is assumed to get this knowledge.

c2   Εἰπεῖν The manuscripts read εἴποι, making οἶμαι parenthetic rather than being the governing verb. If we are not to suppose that Plato forgot that his subject was plural, must we accept either this emendation by Burnet or Stephanus's εἴποιεν? If we must, I would prefer the latter, which is closer to the tradition and for which, as Thompson suggests, the following ἂν or the εἴποι in b9 would offer an explanation for the corruption. But must the subject be plural? It is true that Socrates, having mentioned Eryximachus *or* (ἢ) his father Acumenus in a9, then refers to them again with the plural ἀκούσαντας in b5, seeming to make this an argument between two MDs and one mountebank, but Phaedrus is speaking now. Can he not be allowed to go back to the disjunctive introduction of these two men in a9 and—thinking only of his close friend Eryximachus—let Acumenus slip out of mind? The illustration drawn from the imaginary conversation between the two poets and the poetaster that will follow begins by posing a question to Sophocles and Euripides, but by the time it ends, Socrates gives the reply to Sophocles alone; and when he refers back to the present illustration (269a2–3), he mentions only the man of *his* own generation, Acumenus. I would defend εἴποι. It seems to lie close to the outer edge of the kind of syntactical inconcinnity that Plato allows himself in the name of conversational artlessness, but still within its bounds.

c2   **ἄνθρωπος** The copyists of the manuscript tradition lost the rough breathing, which is obviously necessary.

c2–3   **καὶ . . . ἀκούσας** Compare this with Socrates' description of his discovery of the thought of Anaxagoras in *Phd*. 97b8–c1: Ἀλλ' ἀκούσας μέν ποτε ἐκ βιβλίου τινός, ὡς ἔφη, Ἀναξαγόρου ἀναγιγνώσκοντος, καὶ λέγοντος ὡς . . . ('but having once heard someone reading from a book, as he said, of Anaxagoras mad saying that . . .'). The Classical Greek equivalent of the serendipities of browsing was to chance to overhear someone reading some novel matter aloud.

c3   **φαρμακίοις** "Mild remedies" (LSJ, citing this passage) would have no point here; the diminutive expresses offhand contempt. I like Thompson's "having picked up a nostrum or two."

268c5–269a4: Socrates broadens the discussion by bringing in people who imagine themselves to be tragic poets or musicians, because they have mastered a few techniques that are necessary to those arts. He and Phaedrus agree that genuine physicians, poets, and musicians would tell these pretenders to their several arts that they know not the arts they profess but only some necessary preliminaries to those arts.

268c6–7   ἐπίσταται . . . σμικράς   This is similar to the boast attributed to Tisias and Gorgias in 267a7–8. The term ῥῆσις is proper to a speech in a play (LSJ s.v. III), and Euripides in particular is known for the rhetorical, quasiforensic tone of speeches he puts into the mouths of his characters.

c7–8   ὅταν . . . ἀπειλητικὰς   Understand ῥήσεις with the adjectives; and for another connection between tragedy and rhetoric, compare what was said in 267c–d about Thrasymachus's λόγοι οἰκτρόγοοι and his claim to be able to excite and allay passions.

268d3–5   Καὶ οὗτοι . . . συνισταμένην   With b6–8 this reply leads to the conclusion that Phaedrus is being allowed to display rather more insight in this discussion than we are accustomed to see him show in the dialogue at large.

d4   τούτων refers to the elements of tragedy mentioned and suggested in c6–d1. Since it is they, not the thing composed of them, that must 'stand together by being appropriate to each other and to the whole,' logic would demand that the participles be genitive plural, but they have been attracted into agreement with σύστασιν in the sense 'composition' or 'structure' (LSJ s.v. B.II).

d5   πρέπουσαν is subordinate to συνισταμένην and expresses manner. Compare the similar use of πρέποντα at 264c5 in a passage closely related to this one.

d8   ὅτι δὴ   'just because.' See note on 244a5.

d8–e1   ὀξυτάτην . . . ποιεῖν   'to make a string very high and very low in pitch,' which would involve knowing how to tighten and relax it in the proper degree, presumably an operation requiring skill.

268e1   ἀγρίως is harsher and ruder than ἀγροίκως at d6.

μοχθηρέ is conspicuously rude and ill tempered. Characters in comedy are occasionally so addressed, but in Plato the vocative of this word occurs only in imagined conversations. Perhaps 'you idiot!' might catch the tone.

e2   μελαγχολᾷς is a straightforward medical term for being mad, without any of the romantic associations of melancholia.

μουσικὸς is evidently used in the sense 'cultured' here, whereas in d7 it meant approximately what forms of ἁρμονικὸς mean in d7 and e4, i.e. a musician.

ὅτι   See note on 236c6.

e2–3   Ὦ ἄριστε   See second note on 228d6.

e4   μὴν antithetically balances μὲν in the preceding line like a more emphatic δέ, implying "complete, or almost complete negation" (D. 335).

e4–5   μηδὲ... ἐπαΐειν 'from not understanding even. ...'

e5   τὸν... ἔχοντα 'someone in your state,' i.e. someone who can do what this man claimed to be able to do in d8–e1.

269a1   σφισιν is plural because the man displayed his powers to Euripides too (268c5) and indirect reflexive because it refers to the subject of the main verb, φαίη, but depends on τὸν . . . ἐπιδεικνύμενον, which is the subject of a clause in indirect statements after that verb. The verb in the dependent clause is ἐπίστασθαι, understood from ἐπίστασαι in 268e6.

269a5–c5: Under the guise of reproving Phaedrus and himself for their lack of urbanity, Socrates improvises a courteous but devastating evaluation, such as one of the great practicing orators, like Pericles, might have made, of the rhetorical theorists and their productions.

269a5–b4   Τί δὲ . . . εἰπόντας   Socrates begins as if he is going to ask a word question (the kind that is introduced by an interrogative pronoun, adjective, or adverb and expects some sort of statement in reply), but after the parenthetic explanation in a7–8, he "forgets" to complete his word question and—with πότερον— moves into a sentence question (the kind that is not introduced by an interrogative and expects "yes" or "no" in reply). The result is that when the ἂν . . . εἰπεῖν we have been expecting since a5 finally comes, it still has 'the honey-voiced Adrastus or Pericles' (recalled to the reader by αὐτούς in b1) as its subject, but it has acquired a new object in ῥῆμά τι . . . ἀπαίδευτον, leaving τί stranded high and dry back at the beginning of the sentence. But τί has its revenge in the end; after the sentence question has come to a formal close with ἐπιπλῆξαι, Socrates adds εἰπόντας, which demands as object exactly what τί wanted all along: a statement of what

Pericles or the sweet-voiced Adrastus would say. Burnet seems to have despaired of finding the right place to put a question mark. Although it would create a kind of typographical monstrosity, the logical place to put it is at the end of the paragraph, moving the period inside the quotation marks, since it applies only to the quoted material.

a5   τὸν μελίγηρυν Ἄδραστον   Adrastus, a central figure in the legends about the wars against Thebes in the heroic age, seems to have enjoyed a Nestor-like reputation for eloquence in the poetic tradition. The phrase γλῶσσαν Ἀδράστου μειλιχόγηρυν appears in the fragments of the Spartan elegiac poet Tyrtaeus 12.8 (West, *Elegi et Iambi Cantati ante Alexandrum*, vol. 2), and see the rhetorical skill with which Adrastus manipulates the feelings of Theseus in Euripides' *Suppliants*. In our passage his name is generally thought to stand for some orator contemporary with either Pericles or the dramatic date of the dialogue. Antiphon has been suggested, but that is only a guess. The alternative to identifying him with a contemporary would be to suppose that Pericles so far surpassed other orators of his generation that he could be paired only with a figure out of the heroic age.

a5–6   ἢ καὶ Περικλέα   'or Pericles, if you will' (D. 306).

a7–8   ὅσα ἄλλα   Ἄλλων, which might have appeared in series with βραχυλογιῶν τε καὶ εἰκονολογιῶν, has instead been attracted into the clause and case of the relative ὅσα, which agrees with the verbal adjective σκεπτέα in its personal and passive construction (S. 2149).

a8   ὑπ᾽ αὐγὰς   See note on 268a1–2.

πότερον   At this point we must repeat οἰόμεθα from a5.

269b1   ὑπ᾽ ἀγροικίας expresses internal cause (S. 1698.1b) and tells us why, assuming that they were like Socrates and Phaedrus, they would speak χαλεπῶς.

b3   ὡς introduces a comparison, of which the first term is ταῦτα from the line before, the handbooks of rhetoric with their κομψά.

b3–4   ὄντας σοφωτέρους is in agreement with αὐτούς in b1.

b4   κἂν νῷν ἐπιπλῆξαι   Ἐπιπλήσσω in the sense 'rebuke' can take either accusative or, as here, dative. The καί component of κἂν could be translated 'too,' comparing the case of Socrates and Phaedrus with those of the people censured by Sophocles and the physicians, or it could bear on ἐπιπλῆξαι adverbially and be translated 'even.'

b5   τινες 'certain people.'

b6   ἐγένοντο 'turned out to be.'

b7   ἐκ . . . τούτου τοῦ πάθους   i.e. as a result of being unable to define rhetoric.

b8   ἀναγκαῖα μαθήματα   Compare 268e6.

269c1   ταῦτα is once again the handbooks and their contents.

Σφισιν is dative of agent and an indirect reflexive, because it is part of an indirect statement but refers to the subject of the governing verb, ἡγοῦνται. A shift in tense comes with this verb. These people wrote their handbooks and formulated their faulty notion of what rhetoric is in the past; hence ἀδύνατοι ἐγένοντο ὁρίσασθαι in b6 and ᾠήθησαν ηὑρηκέναι in b8–c1. But they are still propagating those notions, so 'in teaching others they think. . . .'

c2–3   τὸ δὲ . . . συνίστασθαι 'but the effective presentation of each of these devices and the composition of the whole.' The article goes with both infinitives and the whole phrase stands as the object of πορίζεσθαι.

c2   τούτων refers to the tricks and devices of the rhetorical theoretician, into which these students must breathe life.

c3   οὐδὲν ἔργον can stand as an appositive to the infinitive phrase without Hermeias's addition of the participle to make it into an accusative absolute. In either case the relationship is causal; the rhetoricians think that their students can supply these abilities, because it is a negligible task.

αὐτοὺς serves the same function as did αὐτὸν in 268c1, but is much more explicit.

c4   δεῖν is parallel to δεδιδάχθαι in indirect discourse with ἡγοῦνται. σφων is genitive of possession, referring to τινες of b5; it is an indirect reflexive, because not they but their students are the subjects of δεῖν. This exhilarating paragraph deserves repeated reading as an example of Plato's supple and informal handling of Greek. Although it begins as a defense of the rhetoricians against the rough handling they were receiving from Socrates and Phaedrus, before it comes to an end, it has imperceptibly turned into a repudiation of all that was wrong with their practices.

TOWARD AN ART OF SPEAKING

269c6–270a8: Phaedrus concedes that Socrates has made his point about the rhetorical theorists, but observes that the question of how one does acquire the art of persuasive speaking remains unanswered. Socrates replies that becoming an outstanding orator demands the same three prerequisites as does becoming a champion in any other pursuit: innate talent, knowledge, and practice. He warns that the way of Lysias and Thrasymachus will not lead to that happy result. A more liberal education, such as that which Pericles acquired from Anaxagoras, is needed.

269c6–9   Ἀλλὰ μήν . . . ἀλλὰ δὴ   "In the sphere of thought" ἀλλὰ μήν indicates assent (D. 343); ἀλλὰ δὴ dismisses what preceded as being, if not irrelevant, at least of less importance than the point that is to follow (D. 241): 'to be sure (what the rhetorical theoreticians do may be as you say), *but.* . . .'

c6   κινδυνεύει γε   De Vries remarks that Phaedrus is acting in character in putting limitations on his agreement with Socrates.

c7   τὸ τῆς τέχνης   'the case of the art.'

269d2   Τὸ μὲν . . . ὥστε   Δύνασθαι is ordinarily followed directly by an infinitive, but compare 258b10–c2 with note and *Prt.* 338c2–3: ἀδύνατον ὑμῖν ὥστε . . . ἑλέσθαι. The construction implies that δύνασθαι means 'to have so much ability' that (as a result) such and such happens. The whole phrase as far as γενέσθαι is accusative of respect, which then becomes the subject of ἔχειν.

μὲν would appear to be truly solitary, emphasizing the importance of the concept of ability. See further on d6.

ἀγωνιστὴν τέλεον   'an accomplished contender.'

d3   εἰκός   Understand ἐστί.

τἆλλα is another accusative of respect: 'elsewhere,' i.e. in all other pursuits.

d5   προσλαβὼν is a circumstantial participle that imports a proviso.

d5–6   ὅτου . . . τούτων   It will make for easier translation if you make this conditional relative protasis into a pure condition: 'but if you are short any one of them.'

d6   ὅσον δὲ αὐτοῦ τέχνη answers εἰ μέν σοι ὑπάρχει φύσει in d4,

292

not τὸ μὲν δύνασθαι in d2; the power subsumes both nature and art, but Socrates is now coming back to the art after speaking about the artist in the two lines that precede. See LSJ s.v. ὅσος IV.1. Some verbal idea (perhaps 'goes' or 'is concerned') must be understood. Translate αὐτοῦ 'of it,' meaning, as De Vries puts it, "the whole business."

d8   ἡ μέθοδος The metaphor behind this word is reactivated in this context: the road for pursuit of the τέχνη does not seem to Socrates to come to light on the path Lysias and Thrasymachus travel.

269e1–2   Κινδυνεύει . . . γενέσθαι Pericles' ability to persuade is being praised here; nothing is being said about the wisdom of his policies, so the statement does not contradict the condemnation of them in *Grg.* 515e–516d.

e1   εἰκότως modifies γενέσθαι. Hackforth's "I am inclined to think that it is not surprising that . . ." provides a way of translating both it and κινδυνεύει without redundancy by altering the sentence structure.

e2   εἰς τὴν ῥητορικὴν 'in regard to public speaking.' A τέχνη is a body of knowledge that can be either theoretically contemplated or, as is in question here, demonstrated in action.

e4   προσδέονται The prefix is essential: these arts obviously need their own technicalities, but they all need something in addition.

270a1   ἀδολεσχίας . . . πέρι 'idle talk and airy speculation about nature.' These are activities of which philosophers are accused by the common man, and Socrates is taking the bull by the horns and defiantly flaunting them—or, at least, that is how it seems. Notice, however, that natural philosophy is involved, and in particular that of Anaxagoras, from which Socrates carefully disassociates himself in the *Apology* and *Phaedo*. There may be plenty of room left for his typical ironical stance. In any case LSJ's "keenness, subtlety" is not so much a translation for ἀδολεσχία as it is a misleading interpretation; μετεωρολογία must be understood in a generalized sense that also permits it to be taken with φύσεως πέρι.

a1–2   τὸ γὰρ . . . τελεσιουργὸν LSJ's "high-minded" for ὑψηλόνουν gives the wrong impression; even 'highbrow' would be better. For τελεσιουργὸν either 'finished' (in the sense 'polished') or 'effective' (i.e. bringing to a τέλος) would be possible. Hackforth translates τοῦτο with "of which you are thinking." After all,

Phaedrus has asked (269c9–d1) for the source of 'the art of the real and persuasive orator.'

a2   ἐντεῦθέν ποθεν   Compare 229b4 and note on 229b7; it is from somewhere in the neighborhood of the intellectual pursuits in a1 that the distinguished qualities that Phaedrus has in mind come.

a3   ὃ καὶ . . . ἐκτήσατο   Καὶ with the relative pronoun, not with Pericles: Pericles acquired 'this also,' in addition to being talented by nature.

a5   νοῦ τε καὶ διανοίας   This reading gives us two appropriate synonyms, but the reading of B and T is, at the very least, interesting. The phrase would, perhaps, then mean 'having arrived at the nature of mind and what is not mind.' That is not, to be sure, the normal meaning of ἄνοια, but it could have been a presocratic coinage that failed to become current and survives only here.

a6   τὸν πολὺν λόγον   De Vries translates the article as "his well-known." But it simply indicates that Socrates assumes that Phaedrus will have heard about Anaxagoras's teaching and its magnitude. The tense of ἐποιεῖτο makes it likely that λόγον denotes oral teaching, primarily in any case. Rowe's "the very [see D. 218–19 for δή used after a relative pronoun to stress the importance of its antecedent] subjects about which Anaxagoras used to talk so much" is good.

a7–8   τὸ πρόσφορον αὐτῇ   'whatever was relevant to it.'

270a9–c5: Socrates advances the thesis that rhetoric, if it is to be scientific, must determine the nature of the soul as medicine does that of the body. This brings up the question of whether knowledge of the nature of the soul or the body presupposes knowledge of "the nature of the whole."

270b1   Ὁ αὐτὸς . . . ὅσπερ καὶ   'the same as' (S. 1501a).

b4   σώματος   Σῶμα, like ψυχή, is a noun that often lacks a definite article when we would expect to see one (S. 1135).

b5–6   μὴ τριβῇ . . . τέχνη   The historical Gorgias actually claimed that rhetoric was to the mind what medicine was to the body (*Encomium of Helen* 14). It was perhaps in response to such ideas that Plato developed his sharp distinction between τέχνη and ἐμπειρία, which is first found in *Grg.* 463a–466a. A distinguishing feature of ἐμπειρία is that it proceeds in ignorance of the φύσις of its subject matter.

b6–9   **τῷ μὲν . . . παραδώσειν** The structural members of this compound thought exhibit almost mechanical parallelism: viz. τῷ μὲν . . . τῇ δὲ, the two participial phrases, each using προσφέρων with two objects; the two infinitives, each with two objects, which in both cases correspond respectively to the results to be expected from the two objects of προσφέρων. I prefer to translate λόγος 'speeches' rather than 'reasons,' which is favored by a number of translators, because I take πειθὼ ἣν ἂν βούλῃ to refer to producing whatever conviction you want to produce in the assembly and the courts, whereas passing on ἐπιτηδεύσεις νομίμους transmits virtue in that private sphere that Socrates wants to claim for rhetoric in this dialogue despite the doubts of Phaedrus (see καὶ ἐν ἰδίοις in 261a9 with Phaedrus's response). In each of the two clauses the first and second objects of προσφέρων apply respectively to the first and second objects of the infinitives: drugs produce health, proper diet produces strength, speeches produce persuasion, customary practices produce virtue.

b8   **πειθὼ** is accusative. Third-declension stems in οι seem to be exiled from beginning Greek textbooks and are tucked away almost out of sight in S. 279, even though they have the honor of including the poet Σαπφώ. The word here means 'act of persuasion' or 'conviction' rather than the quality of persuasiveness.

270c2   **τῆς τοῦ ὅλου φύσεως** The meaning of this phrase has been debated since at least the time of Galen, and the debate goes outside the bounds of an essentially grammatical commentary. In favor of the opinion that Socrates means that you cannot understand the nature of soul without understanding it 'as a whole' and that Phaedrus in his reply attributes a like view about body to Hippocrates is Socrates' way of testing Hippocrates' view against ὁ ἀληθὴς λόγος, which seems to involve (c10–d7) laying out a method for examining things upward, i.e. in relation to their parts. It seems to be a method for examining the body as a whole and its functions in relation to the liver, let us say, and its functions. In other words, both the physician and the rhetorician must, in Hackforth's words, "know the general character of the object that their art deals with." In favor of the opinion that the phrase means the nature of the whole in the sense 'reality' or, at any rate, something outside the body or the soul that is universal enough to be spoken of as 'the whole' is the tendency of the remarks about the relation between the rhetorical excellence of Pericles and his study of the system of Anaxagoras that has preceded, taken along with Socrates' assertion at b1 that the 'way' of medicine is the same as that of rhetoric. In the end the meaning of the Greek in the passage is insufficiently determined and translations tend to be influenced by the translators' understanding of the larger context, whether that be taken as the argument in which it is embedded, the *Phaedrus*, or "Plato."

c3   τῷ τῶν Ἀσκληπιαδῶν The phrase "constituted a sort of medical degree" (Adam and Adam on *Prt*. 311b6).

c4   τι πιθέσθαι 'to give any credence'; an internal accusative.

οὐδὲ περὶ σώματος is a loose way of putting οὐδὲ δυνατόν ἐστι κατανοῆσαι ἀξίως λόγου σώματος φύσιν. Οὐδὲ, of course, means 'also not' here, rather than 'not even'; there is no hint that this case is any more surprising than the other.

270c6–e6: On the grounds that even Hippocrates must be tested against the reasoned account, Socrates proceeds to give an exposition of what it means to investigate the nature of something. Those who follow this method, he says, will stand to those who do not as the sighted to the blind.

270c6–7   πρὸς τῷ Ἱπποκράτει 'in addition to Hippocrates,' i.e. to the authority residing in his name.

c7   ἐξετάζοντα expresses means.

εἰ συμφωνεῖ sc. ὁ λόγος τῷ Ἱπποκράτει. References to examining, pursuing, or cross-questioning the personified λόγος are not uncommon in Plato, but this sentence puts with unique succinctness the distinction between that process and accepting the *ipse dixit* of authority.

c9   Τὸ . . . φύσεως The exposition begins in a rather loose way with accusative of respect. Also, φύσις is left undefined: it would seem to mean something like 'what a given thing is.' Τοίνυν is transitional: 'now then' (S. 2987).

270d1   περὶ ὁτουοῦν φύσεως is as general as can be.

d2   βουλησόμεθα is future expressing a present intention (S. 1915a).

ἄλλον sc. τεχνικόν.

d4   τίνα . . . ἔχον With τίνα understand δύναμιν. The subject of πέφυκεν . . . ἔχον ('it has by nature') comes from αὐτοῦ, which goes back to the unexpressed antecedent of οὗ in d2. Εἰς expresses goal or capacity with τὸ δρᾶν, as it does with τὸ παθεῖν below.

d6 **ἀριθμησάμενον** must agree with the common subject of διανοεῖσθαι (c10), σκοπεῖν (d3), and ἰδεῖν to follow, all of which depend on δεῖ. Socrates thought of that subject as 'we,' when he said βουλησόμεθα in d2. The singular participle here has more the appearance of a scribal mistake than of the kind of lapse that Plato deliberately employs, especially in long sentences, to give the effect of informality. Stephanus's ἀριθμησαμένους should be read.

 ὅπερ . . . ἑκάστου 'what (we saw) in the case of one, must we not see in the case of each [of the πλείω εἴδη].' See LSJ s.v. ἐπί A.I.2f.

d6–7 **τῷ . . . πέφυκεν** with what follows explicates τοῦτ' in the preceding phrase. Αὐτὸ is subject and refers to the ἕκαστον εἶδος that the reader can infer from πλείω εἴδη in d5 and ἐφ' ἑκάστου in d6. Τῷ is interrogative: 'with what [δυνάμει]?'

d9 **τούτων** i.e. the steps of a procedure just outlined.

d9–e1 **ὥσπερ τυφλοῦ πορείᾳ** The comparison strips the technical veneer from the word μέθοδος and returns it to its semantic origins. Ὥσπερ, as often, is a sign indicating METAPHOR AHEAD and has no syntactical function.

270e1 **ἀλλ' . . . μὴν** A strong adversative to separate this person's route from that of the blind traveler.

e2 **ὁτιοῦν** is the object of μετιόντα. It emphasizes the generality of the assertion.

e2–3 **ἂν τῷ . . . διδῷ** By 'gives words' Socrates means 'teaches rhetoric,' as the context makes clear. The indefinite pronouns flock together.

e3–4 **τὴν ουσίαν . . . τῆς φύσεως** What he will show accurately is 'the real nature.'

e4 **τούτου . . . προσοίσει** The subject is the pupil (τῷ in e3), to whom the teacher will show accurately the nature of the thing to which he will be applying his verbal devices, as a physician applies remedies to the body of his patient, and using the same phrase a physician might use: προσφέρω πρός.

271a1–c9: Socrates maintains that since rhetoric is concerned with producing conviction in the soul, serious theoreticians of it investigate the soul's nature, distinguish its types, and fit them to different kinds of speeches. These rascals, however, keep their procedure to themselves and do not put it into their oral teaching or into handbooks. He agrees to try to describe what these men ought to teach.

271a1   ἡ ἅμιλλα . . . πᾶσα   Once again endeavor is expressed in terms of competition. See first note on 269d2. For τέταται ('is aimed'), see LSJ s.v. τείνω 4.

            αὐτῷ   Dative of agent, refers to the subject of δείξει in 270e3.

            τοῦτο, despite its gender, would seem to mean the soul, as will τούτῳ in the following line and as did τοῦτο two lines above.

a2   πειθὼ . . . ποιεῖν   Producing conviction is more impressive than merely persuading and seems to dignify rhetoric by giving it, like poetry and shoemaking, a product.

a4–5   ἄν . . . διδῷ   Compare on λόγους διδῷ at 270e2–3. This use of δίδωμι in the sense of διδάσκω was missed by LSJ, but compare *Rep.* 365d4–5, where we find διδάσκαλοι σοφίαν δημηγορικήν τε καὶ δικανικὴν διδόντες.

a5   σπουδῇ   'as a profession.'

            πάσῃ ἀκριβείᾳ modifies only γράψει. Compare δείξει ἀκριβῶς at 270e3.

a6   ποιήσει ψυχὴν ἰδεῖν   He will make his pupil see the soul (LSJ s.v. ποιέω A.II.b). Since he will do that by writing very accurately, the force of the τε καί connection is consecutive: 'and by so doing.' The reader must keep in mind the pupil of this τεχνικός teacher, even though he has appeared on the page only as the indefinite τῷ in 270e3, and understand him as the subject of προσοίσει in 270e4 and of ἰδεῖν here.

a6–7   πότερον . . . πολυειδές   As often happens, the subject of the indirect question, which would have been ψυχή, has been extracted and put proleptically into the main clause as object of ἰδεῖν. Again the soul becomes a 'thing'; see third note on a1.

a6   ὅμοιον replaces ἁπλοῦν of 270d1: De Vries suggests "homogeneous."

a7   κατά   "analogously to" (Hackforth).

a10–11   Δεύτερον . . . πέφυκεν   The indirect question is governed by ποιήσει . . . ἰδεῖν from a6.

a10   ὅτῳ   sc. δυνάμει, as with τῷ in 270d6.

τί serves as object of both infinitives.

271b1–2   **Τρίτον . . . αἰτίας**   The tense and voice of διαταξάμενος tell us that the teacher of rhetoric who does his job σπουδῇ (a5) must do all the laborious matching of ψυχή to λόγος himself in advance. Only then will he go through (the future δίεισι) the reasons for his arrangement for his students. Although as recently as a7 (πολυειδές) Socrates was talking about complex structure within the individual soul, the complexity now consists of different kinds of individual souls. By different kinds in this context, however, he merely means having different attributes, through which, as we shall see in b3–4, they are bound to find different kinds of λόγοι persuasive.

b2   **τούτων** refers primarily to the various γένη of soul, although one could also speak of the kinds of speeches having 'experiences'; they either succeed in producing or fail to produce πειθώ.

b3   **ἕκαστον** sc. γένος.

b3–5   **οἵα οὖσα . . . ἀπειθεῖ**   The participle is causal: 'which soul, because it is of the kind it is . . . is convinced . . . and which is not.'

b4   **δι' ἣν αἰτίαν**   For the relative pronoun as an indirect interrogative, see S. 2668.

b7   **μὲν οὖν** is corrective (S. 2901b). Socrates insists that this procedure is not 'very good, at any rate,' as Phaedrus has said; it is absolutely indispensable.

b7–8   **ἐνδεικνύμενον . . . γραφήσεται**   Both participles agree with οὔτε τι ἄλλο οὔτε τοῦτο in b8–c1. The difficulty here lies in the paucity of evidence for arriving at just what ἐνδεικνύμενον means. With De Vries, I endorse Hackforth's suggestion of a rhetorical model or 'fair copy' for use in schools—think of Phaedrus's close attention to and desire to memorize Lysias's speech earlier in the day—as opposed to a speech actually delivered in public, which might be ἐπιδεικνύμενον, but is here simply λεγόμενον. Take τέχνη with both participles and let the first be governed by γραφήσεται and the second by λεχθήσεται in hysteron proteron order (S. 3030).

271c1   **τοῦτο** refers to 'the present subject' in a broad sense: ἔρως.

   ὧν σὺ ἀκήκοας   'whom you have heard.' Once again we see the oral nature of most literary experience. I think De Vries right in saying that the translation "of whom you have heard" (Hackforth and, in substance, Vicaire and Fowler), while grammatically possible, gives Phaedrus too little credit for being the aficionado he is. Of course he has heard of these people! Rowe's "but who now write manuals of rhetoric, the people you have listened to" gets the right idea.

c2   **πανοῦργοί** The kind of moral delinquency denoted by this word varies with the context: 'they are disingenuous' might do here.

c3   **τὸν τρόπον τοῦτον** De Vries thinks that τοῦτον looks forward, "as Phaedrus's next question shows." He is probably right; it is Socrates' way to throw out demonstrative teasers for his interlocutors to throw back.

c4   **μὴ ... γράφειν** 'let's not believe that they write scientifically.' The αὐτοὺς we might expect as subject of γράφειν has been attracted into the dative by the proximity of πείθώμεθα, even though the latter here introduces *oratio obliqua* rather than taking its usual indirect object.

c6   **Αὐτὰ . . . τὰ ῥήματα** i.e. the exact wording of the handbooks that would teach this method.

c7   **μέλλει** The subject is 'the work.'

c8   **ἐθέλω** It is easy to see how misleading 'I want' would be here. Socrates does not represent himself as wanting to undertake the difficult task; his desire to carry the discussion forward compels him to be *willing* to do so.

271c10–272b6: Socrates sketches a vivid outline of a genuinely scientific education in speaking. Phaedrus agrees that it would have to be like that, but seems daunted by the magnitude of the task.

271c10   **ψυχαγωγία** See 261a8 with note.

271d1   **ψυχὴ** is proleptic. Normally the subject of a relative clause pulled forward in this way takes a case determined by its syntactical function in the clause into which it has been drawn, but there is no need to change to ψυχήν. De Vries cites *Meno* 81e2: ζητεῖν ἀρετη ὅτι ἐστίν, where Bluck ad loc. cites *La.* 199e11: οὐκ ἄρα ηὑρήκαμεν ἀνδρεία ὅτι ἔστιν.

d2   **εἴδη** are kinds of soul, like ψυχῆς γένη in b1–2, not parts of soul, as might be mistakenly inferred from the use of the adjective πολυειδές (270d1) in the argument.

    τόσα καὶ τόσα 'so and so many' (LSJ s.v. II).

    τοῖα καὶ τοῖα 'such and such.' This demonstrative is used only

in phrases of this sort in Classical prose. Elsewhere τοιοῦτος is
used, or, as in the following clause, τοιόσδε.

d4   **αὖ** 'in turn.' Having finished for the time being with
compendiously sketching the classification of souls and the
people they produce, Socrates turns to that of rhetorical devices—
presumably all the way from those on the largest scale, like the
disposition of the parts of a work, to the smallest, like figures of
speech. That such is what λόγοι is likely to mean in this context
will emerge as Socrates goes on.

    τοιόνδε 'of a certain sort.'

d6   **διὰ τήνδε τὴν αἰτίαν** Take αἰτίαν in the sense 'cause' (LSJ s.v.
II) and translate 'because of this,' i.e. because both ψυχαί and
λόγοι come in certain discrete kinds, which one who intends
to be a speaker must know and which will produce predictable
results when put together in the right combinations. Hackforth
translates by opening his sentence with "hence," and it is true
that this phrase connects its sentence with what preceded and
serves the same function as a particle such as οὖν, but Helmbold
and Rabinowitz give an explanatory translation: "because of the
qualitative correlation between speech and soul."

    ἐς τὰ τοιάδε 'to positions [or opinions or actions] such as these.'

d7   **διὰ τάδε** is not quite parallel to διὰ τήνδε τὴν αἰτίαν above; the
demonstrative refers, in a more abstract and general way, to the
speaker's arguments and his presentation of them, τῶν τοιῶνδε
λόγων of the preceding clause.

d7–e1   **δεῖ . . . ἐπακολουθεῖν** passes quickly through the three
stages of rhetorical education: (1) understanding theoretical
elements (ταῦτα ἱκανῶς νοήσαντα), (2) coming to recognize the
embodiment of these principles in real-life situations (θεώμενον
. . . πραττόμενα), and (3) being able to respond quickly to those
situations and think on one's feet (ὀξέως . . . ἐπακολουθεῖν). Part
one has already been sketched in generalities; parts two and three
will be treated more dramatically in the two long subordinate
members of the sentence that stretches from e2 to 272a8. Notice
the difference in tense of the two participles: 'when he has come
to understand . . . he must be able . . . when he sees. . . .'

271e1   **τῇ αἰσθήσει** Dative with ἐπακολουθεῖν. The student's response
must follow his perception quickly.

e1–2   **ἢ μηδὲν . . . συνών** 'otherwise he is bound to gain no advantage
from the teaching he heard before, when he was a student.' The

force of δεῖ carries over to govern εἶναι. For the idiom μηδὲν εἶναι πλέον τινι, compare Sym. 217c3–4, where Alcibiades in recounting his attempt to seduce Socrates says οὐδὲν γάρ μοι πλέον ἦν ('I was no further on'). Δεῖ, which has governed δύνασθαι with its masculine subject, can continue to be felt with the impersonal εἶναι. Λόγων, an instrumental dative at heart, has been attracted into the relative clause and the case of the relative pronoun. Σύνειμι is used so frequently of the pupil-teacher relationship that in a context such as this it is easy to supply a dative like τῷ διδασκάλῳ with it.

e2–3   ὅταν . . . πείθεται summarizes c10–d7, the whole first stage of rhetorical education.

e3   εἰπεῖν means 'to say' and governs the indirect question that begins with οἷος.

ὑφ' οἵων   sc. λόγων.

πείθεται is passive; it cannot be translated as 'believes.'

e3–4   παραγιγνόμενον is an attributive participle used as a substantive: 'such a one [from οἷος] nearby,' the object of διαισθανόμενος.

272a1   οὗτός ἐστι   'there he is!'

αὕτη is the subject of the clause that follows, ἡ φύσις the predicate. Predicate nouns that are identical with the subject take an article (S. 1152). Compare 245c4 and note.

a2   ἔργῳ   'in the flesh,' one might say.

οἱ is a pronoun.

a3   τῶνδε is an objective genitive denoting the points or arguments of which the man is to be persuaded.

a3–7   ταῦτα . . . διαγνόντι   As we move into the second member of the long, compound subordinate member of this sentence with the connective δ', the recent graduate in rhetoric on his first field trip, who has been the subject in the first half, is supplanted by the art itself in the forefront of Socrates' thought. As a consequence the person moves into the dative as subject of a series of participles, even though the art itself does not appear as expressed subject until the main clause arrives. There is no formal anacoluthon, and the effect is quite natural. The participles have temporal force, as πρότερον δ'οὐ in a8 indicates, and notice the change in tense; there are a few more lessons he must be assumed to have learned before he is ready to be tested.

a4   τοῦ . . . ἐπισχετέον   A signal example of the substantive-making power of the article.

a5–7   **βραχυλογίας . . . ἀκαιρίαν** The genitives, recapitulated by τούτων, all depend on τὴν εὐκαιρίαν τε καὶ ἀκαιρίαν. Εἴδη has been attracted into the relative clause from agreement with ἑκάστων, perhaps to avoid yet another genitive: 'The apt and inept time for brevity, the arousal of pity, aggressiveness, and all the forms of verbal expressions he has learned.'

a6–7   **τὴν εὐκαιρίαν . . . διαγόντι** Much of the orator's skill in practice lies in timing: times for speaking and times for holding one's peace (a4), and—within the former—proper occasions for using the particular devices of rhetoric effectively.

a7–8   **ἐστὶν . . . ἀπειργασμένη** In Plato the perfect forms of this verb are sometimes active, sometimes, as here, passive in meaning.

a8–b1   **ὅτι . . . ἐλλείπῃ** Very often conditional relative clauses are more easily translated by pure conditionals in English, with 'if' and an indefinite pronoun.

272b1   **λέγων . . . γράφων** These participles are not supplementary, although that is the usual construction with ἐλλείπω; translate 'in speaking,' etc.

b2   **κρατεῖ** 'has the better of it,' 'wins,' as often.

b2–3   **ὁ συγγραφεύς** is the imaginary author of a rhetorical manual along the lines that Socrates has just described. The clause is, of course, not part of the quotation, despite the typographical conventions of Burnet's text.

b3–4   **δοκεῖ . . . τέχνης** Burnet's μὴ, introducing a question that expects a negative reply, is good Greek but not necessary. The ἢ of the manuscripts with the punctuation left as Burnet has it is better; but it would be better yet to eliminate the first question mark as well and—as De Vries suggests—take οὕτως ἢ ἄλλως πως together with the genitive absolute λεγομένης . . . τέχνης, leaving ἀποδεκτέον to stand alone. Ὁ συγγραφεύς would then ask the sensible question: 'What do you think, Phaedrus and Socrates? Should we accept it if an art of rhetoric is described in this way? Or in some other way?'

272b7–273a5: In casting about for some shorter, easier road to good speaking, Socrates and Phaedrus return to a point they had touched on before and discuss the opinion of the professionals that, compared with likelihood, truth has little or nothing to do with the matter.

272c1 αὐτὴν The rhetorical τέχνη.

c2 πολλὴν ἀπίῃ καὶ τραχεῖαν The prefix of the verb connotes futility and loss of time and effort; its subject is 'one,' the subject assumed with μεταστρέφοντα ἐπισκοπεῖν in b8. The adjectives, agreeing with an understood ὁδόν, are accusatives of extent of space (S. 1581).

c5 Ἕνεκα ... ἔχοιμ' ἄν 'if trying could do it, I would be able' (LSJ s.v. ἕνεκα 2). Understand λέγειν from c4 with ἔχοιμ' ἄν.

c6 οὕτως 'as it is,' not quite the same as at 235c2.

c7 Βούλει ... εἴπω See note on 228e4–5.

 τῶν περὶ ταῦτά is partitive with τινων, which depends on ἀκήκοα, in the sense 'have heard from,' unlike the occurrence discussed on 271c1. For the idiom, see note on 248d7.

c10–11 Λέγεται ... εἰπεῖν Even the devil must have his due. Hermeias and other ancient commentators thought that the saying was derived from a fable in which a wolf, seeing some shepherds eating mutton, says εἰ ἐγὼ τοῦτο ἐποίουν, πόσος ἂν θόρυβος ἐγεγόνει.

272d1 Καὶ σύ γε "The effect of γε in καί ... γε is to stress the addition made by καί" (D. 157): 'and you do so too.'

d2 ταῦτα ... σεμνύνειν 'to exalt the importance of these things.' Ταῦτα stands for the fundamental knowledge of φύσις that underlies the procedure that Socrates outlined in 271c10–272b2 and is related to ἀλήθεια.

 οὕτω 'as we have.'

d3 ἀνάγειν ἄνω is a metaphorical restatement of σεμνύνειν (LSJ s.v. ἀνάγω I.6).

 μακρὰν περιβαλλομένους 'going the long way round.' Probably some technical meaning of περιβάλλω is involved, possibly 'to send round a detachment' in warfare, as Thompson suggests. Understand ἡμᾶς as its subject. For μακρὰν (ὁδόν), see note on c2.

 παντάπασι γάρ is all that appears of the main clause of this sentence. Before Socrates says what he is talking about, he embarks on a relative clause to tell Phaedrus that the two of them had said the same thing earlier in the dialogue, and that leads to an indirect statement of what they had said, which more or less imparts what might have been said in the main clause, and renders going back to it an act of mere syntactical tidiness that Plato disdains to perform.

d4   **κατ' ἀρχὰς . . . λόγου** Socrates in proceeding seems to allude to 259e7–260a4, so that what he means by the λόγος must begin with the agreement (259e1ff.) to examine what constitutes good writing and speaking.

d5   **μετέχειν** will have as its subject τὸν μέλλοντα in the following line.

    ἢ καὶ possibly merely adds another item to be kept before the mind, but is more likely to mark a climax: 'or even' (D. 306). Not showing concern for the truth of men's characters may be more shocking than carelessness regarding what is just in events.

d6   **τοιούτων** i.e. δικαίων ἢ ἀγαθῶν.

d8   **μέλειν** Now that the sentence without a main clause is over (see third note on d3), we revert to φασὶ in d2, which governs the *oratio obliqua* to the end of the paragraph.

272e1   **δεῖν** is an infinitive in a relative clause in *oratio obliqua* 'by attraction' (S. 2631).

    προσέχειν sc. τὸν νοῦν, which is omitted as often as it is expressed in this idiom.

e2   **οὐδὲ . . . δεῖν** 'he ought not even,' as the following clause makes clear.

e3   **εἰκότως** 'in a plausible way.'

e3–4   **ἕν . . . ἀπολογίᾳ** Compare 267a2. The phrase is not mere amplification; the two classes of speeches call for different treatments in many respects.

e4–5   **λέγοντα . . . εἶναι** For the agent in the accusative with the impersonal construction of a verbal adjective in -τέος, see S. 2152a. The emphasis given by δή is "often ironical in tone" (D. 229); here the irony underlines the implicit unworthiness of what the orator must nevertheless pursue. For the function of εἶναι, remember that the verbal adjective is normally accompanied by the third-person singular of the copula (although it may be omitted) and we are here in indirect discourse.

e5   **πολλὰ . . . ἀληθεῖ** Πολλὰ is an internal accusative and is best translated adverbially: 'frequently.' Its presence perhaps provides the reason that χαίρειν in the sense 'bid good-bye to,' which is usually followed by an accusative, here takes the less common dative.

273a1   γιγνόμενον is conditional: 'if it is manifested'; τὸ εἰκός must be seen everywhere in the speech.

τὴν ἅπασαν τέχνην   'the whole of the art.' At any rate, it is all the speaker has to remember in a case in which it will not do to mention αὐτὰ τὰ πραχθέντα (272e2).

a3–4   ἀνεμνήσθην γὰρ   As its name implies, the dramatic aorist (S. 1937) is a feature of tragedy and comedy. It is rare in good prose. Γὰρ here—like assentient γάρ (see note on 228c9)—is a trace left behind by something that has been omitted: '(I am saying this now), for I remembered (while you were speaking a moment ago).'

a4   ἐν τῷ πρόσθεν   In 259e–261c.

a5   πάμμεγα   Phaedrus means to protest mildly against the short shrift this opinion, dear to the professionals (τοῖς περὶ ταῦτα), received before.

273a6–c6: Socrates draws an example from the handbook of Tisias in order to show how this theory distorts the pleading in a case of assault and robbery.

273a6   Ἀλλὰ μὴν ... γε   As De Vries points out, Socrates is protesting against the vagueness of Phaedrus's τοῖς περὶ ταῦτα: 'But really, you have read Tisias himself with care,' he says, 'so why not go right to the horse's mouth?' (D. 119).

πεπάτηκας   In a world in which books were pasted together in continuous strips, to speak of 'treading' your author is more natural than to speak of 'thumbing' him. The expression evokes an image of reading as making a journey from one end of a scroll to the other.

a7–b1   μή ... δοκοῦν   Since this sort of indirect question develops from a direct question introduced by μή ('he isn't saying, is he?'), there is an element of apprehension present: 'Whether he means by likelihood anything other than what seems true to the masses (but we are afraid that he does not).' See S. 2676b.

273b3   Τοῦτο δή ... τεχνικόν   Δή is faintly contemptuous here. Hackforth's "that profound scientific discovery" is good. Τοῦτο does not point to what follows. It refers to the principle of the all importance of τὸ εἰκός. Having discovered that, Tisias wrote the example, as he thought, of its validity that follows.

b5   **ἱμάτιον . . . ἀφελόμενος** A mugger who stole clothing (λωποδύτης) could suffer capital punishment. See Demosthenes' amusing speech *Against Conon.*

b7   **μὴ** goes with the prepositional phrase.

    φάναι is governed by δεῖ, as are the two infinitives that follow.

b8   **τὸν δὲ** sc. τὸν ἀσθενῆ καὶ ἀνδρικόν.

    ἐλέγχειν cuts two ways: it refutes the contention of the cowardly man and thereby maintains τοῦτο, namely, that the two of them were alone. See LSJ s.v. II.3.

    ἐκείνῳ is demonstrative with the sentence Πῶς . . . ἐπεχείρησα, which has been turned into a dative substantive by τῷ: 'that well-known argument.'

b8–c1   **καταχρήσασθαι** 'make use of,' not 'abuse,' a sense to which Plato does not apply the word. Socrates does not imply that there is any proper use for this argument.

273c1–2   **ἂν . . . ἐπεχείρησα** is past potential (S. 1784); see LSJ s.v. ἐπιχειρέω II.

c2   **οὐκ ἐρεῖ δὴ** 'will not, of course, admit.'

c2–4   **ἀλλά τι . . . τῷ ἀντιδίκῳ** This, then, is how cases are won and lost. They are like wrestling matches, undecided until one contender slips up and gives an opening to his opponent. Ἔλεγχον means 'opportunity for refutation' here.

c4   **περὶ τἄλλα δὴ** De Vries remarks on the contempt expressed by the "accumulation of δής" (four of them) in the paragraph. Compared to the bantering, essentially good-humored treatment of the rhetorical handbooks in 266d–267d this has been a body blow. Pericles might find a trace of ἀγροικία (269b1) in it.

c5   **τέχνῃ** In this debased sense of the term.

273c7–274b5: With elaborate irony Socrates tells Tisias that, while his discoveries seem impressive, he and Phaedrus had, in fact, agreed that only one who knows the truth can discover what is like the truth. As a consequence they must decline his easier path and go their own long way around to reach excellence in speaking. Their way is hard, but the goal is glorious. The two friends agree that they have said enough about the art of speaking.

273c8–9   **ἢ ἄλλος... ὀνομαζόμενος** More contempt, this time expressed by the offhand manner in which the authorship of this trash is assumed to be a matter of little or no importance. Already in antiquity commentators saw these words as implying that as far as Socrates knows—or cares—the real author might be Tisias's alleged teacher Corax with his ill-omened name. Ὀνομαζόμενος is supplementary: 'he takes pleasure in being named.' As De Vries points out, the end of this sentence offers "a mocking adaptation of a ritual formula." In prayers it was important to call the god by the right name and customary to follow a selection of names with an admission that one had perhaps not hit upon the name he or she prefers.

273d2–4   **πάλαι . . . ἐγγιγνόμενον** The present tense of τυγχάνομεν λέγοντες in combination with πάλαι denotes past time right down to the present: 'have, as it happens, been saying' (GMT 26). They began saying this in 262a5–7. Whereas τυγχάνει ἐγγιγνόμενον, free from the influence of πάλαι, expresses a general truth: 'in fact arises' (GMT 24). That is how the multitude gets its notion of likelihood.

d2   **πρὶν καὶ σὲ παρελθεῖν** Adverbial καὶ cooperates with the accented form of the pronoun to add emphasis: 'before *you* as much as turned up.'

d3   **ἄρα** expresses mild surprise at the thought that what Socrates and Phaedrus had been discussing before Tisias arrived has turned out to shed light on the origin of this method he sets so much store by.

d4–5   **τὰς... ὁμοιότητας** is the object of εὑρίσκειν brought forward into the main clause for the connection it makes with the preceding sentence.

d8–e1   **τις τῶν τε ἀκουσομένων** 'a prospective pupil.'

273e1   **διαριθμήσηται** The prefix indicates that the pupil will classify as well as count, the voice that he will do it for himself. De Vries cites διαταξάμενος from 271b1.

e2   **μιᾷ ἰδέᾳ** Dative of means.

e4   **οὐ μή ποτε κτήσηται** expresses emphatic denial (S. 1804).

e5   **ἕνεκα** takes two objects: τοῦ λέγειν καὶ πράττειν πρὸς ἀνθρώπους and τοῦ θεοῖς κεχαρισμένα μὲν λέγειν δύνασθαι, κεχαρισμένως δὲ πράττειν.

e7   **κεχαρισμένα μὲν . . . κεχαρισμέως δὲ** Although the antithesis, such as it is, contrasts λέγειν with πράττειν, μὲν and δὲ are positioned to emphasize the anaphoric use of the participle and its adverbial derivative.

e8   **εἰς δύναμιν** is a briefer version of καθ' ὅσον δυνατὸν ἀνθρώπῳ at e3–4. In this dialogue Plato is more than usually careful to keep the limitations set by the human condition before the reader.

    γὰρ δὴ ἄρα Δή emphasizes γὰρ, but Denniston (43), who is conservative in these matters, goes out on no limb about the force of ἄρα in this collocation, perhaps wisely. De Vries suggests "as you know," citing from des Places 249 a category of use of ἄρα as a logical connective that insists on the discovery of the connection—here a nuance, that is, to be added to the force of γὰρ.

e9   **οἱ σοφώτεροι ἡμῶν** Hermeias plausibly identified them as οἱ Πυθαγόρειοι. Wherever Plato's Socrates may have stood on their specific teachings, he certainly shared with them a religious worldview that emphasized the humble condition of humanity.

    ὁμοδούλοις In *Phd.* 62bff. the notion that human beings are κτήματα of the gods is used as an argument against suicide.

274a1   **μελετᾶν** followed by an infinitive in the sense 'to make it one's study to . . .' is not uncommon. Particularly memorable is the assertion in *Phd.* 67e5–6: οἱ ὀρθῶς φιλοσοφοῦντες ἀποθνῄσκειν μελετῶσι.

    ὅτι μὴ πάρεργον 'except incidentally' (S. 2765).

a2   **ἀγαθοῖς τε καὶ ἐξ ἀγαθῶν** See note on 246a8.

a2–3   **ὥστ' . . . θαυμάσῃς** When ὥστε introduces a main clause, as with this prohibitive subjunctive, the best translation is usually 'and so.' With μακρὰ ἡ περίοδος Tisias is expected to understand an allusion to things said before his imaginary arrival (272c1–2 and d3).

a3   **οὐχ . . . δοκεῖς** Ast explains correctly as a brachylogy equivalent to οὐ σμικρῶν ἐκείνων ἕνεκα, ὡς σὺ δοκεῖς. It will not be for purposes like getting the better of other people in court. This possibly, as De Vries suggests, marks the end of Socrates' attention to Tisias. The sentence that follows will in part, at least, encourage Phaedrus by telling him that the course Socrates advocates is not entirely otherworldly. There are no guarantees, but prosperity *may* follow piety.

a4–5 ἔσται . . . γιγνόμενα For the periphrastic future, see S. 1961.

a4 μήν An adversative that "balances, denoting that a fact coexists with another fact opposed to it: 'yet,' 'however'" (D. 334).

ταῦτα represents what was implied in ὁμοδούλοις . . . χαρίζεσθαι at 273e9.

a5 κάλλιστα is an adverb.

ἐκείνων are the μεγάλων of a3.

a8–b1 Ἀλλὰ . . . παθεῖν To Phaedrus's by now familiar expression of bemusement over the magnitude of the task, Socrates replies with the sort of gnomic utterance that gets copied into commonplace books.

274b3 Οὐκοῦν Denniston (436–37) detects something of the original interrogative force ('it's true, then, isn't it?') even here with an imperative verb; "a *nicht wahr?*" he says. Perhaps 'that will be *enough* about the subject of the true and false art of speaking,' said with a mild interrogatory lifting of an eyebrow, might convey the nuance he wants. On the other hand, Cooper (69.51.2B) sees the force of οὖν as remaining strong and would take its use as comparable to the supplementary ἄγε, φέρε, or ἴθι that is often found with an imperative to add urgency or excitement. The reader will get another chance to make up his or her mind on this point at 278b7.

Two Cheers for the
Written Word

*274b6–275b2: Socrates and Phaedrus take up the proper use of writing.
Socrates recounts a tradition, which he says was handed down from the
ancients, about the invention of writing and its reception.*

274b6–7   **Τὸ δ' . . . λοιπόν**   As we turn to the subject that remains, δ'
answers the μὲν in b3, and γραφῆς πέρι here provides justification
for translating λόγων there as 'speaking.' Hackforth's "propriety
and impropriety" gets the right mixture of concern for outward
appearance and real values out of εὐπρεπείας . . . καὶ ἀπρεπείας.
When this subject came up before (257cff.), it was discussed
entirely from the point of view of the concern the public man
might feel about the effect becoming known as a λογογράφος
could have on his "image." Now the discussion will take a more
substantive turn.

   πῆ . . . ὅπῆ   A direct interrogative normally precedes an indirect
in introducing the members of an alternative direct or indirect
question (S. 2666).

b9   **θεῷ**   'the divine.' The expression does not point to any particular
god or gods, whether specified or unspecified (Burkert 271–72).
   χαριῆ in this context implies 'you will be in agreement with.'

274c1   **Ἀκοήν** is used of oral tradition. Compare *Tim.* 21a6: κατὰ τὴν
Σόλωνος ἀκοήν, where the genitive, as it does here, indicates the
source.

c1–3   **τὸ δ' ἀληθὲς . . . δοξασμάτων** bears on the uncertainties of
interpreting tradition correctly. Τὸ ἀληθές is the truth of the
matter as passed down in the ἀκοή; δ', a strong adversative, works
with the γε that limits ἀκοήν to emphasize the difference between
merely knowing the traditional story and knowing the truth at its
heart. The ancients alone (αὐτοί, sc. οἱ πρότεροι) knew that; but if
we ourselves could discover it, would the opinion of humans any
longer matter to us at all? The antithesis implicit in ἀνθρωπίνων
depends on the assumption that οἱ πρότεροι were closer to the
gods than we are and more likely to have known what they want.

De Vries cites *Phlb.* 16c7–8: οἱ μὲν παλαιοί, κρείττοντες ἡμῶν καὶ ἐγγυτέρω θεῶν οἰκοῦντες, ταύτην φήμην παρέδοσαν. That this feeling (apart from a general respect for tradition and tendency to exalt the wisdom of ancestors) could find justification in the tales about an age of heroes born from gods can be seen in *Tim.* 40d7–8, where it is said that concerning the generations of the traditional divinities we must trust those who have spoken about the matter in earlier times, on the grounds that they are ἔκγονοι of the gods, although even there, one should note, Plato adds ὡς ἔφασαν. For genitive of thing one feels concern for with μέλοι, see S. 1356.

c5 τοίνυν 'very well.' Note ἤκουσα, echoing Phaedrus's ἀκηκοέναι: when τοίνυν responds to an invitation to speak, a word from the invitation itself is frequently repeated, especially by Plato (D. 571).

περὶ Ναύκρατιν Plato—the tale seems to be his invention—not surprisingly locates Toth around Naukratis in the Delta, because the Greeks, who had traded there from at least the latter half of the seventh century and were given some sort of legal status as a trading colony by Pharaoh Amasis in the sixth (Herodotus 2.178), will have first become acquainted with the god and learned his name in that area. Hermopolis, the Greek name for a city on the west bank of the Nile with which Toth had close ties, shows that he had been identified with Hermes by the Greeks at least as early as the time of Herodotus, who alludes to it in 2.67 and connects it with the cult of the ibis (see c7 with note). Since Toth was the protector of scribes from a time long before Greek contact with Egypt, Plato used, but did not invent, his connection with writing.

c6 οὗ 'to whom' (LSJ s.v. ἱερός II.3 and S. 1414); ἱερὸν is predicate, which is why Burnet and many others omitted the article that B and T give.

c7 Ἶβιν Toth's connection with this marsh bird suggests that he may have been originally a god of the Delta, who conquered and assimilated the baboon god of Hermopolis. He sometimes turns up baboon-headed in effigies. The uppercase iota represents, of course, an editorial decision.

αὐτῷ . . . τῷ δαίμονι As opposed to his sacred bird. Δαίμων here seems to mean a god of subordinate rank; we shall see that he is responsible to the god Ammon, who is personified in the pharaoh.

c8–d2   **Τοῦτον . . . γράμματα**   Plato carefully varies the connectives: τε καὶ with the nearly synonymous pairs that form composite units; καὶ alone to join the more independent γεωμετρίαν and ἀστρονομίαν; ἔτι δὲ to mark the descent from science to gambling; and καὶ δὴ καὶ to usher in with a flourish the point of it all, γράμματα.

274d1   **πεττείας τε καὶ κυβείας**   Skill and acumen were required not only for games involving πεσσοί, which resembled checkers, but also for at least some games involving κύβοι. In *Rep.* 374c5–7 Socrates speaks of both types of games in terms reminiscent of the kind of dedication that is given to chess by some people in the modern world: πεττευτικὸς δὲ ἢ κυβευτικὸς ἱκανῶς οὐδ᾽ ἂν εἷς γένοιτο μὴ αὐτὸ τοῦτο ἐκ παιδὸς ἐπιτηδεύων, ἀλλὰ παρέργῳ χρώμενος. For more on πεττεία as a recognized skill, see Dodds on *Grg.* 450d6.

d2   **καὶ δὴ καὶ γράμματα**   In Greek legend Prometheus is the inventor of writing (see Aeschylus, *Prometheus vinctus* 460), but for Plato's present didactic purpose the remoteness and antiquity of Egypt gives more scope for free invention. Moreover, the hero Palamedes (see note on 261d6) was also associated with the invention of writing, or at least some new letters of the alphabet. All three of the great Athenian tragedians wrote tragedies about him, and perhaps Plato parodies Euripides' treatment in this tale. For an interesting exposition of this thesis and its implications for Plato's view of tragedy, see Nightingale, chap. 4, esp. pp. 149–54.

d3   **τοῦ ἄνω τόπου**   i.e. of what we now call Upper Egypt, along the Nile above the Delta.

d4   **Αἰγυπτίας Θήβας**   The Egyptians called the city Waset. Why the Greeks called it Thebes is a mystery. In any case, they were already doing so by the time *Iliad* 9, with Achilles' reference to "Thebes of the hundred gates" was composed.

    τὸν θεὸν is a second object for καλοῦσι. In order to understand properly, Plato's reader, whether ancient or modern, must know that Pharaoh was a god to the Egyptians and take θεὸν here as a synonym for βασιλέως in d2 without any aid or preparation. This seems to be too much to expect. Τὸν θεὸν is likely to have been a marginal annotation (explaining Ἄμμωνα) that ousted from the text Θαμοῦν, which is restored by Postgate's palmary emendation: 'And they [the Greeks] call Thamous Ammon.'

d6   διαδοθῆναι   sc. αὐτάς as subject.

d7   διεξιόντος   sc. αὐτοῦ; the force is temporal, indicating simultaneity.

d7-e1   ὅτι . . . λέγειν   The object of the king's praise and blame is not the inventions directly, but the validity of Toth's advocacy for them: τὸ μὲν = ὅτι μὴ καλῶς δοκοῖ λέγειν; and τὸ δὲ = ὅτι καλῶς δοκοῖ λέγειν.

274e1   δοκοῖ represents the present indicative in direct discourse; what was in Thamous's mind as he praised or blamed was 'he seems to be speaking. . . .' Note the chiastic arrangement.

e2   ἐπ' ἀμφότερα   'pro and con.'

e3   Θεὺθ is a dative of an indeclinable noun. Egyptian names that could be readily adapted to a Greek declensional type (e.g. Ἄμμων, Ἄμμονος from Amun) were so adapted. Less amenable names were treated in the way in which Medieval Latin, following the advice of Cassiodorus, dealt with Hebrew names: they were treated as indeclinable.

λέγεται is impersonal and equivalent to φασί.

e4   ἐπὶ τοῖς γράμμασιν   'at writing' or 'on the subject of writing,' which is a use of ἐπί + dative with εἰμί or γίγνομαι, for which De Vries gives parallels that KG 1.500 did not find.

e6   μνήμης . . . φάρμακον   For the objective genitive, compare τῆς ἐμῆς ἐξόδου τὸ φάρμακον in 230d5-6 with note.

e7   ηὑρέθη   The subject is Τοῦτο . . . τὸ μάθημα from e4-5, φάρμακον the predicate nominative.

e7-9   ἄλλος μὲν . . . χρῆσθαι is still the position of politicians about ethical questions arising out of science and technology.

275a1   δι' εὔνοιαν   i.e. through his natural partiality for his intellectual children.

a1-2   τοὐναντίον . . . δύναται   'you reversed its capabilities in what you said.' De Vries compares Euthyp. 12a7-8: τὸ ἐναντίον ἢ ὁ ποιητὴς ἐποίησεν.

a4   ὑπ' ἀλλοτρίων τύπων   Impressions—whether on papyrus, wax tablets, or stone—made by others, as opposed to those made ὑφ' αὐτῶν. A reader may be reminded of Socrates' simile in Tht. 191cff., in which he speaks of the block of wax within us upon which we stamp (ἀποτυποῦσθαι) whatever we want to remember of all we see or hear or conceive in our minds.

a4–5   αὐτοὺς . . . ἀναμιμνῃσκομένους   There is a shift in construction: instead of αὐτῶν ἀναμιμνῃσκομένων in agreement with τῶν μαθόντων from a2, as we would expect, the participial phrase, without losing connection with the ἅτε that marks it as causal, gets skewed about into a supplementary participial construction with παρέξει, which has already governed the direct object λήθην: 'because it will make them be reminded. . . .' This is an anacoluthon, but it seems to flow quite naturally and not be in need of textual tampering.

a7   πολυήκοοι . . . γενόμενοι   The etymology of πολυήκοος reveals that the pupils will expect to become 'learned' through hearing books read aloud (compare on 268c3). They do so ἄνευ διδαχῆς, without the personal contact that is so central not only to Socratic dialectic but to humbler educational situations as well, like the handing down of skills. See reference to Nightingale in note to 235d1. By the ethical dative σοι the king indicates Toth's particular interest in and close connection with this fact. As De Vries says, it is tantamount to calling them "your pupils."

275b1   εἶναι δόξουσιν   Not 'they will seem to be' with most translators, but 'they will think or "imagine" [Nehamas and Woodruff] they are' (LSJ s.v. δοκέω I.1). This leads much more naturally into what follows.

        ὡς ἐπὶ τὸ πλῆθος   'for the most part' or 'in the main'; ὡς ἐπὶ τὸ πολύ is more common.

b2   χαλεποὶ συνεῖναι evokes the bumptiousness of the autodidact.

        δοξόσοφοι is probably, as De Vries suggests, a coinage of Plato: 'conceited' is perhaps a bit too general, but its bearing would be clear enough in this context.

275b3–e6: After reproving Phaedrus for caring more about the provenance of his story than about whether it conforms to the way things are, Socrates proceeds to draw from it two conclusions: that anyone who hopes to either transmit or receive an art in writing is rather naïve, and that writing is like painting in that both produce progeny that seem to be alive but cannot defend themselves when questioned.

275b3–4   Ὦ Σώκρατες . . . ποιεῖς implies that Phaedrus assumes that Socrates made up the story he has just told.

b5   δέ γ' is a collocation of particles often used to introduce "retorts and lively rejoinders" (D. 153), including those that pick up what the other speaker has said and express dissatisfaction with it. Contrast 265a9 with note.

b6   δρυὸς is genitive of source (S. 1410). For the antiquity of the shrine at Dodona and the oracular function of the oak there, see Burkert 114.

b7   μὲν οὖν Οὖν is inferential: 'so for the men of that time it sufficed . . .'; μὲν looks forward to σοὶ δ' in c1 (S. 2901c).

b8   πέτρας The rock is added to the oak "for," as Thompson puts it, "the sake of the adage" (see *Iliad* 22.126; *Odyssey* 19.163; Hesiod, *Theogony* 35; Plato, *Ap.* 34d5; *Rep.* 544d7–8). It also helps to emphasize Socrates' point that it does not matter where truth comes from, so long as it is truth. For a similar redundancy that adds amplitude, see περὶ ὄνου σκιᾶς at 260c7 with note.

     ὑπ' εὐηθείας is a positive quality here, contrasted with οὖσι σοφοῖς above. Compare that other set of know-it-alls, οἱ σοφοί at 229c6.

275c2   οὐ γὰρ . . . ἔχει; This sentence can be taken as a mildly reproving statement as easily as it can be taken as a mildly reproving question. Readers should remain alert to how often the punctuation in printed texts of ancient works reflects the judgment of the editor rather than any more objective and demonstrable criterion.

c5   τέχνην need not be taken here in the concrete sense 'a handbook.' One could scarcely be mistaken about whether one had left such a thing behind, but one could easily be mistaken in thinking that one had left behind a rational procedure for learning and practicing some pursuit.

c6–7   ὥς . . . ἐσόμενον 'under the impression that something clear and firm will emerge.'

c8–d1   πλέον τι . . . ὑπομνῆσαι Emendation (editors have altered εἶναι to ἔχειν or ποιεῖν) is not necessary. Supposing that written discourse "is" something more than reminding is equivalent to supposing that it is more efficacious or of more value than reminding. We say, 'It's a great deal that he is even considering the change,' meaning that it is significant or of value. That Greek can use εἶναι with an adjective denoting magnitude in this way is shown by De Vries' parallel from Xenophon's *Oeconomicus* 18. 7 to the effect that 'it is important [πολὺ . . . ἐστιν] that the chaff is carried over the grain into the vacant part of the threshing floor.'

275d4 **Δεινὸν ... τοῦτ'** 'the following strange feature.'

d4–5 **καὶ ... ζωγραφίᾳ** Conjunctional καί often has "an intensive or heightening force as when it joins a part and the whole, the universal and the particular" (S. 2869). Here it joins δεινὸν, an adjective of very wide possible application in this context, with a more exact statement of in just what way the matter at hand is to be considered δεινόν. We might translate, 'really [ὡς ἀληθῶς] like painting, in fact,' as if Socrates had just thought as he was speaking of the way in which writing is δεινόν.

d6 **ἕστηκε** 'stand upright.' The verb conveys not their fixity, which would detract from the antithesis, but their likeness to living creatures.

  σεμνῶς πάνυ σιγᾷ 'they maintain a most haughty silence.'

d7 **ταὐτὸν** It is often difficult to say whether Plato would have felt a neuter pronoun could stand for the content of the previous sentence as the object of an understood transitive verb or as an adverbial accusative modifying an understood intransitive verb; in other words, whether they 'do the same thing' or 'behave in the same way.'

d9 **σημαίνει** Socrates has moved on to imagine questioning some particular item in a particular discourse (τι ... τῶν λεγομένων), so a singular ὁ λόγος can be understood out of οἱ λόγοι in d7.

275e1 **κυλινδεῖται** Like the soul of the calculating and illiberal man at 257a2, written discourse falls prey to aimless motion without purpose or dignity.

e2 **ὡς δ' αὕτως** This, the expression always used by Homer, does not differ materially in meaning from αὕτως alone. Ὡς is being used as in ὡς ἀληθῶς (S. 2988). For the rough breathing, see LSJ s.v. αὕτως II in parentheses at the end.

e3 **λέγειν οἷς δεῖ γε καὶ μή** A double indirect question, condensed from οὐκ ἐπίσταται λέγειν οἷς δεῖ γε λέγειν καὶ μὴ λέγειν οἷς δεῖ μὴ λέγειν. If γε is genuine, it must be emphatic rather than limiting. Many editors have put Hirschig's τε into their texts.

e4 **οὐκ ἐν δίκῃ λοιδορηθείς** Compare ἐλοιδόρησεν μάλ' ἐν δίκῃ at 266a5–6. Here the negative makes it clear that the written discourse cannot defend itself, not even when it is in the right.

  τοῦ πατρὸς ἀεὶ δεῖται βοηθοῦ The father it needs would be, of course, its author. Phaedrus, without realizing what he was doing, offered to serve as stepfather for the speech of Lysias at 234c5.

276a1–c10: In order to illustrate the relationship between the man who writes in ink and the man who writes on the soul in living speech, Socrates compares the first to someone who forces plants in pots for the Adonis festival and the second to a practical farmer. Phaedrus agrees that someone who possesses such seeds as knowledge of justice and other important things will be serious and responsible in how he sows them.

276a1–3   **ἄλλον . . . φύεται** The implication is not that this other λόγος is a legitimate brother (whatever that may be) of writing (τούτου), but that it, unlike writing, is a legitimate son of their father. In order to convey this De Vries wants to put a comma before γνήσιον, which is not necessary but would do no harm. The double indirect question remains convincing; writing is a νόθος by implication in either case. Φύεται carries on the organic metaphor; this legitimate child is from birth better and stronger than his half-brother.

a5–6   **γράφεται . . . ψυχῇ** For the metaphor, see note on 275a4.

a6   **ἀμῦναι ἑαυτῷ** Comparison with 275e5 will show that with this verb choice between use of the active with a reflexive pronoun and the reflexive use of the middle is virtually indifferent.

     ἐπιστήμων . . . λέγειν Since ἐπίσταμαι sometimes means 'know how,' its cognate adjective can take a complementary infinitive.

a8   **Τὸν . . . λόγον** 'the spoken word of one who knows,' as the relative clause makes clear.

276b1–2   **ὁ νοῦν ἔχων γεωργός** The generic use of the article, as with τοῦ εἰδότος in a8 (S. 1122): 'sensible farmers.'

b2–3   **ὧν . . . γενέσθαι** affords another example of a conditional relative clause that is more easily translated as a pure condition. Σπερμάτων has been attracted into the relative clause and into the case of the relative pronoun, which is genitive after the verb of caring (S. 1356). We might expect ἅ to serve as object of βούλοιτο, but the rule in Greek is that if two relative clauses referring to the same antecedent are connected by a copulative conjunction, such as καὶ here, the second relative, if it would stand in a different case from the first, is either omitted entirely (as here) or replaced by the appropriate case of αὐτός (S. 2517). In other words, Greek does not tolerate sentences of the form, 'I saw the woman whose sons he slew and whom he drove mad.' It prefers, 'I saw the woman whose sons he slew, and he drove her mad' or even—misleading as it might seem—'I saw the woman whose sons he slew and he drove mad.'

b3   **θέρους** Genitive of time within which (S. 1444). The indication of time will contrast with the sowing of winter wheat in b7. That the festival took place at a warm time of year is as precise as we need it to be; probably in spring.

           Ἀδώνιδος κήπους were pots planted to be used in the festival of Adonis. Gow (on Theocritus 15. 113) says, "The brief life of the pot-grown plants corresponded to that of Adonis himself, and when he was carried out for burial they were thrown into wells or into the sea." The festival was a private one, celebrated by women on the flat roofs of their houses, where no doubt the potted plants had germinated. Aristophanes gives a lively picture of it in *Lysistrata* 387–98. If we may believe him, it was not uncommon for the women to have a few drinks as part of the festivities. Men tended to be suspicious about what went on in women's festivals without being able to interfere with them because of religious law (Burkert 258).

b4   **ἀρῶν** Ἀρόω is a poetic verb that ordinarily means 'plough,' but it is clearly a synonym for σπείρω here. Planting these pots is, after all, being compared to farming; the word was perhaps chosen as a deliberate incongruity to emphasize the absurdity of substituting this play farming for real farming.

           ἡμέραισιν For the form, see second note on 240b5.

b5–6   **ὅτε καὶ ποιοῖ** 'when he *would* do it,' i.e. if he would do it at all (D. 321–22). See note on b2–3. There is no implication that he ever does.

b6   **ἐφ' οἷς** sc. σπέρμασιν.

b7   **εἰς τὸ προσῆκον** 'in the appropriate way,' referring to both the proper time and the proper place (S. 1686.1d).

b7–8   **ἀγαπῷη . . . λαβόντα** 'would be content with what he had sown if it came to maturity in the eighth month.' The participial construction with ἀγαπάω lacks good parallels, but must be accepted if we are not to emend. For ἐν ὀγδόῳ μηνὶ, it is normal for a substantive modified by an ordinal number used attributively to lack the article (KG 1.639). We need not suppose that the farmer actually waited eight months to see his winter wheat germinate; the number is chosen to correspond with the number of days in b4. The implication is that a serious man engaged in a serious activity will wait as long as it takes.

276c1–2   **ὡς ἑτέρως** 'entirely differently.' See note on 275e2.

c4   **τοῦ γεωργοῦ** Genitive of comparison.

           ἧττον νοῦν ἔχειν εἰς 'shows less forethought for.'

c4–5   τὰ ἑαυτοῦ σπέρματα is to be taken quite literally. It is part of
himself, seeds that have grown within him, that this man sows.

c7   ἐν ὕδατι γράψει μέλανι Writing in water, a practice most
students of the Classics remember from their reading of Catullus,
is proverbial for futility and transience. Although Plato turns the
water to ink by adding μέλανι, he wants us to be aware of the
proverbial associations. Writing may *seem* to be a way to render
discourse permanent, but what is expressed in it is, paradoxically,
more evanescent than speech, because it cannot defend itself.

c8   μετὰ λόγων What this man is sowing (αὐτὰ) are σπέρματα that
in turn represent the ἐπιστήμας of c3. He does so 'together with'
or 'in cooperation with [LSJ s.v. μετά A.II] words that are able
neither to defend themselves by argument nor to teach the whole
truth.' Μετὰ is not as difficult as some commentators would make
it. In *Ap.* 32b9–c2, for instance, Socrates says that he thought it
better to undergo danger 'in the company of law and justice'
(μετὰ τοῦ νόμου καὶ τοῦ δικαίου).

c9   λόγῳ is dative of means.

c10   Οὔκουν δὴ τό γ᾽ εἰκός 'That's at the very least quite unlikely'
(D. 423). Compare 258c9 with note.

*276d1–277a5: Socrates maintains that writing is a sort of pastime that
some men engage in as others go to drinking parties. When Phaedrus
protests that amusing themselves with words rather than in some grosser
fashion is a noble pastime, he agrees in part, but insists that it is much
nobler to be serious about words and, by using dialectic, to plant in
suitable souls words that can defend themselves and bear seeds from
which new words will grow.*

276d1   ἐν γράμμασι probably exhibits the common quasi-instrumental
use of ἐν (S. 1687c), but it would be possible to take it locally, if
we think of γράμματα as the whole field of existing and potential
written discourse, out of which each author marks out and
cultivates his or her own κῆποι.

d2   σπερεῖ τε καὶ γράψει The subject is still the man who has
knowledge about justice and beauty from c3–4.
[δὲ] was bracketed by Bekker, because with it the preceding clause
is an assertion that this man will practice writing, which is not
likely to be what Socrates wants to say. He wants to say that the

man, when he writes, will write with certain ends in view, leaving open the implication that it is very likely that he will not write at all. For its possible origin, see third note on d5.

d3   **τὸ λήθης γῆρας** The genitive is basically possessive. The wide spacing between the letters from λήθης to ἵκηται is a Burnet's typographical convention to tell us that, although he cannot identify it, the editor thinks that these words, with their archaic, poetic ring, are a quotation from a source that Socrates doesn't feel that he needs to identify for Phaedrus.

d4   **καὶ ... μετιόντι** This is a significant concession; for Plato it may have justified writing his dialogues. The notes of students in the Academy or elsewhere might also be meant.

d5   **αὐτοὺς** sc. κήπους. The garden rather than the plants is said to grow, as often in English.

    ἀπαλούς evokes the young plants when they have grown enough to be no longer bristling stubble.

    <δὲ> is likely to have been displaced after the ὅταν in d2 from here, where it is needed if only to avoid a pointless and unlikely asyndeton.

d6–7   **ἄρδοντες αὐτοὺς** Instead of their gardens.

d7   **ὅσα τούτων ἀδελφά** are the customary accompaniments of wine: women (or boys) and song—all the things, in short, that the highbrow gathering in Plato's *Symposium* rejected at the outset. For the adjectival use of ἀδελφός, compare 238b4.

d8   **τούτων** The pleasures of the symposium.

    οἷς Some editors accept Heindorf's ἐν οἷς, making the construction parallel to ἐν λόγοις . . . παίζειν in e2, but dative of means will go with παίζων. Understand ἀντὶ τούτων ἐκείνοις ἃ λέγω παίζων διάξει. The gender of the demonstratives will come from ὅσα . . . ἀδελφά in the preceding line, that being closer than παιδιαῖς ἄλλαις in the line before. One might have expected ἔλεγον, but that would be, as De Vries says, a correction rather than an emendation.

    διάξει 'will pass his time.'

276e1   **παρὰ** 'along side of' and so 'compared with' (LSJ s.v. C.I.7).

e3   **μυθολογοῦντα** Notice the abrupt change of construction; we would expect μυθολογοῦντος. Phaedrus seems to recall that he had used an infinitive but forget that it was complementary to τοῦ . . . δυναμένου and had no accusative subject either stated or implied.

e4–5   πολὺ...καλλίων 'a much finer thing,' attracted into the gender of its predicate, σπουδὴ, which stands in contrast to παίζειν and μυθολογοῦντα in e2–3. Phaedrus, quoting the phrase in 277a5, recalls it as neuter.

e5   αὐτὰ harks back to δικαιοσύνης... πέρι in e2–3.

e6   ψυχὴν προσήκουσαν implies affinity as well as capability; when the philosophical lovers choose their beloveds, πρὸς τρόπου ἐκλέγεται ἕκαστος (252d6).

e7–277a4   οἳ ... μάλιστα The absence of verbs has prompted editors to import various supplements, some of which Burnet deemed worthy of space in his apparatus. Understand ἔσονται with βοηθεῖν... σπέρμα in a1, and again with ἄλλοι... ἱκανοί in a2–3, as well as (if Shanz's deletion of καὶ is rejected) with ποιοῦντες in a3, in this last case not as a copula, but as making a periphrastic future. If the first of these three were on the page, the absence of the others would be unremarkable.

277a2   ἄλλοι sc. λόγοι.
             τοῦτ' sc. σπέρμα.

a3–4   εἰς ... μάλιστα The usual disclaimer on behalf of mere humanity.

277a6–c7: Socrates says that he and Phaedrus are now ready to come to conclusions about the questions that have brought them to this point, since they now know both whether the reproach against Lysias for being a writer was justified and what determines whether a speech is or is not made scientifically. In order to elucidate the latter point, he recapitulates what was said about the application of collection and division to rhetoric.

277a7   τούτων stands for the recently arrived at conclusions about the relative value of living speech and writing.

a8   Τὰ ποῖα; Phaedrus is not sure what Socrates meant by ἐκεῖνα. The article can be used idiomatically with interrogative adjectives; had he so wished, Phaedrus could have said τὰ τίνα (KG 1.625–26). Compare the following fragment of dialogue in English: "I said bring the paint from the attic." "The what?"

a9   Ὧν... ἰδεῖν will be explicated by ὅπως... γράφοιντο, a purpose clause with an indirect question dependent upon it.

a10   τὸ Λυσίου τε ὄνειδος 'the reproach against Lysias,' an objective genitive.

ἐξετάσαιμεν It was precisely the genuineness of the ὄνειδος that Socrates called into question in 257d2–3, so a verb that is used for testing gold against a touchstone is appropriate.

277b1   αὐτοὺς τοὺς λόγους With this second object the ἐξέτασις cuts deeper, from the reproach about writing speeches to the speeches themselves.

b2   γράφοιντο replaces the present indicative in a secondary-sequence indirect question (S. 2677). The indirect question—harkening back to the discussion in 259e—is introduced by an ordinary relative pronoun rather than an interrogative, as we saw in a9 as well (S. 2668). In this use ὅς = οἷος: 'Test the speeches themselves (to see) which are such as to be written with art and which without it.' Socrates is talking about criteria for judging speeches in general, not just those of Lysias or the three that have been delivered in the dialogue.

b4   Ἔδοξέ γε δή 'it certainly *seems* so'; γε δή is emphatic limitative (D. 245). The collocation can add "a sense of prudence, almost of hesitancy" to a response (C. 69.17.5.J). The request that follows shows that, as De Vries observes, Phaedrus is once again assenting to a proposition without fully understanding it.

b5–c6   Πρὶν . . . λόγος The structure of this long sentence is very simple: a series of parallel temporal clauses with πρὶν ἄν and the subjunctive (S. 2444), which are connected with each other by repetitions of τε, takes us all the way to ἁπλῇ in c3. The verb in the main clause will be ἔσεσθαι, rather than the ἔσται we might expect, because Socrates frames the entire sentence in *oratio obliqua*, depending on δεδηλῶσθαι in b3.

b6   πᾶν is to be taken in the limited sense of all that belongs to a given genus and corresponds to τὰ πολλαχῇ διεσπαρμένα at 265d3–4, as κατ᾽ αὐτό corresponds to εἰς μίαν ἰδέαν there.

b7   ὁρισάμενός is temporal: 'after he has. . . .'

πάλιν 'next' (LSJ s.v. III) will not quite do, since it misses the nuance of retracing ground in the opposite direction: 'knows how to go back and. . . .'

μέχρι τοῦ ἀτμήτου τέμνειν was not quite stated but was clearly implied by οὐκ ἐπανῆκεν πρὶν at 266a4.

277c2–3   ποικίλῃ . . . λόγους Notice the interlaced and, in fact, ποικίλος word order.

c3   παναρμονίους Socrates chooses a word for 'complex' that calls to mind his views on the 'new music' in *Rep.* 3.

ἁπλοῦς δὲ ἁπλῇ The Palinode shows all souls as being fundamentally manifold. Presumably the simple ones are those that have been unified under their charioteer.

οὐ πρότερον comes along to remind the reader of πρὶν ἄν so long ago.

c4 τέχνῃ, which modifies μεταχειρισθῆναι, has been drawn forward for emphasis.

καθ' ὅσον πέφυκε is not the customary bow to human limitations, but applies to the subject of the clause, τὸ λόγων γένος: i.e. insofar as it is the nature of human speech to be treated scientifically. The rhetoric contemplated in this dialogue is a τέχνη that is willing to make the compromises necessary in order to act in the city as it is. I doubt that Socrates in Plato's *Gorgias* would consider a rationale for speaking to ψυχαὶ ποικίλαι to be a subject worth investigating.

c5–6 τὸ πεῖσαι is the practice of persuasion, as opposed to that of teaching.

277d1–278b6: In addressing the question of whether writing or delivering composed speeches is a matter for reproach, Socrates thinks that the attitude of the writer will count for much. His writings will bring no reproach if he considers them merely a means for reminding those who already know the truth, and does not confuse them with serious investigations, which are written on the soul of the listener.

277d1 Τί δ' The clause is not formally completed and the interrogative receives no verb. We might say, 'What about the matter of. . . ?'

d1–2 τὸ λόγους . . . γράφειν These articular infinitives serve as the subject of τοῦ . . . εἶναι, where they have καλὸν ἢ αἰσχρόν as a predicate. Fresh from this accusative function, they must turn about and become nominative as subject of λέγοιτ', with ὅπη γιγνόμενον as attribute and ὄνειδος ('cause for reproach') as predicate. Understand εἶναι after λέγοιτ'.

d6 Ὡς picks up from δεδήλωκεν, as if Phaedrus had not interpolated his question.

εἴτε . . . ἤ offers an uncommon but well-attested substitute for εἴτε . . . εἴτε to introduce alternative hypotheses.

d7 ἰδίᾳ . . . τιθείς As a metic, Lysias could do nothing δημοσίᾳ in the strict interpretation, but he could write speeches for the use of citizens.

σύγγραμμα πολιτικὸν is deliberately vague.

d8–9   μεγάλην . . . σαφήνειαν Understand εἶναι.

d9–10   εἴτε τίς φησιν εἴτε μή Is τίς drawn from Λυσίας ἤ τίς ἄλλος, in which case the verb has the sense 'admits' or 'agrees'? Or is τις the anonymous heckler of 257c4 surfacing again, in which case φησιν means 'says' with the force 'points out'? Although making the cross-connection is tempting, the normal usage of the verb favors the former alternative.

d10   ὕπαρ τε καὶ ὄναρ is an adverbial phrase with the sense 'in waking moments and in sleep; and so 'in all conceivable mental states.' Compare *Rep.* 382e9–11: οὔτε κατὰ φαντασίας οὔτε κατὰ λόγους οὔτε κατὰ σημείων πομπάς, οὐθ' ὕπαρ οὐδ' ὄναρ ('[God does not deceive others] by visions or words or the leading of signs either waking or in sleep'). This phrase, taken with εἴτε τίς φησιν εἴτε μή above, shows a Socrates determined to rule out any exceptions to what he is asserting in this paragraph.

277e1–2 οὐκ ἐκφεύγει . . . μὴ οὐκ . . . εἶναι Both of the negatives that introduce a clause following a negated verb of avoiding are redundant (S. 2744.8).

τῇ ἀληθείᾳ is equivalent to ἀληθῶς; the dative indicates accompanying circumstance (S. 1527b). For the language of ὁ πᾶς ὄχλος αὐτὸ ἐπαινέσῃ, reread 258a. Here the δῆμος has been downgraded to ὄχλος, but ἐπαινέω and ἐπαινέτης seem to be terms of art for political approval in the tangible form of votes and supporters.

e5–6   Ὁ δέ γε . . . ἡγούμενος This person, 'the man who believes that . . . ,' will be described elaborately. We will know a great deal about what he believes by the time we reach ἐνέφυσαν in 278b2, but not until all we know about him has been summed up in οὗτος δὲ ὁ τοιοῦτος ἀνὴρ will he finally receive a predicate in 278b3–4. Plato kept the structure of this extensive hanging subject clear by reminding us of this man, when Socrates turns to the positive aspects of his beliefs, by a repetition of ἡγούμενος in 278a4 and by dividing what is said about him into three formal sections with ἐν μὲν τῷ γεγραμμένῳ λόγῳ at the beginning answered by ἐν δὲ τοῖς . . . γραφομένοις at 278a2–3, which is picked up in a5 and carried past Burnet's rather confusing punctuation by δεῖν δὲ, although, as is often the case in Plato, the division in substance is not quite so tidy. For δέ γε, see first note on 265a9.

e6   παιδίαν . . . εἶναι Ἀναγκαῖον, an adjective of two terminations here (S. 289d), is predicate to παιδίαν: 'a great deal of frivolity is bound to occur.' For this personal use of an adjective we are used to seeing used impersonally, compare *Grg.* 449b9–10: εἰσὶ . . . ἔνιαι τῶν ἀποκρίσεων ἀναγκαῖαι διὰ μακρῶν τοὺς λόγους ποιεῖσθαι ("some answers require lengthy exposition," Dodds) and the common personal use of δίκαιος illustrated by δίκαιός εἰμι ἀπολογήσασθαι at *Ap.* 18a7.

e8   **οὐδὲ λεχθῆναι ὡς** Understand ἄξιον σπουδῆς with this infinitive too: 'nor has any discourse worthy of serious consideration been spoken in the same way as . . . are spoken.'

       οἱ ῥαψῳδούμενοι sc. λόγοι. The point Socrates is making here seems to have been widely misunderstood. The main subject here is the value of writing, but in οὐδὲ λεχθῆναι . . . ἐλέχθησαν (parts of which a number of editors and commentators have wanted to jettison) Socrates is including in his description speeches that have been memorized from written texts, either verbatim or more loosely, and then delivered in court or the assembly more or less as rhapsodes performed the Homeric poems. But the implications reach further: reading books has been excluded from serious occupations; now hearing them read or commented upon aloud—a common experience in antiquity, as we have seen—meets with the same fate.

e9   **ἀνακρίσεως καὶ διδαχῆς** Two aspects of one process for Socrates. Homer may have been called the teacher of Hellas, but obviously neither of these activities, in their Socratic sense, has any place in a rhapsode's performance.

       ἐλέχθησαν is a gnomic aorist.

       ἀλλὰ does not answer μὲν in e5; it merely introduces a partial exception to the general tendency expressed in the context.

278a1   **αὐτῶν** is partitive with τοὺς βελτίστους (λόγους).

       εἰδότων is objective genitive with ὑπόμνησιν.

       γεγονέναι Note the tense; what is at issue is the whole past of the written word.

a2   **ἐν δὲ** answers ἐν μὲν in 277e5 and marks a pivotal point in the sentence.

a4   **[ἐν]** was probably written by a scribe who forgot about ἐν in a2, unless a resumptive τούτοις has dropped out before μόνοις, which is possible but not likely.

a4–5   **τό . . . σπουδῆς** The article turns the two adjectives and one adjectival phrase into substantives: 'clarity and wholeness and substance,' all as subject of εἶναι in its strong sense 'exist.'

a6   αὐτοῦ takes us back, as a direct reflexive should, to the subject of the main verb, ὁ . . . ἡγούμενος of 277e5–6.

εἶναι is not redundant, but depends on λέγεσθαι to make not exactly a verb of naming, but a verb of accepting, in the sense a father formally accepted his children and acknowledged their legitimacy.

a7   ἐὰν εὑρεθεὶς ἐνῇ 'if he [i.e. the λόγος that is this man's υἱός] is in there and he [the man] has discovered him.' The leading idea resides in the participle. To elucidate this and the context in which it is embedded I quote Hackforth 162: "A man's legitimate spiritual children are primarily those that he himself has discovered by a process of dialectic, and secondarily those that, while logically consequent upon the former, are actually reached, again dialectically, by others."

a7–b2   ἔπειτα . . . ἐνέφυσαν Some, the ἔκγονοι, will be consequences of the man's own λόγοι that will be drawn by other minds in which he has planted the seed for them; others, the ἀδελφοί, will perhaps be λόγοι that are born in the intellectual milieu that this man is thought of as influencing. The literal meaning of ἅμα must not be pressed too hard. Notice the pleonastic amplitude of ἐν ἄλλαισιν ἄλλων ψυχαῖς. For the Ionic dative plural, see third note on 240b5.

278b1   κατ' ἀξίαν 'according to their worth,' 'as they deserve.' This qualification probably, as De Vries observes, relates to ψυχὴν προσήκουσαν in 276e6.

b2   ἐνέφυσαν This is a second aorist form (S. Appendix: List of Verbs s.v. φύω); consequently, it is intransitive: 'took root,' not 'implanted.'

τοὺς δὲ . . . οὗτος δὲ The first δὲ is adversative, rejecting respect for τοὺς ἄλλους (sc. λόγους). The subject of ἐῶν being the same as that of ἡγούμενος in a4, Socrates is now contrasting his conclusions about writing in ink with writing on the soul. The second δὲ is resumptive, of the kind used after a demonstrative that stands in apposition to a preceding substantival phrase, here technically τοὺς . . . ἐῶν, but actually the whole paragraph from 277e5 (D. 184–85).

Epilogue

278b7–279b3: Socrates directs Phaedrus to convey the conclusions they have reached to Lysias and concedes that there is also a message in them for his own young friend Isocrates, who may in the future become dissatisfied with the kind of writing he practices and follow a nobler path.

278b7   **Οὐκοῦν**   For the possibility of either an interrogative nuance or a note of urgency, see note on 274b3.

   πεπαίσθω ... ἡμῖν   See note on 250c7 for the force of the perfect passive imperative. Austin and Olson suggest "in appropriate measure, i.e. long enough" for μετρίως at Aristophanes' *Thesmophoriazusae* 1227, where these same three words set the final sentence of the play in motion.

b8   **καὶ σύ τε** exhibits an odd collocation of connectives, which turns up occasionally in Plato, whose editors often emend the τε to γε or δέ. If our text is sound, take τε as connecting this to the preceding clause and καὶ as adverbial 'also,' modifying ἐλθὼν φράζε.

   καταβάντε   In this context the verb evokes the practice of consulting oracles in caves, like that of Trophonius at Lebadeia.

b9   **ἠκούσαμεν**   A plural used freely with the dual pronoun and participle.

b9–c1   **ἐπέστελλον λέγειν**   For ἐπιστέλλω in the sense 'command' or enjoin,' see LSJ s.v. 2. Understand ἡμῖν or νῷν.

278c2   **ποίησιν ψιλὴν** is poetry that, like epic, is recited rather than sung (LSJ s.v. ψιλός IV.2).

c3–4   **καὶ ὅστις ... ἔγραψεν** 'and if anyone is the author of compositions in the form of political discourses that he calls laws.' See 257e–258c. The gnomic aorist is used parallel to the perfect συντέθηκε and the present συντίθησι: Lysias and λογόγραφοι like him belong in the present, the great epic and lyric poets in the past, the politicians are always with us. And there is typically Platonic variation in the καὶ ὅστις clause parallel to the two introduced by εἴ τις ἄλλος.

c4–5   **εἰδὼς ... ἔχει**   The content of the message begins with an

328

indirect question involving ἔχειν with an adverb in place of εἶναι with an interrogative pronoun.

c6   **λέγων αὐτός** 'by speaking in person.' The participle is subordinate to δυνατός, with which we must understand ἐστί, just as ἰών is subordinate to ἔχων βοηθεῖν, both expressing means.

c6–7   **τὰ γεγραμμένα φαῦλα ἀποδεῖξαι** 'to demonstrate the inferiority of written discourse.' For ἀποδείκνυμι in the sense to show a thing as having some quality expressed by a predicate adjective, see LSJ s.v. II.

c7   **τῶνδε** sc. τῶν γεγραμμένων: genitive of source. Perhaps the scroll containing the speech of Lysias is pointed to here for the last time.

    ἐπωνυμίαν Here his appellation—the designation of what he is and does in the world.

278d1   **τὸν τοιοῦτον** 'such a man,' i.e. one who knows the truth and can defend what he says—the man who has just been described.
    ἐκείνων (sc. ἐπωνυμίαν ἔχοντα δεῖ λέγεσθαι) is parallel to τῶνδε. The reader may be reminded of the serious farmer in 276b–c.

d3   **Τὸ μὲν ... καλεῖν** The article goes with καλεῖν, and σοφόν is predicate adjective to its unexpressed object, τινά.
    μέγα suggests arrogance and overstepping the bounds of humanity, as when Socrates, in *Phd.* 95b5, says μὴ μέγα λέγε to Cebes, who has suggested that he (Socrates) will be able to prove the indestructibility of the soul with ease.

d4–5   **τὸ δὲ ... τοιοῦτόν τι** Understand καλεῖν again, but this time its object, if expressed, would be αὐτόν, the same person as τινα in the first note on d3. Or perhaps it would be simpler and more direct to understand καλεῖσθαι: 'being called a philosopher or something like that' as subject of ἁρμόττοι.

d5–6   **ἐμμελεστέρως ἔχοι** 'would be in better taste' (LSJ s.v. ἐμμελής II.2). Compare πλημμελούμενος at 275e3: the root notion is musical, in or out of tune.

d7   **ἀπὸ τρόπου** 'out of the way,' i.e. departing from what it is proper and reasonable to say or do. At *Tht.* 143c7 Terpsion uses Phaedrus's exact words to respond with approval to a proposal of his friend Euclides.

d8   **τὸν ... τιμιώτερα** For the qualities this man lacks, look back at c4–5: he does not know the truth and he cannot come to the aid of what he has written.

d9–e1   **ἄνω κάτω ... ἀφαιρῶν** Dionysius of Halicarnassus (*On Literary*

Composition 25) tells us that after Plato's death a tablet was found with the opening words of the *Republic* arranged and rearranged in various ways. He asserts that Plato, even at eighty years of age, never stopped "combing and curling his dialogues and braiding them in every way" (τοὺς ἑαυτοῦ διαλόγους κτενίζων καὶ βοστρυχίζων καὶ πάντα τρόπον ἀναπλέκων). Hackforth makes the interesting suggestion that what we see here is the irritation Plato the philosopher felt with Plato the literary artist. Κολλῶν τε καὶ ἀφαιρῶν can be taken literally of cutting out and pasting in individual columns (σέλιδες) of a papyrus roll.

278e4   τῷ ἑταίρῳ   See note on 257b4–5.

e5–6   οὐδὲ γὰρ οὐδὲ . . . παρελθεῖν   'for you must not overlook *your* friend either' (S. 2938).

e8   Ἰσοκράτη   Isocrates, whose very long life (436–338 B.C.E.) extended beyond that of Plato at both ends by roughly a decade, was a writer of essays in the form of speeches and an educator. (I call them essays, because he was too lacking in confidence to actually speak before a crowd.) This is the first and only time he is mentioned by name in the *Phaedrus*, but perhaps he can be seen in the background elsewhere in the dialogue (see note on 279a9).

e8–9   ᾧ . . . εἶναι;   What message Socrates will deliver to Isocrates depends on the answer to Phaedrus's second question: 'What are we going to say that he is?' i.e. of the two possibilities that have emerged: a συγγραφεύς or a φιλόσοφος?

e10–279a1 Νέος . . . ἐθέλω   Socrates discreetly avoids giving a direct answer.

279a1   κατ᾽ αὐτοῦ   'about him' (LSJ s.v. κατά A.II.7).

a3   ἀμείνων . . . εἶναι   'too good to be put on a level with the speeches of Lysias and his circle.' Compare *Ap.* 17b6: ὁμολογοίην ἂν ἔγωγε οὐ κατὰ τούτους εἶναι ῥήτωρ.

a3–4   τοὺς περὶ Λυσίαν . . . λόγους   are the speeches one hears in his vicinity, which would naturally be his own and those of people with whom he associates.

a4   τὰ τῆς φύσεως   is accusative of respect.

ἤθει refers to his character as opposed to his talents.

κεκρᾶσθαι denotes the mingling of talents and qualities in his character and abilities without drawing on any specific medical theory.

a6–7   πλέον ἢ . . . λόγων   Λόγων is partitive with τῶν πώποτε ἁψαμένων, which is genitive of comparison following διενέγκοι;

παίδων is genitive of comparison with πλέον ἤ. From προϊούσης τῆς ἡλικίας in a5 understand ἀνήρ in apposition to the subject of διενέγκοι: 'If . . . as an adult he should excel all those who engaged in literature in the past more than (he would excel) children.'

a7–9   ἔτι τε εἰ . . . θειοτέρα   These two clauses continue to depend on οὐδὲν . . . θαυμαστὸν in a5.

a8   ταῦτα   The literary preeminence for which he is destined.

a9   θειοτέρα   i.e. more divine than the ὁρμὴ that will have led to his literary eminence. There are two steps in what would not surprise Socrates (a5). First comes simply the future success of Isocrates in his present pursuits. The second itself consists of two steps: his dissatisfaction with that success and (δέ) the ὁρμὴ θειοτέρα that may someday spur him on to greater things.

φύσει   Instrumental dative. At any likely dramatic date for the dialogue Isocrates could have been seen as a young friend of Socrates, who might be thought to have a ὁρμὴ θειοτέρα lying in wait for him; by any likely date for its composition and publication it had become clear that the time for achieving the greater things his philosophical nature fitted him for had passed him by. To a reader who would understand his place in the *Phaedrus* I warmly recommend two articles. Coulter and Brown, although they do not assert definitely that Socrates' first speech is a pastiche of Isocrates, show convincingly that it embodies the rhetorical-sophistic culture and shallow notion of φιλοσοφία he taught, and that it is Isocrates whom Socrates is hiding behind, when he covers his head in 237a. Asmis, building a larger structure on this foundation, finds the presence of Isocrates throughout the dialogue and argues that, for Plato, his work represents something much more dangerous than does that of Lysias. Remember that Lysias was not a citizen and was certainly dead when the *Phaedrus* was written. No one was going to object if he received satiric treatment by name. Isocrates, on the other hand, was very much alive and widely respected.

279b1–2   τῶνδε τῶν θεῶν is fully deictic: the Nymphs, Achelous, and Pan. Socrates will have gestured broadly toward his surroundings.

b2   ὡς essentially denies the connection implied in παιδικοῖς.

ἐξαγγέλλω is a present of anticipation, this time denoting not (as ἄγομεν did at 267a3) what is going to happen immediately, but what is, as Socrates pretends, certain to happen (S. 1879).

279b4–c8: After praying to Pan and the other deities of the place, Socrates and Phaedrus depart.

279b4 **ἐπειδὴ καὶ** 'especially since'; the καί of balanced contrast (S. 2886). At 242a3 the oppressive heat had been advanced by Phaedrus as a reason for remaining in the shade and continuing the conversation; its abatement now offers an additional reason for ending it.

b6 **εὐξαμένῳ** Here the temporal participle carries the main idea of the sentence. Bekker's dual form turns up in some texts and is implied in the translations of Hackforth and Rowe, but why would Phaedrus ask to be associated in the prayer at c6 if it had already been made in his name as well as that of Socrates?

  τοῖσδε See note on b1–2.

b8 **δοίητέ** Optatives of wish in place of imperatives make prayers a bit more respectful.

279c2 **δύναιτο** is optative by assimilation of a verb in an indirect question dependent on an optative of wish (S. 2186d).

c5 **ηὖκται** Many deponent verbs are sometimes used with passive meaning in the perfect system (S. 813d).

c8 **Ἴωμεν** "One of the most felicitous closing sentences in literature," in De Vries' words. Certainly one of the shortest.

INDEX OF GREEK TERMS

Note: This is an index to the commentary, not to the text.

impatient questions, 236d10–e1; in
questions expecting "yes," 229b4
μετά: with gen., 276c8
μεταβάλλω, 241a2–3 & b5
μεταμέλει, 231a2
μεταξύ 234d3-4
μή, redundant after verbs of
hindering, 251b4–5
μὴ ὅτι, 240e1
μὴ οὐ, redundant after negated verb of
avoiding, 277e1–2
μήν, adversative, 244b6, 274a4

νοέω, 235c7
νοσέω, 228b6–7
νυμφόληπτος, 238d1
νῦν δέ, 244a6
νῶτον, 247b7–c1

ὁδός, 263b7–8
οἶδα, 264a8
οἰκονομέω, 256e5–6
οἷος, 239b7–8
ὄνομα, 234e8
ὄνου σκιά, 260c7
ὅπως, with future indicative, 252e4–5
ὅς, as demonstrative pronoun, 258a5
ὅσον, 229c1
ὅτι, pleonastic, 236c6
ὅτι (or διότι) δή, 244a5
ὅτι μή, 274a1
οὐ μὲν δή, 266c6
οὐ μή: in emphatic negative
prediction with subj., 227d5,
260e5–7; with future ind., 262b9;
redundant after negated verb of
hindering or avoiding, 277e1–2
οὐκ οἶδ' ὅντινα τρόπον, 227c4–5
οὐκοῦν, 274b3
οὖν: confirmatory, 242e2; weakly

inferential, 229a8
οὖν δή (δὴ οὖν), 227b6
οὐρανός, 245d8
οὕτω, 237b2

πάλιν, 277b7
παντὸς μᾶλλον, 228d1–2
πάντως, 228c4–5
πάνυ μὲν οὖν, 238c7, 258b9
παρά: with acc., 235b3, 276e1; with
dat., 227b4; with gen., 245c1
παράδειγμα, 262c8–9 & d1
παρακινέω, 249d2
παρασκευάζω, 238e4
παρέχω, 238a5, 257a2
παρίστημι, 233c6
παύω, 228e3, 231a3
πάσχω, 264d1
πείθομαι, 235b6
πειθώ: declension of, 270b8
πειράω, 227c5
περί, in anastrophe, 259e6
περὶ πολλοῦ ποιεῖσθαι, 231c1, 232c1
πεττεία, 274d1
πλάτανος, 229a8
ποιέω, 271a6
ποιητής, 234e6, 236d5
πολλάκις, 238d1
πολύς, 234e3, 244b1, 261b5
πονέω, 232a3–4
πρᾶγμα, 230e6
πρέπω, 264c5, 268d5
πρίν, 242a3
προβάλλω, 241e4
πρός: with dat. 257b6; with acc.,
236a5, 227a3, 231a5–6, 240c6,
255b6;πρός, as adverb, 260b9
πρὸς ἄναντες, 247b1
προσαιτέω 233e7
προσήκοντες, 231b4

INDEX OF ENGLISH TERMS

Note: This is an index to the commentary, not to the text.

INDEX OF PROPER TERMS

Note: This is an index to the commentary, not to the text.

CPSIA information can be obtained at www.ICGtesting.com
Printed in the USA
LVOW132033270712

291939LV00003B/4/P

9 780806 142593